FAST TRACK TO A 5

Preparing for the AP® United States History Examination

To Accompany

The American Pageant

14th and 15th Editions

by David M. Kennedy, Lizabeth Cohen, and Thomas A. Bailey

Stacie Brensilver Berman
Edward R. Murrow High School, Brooklyn, New York

Bobbi Rodriguez
A&M Consolidated High School, College Station, Texas

Mark Epstein
Greenwich High School, Greenwich, Connecticut

Australia • Brazil • Japan • Korea • Mexico • Singapore • Spain • United Kingdom • United States

National Geographic Learning/Cengage Learning is pleased to offer our college-level materials to high schools for Advanced Placement®, honors, and electives courses. To contact your National Geographic Learning representative, please call us toll-free at **1-888-915-3276** or visit us at **http://ngl.cengage.com**.

For permission to use material from this text or product, submit all requests online at **www.cengage.com/permissions** Further permissions questions can be emailed to **permissionrequest@cengage.com.**

ISBN: 978-1-285-08721-4

Cengage Learning
20 Channel Center Street
Boston, MA 02210
USA

Cengage Learning is a leading provider of customized learning solutions with office locations around the globe, including Singapore, the United Kingdom, Australia, Mexico, Brazil, and Japan. Locate your local office at: **www.cengage.com/global**.

Cengage Learning products are represented in Canada by Nelson Education, Ltd.

To learn more about Cengage Learning Solutions, visit **www.cengage.com**.

To find online supplements and other instructional support, please visit **www.cengagebrain.com**.

Printed in the United States of America
Print Number: 02 Print Year: 2014

CONTENTS

Period 4: 1800–1848
The Rise of the American Republic 145

Period 5: 1844–1877
Manifest Destiny, Civil War, and Reconstruction 198

About the Author

Stacie Brensilver Berman taught United States History for ten years, and AP United States History for seven years, at Edward R. Murrow High School in Brooklyn, New York. She is now in the third year of a doctoral program at NYU in Teaching and Learning Social Studies where she is writing her dissertation on LGBTQ issues in high school U.S. history classes. Stacie presents annually at the AP Annual Conference, most recently conducting a full day workshop on implementing project based units in AP classes. She has also presented curricula at the Organization of American Historians Annual Conference and the National Council for the Social Studies Annual Conference. Stacie edited and wrote end-of-chapter questions for the 15th edition of *The American Pageant.* She co-authored a chapter on teaching the Civil Rights Movement in *Teaching US History: Dialogues among Social Studies Teachers and Historians,* a chapter on teaching war crimes in a comparative perspective in *Teaching Recent Global History,* and a chapter on strategies for teaching the Port Huron Statement in Tom Hayden's *Inspiring Participatory Democracy.*

Bobbi Rodriguez, a teacher at A&M Consolidated High School in College Station, Texas, has been teaching AP U.S. History for seven years, during which time she has been a contributing author on several projects designed to improve student performance on the AP U.S. History exam. This includes work on the original roll-out of PrepU for AP U.S. History and the alignment of *The American Pageant* (15th edition) with the State of Texas Essential Knowledge and Skills. She has also led the development of AP U.S. History curriculum for her school district, work that has been shared with other districts in the state.

Mark Epstein, a teacher for twenty-six years at Greenwich High School in Greenwich, Connecticut, has over the years taught nearly every course in the social studies curriculum. He began teaching AP U.S. History fifteen years ago, and since then his students have compiled a 4.6 group average on the examination. In 2002 he was named a Greenwich Public Schools Distinguished Teacher.

PREFACE

History provides the context for everything we do and all that we will become. Knowing what happened in the past helps us understand the mistakes and triumphs of the present. As monumental events unfold around the world—news to us, but the history that my daughter and my students' children will read in a textbook—it becomes even more important that we acknowledge the value of history and our place in it.

This updated edition includes recent events including the prolonged economic crisis, the battle over a national healthcare plan and the Patient Protection and Affordable Care Act, the rise of the "Tea Party," the election of 2012, and issues facing the nation in President Obama's second term. The chapter organization and diagnostic and practice tests have been updated to include recent United States History as well as to reflect changes to the College Board's AP U.S. History curriculum and exam.

I had wonderful allies in my co-author, Bobbi Rodriguez, and in our editor, Craig Leonard. We also had a marvelous foundation courtesy of Mark Epstein, whose previous editions included detailed and well-contextualized information. Jim Fraser and Diana Turk, my colleagues at NYU, push me to explore projects outside of the classroom and continue to develop innovative ways to bring content into AP U.S. History classes.

This book is dedicated to the teachers, staff, and students of Edward R. Murrow High School, who will always be more important to me than I can express. I would not be able to pursue my passion for history and learning without the unwavering support of my husband, Jeff, and the inspiration provided by my daughter, Mia. Lastly, I am eternally grateful for the opportunities made available by and the encouragement of my parents Vicki and Alvin Brensilver and my brother, Peter.

Stacie Brensilver Berman
Steinhardt School of Culture, Education, and Human Development
New York University
New York, NY

PREFACE

Why study history? The answer is one that is as simple as it is significant: Because history matters. History matters as we seek to avoid mistakes of the past in making our decisions of the future. History matters as we attempt to understand the dynamics of the world around us in hopes of better predicting the impact of decisions made today. History matters because it demonstrates the capacities of our nation, and the human race, giving hope to times of uncertainty and whispering words of caution when power moves towards excess.

This updated edition seeks to broaden our approach to U.S. history—beginning in the Pre-Columbian Era and extending through what many of us would consider current events. At the same time, history educators and students alike must appreciate that breadth of knowledge is nearly useless without depth of understanding. To this end, we have also worked to align this book with the College Board's new curriculum framework for AP U.S. History. There are some major changes in store for AP teachers and students, but the new format, new questions, and new standards are intended to encourage students of history to not simply memorize facts, but to use the facts they know to build a cohesive understanding about history.

I am deeply grateful for the support of Margaret Lannamann and Craig Leonard at O'Donnell Learn, and for the contributions of Stacie Berman with whom I had the privilege of working on this latest update. Moreover, it is the support of my colleagues at A&M Consolidated High School and of my incredibly talented students that enables me to continue to pursue new ideas in teaching AP U.S. History.

This book is dedicated to husband, Roy, without whose encouragement and patience this project could never have been completed; to my children, Nate and Dorothy, in whose futures I see the promises of the past; and to my parents, Sam and Fletcher Kelly, who taught me to love history and to love learning without ever losing sight of the people who are individually affected by the events that surround us all.

Bobbi Rodriguez
A&M Consolidated High School
College Station, Texas
January 2014

Part I

Strategies for the AP Test

PREPARING FOR THE AP® EXAM

Advanced Placement is a challenging yet stimulating experience. Whether you are taking an AP course at your school or you are working on AP independently, the stage is set for a great intellectual experience. As the school year progresses and you burrow deeper and deeper into the coursework, you can see the broad concepts, movements, conflicts, resolutions, and personalities that have shaped the history of the United States. Fleshing out those forces with a growing collection of nuances is exciting. More exciting still is recognizing references to those forces in the media.

But as spring approaches and the College Board examination begins to loom on the horizon, Advanced Placement can seem downright intimidating given the enormous scope and extent of the information that is required to score well. If you are intimidated by the College Board examination, you are certainly not alone.

The best way to deal with an AP examination is to master it, not let it master you. If you manage your time effectively, you will eliminate one major obstacle—learning a considerable amount of material. In addition, if you can think of these tests as a way to show off how your mind works, you have a leg up: attitude *does* help. If you are not one of those students, there is still a lot you can do to sideline your anxiety. This book is designed to put you on a fast track. Focused review and practice time will help you master the examination so that you can walk in with confidence and get a 5.

WHAT'S IN THIS BOOK

This book is keyed to *The American Pageant*, 14th and 15th editions, by David M. Kennedy, Lizabeth Cohen, and Thomas A. Bailey, but because it follows the College Board Topic Outline, it is compatible with all textbooks. It is divided into three sections. Part I offers suggestions for getting yourself ready, from signing up to take the test and sharpening your pencils to organizing a free-response essay. At the end of Part I you will find a Diagnostic Test. This test has all of the elements of the U.S. History examination, but the fifty-five multiple-choice questions are organized according to the College Board Concept Outline. When you go through the answers at the end of the test, a cluster of wrong answers in one content area will show you where you are weak. Page references at the end of each answer indicate where you will find the discussion on that particular point in

---

AP® and Advanced Placement Program® are trademarks registered and/or owned by the College Board, which was not involved in the production of, and does not endorse, this product.

both the 14th and 15th editions of *The American Pageant.* Scoring is explained, so you will have some idea of how well you can do.

Part II is made up of twenty-one chapters organized chronologically by topic. These chapters are not a substitute for your textbook and class discussion; they simply review the U.S. History course. At the end of each chapter you will find fifteen content review questions, two long-essay questions, and two short-answer questions based on the material in that chapter. Again, you will find page references at the end of each answer directing you to the discussion on that particular point in *The American Pageant.* It is important to note that the content review questions at the end of each chapter, although in a multiple-choice format, are intended for content review—not as direct preparation for the multiple-choice section of the AP U.S. History exam. One of the biggest advantages to using these, fairly specific, content review questions is that it will help you to internalize details that you will need to use in your essays and short-answer responses. For practice multiple-choice questions that model the style of the AP exam, work through the diagnostic and practice exams.

Part III has two complete AP U.S. History examinations. At the end of each test you will find the answers, explanations, and references to *The American Pageant* for the 55 multiple-choice questions and comments on what essays for the document-based question (DBQ), the four short-answer, and the two long-essay questions should cover.

SETTING UP A REVIEW SCHEDULE

If you have been steadily doing your homework and keeping up with the coursework, you are in good shape. The key to preparing for the examination is to begin as early as possible; do not wait until the exam is just a week or two away to begin your studying. But even if you've done all that—or if it's too late to do all that—there are some more ways to get it all together.

To begin, read Part I of this book. You will be much more comfortable going into the test if you understand how the test questions are designed and how best to approach them. Then take the Diagnostic Test and see where you are right now.

Take out a calendar and set up a schedule for yourself. If you begin studying early, you can chip away at the review chapters in Part II. You'll be surprised—and pleased—by how much material you can cover with half an hour a day of study for a month or so before the test. Look carefully at the sections of the Diagnostic Test; if you missed a number of questions in one particular area, allow more time for the chapters that cover that area of the course. The practice tests in Part III will give you more experience with different kinds of multiple-choice questions and the wide range of long-essay and short-answer questions.

If time is short, skip reading the review chapters. Look at the Key Concepts at the beginning of each chapter to make sure you know the broad concepts, and work on the content review and free-response questions at the end of each review. This will give you a good idea of your understanding of that particular topic. Then take the tests in Part III.

If time is *really* short, go straight from Part I to Part III. Taking practice tests over and over again is the fastest, most practical way to prepare.

BEFORE THE EXAM

By February, long before the exam, you need to make sure that you are registered to take the test. Many schools take care of the paperwork and handle the fees for their AP students, but check with your teacher or the AP coordinator to make sure that you are on the list. This is especially important if you have a documented disability and need test accommodations. If you are studying AP independently, call AP Services at the College Board for the name of the local AP coordinator, who will help you through the registration process.

The evening before the exam is not a great time for partying. Nor is it a great time for cramming. If you like, look over class notes or drift through your textbook, but concentrate on the broad outlines, not the small details, of the course. You might also want to skim through this book and read the AP tips. However, the evening before the exam *is* a great time to get your things together for the next day. Sharpen a fistful of no. 2 pencils with good erasers for the multiple-choice section of the test; set out several black or dark-blue ballpoint pens for the free-response questions; bring a watch as no cell phones are allowed in the testing room; get a piece of fruit or a snack bar and a bottle of water for the break; make sure you have your Social Security number and whatever photo identification and admission ticket are required. Then relax. And get a good night's sleep. An extra hour of sleep is more valuable than an extra hour of study.

On the day of the examination, make certain to eat breakfast—fuel for the brain. Studies show that students who eat a hot breakfast before testing get higher grades. Be careful not to drink a lot of liquids, necessitating trips to the bathroom during the test. You need energy to power you through the test—and more. You will spend some time waiting while everyone is seated in the right room for the right test. That's before the test has even begun. Including the brief break and all four parts of the test, the U.S. History exam lasts for over three hours. So be prepared for a long morning. You do not want to be distracted by a growling stomach or hunger pangs.

Be sure to wear comfortable clothes, taking along a sweater in case the heating or air-conditioning is erratic—and by all means wear your lucky socks if you have some.

You have been on the fast track. Now go get a 5.

TAKING THE AP® U.S. HISTORY EXAM

The AP U.S. History exam consists of four parts in two sections. Section 1 includes Parts A and B. Section 1 Part A has 55 multiple-choice questions for which you will have 55 minutes to answer; all questions will be organized into sets of two to five questions that will follow along with a stimulus material (a primary or secondary source). Section 1 Part B consists of four short-answer questions that you will answer in 45 minutes. Section 2 includes its own Part A and Part B. Section 2 Part A contains a document-based question assessing continuity and change over time as well as your ability to apply your understanding of the documents using the historical thinking skills. You will be given 60 minutes to read the documents and answer the question. Section 2 Part B consists of two long-essay questions that focus on the same historical thinking skill as it applies to two time periods; you will choose to respond to one of these in the allotted 35 minutes. Keep an eye on your watch. Watch alarms are not allowed.

The College Board has identified seven themes that run through a U.S. history course: *Identity (ID)*—how American national identity has been shaped, debated, and defined over time; *Work, Exchange, and Technology (WXT)*—how changes in markets, transportation, labor systems, and technology have been debated and what impact they have had in the role of government, the economy, and society; *Peopling (PEO)*—the effects of migrations to, from, and within North America; *Politics and Power (POL)*—the debate and competition among different political and social groups seeking to influence American values and government; *America in the World (WOR)*—the interaction between events in North America/the United States and contemporary developments in the rest of the world; *Environment and Geography, Physical and Human (ENV)*—the impact of the natural environment on the institutions and values of Americans, as well as the impact of political, economic and demographic changes within the United States on the environment itself; *Ideas, Beliefs, and Culture (CUL)*—reasons for and impacts of the changes in moral, philosophical, and cultural values among the people of the United States (and their colonial predecessors). A theme won't appear in every chapter of the textbook, but it will turn up over and over again in the course. For example, American identity evolved throughout the Revolutionary era, during Westward Expansion, in the build-up to and aftermath of the Civil War, as Americans turned toward imperialism, and throughout the twentieth century as America contended with

---

AP® and Advanced Placement Program® are trademarks registered and/or owned by the College Board, which was not involved in the production of, and does not endorse, this product.

conflicts in the wider world. The themes can give you a real assist in writing free-response essays; they provide the big idea, which you support with your historical facts.

STRATEGIES FOR THE MULTIPLE-CHOICE SECTION

Here are some rules of thumb to help you work your way through the multiple-choice questions—your score on this section will make up 40% of your final score:

- **Multiple-Choice Scoring** Each correct answer is worth 1 point; you will not lose points for incorrect answers. Therefore it is worthwhile to answer every question, even if you have to guess. There are four possible answers for each question. If you cannot narrow down the choices at all, you have a 25 percent chance of guessing correctly. If you can eliminate even just one response, it will always improve your chances of guessing correctly. Your best strategy is to go through the entire multiple-choice section, answering all questions to which you know the answers. If you skip a question, be careful to skip that line on the answer sheet as well. Then go back and work on the questions you skipped. Leave yourself enough time to fill in answers—even guesses—on all unanswered items before the time expires.
- **Read the question and stimulus material carefully** Pressured for time, many students make the mistake of reading the questions too quickly or merely skimming them. By reading a question carefully, you may already have some idea about the correct answer. You can then look for it in the responses. Be sure to use the stimulus material to help inform your thoughts as you work through each set of questions, and pay attention to connections among test questions within a set for cues to other questions.
- **Eliminate any answer you know is wrong** You can write on the multiple-choice questions in the test book. As you read through the responses, draw a line through any answer you know is wrong.
- **Read all of the possible answers, then choose the most accurate response** The AP exam is written to test your ability to reason about the document you are given as it relates to your knowledge of history. Sometimes there are a few probable answers but one of them is more specific. For example, a question dealing with the Open Door policy in 1899 may have an answer that seems correct: "It sought to promote U.S. interests overseas." However, there may be an even better answer, one that is more specific to the topic: "To provide the United States access to trade in Asia."
- **Avoid absolute responses** These answers often include the words "always" or "never." For example, the statement "Jefferson always rejected the Hamiltonian economic program" is an overstatement in that Jefferson never attempted to eliminate one of the key features of Hamilton's economic program, the Bank of the United States.

TYPES OF MULTIPLE-CHOICE QUESTIONS

There are various kinds of multiple-choice questions and all will require you to review a primary or secondary source to supplement the question itself. Here are some suggestions for how to approach each kind of stimulus:

CHART/GRAPH QUESTIONS

These questions require you to examine the data on a chart or graph. While these questions are not difficult, spending too much time interpreting a chart or graph may slow you down. To avoid this, first read the question and all of the possible answers so that you know what you are looking for. Before you look at the chart, you may be able to eliminate some obviously incorrect responses. For example:

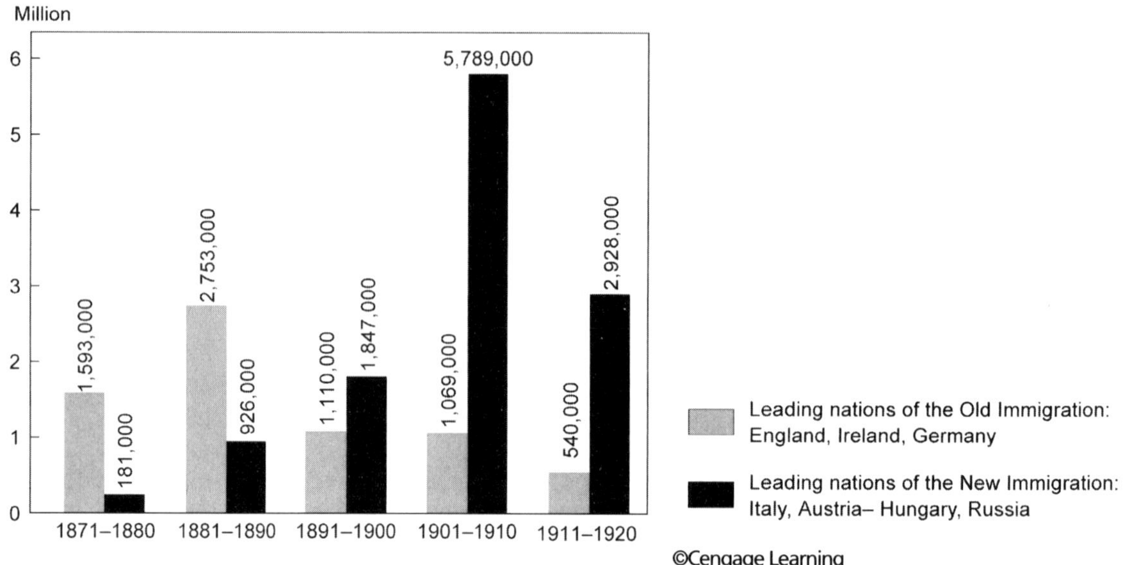

©Cengage Learning

1. Which of the following statements does the table above best support?
   (A) Immigration remained at the same level from 1871 to 1920.
   (B) The period 1871–1880 witnessed the largest immigration of New Immigrants in the late nineteenth century.
   (C) Most immigrants came from Italy and Germany.
   (D) The period 1891–1900 was the first decade in the late nineteenth century in which the number of New Immigrants exceeded the number of Old Immigrants.

ANSWER: **(D)** After analyzing the table, option A can be eliminated because the measurement bars are not level in *any* period. Option B is incorrect because the total number of New Immigrants in 1871–1880 is the lowest of any decade represented. Option C is incorrect in that there is no way to tell from the table what percentage of the immigrants came from a specific country. Option D therefore is correct because the bar for New Immigrants is higher for the first time than the bar for Old Immigrants.

POLITICAL CARTOON QUESTIONS

These questions require you to interpret a political cartoon. Every political cartoon contains symbolism and a point of view. Examine the cartoon before you read the question and possible responses to determine what each part of the drawing represents and to identify the artist's viewpoint. For example:

The Granger Collection, New York

1. What is the viewpoint expressed in the above cartoon?
   (A) The United States rejected the Roosevelt Corollary to the Monroe Doctrine.
   (B) Under Roosevelt the United States allowed European nations to take part in the colonization of South America.
   (C) Roosevelt brought the Caribbean under the control of the United States.
   (D) Roosevelt was protecting the Caribbean nations from U.S. intervention.

ANSWER: (C) Roosevelt actually strengthened the Monroe Doctrine with his Roosevelt Corollary. Therefore A and B are incorrect because one of the primary purposes of the Monroe Doctrine and the Roosevelt Corollary was to prevent European intervention in the Western Hemisphere. Because the United States consistently intervened in South American affairs, answer D is incorrect.

INTERPRETING A MAP

For history students, maps are used to describe not just geography but social and political organization as well. Asked to interpret a map, you can pick up a lot of information just by looking at the key.

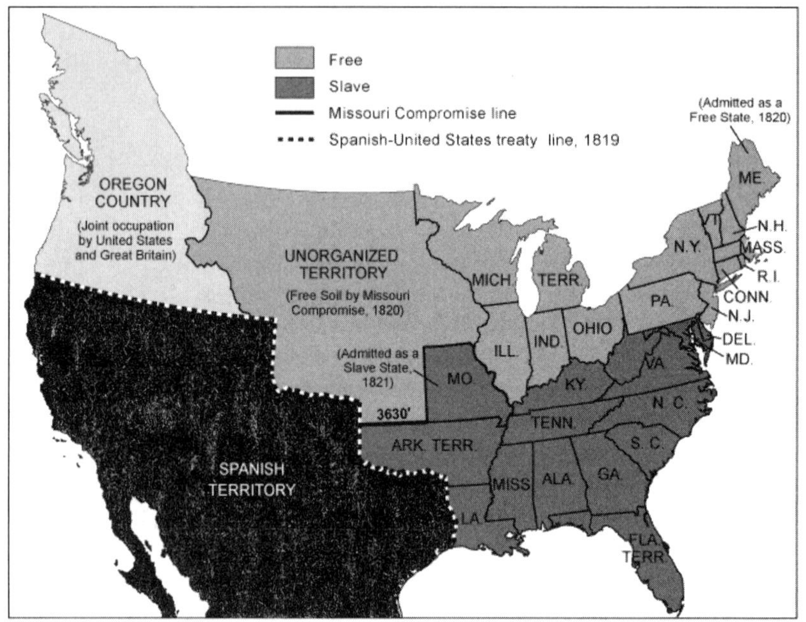

©Cengage Learning

1. The map above shows the United States
   (A) at the end of the Revolutionary War.
   (B) following the end of the Mexican-American War.
   (C) after all of the Eastern Native American tribes had been moved to reservations in the West.
   (D) after the passage of the Missouri Compromise.

ANSWER: **(D)** At the end of the Revolutionary War the United States comprised the thirteen original colonies; therefore answer A is incorrect. B is incorrect for several reasons, foremost being the absence of Texas and the Mexican Cession on the map. There is no information on the map that indicates it has anything to do with Native American removal, thus answer C is incorrect.

INTERPRETING A PRIMARY SOURCE

Primary sources are a historian's best window on the past and should be read carefully. Particularly when dealing with sources from the sixteenth or seventeenth century, be sure that you understand the author's meaning. Give careful consideration to the intended audience and, if you are familiar with the author listed, be aware of their actions, beliefs, and motivations. Take any dates given to help you place the passage in context.

> "While we have land to labor then, let us never wish to see our citizens occupied at a work-bench, or twirling a distaff... For the general operations of manufacture, let our workshops remain in Europe...The

mobs of great cities add just so much to the support of pure government, as sores do to the strength of the human body."

Thomas Jefferson, 1784

1. Which of the following eighteenth-century political debates is most likely the topic of Jefferson's writing?
   (A) whether or not to replace the Articles of Confederation with a stronger central government
   (B) whether or not to declare independence from Britain
   (C) whether or not to involve the federal government in supporting the national economy
   (D) whether or not to allow slaves to work in factories in the South

ANSWER: (C) In this passage, Jefferson is discussing the problems with industrial work, in line with his belief in the virtue of agricultural work. Jefferson believed that there was little desirability in developing an industrial economy such as Britain's. In 1784, the United States was operating under the Articles of Confederation as an independent nation, a stronger national government was not seriously considered until 1787 and even then Jefferson preferred the decentralized government of the Articles; therefore A and B are incorrect. Even by the language of the time ("such persons" held to labor, for example, from the Constitution), no mention is made of slavery in this passage.

INTERPRETING A SECONDARY SOURCE

Secondary sources reveal historian's thoughts about the past, and often present an argument about causes or impacts of historical events. When presented with one (or a pair of sources), first identify the author's argument, then try to contextualize the issue. What era is being discussed? What was happening at that time?

"The function of the ideology of mobility was to supply the citizens of nineteenth century America with a scheme for comprehending and accommodating themselves to a new social and economic order... The defining characteristic of this open society was perfect competitiveness, which guaranteed a complete correspondence between social status and merit...A general acceptance of the mobility ideology by the lower class would have served to integrate workmen into the social order, minimizing discontent and directing it at targets other than the society itself."

—Stephan Thernstrom, *Poverty and Progress: Social Mobility in a Nineteenth Century City* (1964) pp. 58–59

1. Which of the following groups most clearly did not buy into the ideology of mobility that Thernstrom discusses?
   (A) Labor unions
   (B) Industrial leaders
   (C) Urban reformers
   (D) Believers in Social Darwinism

ANSWER: **(A)** Clues about the "new social and economic order," "competitiveness," and "workmen" help reveal that Thernstrom is discussing the industrial changes in the nineteenth century. The argument he is making is, generally, that society was inherently fair and that the best would rise to the top. This was the basic tenet of Social Darwinism, making D incorrect. Of the groups listed, labor unions most clearly disagreed with this idea; they argued, in fact, that the economic system in place unfairly gave benefits to those who owned capital, thus A is correct. Many industrial leaders believed that they were deserving of their wealth because of superior talent (more Social Darwinism, or the Gospel of Wealth), therefore B is incorrect. Urban reformers (early progressives seeking to improve industrial conditions) focused on bettering the lives of those at the bottom of the social ladder rather than debating their ability to improve their station, making C a poor choice.

SHORT-ANSWER QUESTIONS

You are required to write responses to a total of four short-answer question in the provided 45 minutes. Your score on this portion will count for 20 percent of your final score. Each question will consist of two or more parts and at least two of the four questions will contain elements of internal choice, allowing you to demonstrate the knowledge that you know best. Each question will require you to use your knowledge about American history to respond to a stimulus such as a primary or secondary source, a map or image, or a general statement about U.S. history. **You do not need to develop and defend a thesis—however, bulleted answers will automatically receive a zero**. Instead, focus on answering them fully (and in complete sentences) and on including evidence or examples to support your response. The questions are designed to give you the freedom to choose from a wide range of possible examples. This means that you can pick from what you might have studied in-depth in class or what you might have read more about, rather than worrying about knowing one, specific fact or event.

FREE-RESPONSE SECTION II: FREE-RESPONSE QUESTIONS

You are required to write essays for two free-response questions on Part 2 of the United States History examination. Section II Part A presents the Document-Based Question. It is mandatory and will count as 25 percent of your final score. For the DBQ, you are given 60 minutes to read the documents, organize your answer, and write your response. The essay will ask you to use your historical thinking skills in addition to analysis of one or more of the themes of American History. In Section II Part B you will respond to one of two Long-Essay Questions, both of which will focus on the same historical thinking skill as applied to different time periods. You will be asked to choose one question to answer in the given 35 minute time period. Your score on this portion will count for 15 percent of your final score.

The Document-Based Question (DBQ)

The DBQ is considered by many students to be the most complex and challenging component of the AP examination. As its name implies, the DBQ presents you with a wide variety of primary-source information in the form of a series of documents. Primary sources are contemporaneous with a time period or event and include everything from maps, political cartoons, photographs, and illustrations to speeches, essays, books, documentaries, and editorials. Documents will *not* be taken from secondary sources such as textbooks.

All free-response essays require you to utilize your knowledge of the topic, but with the DBQ your essay needs to be grounded on the documents. Your goal is to demonstrate your ability to tease out the thrust and substance of each document, then combine this information with your own general knowledge in an analytical and evaluative essay. The following are necessary for a quality DBQ essay:

- Background—your own knowledge of the topic
- Analysis—your ability to interpret and explain the documents and identify patterns across time periods
- Contextualization—your ability to link your argument to broader historical events and/or processes
- Synthesis—your ability to blend your outside information with the information provided in the documents to explain an issue

There are three DBQs in this book, one in the Diagnostic Test and one in each of the practice tests. In addition, you will find fifteen DBQs at the end of both the fourteenth and fifteenth editions of *The American Pageant*.

Take a look at an abbreviated DBQ, one that contains only four documents for explanation purposes. (You will have the opportunity to practice on full DBQs when you work on the diagnostic and practice tests.)

Question: Using the documents provided and your knowledge of the period, write an answer to the following question:

Analyze the factors that determined the degree of success that labor unions had in securing the goals that American workers desired during the years 1865–1900.

Document A: The Address of the National Labor [Union] Congress to the Working Men of the United States

Andrew C. Cameron, August 1867

The question of all others which at present engrosses the attention of the American workman, and, in fact, the American people, is the proposed reduction of the hours of daily labor and the substitution of the eight- for the ten-hour system. . . . As might have been expected, the employing capitalists, aided by a venal press, have set up a howl of rage and protested the adoption of such [an] innovation. . . .

There are, probably, no organizations upon the nature of which so much ignorance exists, even among workingmen, or against which such persistent and systematic opposition has been urged, as trades unions. . . . [T]heir establishment has been beneficial to the community in general and the working classes in particular. . . .

Source: excerpted from The Annals of America, *Vol. 10*

Document B: The Preamble to "The Constitution of the Knights of Labor," adopted 3 January 1878

[We] submit to the world the objects sought to be accomplished by our organization . . . .

. . . .

2. To secure to the toilers a proper share of wealth they create. . . .

. . . .

6. . . . the adopting of measures providing for the health and safety of those engaged in mining, manufacturing, or building pursuits.

. . . .

11. The prohibition of the employment of children in workshops, mines, and factories. . . .

. . . .

14. The reduction of the hours of labor to eight per day, so that the laborers may have more time for social enjoyment and intellectual improvement. . . .

Source: excerpted from The Annals of America, *Vol. 10*

Document C: Earnings, Expenses and Conditions of Workingmen and Their Families

No. 51 [Family number], Machinist, American [birthplace]

EARNINGS

Of father	$540
Of mother	255
Of son, aged sixteen	255
Total	$1050

CONDITION

Family numbers 10—parents and eight children, five girls and three boys, aged from two to sixteen. Four of the children attend school. Father works only 30 weeks in the year, receives $3 per day for his services. They live in a comfortably furnished house, of 7 rooms, have a piano, take an interest in society and domestic affairs, are intelligent, but do not dress very well. Their expenditures are equal to, but do not exceed their income. Father belongs to trades union, and is interested and benefited by and in it.

FOOD

Breakfast—Bread, meat and coffee.
Dinner—Bread, meat, vegetables and tea.
Supper—Bread, meat, vegetables and coffee.

COST OF LIVING

Rent	$300
Fuel	50
Meat	100
Groceries	200
Clothing	160
Boots and shoes	50
Dry goods	25
Books, papers, etc.	15
Trades union	10
Sickness [insurance]	50
Sundries	90
Total	$1050

No. 112 [Family number], Coal Miner, American [birthplace]

EARNINGS

Of father	$250

CONDITION

Family numbers 7—husband, wife, and five children, three girls and two boys, aged from three to nineteen years. Three of them go to the public school. Family live in 2 room tenement, in healthy locality, for which they pay $6 per month rent. The house is scantily furnished, without carpets, but is kept neat and clean. They are compelled to live very economically, and every cent they earn is used to the best advantage. Father had only thirty weeks work during the past year. He belongs to trades union. The figures for cost of living are actual and there is no doubt the family lived on the amount specified.

FOOD

Breakfast—Bread, coffee and salt meat.
Dinner—Meat, bread, coffee and butter.
Supper—Sausage, bread and coffee.

COST OF LIVING

Rent	$72
Fuel	20
Meat	20
Groceries	60
Clothing	28
Boots and shoes	15
Dry goods	20
Trades union	3
Sickness [insurance]	10
Sundries	5
Total	$253

Source: 1884, Illinois Bureau of Labor Statistics, Third Biennial Report, 1884 (excerpted from Hollitz, Thinking Through the Past, *2nd ed., Boston: Houghton Mifflin Co.)*

Document D: Debs's Claim Is Puerile: Violence the Strikers' Main Reliance to Insure Success

President Debs of the American Railway Union, President Gompers of the American Federation of Labor, and other labor leaders who are responsible for strikes, have repeatedly affirmed that during the present [Pullman] strike and in strikes in the past[,] all violent acts were done by men [who were] not strikers. . . . When several persons were shot by the United States troops, he claimed none of them was a member of the American Railway Union and instanced this fact to prove that the strikers were not the ones who were committing overt acts [of violence] . . . and are not accountable for the bloodshed, arson, destruction of property in other ways, hindrance to business, and other losses which the [state] always suffers when a big strike is in progress.

That the contrary is true is proved beyond cavil [frivolous objection] by reference to the history of every big strike ever ordered in this country. In a railway strike success can only be achieved by the forcible detention of trains . . . , and the forcible detention of trains means rioting, and perhaps bloodshed.

. . . .

It is because Debs and his ilk cannot, and know they cannot, achieve their communistic ends by the ballot or in any other lawful way that they resort to the use of hurled rocks, blows with clubs, shots fired from ambush, and all the other base acts of a relentless and bloodthirsty guerilla warfare.

Source: New York Times, 11 July 1894 (excerpted from the Times *through Proquest, an electronic database)*

Steps in organizing and structuring the DBQ essay:

Step 1: Brainstorm ideas that relate to the question.

Step 2: Consider a structure for your response.

Step 3: Analyze each document. What is the meaning of the document? What or who is the source—the Supreme Court, a presidential candidate, a labor leader, a capitalist? The source provides important clues to the position being put forth in the document. As you analyze the meaning or significance of the document, jot down margin notes—generalizations that relate to the document. For example:

- **Margin note for Document A** Address to the NLU (National Labor Union) in support of the eight-hour day.
- **Margin note for Document B** Extract from the Knights of Labor constitution regarding higher wages, improved working conditions, and a shortened workday.
- **Margin note for Document C** Bureau of Labor Statistics cost-of-living figures for union members equals the amount paid in salary for the machinist, slightly less for the coal miner.
- **Margin note for Document D** Criticism of claim by Eugene Debs, president of the American Railway Union, that acts of violence were not perpetrated by union members and that Debs's union was interfering with the railroads. Suggestion that Debs is communistic.

When you begin to map out your essay, remember that the DBQ calls for a synthesis of the document information and your own knowledge of the topic. With that in mind, start with your own knowledge that the period 1865–1877 was characterized by tensions between labor and the business owners, or capitalists. You will need to point out the conditions—low pay and dangerous work environments—faced by workers. Documents A, B, and C provide the grist for this point; you might note that the sources for Documents A and B were partisan, while the source for Document C was nonpartisan. To assess the level of success for workers in achieving their objectives, you will need to address factors—in this case, obstacles—such as the role played by government in assisting the capitalist class to put down strikes (for example, the Railroad Strike of 1877); the influx of millions of immigrants, which drove down wages; and the methods used by businesses and government to undermine union efforts. As you discuss these features, you should refer to the documents that support your own analysis. For example the degree of success for the American workers in general and unions specifically was in part determined by the attitudes expressed in Document D, which portrays unions as violent. This turned public opinion against labor unions, therefore limiting their success.

AP Tip

Do not wait until you've read the documents to develop your own personal knowledge. Even before reading the documents take a few minutes to brainstorm information that you can recall about the topic. If time permits, organize this information so that you can construct the essay while incorporating the documents into the essay. When the document information is similar to what you have brainstormed, present that knowledge as it is expressed in the documents. Possibly the document material can be used to help you analyze other issues.

STRUCTURE OF A FREE-RESPONSE ESSAY

In writing a free-response essay, whether a DBQ or a general long-essay question, you need the following:

- a well-developed thesis that sums up your perspective
- an effective analysis and appropriate use of information
- a lucidly cogent essay that is well-structured and lucidly written

Below is one model for organizing your thoughts in preparation for writing the free-response and DBQ essays:

Thesis (Opinion)

Supporting Arguments (major reasons, to be developed in the body paragraphs, that defend or support your thesis)

Structured Body Paragraphs

- Topic Sentence
    - supports the thesis
    - introduces the topic of the paragraph

- Historical and Factual Information
  - facts
  - details
  - statistics
  - quotes
- Analysis
  - explains the separate parts of your arguments
  - explains the significance of the information you present as it relates to the thesis

FRAMING THE DEBATE To demonstrate an understanding of the complexity of the issue or question, you need to show that you are aware of both sides of the argument or perspective. This frames the debate for the reader. Thus in the introduction, you want to present the "other" view—the one you are *not* supporting. Make certain, however, that you do not develop the other perspective so fully that the reader is unclear about your thesis. Your objective is to convince the reader that you have a strong thesis and that it is well developed with historical information and analysis.

OUTLINING For each essay in Section II, the AP examination has built in time for you to develop an outline. Time spent on your outlines is important for a number of reasons:

- It prevents you from writing an essay that is unorganized because you begin writing whatever comes into your head at the moment.
- It helps you determine your perspective on the issue. If after completing an outline you realize that your information tends to support one view over the other, then this is the perspective you should develop.
- It provides you with a brief brainstorming opportunity before writing the essay.

Once you have outlined your essay, it is time to put pen to paper. Remember that examination readers are looking for a clear thesis backed up with specifics. Concentrate on setting out accurate information in straightforward, concise prose. You cannot mask vague information with elegant prose.

A LONG-ESSAY QUESTION AND THREE SAMPLE ESSAYS

Having established the ingredients of a free-response answer, let us now look at three essays—one excellent, one good, and one poor. Comments following each essay explain ways in which each essay succeeded or failed. All three essays respond to the following long-essay question that focuses on the skill of Historical Argumentation:

Question: Analyze the extent to which compromise was no longer possible between the North and South by the 1850s.

SAMPLE ESSAY 1

By the time Abraham Lincoln was elected president in 1860, the time for compromise between the North and South had passed. Lincoln's election was the spark that ignited secession. Throughout the antebellum period political leaders had attempted to preserve the Union through compromise and by maintaining the political balance in the Senate. As early as the Constitutional Convention there were indications that the conflicting economies and cultures of the regions would ultimately have to be resolved, either through ongoing political compromise or through war. As late as 1858, just two years before secession, Lincoln had said "a house divided against itself cannot stand." The outbreak of the Civil War was the tragic resolution to the sectional differences and the inability to maintain two different economic, political, and cultural systems under one government.

Territorial expansion played a significant role in straining sectional relations because it involved the debate over the expansion or containment of slavery. In 1820 Congress seemed to have resolved this problem when it passed the Missouri Compromise, which prevented the expansion of slavery north of the 36° 30′ line. For a time, Congress was able to balance representation in the Senate by admitting both a slave state and a free state into the Union. For example, Missouri, a slave state, was admitted at the same time as Maine, a free state.

Compromise could only address the symptoms of the problem; it could not resolve the basic economic, moral, and cultural differences, especially because the two regions had completely different economic systems dominated by opposing dominant social, economic, and political classes: the planter-slaveholder in the South and the industrial capitalist in the North. Economically, Northern manufacturers and the Northern economy required a protective tariff, internal improvements, and a national bank to facilitate commerce, whereas the South wanted low tariffs, state banks, and was opposed to internal improvements. The North's economy and culture rested on the wage-labor system, which was, of course, inconsistent with the South's slave economy and culture. Both sought to expand their systems for a variety of reasons: politically the North and South quarreled over the extension of slavery because the addition of a new slave state or free state meant greater political representation in Congress. This in turn meant that either region, if given the political advantage, could pass legislation that affected not only the future expansion of slavery, but other burning political issues as well, such as the tariff.

Furthermore, the North maintained that the Union had been established as a contract between the people of the United States. Southern political leaders responded that the Union was the result of a compact between the states, and that a state had the authority to nullify federal laws and even secede from the Union. These conflicting political theories made compromise even more difficult to achieve because the South claimed to have the authority to reject any federal law it deemed unconstitutional or a threat to states' rights.

Added to this was the role of Northern abolitionists and Southern defenders of slavery whose justifications for or against the peculiar institution added a moral element to the already significant differences. Thus by the time Congress passed the Kansas-Nebraska Act in 1854 and the Supreme Court handed down the Dred Scott decision in 1857, the possibility of maintaining the Union became increasingly tenuous.

Politically, by the 1850s the two major political parties represented, for the most part, different sections: the Democrats articulated the South's objectives, whereas the Republicans represented an adversarial view. Up until the election of Lincoln, the presidency was occupied either by a Southerner or a Northerner who tended to favor the South's position. Lincoln, a Republican and an advocate of the containment of slavery, represented to the South that the executive branch would now become an obstacle to the South's political objectives, and that its political and economic influence would therefore wane over time. Thus, by the 1850s, conditions for secession were already present, and the time for compromise had, for all intents and purposes, passed.

COMMENT This essay effectively outlines the divisions that prevailed between the North and South in the antebellum period. While it by no means completely addresses the issue, given the time constraint (35 minutes) it successfully indicates that while Lincoln's election was the event that finally shattered the Union, deep social, economic, and political divisions had already been festering for decades. The writer articulates the view that the Civil War was the result of irreconcilable differences that could no longer be resolved through compromise. Although listing the features of the *Dred Scott* case would certainly help, the writer successfully synthesizes selective historical content with effective analysis to support the thesis. (Excellent)

Sample Essay 2

Although there were many disputes, differences, and events that made compromise in the decades before the 1850s very difficult, political leaders such as Clay and Calhoun were able to work out solutions that politically resolved the differences between North and South and therefore prevented secession and war. Unfortunately the nation's political leaders were not up to the task in the 1850s. As early as the Constitutional Convention the Framers developed solutions to sectional problems such as the Three-fifths Compromise and the Assumption Bill. In the early nineteenth century, with tensions high over the attempt to expand or limit the spread of slavery, congressional leaders were able to work out the Missouri Compromise, which defined where slavery could and could not expand. In 1850 the United States could have experienced civil war had not political leaders worked out the Compromise of 1850, which strengthened the Fugitive Slave Act in the South's favor but allowed California to enter as a free state. True, the Dred Scott decision effectively eliminated the Missouri Compromise, but political leaders such as Senator Stephen Douglas could not create compromises that would reduce tensions. Instead, they offered the controversial Kansas-Nebraska Act.

The idea of popular sovereignty made compromise almost impossible because Congress could no longer establish areas where slavery could expand and where it could not. Besides, the Kansas-Nebraska Act further enforced the Fugitive Slave Act, which angered Northerners immensely. The only thing holding the Union together at this point was the hope on the part of the South that it could in the future continue to expand slavery. Lincoln, who was opposed to the expansion of slavery, concerned the South so much that no one in 1860 could find any way to compromise. With Lincoln's election the South seceded. But it didn't have to come to that. The nation's political leaders had failed to do what their predecessors in Congress had been able to achieve: effective compromises.

COMMENT This essay has a clear thesis: the nation's political leaders in the 1850s were responsible for failing to reduce or resolve the sectional tensions through effective compromises that earlier political leaders had accomplished. The writer cites several important political compromises. The scope of this essay could be broader, however, in that the author does not incorporate the role of territorial expansion into the discussion. Further, the discussion is limited in that no clear differences between the sections are established. Thus the essay focuses only on the controversy over the expansion of slavery and not on its economic and political consequences for the sections. It also depicts the Compromise of 1850 as a workable solution that had no subsequent repercussions. In fact the North was outraged by the Fugitive Slave component of the act. There is also a factual error: the Kansas-Nebraska Act did not strengthen the Fugitive Slave Act. An explanation of popular sovereignty would also add to the quality of this essay. Nevertheless, the writer exhibits a good understanding of the topic and uses information that sustains the thesis throughout the essay. (Good)

SAMPLE ESSAY 3

Compromise in the 1850s was impossible because the North and South no longer wanted to negotiate. They believed that only through war would their differences be settled. The Missouri Compromise was more effective than the Kansas-Nebraska Act. It prevented war, whereas the Kansas-Nebraska Act made war more possible. Popular sovereignty was not an effective solution either. Now slavery could spread anywhere and the North would be opposed to this. Lincoln was opposed to the spread of slavery, but he was not willing to break up the Union for it. Therefore a better solution to the problem could not be found. If Lincoln opposed the spread of slavery, what other option did the South have but to leave the Union? Also, the North and South viewed slavery differently. The North opposed it as inhumane, but the South claimed it was an institution that benefited both Southern whites and slaves. Had the Framers at the Constitutional Convention addressed the issue of slavery, future generations would not have to find solutions and compromises to this problem. But even if Congress did work out compromises, such as the

Missouri Compromise, no one could determine what the Supreme Court would do, such as the Dred Scott case. Lincoln's election was not the cause of the war. True, he was a Northerner, but so were other presidents. Put simply, neither the North nor the South favored compromise by the 1850s because they could not resolve their political differences.

COMMENT This essay is weak in a number of areas. While it has a thesis, it is rudimentary; the thesis is not developed in the essay effectively. The writer strings together generalizations that have little connection to one another. Important issues are not explained. For instance the writer contends that the Missouri Compromise was more effective than the Kansas-Nebraska Act but does not explain how or why the former prevented war. This essay lacks focus, analysis, and sufficient historical information to defend the thesis. (Poor)

A Historiographical Approach

One misconception about historical study is that it is merely a string of facts, meaningless dates, and the names of often long-dead individuals, with little relevance to our lives and the times. Nothing could be further from the truth. Historians study the nature of change. To be sure, facts are an integral component of historical study and discourse, but equally important is the meaning we give to historical information. One interesting approach to the study of history is historiography—the interpretation of information. There are two dominant schools of historiography. One historiographic perspective argues that change is the result of consensus among groups, classes, ethnicities, races, and genders that change is needed; strains, divisions, and class interests exist, but they are not fundamental and have not interfered with the process of consensual change. Those who subscribe to this view are called consensus or traditional historians. Other historians, referred to as revisionist or conflict historians, view conflict among groups, classes, ethnicities, races, and genders as fundamental to change, its wellspring. As you become immersed in the study of U.S. history at the Advanced Placement level, filtering the information you learn through the lens of historiographic analysis can make for a richer experience and provide you with the analytical tools to interpret the nature of change. Analyzing, synthesizing, and evaluating the forces that shaped this nation are important aspects of any student's intellectual growth, and they are essential tools for achieving a 5 on the Advanced Placement U.S. History examination when you take it in May.

Thematic Learning Objectives

As indicated earlier, the College Board has identified seven themes, or topics, that can guide our exploration of history. Importantly, they have also identified a series of learning objectives, categorized by theme, to help identify important understandings that they expect students to grasp. As you study U.S. History, refer often to these themes and objectives and ensure that you can offer analysis and factual details for each. On the AP exam, every question will measure your understanding of one of these objectives. To assist you, references to the tested objectives have been included in the answer keys to all multiple-choice questions in this guide.

Identity (ID)

Essential Understanding	In particular, students can...
Students demonstrate understanding of ways that debates over national identity have changed over time.	**ID-1** Analyze how competing conceptions of national identity were expressed in the development of political institutions and cultural values from the late colonial through the antebellum periods.
	ID-2 Assess the impact of Manifest Destiny, territorial expansion, the Civil War, and industrialization on popular beliefs about progress and the national destiny of the United States in the nineteenth Century.
	ID-3 Analyze how U.S. involvement in international crises such as the Spanish-American War, World Wars I and II, the Great Depression, and the Cold War influenced public debates about American national identity in the twentieth century.
Students demonstrate understanding of ways that gender, class, ethnic, religious, regional, and other group identities changed in different eras.	**ID-4** Explain how conceptions of group identity and autonomy emerged out of cultural interactions between colonizing groups, Africans, and American Indians in the colonial era.
	ID-5 Analyze the role of economic, political, social, and ethnic factors on the formation of regional identities in what would become the United States from the colonial period through the nineteenth century.

Essential Understanding	In particular, students can...
	ID-6 Analyze how migration patterns to, and migration within, the United States have influenced the growth of racial and ethnic identities and conflicts over ethnic assimilation and distinctiveness.
	ID-7 Analyze how changes in class identity and gender roles have related to economic, social, and cultural transformations since the late nineteenth century.
	ID-8 Explain how civil rights activism in the twentieth century affected the growth of African American and other identity-based political and social movements.

Work, Exchange, and Technology (WXT)

Essential Understanding	In particular, students can...
Students demonstrate understanding of ways that changes in markets, transportation, and technology have affected American society.	**WXT-1** Explain how patterns of exchanging commodities, peoples, diseases, and ideas around the Atlantic World developed after European contact and shaped North American colonial-era societies.
	WXT-2 Analyze how innovations in markets, transportation, and technology affected the economy and the different regions of North America from the colonial period through the end of the Civil War.
	WXT-3 Explain how changes in transportation, technology, and the integration of the U.S. economy into world markets have influenced U.S. society since the Gilded Age.
Students demonstrate understanding of ways that different labor systems have developed over time.	**WXT-4** Explain the development of labor systems such as slavery, indentured servitude, free labor, and sharecropping from the colonial period through the end of the eighteenth century.
	WXT-5 Explain the development of labor systems that accompanied industrialization since the nineteenth century and how industrialization shaped U.S. society and workers' lives.

Essential Understanding	In particular, students can...
Students demonstrate understanding of debates over economic values and the role of government in the U.S. economy and how these debates affected politics, society, the economy, and the environment.	**WXT-6** Explain how arguments about market capitalism, the growth of corporate power, and government policies influenced economic policies from the late eighteenth century through the early twentieth century.
	WXT-7 Compare the beliefs and strategies of movements advocating changes to the U.S. economic system since industrialization, particularly the organized labor, Populist, and progressive movements.
	WXT-8 Explain how and why the role of the federal government in regulating economic life and the environment has changed since the end of the nineteenth century.

Peopling (PEO)

Essential Understanding	In particular, students can...
Students demonstrate understanding of why people have migrated to, from, and within North America.	**PEO-1** Explain how and why people moved within the Americas (before contact) and to and within the Americas (after contact and colonization).
	PEO-2 Explain how changes in the numbers and sources of international migrants in the nineteenth and twentieth centuries altered the ethnic and social makeup of the U.S. population.
	PEO-3 Analyze the causes and effects of major internal migration patterns such as urbanization, suburbanization, westward movement, and the Great Migration in the nineteenth and twentieth centuries.
Students demonstrate understanding of how changes in migration and population patterns have affected American life.	**PEO-4** Analyze the effects that migration, disease, and warfare had on the American Indian population after contact with Europeans.
	PEO-5 Explain how free and forced migration to and within different parts of North America caused regional development, cultural diversity and blending, and political and social conflicts through the nineteenth century.

Essential Understanding	In particular, students can...
	PEO-6 Analyze the role of both internal and international migration on changes to urban life, cultural developments, labor issues, and reform movements from the mid-nineteenth century through the mid-twentieth century.
	PEO-7 Explain how and why debates over immigration to the United States have changed since the turn of the twentieth century.

Politics and Power (POL)

Essential Understanding	In particular, students can...
Students demonstrate understanding of how different political and social groups competed for influence over society and government in colonial North America and the United States.	**POL-1** Analyze the factors behind competition, cooperation, and conflict among different societies and social groups in North America during the colonial period.
	POL-2 Explain how and why major party systems and political alignments arose and have changed from the early Republic through the end of the twentieth century.
	POL-3 Explain how activist groups and reform movements, such as antebellum reformers, civil rights activists, and social conservatives, have caused changes to state institutions and U.S. society.
	POL-4 Analyze how and why the New Deal, the Great Society, and the modern conservative movement all sought to change the federal government's role in U.S. political, social, and economic life.
Students demonstrate understanding of how Americans have agreed on or argued over the values that guide the political system, as well as who is a part of the political process.	**POL-5** Analyze how arguments over the meaning and interpretation of the Constitution have affected U.S. politics since 1787.
	POL-6 Analyze how debates over political values (such as democracy, freedom, and citizenship) and the extension of American ideals abroad contributed to the ideological clashes and military conflicts of the nineteenth century and the early twentieth century.
	POL-7 Analyze how debates over civil rights and civil liberties have influenced political life from the early twentieth century through the early twenty-first century.

America in the World (WOR)

Essential Understanding	In particular, students can...
Students demonstrate understanding of the relationship among events in North America and the United States and contemporary events in the rest of the world.	**WOR-1** Explain how imperial competition and the exchange of commodities on both sides of the Atlantic Ocean influenced the origins and patterns of development of North American societies in the colonial period.
	WOR-2 Explain how the exchange of ideas among different parts of the Atlantic World shaped the belief systems and independence movements into the early nineteenth century.
	WOR-3 Explain how the growing interconnection of the U.S. with worldwide economic, labor, and migration systems affected U.S. society since the late nineteenth century.
	WOR-4 Explain how the U.S. involvement in global conflicts in the twentieth century set the stage for domestic social changes.
Students demonstrate understanding of how different factors have influenced U.S. military, diplomatic, and economic involvement in international affairs and foreign conflicts, both in North America and overseas.	**WOR-5** Analyze the motives behind, and results of, economic, military, and diplomatic initiatives aimed at expanding U.S. power and territory in the Western Hemisphere in the years between independence and the Civil War.
	WOR-6 Analyze the major aspects of domestic debates over U.S. expansionism in the nineteenth century and the early twentieth century.
	WOR-7 Analyze the goals of U.S. policymakers in major international conflicts, such as the Spanish-American War, World Wars I and II, and the Cold War, and explain how U.S. involvement in these conflicts has altered the U.S. role in world affairs.
	WOR-8 Explain how U.S. military and economic involvement in the developing world and issues such as terrorism and economic globalization have changed U.S. foreign policy goals since the middle of the twentieth century.

Environment and Geography—Physical and Human (ENV)

Essential Understanding	In particular, students can...
Students demonstrate understanding of the various ways in which interactions with the natural environment shaped the institutions and values of various groups living in North America from prior to European contact through the Civil War.	**ENV-1** Explain how the introduction of new plants, animals, and technologies altered the natural environment of North America and affected interactions among various groups in the colonial period.
	ENV-2 Explain how the natural environment contributed to the development of distinct regional group identities, institutions, and conflicts in the precontact period through the independence period.
	ENV-3 Analyze the role of environmental factors in contributing to regional economic and political identities in the nineteenth century, and how they affected conflicts such as the American Revolution and the Civil War.
Students demonstrate understanding of how economic and demographic changes affected the environment and led to debates over use and control of the environment and natural resources.	**ENV-4** Analyze how the search for economic resources affected social and political developments from the colonial period through Reconstruction.
	ENV-5 Explain how and why debates about policies concerning the use of natural resources and the environment more generally have changed since the late nineteenth century.

Ideas, Beliefs, and Culture (CUL)

Essential Understanding	In particular, students can...
Students demonstrate understanding of how and why moral, philosophical, and cultural values changed in what would become the United States.	**CUL-1** Compare the cultural values and attitudes of different European, African American, and Native peoples in the colonial period and explain how contact affected intergroup relationships and conflicts.
	CUL-2 Analyze how emerging conceptions of national identity and democratic ideals shaped value systems, gender roles, and cultural movements in the late eighteenth century and the nineteenth century.
	CUL-3 Explain how cultural values and artistic expression changed in response to the Civil War and the postwar industrialization of the United States.

Essential Understanding	In particular, students can...
Students demonstrate understanding of how and why changes in moral, philosophical, and cultural values affected U.S. history.	**CUL-4** Analyze how changing religious ideals, Enlightenment beliefs, and republican thought shaped the politics, culture, and society of the colonial era through the early Republic.
	CUL-5 Analyze ways that philosophical, moral, and scientific ideas were used to defend and challenge the dominant economic and social order in the nineteenth and twentieth centuries.
	CUL-6 Analyze the role of culture and the arts in the nineteenth- and twentieth-century movements for social and political change.
	CUL-7 Explain how and why "modern" cultural values and popular culture have grown since the early twentieth century and how they have affected American politics and society.

A Diagnostic Test

The purpose of this diagnostic test is to provide you with an indication of how well you will perform on the AP U.S. History examination. Keep in mind that the exam changes every year, so it is not possible to predict your score with certainty. For this diagnostic exam, the questions are organized by historical periods, with each represented by one or two sets of questions. You can thus identify which periods to concentrate on when preparing for the AP exam.

AP UNITED STATES HISTORY EXAMINATION
Section I
Part A: Multiple-Choice Questions
Time—55 minutes
Number of Questions—55

Directions Each question below is part of a set of 2–5 questions that focus on a primary source, secondary source, or other historical issue. Each individual question has four possible answers. For each question, select the best response.

Questions 1–3 refer to the following diagram.

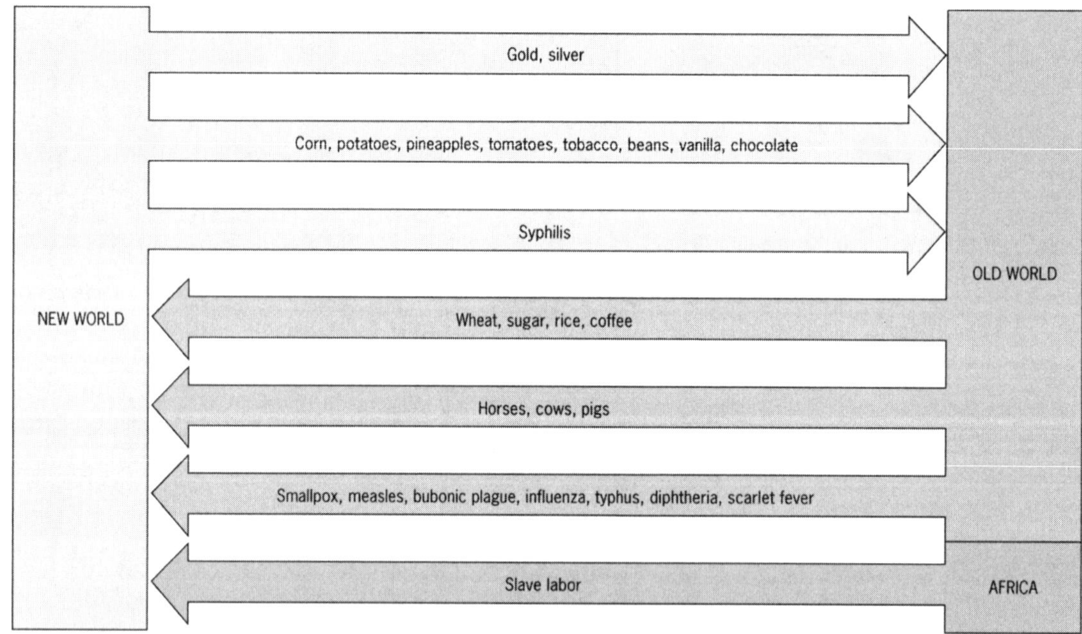

Cengage Learning

1. Which of the following statements best explains one of the changes that occurred as a result of the phenomenon depicted in the diagram?
   (A) Violent conflict emerged between European explorers and the Native Americans, who they perceived as racially and culturally inferior.
   (B) The rise of the slave trade in the Caribbean supplied forced labor to conquering Europeans in the wake of the near annihilation of

Native populations as a result of disease.
(C) Improved economic and political stability in Europe paved the way for more rapid exploration and settlement of the New World.
(D) In search of power and profit for themselves and their nation, conquering European explorers laid waste to large parts of Central and South America, disrupting long-standing civilizations.

2. Which of the following events was most directly caused by the phenomenon depicted in the diagram?
(A) The development of the *encomienda* system
(B) The spread of Christianity across the Americas
(C) The intermarriage of Spanish conquerors with Native women
(D) The rise of capitalism among European nations

3. Which of the following most accurately describes the impact in Europe of the phenomenon depicted in the diagram?
(A) Economic connections reduced imperial competition.
(B) The rise of the slave trade led reformers to challenge the government.
(C) The arrival of new goods allowed for population growth.
(D) New diseases caused social unrest and instability.

Questions 4–6 refer to the following quotations.

"...for having protected, favored, and emboldened the Indians against His Majesty's loyal subjects, never contriving, requiring, or appointing any due or proper means of satisfaction for their many invasions, robberies, and murders committed upon us."

Declaration of Nathaniel Bacon, leader of a rebellion of freemen (former indentured servants) against Royal Governor William Berkeley (1676)

"I have lived thirty-four years amongst you [Virginians], as uncorrupt and diligent as ever [a] Governor was, [while] Bacon is a man of two years amongst you, his person and qualities unknown to most of you, and to all men else, by any virtuous act that ever I heard of...I will take counsel of wiser men than myself, but Mr. Bacon has none about him but the lowest of the people."

Response of Governor William Berkeley to news of the grievances of Nathaniel Bacon (1676)

4. Which of the following best explains the role of Native Americans in the conflict at the heart of Bacon's Rebellion and other flare-ups among colonial settlers?
(A) Faced with dwindling resources and violent, discriminatory actions by colonists, Native Americans often raided border settlements.
(B) Native Americans fought on the side of the colonists against royal authorities.
(C) Native Americans often allied and intermarried with British colonial settlers, forcing the British government to ban the practice out of fear and racial prejudice.
(D) The threat of a Native American-Slave alliance in the southern colonies increased tensions among white settlers.

5. Which of these major developments was caused in part by conflicts between former indentured servants and the landed gentry?
(A) The rise in the regulation of trade among the colonies
(B) Uprisings by confederations of Native Americans against the colonists
(C) An increase in the importation of enslaved African laborers
(D) A general movement towards support of Republicanism

GO ON TO NEXT PAGE

6. In which of the colonial regions was indentured servitude a major source of labor in the seventeenth century?
   (A) The New England colonies (like Massachusetts Bay)
   (B) The Chesapeake Bay and Middle colonies (like Virginia)
   (C) The southern colonies (like South Carolina)
   (D) The British West Indies (like Barbados)

Questions 7–9 refer to the following map.

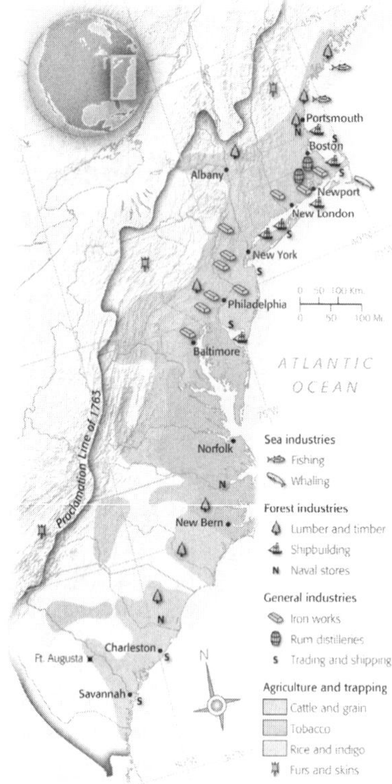

Cengage Learning

7. Which of the following helped to counteract the great diversity among the British colonies apparent in this map?
   (A) The slow but steady rise of manufacturing
   (B) The rapid increase in the use of chattel slavery
   (C) The arrival of religious dissidents seeking a haven from persecution
   (D) The growth of cultural movements steeped in religion and education

8. Which of the following conclusions can best be drawn from the map's depiction of the development of the colonial economy?
   (A) The British colonies were of significant economic value to Great Britain.
   (B) The British colonies had quickly developed a sense of nationalism based on their productivity.
   (C) Very early, the British colonies worked to establish their own manufacturing centers as a means of self-sufficiency.
   (D) Trade with the West Indies helped to support the fledgling economy of the British colonies.

9. The British issue of the Proclamation of 1763, as depicted in the map, sought to prevent colonial expansion west of that point. What motivated the British to make such an assertion?
   (A) Their desire to increase colonial productivity
   (B) An open hostility towards settlers of the west, who tended to harbor resentment towards the Crown
   (C) A desire to consolidate imperial control and limit further conflict with the Native Americans
   (D) The slow growth of the colonial population

Questions 10–12 refer to the following cartoon.

The Print Collection, Lewis Walpole Library, Yale University

Britain is symbolized as a lady of fashion; her rebellious daughter, America, as an Indian princess. Their shields of Obedience and Liberty seem mutually exclusive standards.

10. Which of the following events most likely inspired the sentiment of this 1776 cartoon?
    (A) The passage of the Coercive (or Intolerable) Acts to punish Boston colonists for damage done in acts of protest against new duties on tea
    (B) The levying of direct taxes to help pay debts from the Seven Years (French and Indian) War and provide for British defense of the colonies
    (C) The establishment of colonial assemblies under royally appointed governors
    (D) The formation of committees of correspondence to broadcast grievances of the colonists against the British throughout the North American colonies

11. Which of the following most strongly influenced the development of the American ideology expressed in this cartoon?
    (A) The French Revolution
    (B) The Enlightenment
    (C) The Seven Years' War
    (D) Conflict with the Native Americans

12. The conflict between ideals depicted in the cartoon is also apparent in which of the following?
    (A) The conflict between abolitionists and Southerners over the morality of slavery
    (B) The debate over the powers of the national government to enforce laws that seemed to benefit one group over others
    (C) The clash between Federalists and Anti-federalists over the desirability of a stronger central government
    (D) The continued clash between Western settlers and British troops, whose presence was seen as a violation of American independence

Questions 13–15 refer to the following two documents.

"Be it enacted . . ., That if any person shall write, print, utter. Or publish ...any false, scandalous and malicious writing or writings against the government of the United States, or either house of the Congress of the United States, or the President of the United States, with intent to defame the said government... or to bring them... into contempt or disrepute; or to excite against them...the hatred of the good people of the United States... or to resist, oppose, or defeat any such law or act, or to aid, encourage or abet any hostile designs of any foreign nation against the United States...then such person, being thereof convicted before any court of the United States having jurisdiction thereof, shall be punished by a fine not exceeding two thousand dollars, and by imprisonment not exceeding two years."

The Sedition Act of 1798

"RESOLVED, ...That the General Assembly [of Virginia] doth particularly protest against the palpable and alarming infractions of the Constitution, in the two late cases of the "Alien and Sedition Acts" passed at the last session of Congress; the first of which exercises a power no where delegated to the federal government...and the other of which acts, exercises in like manner, a power not delegated by the

GO ON TO NEXT PAGE

constitution, but on the contrary, expressly and positively forbidden by one of the amendments thereto;_a power, which more than any other, ought to produce universal alarm, because it is levelled against that right of freely examining public characters and measures, and of free communication among the people thereon, which has ever been justly deemed, the only effectual guardian of every other right. ...the General Assembly doth solemenly appeal to the like dispositions of the other states, in confidence that they will concur with this commonwealth in declaring, as it does hereby declare, that the acts aforesaid, are unconstitutional..."

James Madison, Virginia Resolution (1798)

13. The national debate over the Alien and Sedition Acts of 1798, as highlighted by James Madison's response, most directly reflects which of the following enduring controversies in United States history
    (A) Debates about the nature of federalism
    (B) Debates about the role of the national government in the economy
    (C) Debates about the nature of American involvement in foreign affairs
    (D) Debates about the application of the Bill of Rights to the states

14. Which of the following best explains the direct impact of this and similar debates during the presidencies of Washington and Adams?
    (A) The development of a political consensus and a long period of national unity
    (B) The adoption of a secessionist doctrine by many states
    (C) The rise of competing political parties
    (D) The shift in power from the political elites to the "common man"

15. Which of the following political controversies of the twentieth century most closely mirrors the debate over the Alien and Sedition Acts of 1798?
    (A) The scandal that erupted over charges of corruption during the Republican administrations of the 1920s
    (B) The outcry over the limitations of civil liberties during World War I
    (C) The public protest over American foreign policy decisions related to the conflict in Vietnam
    (D) The deep divisions that emerged over attempts at integration during the 1950s and 1960s

Questions 16–19 refer to the following quotation.

"[The laws of our national government], when made in pursuance of the Constitution, form the supreme law of the land... Although, among the enumerated powers of Government, we do not find the word "bank" or "incorporation," we find the great powers, to lay and collect taxes; to borrow money; to regulate commerce; to declare and conduct a war; and to raise and support armies and navies. ... it may with great reason be contended that a Government entrusted with such ample powers, ... must also be entrusted with ample means for their execution.

...The power to tax involves the power to destroy [therefore, such a tax]... on the operations of the [national] bank... must be unconstitutional."

McCulloch v. *Maryland* (1819)

Majority Opinion of the Supreme Court delivered by Chief Justice John Marshall, addressing the Constitutionality of the National Bank and of a tax levied by Maryland upon the bank

16. Which of the following groups would be most likely to support the perspective offered by Chief Justice Marshall in this opinion?
    (A) Members of the Democratic-Republican Party (of Thomas Jefferson)
    (B) Members of the Democratic Party (of Andrew Jackson)

(C) Members of the Radical Republican Party (of Thaddeus Stevens)
(D) Members of the Federalist Party (of Alexander Hamilton)

17. Which of the following best explains the ideology used by Marshall in this decision?
(A) Preservation of states' rights in the face of a growing federal government is the most important end of the Court.
(B) A narrow interpretation of the Constitution is necessary to protect liberty and avoid the tyranny of the national government.
(C) Federal power must be expanded into every possible outlet in order to build up the prestige of the nation.
(D) Created by the people through the Constitution, the federal government must be able to exercise its power to maintain the nation.

18. What rationale was given in support of the nation's charter of a national bank, the object at the center of the controversy here addressed?
(A) Unification and added efficiency for the national economy
(B) Protection of the interests of the land and factory owners
(C) Favorable conditions for increased international trade
(D) Limitation of the power of the British commercial interests

19. Although the Bank's constitutionality was upheld in *McCulloch* v. *Maryland*, the Second Bank of the United States was later dissolved by Andrew Jackson amidst great popular support because
(A) it negatively affected the nation's manufacturers.
(B) it made credit too widely available.
(C) it had become a place for spoils-system appointments.
(D) it was seen as a regional and elite interest.

Questions 20–24 refer to the following quotation.

> *"Have not results in Mexico taught the invincibility of American arms?...The North Americans will spread out far beyond their present bounds. They will encroach again and again upon their neighbors. New territories will be planted, declare their independence, and be annexed. We have New Mexico and California! We will have Old Mexico and Cuba! The isthmus cannot arrest--nor even the Saint Lawrence!! Time has all of this in her womb. A hundred states will grow up where now exists but thirty."*
>
> DeBow's *Commercial Review,* 1848

20. Which of the following ideas from the mid-nineteenth century is best reflected in the sentiments expressed by the *Commercial Review?*
(A) Nationalist fervor for the continued expansion of the United States
(B) Agitation for war based on the assumed racial inferiority of opposing groups
(C) Nativist campaigning against the assimilation of new groups
(D) Abolitionist rhetoric supporting the exclusion of slavery from all new territories

21. Which of the following debates made the most significant impact on national politics during the expansionism of the 1840s and 1850s?
(A) How best to assimilate the Mexican people into American culture
(B) Whether federal funds should pay for the development of infrastructure in new territories
(C) Which of the many contested territories ought to be sought after by the United States
(D) Whether slavery ought to be allowed in territory taken via conquest

GO ON TO NEXT PAGE

22. Amidst a desire to acquire territory for new resources and land to settle, many Americans felt that
   (A) American claims against Mexico and Britain made likely the diplomatic transfer of territory in the West and Southwest.
   (B) American settlements in the West were so vast by 1848 that no other nation could legitimately claim the land.
   (C) American cultural superiority made the nation's triumph over Mexico inevitable.
   (D) the nation's future lay in the expansion of agriculture, which could only be done in the West.

23. One of the groups least likely to agree with the jubilant tone of the passage above was
   (A) white Southern planters who desired the extension of their way of life.
   (B) Western Democrats who sought to expand their influence.
   (C) the Californios and Native Americans who inhabited the territory.
   (D) urban industrialists who prioritized developing new markets.

24. Chief among the benefits of expansionism in the mid-nineteenth century was
   (A) the acquisition of valuable new resources.
   (B) relieving the extreme population pressures faced by eastern cities.
   (C) the addition of several new states to the union.
   (D) the assimilation of new groups into the American identity.

Questions 25–28 refer to the following quotation.

"Many people in both North and South sometimes faltered in the face of the war's terrible cost in lives and resources. But...the war continued four long years, ending only when Southern resources and Confederate armies had been so eviscerated that they were no longer capable of fighting. ...Both sides were willing to sustain such punishment and keep fighting because the stakes were so great: nationality and freedom. If the Confederacy lost the war, a clerk in the Confederate War Department declared in 1863...[they would] "lose their property, country, freedom, everything..." But [Northerners]... believed [that if they were defeated] they would no longer have a country worthy of the name."

James McPherson, *The Civil War Remembered* (2012)

25. Which of the following pre-War developments led Southerners to believe that defeat would result in the loss of "everything"?
   (A) Booming cotton prices due to the growth of the textile industry
   (B) Population growth in Northern, industrial cities
   (C) The victory of an anti-slavery party at the national level
   (D) Opposition in the North to the annexation of Texas

26. Which of the following best explains the Union's eventual victory in the Civil War?
   (A) The Union's superior military leadership
   (B) The lack of opposition to the war effort in the Union
   (C) The Union's superior economic and demographic resources
   (D) The Union's diplomatic victory in securing the support of the British and French

27. Which of the following resulted from the ideological conflict of the Civil War?
   (A) A universal rejection of slavery as an institution
   (B) A unification of the economic interests of North and South
   (C) A balanced, political approach to Reconstruction based on mutual respect
   (D) An acceptance of the supremacy of federal law and a rejection of secession

28. Before resorting to war, which of the following remedies was tried in attempting to mediate the conflict between North and South?

(A) Commitment to the bounds of "slave" and "free" territory as set forth by the national legislature
(B) Allowing free blacks to enjoy the rights of citizenship
(C) The passage of a stronger law requiring the return of fugitive slaves to their masters
(D) Resolutions passed in both the Whig and Democratic parties taking strong positions on the issue of slavery

Questions 29–30 refer to the following quotation.

This is a free country, we are told -- every man has a vote and every man has a chance. ...The inequalities in condition result from the inequalities of human nature...This, in substance, is the teaching which we constantly hear. It is accepted by some because it is flattering to their vanity,... by others, because it is dinned into their ears ... [And yet] the head of one of the largest manufacturing firms in the United States said to me recently, 'It is not on our ordinary business that we make our money; it is where we can get a monopoly.' And this, I think, is generally true.

I am not ...seeking... to excite envy and hatred; but if we would get a clear understanding of social problems, we must recognize the fact that it is due to monopolies which we permit and create...that some men are enabled to get so enormously rich while others remain so miserably poor

Henry George, *Social Problems* (1883) pp. 68, 71, 78

29. Which of the following individuals would most likely agree with the sentiments expressed by George?
(A) A leading capitalist
(B) A reformer fighting for better urban conditions
(C) A labor union organizer
(D) An immigrant from eastern Europe

30. Which of the following Gilded Age policies attempted to mitigate the problems described by George?
(A) Regulation of the railroad companies
(B) Raising the tariff
(C) Maintenance of the gold standard
(D) Civil-service laws like the Pendleton Act

Questions 31–33 refer to the following quotation.

"The great common people of this country are slaves, and monopoly is the master. The West and South are bound and prostrate before the manufacturing East.

The parties lie to us and the political speakers mislead us. We were told two years ago to go to work and raise a big crop...and what came of it? Eight-cent corn, ten-cent oats, two-cent beef, and no price at all for butter and eggs...

We want money, land, and transportation. We want the abolition of the national banks, and we want the power to make loans direct from the government. We want the accursed foreclosure system wiped out."

Mary E. Lease, lawyer, speech (1890)

31. Which of the following best explains the cause of some of the farmers' problems listed here?
(A) Conservationism and protectionism
(B) Union organization
(C) Racism and the sharecropping system
(D) Industrialization and mechanization

32. Which of the following groups formed in response to the problems described by Lease?
(A) Social Darwinists
(B) The Populists
(C) Suffragists
(D) The progressives

33. The ideas expressed in the passage reflect which of the following continuities in United States history?
(A) Conflict over corporate influence in government
(B) Conflict between agrarian and industrial interests
(C) Conflict about the role of the national government in the economy
(D) Conflict over federal responsibility for social welfare

GO ON TO NEXT PAGE

Questions 34–38 refer to the following graph.

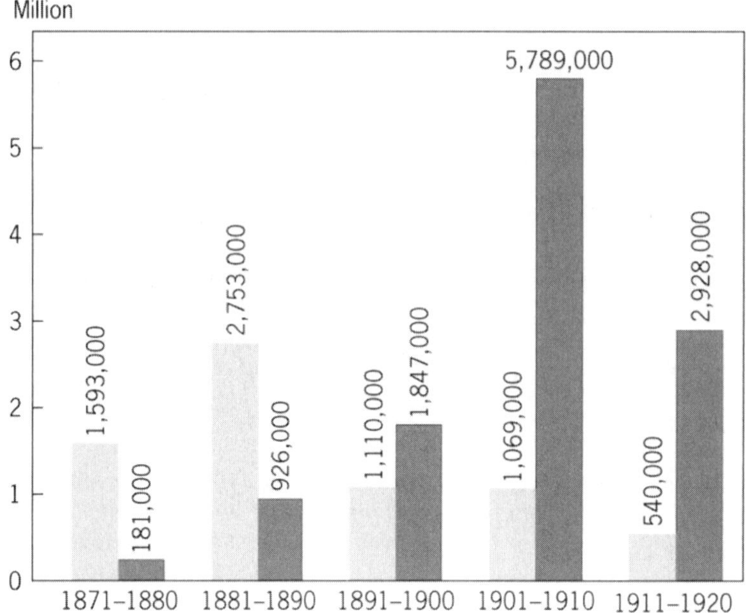

Cengage Learning

34. Which of the following best explains the growth of immigration to the United States as seen between 1871 and 1920?
   (A) A well-known warmth and openness in America towards immigrants
   (B) The steady growth of industry in the United States
   (C) Warfare throughout the European continent
   (D) The abolition of slavery in the years following the Civil War

35. The trend revealed in this graph helps to explain the rise in America of feelings of
   (A) nativism.
   (B) abolitionism.
   (C) socialism.
   (D) isolationism.

36. All of the following are true of the experiences of immigrants to the United States during the period between 1871 and 1920 EXCEPT
   (A) immigrants often found themselves living in ethnic enclaves, deep in the slums of Eastern cities.
   (B) despite discrimination, immigrants found significant economic opportunities available to them in both urban factories and Western settlements.
   (C) in the face of nativist pressure, most immigrants worked quickly to assimilate and abandoned all ties with their native cultures.
   (D) largely due to their very numbers, most immigrants found work in very low-paying, low-skilled industries.

37. Which of the following groups' experiences were most unlike those of immigrants to America during this time period?
    (A) Working-class women
    (B) Urban blacks
    (C) Union organizers
    (D) Low-level government employees

38. Which of the following resulted from tensions surrounding immigration in both the Gilded Age and the Roaring Twenties?
    (A) Laws were passed excluding or greatly reducing the number of immigrants from "undesirable" groups.
    (B) Fear of socialist influences led to violence against various immigrant groups.
    (C) New homesteading provisions were made to encourage a reduction in the number of immigrants concentrated in cities.
    (D) Legal provisions were made to protect the political rights of immigrants.

Questions 39–41 refer to the following quotation.

> *"...Nearly all are agreed that private enterprise in times such as these cannot be left without assistance and without reasonable safeguards lest it destroy not only itself but also our processes of civilization. The underlying necessity for such activity is indeed as strong now as it was years ago when Elihu Root said...*
>
> *'Instead of the give and take of free individual contract, the tremendous power of organization has combined great aggregations of capital in enormous industrial establishments... so great in the mass that each individual concerned in them is quite helpless by himself. ... And in many directions, the intervention of that organized control which we call government seems necessary to produce the same result of justice and right conduct ...'"*
>
> Franklin D. Roosevelt, Fireside Chat (September 30, 1934)

39. Which of the following movements from American history most directly inspired the sentiments offered here by President Franklin Roosevelt?
    (A) The work of the progressives to address the problems brought on by the new industrial order of the 1890s
    (B) The work of the abolitionists to combat the great evil of slavery that was defended in the South on an economic basis
    (C) The work of the suffragists to expand the vote by national amendment, after the failure of a state-by-state approach
    (D) The work of the Federalists to expand the powers of the national government in order to reduce divisions among states

40. Which of the following groups would most likely have disagreed with Roosevelt's approach?
    (A) African American industrial workers concerned with unemployment
    (B) Western farmers concerned with plummeting prices
    (C) Eastern capitalists concerned with the national debt
    (D) Immigrant families concerned with protecting their meager savings

41. One of the most significant results of the New Deal as advocated by Roosevelt here was...
    (A) long-term political re-alignment among class-based and racial groups.
    (B) an aversion towards social welfare spending among the vast majority of American voters.
    (C) a quick end to the economic catastrophe of the Great Depression.
    (D) unprecedented levels of regional stability and a decline in internal migration.

GO ON TO NEXT PAGE

Questions 42–44 refer to the following image.

Library of Congress

42. Which of the following events most directly contradicts the ideas presented by Rockwell's poster?
    (A) African American's "Great Migration"
    (B) American movement away from neutrality in the 1930s
    (C) Anti-strike laws passed to govern wartime union activity
    (D) Use of the atom bomb in 1945

43. Which of the following generalizations best represents the assertion of Rockwell's poster as it applies to American rhetoric surrounding its involvement in conflicts from the Spanish-American War, the Great War, and World War II?
    (A) Americans fight to preserve liberty and democracy.
    (B) The United States fights only to defend itself from an attack.
    (C) America always fights to overthrow colonialism.
    (D) America never gets involved in a fight it cannot win.

44. Which of the following groups struggled to attain another kind of freedom during their wartime experiences?
    (A) Women seeking roles in the armed forces
    (B) African American workers seeking war jobs
    (C) Mexican immigrants seeking admission to the United States
    (D) Japanese Americans seeking to protect property rights

Questions 45–47 refer to the following quotation.

"It was also inevitable that the policy of containment would develop a political-military dimension...President Truman had already applied the principles of containment to Latin America. The Rio Pact, signed in September 1947, provided that "an armed attack by any State shall be considered as an attack against all the American States and, consequently, each one of the said Contracting Parties undertakes to assist in meeting the attack." Collective security was invoked again in the North Atlantic Treaty. Signed in Washington in April 1949, it created the North Atlantic Treaty Organization (NATO)...[which] formally marked the end of George Washington's policy of no entangling alliances. Economic assistance and collective defense agreements became the bulwark of Western containment policy."

"Containment and the Collective Defense," US Department of State, Office of the Historian (2013)

45. Which of the following actions of the United States follows most closely from the perspective offered by the U.S. Department of State?
(A) The division of Germany between the Soviets, the British, the French, and the Americans following World War II
(B) The establishment of alliances and trade agreements among the newly independent Middle Eastern countries
(C) The involvement of American military forces in support of the Republic of Korea (South Korea) in 1950
(D) The development of the hydrogen bomb and the continued testing of nuclear weapons

46. Which of the following features of American Cold War policy most strongly led many to question whether America was truly fighting to protect democracy and freedom?
(A) American financial aid to European nations ravaged by war
(B) United States support of anti-communist military dictatorships in Latin America
(C) American leadership in the creation of the North Atlantic Treaty Organization, uniting Western powers
(D) President Nixon's attempts to restrain the conflict of the Cold War through periods of détente

47. Based on the passage above, American foreign policy served most directly to
(A) inflame conflict with the Soviets to the point of war
(B) undermine civil liberties in the United States
(C) solidify the American desire for isolationism
(D) bolster smaller democracies around the world

Questions 48–50 refer to the following quotation.

"For better or for worse, your generation has been appointed, by history, to deal with those problems and to lead America toward a new age... So will you join in the battle to give every citizen the full equality which God enjoins and the law requires, whatever his belief, or race, or the color of his skin? Will you join in the battle to give every citizen an escape from the crushing weight of poverty? Will you join in the battle to make it possible for all nations to live in enduring peace as neighbors and not as mortal enemies?... There are those timid souls that say this battle cannot be won; ...I do not agree. We have the power to shape the civilization that we want..."

Lyndon B. Johnson, Speech at the University of Michigan (1964)

48. Which of the following government actions followed directly from the ideology put forth by President Johnson?
(A) Expanded American involvement in the conflict in Vietnam
(B) The growth of the conservative movement
(C) Passage of legislation under the Great Society
(D) Significant migration into the Sun Belt

49. Which of the following movements helped to spark the activism proposed by Johnson here?
(A) The civil rights movement
(B) The anti-war movement
(C) The women's liberation movement
(D) The anti-communist movement

50. Which of the following movements in American history most closely parallels the call to action here issued by Johnson?
(A) The labor movement of the 1890s
(B) The progressive movement of the 1900s
(C) The abolition movement of the 1850s
(D) The temperance movement of the 1880s

GO ON TO NEXT PAGE

Questions 51–53 refer to the following political cartoon.

Jim Borgman. Reprinted with permission of Universal Press Syndicate. All rights reserved.

51. Which of the following best explains the growth of the power of conservatives in the 1980s?
    (A) Increasing confidence in the effectiveness of the national government
    (B) A decline in political participation among evangelical Christians
    (C) Strong economic performance, particularly in the industrial sector
    (D) An increase in the popular opposition to national social and economic policies

52. Which of the following most strongly limited the policy successes of the neo-conservatives?
    (A) Opposition to deregulation by small business owners
    (B) The filibuster efforts of House Democrats that impeded changes to the tax code
    (C) The escalation of international conflict, threatening U.S. national security
    (D) Widespread voter support for social insurance programs

53. The political shift depicted by this cartoon mirrors in many ways the changes that occurred
    (A) in the wake of the Great Depression.
    (B) after the signing of the U.S. Constitution.
    (C) at the conclusion of Reconstruction.
    (D) at the conclusion of the Mexican War.

Questions 54–55 refer to the following cartoon.

Pismestrovic, Klene Zeitung, Cartoon Arts International, Inc.

54. Which of the following best explains the conflict depicted in this cartoon?
    (A) Debate over the right of the United States to respond to threats to its national security abroad
    (B) Disputes over America's use of its power to promote economic growth
    (C) Disagreement over the United States' ability to protect its allies

(D) Disagreement over the leadership and decisions of the United States in international affairs

55. Which of the following most strongly contributed to international mistrust of American foreign policy in Iraq and elsewhere?
(A) Questions over the United States' motives and intelligence in building the case for war
(B) Debate over the desirability of maintaining Saddam Hussein's regime
(C) Fears about the United States' role as the largest remaining superpower in the post–Cold War era
(D) Widespread sympathy for Islamic fundamentalist groups that protested the United States' involvement in the Middle East

STOP
END OF SECTION I, PART A

IF YOU FINISH BEFORE TIME IS CALLED, YOU MAY CHECK YOUR WORK ON THIS SECTION. DO NOT GO ON TO SECTION I, PART B UNTIL YOU ARE TOLD TO DO SO.

AP UNITED STATES HISTORY EXAMINATION
Section I
Part B: Short-Answer Questions
Writing Time—45 minutes

Directions: Part B of the examination contains 4 questions. You will have 45 minutes to respond to all questions. You are not required to develop and support a thesis statement in your response. Rather, focus on directly answering each question using evidence from your study of history.

1. Answer a and b.
   a) Choose ONE of the groups listed below, and explain the impact of United States westward expansion on that group.
      Asian Immigrants
      African Americans
      Native Americans
      Homesteaders
   b) Compare your choice to ONE of the other options and explain which group was more affected by the course of American expansion.

Library of Congress

2. Use the image on the previous page and your knowledge of United States history to answer Parts a, b, and c.
   a) Explain the significance of the image as it reveals changes in the United States after World War II with respect to ONE of the following:
      Transportation
      Family life
      Consumerism
   b) Provide ONE piece of evidence that contrasts the change you explained in Part a with life in the United States before 1950.
   c) Explain the long-term impact of the change you identified in Part a on the American culture, economy, *or* government.

"That this Assembly doth explicitly and peremptorily declare, that it views the powers of the federal government, as resulting from the compact, to which the states are parties; as limited by the plain sense and intention of the instrument constituting the compact; as no further valid than they are authorized by the grants enumerated in that compact; and that in the case of a deliberate, palpable, and dangerous exercise of other powers, not granted by the said compact, the states who are parties thereto, have the right, and are in duty bound, to interpose for arresting the progress of the evil, and for maintaining within their respective limits, the authorities, rights, and liberties appertaining to them."

James Madison, "Virginia Resolutions" (1798)

3. Using the passage above, answer a, b, and c.
   a) Briefly explain the argument made by Madison about the power of the national government.
   b) Offer ONE piece of evidence from American political history between 1781 and 1820 that would lead some to make claims like that of Madison.
   c) Provide ONE piece of evidence of a similar political protest made in the United States after 1820, explaining the similarities as you see them.

4. Answer a and b.
   a) Defend or refute the identification of September 11, 2001 as a turning point in American history with respect to ONE of the following:
      American military engagements
      Civil liberties and domestic security measures
      American political unity
   b) Identify another major event that has significantly changed the politics, economy, or culture of the United States after the end of the Cold War. Briefly explain the changes brought about by this event.

STOP
END OF SECTION I

IF YOU FINISH BEFORE TIME IS CALLED, YOU MAY CHECK YOUR WORK ON THIS SECTION. DO NOT GO ON TO SECTION II UNTIL YOU ARE TOLD TO DO SO.

Section II: Free-Response Essays

Section II of the examination has two kinds of questions. Part A is the Document-Based Question, which includes a series of primary source documents organized around a central question. Part B will present a pair of long-essay questions, both focusing on the same historical thinking skill. Each of the two long-essay prompts will apply the skill to a different time period and you will choose ONE of the two prompts to answer. You will have a total of 95 minutes to complete the document-based essay and the long essay.

Part A: Document-Based Question (DBQ)
Time—60 minutes

Directions: Question 1 is based on the accompanying documents. The documents have been edited for the purpose of this exercise. You are advised to spend 15 minutes planning and 45 minutes writing your answer.

In your response you should do the following.

- State a relevant thesis that directly answers all parts of the question.
- Support the thesis or a relevant argument with evidence from all, or all but one, of the documents.
- Incorporate analysis of all, or all but one, of the documents into your argument.
- Focus your analysis of each document on at least one of the following: intended audience, purpose, historical context, and/or point of view.
- Support your argument with analysis of historical examples outside the documents.
- Connect historical phenomena relevant to your argument to broader events or processes.
- Synthesize the elements above into a persuasive essay.

Question 1. Was U.S. imperialism at the turn of the twentieth century based on arrogance and superiority or did it reflect a humanitarian concern for the nations of South America and the Pacific?

Document 1: American Anti-Imperialist League Program, 1899

We hold that the policy known as imperialism is hostile to liberty and tends toward militarism, an evil from which it has been our glory to be free. We regret that it has become necessary in the land of Washington and Lincoln to reaffirm that all men, of whatever race or color, are entitled to life, liberty, and the pursuit of happiness. We maintain that governments derive their just powers from the consent of the governed. We insist that the subjugation of any people is "criminal aggression" and open disloyalty to the distinctive principles of our government.

We earnestly condemn the policy of the present national administration in the Philippines. It seeks to extinguish the spirit of 1776 in those islands. We deplore the sacrifice of our soldiers and sailors, whose bravery deserves admiration even in an unjust war. We denounce the slaughter of the Filipinos as a needless horror. We protest against the extension of American sovereignty by Spanish methods.

Document 2

The Granger Collection, New York

Document 3

Uncle Sam Gets Cocky

European chickens: “You’re not the only rooster in South America.”

Uncle Sam rooster: “I was aware of that when I cooped you up.”

Library of Congress

GO ON TO NEXT PAGE

Document 4: Alfred Taylor Mahan Defines Security in Terms of Sea Power, 1897

. . . The interesting and significant feature of this changing attitude is the turning of the eyes outward, instead of inward only, to seek the welfare of the country. To affirm the importance of distant markets, and the relation to them of our own immense powers of production, implies logically the recognition of the link that joins the products and the markets,—that is, the carrying trade; the three together constituting that chain of maritime power to which Great Britain owes her wealth and greatness. Further, is it too much to say that, as two of these links, the shipping and the markets, are exterior to our own borders, the acknowledgment of them carries with it a view of the relations of the United States to the world radically distinct from the simple idea of self-sufficingness? We shall not follow far this line of thought before there will dawn the realization of America's unique position, facing the older worlds of the East and West, her shores washed by the oceans which touch the one or the other, but which are common to her alone. . . .

Document 5

Library of Congress

Document 6: Roosevelt Corollary to the Monroe Doctrine

Roosevelt, Theodore
1904

It is not true that the United States feels any land hunger or entertains any projects as regards the other nations of the Western Hemisphere save such as are for their welfare. All that this country desires is to see the neighboring countries stable, orderly, and prosperous. Any country whose people conduct themselves well can count upon our hearty friendship. If a nation shows that it knows how to act with reasonable efficiency and decency in social and political matters, if it keeps order and pays its obligations, it need fear no interference from the United States. Chronic wrongdoing, or an impotence which results in a general loosening of the ties of civilized society, may in America, as elsewhere, ultimately require intervention by some civilized nation, and in the Western Hemisphere the adherence of the United States to the Monroe Doctrine may force the United States, however reluctantly, in flagrant cases of such wrongdoing or impotence, to the exercise of an international police power. . . .

End of documents for Question 1.
Go on to the next page.

GO ON TO NEXT PAGE

Part B: Long-Essay Questions
Writing Time—35 minutes

Directions Answer ONE of the following questions. It is recommended that you spend 5 minutes planning your essay and 30 minutes for writing. Write a well-structured, clearly written essay that provides sufficient evidence to support your thesis. Make certain to identify in the test booklet which essay questions you have selected.

Question 1. To what extent were the Jeffersonian Democrats and the Jacksonian Democrats similar in their political views and goals?

Question 2. To what extent were the Democratic Party of the 1930s and the Democratic Party of the 1960s similar in their political views and goals?

END OF EXAMINATION

ANSWERS FOR SECTION I

ANSWER KEY FOR MULTIPLE-CHOICE QUESTIONS

1. B	12. B	23. C	34. B	45. C
2. D	13. A	24. A	35. A	46. B
3. C	14. C	25. C	36. C	47. D
4. A	15. B	26. C	37. D	48. C
5. C	16. D	27. D	38. A	49. A
6. B	17. D	28. C	39. A	50. B
7. D	18. A	29. C	40. C	51. D
8. A	19. D	30. A	41. A	52. D
9. C	20. A	31. D	42. C	53. A
10. A	21. D	32. B	43. A	54. D
11. B	22. C	33. B	44. D	55. A

PART A: EXPLANATIONS FOR THE MULTIPLE-CHOICE ANSWERS

Questions 1–3 cover Period 1, Pre-Columbian America and Initial European Exploration (*The American Pageant,* 14th and 15th eds., Chapter 1).

1. **(B)** Although all of these changes occurred, the diagram depicts the Columbian Exchange. One of the impacts of this exchange was the devastation of the populations of Native Americans. In the absence of a Native labor force, conquerors turned to imported slave labor (*The American Pageant,* 14th ed., p. 13/15th ed., p. 12; Learning Objective WXT-1).

2. **(D)** Mineral wealth—in the form of gold and silver from the Americas—facilitated the European shift from feudalism to capitalism (*The American Pageant,* 14th ed., p. 17/15th ed., p. 16; Learning Objective WOR-1).

3. **(C)** Nutrient and calorie-dense foods brought from the New World supported European population growth and economic expansion (*The American Pageant,* 14th ed., p. 13/15th ed., p. 14; Learning Objective ENV-1).

Questions 4–8 cover Period 2, English Settlement of North America (*The American Pageant,* 14th and 15th eds., Chapters 2–4).

4. **(A)** The large number of British settlers combined with poor relations led to violence between Native Americans and colonists, especially along the vulnerable frontier (*The American Pageant,* 14th ed., p. 70/15th ed., p. 62; Learning Objective POL-1).

5. **(C)** Because of frustrations over the shortages of indentured servants and the challenges of accommodating the newly independent freedmen, the Chesapeake colonies eventually turned

to slave labor (*The American Pageant,* 14th ed., p. 70/15th ed., p. 62; Learning Objective WXT-4).

6. **(B)** Particularly in Virginia, indentured servants were initially a significant source of labor under the headright system, unlike in the Southern colonies that had adopted the chattel slavery institution as modeled by colonists in Barbados (*The American Pageant,* 14th ed., pp. 69–70/15th ed., p. 61; Learning Objective ID-5).

7. **(D)** Though economic differences continued to exist, the development of a uniquely American culture, spurred on in part by movements like the Great Awakening, helped to unify the colonies in the decades before the American Revolution (*The American Pageant,* 14th ed., pp. 98–100/15th ed., pp. 87–88; Learning Objective CUL-4).

8. **(A)** Although their attempts to pursue mercantilism often frustrated the colonists in North America, the growth of an Atlantic economy (particularly as a source of raw materials and market for European goods) in North America was of great interest to the British (*The American Pageant,* 14th ed., pp. 93–96/15th ed., pp. 82–85; Learning Objective WOR-1).

Questions 9–15 cover Period 3, The Rise of the American Republic (*The American Pageant,* 14th and 15th eds., Chapters 6–10).

9. **(C)** Following the French and Indian War, the British wanted to reduce the cost of governing the colonies and hoped to prevent expensive military action (*The American Pageant,* 14th ed., pp. 122–124/15th ed., p. 111; Learning Objective POL-1).

10. **(A)** Britain attempted to punish the Americans back into cooperation via shows of force and the hated Intolerable Acts (*The American Pageant,* 14th ed., p. 136/15th ed., p. 122; Learning Objective CUL-4).

11. **(B)** The Enlightenment introduced Americans to ideas about liberty, individualism, and republican government (*The American Pageant,* 14th ed., pp. 98–102/15th ed., p. 91; Learning Objective CUL-4).

12. **(B)** Even after the ratification of the Constitution, many Americans continued to struggle against the national government when it overstepped its bounds as they saw them—a fundamental debate between ideals of liberty and obedience (*The American Pageant,* 14th ed., pp. 204–205/15th ed., p. 185; Learning Objective ID-1).

13. **(A)** Madison challenged the constitutionality of the Alien and Sedition Acts, arguing that the powers of the Alien Act went beyond the scope of federal power and calling upon all states to likewise condemn the overreach of the national government (*The American Pageant,* 14th ed., pp. 218–219/15th ed., pp. 197–198; Learning Objective POL-5).

14. **(C)** Partisanship had in part accounted for the original enacting of the Alien and Sedition Acts; this and other controversies (such as those over the tariff and American foreign policy) fueled the growing partisan divide between Federalists and Jeffersonian Republicans (*The American Pageant,* 14th ed., pp. 219–221/15th ed., pp. 198–200; Learning Objective POL-2).

15. **(B)** The outcry against the Espionage and Sedition Acts of 1918 closely mirrored the debate of 1798, with opponents charging that the laws put undue restrictions on freedom of speech in the name of national security (*The American Pageant,* 14th ed., p. 750/15th ed., pp. 681–682; Learning Objective POL-6).

Questions 16–19 cover Period 4, The Growth of America (*The American Pageant,* 14th and 15th eds., Chapters 11–17).

16. **(D)** Marshall himself was a staunch Federalist and the last remaining member of that party in power after the collapse of the Federalists following the War of 1812 (*The American Pageant,* 14th ed., pp. 231–232, 263/15th ed., pp. 208–209, 238; Learning Objective POL-5).

17. **(D)** Many of Marshall's rulings, including this one, focused on expanding the power of the federal government through a broad interpretation of its rights and a dedication to the supremacy clause (*The American Pageant,* 14th ed., pp. 231–232/15th ed., pp. 208–209; Learning Objective POL-5).

18. **(A)** Championed by Alexander Hamilton and later Henry Clay's American System, the Bank of the US (BUS) was designed to improve the stability of the national economy and allow for growth (*The American Pageant,* 14th ed., pp. 204, 256–257/15th ed., pp. 184–185, 231; Learning Objective WXT-6).

19. **(D)** Despite hopes of creating a unified national economy, the Bank was associated with the commercial interests of the elite in the Northeast and, after vetoing its recharter, Jackson withdrew federal funds from the 2nd Bank of the US and "killed" it (*The American Pageant,* 14th ed., pp. 286–290/15th ed., pp. 259–262; Learning Objective ID-5).

Questions 20–28 cover Period 5, Manifest Destiny, Civil War, and Reconstruction (*The American Pageant,* 14th and 15th eds., Chapters 17–22).

20. **(A)** The very definition of "Manifest Destiny," this selection reveals the extent of the belief that America's conquest of new lands was assured and preordained (*The American Pageant,* 14th ed., pp. 403–404/15th ed., p. 366; Learning Objective CUL-2).

21. **(D)** Though discussion was opened about how, when, and where to acquire and integrate new territories, the most significant debate that emerged was that over the expansion of slavery—beginning with the debate over the Wilmot Proviso (*The American*

Pageant, 14th ed., p. 414/15th ed., pp. 373, 376; Learning Objective CUL-5).

22. **(C)** Central to the idea of Manifest Destiny was the notion of white racial superiority and the certainty that American democracy would triumph over all (*The American Pageant,* 14th ed., pp. 403–404/15th ed., p. 366; Learning Objective WOR-5).

23. **(C)** As more white settlers moved into the region, the West's earlier inhabitants—like the Californios and the Native Americans—faced losing their land and, in the case of former Mexican citizens, their rights to participate in government (*The American Pageant,* 14th ed., pp. 412–413/15th ed., pp. 374–375; Learning Objective PEO-5).

24. **(A)** Though the new territories brought about much controversy—especially as several sought statehood and questions arose about how to integrate the existing populations into the United States—the access to the vast farm lands and valuable resources (like gold) stood out as the most important benefit of expansion (*The American Pageant,* 14th ed., p. 411/15th ed., p. 373; Learning Objective ENV-4).

25. **(C)** Given that the South was tied economically, politically, and socially to slavery, the success of Republican Lincoln—running on a free-soil platform—led the South to believe that its interests could no longer be protected by the U.S. government (*The American Pageant,* 14th ed., pp. 458–459/15th ed., pp. 414–415; Learning Objective POL-6).

26. **(C)** More manpower (owing to significant immigration) and more industrial and financial resources allowed the North to outlast the South (*The American Pageant,* 14th ed., pp. 479, 502–503/15th ed., pp. 433, 453–454; Learning Objective ENV-3).

27. **(D)** Despite enormous challenges facing the still divided nation at the end of the Civil War, the war itself had decided the question of federal supremacy for good (*The American Pageant,* 14th ed., p. 509/15th ed., p. 461; Learning Objective POL-5).

28. **(C)** As part of the Compromise of 1850, the Fugitive Slave Act added teeth to the constitutional requirement that escaped slaves be caught and returned to their masters—hoping to placate the South and convince Southerners that the federal government respected their interests (*The American Pageant,* 14th ed., pp. 423–427/15th ed., pp. 384–387; Learning Objective POL-6).

Questions 29–33 cover Period 6, The Gilded Age (*The American Pageant,* 14th and 15th eds., Chapters 23–26).

29. **(C)** Rejecting the idea that capitalists had earned and deserved their immense wealth, union organizers fought for restrictions on the power of large corporations to dictate prices and wages (*The American Pageant,* 14th ed., pp. 586–587/15th ed., pp. 530–532; Learning Objective CUL-5).

30. **(A)** In passing the Interstate Commerce Act, early reformers hoped to increase the fairness of the railways making room for more industrial competitors and improving farm shipping rates (*The American Pageant,* 14th ed., p. 573/15th ed., p. 519; Learning Objective POL-6).

31. **(D)** Overproduction due to large numbers of new farmers in the West and the mechanization of agriculture lay at the heart of the farmers' problems, though the rise of industrial powers reduced their political voice (*The American Pageant,* 14th ed., pp. 651–656/15th ed., pp. 594–596; Learning Objective WXT-7).

32. **(B)** Developing from economic cooperatives like the Farmers' Alliance, the Populist party represented the interests of the agricultural workers and sought (fairly unsuccessfully) political influence on the state and national scale (*The American Pageant,* 14th ed., pp. 657–658/15th ed., p. 598; Learning Objective WXT-7).

33. **(B)** Because of the differences in the economic and political desires of rural farmers who were often in debt and urban manufacturers who competed with international imports, conflict among agrarian and industrial interests has pervaded American history (*The American Pageant,* 14th ed., pp. 536–537/15th ed., pp. 486–487; Learning Objective ID-5).

Questions 34–44 cover Period 7, The US Becomes a World Power (*The American Pageant,* 14th and 15th eds., Chapters 27–35).

34. **(B)** The economic opportunities in the United States—a result of growing industrialism—made the United States a magnet for immigration throughout this period, despite widespread nativism and racism (*The American Pageant,* 14th ed., pp. 601, 604/15th ed., pp. 544–545; Learning Objective WOR-3).

35. **(A)** The "New Immigrants" from southern and eastern Europe were so culturally, linguistically, and ethnically different from so-called "Native" Americans that anti-immigrant feelings rose dramatically during this time (*The American Pageant,* 14th ed., pp. 599–601/15th ed., pp. 542–544; Learning Objective PEO-6).

36. **(C)** Though many assimilation attempts were made by mostly well-intentioned Americans, most immigrants maintained ties to their native cultures while also adopting some American ways (*The American Pageant,* 14th ed., pp. 600–601/15th ed., p. 544; Learning Objective ID-6).

37. **(D)** Many groups faced similar discrimination in wages, political representation, and popular opinion, but most government employees were part of the accepted middle class (*The American Pageant,* 14th ed., pp. 583–587/15th ed., pp. 537, 545, 547; Learning Objective WXT-5).

38. **(A)** In the Gilded Age, the Chinese Exclusion Act sought to reduce the influence of Chinese immigrants in Western communities. In the 1920s, the Emergency Quota Act and National Origins Act

sought to reduce the number of "New Immigrants" coming to America (*The American Pageant,* 14th ed., pp. 608–609, 773–774/15th ed., pp. 551, 703; Learning Objective PEO-6).

39. **(A)** Roosevelt was inspired by the multifaceted, government-led approach to solving structural economic problems that caused suffering that was not the fault of individual citizens (*The American Pageant,* 14th ed., pp. 826–843/15th ed., pp. 754–769; Learning Objective WXT-8).

40. **(C)** Roosevelt built a broad coalition of supporters for the New Deal, but some radical liberals charged him with not doing enough while many conservatives felt that government increases in spending and power were out of control (*The American Pageant,* 14th ed., pp. 847–848/15th ed., pp. 773–774; Learning Objective CUL-5).

41. **(A)** Though it did help to mitigate economic suffering, the New Deal's greatest legacy was political change—change in the Democratic coalition being one of the most significant (*The American Pageant,* 14th ed., p. 844/15th ed., p. 770; Learning Objective PEO-6).

42. **(C)** Though significant changes were to be expected during wartime, government limits on the rights of unions contradicted Roosevelt's insistence (and Rockwell's characterization) that the United States was fighting for absolute freedom (*The American Pageant,* 14th ed., p. 880/15th ed., pp. 802–803; Learning Objective POL-6).

43. **(A)** Though not always the end result, rhetoric surrounding all three major wars listed focused on America's role as the defender of democracy and freedom—against Spanish colonialism, German aggression, and fascism (*The American Pageant,* 14th ed., pp. 700–701/15th ed., pp. 636–637; Learning Objective WOR-7).

44. **(D)** Though World War II presented opportunities for many historically disadvantaged groups, Japanese Americans were forced into internment camps in the post–Pearl Harbor hysteria (*The American Pageant,* 14th ed., pp. 878–886/15th ed., pp. 800–807; Learning Objective WOR-4).

Questions 45–50 cover Period 8, Domestic and International Challenges in Cold War America (*The American Pageant,* 14th and 15th eds., Chapters 36–39).

45. **(C)** Collective security and the general idea of containment led the United States into several military conflicts to support nations where communist forces threatened to take over (*The American Pageant,* 14th ed., pp. 937–939/15th ed., pp. 854–856; Learning Objective WOR-8).

46. **(B)** Particularly in Latin America—but also in Vietnam—America's commitment to oppose communism often led it to support regimes that bore little resemblance to the democratic ideals the

United States claimed to defend (*The American Pageant,* 14th ed., pp. 963–964/15th ed., pp. 878–879; Learning Objective ID-3).

47. **(D)** Collective security agreements like NATO lent American strength to weaker nations, helping to prevent Communist attempts at spreading (*The American Pageant,* 14th ed., p. 932/15th ed., p. 849; Learning Objective WOR-7).

48. **(C)** The Great Society was the name for Johnson's domestic policies, including civil rights and anti-poverty legislation (*The American Pageant,* 14th ed., pp. 986–989/15th ed., pp. 901–904; Learning Objective POL-4).

49. **(A)** Since the 1950s—and even earlier—civil rights activists had been calling for increased government activism in support of equal rights and equal opportunities for all citizens, no matter their race (*The American Pageant,* 14th ed., pp. 979–984/15th ed., pp. 895–900; Learning Objective ID-8).

50. **(B)** In both scope and aim, the Great Society closely parallels the progressive movement's desire to improve Americans' political, economic, and social well-being (*The American Pageant,* 14th ed., p. 986/15th ed., p. 902; Learning Objective POL-3).

Questions 51–55 cover Period 9, The United States in a Changing World (*The American Pageant,* 14th and 15th eds., Chapters 40–42).

51. **(D)** Together with the rise of Christian fundamentalism and a decline in public faith in the government's ability to solve problems, the 1980s revealed a strong growth in the opposition to government policies related to spending, affirmative action, and abortion (*The American Pageant,* 14th ed., pp. 1043–1044/15th ed., pp. 951–954; Learning Objective POL-3).

52. **(D)** Despite strong success in cutting taxes and reducing governmental regulation in industry, popular support for Medicare, Medicaid, and Social Security limited conservatives' ability to dramatically reduce the scope of government (*The American Pageant,* 14th ed., pp. 1041–1042/15th ed., p. 951; Learning Objective WXT-8).

53. **(A)** Just as the policies of the Republican Party during the 1920s had led to a reactionary shift in favor of activist Democratic policies in the 1930s, the activism of the Democratic Party during the 1960s and 1970s—along with their own missteps—had provoked a conservative backlash in the 1980s (*The American Pageant,* 14th ed., pp. 1031–1033/15th ed., pp. 943–944; Learning Objective POL-4).

54. **(D)** Although there was widespread international support for the United States' response to 9/11 in Afghanistan, U.S. leadership in the war in Iraq has been questioned both at home and abroad due to faulty evidence and the protracted conflict (*The American Pageant,* 14th ed., p. 1078/15th ed., p. 982; Learning Objective WOR-8).

55. **(A)** Despite its generally strong support from European allies, the United States struggled to build a coalition for the invasion of Iraq, in part because many were skeptical of the case for war presented by President George W. Bush and Colin Powell (*The American Pageant,* 14th ed., pp. 1070–1071/15th ed., pp. 976–977; WOR-7).

Section I, Part B: Short-Answer Questions

Question 1

Your response should identify the positive and negative impacts on your group of choice. In Part B, you should identify a second group and compare them to your original choice, explaining which was more significantly affected (Learning Objectives PEO-5, ENV-3).

Asian immigrants experienced severe discrimination and were greeted with hostile legislation, such as the Chinese Exclusion Act of 1882. They began as miners and service workers among mining communities, but were eventually pushed out and into the only remaining opportunity: railway work. Many Chinese immigrants worked for the Central Pacific railway building the transcontinental railroad under dangerous conditions.

African Americans saw the West as an opportunity to escape the Jim Crow South with its Black Codes. Some, the Exodusters, managed to take advantage of the Homestead Act and began life as independent farmers. Many more, however, were unable to afford the capital outlay required for such a trip. From another perspective, the emancipation of African Americans has its roots in Westward expansion, as the annexation of new territories accelerated the conflict that resulted in the Civil War.

Native Americans, already pushed out of the land East of the Mississippi River, faced dire consequences as the United States expanded. Particularly after the onset of the Gold Rush, Native Americans found themselves in conflict with settlers whose way of life competed directly with their own. A series of violent conflicts (like the Battle of Little Big Horn) led ultimately to the military subdual of all major tribes and their forced removal from the Great Plains to small, desolate reservations.

Homesteaders, mostly middle-class families, took advantage of the national government's promise of 160 acres of free land under the 1862 Homestead Act. Many struggled to adapt to the new climate, and the difficulties of Western life impacted the culture of the hardy settlers. Over time, the dominance of the railroads would lead to difficulties.

Question 2

Your response should explain one of the social or economic changes revealed by this advertisement and contrast that change with life before World War II. In Part C, explain how that post-war change impacted America in the long term (Learning Objectives ID-7, CUL-7).

In terms of transportation, the ad reveals the increasing availability of the automobile to middle-class families. Due to high savings rates during the war and an increase in average family income after the war, more families owned cars than ever before, increasing their ability to travel and changing the American countryside. The Interstate Highway Act expanded the influence of the automobile. Suburbanization and pollution concerns are both long-term impacts of increased auto use.

The ad also depicts the large families that were common in the postwar Baby Boom. Economic security and a cultural emphasis on family life led to the idealization of parenting as the epitome of middle-class living. Unlike the cautious perspective of the war years, the Baby Boom revealed a newfound optimism (and newfound disposable income). Long term, the Baby Boom paved the way for skyrocketing productivity in later decades and, more recently, impending crisis for the nation's Social Security system.

Consumerism climbed to new heights after World War II due to high savings rates and postwar prosperity. With a college education paid for by the American GI Bill (Serviceman's Re-adjustment Act) more families could claim membership in the middle class. Buying cars fell in line with increases in ownership of convenience appliances and matched other ads of the time period. In the long-run, consumerism became motivation for spending beyond means and high levels of personal debt which contributed to the economic crises of the late twentieth and early twenty-first century.

Question 3

Your response should summarize the argument made by Madison, place his argument in historical context by explaining an event that would have led to such a controversy, and finally connect that debate over the just use of governmental power to a more recent example of political conflict (Learning Objectives POL-5, POL-6).

Madison is writing specifically in response to the Alien and Sedition Acts passed by the government of Federalist president John Adams. Along with that of Kentucky, the Virginia legislature wrote a resolution condemning what it saw as an abuse of the power granted to the national government by the state governments. Madison is arguing that, if the national government's exercise of power exceeds the bounds of the Constitution, then the states may rightfully view those actions as null and void (and not follow them).

Besides the controversy over the Alien and Sedition Acts (which were ostensibly passed to protect against supposed French aggression but were widely seen as a political move to reduce the power of the Democratic-Republicans), other early conflicts over the just exercise of national power include the creation of the national bank (which faced particular opposition in Maryland, culminating in the *McCulloch* v. *Maryland* decision in 1819), Hamilton's financial plan for the funding and assumption of state debts and for the creation of a tariff, or the Whiskey Rebellion (which protested the federal tax on whiskey that hurt the economic prospects of frontier farmers). Later, the Federalists would cry foul at the Hartford Convention over anti-British policies of the Jeffersonian administration.

In the time after 1820, the most obvious parallel to this conflict is the Nullification Crisis of 1832 (whereby South Carolina tried to nullify the so-called Tariff of Abominations before being stopped by the forceful President Jackson). Other conflicts related to the protection (or prohibition) of slavery followed similar veins—especially the *Dred Scott* decision and the debates over the Fugitive Slave Act. Though not going as far as nullification, modern protests over moral-political issues like abortion and gay marriage have inspired similar protests.

Question 4

Your response should explain why September 11th did (or did not) cause a significant change in American policies with respect to one of the categories. In Part B, you should identify and explain the cause of another significant change in the United States since 1991 (Learning Objectives WOR-8, CUL-7).

After 9/11, the United States has seen direct military action in both Afghanistan and Iraq, as well as significant covert engagements in places like Pakistan and Yemen. Fears about international terrorism have also heightened tension between the United States and nations such as Iran and Syria. Even so, the United States had been militarily involved in the Middle East since the 1991 Gulf War.

Debates about the relative value of civil liberties and domestic security have raged since 9/11, especially with respect to the controversial USA PATRIOT ACT. Other concerns have focused on increased screenings in airport security lines. Still others have highlighted the rise of discriminatory profiling for immigrants and travelers. On the other hand, racial and ethnic discrimination were hardly unknown in the country before 9/11.

Americans were politically and culturally united in the wake of the 9/11 crisis with widespread displays of patriotism common in the weeks and months after the attack. Nevertheless, defense against terrorism and the position of the United States in international affairs has quickly become a significant source of division between Republicans and Democrats.

Section II, Part A: Document-Based Question (DBQ)

Below are short analyses of the documents. The italicized words suggest what your margin notes might include:

Document 1 This statement by the American Anti-Imperialist League harshly *criticizes U.S. imperialism* as an affront to the principle of self-determination as well as *contradicts American political and cultural values.*

Document 2 This political cartoon depicts Uncle Sam's *voracious appetite for colonial possessions.* President McKinley, the waiter, is obviously intent on satiating the nation's hunger for an *international empire.*

Document 3 Although this political cartoon shows the *aggressive nature of U.S. foreign policy* at the turn of the twentieth century, it *also represents the United States* as a *protector of South American nations* from the imperialistic European powers. The "cooped-up" chickens represent European powers whose designs on the Western Hemisphere are contained by the *Roosevelt Corollary to the Monroe Doctrine.*

DOCUMENT 4 In this passage, *Mahan* articulates the *need for international markets,* the protection of which would be the responsibility of the *U.S. Navy*. The navy, in turn, would require access to colonies, which would serve as *coaling and supply stations,* as well as *markets for U.S. commodities.*

DOCUMENT 5 This political cartoon depicts an athletic and robust Theodore Roosevelt flexing his muscles in a *demonstration of U.S. hegemony in South America.*

DOCUMENT 6 *Roosevelt* portrays *U.S. hegemony in the Western Hemisphere* as *benevolent* and paved with good intentions. *Yet,* the passage *implies a sense of moral, political, and cultural superiority* in that "wrongdoing" on the part of the South Americans is tantamount to being uncivilized.

Documents that reflect arrogance or superiority on the part of the United States in its relationship with South America and the Pacific are grouped as negative; those documents that suggest a humanitarian concern on the part of the United States are grouped as positive. Documents that are not necessarily identified with one perspective or another can nonetheless be used to defend your perspective. The following is a categorization of the documents:

Negative Documents	**Positive Documents**	**Neutral Documents**
A	C	D
B	F	
E		

In developing the essay, you should incorporate the following historical information:

- The "New Imperialism" paved the way for the adoption of expansionist policy by the United States with the intention of establishing international markets for domestically produced commodities as well as providing raw materials necessary for industrialization. Furthermore, colonies could ostensibly provide a "safety valve" for those discontented with domestic conditions in the United States.
- Social Darwinism was used as a justification for imperialism. Social Darwinists claimed that certain civilizations had evolved faster than others. In other words, some societies were civilized and others were "barbaric." The implication was that Western cultures, being more advanced than other generally non-Western cultures, had the right and duty to expand and "uplift" other "less developed" people.
- President Roosevelt's "Big Stick" policy in South America called for U.S. military and political intervention in Venezuela and other South American nations that could default on loans to European nations and therefore risked European intervention in violation of the Monroe Doctrine. This convinced Roosevelt to extend the authority of the United States under the Monroe Doctrine. By this Roosevelt Corollary, the United States claimed the right to intervene in South American countries whenever the United States deemed it necessary to do so.

- The United States supported Panamanian independence as part of an arrangement to build the Panama Canal and ultimately to provide the United States with long-term control of the canal.

The causes and effects of the Spanish-American War played an important role. Make certain to include the following:

- Teller Amendment
- Platt Amendment
- Insular Cases

A Sample Essay

An essay that takes the position that the United States was arrogant and felt superior to those in South America and the Pacific might look something like this:

By the late nineteenth century the United States had embarked on a policy of international territorial expansion based on its own ideas of superiority. Having expanded to the Pacific Ocean, it now looked to establish a world empire (Document B), first by gaining new colonies, and second by preventing the European imperial powers from colonizing the Western Hemisphere. This would allow America to comfortably maintain authority over her own "house". The United States, like other imperial powers, had certain assumptions regarding those nations in which it had either direct or indirect control. For example, in 1823 the United States adopted a hegemonic policy in the Western Hemisphere, warning Europe not to take steps to recolonize South America. This pivotal foreign policy statement, the Monroe Doctrine, has been the cornerstone of U.S. foreign policy, not only in the Western Hemisphere, but as applied to Asia, Europe, and Africa as well. For, though the initial document applied to the Western Hemisphere, the United States has used it to justify its intervention in other areas of the world where Americans felt that they could better manage the conflict or challenge facing a developing nation. This same ideology would serve to guide American intervention in the Cold War era as the nation sought to project its "superior" ideas about government and the economy to nations that might be influenced by Communism.

At the turn of the twentieth century, the United States was arrogant and condescending in its treatment of South American nations. In order to justify its feeling of superiority, U.S. political leaders rationalized that the application of the Monroe Doctrine (Document F) by means of periodic U.S. interventions in the internal affairs of these nations was based in large part on the ideas associated with Social Darwinism. Those who advocated this perspective claimed that nonmodern or less developed nations were simply less evolved than, for example, the United States, which had over time developed into a modern nation. This perspective was held by many political leaders such as President Theodore Roosevelt, who maintained that U.S. hegemony was beneficial to less developed cultures. For example, in his Corollary to the Monroe Doctrine (Document F) he claimed the United States had the right to intervene when South American nations acted "irresponsibly." We see this attitude conveyed in the political cartoon "His Foresight" (Document E), in which the United States (Roosevelt) is depicted as the protector of South American nations, which could fall prey to the European powers were it not for the United States. In the Corollary President Roosevelt further articulated the view that the United States would intervene in South American nations if "it became evident that their inability or unwillingness to do justice at home and abroad had violated the rights of the United States or had invited foreign aggression to the detriment of the entire body of American nations" (Document F), placing American interests above respect for other nations' integrity. This view of superiority was expressed in the Platt Amendment following the Spanish-American War, which legitimized U.S. intervention in order to maintain political stability in Cuba, as well as to establish a U.S. military presence in Cuba (the naval base at Guantanamo) and restricted Cuba's diplomatic autonomy. By establishing a strategic naval base in Cuba, the United States was fulfilling the recommendation of Captain Alfred Thayer Mahan (whose <u>The Influence of Sea Power upon History</u> had a profound influence on Roosevelt). In Document D Mahan articulates the view that the United States needed to protect its international trade and markets by establishing a powerful navy, as well as by obtaining naval bases and coaling stations to supply the navy's ships. Together with the ideas about American racial superiority, this was enough to motivate the nation to secure territory around the globe in order to promote American interests. No thought was given to the idea of Cuban self-determination, which had been one reason why the United States claimed it fought against Spain in the war.

COMMENT: This essay synthesizes outside information—the reader's knowledge and use of Social Darwinism, the Roosevelt Corollary to the Monroe Doctrine, the Platt Amendment, and Mahan's thesis—with information gleaned from the documents—a political cartoon, two quotes from the Roosevelt Corollary, and Mahan's view on sea power. Together, the information from the documents and the outside information sustain a defense of the thesis.

SCORING: Based on the AP U.S. History Document-Based Question Rubric as established by the College Board, you should score your essay as follows (with a maximum possible score of 7).

A. Thesis: 0–1 point

Give 1 point for a stated thesis that directly answers all parts of the question. It must do more than simply restate the question.

B. Analysis of historical evidence and support of argument: 0–4 points

Give 1 point for an essay that offers plausible analysis of the content of a <u>majority</u> of the document, explicitly using that analysis to support the stated thesis or a relevant argument, OR

Give 2 points for an essay that offers plausible analysis of BOTH the content of a majority of the documents, explicitly using this analysis to support the stated thesis or a relevant argument; AND at least one of the following for the majority of the documents: intended audience, purpose, historical context, and/or the author's point of view, OR

Give 3 points for an essay that offers plausible analysis of BOTH the content of all or all but one of the documents, explicitly using this analysis to support the stated thesis or a relevant argument; AND at least one of the following for all or all but one of the documents: intended audience, purpose, historical context, and/or the author's point of view.

PLUS: **Add 1 additional point** for an essay that offers plausible analysis of historical examples beyond or outside of the documents to support the stated thesis or a relevant argument.

C. Contextualization: 0–1 point

Give 1 point for an essay that accurately and explicitly connects historical phenomena relevant to the argument to broader historical events and/or processes.

D. Synthesis: 0–1 point

Give 1 point for an essay that appropriately extends or modifies the stated thesis or argument, OR

Give 1 point for an essay that effectively accounts for disparate, sometimes contradictory evidence from primary sources and/or secondary works in crafting a coherent argument, OR

Give 1 point for an essay that appropriately connects the topic of the question to other historical periods, geographical areas, contexts, or circumstances.

Section II, Part B: Long-Essay Questions

Question 1

At the heart of a discussion on Jeffersonian democracy and Jacksonian democracy is the nature of reform—the democratization of the nation's socioeconomic and political institutions and rights. Pointing out that some historians refer to Jefferson's election as the "Revolution of 1800" sets the tone of this part of the answer. Thus an explanation of the ways in which Jefferson's election promoted the interests of the common man over the interests of bankers and manufacturers is needed. You should also take up Jefferson's attempt to implement the ideals of limited government and strict constructionism. Like Jefferson, Jackson claimed to represent the common man. He too claimed to attack the expansive nature of government. Thus a discussion of the Bank War is essential, as is an analysis of Jackson's political responses, such as the spoils system and the kitchen cabinet, to entrenched elitism.

An effective essay is one that addresses how the two administrations viewed the nature of reform and liberalism. However, a fuller discussion should indicate that reform did not emanate exclusively from the federal government; state governments also sought to address abuses in government, society, and the economy that were not democratic. Also, a discussion of grassroots movements—that is, citizens at the local level engaged in improving and democratizing American institutions and social life, such as urban decay, abolition of slavery, education, and women's rights—is essential to an excellent essay on this topic. A first-rate essay might also incorporate the inconsistencies and contradictions of Jeffersonian and Jacksonian reform—for example, the treatment of Native Americans under both governments, the fact that both presidents were slave owners, and the territorial expansion that sought to expand American democracy at the expense of Native Americans.

QUESTION 2

Key to an effective essay on the evolution of the Democratic Party is a discussion of the Democratic coalition and that party's stance on civil rights. No discussion of the Democratic Party of the 1930s would be complete without reference to Franklin D. Roosevelt and the New Deal. By emphasizing a role for the national government in the country's economic and social well-being, the New Dealers initiated the Democratic Party's advocacy for an activist national government. Furthermore, it was the New Deal and Roosevelt's willingness to include black Americans (at least to some extent) in the relief programs that brought about the historic shift in voting patterns whereby African Americans switched their support from the Republican Party of Lincoln to the Democrats under Roosevelt. Though the New Deal was not a civil rights initiative, Roosevelt did make some concessions to African American leaders, such as presidential appointments and, when threatened with a wartime protest, the prohibition on discrimination in defense industry hiring. Nevertheless, the South remained part of the Democratic coalition as it made secure protections for agriculture and as Roosevelt was politically cautious not to alienate segregationists in the South.

Advances in the Democratic Party on the issue of civil rights, however, began fairly quickly after Roosevelt's death. President Truman desegregated the military with EO 9981. When Kennedy was elected, he promised black voters federal support for changes to the Jim Crow South. Though he moved fairly slowly, Kennedy set in motion the historic Civil Rights Act of 1964, signed by President Johnson. Upon signing, Johnson remarked that the Democrats had "lost the South for a generation." Indeed, the Solid South changed its tune quickly and, by 1968, voted firmly for the Republican Party (Nixon's Southern Strategy and courting of segregationist interests didn't hurt). This served to further liberalize the Democratic Party, which continued to advance significant reforms throughout the 1960s. Johnson's Great Society was reminiscent of the New Deal in scope and aim, and increased the reach of the federal government to the fields of education and health care.

SCORING: Based on the AP U.S. History Long Essay Question Rubric as established by the College Board, you should score your essay as follows (with a maximum possible score of 6).

A. Thesis: 0–1 point

Give 1 point for a stated thesis that directly answers all parts of the question. It must do more than simply restate the question.

B. Support for argument: 0–2 points

Give 1 point for an essay that supports a stated thesis or makes a relevant argument using specific evidence, OR

Give 2 points for an essay that supports the stated thesis or makes a relevant argument using specific evidence, clearly and consistently stating how the evidence supports the thesis or argument, and establishing clear linkages between the evidence and the thesis or argument.

C. Application of targeted historical thinking skill: 0–2 points

This is a COMPARISON Essay, therefore:

Give 1 point for an essay that describes similarities AND differences among historical developments, OR

Give 2 points for an essay that describes similarities AND differences among historical developments, providing specific examples AND analyzes the reasons for their similarities AND/OR differences OR evaluates the relative significance of the historical developments.

D. Synthesis: 0–1 point

Give 1 point for an essay that appropriately extends or modifies the stated thesis or argument, OR

Give 1 point for an essay that explicitly employs an additional appropriate category of analysis (e.g., political, economic, social, cultural, geographical, race/ethnicity, gender) beyond that called for by the prompt, OR

Give 1 point for an essay that appropriately connects the topic of the question to other historical periods, geographical areas, contexts, or circumstances.

It is important that you be as objective as possible when evaluating your essays. You might ask a teacher, parent, fellow student, or friend to evaluate your essays for you and to offer advice on areas for improvement.

Part II

A Review of AP U.S. History Exam

Period 1: 1491–1607

Pre-Columbian America and Initial European Exploration

The America that was "discovered" by the Spanish crew of Christopher Columbus in 1492, had in fact been occupied for thousands of years by a diverse group of Native American tribes and civilizations. The arrival of Europeans marked the beginning of a new age and the description of the discovered lands as the "New World" seems appropriate. In fact, it would be the contact among the peoples of Europe—the Spanish the first to arrive in large numbers—the Americas, and West Africa that would give birth to an entirely new world, full of new promise and new devastation.

Key Concepts from the College Board

1.1 Before the arrival of Europeans, native populations in North America developed a wide variety of social, political, and economic structures based in part on interactions with the environment and each other.

1.2 European overseas expansion resulted in the Columbian Exchange, a series of interactions and adaptations among societies across the Atlantic.

1.3 Contacts among American Indians, Africans, and Europeans challenged the worldviews of each group.

1

INITIAL CONTACTS: 1491–1607

Thirty to forty thousand years before Christopher Columbus—or any western European, for that matter—found his way to the New World (the Western Hemisphere), the continent had already been settled by migrants who had crossed a land bridge that once connected Alaska with Russia. Much later, in the early eleventh century, Viking ships entered the Western Hemisphere intent on establishing colonies in North America, but the Norse venture failed. In the latter stages of the feudal era, powerful western European nations such as Spain and Portugal were emerging, and they too were bent on expanding their political and economic advantages through colonization. As Europe emerged from its feudal period around the fifteenth to sixteenth century, commerce and exploration increased in intensity, stimulated by new navigational developments such as the compass and better shipbuilding techniques, as well as nonmaritime discoveries and advancements such as the printing press. In the feudal age, power had been diffused and often decentralized, but with the rise of the modern nation-state, powerful monarchs and wealthy merchants were willing to finance explorations of discovery. Colonization ultimately followed these explorations, and it was not long before France, Holland, and England set covetous eyes on the New World as well. In fact, the expansion of commerce was an essential element in the explorations that took place in the fifteenth and sixteenth centuries. Leading the way were Spain and Portugal, but England, the latecomer, would gain the upper hand in North America and set the stage for the unfolding of United States history.

KEY CONCEPTS

- The Americas were richly populated with diverse groups before the arrival of European explorers.

- The Columbian Exchange set off a series of economic, cultural, social, and political changes that would revolutionize the world.
- The rise of nation-states in Europe was a factor in stimulating explorations to the New World and dictated the goals of settlers and explorers.
- Contact between Native Americans, enslaved Africans, and European explorers led to intense competition and to the development of ideas about race and class that would permeate colonial society and beyond.

The exploration of the New World and colonial life in North America are discussed in depth in *The American Pageant,* 14th and 15th eds., Chapter 1.

Pre-Columbian Settlements in North America

Long before the arrival of permanent European settlers, a wide variety of complex Native American societies had developed on the North American continent. American Indian civilizations were diverse in their structure, culture, and lifestyle and most differences can be traced to their interactions with the environment across a broad range of climates. In adapting to local conditions, Native American communities transformed their environment—a theme that would only accelerate with the arrival of the first colonists in the New World. The Natives of North America can be divided into four major groups as follows:

- **The American Southwest** After the advent of maize cultivation, many of the nomadic tribes of the American Southwest began to develop complex, urban settlements characterized by large, apartment-like stone and adobe structures. While never giving up hunting completely, these groups began to rely on highly organized systems of agriculture supported by well-engineered irrigation systems. Despite the challenges of the arid Southwest, tribes such as the Pueblo were able to grow enough food to sustain fairly large population centers that, in some places, may have numbered in the thousands.
- **The American Northwest (and California)** In the resource–rich areas of modern day Oregon, Washington, and northern California, other groups of Native Americans, like the Chinook, were able to establish sedentary communities by developing sophisticated methods for hunting and fishing, combined with some foraging. Because of their use of fixed settlements, American Indians in this region rarely experienced conflict or competition among tribal groups. Their resulting prosperity also allowed for the development of a highly structured system of social stratification.
- **The Great Basin and the Great Plains** Unlike other regions, the Great Basin (between the Rocky Mountains and the Sierra Nevadas) and the Great Plains posed such significant challenges to native inhabitants that permanent settlements were impossible. Relying on large, migratory game, the American Indians of these regions lived as nomads in fairly small groups scattered across the vastness of the land. Some of the archetypes of Native Americans are based on the lives of those who lived in this region; the Plains Indians, like the Pawnee, hunted bison and built highly mobile dwellings that

could be transported easily (like the teepee). These groups were particularly astute at using every bit of any animal they killed—including organs, bones, hide, and hair.

- **American Northeast and Atlantic Seaboard** Because of the variety of available resources, weather patterns, and game, the Native peoples of the East Coast of North America—like the Iroquois and the Algonquian—utilized multi-crop patterns of cultivation (like maize, beans, and squash planted together) to provide for more stable, permanent villages. Although the nature of the terrain lent itself to fairly small communities, connections among tribes that were part of confederacies like the Iroquois nation were highly complex. By forming self-governing bodies, the American Indian inhabitants of the Eastern Seaboard capitalized on and made efficient use of the resources of the territory they occupied.

THE COLUMBIAN EXCHANGE

When Christopher Columbus returned to Spain after having discovered the New World, he initiated a system of trade that would revolutionize the world.

Once brought back by Columbus and other explorers, New World goods like corn and potatoes quickly became staples in the diets of people all over Europe and Africa, enabling population growth. Old World transplants such as sugar and coffee thrived in the rich soil and warm weather of Central and South America, a fact that led to their rapid development as cash crops in the plantation system that relied upon forced labor. Furthermore, the introduction to the New World of cattle and horses dramatically changed the lifestyle of Native Americans, such as the Plains Indians, like the Apache and Sioux, whose nomadic culture quickly embraced the horse's ability to expand their hunting grounds and further increase their mobility.

Most dramatic of all, however, was the result of the introduction of European diseases to populations of Native Americans with no natural resistance. Though usually unintentional, deadly epidemics of yellow fever and smallpox reduced Native American populations by as much as 90 percent in a single century. Many of those infected had never even seen a European.

Over time, the pace of these changes only accelerated as new technologies and new methods for raising the funds required for exploration made the exploration of the New World much easier. These developments, in turn, opened the door for colonization and settlement, a change that would literally turn the course of history.

EXPANSION INTO THE NEW WORLD

The Treaty of Tordesillas, drafted in 1494 with influence from the pope, had drawn a line of demarcation to divide the world between Catholic Spain and Portugal. All of the Western Hemisphere except Brazil was assigned to Spain; Portugal was permitted to colonize Asia. Although other nations did not take this agreement seriously, Spain and Portugal were in the forefront of exploration, spurred on by new technological developments in navigation and the consolidation of power by their respective royal families.

Initially, the Spanish journeyed to North and South America in search of precious metals and gave little thought to colonizing the areas they explored. The gold and silver that they discovered and mined provided the capital necessary for a host of political changes among European powers, among which is counted the shift from feudalism to capitalism. On the heels of the early explorers and settlers came Catholic missionaries, who viewed the Western Hemisphere as fertile ground for proselytizing their religious views. Furthermore, as competition among European monarchies heated up, the New World offered fertile ground for the seizure of territory (and power) in hopes of beating out Old World rivals.

AP Tip

Information in this chapter can be used in a free-response question that deals with the causes of imperialism, inter-imperialist competition, and the clash of cultures.

INTERACTION BETWEEN THE EUROPEANS, NATIVE AMERICANS, AND AFRICAN SLAVES

First to lay claim to the New World, the Spanish sought to subdue the vast new territory claimed for it by explorers such as Francisco Coronado, Francisco Pizzaro, and Hernán Cortés. Though the Americas were full of rich resources, labor was required to extract them. Initially, the Spanish developed an institution known as the *encomienda* system, which granted colonists the rights to the labor of Native Americans in exchange for providing for their food, shelter, and, above all, for Christianizing them. Little more than slavery, this system powered sugar plantations and silver mines for a short time, until the many thousands of Natives who had been present at the time of Spanish colonization were all but annihilated by disease. Though there were some voices of protest—most notably that of missionary Bartolomé de Las Casas—most of the conquistadors felt that the American Indians' lack of "civilization" was an indicator of their inferiority and made natural their subjugation. Despite being vastly overpowered, Native Americans who remained under Spanish rule—in *encomiendas* or on Spanish missions—resisted the changes forced upon them and some rebelled violently (as did the Pueblo Indians in Popé's Rebellion in 1680). Over time, however, intermarriage led to the creation of new cultural identities and to the development of a caste-like system defined by race and power.

In response to the issues that developed with the use of Native labor, the Spanish quickly turned to African forced labor. In partnership with the Portuguese (who controlled the European trade in slaves along the West African coast), Spanish slave ships brought hundreds of thousands of slaves to work in sugar plantations and silver mines in the Americas. Though Arab and African traders had practiced the sale of slaves for centuries, the scale of the importation of slaves to the New World dwarfed any prior model. Furthermore, the institution of slavery that developed in the New World—with its permanency and basis in race, not conquest—created tensions that would set up racial conflicts in the centuries to come. However, despite every attempt to confound slave organization and cooperation, African slaves nevertheless managed to maintain some cultural autonomy, particularly on plantations where incredible numbers of slaves toiled together. Though many adopted the religion of their captors, slave communities often preserved tribal traditions and blended them into their practice of Christianity.

Content Review Questions

1. Which of the following best describes the impact European colonization had on the Western Hemisphere's native population?
   (A) The native population was highly respected in terms of territorial possessions and religious beliefs.
   (B) The Europeans for the most part did not interact with the native population.
   (C) Spain was the only European country to successfully create an alliance with the native population.
   (D) Native populations were often killed off or driven away by the Europeans.
2. Which of the following regions was home to bands of nomadic Native Americans who relied on their game for the vast majority of their needs?
   (A) The Southwest
   (B) The Northwest
   (C) The Great Plains
   (D) The Eastern Seaboard
3. Which of the following shows how Native Americans adapted to and transformed the environment in which they lived?
   (A) The creation of large-scale irrigation works to promote the growing of maize
   (B) The development of highly structured systems of social stratification
   (C) The construction of monuments to nature-based deities
   (D) The organization of self-governing confederacies among disparate tribes
4. Which of the following tribes was encountered by English settlers and best known for their highly evolved system of government?
   (A) The Pueblo
   (B) The Chinook
   (C) The Sioux
   (D) The Iroquois

5. As a result of the Columbian Exchange, the New World gained
   (A) a significant new source of staple food crops.
   (B) an influx of gold and silver capital for the construction of new urban centers.
   (C) advanced medical techniques that extended the life span of Native Americans.
   (D) new animals as sources of food and to serve as beasts of burden.

6. European diseases that arrived in the New World were particularly deadly because
   (A) little medical aid was available so far from European urban centers.
   (B) the European conquerors deliberately accelerated the spread of the most deadly strains.
   (C) the Native Americans had no natural resistance to these diseases.
   (D) the vast devastation of warfare with the Europeans left few to care for the sick.

7. One significant impact of the Columbian Exchange on the Old World was
   (A) the growth of the food supply and subsequent population increase.
   (B) the introduction of slavery as a significant source of labor for European landowners.
   (C) the widespread devastation of new diseases among the poor.
   (D) a draining of capital from the royal families and a shift of wealth to the hands of the merchant class.

8. Which of the following explains the impact of the Treaty of Tordesillas (1494)?
   (A) It offered eternal life to anyone who would convert the natives of North America.
   (B) It encouraged Spanish exploration of the New World.
   (C) It banned the Portuguese slave trade.
   (D) It condoned the use of the *encomienda* system.

9. Which of the following served as the initial motivation for Spanish exploration?
   (A) Desires to convert the Native Americans to Catholicism
   (B) Hopes of establishing permanent colonies for settlement
   (C) The desire to beat out European rivals in the land-grab for North America
   (D) The need for new sources of wealth to support the growth of the nation

10. All of the following contributed to European expansion into the New World EXCEPT
   (A) the development of new navigational technology.
   (B) an end to European wars between competing royal families.
   (C) a rise in nationalism among European states.
   (D) the desire to spread Christianity.

11. Which European nation was first to lay claim to the New World?
    (A) Portugal
    (B) Spain
    (C) France
    (D) England

12. In the view of the *encomienda* system, Native Americans were seen primarily as
    (A) a source of labor.
    (B) a group to be protected.
    (C) a focus of evangelization.
    (D) outcasts to be excluded from Spanish settlement.

13. What aspect of Spanish colonization did missionary Bartolomé de Las Casas famously protest?
    (A) The refusal of explorers to tithe of the wealth they discovered
    (B) The lack of missionary zeal among the *conquistadors*
    (C) The treatment of Native Americans as subhuman and expendable
    (D) The focus of the Spanish Crown on Latin America, while neglecting the *Reconquista* at home

14. All of the following encouraged the growth of African slavery EXCEPT
    (A) the cooperation of Portuguese, Arab, and African merchants.
    (B) the cultural unwillingness of the Spanish to work alongside the Native Americans who they perceived to be pagan.
    (C) the success of the slave-based labor system in the English colonies.
    (D) the dramatic reduction in the population of able-bodied Native Americans due to disease.

15. One new feature of the institution of slavery as developed by the Spanish in the New World was
    (A) its basis in race.
    (B) the use of slave labor in agriculture.
    (C) its ability to essentially erase the home culture of captured slaves.
    (D) the use of violent coercion to force labor.

Short-Answer Questions

1. The arrival of Europeans in the New World greatly impacted the American Indian populations.
    A) Of the choices below, choose ONE and explain the results of that particular development for the Native Americans.
    The exchange of crops and animals
    The spread of diseases
    The political and social interaction between Native Americans and Europeans
    B) Explain the impact of the change you chose in Part A on the Europeans.

Question 2 is based on the following map.

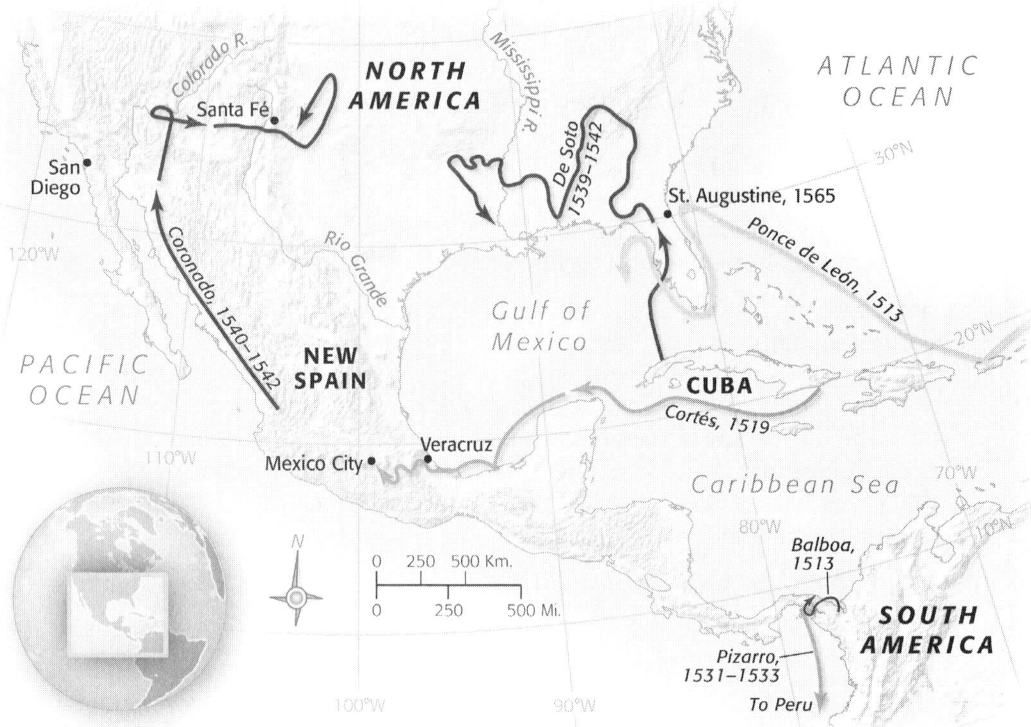

Cengage Learning

2. Use the map and your knowledge of United States History to answer Parts A and B.
   A) Briefly explain the culture of one of the groups of Natives encountered by Spanish explorers in the 16th century.
   B) Briefly explain the interaction between the Native Americans and Spanish explorers in the New World.

Long-Essay Questions

1. Explain how contact between Europeans, Native Americans, and the people of West Africa created a new world.
2. What role did competition over resources play in the conflicts that emerged in the Americas after European exploration and settlement?

Answers

Content Review Questions

1. **(D)** The impact of European colonization on the native populations of both North and South America and the Caribbean was devastating (*The American Pageant,* 14th ed., pp. 15–16/15th ed., pp. 15–16; Learning Objective PEO-4).

2. **(C)** Low levels of rainfall and large herds of buffalo encouraged the nomadic lifestyle of the Plains Indians (*The American Pageant,* 14th ed., pp. 8–10/15th ed., p. 8; Learning Objective ENV-2).

3. **(A)** In light of scant rainfall, the Pueblo developed irrigation to support the maize farming that sustained their large urban populations (*The American Pageant,* 14th ed., pp. 8–10/15th ed., p. 8; Learning Objective ENV-1).

4. **(D)** The Iroquois Confederacy was noted by English settlers for its advancement in self-government and democratic principles (*The American Pageant,* 14th ed., pp. 8–10/15th ed., p. 8; Learning Objective CUL-1).

5. **(D)** Cattle and horses revolutionized the lifestyles of many groups of Native Americans in the New World within a few centuries of their introduction by Columbus (*The American Pageant,* 14th ed., p. 15/15th ed., p. 14; Learning Objective WOR-1).

6. **(C)** Isolated for millennia from such strains as smallpox and yellow fever, the Native Americans had almost no way to fight off the dread diseases (*The American Pageant,* 14th ed., p. 16/15th ed., p. 15; Learning Objective PEO-4).

7. **(A)** The arrival of such crops as maize and potatoes provided an easy-to-grow source of more calories to support the growth of the European population (*The American Pageant,* 14th ed., p. 15/15th ed., p. 14; Learning Objective WOR-1).

8. **(B)** By ceding rights to the exploration of Asia to the Portuguese, the Treaty opened the doors to Spanish exploration and profit-seeking in the Americas (*The American Pageant,* 14th ed., p. 17/15th ed., p. 15; Learning Objective PEO-1).

9. **(D)** Though all certainly played a role in Spanish exploration, the search for gold and silver—a valuable trading commodity in the Eastern world—was paramount (*The American Pageant,* 14th ed., pp. 16–18/15th ed., pp. 15–17; Learning Objective POL-1).

10. **(B)** Competition and conflict continued in Europe as each of the major powers sought to lay claim to the wealth of the New World (*The American Pageant,* 14th ed., p. 14/15th ed., p. 13; Learning Objective WOR-1).

11. **(B)** Columbus' discovery, an early unification, and the Treaty of Tordesillas gave Spain the head start in the exploration of the New World (*The American Pageant,* 14th ed., pp. 16–17/15th ed., p. 15; Learning Objective PEO-1).

12. **(A)** Though recipients of the grants of rights to the Native Americans were encouraged to provide for the sustenance of the Natives and to attempt to Christianize them, they were primarily a source of semi-slave labor for mining and plantation style agriculture (*The American Pageant,* 14th ed., p. 18/15th ed., p. 17; Learning Objective WXT-4).

13. **(C)** De Las Casas was one of the only voices condemning the treatment of Native Americans (*The American Pageant,* 14th ed., pp. 18–19/15th ed., p. 17; Learning Objective ID-4).

14. **(C)** The Spanish followed the Portuguese in the use of slave labor in mines and on plantations, to be adapted first by English colonists in the Barbados and then by English colonists in North America (*The American Pageant,* 14th ed., p. 12/15th ed., p. 12; Learning Objective WXT-4).

15. **(E)** Although a step in the right direction in regard to religious freedom, the act protected only Christians. Non-Christians and atheists could suffer the death penalty for their beliefs (*The American Pageant,* 14th ed., pp. 72–75/15th ed., pp. 62–65; Learning Objective ID-4).

Short-Answer Questions

1. A) **The exchange of crops and animals** changed the lifestyle of Native groups by providing additional sources of food and beasts of burden. In particular, the hunting and migration patterns of the North American Plains Indians were affected by their adoption of the horse in the seventeenth century. **The spread of diseases** devastated Native American communities who had no immunity to diseases like smallpox and yellow fever. By some accounts, their population was reduced by 90 percent. **The political and social interaction between Native Americans and Europeans** resulted in the creation of a distinct hierarchy among racially mixed populations with Europeans serving as the ruling class, followed by a *mestizo* class that oversaw the Native and African slave labor. In some places, these relationships played out in the *encomienda* system.

   B) **The exchange of crops and animals** provided the Old World with new staple crops like corn and potatoes that provided a much-needed boost to the food supply and allowed for a growing population. **The spread of diseases** affected

Europeans to a lesser extent, though syphilis did arrive in the Old World as part of the Columbian Exchange. To a greater degree, the devastation of Native populations eased the path of conquest for European settlers and necessitated the use of African slave labor. **The political and social interaction between Native Americans and Europeans** led to a distinct, New World culture that in many cases would ultimately lead to differences in the views of colonial and European leaders. Ideas of superiority further developed racial conflict among New World settlers.

2. A) The Pueblo of the Southwest (encountered by Coronado) created large urban centers based on irrigated agriculture. He, along with Hernando de Soto, also encountered some of the Plains Indians, nomadic people who relied on their skill in hunting vast herds of buffalo. Ponce de León encountered groups of Natives along the Eastern Seaboard that lived in highly organized, though small, bands that relied on a combination of agriculture and hunting and gathering for their survival.

   B) Discuss the violence of conquest and the cultural misunderstandings and perceived inferiority of Native American groups. Explain the role of disease in reducing the strength of the American Indian population. Include a discussion of the *encomienda* system of forced labor combined with Christianization as a model for Spanish conquest.

Long-Essay Questions

1. You should address the nature of the interaction among these groups—with Europeans as conquerors exploiting the labor of West African slaves and subjugating Native American groups they encounter. Discuss the results of these contacts for all involved, including the impact of the Columbian Exchange (especially the impact of European diseases among Native Americans and the value of New World staple crops for expanding the global food supply). (Historical Thinking Skill I-1: Historical Causation)

2. You should point out that the accumulation of resources (particularly gold and silver, but also new cash crops) served as a primary motivator for the Spanish conquerors. Include a discussion of the role of religion in Spanish *encomiendas* and missions and the reactions of the Native Americans. Explain the additional role of race and culture as factors that further complicated the interaction between the Spanish and the Native American groups they perceived as inferior and savages. (Historical Thinking Skill II-5: Contextualization and III-6: Historical Argumentation)

Period 2: 1607–1754

The Settlement of North America

On the heels of the Spanish explorers, the French, Dutch, and English each made their way to the New World of North America. Based on their unique resources, goals, and on the varied environments encountered by each group, the European colonies were in every way diverse. As each maneuvered to reap the greatest possible gain from their American settlements, they in turn created distinctive societies that would find their identity in their survival (and thriving) in the New World. Nevertheless, these changes would not come without conflict: conflict between intercolonial rivals and between settlers and the Native Americans who desperately wanted to maintain their way of life.

Key Concepts from the College Board

2.1 Differences in imperial goals, cultures, and the North American environments that different empires confronted led Europeans to develop diverse patterns of colonization.

2.2 European colonization efforts in North America stimulated intercultural contact and intensified conflict between the various groups of colonizers and native peoples.

2.3 The increasing political, economic, and cultural exchanges within the "Atlantic World" had a profound impact on the development of colonial societies in North America.

2

COLONIZATION OF NORTH AMERICA: 1565–1754

After the initial establishment of a colonial foothold by the Spanish, other European powers scrambled to seize a piece of the New World for themselves. In the subsequent century, the Spanish, French, Dutch, and English each developed their own unique patterns of colonization. Differing decisions about how to interact with Native populations and how best to profit from the development of colonies produced distinctive settlement patterns and defined much of their ultimate success. Geography played an important role, particularly among the British colonies, whose individual situations were so different as to form four distinct regions with diverse needs, values, and challenges. Over time, the rise in the trade system of the Atlantic world helped to unify colonists and, among other developments, contributed to the growth of a unique, American identity.

KEY CONCEPTS

- Spain and Portugal initially colonized the Western Hemisphere and used a mixture of intermarriage and subjugation to dominate the Native people of Central and South America.
- The Dutch colonized the Hudson River Valley, while the French settled in parts of Canada and the Ohio River Valley, both developing significant trade alliances with the American Indians in order to establish a profitable export industry.
- The English ultimately established a strong foothold of permanent settlements on the Eastern Seaboard, where they developed hostile relationships with the Indians who occupied territory they desired. The origins of the English colonies varied, as did their social and political systems.
- The British pursuit of mercantilist policies in the Americas was fairly unsuccessful in light of strong colonial resistance.

The exploration of the New World and colonial life in North America are discussed in depth in *The American Pageant,* 14th and 15th eds., Chapters 2–5.

SPAIN COLONIZES THE NEW WORLD

Initially, the Spanish journeyed to North and South America in search of precious metals and gave little thought to colonizing the areas they explored. Only when other European powers such as France took an interest in North America did Spain make a concerted effort to establish permanent settlements, first at St. Augustine, Florida (1565), later in South America, the American Southwest, and as far west as California. On the heels of the early explorers and settlers came Catholic missionaries, who viewed the Western Hemisphere as fertile ground for proselytizing their religious views. The goal of the Spanish monarchy, however, was to establish and defend a mercantilist policy that would reserve to Spain all the rewards the New World had to offer. In North and South America, the authority of the king and his representatives was supreme. By the 1640s the economic benefits accrued by Spain in the New World began to seriously decline. There were many causes: increased pressure from the other imperial nations, especially from the Dutch; domestic problems in Spain itself; declining profits because of the expense of maintaining its colonies, particularly after the Pueblo Revolt in 1680; enormous military expenditures for the protection of its colonies; and a fleet to defend its trade ships. Spain was left a second-rate power. In its colonies that remained, Spain was forced to accommodate—in some respects—the culture of the American Indians they encountered, intermarrying with them in many cases and creating an entirely new society.

AP Tip

Information in this chapter can be used in a free-response question that deals with the effects of geography on the development of social, economic, and political systems.

DUTCH SETTLEMENTS AND A FRENCH EMPIRE IN NORTH AMERICA

The Dutch entered the race for colonies in the late sixteenth century, exploring what later became known as the Hudson River, where they established a colony, New Netherland. Shortly thereafter another major colony, New Amsterdam, was founded on Manhattan Island. The Dutch, like the French, sought to exploit the lucrative fur trade. And like the French colony in Quebec, New Amsterdam did not receive support from the government at home. Despite enticing settlers with patroonships (large tracts of land given in return for settling an area), few Dutch emigrants arrived, and the colony suffered incessant attacks by Native Americans and incursions by other European nations.

While the Spanish settled colonies in warmer climates, the French established their first permanent settlement in the less hospitable climate of Quebec and Nova Scotia, collectively referred to as New France in the seventeenth century. Not surprisingly, the colony was at first sparsely settled. The French government provided little incentive for its citizens to resettle in the frigid areas in and around Quebec, and it forbade French citizens who were looking for a way out of France, the Huguenots (Protestant reformers persecuted for their break from the Catholic Church), from emigrating. Not surprisingly, the vast majority of French citizens who settled in Canada returned home. Not until 1608 would the French make inroads into acquiring lucrative North American resources such as beaver pelts. The French (like the Spaniards) would experience some success in the New World because of the alliances they established with various Native American tribes. In fact, the French had earlier joined with two tribes, the Algonquian and the Huron, in a fight with the powerful Iroquois. Unfortunately for all Native Americans, regardless of their tribe, the Europeans brought with them diseases to which the Native Americans had no immunity. The mortality rate was staggering.

Later in the century (1682), the French laid claim to the Mississippi Valley, calling it Louisiana after their king, Louis XIV. Thirty years later the city of New Orleans was established; it would eventually become an important military and economic strategic location. By the second decade of the eighteenth century, the French had settled as far west as present-day New Mexico and South Dakota.

As a consequence, the English colonies that had been settled in the early seventeenth century along the East Coast were restricted to territory east of the Appalachian Mountains by French control of the area from the Ohio River Valley to Louisiana. The turning point, however, for French expansion in North America came with the Treaty of Utrecht (1713). Having been on the losing side in the War of Spanish Succession (Queen Anne's War, as it was known in the colonies), France lost Newfoundland, Hudson Bay, and Acadia (Nova Scotia) to Britain. While France could ostensibly afford to lose territory—though of course it preferred not to, especially to its rival Britain it was the lack of French inhabitants there that hampered the development of its empire in the New World; British settlers outnumbered French settlers in the mid-eighteenth century by a ratio of 3:1. Both Britain and France had Native American allies to swell their numbers as far as defense was concerned, but in 1763, when France was defeated by Britain and its American colonists in the French and Indian War, France temporarily had no major territorial possessions in North America. The Louisiana Territory had been ceded to Spain in 1762, and while Napoleon Bonaparte regained it in 1800, this vast territory was sold to the United States in 1803. Simply stated, by 1763 Great Britain controlled nearly all of North America from the Eastern Seaboard to the Mississippi River as well as Canada.

The British Empire in the New World

England had established a colony, the doomed Roanoke Island settlement in Virginia, as early as 1585, but grander forays into the New World had been slowed by the need to resolve religious division between Catholics and Protestants, a result of King Henry VIII's decision to separate from the Catholic Church. With that settled, and buoyed by the defeat, under Queen Elizabeth I, of the invading Spanish Armada, in 1588, the English caught up with the other European imperial powers in exploring and settling the New World. As with the Dutch and French, the English sailed to North America in search of a Northwest Passage to Asia. But the English had other motives as well: exploration could yield lucrative benefits for investors who bought into joint-stock companies in the hopes of realizing a profit. The lure of raw materials was an important incentive as well, especially as these resources were vital to England's expanding manufacturing sector. At the heart of the government's desire for colonies was mercantilism; the need to accumulate gold, silver, and other precious resources; the establishment of a favorable balance of trade between the mother country and its colonies; and the establishment of colonies to act as a counterbalance to the influence of other imperial nations. The major early English colonies included the following:

- **Jamestown** England's first permanent colony in North America, Jamestown was established by the Virginia Company after receiving a charter from King James I in 1606. The original settlers suffered from disease (especially malaria because the colony was established near swampland), internal strife, and starvation, and they were heavily dependent on supplies from the mother country and assistance from Native Americans. The colony's economy finally stabilized when tobacco was successfully cultivated after its introduction by John Rolfe. In 1676 Jamestown was burned to the ground during Bacon's Rebellion. Rebuilt a number of years later, it was again destroyed by a fire in 1698.
- **Plymouth** Whereas the settlers who established Jamestown did so for predominantly economic reasons, Plymouth Colony was established by religious separatists seeking autonomy from the Church of England (Anglican Church). In 1620 these "Pilgrims" sailed on the *Mayflower* to New England after receiving a charter from the Virginia Company. When they arrived, they created a document known as the Mayflower Compact—the first form of self-government in the British colonies. By the end of the century, Plymouth, where the Pilgrims settled first, had become part of the colony of Massachusetts.
- **Massachusetts Bay Colony** Started in 1630, the Massachusetts Bay Colony was home to many Puritans, who left England because of the persecution they faced from the Crown and the Anglican Church. Under Calvinist religious leaders such as John Winthrop, the colony almost immediately developed into a theocracy in which the church was paramount in all decisions, political as well as religious. Though far from democratic, it became the first English colony to establish the basis of a representative government when residents demanded representation if they were to be taxed.
- **Other New England colonies** Major colonies were also established in Connecticut, Rhode Island, New Hampshire, and Maine. In the former, a productive fur trade operated in the Connecticut River Valley. Unlike the Massachusetts Bay Colony, religion was less important than commerce in Connecticut. Importantly, Connecticut colonists were the first in America to

write a constitution. The New Hampshire and Maine colonies originated when two Englishmen, given a government grant to the areas north of Massachusetts, divided the land. Both colonies eventually were absorbed into the Massachusetts Bay Colony, but New Hampshire became an independent royal colony in 1679. Maine remained a part of Massachusetts until 1820. Rhode Island's colonial history is very much tied to the trials and tribulations of Roger Williams, whose advocacy of separation of church and state and complete individual religious freedom convinced Boston's Puritan leaders to banish him from the Massachusetts Bay Colony. Undeterred, Williams went on to establish the colony of Providence. Other religious refugees, among them Anne Hutchinson, soon found their way to Rhode Island, and in 1663, Parliament granted the colony a new charter that guaranteed religious freedom.

- **The middle colonies** New York became an English colony through conquest. In the seventeenth century, England and Holland had engaged in a series of commercial wars in which the North American fur trade became increasingly important. To eliminate Dutch competition, the Duke of York was provided a fleet by his brother, King Charles II, to capture New Netherland, which he did in 1664. Under the duke, democracy was, at best, limited in the colony now named for him—New York. New Jersey originally belonged to the duke as well, but he transferred parts of it to other nobles. Quakers inhabited parts of east and west New Jersey, but in 1702 the colony was unified and granted a royal charter. Its neighbor to the west, Pennsylvania, was founded as a sanctuary for Quakers when William Penn was provided a grant to establish a settlement. It would be home to Germans, Quakers, and a wide variety of settlers who wanted good farmland in a colony that was, by and large, democratic for the time. Delaware—once Sweden's colony, then taken by the Dutch, and finally lost to the English—was also owned by the Duke of York. Concerned that Pennsylvania was landlocked, Penn purchased Delaware to provide his settlers access to the sea.
- **The southern and Chesapeake Bay colonies** Despite its rocky start, Virginia would become an economic powerhouse by the dawn of the eighteenth century—supported by a profitable trade in tobacco and other labor intensive crops. Maryland was conceived as a refuge for Catholics by Lord Baltimore, a recent convert to Catholicism and a London Company stockholder. After his death, the English Crown granted his son, the second Lord Baltimore, a charter to administer the colony. For all intents and purposes, Lord Baltimore ran Maryland as if it was a fiefdom, giving vassals land in return for their loyalty and assistance. Over time, republican features seeped into Maryland's political system and a bicameral legislature was established. Religious problems ensued, however, between Protestants, who settled the area in increasing numbers, and Catholics, for whom the colony was originally established. In 1649 the Maryland Toleration Act guaranteed freedom of worship for Christians while punishing those who made blasphemous remarks and committed other religious transgressions. In the Carolinas, land was granted as a reward for those who had helped

in the restoration of the monarchy, following the English Civil War and parliamentary rule. The Carolinas were similar to the middle colonies, which had for the most part been founded by proprietors, not (stock) companies. However, like Maryland, they were initially reminiscent of feudal kingdoms. Over time the Carolinas came to be identified with religious and political freedom, but, paradoxically, slavery was introduced almost immediately because the proprietors also had investments in the slave trade. Thus while indentured servants were represented in the labor force of other colonies, the Carolinas embraced slavery. Not until 1729 was the huge colony divided into North and South Carolina. Georgia, as already mentioned, began its history as a penal colony (where originally rum, Catholics, and blacks were prohibited) and as a first line of defense against Spanish-held Florida. When the number of convicts was found to be insufficient to sustain a viable colony, Georgia welcomed Protestants and skilled craftsmen from England, Scotland, and Germany.

By the eighteenth century the American colonies were on the way to developing their own unique cultures while maintaining the essence of their Old World customs. Some colonies were more theocratic and politically elitist than others; a few had some of the political rights found in a democracy—or anywhere in Europe, for that matter—such as freedom of religion and political expression. For their part, typical English colonists came to the New World in the hopes of improving their economic status or to seek greater political and religious autonomy—the goal of Quakers, Puritans, and Catholics. Once in North America, some sought to convert the Native American population to Christianity. Some arrived as indentured servants, others as refugees from persecution, some as slaves, and still others as castoffs because of criminal records or, more often, indebtedness. Some found success and freedom in the New World; others sank into poverty and despair. As in Europe, the wealthy colonists were generally politically powerful, their interests and concerns not necessarily consistent with those of their less fortunate fellow colonists.

Despite significant economic, political, social, and racial divisions, the American colonies' common British heritage and the unique challenges (like coming to terms with hostile Native Americans) and experiences (like the religious revival movement known as the Great Awakening) that they encountered in the New World led slowly to the emergence of an American identity. This common culture would, with the added motivation of Enlightenment ideals of self-government and liberty, help establish the foundation of the United States as an independent country.

British Policy in the Colonies

Despite the reality of the colonies' ultimate revolution for independence, many historians view the British-colonial relationship as initially benign. In other words, while the British sought to regulate trade and influence the colonial governments overall, it generally limited its intervention and management. During what is often referred to as a period of "salutary (benign) neglect," the years from about 1650 to the end of the French and Indian War in 1763, the Americans were largely left alone to develop their economy without serious British intervention. But some historians question this view, especially given that mercantilism was the prevailing economic system, one that emphasizes that a nation's economic power expands by maintaining a favorable balance of trade and controlling hard currency—specie. As with other imperial powers, Britain viewed the American colonies as a reliable source of raw materials and a viable market for British goods, as well as a place for profitable investment opportunities. For example, by the eighteenth century large swaths of Britain had been deforested, a serious concern for a nation that relied heavily on its wooden naval ships to control the seas. North America, on the other hand, had millions of acres of forest that could be harvested for British use.

British mercantilist policies were generally not challenged by the colonists, in part because they were difficult to implement and often infrequently enforced. As long as competition from the Americans wasn't significant and Britain wasn't experiencing an economic or fiscal crisis, there was little need or incentive to abandon the policy of salutary neglect. The major British mercantilist policies in the pre-1760 period include the following:

- **The Navigation Laws** These were a series of strict British trade policies designed to promote English shipping and control colonial trade in regard to important crops (such as tobacco) and resources, which had to be shipped exclusively in British ships. In order for the Americans to trade certain enumerated items with other nations, their ships had to stop in England first. The Navigation Law of 1660 would have had a devastating effect on the American economy had the British enforced the law. The British added further requirements in subsequent Navigation Laws in 1663, 1673, and in 1696, the latter allowed British customs officials using writs of assistance—search warrants—to search for and seize smuggled commodities.
- **The Wool (1699), Hat (1732), and Iron (1750) Acts** These acts were intended to subordinate American capital to British capital by preventing American businessmen from turning raw materials into finished commodities. For example, the fashion fad of the eighteenth century was beaver hats. The Hat Act prevented Americans from turning the beaver pelts into hats and selling them on the open market. Instead, as with many raw materials, the pelts were to be sold to English manufacturers, who then used them to make hats, which in turn were sold on the international market, including to the Americans. This type of legislation helps you see why some members of the colonial merchant class, those who had the most to lose financially, took up arms against Great Britain.
- **The Molasses Act (1733)** Molasses, an important sweetener—and an important component of the triangle trade—was used primarily in this era as an essential ingredient in the making of rum, an enormously popular beverage in the colonial period. In an attempt to control the lucrative sale of sugar cane to the colonies, the British government established regulations and restrictions, again not well enforced. Besides, the Americans often purchased sugar from the non-British sugar-producing Caribbean islands.

Discontent on the Frontier

In 1763, a band of western Pennsylvania frontiersmen, the Paxton Boys, attacked Native Americans whom they believed had been part of Pontiac's rebellion. When the Native Americans took refuge in Philadelphia, the Paxton Boys, numbering in the hundreds, descended on the city to demand funding to support their defensive needs on the frontier. It was not until Benjamin Franklin convinced the belligerent frontiersmen that financial aid would be forthcoming that the Paxton Boys returned home. This event, however, was not the first occasion in which settlers living on the frontier of their colonies took up arms to address grievances they claimed were being ignored by the colonial government. Nearly a hundred years before the Paxton Boys marched on Philadelphia, discontent on Virginia's frontier erupted into armed insurrection. In 1676 the royal governor of Virginia, William Berkeley, became the focus of discontent for those Virginians on the colony's frontier. It had become obvious to them that Berkeley was concerned more with the wealthy planters on Virginia's eastern seaboard (called the Tidewater region) than with those in western Virginia whose lives were considerably more tenuous because of constant fighting with Native Americans. Taking matters into their own hands, the Virginians, led by Nathaniel Bacon, attacked the Native Americans, whereby Governor Berkeley, after promising some needed reforms, organized an attack on Bacon's forces. Bacon and his men retaliated by marching on Jamestown and burning it. Then, unexpectedly and fortuitously for Berkeley, Bacon died. The revolt came to an end, and many of Bacon's followers were hanged. Nevertheless, the event was a harbinger of what would happen a century later. Further, many Americans saw that they had a common perception: colonial governments favored the aristocracy over the needs of the masses. Another impact of the rebellion unforeseen by Bacon and his men: a hastening of the move away from the use of indentured servants and toward increased reliance on African slaves (who would never become free and demanding of their rights).

Content Review Questions

1. Which of the following distinguished British settlement patterns from those of the other major European powers?
   (A) Their respect for Native cultures
   (B) Their establishment of widespread missions
   (C) Their focus on extracting gold and silver for export
   (D) Their creation of larger-scale colonies with permanent settlers

2. Which of the following imperial powers originally settled the Hudson River Valley?
   (A) Holland
   (B) England
   (C) France
   (D) Sweden

3. The colony of Georgia was
   (A) comparatively the most democratic English colony.
   (B) established by Spain in order to protect its colony of Florida.
   (C) established by England as a penal colony.
   (D) eventually ceded to Spain in return for Florida.

4. The Duke of Baltimore established the colony of Maryland
   (A) as an opportunity to invest in that colony's maritime industry.
   (B) in order to prevent France from seizing that territory.
   (C) as a haven for persecuted English Catholics.
   (D) for Quakers who had been evicted from Pennsylvania.

5. French immigrants to the New World tended to inhabit
   (A) Canada.
   (B) Florida.
   (C) territory east of the Appalachian Mountains.
   (D) southern colonies.

6. As the founder of Rhode Island, Roger Williams
   (A) established religious freedom for Jews and Catholics.
   (B) supported freedom of religion for the Huguenots.
   (C) established complete religious freedom for all of the colony's settlers.
   (D) established mandatory church attendance.

7. Which of the following stunted the physical growth of the English colony of New York?
   (A) Most settlers refused to recognize the Anglican Church.
   (B) New York relied almost exclusively on imports from Britain.
   (C) Few colonists wanted to settle in the western part of the colony.
   (D) Aristocrats controlled vast tracts of land.

8. Which of the following sought to exploit the lucrative fur trade in North America?
   (A) The French
   (B) The British
   (C) The French and Dutch
   (D) The Spanish and the French

9. John Winthrop is associated with which colony?
   (A) New Amsterdam
   (B) Massachusetts Bay Colony
   (C) Jamestown
   (D) Quebec

10. The English law decreeing that only the eldest son was eligible to inherit family lands concerns
    (A) a charter.
    (B) an entail.
    (C) a confederation.
    (D) primogeniture.

11. A major consequence of the Second Anglo-Powhatan War was
    (A) the repudiation of peaceful coexistence between the English and the Indians.
    (B) the territorial expansion of Indian tribes east of the Appalachian Mountains.
    (C) the complete destruction of Indian tribes in Virginia.
    (D) the collapse of English colonies in Virginia.

12. In the seventeenth century, the colony of Maryland became a safe haven for
    (A) runaway slaves.
    (B) runaway indentured servants.
    (C) Catholics.
    (D) Indians who had been chased from their ancestral lands.

13. The Maryland Act of Toleration (1649) granted religious toleration to
    (A) only those colonists who had settled in Maryland before the statute was ratified.
    (B) all residents of Maryland except Indians.
    (C) Protestants only.
    (D) all Christians, but no Jews or atheists.

14. Under Britain's mercantilist policy
    (A) Britain and the other imperialist powers worked out a trade agreement that would prevent conflict.
    (B) the colonies were expected to export more finished goods than they imported.
    (C) the colonies were expected to supply Great Britain with raw materials.
    (D) the colonies enjoyed considerable political and economic growth.

15. The primary goal of the Hat Act, Iron Act, and Wool Act was to
    (A) subordinate American capitalism to British capitalism.
    (B) increase production levels of these items in the colonies.
    (C) prevent British manufacturers from shipping raw materials to America.
    (D) raise revenue to pay for the salaries of British officials serving in the American colonies.

Short-Answer Questions

1. The French, Dutch, and English each laid claim to various parts of North America in the 17th century.
   A) Explain a major difference between the colonial settlements of the French, the Dutch, and the English regarding ONE of the following:
      - Relations with the Native Americans
      - Settlement patterns
      - Economic initiative
   B) Explain one cause and one effect of the difference you identified in Part A.

2. The mercantilist principles of the British Empire shaped the development of the American colonies.
   A) Briefly describe the principle of mercantilism.
   B) Provide ONE piece of evidence that demonstrates how the British exercised mercantilism in their governance of the American colonies.
   C) Provide ONE example of a conflict that developed as a result of the British pursuit of mercantilism.

Long-Essay Questions

1. Compare the English colonies in the New World in terms of government, population, and origin.
2. What role did religion play in the establishment of English colonies in North America?

Answers

Content Review Questions

1. **(D)** In fact, the scale and permanency of the British colonies often exacerbated their relationships with Native Americans, with whom they refused to associate (*The American Pageant*, 14th ed., pp. 15–16/15th ed., pp. 15–16; Learning Objective PEO-5).
2. **(A)** The Dutch established New Netherland and later New Amsterdam (*The American Pageant*, 14th ed., p. 57/15th ed., p. 50; Learning Objective PEO-1).
3. **(C)** Another reason the English established the Georgia Colony was to act as a barrier to potential incursion by the Spaniards in Florida (*The American Pageant*, 14th ed., p. 41/15th ed., p. 38; Learning Objective PEO-5).
4. **(C)** The duke was a recent convert to Catholicism and wanted to establish a colony for English colonists who were mistreated by the Anglican Church (*The American Pageant*, 14th ed., p. 36/15th ed., p. 32; Learning Objective CUL-1).
5. **(A)** The French settled mainly in Canada. After the French and Indian War Canada became part of Britain's North American empire (*The American Pageant*, 14th ed., pp. 109–110/15th ed., p. 98; Learning Objective PEO-1).
6. **(C)** Williams established total religious freedom, even for Jews and Catholics (*The American Pageant*, 14th ed., p. 52/15th ed., p. 46; Learning Objective CUL-1).
7. **(D)** For example, along the Hudson River, aristocrats owned immense landholdings (*The American Pageant*, 14th ed., p. 59/15th ed., pp. 52–53; Learning Objective POL-1).
8. **(C)** New Netherland was established as the base for the Dutch fur trade, and the French traveled across North America in search of beaver pelts (*The American Pageant*, 14th ed., pp. 111–112/15th ed., pp. 99–100; Learning Objective WOR-1).
9. **(B)** A Calvinist, Winthrop helped to establish a theocracy in the Massachusetts Bay Colony (*The American Pageant*, 14th ed., p. 49/15th ed., p. 44; Learning Objective CUL-1).
10. **(D)** Primogeniture was criticized as a method of concentrating land—and therefore wealth—in the hands of the few. It took

root in America but died out in the early nineteenth century (*The American Pageant,* 14th ed., p. 30/15th ed., p. 27; Learning Objective PEO-1).

11. **(A)** The Chesapeake Indians failed to defeat the Virginia colonists and were consequently driven out of their ancestral homes (*The American Pageant,* 14th ed., p. 33/15th ed., p. 29; Learning Objective PEO-4).
12. **(C)** Catholics were persecuted in Protestant England following the English Civil War; Maryland was founded by Lord Baltimore in 1634 in part as a refuge for Catholic émigrés (*The American Pageant,* 14th ed., p. 36/15th ed., p. 32; Learning Objective CUL-4).
13. **(D)** Although a step in the right direction in regard to religious freedom, the act protected only Christians. Non-Christians and atheists could suffer the death penalty for their beliefs (*The American Pageant,* 14th ed., p. 36/15th ed., p. 32; Learning Objective CUL-4).
14. **(D)** Under mercantilism, the colonies supplied the center (or mother country) with raw materials and became a market for finished goods (*The American Pageant,* 14th ed., pp. 127–128/15th ed., p. 114; Learning Objective WXT-1).
15. **(A)** The acts prevented American businessmen from turning raw materials into finished commodities. British manufacturers made considerably larger profits by producing finished goods and selling them on the open market (*The American Pageant,* 14th ed., pp. 127–128/15th ed., p. 114; Learning Objective WOR-1).

Short-Answer Questions

1. The regions available for analysis here are the British New England and Chesapeake colonies, the Dutch settlements around New Amsterdam, and the French settlements along the St. Lawrence River. You could discuss the reasons for the British colonists' rocky relationships with the Native Americans—including their goals for permanent settlement and refusal to accept Native cultural and religious practices. Discussing the relative sizes of the various nations' settlements will require an explanation of their respective goals for settlement. Noting the geographic challenges and advantages of each area will help to explain the ultimate outcomes of each settlement.
2. Mercantilism is an economic idea that claims that a positive balance of trade (exporting more than one imports) and a ready supply of specie are central to a nation's economic and military security. A strong answer must include a discussion of any of the early British laws restricting colonial trade—foremost among them the Navigation Acts—and the colonists' propensity towards smuggling in defiance of those laws.

Long-Essay Questions

1. You should address the differences by explaining that some colonies were started for religious reasons, others as economic ventures, some as grants from the monarch, and Georgia as a penal colony. Some were more democratic than others, and some were more religiously tolerant that others. Massachusetts and the mid-Atlantic colonies tended to have a higher population density than those in the south. (Historical Thinking Skill II-4: Comparison)

2. You should point out that religion was one of several important motives for colonization. Explain the role religion played in the establishment of colonies such as Plymouth and Maryland. Discuss the theocracy that was established in the Massachusetts Bay Colony, and contrast this with the freedom of religion that prevailed in Rhode Island. Important to this question is the establishment of Pennsylvania by the Quaker William Penn, whose colony tolerated religious freedom. (Historical Thinking Skill II-5: Contextualization and III-6: Historical Argumentation)

Period 3: 1754–1800

The Rise of the American Republic

By the middle of the eighteenth century, the British and the French were in the midst of a duel for dominance on the continent of North America. Meanwhile, the settlers of the North American colonies had themselves begun to forge a new identity. Although the final battles between the great European powers would result in a British victory—and the loss of all French territory in North America—the conflict over who would rule the land had only just begun. When Great Britain, reeling from her costly victory over France, attempted to force the colonies to live up to the spirit of mercantilism under which they had been founded, trouble arose. In the end, the American colonists had so strongly formed their self-image in liberty and prosperity that the idea of surrendering it to anyone, even their king, seemed unthinkable. After the American Revolution secured for the colonists their independence, they then commenced the real work of creating a nation that could last. It took two attempts, but the final Constitution has since stood the test of time, lasting more than 200 years.

Key Concepts from the College Board

3.1 Britain's victory over France in the imperial struggle for North America led to new conflicts among the British government, the North American colonists, and American Indians, culminating in the creation of a new nation, the United States.

3.2 In the late eighteenth century, new experiments with democratic ideas and republican forms of government, as well as other new religious, economic, and cultural ideas, challenged traditional imperial systems across the Atlantic World.

3.3 Migration within North America, cooperative interaction, and competition for resources raised questions about boundaries and policies, intensified conflicts among peoples and nations, and led to contests over the creation of a multiethnic, multiracial national identity.

3

Causes of the American Revolution: 1760–1774

When thinking about the causes of American colonial independence, many people often give little thought to factors other than the desire for liberty. All agree that the Revolution began because the colonists wanted independence, but they don't always trace this desire back to the imperialistic foreign policy adopted by the British long before the struggle for independence began. There are essentially two types of revolution: anti-imperialist and social or domestic. The objective of the first is self-determination, or autonomy. Profound social change, as in democratization, is the goal of the second type. Ultimately, when you study the causes of the American Revolution, you will need to interpret whether there were one or two revolutionary impulses.

Key Concepts

- Prior to 1763, the British subordinated American capital to British capital.
- The British success in the French and Indian War transformed the relationship between Britain and the American colonies.
- British policies after 1763 were designed to raise revenue to pay for the cost of the empire.
- The American colonists were divided over what course of action to take in response to British policies.
- The Americans created a government, the Continental Congress, to address the deteriorating relationship between Britain and the colonies.

The causes of the American Revolution are discussed in depth in *The American Pageant,* 14th and 15th eds., Chapters 6 and 7.

Competition between the British and French in the New World

By the middle of the eighteenth century, two powerful competitors, Britain and France, continued to vie for dominance in North America. In the seventeenth and early eighteenth centuries, Great Britain dominated the Eastern Seaboard of what would become the United States. The French were in control of Canada and also laid claim to an enormous swath of land that stretched west well beyond the Mississippi River and south to present-day Texas. Actually, both Britain and France had been fighting intermittently for centuries before they engaged each other militarily and diplomatically over the potential rewards of the North American continent.

French and British interimperialist rivalry was most intense between 1689 and 1763, when the French were finally defeated. Before this, however, Great Britain and France fought a series of wars. The final and most famous of which that was fought in North America (before spreading to Europe) was the French and Indian War, commonly referred to in Europe as the Seven Years War. The focal point of the struggle in North America was the Ohio Valley, where the French began constructing forts to stop the westward expansion into what they called New France by British colonists. Eventually, British and colonial forces, under the leadership of a youthful planter from Virginia named George Washington, engaged the French in the Ohio Valley. They were defeated. It was apparent that the war would last a bit longer than the British and their colonists had anticipated. In order to prepare for the ensuing warfare, the colonists, with encouragement from Britain, organized the Albany Congress. The immediate objective of this meeting was to keep the Iroquois tribes loyal to Britain. This would be accomplished by involving the Iroquois in discussions about issues affecting both the Iroquois and the American colonists and their British government officials. Under the leadership of Benjamin Franklin, the delegates drew up an American colonial response to the French, which became known as the Albany Plan of Union. This coalition would have provided for an American Congress, which would in turn have the authority to

- carry out diplomatic relations with the Native American tribes
- control public territory
- raise an army
- tax colonial citizens

Unfortunately, the colonists were too concerned about their own interests and unwilling to relinquish control to a provincial congress, so the Albany Plan was not accepted. Still, it created a foundation for future colonial cooperation, especially when it mattered even more, in the war against Britain.

Early on in the French and Indian War, the British suffered serious setbacks—for example, General Braddock's defeat at the hands of the French and their Native American allies near Ft. Duquesne, the worst British defeat in North America up to that time. But many French colonists were suffering hardships as well, despite their countrymen's military successes. French-Canadians living in Acadia (present-day

Nova Scotia) were driven out, ultimately settling in New Orleans (where their culture is commonly called Cajun). In 1756 the two imperialist rivals took their war global, each attacking its enemy's colonies in the Caribbean, the Pacific, and in India. Not until 1758 did British fortunes improve. Under a new British secretary of state, William Pitt, the British and Americans found common ground to address the military and economic demands of the war. Successes followed on the battlefield. The capture of the major French stronghold, Ft. Duquesne, by troops under the command of George Washington along with major British victories in New York drove the French out of most of the area they previously controlled. Retreating to Quebec, the French commander, General Montcalm, was decisively defeated by Britain's General Wolfe on the Plains of Abraham, outside of Quebec. Militarily and financially exhausted, the French sued for peace.

The Peace of Paris brought hostilities to a close, and with it French control of North America. The parts of the treaty that relate to North America include the following:

- Britain received all of French Canada and all territory south of Canada and east of the Mississippi River.
- France and its ally, Spain, lost their West Indian colonies.
- Britain received Florida from Spain.
- Spain received from France its territory west of the Mississippi, including control of the port city of New Orleans, as compensation for its loss of Florida.

Problems Inherited by Britain Following the War

With military victory came political and economic problems for the British. While they defeated their long-time rival in a pivotal campaign for territorial expansion and colonization, the British government had incurred a large debt. Prosecuting the war had been expensive. That and the huge cost of maintaining and controlling its expanded empire created a fiscal crisis, forcing the British to address important political and economic concerns that came with empire building:

- The newly won land, which doubled the size of Britain's North American territory, must be governed.
- Revenue must be raised to help absorb the costs of maintaining and controlling this vast territory. To make matters worse, citizens in Great Britain were already heavily taxed.
- Hostile Native Americans in the Appalachian region, who felt threatened by American westward expansion into the Ohio River Valley, needed to be controlled. (In 1763, under the leadership of Chief Pontiac, Native Americans in the Ohio Valley responded to these encroachments on what they considered to be their land by destroying forts and homes. The British, wary of their colonists' fighting capabilities, sent their own redcoats, not the colonial militias, to put down Pontiac's rebellion.) That year, the British government imposed restrictions on westward settlement.
- French Canadians needed to be assimilated into the British Empire.
- Opening new trade channels posed difficulties.

- Intractable American colonists were not about to accept restrictions on their activities. Some colonists, in fact, were beginning to compete effectively with British capitalists and refused to subordinate their economic interests to those of British manufacturers.

So extensive were these problems, so aggravating to colonial-British relations, that it can be rightly stated that Britain's eventual loss of its American colonies paradoxically began with its interimperialist victory in the French and Indian War.

Not surprisingly, with the defeat of the French, American colonists no longer felt threatened by French attacks, but an unanticipated consequence of the war soon became apparent. The British and Americans had taken away from the conflict contrary views of their relationship during the course of the conflict. For its part, Britain was highly critical of the American military contribution to the war effort. The American militia, they claimed, had fared poorly—in fact, not all colonies had sent troops to help. To the British, it was obvious that the Americans would be incapable or unwilling to defend the mother country's newly acquired territories. Further, throughout the war the Americans had continued to engage in illegal smuggling, which was harmful to the British economy. The American colonists, however, were equally disappointed with the British. Convinced they had indeed fought well, they were highly critical of Britain's military, which seemed more suited for European-style warfare than for warfare in the dense woodlands of North America. Politically and economically, the outcome of the war was to forever change the relationship between the center, Britain, and its periphery, the colonies. Eventually that outcome took both to a point hardly imaginable at the end of the French and Indian War, a fight for colonial independence.

British Attempts to Exert Authority

While annoying to some Americans, British mercantilist policy before the French and Indian War was not as irritating to them as what was to follow. The year 1763, while not as indelible as, say, 1776, is no less as fateful for two significant events that would profoundly shape the American colonists' relationship with Britain. The French and Indian War had created a fundamental change in the relationship between the American colonies and Great Britain. In some ways, 1763 can be considered a turning point in the association between Britain and its American colonies. It was in that year that King George III appointed George Grenville as prime minister. Under Grenville, the British devised a solution to their economic woes by fundamentally transforming their political, economic, and trade relationship with the American colonies. As a result, the policy of salutary neglect was abandoned. From then on, the British government would play a considerably enlarged (and, to some colonists, exploitative) role in the colonies. The first major controversial measure was the Proclamation of 1763.

One especially undesirable consequence of sustaining an imperialist policy is the cost of empire exceeding its benefits. Britain in the mid-eighteenth century was sensitive to this. Given the limited military resources the Crown had in the colonies and the large size of its territory after the French and Indian War, the British were already stretched thin. Allowing colonists to move farther west beyond British control (though Parliament would use the word "protection" instead) would only aggravate their already evident difficulties in governing the American colonies. Having to constantly fight Native Americans out West (for example, Pontiac's rebellion) would be a further drain on Britain's military and financial resources. Out of this concern came the Proclamation of 1763, which prohibited colonial migration and settlement west of the Appalachian Mountains. Americans were incensed by the act, but it didn't prevent them from streaming across the Appalachian Mountains—and the proclamation line. The colonists believed that the Proclamation had little to do with preventing colonial–Native American hostilities and almost everything to do with political, military, and economic control of them. The Proclamation effectively closed the area to Americans who wished to invest in the economic opportunities—fur and timber, land speculation—that the West offered.

Over the two years following the Proclamation of 1763, Parliament would enact a series of revenue-raising acts that infuriated many American colonists, especially as the British began to enforce their colonial laws. The following controversial legislation was passed:

- **Sugar (or Revenue) Act of 1764** With the first Navigation Law passed by Parliament in the previous century, Britain established its authority to regulate colonial trade. In 1733 it attempted to control the lucrative sugar trade between the colonies and the Spanish and French West Indies. The Sugar Act of 1764, which replaced the ineffective Molasses Act of 1733, actually reduced the duties on imported sugar (possibly as an enticement to colonial importers to stay within the law), but the British made a concerted effort to enforce the act and punish smugglers.
- **The Currency Act of 1764** Superseding the Currency Act of 1751 (which applied only to New England), this act forbade the colonists from printing their own currency and instead required them to use hard currency (gold and silver), which was in short supply in the colonies. All taxes had to be paid in hard currency as well.
- **The Quartering Act** Instituted in 1765, this act required Americans to provide food and supplies to British troops stationed in the colonies—going so far as to allow troops to be stationed in colonists' homes and businesses if no other facilities were available.
- **Stamp Act (1765)** Few acts of Parliament angered the American colonists as much as this attempt to raise revenue by taxing virtually all printed material, from newspapers and wills to marriage licenses and even playing cards. American opposition to this direct, or internal, tax was vociferous. Many colonists did not challenge Parliament's right to tax its citizens (and most Americans at this point believed themselves to be British citizens). What they wanted, as Virginia's Patrick Henry so passionately declared, was the right accorded other British subjects—namely, no taxation without representation. Many colonists were directly affected by the act, especially those who relied on the use of legal documents, such as attorneys and businessmen. It is not surprising, then, that the colonial middle class was so actively involved in organizing

resistance to this act and subsequent legislation. In the case of the Stamp Act, they organized almost immediately. In the fall of 1765, delegates from nine colonies met in New York City for what was referred to as the Stamp Act Congress. They issued a Declaration of Rights, the essence of which was the contention that Britain could not tax the colonists because they lacked representation in Parliament. Recalcitrant Americans responded to the Stamp Act with noncompliance—not using items that were affected by the tax (a boycott). Some used force and coercion. For example, the Sons (and Daughters) of Liberty and the Loyal Nine organized to attack and intimidate tax agents as well as fellow colonists who used the stamps. By the following year the British government realized that the act was a political and economic debacle—made abundantly clear when they could find no one willing to risk his life collecting the tax—and repealed it. But the act had allowed individuals and organizations—for example, Sam Adams's the Loyal Nine and the Sons of Liberty—to suggest that a complete break with Britain was essential to the colonies' future.

- **Declaratory Act (1766)** Britain professed the right to tax the colonists without challenge (or, in the language of the document, "in all cases whatsoever") even as it repealed the Stamp Act. Britain's response to the cry of no taxation without representation was that in fact the Americans possessed *virtual representation*. That is, members of Parliament were representatives of all British subjects wherever they lived.

Class Conflict in Colonial America

The contrast in the colonists' reactions to the hardly noticed Sugar Act (that taxed a good purchased nearly exclusively by the elites) and the Stamp Act (that taxed goods purchased by members of all classes) is revealing. Though the American Revolution would ultimately be fought for liberty and equality, strong elements of classism already existed in the colonies.

In 1771, just a few years before the American Revolution, Carolinians calling themselves Regulators revolted against what they believed were unfair taxes and a lack of representation in their state legislature. Although the rebellion was put down, it personalized the assertion that taxation without representation is tyranny. Some historians believe that the Revolution was needed to not only win independence but also to democratize American society and government.

Many British elites criticized Parliament for appeasing the colonies and expected the government to compel the colonists to pay their share of taxes. Under the new prime minister, Charles Townshend (called Champagne Charley for his ability to make speeches in Parliament while drunk), the British looked for new ways to address their revenue problem. The result was the Townshend Acts (1767).

In order to bring revenue into the Exchequer (British treasury), Townshend proposed that items produced in Britain and sold in America—such as paper, glass, lead, paint, and tea—be taxed. But this was not a direct levy in that it did not immediately come out of the individual consumer's pocket; it was to be paid at American ports. One way or another, however, the price of these commodities would be inflated. Further, Townshend suspended the New York Assembly for refusing to provide British troops with supplies, as required by the Quartering Act. The suspension was also meant as a warning to other disobedient colonies. To prevent further smuggling, Townshend established an American Board of Customs and admiralty courts to hear such cases. Writs of assistance were again issued to prevent smuggling. To make matters worse, some of the revenue raised from the act would go to pay for the salaries of the colonial royal governors, those very same individuals who were charged with the responsibility of governing the colonists and therefore enforcing the Townshend Acts.

The colonial response was immediate: boycott. In Massachusetts, the legislature condemned the Townshend Acts in a circular letter—that is, a letter disseminated in all the colonies. It stated that "a taxation of their constituents, even without their consent, grievous as it is, would be preferable to any representation that could be admitted for them there." The British maintained that the circular letter was treasonous, but it was not long before other colonies had adopted their own circular letters. Dissent was spreading, and even individual citizens took quill to paper to express their concerns. In Pennsylvania, John Dickinson published his *Letters from a Pennsylvania Farmer* (1767) in which he attacked Britain's assertion of the right to tax the colonists to raise revenue—Dickinson, like most Americans, had no argument with Britain's right to regulate colonial trade. Other colonial leaders such as Benjamin Franklin and Sam Adams weighed in as well, Franklin through the use of reasoned oratory and Adams via intimidation and belligerence. One coercive and humiliating tactic designed to send a message to officials in the colonies and in Britain was to tar and feather customs officers. Still, many colonists were not terribly affected by this indirect tax, especially because they could purchase smuggled items, such as tea, at a lower, nontaxed price. From the British perspective, these actions could not be tolerated. In haste, more British troops were sent to the center of discontent, Boston. It was there on a winter's day in March 1770, that one of the most famous and incendiary events in our story took place, the Boston "Massacre."

The Boston "Massacre"

For enlisted men, serving in the British army was often an act of desperation. They were paid subsistence wages, and discipline was maintained through the use of physical punishment and intimidation. In the American colonies, most notably in Boston, these lobsterbacks (as they were derisively referred to because of their scarlet coats) sometimes took spare jobs when they were off-duty for a fee lower than colonial workers would accept. This only added to the tension that prevailed in Boston—already a tinderbox in 1770. On March 5, a crowd of Bostonians attacked a squadron of British troops. The redcoats opened fire, killing and wounding about eleven of the provocateurs, including a black or mulatto mob leader, Crispus

Attucks. John Adams defended the British soldiers, winning an acquittal for most of them. But American propagandists wasted little time in presenting the event as an unprovoked attack on Americans. A Boston silversmith named Paul Revere created a powerful and widely distributed engraving whose imagery left no doubts as to the nature of the event. Long after the deadly volley had ceased, it would be referred to as the Boston Massacre. And it took the colonies one step closer to a formal separation with Britain, five years later.

In the months following the Boston Massacre, the colonies settled into a period of comparative calm after Parliament agreed with the new prime minister, Lord North, that the Townshend duties, except the tax on tea, should be repealed. Although this was a significant victory for the colonies, activists and radicals such as Sam Adams nurtured the revolutionary spirit by creating committees of correspondence. The committees acted as a conduit for the exchange of ideas and for disseminating the goal of a unified response by the colonial governments.

The Tea Tax

In the midst of this period of calm, two incidents revealed that the tranquility was deceptive. On a summer night in 1772, a British customs schooner, *Gaspee*, ran aground near Providence, Rhode Island. Residents in the area led by a merchant named John Brown wasted no time in burning the *Gaspee* to the waterline, but not before putting its crew ashore and looting the ship. Although a board of inquiry was established, the British never were able to establish guilt, in large part because of uncooperative Rhode Islanders. The looting of the *Gaspee*, while serious, pales in comparison with the plundering of a British commercial ship by Bostonians the following year. That ship carried tea in its holds.

In some areas, many colonists continued to boycott British tea. Yet by 1773 most Americans had begun once again to purchase tea from British merchants. In fact the opposition to paying the tea tax had withered, mainly because of the abundance of tea for sale, which made British tea cheaper than smuggled tea. The supply of tea became so great that the powerful British East India Company had an enormous surplus, which brought it to the brink of bankruptcy. But the company had powerful friends in high places in the British government, and they too were not eager to see the lucrative tea tax dry up should the company go under. The British government's solution to the problem was to grant the company a monopoly of the colonial tea trade. New England merchants who sold non-British tea believed this legislation placed them at a competitive disadvantage. Then tea prices came down even more as the company sought to unload its surplus. But most colonists would have none of it. True, they could purchase tea at a cost lower than ever, but the Americans believed the British government was duplicitous, getting the Americans to pay the tea tax by enticing them with lower prices. Incensed, individual consumers, merchants, and even colonial assemblies throughout the colonies responded, in some cases with violence, in others with noncompliance. Some of the tea was in fact confiscated and sold, the money eventually—and ironically—going to fund the Continental Army.

THE BOSTON TEA PARTY AND THE BRITISH RESPONSE

Our story returns to Boston, where residents by this point had had considerable experience with acts of civil disobedience, protest, and violence. One victim was the royal governor of Massachusetts, Thomas Hutchinson. After he confronted the mob in the Stamp Act crisis of 1765, his home was burned by the protestors. Hutchinson was resolute: he would enforce the letter of the law. Bostonians, however, were resolved not to pay the tea tax. The British government was determined to unload the tea in Boston despite strong opposition; they even considered suspending some civil liberties, which further enraged some Bostonian radicals such as Sam Adams. In response Bostonians, disguised to look like Native Americans, boarded the tea ships on the evening of December 16, 1773, and proceeded to throw the cargo into Boston Harbor as citizens of the city looked on silently and, more often than not, sympathetically. Governor Hutchinson returned to England in disgust. He had had enough of Boston.

The British government now faced an important dilemma. A strong response might only exacerbate the situation; no response was tantamount to appeasement and tolerance of the destruction of private property. By spring the British had decided on their answer. They would punish not just those who destroyed the tea, and not the city of Boston alone, but the entire state of Massachusetts, to show other colonies the consequences of challenging British authority. Collectively the British response is referred to as the Intolerable Acts (or Coercive Acts) of 1774, which included

- **The Boston Port Bill**, which closed the port of Boston and relocated the customs house so that some important supplies could enter Massachusetts.
- **The Administration of Justice Act**, which required that trials of royal officials accused of serious crimes in the colonies while carrying out their duties be held in Britain.
- **The Massachusetts Government Act**, which greatly limited citizens' rights to organize freely. It also replaced the election of Massachusetts judiciary and council members with Crown appointees.

In addition, the Quartering Act was expanded to require all colonists to house British troops when ordered.

To make matters even worse, in 1774 the British passed another act that was considered nothing short of contemptible by the Americans. The Quebec Act was designed to facilitate the incorporation of French Canadians and their land into Britain's colonial American empire. Quebec's boundary was extended to the Ohio River, Catholicism was recognized as Quebec's official religion, and a nonrepresentative government was established for its citizens. The Quebec Act was roundly condemned by the American colonists because they

- feared a precedent had been established in regard to the type of government (nonrepresentative) that was created in Quebec
- resented the expansion of Quebec's (French Canadian) colonial territory, to which they had been denied access by the Proclamation of 1763

- were offended by the Crown's recognition of Catholicism, given that most American colonials were Protestants

When it passed the Intolerable Acts in 1774, Parliament did not know that in just one year its troops and its colonists would exchange gunfire that would open the floodgates to a full-scale war for independence.

The First Continental Congress

In September 1774 delegates from twelve of the colonies sent representatives to Philadelphia to discuss a response to the Intolerable Acts. The eventual rejoinder from this body, later known as the First Continental Congress, ultimately took the form of a series of radical resolutions.

The vast majority of delegates reflected the views of those in their home colonies—namely, that conditions did not yet warrant a complete break with Great Britain. A distinct minority, however, did see this as the only viable alternative to what they viewed as a long series of British abuses. Others looked back, hoping to find a solution to the crisis in the pre–French and Indian War relationship. All had confidence in the American colonies' long history of self-government, through institutions as varied as the Virginia House of Burgesses and the Fundamental Orders of Connecticut. The tyrannical actions of the British towards the colonies could not be allowed to continue unchecked. The delegates then fell into three distinct groups:

- **Radicals** (such as Virginia's Patrick Henry, Massachusetts's Sam and John Adams, and Pennsylvania's Charles Thomson) believed that the colonies' relationship with Britain had already passed a point of no return. For them there were only two alternatives: force Britain to accede to their demands or declare independence.
- **Moderates** (such as Pennsylvania's John Dickinson and Virginia's George Washington) believed that the relationship between the colonies and Great Britain could be repaired.
- **Conservatives** (such as New York's John Jay and Pennsylvania's Joseph Galloway) were not prepared to make an aggressive response but did favor a mild rebuke of the British. In fact, Galloway proposed a union of colonies under British authority similar to that proposed in the ill-fated Albany Plan of the French and Indian War. If adopted, the relationship would return Britain and the colonies essentially to what had been the situation before the dramatic changes that took place in 1763 and the years since. There was one substantial addition, however: a colonial "grand council" would have the power to veto British acts. The Galloway Plan was narrowly defeated, setting the stage for the radicals to guide the direction of events and actions.

Using as their philosophical inspiration the ideas set forth by Thomas Jefferson in his pamphlet, *A Summary View of the Rights of British America,* the more radical delegates applied the following ideas to their response:

- Parliament possessed no inherent authority to tax the colonists.

- The British Empire was a compact (or loose union) between the center (the mother country) and its colonies, not one unit dominated by Britain.
- Each colony possessed its own legislature independent of Britain's legislative authority.
- Holding together this loose-knit union was a collective allegiance to the king.

The delegates adopted a statement of rights, the Declaration and Resolves, which had originally been enacted in Massachusetts as the Suffolk Resolves. In it the delegates took the following actions:

- They declared the Intolerable Acts null and void.
- They recommended that colonists arm themselves and that militias be formed. (In fact, Massachusetts residents had already taken this step, forming militia units ready to respond at a moment's notice—the Minute Men.)
- They recommended a boycott of British imports. ("Associations" were established in every colony to make sure the boycott was enforced.)

After a month of deliberations and squabbling, the delegates adjourned in late October, agreeing to reconvene in the spring. As they made their way home from Philadelphia, few delegates could have anticipated that in April 1775, an exchange of gunfire in a small Massachusetts town would take the Americans and the British to a crossroad in their rocky relationship. The road to Lexington and Concord had already begun.

Content Review Questions

1. A major goal of the French in wanting to maintain control over the Ohio Valley was to
   (A) prevent attacks by Native Americans on their forts and outposts.
   (B) eventually expand into Canada.
   (C) merge their landholdings from Canada to the Mississippi Valley.
   (D) exploit the lumber trade.

2. The most immediate objective of the Albany Congress was to
   (A) bring to an end the French and Indian War.
   (B) convince American colonists to boycott British-made goods.
   (C) end hostilities between Native Americans and French settlers in the Ohio Valley.
   (D) improve relations with the Iroquois tribes.

3. As a result of the French and Indian War
   (A) relations between French and American colonists improved dramatically.
   (B) France was able to hold on to Canada but lost the rest of its North American empire.
   (C) the Americans and British developed a mutual respect for each other's military abilities.
   (D) Britain felt it necessary to abandon the practice of salutary neglect.

> tacit trust, that it shall be employed for their good, and the preservation of their property;... and so [it] cannot be an absolute, arbitrary power over their lives and fortunes ...And this power has its original only from compact and agreement, and the mutual consent of those who make up the community."
>
> John Locke, "Second Treatise on Civil Government," Section 121 (1690)
>
> "...Whenever the legislators endeavour to take away, and destroy the property of the people, or to reduce them to slavery under arbitrary power, they put themselves into a state of war with the people... by this breach of trust they forfeit the power the people had put into their hands ...and it devolves to the people, who have a right to resume their original liberty, and, by the establishment of a new legislative, (such as they shall think fit) provide for their own safety and security."
>
> John Locke, "Second Treatise on Civil Government," Section 222 (1690)

1. Based on the two passages from John Locke's "Second Treatise on Civil Government," complete the following three tasks:
   A) Briefly explain the main point made by Passage 1 (from section 121).
   B) Briefly explain the main point made by Passage 2 (from section 222).
   C) Provide ONE piece of evidence from the period between 1763 and 1775 in support of the argument of some colonists that the British had violated the rights of the colonists as here explained by John Locke.
2. United States historians have proposed various events to mark the beginning of the American Revolution.
   A) Choose ONE of the events listed below, and explain why your choice best represents the beginning of the American Revolution. Provide at least ONE piece of evidence to support your explanation.

      The passage of the Stamp Act

      The First Continental Congress

      The Battle of Lexington and Concord
   B) Contrast your choice against ONE of the other options, demonstrating why that option is not as good as your choice.

Long-Essay Questions

1. In the decision to rebel against Britain, was the American Revolution fought strictly for independence, or did a desire for democratization play a role?
2. Compare the positions of moderates, radicals, and conservatives at the Continental Congresses. Which group was most effective in achieving its goals?

Answers

Content Review Questions

1. **(C)** The French sought to control territory west of the Appalachian Mountains, which would counterbalance Britain's landholdings along the Eastern Seaboard (*The American Pageant,* 14th ed., pp. 111–112/15th ed., pp. 102–103; Learning Objective WOR-1).

2. **(D)** Though the Albany Congress addressed other concerns, such as coordinating a united response to the French, its most immediate objective was keeping the powerful Iroquois nation loyal to Great Britain (*The American Pageant,* 14th ed., pp. 116–117/15th ed., p. 106; Learning Objective POL-1).

3. **(D)** The war strained American-British relations, particularly because of the resulting increase in taxation (and crackdown on smuggling) that Britain felt was necessary to finance the colonies' defense (*The American Pageant,* 14th ed., pp. 119–120/15th ed., pp. 107–109; Learning Objective WOR-1).

4. **(B)** Keep in mind that the Navigation Laws were poorly enforced and of almost no consequence. It wasn't until after the French and Indian War (during which the colonists met at the Albany Congress) had been concluded by the Peace of Paris that the British began raising significant taxes on the colonists. Though the Molasses Act met little resistance, the Tea Act caused much uproar (*The American Pageant,* 14th ed. and 15th ed., Chapters 6–7; Learning Objective WOR-1).

5. **(D)** In fact, the success of the colonial economy led many American colonists to begin to question Britain's insistence upon mercantilism and to see themselves as self-reliant (*The American Pageant,* 14th ed., p. 128/15th ed., p. 115; Learning Objective WOR-1).

6. **(C)** Prior to the 1760s Americans avoided the Navigation Laws through such illegal activities as smuggling. The British did not yet have a financial need to enforce the acts (*The American Pageant,* 14th ed., pp. 127–128/15th ed., p. 49; Learning Objective WXT-1).

7. **(A)** Though only killing five and wounding 6 others, the graphic engraving made by Paul Revere helped to solidify in many American minds the idea that the British were bent on attacking the innocent colonists (*The American Pageant,* 14th ed., pp. 132–133/15th ed., pp. 118–119; Learning Objective ID-1).

8. **(B)** The "Intolerable Acts" were a group of acts passed by Parliament to punish the colonies after the Boston Tea Party

(*The American Pageant,* 14th ed., p. 137/15th ed., p. 123; Learning Objective ID-1).

9. **(A)** Most American colonists rejected the Quebec Act for the reasons expressed in answers B–D. E is the primary reason the Quebec Act was passed (*The American Pageant,* 14th ed., pp. 137–138/15th ed., p. 122; Learning Objective POL-1).

10. **(C)** Though more radical delegates like John Adams succeeded in swaying many of the colonial representatives, conservatives advanced plans like the Galloway Plan, which proposed a return to the governing style of the British before 1763 (*The American Pageant,* 14th ed., pp. 137–138/15th ed., pp. 122–123; Learning Objective POL-1).

11. **(A)** The Fundamental Orders became the foundation for Connecticut's constitution (*The American Pageant,* 14th ed., p. 52/15th ed., p. 47; Learning Objective CUL-4).

12. **(C)** The Navigation Laws prohibited American trade with nations, such as France, that were not controlled by England. Naturally, many Americans resented the laws and sought to circumvent them through smuggling (*The American Pageant,* 14th ed., p. 55/15th ed., p. 49; Learning Objective WXT-1).

13. **(E)** Zenger's newspaper had criticized the colony's royal governor, and Zenger was arrested for libel. The court's decision was essential to the development of a free press (*The American Pageant,* 14th ed., p. 104/15th ed., p. 92; Learning Objective WOR-2).

14. **(C)** Radical agitators such as Sam Adams organized Committees of Correspondence throughout the colonies in order to incite the colonists to challenge the decisions and policies of the British government (*The American Pageant,* 14th ed., p. 134/15th ed., pp. 119–121; Learning Objective ID-5).

15. **(B)** Considered the most significant achievement of the First Continental Congress, the Association sought to convince the British government to address colonial grievances, many of which were economic in nature (*The American Pageant,* 14th ed., p. 138/15th ed., p. 123; Learning Objective WOR-2).

Short-Answer Questions

1. Understanding the first passage's point about the purpose of government and the origins of power is key to a strong answer. In the second passage, you must include an explanation of the just cause of a revolution. For your example, choose an event (like the Intolerable Acts) where the British were perceived by the colonists as abusing their power and, most importantly, failing to protect the property of the colonists.

2. Each of these three events represents the beginning of some new phase of the road to Revolution (though indeed, the colonists did not declare independence until 1776, more than a year after the first shots were fired at Lexington). Focus your answer on what element of the Revolution "began" at the event of your choice. Was it the beginning of the feeling that the British were abusing the rights of the colonists? The beginning of a concerted colonial effort to condemn the British? The point of no return after which political solutions to the conflict seemed unworkable?

LONG-ESSAY QUESTIONS

1. A discussion of the causes of the American Revolution must focus on the desire for independence, but another dimension can be added depending on your perspective: the war was also fought to democratize American society by removing the British, who were content to maintain the status quo in the colonies. For the first revolutionary impulse, you should address pre- and post-1763 policies. For the second, discuss the features of colonial America that were not particularly democratic. (Historical Thinking Skill III-6: Historical Argumentation)

2. Be sure to point out that twice as many Americans were opposed or indifferent to independence as favored liberty. This is reflected in the First and Second Continental Congresses: conservatives favored a return to the relationship that existed before the French and Indian War. Moderates maintained that events had not yet necessitated a break from Britain, and radicals favored immediate independence. Later events would satisfy the radicals' goals. (Historical Thinking Skill II-4: Comparison)

THE AMERICAN REVOLUTION: 1774–1783

Debate over the rights of the colonists had been raging since the close of the French and Indian War. Even in England, the radical British Whigs lamented the arbitrary use of power by the aristocratic Parliament and power-hungry king. Nevertheless, when the First Continental Congress's appeal to King George III, the Declaration of Rights, reached Britain in 1774, it was, to put it mildly, poorly received. Massachusetts was now considered to be in open rebellion, and soon fresh troops began arriving to enforce British laws and policies.

KEY CONCEPTS

- Both the British and the Americans had military, political, and economic advantages and disadvantages in the war.
- The Battle of Saratoga was the turning point in the war, for it persuaded the French to give what proved to be significant help to the Americans in the war for independence.
- Black Americans played an important role in the war.
- The American victory did not fundamentally change the condition or status of blacks or women.

The American Revolution is discussed in depth in *The American Pageant*, 14th and 15th eds., Chapters 7 and 8.

Massachusetts met this escalation of hostilities with its own call to arms. In April 1775, General Thomas Gage, who had replaced Hutchinson as royal governor of Massachusetts, dispatched troops to seize military supplies that militiamen had stored in Lexington. Upon meeting the Minute Men (militiamen who could be mobilized at a moment's notice) in Lexington, shots were exchanged between the two forces, killing eight of the Massachusetts combatants. The British then proceeded to Concord to continue their futile search for gunpowder and weapons. On their return from Concord, the British were ambushed time and again as they attempted to make their way back to Boston. Their losses were staggering, almost three hundred casualties. Even more damaging, however, was that the events at Lexington and Concord had a lightning-rod effect. Soon colonists were organizing to confront the British. As planned, the following month the Second Continental Congress assembled in Philadelphia. This time there were but two conflicting groups: those who sought immediate independence and those who still hoped for a negotiated settlement. Both sides had their say. The Congress then drew up military plans, in the Declaration of the Causes and Necessities for Taking Up Arms, which called for

- an American army to be organized and led by George Washington
- an American navy to be created to disrupt British shipping
- a military expedition to be led by Benedict Arnold to wrest Canada from the British Empire

By this time, Ethan Allen and his Green Mountain Boys had already seized Fort Ticonderoga in New York. But the center of hostilities continued to be Massachusetts, specifically Boston, the hotbed of radical dissent.

The War Begins in Earnest: Bunker Hill

For weeks after Lexington and Concord, both British and American troops poured into the Boston area, anticipating a major conflict. The Americans, under General Israel Putnam, occupied two strategic areas overlooking Boston, Breed's Hill and Bunker Hill, in advance of the British, who also wanted to control the high ground around Boston. On June 13, 1775, British troops, in their distinctive, conspicuous scarlet uniforms and weighed down with heavy supplies, attacked. After launching several assaults in which over one thousand British and some four hundred Americans were killed, the redcoats drove the Americans, who were nearly out of supplies, from their positions. Importantly, the colonists had stood their ground against what was considered the best European fighting force at that time. But even then there were still some colonial leaders who firmly believed that a peaceful solution could be found. The month after the Battle of Bunker Hill, Congress sent the Olive Branch Petition to King George III. Reaffirming their loyalty to him, they implored him to intercede on their behalf. Their appeal fell on deaf ears; the king would not negotiate with his own subjects, especially those who had taken up arms and clashed with his forces. In August, Parliament issued the Prohibitory Act, declaring all of the colonies in open rebellion and suspending all trade between Britain and the American colonies.

The Declaration of Independence

In early June of 1776, Virginia's representative to the Second Continental Congress, Richard Henry Lee, introduced a resolution in Congress that declared the colonies free and independent states. A committee that included John Adams and Benjamin Franklin was established to write a draft declaring this sentiment and the justifications for it. Thomas Jefferson, a gifted writer and brilliant thinker, was given the task of writing the document, which was then to be edited by the committee. Jefferson was influenced by the Enlightenment philosophers of his day, whose ideas can be found in the document he presented. By early July, all of the colonies except New York, which had a large percentage of its population still loyal to the king, adopted Lee's call for independence as articulated in Jefferson's draft. On July 4, 1776, the Declaration of Independence was formally approved by Congress.

Tom Paine's *Common Sense* (January 1776)

Whereas some colonists viewed the king's response to the Olive Branch Petition with dismay and foreboding, a recent English immigrant to Philadelphia, Thomas Paine, was resolute in his demands for independence. Considered incendiary and radical, Paine's forty-seven-page pamphlet, *Common Sense,* made some bold assertions. Foremost among them was his condemnation of monarchy and aristocracy and his advocacy for republican self-government based on the natural rights of the people. Moreover, Paine viewed the American cause as one that had historical impact for all people under the thumb of foreign domination. Obviously the themes of the pamphlet resonated with those who advocated a republican form of government, one deriving its power from the people. Over 150,000 copies were sold, an astounding number for its day. But the pamphlet, like the revolution it espoused, has lived on as a political inspiration ever since.

In the first part, which includes the Preamble (an introduction), Jefferson explains the necessity of independence for the preservation of basic natural laws and rights. These were John Locke's thoughts about the social contract, articulated in his *Two Treatises of Government,* and Jean-Jacques Rousseau's *Social Contract.*

> We hold these truths to be self-evident: That all men are created equal; that they are endowed by their Creator with certain unalienable rights; that among these are life, liberty, and the pursuit of happiness.

The second part of the Declaration of Independence lists the grievances of the colonies, a series of "abuses and usurpations" by the king and his government. This maltreatment, claimed Jefferson, violated the social contract the British monarch had with his colonies, thereby justifying the actions his American subjects felt compelled to take. The document ends with what is tantamount to a formal declaration of war. Even before signing the Declaration of Independence, the Second Continental Congress appointed a committee to draft the first constitution of the United States—the Articles of Confederation.

The Military Phase of the Revolutionary War

For upstart colonists to challenge the formidable British army and the even more potent Royal Navy in the late eighteenth century was an intimidating task. But as in all wars, both sides had their strengths and weaknesses.

- British Advantages
  - The British had a considerably larger population from which to draw for troops. However, they relied on volunteers and mercenaries (such as hired Germans called Hessians).
  - The British possessed considerable financial resources.
  - Britain had a highly trained and experienced professional fighting force.
  - Britain's Royal Navy controlled the seas, and therefore trade.
  - Native American tribes, eager to see an end to colonial westward expansion, generally allied themselves to the British.
  - Many Americans opposed to independence, called Tories or Loyalists, fought against the Continental Army. Among these were many immigrants from Germany, the Netherlands, and France who believed that the British offered greater religious tolerance than the at times puritanical Americans.
  - Black American slaves were offered freedom if they helped the British and some served in the British army.
- British Disadvantages
  - Britain needed a substantial part of its military to maintain its global empire. In fighting the Americans it eventually battled Holland, Spain, and France, nations all eager to see Britain defeated.
  - The European style of fighting practiced by the British army was not suitable for the North American wilderness.
  - The British had considerable logistical problems as their lines of communication and supplies stretched across the Atlantic Ocean.
  - The British army had to crush the rebellion by destroying Washington's army.
- Colonial (Patriot) Advantages
  - Americans were fighting for a lofty ideal—liberty—as well as for their homes and way of life.
  - By and large, the Americans had excellent officers, such as George Washington, as well as foreigners who came to assist the Americans, such as Thaddeus Kosciusko and Casimir Pulaski of Poland, Germany's Baron von Steuben, and, most famously, the Marquis de Lafayette from France.
  - The Americans were able to utilize guerrilla warfare, which often effectively counteracted Britain's disciplined troops and greater firepower.

  - The Americans received financial support from France and greatly benefited from direct French military intervention after 1778.
  - The Americans hoped that a protracted war would convince the British public and allies of the American cause in Parliament that continuing the war was senseless.
- Colonial Disadvantages
  - George Washington's army was considerably smaller than Britain's military forces in North America.
  - The Continental Congress had no real political authority. It had no power to tax or to create a sound currency.
  - Most Americans were loyalists or were indifferent or neutral about the war and so did not support it. Many Tories actually took up arms to crush the rebellion.
  - The Continental Army frequently suffered from supply shortages.
  - As with their foe, the Americans were vulnerable to war weariness and a sense of futility, possible consequences of a long war.

MAJOR MILITARY EVENTS OF THE WAR

Though they suffered significant losses at the Battle of Bunker Hill, the Americans, under the command of George Washington, forced the British out of Boston in 1776. The British commander, Lord Howe, relocated his center of operations to New York. Washington's forces attempted to drive the British out of New York in 1776, but they were decisively defeated at the battles of Long Island and Washington Heights. Retreating to New Jersey, the Continental Army launched successful attacks on Hessian troops at Trenton and on the British at Princeton. The British then devised a plan that, if successful, would strategically divide the New England colonies from the rest. It called for a coordinated pincer movement requiring British Generals Burgoyne in Canada, St. Leger in the Great Lakes region, and Howe in the South to unite their forces in central New York, near Albany. Unfortunately for the British, Howe inexplicably moved south to Philadelphia instead of north, and St. Leger was forced to retreat to Canada. Howe did manage to capture Philadelphia and defeat Washington's army at the battles of Brandywine and Germantown in Pennsylvania, but these actions left Burgoyne isolated north of Albany. Washington's troops then retreated to Valley Forge, Pennsylvania, where, despite a serious shortage of supplies and in critical condition, they bravely endured a miserable winter. ("These are the times that try men's souls," declared Thomas Paine.)

But despair was soon to turn to victory for the Continental Army. Upon reaching Albany, Burgoyne's army was surrounded and defeated at the Battle of Saratoga (1777) by American forces under General Horatio Gates. More than just a decisive military victory, Saratoga was the turning point in the war. It convinced the French, still bitter about their defeat in the French and Indian War, to help the Americans. There is considerable speculation among historians as to the likelihood of American military success had the French not provided military and economic aid.

Following the debacle at Saratoga, British morale improved when Howe's replacement, Sir Henry Clinton, launched a major military campaign in the southern states. But in 1781, the sixth year of the war, fortunes in the South again changed as American forces began to win a series of military engagements. A British army under General Cornwallis's command marched to Yorktown, on the coast of Virginia, so that it could be protected by the Royal Navy. By this time, the British controlled only New York City and several southern ports. Their future success was tied to Cornwallis's army in Virginia.

Unfortunately for Cornwallis, Washington's army was closing in on him from the north, General Lafayette's combined French and American force was on the move in Virginia, and French Admiral DeGrasse's flotilla of warships cut Cornwallis off from supplies, reinforcements, and finally even retreat. There was only one option left to the British general. On October 17, 1781, with the British band playing "The World Turned Upside Down," Cornwallis's army surrendered. Upon hearing of the defeat, the British public demanded an end to the war, Lord North resigned as prime minister, and before long the British and Americans convened peace negotiations in Paris.

The Treaty of Paris

The three principal American diplomats—Benjamin Franklin, John Jay, and John Adams—were directed to work closely with the French to bring about a suitable resolution. Whereas the Americans and French had been effective military allies, their diplomatic relationship soon revealed weaknesses. Both had been unified in their effort to defeat the British, but it became apparent that the French had further objectives; for instance, they stipulated that Britain return Gibraltar to its ally, Spain, as a prerequisite to an agreement. The Americans were also concerned that France might negotiate an independent settlement with Britain that would exclude American independence. Thus the three American delegates chose to carry out their negotiations independent of the French. In September 1783, the British and American delegates reached an agreement that effectively ended all hostilities between the two. On January 14, 1783, Congress ratified the Treaty of Paris. Two weeks later, Britain, France, and Spain agreed to their own provisional peace treaty.

The Terms of the Treaty of Paris were as follows:

- Britain formally and unconditionally recognized the independence of the United States.
- The boundaries of the new nation were established: north at the Canadian border and along the Great Lakes, west to the Mississippi River, and south to Florida (which in a separate treaty had been returned by Britain to Spain).
- American fishing ships were given unlimited access to the waters off Newfoundland.
- The government of the United States agreed it would not interfere legally with British creditors and merchants seeking to collect debts owed to them by Americans.
- The United States would compensate loyalists whose property had been confiscated during the war.

The success of the United States in securing its liberty from the tyrannical rule of Great Britain had impacts far beyond the borders of the North American colonies. In Haiti and France and elsewhere, the ideals of the American Revolution as articulated by Thomas Jefferson inspired revolutionary movements around the world.

WOMEN AND THE REVOLUTION Women's rights would not be addressed by a major reform movement until the mid-nineteenth century, and even then, women would have to wait until 1919 just for the right to vote. (Though New Jersey did enfranchise women after the American Revolution, this right was repealed early in the nineteenth century.) American women were certainly conscious of the revolutionary goals their male family members were fighting for: liberty and the "rights of man." But some women wondered whether their own rights could be enhanced as well. Abigail Adams counseled her husband that when writing the "new code of laws . . . I desire you would remember the ladies [and] do not put such unlimited power in the hands of husbands." Some enlightened leaders such as Benjamin Franklin were even supportive of female education; however, women at the end of the American Revolution were no better off than before—this despite the fact that women played a major role in maintaining the colonial economy. They had run the family farms and businesses while their husbands, sons, and brothers were away fighting the war. Women also contributed to the war effort by providing essential supplies, serving as nurses, and, in rare cases, even as soldiers. Ideologically, a new concept of "republican motherhood" emerged, which exhorted women to maintain and teach the values of democratic rule and citizenship to their children—an important role in the nascent republic. In some ways a step forward, the idea of republican motherhood added cultural value to women and their role in the nation. Yet, in every practical sense of the word, they continued to be subordinated to men. The patriarchal society that defined gender roles in the colonial period would survive for many more decades.

BLACKS AND THE REVOLUTION In the first draft of the Declaration of Independence, Thomas Jefferson actually blamed King George III for the existence of slavery in the colonies. Thankfully, Benjamin Franklin and the other editors of the document removed that allegation. Still, it is one of the tragic ironies of U.S. history that some of the most famous leaders of the war for independence—among them Washington and Jefferson—owned slaves. This did not go unnoticed by Dr. Samuel Johnson, the famous British author and contemporary of the American Revolution. "How is it that the loudest yelps for liberty," he asked, "come from the drivers of slaves?" Even more ironic is that black Americans contributed to both sides during the war, and for basically the same reason: their own independence. Some black colonists actually fought as redcoats because they were promised their freedom if they joined the British. As for the American side, blacks had actually been in northern militia units before the war and could rightly be called Minute Men. Some were even veterans of the French and Indian War. At the outbreak of hostilities in 1775, due in large part to pressure from the southern colonies (who feared that blacks would seek their own freedom), the Continental Congress prohibited blacks from serving in the Continental Army, whether they were free men or slaves. As the war dragged on, however, blacks began to enter the Continental Army from both northern and some southern colonies. By the end of the war, approximately 5,500 black colonists fought for the American side, though frequently they were segregated from white troops. They had hoped that their contribution to American independence would entitle them to their own freedom, but many black soldiers were returned to slavery at the end of the war. They had been considered patriots in name only.

Two Revolutions?

The primary goal of those who took up arms against Britain was to end British control of their colonies. To this end, the war was an anti-imperialist revolutionary struggle. But did the war have another dimension, one that also sought to democratize America socially and politically? Some historians contend that this is not the case, that the war was in fact a conservative revolution. In their view, America was qualitatively and comparatively democratic already and the revolutionaries of all classes consequently were seeking to preserve the social, economic, and political order, not transform it. These historians point to the democratic features already in place in the colonies in the eighteenth century, such as basic political, economic, and religious freedoms. For example, they argue, there were few obstacles to white male enfranchisement. Given the vast amount of land, most Americans had the ability to purchase inexpensive property and therefore meet any land-ownership requirements for voting. What is more, social mobility was indeed open to nearly all white males; thus social conflict in colonial society was minimal.

Other historians see a dual impulse: win independence in order to further democratize society, government, and the economy. Independence was the precondition for this goal because it was in Britain's interest to preserve the status quo in the colonies. This in turn permitted the colonial elites to maintain their dominance and control over the rest of colonial society through, for example, voting qualifications based on property ownership (substantial in some colonies, especially New York, where thirty families controlled three-quarters of the land), and the merchant class's monopoly of the retail trade. The outbreak of violence against entrenched elites—for example, the hostility expressed in the Regulator Movement in the late eighteenth century and Bacon's Rebellion in the mid-seventeenth century—demonstrate class tensions in pre-Revolutionary America. There are other examples as well; in Boston, over 40 percent of the city's wealth was controlled by just 1 percent of the population. There are many points to support both perspectives.

As you reflect on the causes and impact of the American Revolution, it is important to remember that there were members of society who, even after independence had been won, were just as concerned about the effects of too much democracy as there were those who believed the war had in part been fought to expand it. The creation of a permanent government in the postwar years would reveal the nature of this debate as well as concerns over the constitutional powers and limitations that should be accorded the new government of the United States.

Content Review Questions

1. The Declaration of Rights
   (A) was issued by Parliament to grant greater autonomy for colonial governments.
   (B) was a formal declaration of war issued by the First Continental Congress.
   (C) was written by George Washington.
   (D) was rejected by the British Parliament.

2. The opening shots of the American Revolution occurred at
   (A) the Battles of Lexington and Concord.
   (B) the Battle of Bunker Hill.
   (C) the Boston Massacre.
   (D) the Battle of Saratoga.

3. Which one of the following was NOT an advantage the British had in their war effort to suppress the American rebellion?
   (A) A larger military
   (B) Shorter supply lines
   (C) A larger and stronger navy
   (D) Greater financial resources

4. The Olive Branch Petition
   (A) was an attempt by the British to reach a political settlement after their defeat at the Battle of Saratoga.
   (B) was issued by France in an attempt to bring hostilities between the British and Americans to an end.
   (C) was offered to Native American tribes by the First Continental Congress to gain their support in the war against the British.
   (D) was an attempt by the First Continental Congress to prevent further hostilities after the Battle of Bunker Hill.

5. Which of the following British measures declared that because the American colonies were in open rebellion against the British Crown, all trade would be suspended?
   (A) The Intolerable Acts
   (B) The Quartering Act
   (C) The Declaration of Rights
   (D) The Prohibitory Act

6. Thomas Paine
   (A) was Britain's prime minister during the early stage of the American Revolution.
   (B) was president of the First Continental Congress.
   (C) wrote *Common Sense*, an appeal to the colonists to resist the British and establish a republican form of government.
   (D) was the leader of the radicals in the Second Continental Congress.

7. The Battle of Saratoga was the turning point of the American Revolution because
   (A) the French entered the war on the American side.
   (B) the last major British army in North America surrendered to Washington's army.
   (C) most Americans who had been Tories decided to switch sides and fight for independence.
   (D) the British issued the Olive Branch Petition, in which they agreed to open peace negotiations with the Americans.

8. The argument that "abuses and usurpations" by King George and his government violated the social contract that had existed between Britain and its American colonies was articulated in
   (A) the Treaty of Paris.
   (B) the Declaration of Rights.
   (C) the Declaration of the Causes and Necessities for Taking Up Arms.
   (D) the Declaration of Independence.

9. The Regulator Movement, Bacon's Rebellion, and the Paxton Boys
   (A) were the names of Tory militia units who fought against the American revolutionaries in the war.
   (B) indicate to some historians the undemocratic nature of pre-Revolutionary American society.
   (C) were Massachusetts radicals who participated in the Boston Tea Party.
   (D) were black American military units who fought for American independence.

10. The Treaty of Paris included the following terms EXCEPT
    (A) Britain formally recognized American independence.
    (B) Britain was allowed to maintain several forts in the area west of the Appalachian Mountains in order to protect its trading posts.
    (C) American fishing ships were given permission to fish off the coast of Newfoundland.
    (D) the Americans promised to compensate loyalists whose property had been confiscated during the war.

11. Which of the following colonies did not send delegates to the First Continental Congress?
    (A) New York
    (B) Georgia
    (C) South Carolina
    (D) Pennsylvania

12. One significant consequence of the Treaty of Paris, signed in 1783, was that Great Britain
    (A) formally recognized American independence.
    (B) ceded Quebec to the Americans.
    (C) declared war on France once the war with the Americans was concluded.
    (D) paid the new United States millions of dollars in war damages.

13. Some Americans who allied themselves with the British Crown
    (A) found themselves in a distinct minority, as most colonists favored independence.
    (B) believed they would receive greater religious freedom under British rule.
    (C) were forced into supporting the British war effort for fear of losing their land and possessions.
    (D) did so primarily because they believed the independence movement would not be successful.

14. Which of the following statements best represents the position of British Whigs toward American independence?
    (A) Britain should impose a naval blockade on all American ports until the colonists capitulate.
    (B) The American colonies and Canada should be unified and ruled as one nation.
    (C) The American colonies were the property of Britain and any rights granted to them could come only from the British Crown.
    (D) The American independence movement was a battle for freedom against a tyrannical monarchy.

15. In order to supplement the troops it had fighting in the American colonies, Britain
    (A) instituted the first military draft in its history.
    (B) forced American colonists into the British army.
    (C) hired Hessian mercenaries.
    (D) forced runaway slaves into the army.

Short-Answer Questions

Question 1 is based on the following passage.

> The American Revolution was integral to the changes occurring in American society, politics, and culture at the end of the eighteenth century. These changes were radical, and they were extensive. To focus, as we are today apt to do, on what the Revolution did not accomplish—highlighting and lamenting its failure to abolish slavery and change fundamentally the lot of women—is to miss the great significance of what it did accomplish; indeed, the Revolution made possible the anti-slavery and women's rights movements of the nineteenth century and in fact all our current egalitarian thinking. The Revolution not only radically changed the personal and social relationships of people, including the position of women, but also destroyed aristocracy as it had been understood in the Western world for at least two millennia. The Revolution brought respectability and even dominance to ordinary people long held in contempt and gave dignity to their menial labor in a manner unprecedented in history and to a degree not equaled elsewhere in the world.
>
> Gordon S. Wood, *The Radicalism of the American Revolution* (2001)

1. Based on the argument advanced by Gordon S. Wood in the above passage, complete the following two tasks.
   A) Provide ONE piece of evidence from American Revolutionary history that supports the argument made by Wood.
   B) Provide ONE piece of evidence from American Revolutionary history that challenges the argument made by Wood.
2. The American Revolution helped to establish many American values.
   A) Choose ONE of the values listed below and provide at least ONE piece of evidence demonstrating how Americans embodied that ideal during the struggle for independence from Britain.
      Liberty
      Equality
      Justice
   B) Based on the value you chose in Part A, identify one source of inspiration for the colonists and explain how they came to esteem that principle.

Long-Essay Questions

1. What caused the American colonists to move towards independence in the period between 1763 and 1776?
2. Compare the relative advantages of the American Continental Army and Great Britain's regulars when war broke out in 1775.

Answers

Content Review Questions

1. **(D)** The king's government rejected the appeal, which led to an intensification of hostilities (*The American Pageant*, 14th ed., p. 138/15th ed., p. 123; Learning Objective POL-1).
2. **(A)** British redcoats and Massachusetts Minute Men fired the first shots at Lexington and later at Concord. They have been called "the shots heard 'round the world" (*The American Pageant*, 14th ed., p. 138/15th ed., p. 124; Learning Objective POL-1).
3. **(B)** Great Britain had to wage war and therefore supply its troops from three thousand miles away (*The American Pageant*, 14th ed., p. 139/15th ed., pp. 124–125; Learning Objective WOR-1).
4. **(D)** Even after a major battle, Bunker Hill, had been fought, the First Continental Congress appealed to King George III to end hostilities. The petition was summarily rejected (*The American Pageant*, 14th ed., pp. 147–148/15th ed., p. 133; Learning Objective POL-1).

5. **(D)** The Prohibitory Act (1775) was an attempt to stop the rebellion by crippling the American economy (this material does not appear in the text; Learning Objective POL-1).

6. **(C)** Thomas Paine's widely read pamphlet *Common Sense* was influential in generating support for the American war effort. Paine rejected monarchy and favored its replacement with a republican—representative—form of government (*The American Pageant*, 14th ed., pp. 149–150/15th ed., pp. 134–136; Learning Objective CUL-4).

7. **(A)** Not only was the Battle of Saratoga a major American victory; it convinced the French to provide financial and military assistance to the Americans (*The American Pageant*, 14th ed., pp. 159–160, 179/15th ed., p. 145; Learning Objective WOR-1).

8. **(D)** Borrowing from Locke's social contract theory, Jefferson asserted in the Declaration of Independence that British violations of American rights had voided the contract between the king and his American subjects (*The American Pageant*, 14th ed., pp. 151–152/15th ed., p. 137; Learning Objective CUL-2).

9. **(B)** The Regulators, Bacon's supporters, and the Paxton Boys rose up against their colonial governments to protest the lack of representation and the claim that these governments served the interests of colonial America's elites (*The American Pageant*, 14th ed., pp. 70, 90/15th ed., pp. 62, 80; Learning Objective ID-5).

10. **(B)** Great Britain removed all of its troops from the area south of Canada. However, Britain still held political and military control of Canada (*The American Pageant*, 14th ed., pp. 166–167/15th ed., pp. 151–152; Learning Objective WOR-2).

11. **(B)** Georgia failed to send delegates for several reasons: the state's considerable distance from Philadelphia, the poor condition of southern roads, and the benefits Georgia had received from British protection against Spanish-controlled Florida (*The American Pageant*, 14th ed., p. 137/15th ed., p. 123; Learning Objective ID-5).

12. **(A)** The Americans became the first nation to successfully break away from the British Empire (*The American Pageant*, 14th ed., p. 167/15th ed., pp. 151–152; Learning Objective WOR-2).

13. **(B)** Some members of German, Dutch, and French religious sects had already been confronted with religious persecution in America and believed they would experience greater tolerance under British rule (*The American Pageant*, 14th ed., p. 154/15th ed., p. 140; Learning Objective PEO-5).

14. **(D)** At least initially, many British Whigs viewed the American independence movement as a conflict that would enhance their

own struggle against the powers of King George III (*The American Pageant*, 14th ed., p. 139/15th ed., p. 113; Learning Objective POL-1).

15. **(C)** King George III arranged with six German princes to hire German soldiers (most of whom came from the principality of Hesse). Interestingly, a number of Hessians stayed in America after the war ended (*The American Pageant*, 14th ed., pp. 148–149/15th ed., p. 133; Learning Objective WOR-1).

Short-Answer Questions

1. Given that Wood argues that the Revolution was, in fact, revolutionary—even at the socio-political level—you must identify examples of radical changes being made to colonial society (or colonial values) in order to support Wood's argument. One possible example: the shift in the perception of the value of women. On the contrary, identifying examples of the preservation of elements of aristocracy or of contempt for the common man would help to challenge his argument. An analysis of the property-based motivation for the war itself may serve as fertile ground for this side of the argument.

2. You might draw heavily from the rhetoric of Thomas Jefferson (in the Declaration of Independence) or Thomas Paine (in *Common Sense*) in your answer. In order to identify inspiration, consider the works of the Enlightenment philosophers like John Locke and Jean Jacques Rousseau or the cultural impact of the Great Awakening in the colonies.

Long-Essay Questions

1. You should incorporate in your essay the idea of taxation without representation versus the British policy of virtual representation. Also, royal governors were appointed to oversee the colonies, which diluted the colonial governments. As for the economic relationship, you should discuss the reasons for specific British economic acts and whether the American responses to these acts were based on moderation or inspired by radicals. (Historical Thinking Skill I-1: Historical Causation)

2. You should discuss the fact that American colonists were divided. Many on the frontier and more remote areas were unaffected by the British government's acts and policies. Point out that the Americans faced serious economic, political, and military disadvantages. On the other hand, point out the political and military advantages on the American side, and be sure to include French intervention. (Historical Thinking Skill II-4: Comparison)

5

Creation of the U.S. Constitution: 1781–1791

When Virginia's Richard Henry Lee introduced a resolution in the Second Continental Congress on June 7, 1776, in favor of American independence, he also proposed that a government be established based on an accord of confederated states—an association of sovereign states. Within a month, under the direction of John Dickinson, a committee established by the Congress had devised a plan of government called the Articles of Confederation and Perpetual Union.

The Articles of Confederation were adopted by the Congress the next year and were finally approved by all the states in 1781. But by 1787, it was clear that the Articles were insufficient for the young nation. A convention charged with revising the Articles concluded that an entirely new structure was needed. The Constitution was the result. In this chapter we will take a closer look at the Founding Fathers and how they came to write the Constitution.

Key Concepts

- The Articles of Confederation were unable to address the economic and political problems facing the new nation.
- The Constitution was completed only because the delegates to the Constitutional Convention were able to reach a number of major compromises.
- Opposition to ratification of the Constitution came from antifederalists, who feared a strong central government.
- Promise of a bill of rights was important to ratification of the Constitution.

The Articles of Confederation and the Constitution are discussed in depth in *The American Pageant,* 14th and 15th eds., Chapter 9.

Creating the Nation's First Government: Issues and Concerns

Not unexpectedly, problems developed as the committee drawing up the Articles of Confederation worked out the details of this newly independent political system. One critical concern was the issue of where, in this new government, power should reside. Would the states be autonomous and more powerful than the central government? Would the central government be paramount in its dealings with the states? Or would there be a sharing of powers and responsibilities? Keep in mind that Americans were then fighting a war against what they perceived to be a tyrannical government, autocratic and seemingly insensitive to the rights of American colonists. As a consequence, Americans were deeply suspicious about placing too much authority in the hands of a central power. But if the central government had little authority compared with the states, then what was the purpose of even having one? Other questions soon arose as well. Would this new government be bicameral (a two-house legislature) or unicameral (a one-house legislature)? How would representation be apportioned? Would larger states with larger populations have more representation than smaller states? Would larger states pay more in taxes? What about the relationship between the powers of the government and the rights of citizens? These were questions that could be answered only if the delegates were able to agree on what was arguably the most pivotal question: What did they actually intend when they created a *United States* of America?

In most cases, these questions were adequately addressed by the delegates in their deliberations and in the ultimate ratification of the Articles of Confederation. Other key issues, however, would go unresolved for decades. In fact, it took the Civil War to conclusively determine the relationship between the states and federal government. But what delayed ratification of the Articles for nearly four years had little to do with issues relating to the nature of the government or the powers of the states, but rather disputes over western land claims. Some states—Rhode Island, for one—insisted that jurisdiction over disputed western lands should be a responsibility of the central government. But settling land claims was an especially difficult task because western state boundaries were often not clearly delineated. This led to claims by more than one state for the same territory. In fact, some states insisted that their western boundaries stretched to the Mississippi River and even as far as the Pacific Ocean. Some land claims were seemingly arbitrary, such as Virginia's claim to land in what is present-day Wisconsin. Only when the two states that had been obstacles to a compromise, New York and Virginia, agreed to relinquish their western land claims was the new government, embodied in the Articles of Confederation, ratified by the Continental Congress, in March 1781.

THE MAJOR FEATURES OF THE ARTICLES OF CONFEDERATION (AOC)

Under the AOC, the central government was extremely ineffective and impotent; most authority remained with the individual states. To many, the decentralization of authority was important to the maintenance of democracy. Further, it protected against potential tyrannical abuses by a strong central government. The Articles of Confederation had the following features, many of which were considered weaknesses by those favoring a stronger central government:

- a unicameral legislature
- no authority for Congress to impose taxes
- one vote in Congress for each state
- no national court system
- no provision for a uniform national currency
- no chief executive
- a requirement that nine of the thirteen states approve passage of certain legislation
- unanimity for amendment of the AOC
- no authority for Congress to regulate either interstate or foreign commerce

AP Tip

Many of the problems and abuses that occurred in the years immediately following the end of the American Revolution can be traced to the weaknesses of the AOC in addressing these concerns. Making this connection is important in understanding why the AOC were inadequate for the new nation and why early on some questioned the new government's usefulness.

As the United States emerged from the turmoil of war, it was immediately faced with serious economic concerns. These were some of the problems afflicting American society in the 1780s:

- The infant manufacturing sector of the economy was adversely affected by Great Britain's practice of flooding the American market with British goods. The consequent unfavorable balance of trade had a negative effect on the nation's economy in general and on many of the new American industries and businesses that emerged in the postwar years.
- Infrastructure (roads, bridges, highways) had been neglected, so the transportation system was inadequate for commerce and trade.
- Inflation was rampant because of the absence of a uniform currency and also because notes were often given an arbitrary value by private banks and state governments. This had a direct impact on business transactions within a state and between states.
- Interstate trade was adversely affected by state trade barriers and a vast assortment of currencies.

- The government could do little to address the effects of a depression that struck following the war.

Because the new government could not address the economic needs of the nation and the individual states, the AOC could do nothing to remedy the maladies of inflation and depression. Individual states had to solve their economic problems. Some states imposed heavy taxes on their citizens to tackle inflation and address their infrastructural needs. For example, Massachusetts imposed a 30 percent tax on the average farmer. Overburdened by the weight of this levy, many farmers lost their farms or went to debtor's prison. It was not long before farmers in Massachusetts organized and petitioned their state legislature to enact stay laws (which would stay, or keep, them from prison for indebtedness). They also wanted their state government to issue more money in order to inflate the economy, thereby expanding the credit system and inflating prices. The Massachusetts state legislature rejected their demands in favor of a deflationary policy (less money in the system), which they expected would strengthen the economy and therefore enhance the public's confidence; this in turn would allow for a more viable credit system. As it turned out, that approach did not work. The depression intensified, and deflation replaced inflation as more and more money was taken out of the system. Believing their government was insensitive to their economic predicament, some farmers engaged in an open revolt known as Shays' Rebellion.

Shays' Rebellion

The most famous example of agrarian discontent in the postwar years occurred in Massachusetts in 1786. An armed band of farmers numbering in the hundreds and led by Daniel Shays, a former officer in the Continental Army, sought to shut down the courts as a form of protest and to prevent the continued foreclosure of their farms and the collection of taxes. The farmers were met by an equally large state militia force, but they still managed to close the courts. However, when Shays and his men marched on the Springfield arsenal, they were routed. In the end, Shays and his men were pardoned and the state of Massachusetts did modify its tax laws. But the rebellion made an indelible impression on the minds of some Americans and their political leaders: civil disobedience could spread easily from county to county and state to state.

As delegates began arriving in Philadelphia in the late spring of 1787 to amend the AOC, the events in Massachusetts weighed heavily on their minds, particularly the nation's conservative political leaders, who believed that a strong central government with the authority to suppress domestic disturbances was necessary. When the delegates wrote a new constitution for the nation, they had the symbolic importance of Shays' Rebellion in mind when they gave to the national government the authority to "protect each of them [states] against invasion; and . . . against domestic violence" (Article IV, Section IV). For others, the strengthening of the national government would lead to tyranny; it would allow those in power to maintain the status quo by preventing fundamental changes to society, the economy, and government. No wonder, then, that in refusing to attend the Constitutional Convention, the famous patriot Patrick Henry exclaimed, "I smelt a rat."

ACHIEVEMENTS OF THE ARTICLES OF CONFEDERATION

In its short life as the government of the United States (1777–1789), the AOC did achieve some noteworthy successes. The AOC was, after all, the government during the American Revolution and negotiated peace terms with the British at the end of the war. In addition, two very important land policies that would shape the future of the nation, the Land Ordinance of 1785 and the Northwest Ordinance of 1787, came about in this period. Both were significant achievements in that they facilitated the settlement of western territories and made expansion systematic.

- **Land Ordinance of 1785** In 1784 Congress decided that western lands would be organized into states roughly the size of each of the original thirteen states. This area would first be divided into sovereign districts, which in due course would become states. However, the plan was not instituted, in large part because of the political clout of land speculators, who wanted to increase the amount of acreage that an individual or company could purchase. Instead, a new plan, the Land Ordinance of 1785, was enacted to provide for the systematic sale and organization of the territories, including the following provisions:
  - Townships six miles square would be surveyed. These in turn would again be divided into sections equaling one square mile.
  - The sections were to be sold in lots of 640 acres at no less than $1 an acre. Land speculators found this agreeable; they had large amounts of ready cash. The average buyer did not have $640 in disposable wealth, nor was credit made available as part of the plan.
  - The revenue from the sale of one section for each township would be used to develop public education.

The Land Ordinance of 1785 established a precedent for subsequent surveys of public land and federal support for public education.

- **The Northwest Ordinance** (also known as the Land Ordinance of 1787) sought to address the government of the territories, and embodied two of the nation's guiding political principles: federalism and republicanism. It provided for the following:
  - The Northwest Territory would be divided into three to five separate territories.
  - A methodical process would advance each territory to statehood.
  - Unorganized territories would be overseen by officials appointed by Congress.
  - Once the population of the territory reached 5,000 it could be organized as a territory. Residents would then elect members to a state legislature and send a delegate to Congress.
  - Once the population reached 60,000 a constitution would be written and the territory would apply to Congress for statehood.

From the region that was the Northwest Territory, five states emerged between 1803 and 1848: Ohio, Indiana, Illinois, Michigan, and Wisconsin.

The AOC Attempt to Confront Foreign Affairs Problems

Problems for the new government were not limited to domestic issues and concerns. Difficulties with foreign affairs were another burden. After the war, relations with European powers quickly deteriorated, especially with the new nation's former nemesis, Great Britain. In some cases the United States brought the problems on itself, as it failed to abide by the Treaty of Paris. Remember that the U.S. government had promised to compensate loyalists whose property was confiscated during the war and to pay foreign debts. Both promises were not met. But the British violated the treaty as well. King George III, who was never impressed with American military power (and now especially since the AOC had to rely on the states to provide troops to protect the nation), broke Britain's treaty obligations by maintaining forts in the Northwest Territory. The United States could do nothing about the forts except vehemently protest. The British also placed various trade restrictions on the United States, which further damaged its already weak economy. To make matters worse, the disunity that plagued the nation under the AOC raised eyebrows in Europe's political circles and threatened the reputation of the United States. European nations reasoned that since the individual states were themselves embroiled in trade disputes, commercial agreements with the United States would certainly be questionable.

Even a former wartime ally, Spain, saw an opportunity to exploit the new nation. The monarchical government of Spain, always wary of the potential for the United States to expand its power, was perhaps even more wary of the democratic ideals emanating from the United States. The two countries quarreled over the undefined northern boundary of Florida (which Britain had ceded back to Spain in 1783), called the Yazoo Strip. There was friction, too, over navigation rights to the Mississippi River—the Spanish controlled the lower river, which was vital to American commerce. Still another problem was Spain's relationship with Native American tribes in the West. Both wanted to contain American western expansion, especially in the South, which interfered with Georgia's desire to expand. In 1785 war broke out between the state of Georgia and the Creeks. Despite the enmity of the Native Americans and Spanish, Americans flooded into what would eventually become Tennessee and Kentucky. Some of these settlers did not hold deeds to this land, which often was owned by eastern speculators. In eastern Tennessee, a group of settlers organized a new state, which they named Franklin in honor of their celebrated compatriot Benjamin Franklin. They then petitioned Congress to admit Franklin into the United States but were rejected. Spain saw its chance. Secret agents were employed to bring Franklin under Spain's control. (It seems that Daniel Boone was one of the agents, but he did nothing to help the project, even though he was paid by Spain.) The effort ultimately collapsed, but not because of any response by the United States.

Given the inability of the AOC to address troublesome domestic and foreign affairs problems, it is not surprising that some of the nation's foremost political leaders wanted to revise the AOC. In 1787, delegates met in Philadelphia to do just that. Before they were through, however, they had in fact created an entirely new government.

Early Attempts to Revise the AOC

By the time the delegates met in Philadelphia, two attempts had already been made to revise the AOC.

- **Alexandria Conference (1785)** Delegates from Virginia and Maryland met to discuss ways to improve navigation and commerce on the Potomac River. They decided to invite delegates from the other states to a meeting in Annapolis, Maryland, to discuss commerce on a national level.
- **Annapolis Conference (1786)** Eight states sent delegates to this conference, but only five arrived on time. Nevertheless, while attendance was poor, there was obviously strong sentiment across the nation that the AOC had to be revised. Important leaders such as James Madison of Virginia and Alexander Hamilton of New York took it upon themselves to invite states to send delegates to a national convention in Philadelphia.

THE CONSTITUTIONAL CONVENTION

By May 1787, fifty-five delegates from twelve states (Rhode Island chose not to participate) had arrived in Philadelphia to begin work on revising the government of the United States. The list of delegates was a veritable "who's who" in America at that time, among them George Washington and James Madison (both future presidents), Benjamin Franklin, George Mason, and Roger Sherman. Those who were absent were just as formidable: radical leaders Patrick Henry, Sam Adams, and Thomas Paine chose not to attend, for they were wary of any attempt to increase the power of the central government. Future presidents Thomas Jefferson and John Adams were serving overseas as U.S. ambassadors. Generally, the delegates to the Constitutional Convention were men of wealth and property. To a large extent, their motives were twofold: to create a government that would protect the nation and at the same time to protect their investments. The difficulty they faced was in designing a strong central government while safeguarding individual liberties. They knew that a new government would not be ratified by the people unless it balanced authoritarian rule and democratic rule. Rest assured that both extremes concerned them.

To be sure, most delegates concluded that the old form of government was no longer suitable. In retrospect, the Framers had four general goals in mind when they deliberated on how best to revise the government. It must be able to

- prevent a tyranny of the majority
- prevent a tyranny of the minority
- have sufficient powers to create conditions for both short- and long-term economic development
- formulate and conduct a more effective foreign policy

Historians Interpret the Intent of the Framers

Which concerns, issues, and hopes motivated the delegates as they left the comfort of their homes in late spring 1787 and headed for Philadelphia to revise the AOC? Historians have contemplated this question for over a century. One of the earliest views held that the Framers did what was necessary and appropriate given the domestic and foreign affairs problems that were plaguing the nation under the AOC.

Not until the early decades of the twentieth century was this view challenged. Most significantly, historian Charles Beard powerfully rejected this view in his highly influential book *An Economic Interpretation of the Constitution of the United States*. Beard's thesis was simple and devastating: the Framers had their own self-interest at heart when they met in Philadelphia. As men of property and wealth, they wanted a government that would stimulate trade and industrial growth, protect private property against "mob rule," and recover loans owed to them in the form of public debts. According to Beard, the AOC government, had it been given a chance to develop, could have become a perfectly suitable system of government. Forty years later, Beard's thesis was in turn refuted by other historians who claimed that there was no correlation between support for the Constitution and one's financial status. Instead, a delegate's regional interests and concerns were the key to their support. Beard's thesis has so eroded that many historians have serious reservations about it. But other historians, with Beard's view in mind, have added to the debate by claiming, for example, that the delegates' views on ratifying the new Constitution were certainly based on their economic outlook. On the one hand, agrarian interests were cautious about creating a centralized government, whereas more commercially minded delegates considered centralization necessary for the sustained economic growth of the nation. Regardless of one's view, the debate over the Framers' rationale continues to be a lively and vital part of any debate on the Constitution.

It was not long, however, before core conflicts emerged between different interest groups:

- bankers (hard money advocates) versus debtors (cheap money advocates)
- northern (commercial) versus southern (rural slave) economic interests
- economic competition between states
- conflicts between states over western land ownership
- large states (representation by population) versus small states (equal representation for each state)
- supporters of a strong central government versus supporters of individual and states' rights

- those with democratic ideals versus those with aristocratic leanings
- slave states, which wanted to include slaves in the population count (for purposes of representation in Congress) versus nonslave states, which sought to omit them from the count (thereby reducing the South's representation in Congress)

Despite the enormous chasm between advocates of the differing approaches, a number of important compromises were worked out:

- The Commerce Compromise (regulating trade and commerce)
  - The South agreed to federal control over foreign and interstate trade.
  - The importation of slaves would be permitted for twenty years, until 1808.
  - The federal government was given the authority to collect import taxes, but there would be no duties on exports.

Two Proposals for Representation

Large states, which favored a bicameral legislature with representation based on population, put forward the Virginia Plan. It called for a lower house of Congress elected by the people, which in turn would elect members to an upper house. Both houses would then elect an executive—president—who could serve only one term. A judiciary system would also be established. This plan granted more power to the central government while maintaining some features of the AOC. The smaller states favored a unicameral legislature with each state receiving one vote (as it was with the AOC), an executive with no veto power, and a judiciary that could arbitrate cases that had originated in state courts. The smaller states would support the New Jersey Plan.

- The Great (or Connecticut) Compromise (dealing with representation in Congress)
  - A state's representation in the House of Representatives was to be based on population.
  - The states' representation in the Senate would be equal (two senators for each state).
  - All money bills would originate in the House.
  - Direct taxes on states were to be assessed according to population.
- The Three-fifths Compromise (counting slaves for representation in Congress)
  - Three-fifths of a state's slave population would be counted for purposes of taxation and representation.
  - A fugitive slave law required that runaway slaves who escaped to a free state must be returned to their owners.

AP Tip

The Constitution is at the heart of American history. You must be able to identify the ways in which the Constitution was designed to allow the government to meet changing conditions and attitudes.

The delegates also divided power within the national government, creating three branches: the legislative (Congress), the executive (the president), and the judicial (the courts). There was considerable disagreement about the powers of the executive branch, which was given a good deal of power; the AOC had had no executive. Much less discussion was devoted to the judiciary. There was no mention of judicial review, an essential part of the system of checks and balances. That would be established under Chief Justice John Marshall, who served on the Court from 1801 to 1835.

- Powers of the legislative branch
  - Congress has the power of the purse—power to set and collect taxes, borrow money, regulate trade, coin money.
  - Congress was to set up a postal service and issue patents and copyrights.
  - War must be authorized by Congress.
  - Congress is responsible for raising and maintaining an army and a navy.
- Powers of the executive branch
  - The president carries out and enforces laws passed by Congress.
  - The president can veto congressional bills (though Congress can override an executive veto with a two-thirds vote, considerably more difficult than the majority need to pass a bill).
  - The president makes treaties (though the Senate has the authority to accept or reject treaties).
  - The president is commander in chief of the U.S. military.
  - The president appoints federal officials, such as federal judges; however, the Senate must consent to the appointments.
- Powers of the judicial branch
  - Congress was to establish a Supreme Court and lower courts.
  - The kind of cases that could be heard in federal courts was specified.
  - The Supreme Court's jurisdiction was outlined.
  - Treason was defined; requirements for conviction were set; and punishment was to be in the hands of Congress.

The Ratification Debate: Federalists Versus Antifederalists

At last, the delegates to the Constitutional Convention had come to an agreement—signing the Constitution in 1787—but the debate had truly only just begun. Before going into effect, the Constitution had to be ratified by a convention in 9 of the 13 states. Ratifying the new government was not easy. For nine months heated exchanges flew back and forth between supporters and opponents of the new constitution. Those who advocated for the new government were known as Federalists; opponents were called Antifederalists.

Federalists	**Antifederalists**
Support came mainly from coastal and urban areas and from the upper classes—merchants, financiers, shippers, planters, though not all upper-class citizens were Federalists.	Support came mainly from backcountry and agricultural areas, debtors, and people philosophically opposed to a strong central government.
Prominent leaders included Washington, Hamilton, Madison, and Franklin.	Prominent leaders included Patrick Henry, John Hancock, and George Mason.
They favored a strong central government to maintain peace and stability and to strengthen the Union in ways that the AOC could not.	They opposed a central government that did not guarantee protection of individual rights. They believed the Constitution subordinated states' rights.

In order to convince the voting public in the crucial state of New York to support ratification, key advocates of the Constitution composed a series of essays for publication in a New York newspaper. Written by James Madison, Alexander Hamilton, and John Jay, the *Federalist Papers* went beyond merely pointing out the inadequacies of the AOC. The underlying premise of their argument was that because man is corruptible he cannot always be trusted to govern himself. What is needed, therefore, is an elaborate constitutional system to prevent rulers from acting in an arbitrary and abusive manner, as well as to control the passions of the masses. One of the most famous of the essays was *Federalist* No. 10, which argues that a republican form of government can effectively and fairly operate in a large and heterogeneous nation in which there are many factions and power is diffused. The authors also addressed claims that too much power would be concentrated in the executive branch, that there would not be enough powers reserved to the states, and that power would be diffused in the federal government as well so that both a "tyranny of the majority" and a "tyranny of the minority" would be prevented. In other words, the delegates were as concerned with a faction of elites (for example, commercial interests or agrarian interests) dominating the government as they were about the masses gaining too much influence.

The Bill of Rights and Ratification of the United States Constitution

Many citizens opposed ratification unless a list of rights was added to the Constitution. Federalists argued that this was unnecessary because members of the House of Representatives would be elected by the people. Further, they argued that by defining the delegated powers of government, they had drastically limited the potential for abuse of power. But if the rights of citizens were enumerated, that would in effect place limitations on their rights. Opponents, the Antifederalists, contended that only a list of basic civil rights could protect citizens from a tyrannical government. The deadlock was resolved when the Federalists promised to add a bill of rights once the Constitution was ratified. (Honoring that promise, the first congressmen elected under the Constitution proposed twelve amendments, ten of which were ratified and adopted in 1791 and make up what we know as the Bill of Rights. They provide for various protections, among them freedom of religion, speech, and the press. There are also protections for the rights of the accused. The Ninth Amendment affirms that citizens have rights that, even if not mentioned, are protected. The Tenth Amendment reserves to the states and the people rights not delegated or prohibited by the Constitution.)

Despite strong opposition, by various states, classes, and regions, the supporters of the new government were able to win over the nine states necessary for ratification by July 1788. North Carolina eventually ratified the Constitution once the Bill of Rights was added. As for the last state, Rhode Island, coercion was needed. Congress threatened to boycott the state if it did not follow the other twelve in ratifying the new government. The following year, 1789, George Washington became the first president of the United States under the new form of government. Though the Framers had put together a document and system of government that was certainly more formidable than the AOC, fissures and divisions that had been present during the Constitutional Convention would soon emerge. Subsequent political leaders in all branches of the government, as well as emerging political parties, would transform the nation's political system, and therefore its economy and society. What is certain, however, is that the U.S. Constitution, despite its inadequacies and limitations, has stood the test of time. It is the world's oldest living written constitution.

The Intellectual Influences on the Framers

The Framers did not write the Constitution in a political or intellectual vacuum. They were very much shaped by the ideas of the previous two centuries, most especially the Scientific Revolution of the seventeenth century and the Enlightenment of the eighteenth century. Profoundly important scientific inventions such as Galileo's astronomical telescope and Leeuwenhoek's microscope allowed thinkers to view the functioning of planetary and human bodies. Their empirical evidence led them to conclude that everything in the universe—for example, the planets revolving around the sun—operated according to certain natural laws. Human anatomy also functions according to anatomical laws. Consider the chambers of the heart, each with a separate function that is necessary for the entire organ to function. Eighteenth-century thinkers such as Jefferson and Franklin believed that God created the universe but left it to man to identify the laws of the universe. They concluded that since God defined perfection, everything he created would be in a state of equilibrium. Therefore, since humans were created in God's image, everything they created, such as a political system, should also reflect this equilibrium.

Enlightenment thinkers added to the Framers' understanding of natural law and human behavior. Take, for instance, Newton's laws of motion: for every action there is an equal and opposite reaction. Or John Calvin's contention (based in large part on Protestantism) that human nature could not be trusted because men were selfish, greedy, and evil, supplemented by Thomas Hobbes's argument that since man was basically evil, he required a strong and powerful government to control his inclinations. Consequently, we see here a direct correlation between these ideas and the principles and mechanisms of the Constitution that reflect bicameralism, separation of powers and checks and balances, and federalism.

- **Bicameralism** A two-house legislature allows for the upper and lower houses to check each other's authority.
- **Separation of powers and checks and balances** Each branch has its own powers and responsibilities, but the three branches of government are compelled to interact. For example, Congress passes a bill, which then goes to the president, who may veto it or sign it into law. In turn, the law may be ruled unconstitutional by the judicial branch. These principles were seen as a safeguard against tyranny—by which was meant one branch, especially the executive, gaining too much power.
- **Federalism** Power is divided between the central government and the states. Although federal law is paramount, states have reserved, or enumerated, powers under the Tenth Amendment—for example, overseeing elections and driving ages. The powers of the federal government, which are delegated powers, include declaring war, borrowing money, and establishing a post office, as well as making all laws "necessary and proper." Yet it took the Civil War to determine conclusively the relationship between the central government's powers and the states' rights.

Content Review Questions

1. Which one of the following was a major success of the Articles of Confederation?
   (A) They ended the French and Indian War.
   (B) They led to the creation of a powerful U.S. military.
   (C) They paved the way for closer economic ties with Great Britain.
   (D) They devised land policies that would allow for the systematic incorporation of new states.

2. Of the following list of political leaders, which one was strongly opposed to the plan of government created by the delegates at the Philadelphia convention?
   (A) Patrick Henry
   (B) George Washington
   (C) James Madison
   (D) Benjamin Franklin

3. Which of the following was NOT a feature of the Articles of Confederation?
   (A) They called for a bicameral legislature.
   (B) Unanimity was required to amend the AOC.
   (C) Nine of thirteen states were required to pass legislation.
   (D) There was no national court system.

4. Shays' Rebellion
   (A) convinced many political leaders of the destructive consequences of a strong central government.
   (B) was eventually suppressed when the federal government sent troops to Massachusetts.
   (C) convinced some political leaders of the necessity of giving more power to the central government.
   (D) came about when American settlers clashed with the British over western land claims.

5. Which important controversy was resolved by the Great (or Connecticut) Compromise?
   (A) Western land claims
   (B) Representation in Congress
   (C) No national currency
   (D) No national military

6. Powers granted to the federal government under the U.S. Constitution are expressed as
   (A) enumerated powers.
   (B) checks and balances.
   (C) reserved powers.
   (D) executive powers.

7. All of the following are true regarding the Antifederalists EXCEPT
   (A) their important leaders included John Hancock and Patrick Henry.
   (B) their political support came mostly from backcountry and agricultural areas.
   (C) debtors were supporters of the Antifederalists.
   (D) they maintained there was no need for a bill of rights.

8. The *Federalist Papers*
   (A) were written by opponents of the Constitution, who feared that a tyrannical government would be a consequence of ratification.
   (B) were the intellectual ideas that shaped the creation of the AOC.
   (C) were written by those who advocated maintaining the AOC.
   (D) attempted to calm the anxieties many had about the powers granted to the central government under the Constitution.

9. North Carolina refused to ratify the Constitution
   (A) because the government under the AOC had not yet determined the status of its western land claims.
   (B) until Congress imposed a boycott on the state.
   (C) until the government removed British forts from its western frontier.
   (D) unless a bill of rights would eventually be added.

10. Which part of government was not as fully developed as the others by the delegates to the Constitutional Convention?
    (A) Judicial branch
    (B) House of Representatives
    (C) Senate
    (D) Executive branch

11. Which of the following was NOT taken up by the delegates to the Constitutional Convention?
    (A) New Jersey Plan
    (B) Virginia Plan
    (C) Albany Plan
    (D) Three-fifths Compromise

12. In extolling republican ideology in the years following the Revolution, the concept that democracy depends on citizens subordinating their own needs to the common good was advanced. This concept is known as
    (A) primogeniture.
    (B) fundamental law.
    (C) civic virtue.
    (D) constitutionalism.

13. Which of the following would NOT be considered the roots of the creation of a federal union, as established by the U.S. Constitution?
    (A) Albany Congress
    (B) Kentucky and Virginia Resolutions
    (C) First Continental Congress
    (D) Committees of Correspondence

14. In *The Federalist* No. 10, Madison extolled the virtues of
    (A) a republican form of government.
    (B) a confederation.
    (C) nullification.
    (D) political parties.

15. In opposing ratification of the U.S. Constitution, Antifederalists claimed that
    (A) the federal government would be weakened by the granting of too many powers to the states.
    (B) the Constitution would grant states the power to nullify federal laws.
    (C) individual freedoms would be endangered by the absence of a bill of rights.
    (D) it did not outlaw slavery.

Short-Answer Questions

Question 1 is based on the following political cartoon.

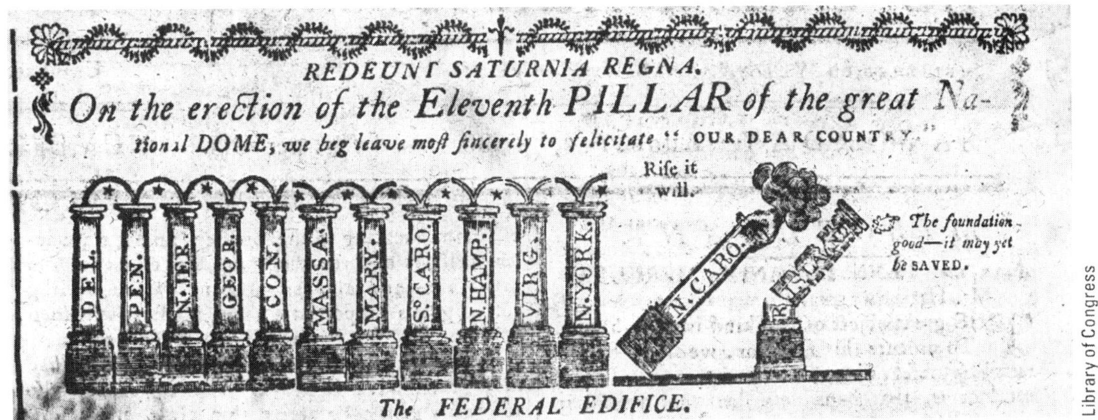

"On the erection of the Eleventh PILLAR of the great National DOME, we beg leave most sincerely to felicitate OUR DEAR COUNTRY" "Rise it will." "The foundation good—it may yet be SAVED." "The FEDERAL EDIFICE."

1. Use the cartoon and your knowledge of United States history to answer Parts A, B, and C.
   A) Explain the purpose or viewpoint of this cartoon as published in 1788.
   B) Explain how ONE element of the cartoon expresses the purpose you identified in Part A.
   C) Describe ONE argument that could be made against the viewpoint of the cartoonist, making sure to identify what type of person might have opposed this cartoon and why.
2. It can be said that the United States Constitution is composed of a series of compromises designed to hold together the diverse interests of the states.
   A) Name and describe the final decision made in ONE of the compromises that became part of the U.S. Constitution.
   B) Explain the position of both sides in relation to the compromise you selected.

Long-Essay Questions

1. Discuss the relative strengths and weaknesses of the U.S. government under the Articles of Confederation.
2. Compare the positions of the Federalists and Antifederalists.

Answers

Content Review Questions

1. **(D)** The Land Ordinance of 1785 and the Northwest Ordinance were considerable achievements of the AOC (*The American Pageant,* 14th ed., pp. 182–183/15th ed., pp. 165–166; Learning Objective ENV-4).

2. **(A)** Wary that the delegates might create a tyrannical government, Patrick Henry refused to attend the Constitutional Convention and later opposed ratification (*The American Pageant,* 14th ed., p. 193/15th ed., p. 169; Learning Objective CUL-5).

3. **(A)** The AOC had a unicameral legislature, which critics claimed did not allot sufficient power to states that had large populations (*The American Pageant,* 14th ed., pp. 187–188/15th ed., pp. 164–165; Learning Objective POL-2).

4. **(C)** Some delegates were alarmed that the federal government possessed no authority to raise an army to defend the nation or suppress domestic violence (*The American Pageant,* 14th ed., pp. 184–185/15th ed., p. 167; Learning Objective ENV-2).

5. **(B)** The Great Compromise created a bicameral legislature. In the Senate, representation would be equal. Representation in the House of Representatives would be based on population (*The American Pageant,* 14th ed., p. 188/15th ed., p. 170; Learning Objective POL-2).

6. **(A)** Enumerated powers include making treaties, raising an army, and creating a postal service, among many others (*The American Pageant,* 14th ed., p. A7/15th ed., p. A7; Learning Objective POL-5).

7. **(D)** The potential for tyrannical abuses by the central government under the Constitution was always on the minds of the Antifederalists. They therefore insisted that a bill of rights be included that would protect citizens from the possible abuses of government (*The American Pageant,* 14th ed., pp. 192–193/15th ed., pp. 172–174; Learning Objective ID-5).

8. **(D)** The *Federalist Papers* attempted to convince critics and doubters that the Constitution had in place various checks on the concentration of power (*The American Pageant,* 14th ed., p. 193/15th ed., p. 175; Learning Objective CUL-2).

9. **(D)** Concerned that the Constitution deposited too much power in the executive branch, voters in North Carolina were adamant about the inclusion of a bill of rights (this material does not appear in the text; Learning Objective ID-5).

10. **(A)** Not until the Marshall Court in the first few decades of the nineteenth century would the Supreme Court's powers be articulated (this material does not appear in the text; Learning Objective POL-5).

11. **(C)** The Albany Plan of Union, proposed in 1754, at the beginning of the French and Indian War, aimed to strengthen the bonds among the colonies (*The American Pageant,* 14th ed., p. 187/15th ed., pp. 170–172; Learning Objective POL-2).

12. **(C)** Educating young Americans about the virtues of civic responsibility, or civic virtue, became a feature of "republican motherhood," which encouraged women to teach the values of American democratic-republicanism (*The American Pageant,* 14th ed., p. 176/15th ed., p. 159; Learning Objective CUL-2).

13. **(B)** Not only were the Kentucky and Virginia Resolutions written after the ratification of the U.S. Constitution, but they articulated the doctrine of nullification and states' rights (*The American Pageant,* 14th ed., pp. 218–219/15th ed., p. 198; Learning Objective POL-2).

14. **(A)** Most of Madison's contemporaries believed it was impossible to expand republicanism as the nation expanded its geographical size, a notion effectively challenged in No. 10 (*The American Pageant,* 14th ed., p. 194/15th ed., p. 175; Learning Objective CUL-4).

15. **(C)** The Antifederalists were deeply concerned that not only would the Constitution relegate the authority of the states to the federal government, but that civil liberties would be endangered by a strong central government—thus the need for a bill of rights (*The American Pageant,* 14th ed., p. 190/15th ed., p. 175; Learning Objective POL-5).

Short-Answer Questions

1. This cartoon, celebrating the eleventh state to ratify the (already in operation) constitutional government, puts strong pressure on North Carolina and Rhode Island to do the same. Pay careful attention to the words used by the cartoonist—"the great National Dome," "Our Dear Country," "Rise it Will," "The Federal Edifice"—as you attempt to explain how the cartoon represents this point of view. In Part C, identify an argument of an Antifederalist, remembering that they tended to be men of rural or agricultural background with less of a stake in the capital economy than their Federalist opponents.

2. The most famous compromises are the Great Compromise (over representation), the Commerce Compromise (over taxes and tariffs), and the 3/5ths Compromise (over slavery). Identifying the interests of the two sides—usually North and South or merchant/industrial and agrarian—will require that you understand the competing fears of tyranny and anarchy.

Long-Essay Questions

1. You should first point out that the very nature of a confederation government is one that has a weak central government and that most power resides in the states. This ultimately became a problem for the new nation under the AOC. In foreign affairs the AOC government had to request troops from the states, and it had no chief executive or state department to conduct foreign affairs. Domestically, the government did not have the authority to tax, establish a uniform currency, or regulate trade (domestic and international). Your essay should address the impact this had on the nation's economy at the end of the Revolutionary War. (Historical Thinking Skill IV-8: Interpretation)

2. You can begin by pointing out that both sides of the debate were wary of tyranny. For the Antifederalists tyranny meant a powerful central government that could potentially deny certain basic rights to the individual and autonomy to the states. This is why the Bill of Rights, which stated certain basic rights of citizens as well as powers reserved to the states, was later added to the Constitution. Federalists believed that, for example, checks and balances and a bicameral legislature would prevent tyranny of the majority and tyranny of the minority. These proponents of the Constitution believed that the AOC was inadequate to address the problems facing the nation after the war. Further, you should address some of the forces that shaped this view, such as Shays' Rebellion, which convinced some of the need for a strong central government that would have the power to defend the nation, but also be prepared to suppress domestic uprisings. (Historical Thinking Skill II-4: Comparison)

Period 4: 1800 –1848

The Rise of the American Republic

Though the constitutional foundation of the nation had been set, the United States had a lot of growing to do in the first half of the nineteenth century. Above all, the country was struggling to define itself in a world where no other country could rightfully call itself a true republic. Furthermore, the country had its eyes on new territory to the West—land that would bring extraordinary economic opportunities, and also lead to significant turmoil amidst a population with diverse and deeply held, often regionalized beliefs.

Key Concepts from the College Board

4.1 The United States developed the world's first modern mass democracy and celebrated a new national culture, while Americans sought to define the nation's democratic ideals and to reform its institutions to match them.

4.2 Developments in technology, agriculture, and commerce precipitated profound changes in U.S. settlement patterns, regional identities, gender and family relations, political power, and distribution of consumer goods.

4.3 U.S. interest in increasing foreign trade, expanding its national borders, and isolating itself from European conflicts shaped the nation's foreign policy and spurred government and private initiatives.

6

The New Nation: 1789–1800

In March 1789 the first Congress to serve under the new Constitution assembled in what was then the nation's capital, New York City. They immediately set to work counting the presidential electors' ballots and declared that George Washington and John Adams had been unanimously elected. One month later, Washington and Adams were sworn in as the nation's first president and vice president. Thomas Jefferson, Alexander Hamilton, and Henry Knox were appointed to newly created departments in the executive branch: secretary of state, secretary of the treasury, and secretary of war. These appointments gave birth to the cabinet system, whereby the president appoints individuals to head the different departments of the executive branch of government. For its part, the Congress made good on its promise to incorporate a Bill of Rights into the Constitution. Also, believing it had a mandate to address the nation's pressing economic needs and, in the process, facilitate capital accumulation, the Congress also passed a protective tariff to raise revenue and protect the nation's infant manufacturing. In order to give greater definition to the judicial branch, they passed the Judiciary Act of 1789, which set up the Constitutionally established Supreme Court with John Jay as chief justice, and a lower federal court system. Obviously, Congress was taking steps to make certain that the federal government would be, if anything, more active than the previous one. But the political disputes that shaped the constitutional ratification debate would soon spill over into the federal government and ultimately lead to the rise of political parties.

Key Concepts

- Hamilton's economic plan promoted manufacturing and enlarged the role of government.
- The Bank of the United States and the tariff were opposed in rural areas and southern states.
- There were both differences and similarities between the Hamiltonian and Jeffersonian movements.
- The election of Jefferson is referred to as the "Revolution of 1800."
- Relations with France and Britain were strained under Adams.

These topics are discussed in depth in *The American Pageant,* 14th and 15th eds., Chapter 10.

The Hamiltonian Vision Versus the Jeffersonian Vision

Alexander Hamilton was one of the most influential members of the new government. As a strong supporter of ratification and as an author of the *Federalist Papers,* he had advocated a commercial and manufacturing vision for the nation that was at odds with the vision of those, such as Jefferson, who saw an agrarian future for the nation. Under Secretary Hamilton's guidance, the federal government became increasingly involved in the promotion of capital accumulation and economic growth and expansion. In a strong attempt to address the impediments to commerce and trade inherent in the AOC, Hamilton created a mercantilist plan that would facilitate economic expansion by, in part, protecting and nurturing the nation's manufacturing sector. Rather than being an obstacle to capital growth, the new government would become a catalyst to an ever-expanding economy and a midwife for economic development. Hamilton's program had four major features:

- **The Tariff of 1789** Designed to provide the government with much needed revenue, it nonetheless served to protect domestic manufacturing by discouraging competition from abroad and compelling foreign competitors to raise prices on their commodities.
- **Report on Public Credit** At the time, the United States owed an enormous amount of money to creditors: $20 million to individual states, $11 million to foreigners, and $40 million to private individuals. Hamilton used this report to suggest that the United States pay off its domestic and foreign debts. Paying off its debts would improve the credit rating of the nation; then additional loans could be obtained, and the economy could be expanded by offering credit (loans) to start new businesses and expand others.

  Southern states were opposed to having the central government pay off the debts at face value, because most of it had been incurred by the northern states. The latter's rejoinder was that all states must share the burden of debt, because all would enjoy the fruits of an improved economy; further, the North had sustained considerably more damage in the American Revolution. Yet other critics saw this aspect of Hamilton's plan as an opportunity to transfer money to self-centered speculators. In the end, an agreement was worked out, the Assumption Bill: Southerners agreed to support Hamilton's proposal if the capitol of the United States was relocated to the South.

The Elastic Clause: Loose Versus Strict Interpretations of the Constitution

The creation of a Bank of the United States raised a serious constitutional question. Because the Constitution did not explicitly state that the federal government had in its enumerated powers the authority to create such an institution, was the Bank constitutional? Although the defenders of the Bank cited the elastic clause as their "loose" constitutional justification ("necessary and proper") for creating this financial institution, opponents, such as Jefferson, claimed in their "strict" interpretation of the Constitution that there was nothing "necessary" about the creation of the Bank. To which Hamilton responded that the enumerated powers of the federal government gave to it the authority to coin and borrow money. The Bank, he argued, was certainly necessary for maintaining the nation's financial stability and so was indeed constitutional. To this day, political leaders and jurists are divided over how best to interpret the Constitution: strictly ("original intent" of the Framers) or loosely (necessary and proper).

- **Report on Manufactures** Hamilton envisioned a government program that had as its precise objective the growth and development of manufacturing. This would be accomplished through
  - tariffs, loans, and grants for businesses.
  - excise taxes (taxes on certain manufactured goods) to raise revenue to finance the government and to aid businesses and manufacturing.
  - infrastructural development—aid in the construction of those facilities that are necessary for economic development, such as transportation and communication networks. Public taxes would help finance many of these programs.
- **Creation of a national bank (the Bank of the United States)** A national bank, reasoned Hamilton, would aid the capitalist class by extending credit to them. This credit would allow for expanded employment opportunities, which in turn would further stimulate economic growth. The government could also address economic problems, such as reckless speculation, by controlling the amount of credit available at any one time and by issuing sound currency. This would contribute to a steady and balanced growth of the economy. The Bank of the United States, though chartered by the United States, would be controlled by the following:
  - U.S. government: 20 percent
  - private U.S. citizens: 60 percent

- private foreign citizens: 20 percent (although many Americans were opposed to any foreign control of the bank)

After considerable squabbling, and vocal opposition by Secretary of State Thomas Jefferson, Congress adopted Hamilton's economic program.

FOREIGN AND DOMESTIC AFFAIRS

In his two terms as president, Washington's administration faced international and domestic tribulations. In his first term, revolution broke out in France and Washington was faced with a crucial decision whether to provide assistance to the French monarchy or to the revolutionaries who were attempting to overthrow King Louis XVI. After all, the revolutionaries were attempting to establish what the Americans in their revolution had recently achieved: a republic. Many Americans, including Thomas Jefferson, therefore sympathized with the revolutionaries, especially because France was at war with Britain, which had been interfering with American merchant ships sailing to French ports. To put the matter to rest, President Washington issued the Neutrality Proclamation, claiming that the new American republic was in no position to confront European powers such as Great Britain. In protest, Jefferson resigned as secretary of state. But the issue did not end there. The French minister to the United States, Edmond Genêt, broke all diplomatic protocol by appealing directly to the American public to persuade their government to intervene on France's behalf in its war against Britain. Washington demanded that the minister be recalled, but the incident hurt the pro-French faction in the American government. In other aspects of foreign affairs, the United States agreed to two major treaties during Washington's second term:

- **The Jay Treaty (1794)** Chief Justice John Jay was sent by Washington to negotiate with the British an end to their practice of seizing American ships and impressing American sailors into the British navy. The British did agree to remove their forts on America's western frontier, but made no guarantees that seizures and impressments would end. The U.S. Senate narrowly ratified the treaty, but the American public was so incensed by Britain's disdain for American neutral rights that support for the French cause in the United States swelled. Nevertheless, the United States was able to maintain its neutrality in the Anglo-French war.
- **The Pinckney Treaty (1795)** Concerned that the animosity between Britain and the United States was thawing, Spain made a series of concessions in negotiations with the U.S. ambassador to Spain, Thomas Pinckney. The treaty opened up the lower Mississippi and the important port city of New Orleans to American trade and shipping. It also granted Americans the right of deposit—a transfer of goods—in New Orleans without having to pay a tax to the Spanish. Spain further agreed to accept the 31st parallel as Florida's northern border, and to stop inciting Native American tribes.

In 1794 farmers in western Pennsylvania tested the new powers of the federal government under the Constitution. As you will recall, one of the weaknesses of the central government under the AOC was its inability to confront domestic challenges. When the farmers refused to pay a federal excise tax, part of Hamilton's economic program, on whiskey and even attacked federal tax collectors, Washington called on the states to assist the government in putting down the uprising, the Whiskey Rebellion. With the collapse of the revolt, the federal government had demonstrated its newfound strength in dealing with domestic challenges to its authority. As for the farmers, who were generally destitute and saw little value in Hamilton's programs, the suppression of the uprising drove them further into the Antifederalist camp.

When his second term expired, Washington chose not to seek reelection, a precedent that would stand for over a century until Franklin D. Roosevelt was elected to four terms. (The Twenty-second Amendment, adopted in 1951, limits the president to two terms.) Prior to leaving office, Washington provided the nation with advice in the form of a Farewell Address. In it the first president counseled the American people about

- maintaining national unity despite the discord that prevailed between divergent regions, groups, and classes
- obeying and supporting the principles and authority of the Constitution
- the dangers inherent in creating political parties
- avoiding the creation of permanent alliances with foreign nations and not becoming embroiled in European affairs

The division between the Federalists and Antifederalists and between Jefferson and Hamilton had made Washington wary of intense political allegiances. But by the time he left office, Washington had become identified with Hamilton's Federalist faction. He was not alone in his political party affiliations. By 1796, despite his warnings about creating political parties, his vice president and successor to the presidency, John Adams, and his former secretary of state, Thomas Jefferson, had rapidly identified themselves as either members of the Federalist Party (led by Hamilton and Vice President John Adams) or of the Democratic-Republican Party (led by Jefferson).

The Presidency of John Adams

The presidential election of 1796 was particularly vitriolic. Adams emerged with a very narrow Electoral College victory, and peculiarly enough Jefferson, the second-place winner, became his vice president. (This unlikely and awkward situation was rectified in 1804 with the passage of the Twelfth Amendment, which changes the procedures followed by the Electoral College so that presidential candidates are chosen along with their vice-presidential running mates.) Upon assuming the office of president, Adams faced foreign and domestic problems and even discord in his own party ranks, as many Federalists looked to Hamilton, not Adams, for their ideological inspiration. Shortly into Adams's only term as president, U.S.-French relations began unraveling as it became abundantly clear to the

French, from a reading of the Jay Treaty, that the Federalists were pro-British. Disregarding American neutrality, the French attacked American shipping—a conflict known as the Quasi-War. In an attempt to reduce tensions, Adams sent a special mission to France in 1794. Upon arriving in France the three U.S. commissioners, John Marshall, Elbridge Gerry, and Charles Cotesworth Pinckney, were asked by the French Minister Talleyrand (through his agents, who became known as X, Y, and Z) for a bribe of $250,000 and millions in loans even before negotiations could begin. Pinckney purportedly declared: "No, no, not a sixpence." Later, the outraged American public and government memorialized the U.S. response with the slogan "Millions for defense, but not a cent for tribute." Again, the nation geared up for war. Hamilton, never far from the center of the action, pressed Adams to arm American merchant ships and raise an army. His rationale was that the further the United States moved away from France the closer it moved to a more lucrative commercial relationship with Britain. But Adams refused to declare war on France, a move which likely cost him his second term as president.

Two years later, Adams sent another mission to France, despite being admonished by members of his own party. This time an agreement was worked out, mainly because Emperor Napoleon wanted to focus on European domination. In the Convention of 1800, the 1778 treaty between the two nations was canceled and relations between the two nations improved.

The Federalists, in the meantime, had sought to silence opposition to their policies from the Democratic-Republicans. Inspired by the ideas of Hamilton, the Federalists drafted a series of acts, the Alien and Sedition Acts, designed to neutralize any challenges to their dominance.

- **The Naturalization Act** An attempt to curb criticism emanating from immigrants—especially the French and Irish—whom Federalists assumed were identified more closely with the Democratic-Republicans, the act raised the residency requirement for citizenship from five to fourteen years. As expected, the act limited the growth of Democratic-Republican voters because of the residency requirement.
- **The Alien (Friends) Act** This gave the president the authority to deport individuals whom he considered a threat to the United States.
- **The Alien Enemies Act** This provided for the deportation or imprisonment of any individuals in a time of declared war.
- **The Sedition Act** Probably the most insidious of the acts, this legislation stated that speaking, writing, or publishing criticisms of the government were at the very least misdemeanors and possibly treasonous.

Without question, the four acts violated the First Amendment and established a precedent more consistent with authoritarian governments than with a democratic republic. Unfortunately, President Adams signed the Alien and Sedition Acts into law. Though they temporarily silenced political opposition, the acts backfired on the Federalists as disgusted Americans gravitated to the Democratic-Republicans. This crisis in constitutional rights, however, would not end until the Federalists lost the White House in the election of 1800. Judicial review would ultimately decide the fate of controversial laws, but that would have to wait for the Marshall Court. Nevertheless, the Alien and Sedition Acts did not go unchallenged. The same year the acts were passed, 1798, the Kentucky and Virginia Resolutions were passed by their respective states. In Kentucky, the state legislature adopted a resolution by Thomas Jefferson questioning the federal government's authority to pass such legislation. The Virginia legislature, guided by James Madison, went even further and articulated what has become known as the "compact" theory of government (or states' rights). The logic of the argument tends to negate the Constitution's supremacy clause and is as follows:

The federal government was created by the states.

There are instances when conflicts arise between the rights and laws of the states and the authority of the federal government.

When such conflicts arise, the interests of the states take precedence over the laws and actions of the federal government.

Therefore, a state has the right to declare national laws null and void.

After the 1800 election, the new Democratic-Republican congressional majority repealed the laws or allowed them to expire. Despite the stain on their reputation that came with the Alien and Sedition Acts, the Federalists had

- strengthened the federal government
- established a sound fiscal system
- formulated policies and programs that stimulated capital accumulation and therefore diversification of the economy

As for John Adams, his presidency was limited to one term. The 1800 election ended the supremacy of the Federalists and led to the nation's first peaceful transition from one political party to its adversary, which is one reason why some historians refer to the election of Jefferson as a political revolution.

"The Revolution of 1800"

In the election of 1800, Democratic-Republicans Thomas Jefferson and Aaron Burr tied. The election eventually went to the House of Representatives, where, oddly enough, Hamilton's support for Jefferson made the Virginian president. Hamilton apparently considered Jefferson less objectionable than Burr. Yet the divisions between the philosophies of Hamilton and Jefferson remained. Many historians see the following distinctions inherent in the outlook of their respective movements:

AP Tip

A free-response question that relates to the Jeffersonian movement, presidency, or the "Revolution of 1800" may in part ask you to relate the meaning of these terms in relation to the alternative perspective, the Hamiltonian movement. Historians have debated the two perspectives for decades, and their observations will help you make a thorough analysis. The contrasts between the Jeffersonian and Hamiltonian movements listed above represent one way of looking at the issue. Historians who see these distinctions go on to contend that the Jeffersonian movement was one that advanced democracy in the United States. Further, it was the first example of political liberalism—reforming the political and economic system—in the nineteenth century: under Jefferson, the government was viewed as the guardian of the people against the abuses of the upper classes. Conversely, Hamilton is often seen as wanting to further the privileges and objectives of the northern commercial/capitalist interests. Consequently, Hamilton and Jefferson inhabit opposite ends of the political spectrum.

Other historians do not see it this way. To them, there are basically no substantial differences between Hamilton and Jefferson or between the Federalists and Democratic-Republicans, because both represented the interests of the upper classes, whether northern capitalists or southern planters. What is more, Jefferson was a pragmatist who was not tied to any particular philosophical approach to government but adjusted to what was expedient, as expressed in his first inaugural address: "We are all Republicans, we are all Federalists." Some would argue that he was attempting to provide a smooth transition from one political party to another. Other historians point to two important examples that show Jefferson was not consistent with the ideals he preached. The first was an abandonment of his strict interpretation of the Constitution when he purchased the Louisiana Territory from France. No clause in the Constitution gave him the authority to do so; he did what was "necessary and proper," the argument of those holding a loose interpretation. The second example is that despite his opposition to the Bank of the United States, upon becoming president he did not seek to eliminate it but simply allowed its charter to expire. Taking into account these conflicting opinions will make for a more compelling free response essay.

- The Jeffersonian Movement
  - The spirit of the movement was embodied in the Democratic-Republican Party, which represented the interests of the common man, the farmer, and was therefore a movement that further democratized the United States.
  - It was anti-capitalistic (favoring the subsistence farmer).
  - It favored limitations on the power of the federal government and a strict interpretation of the Constitution.
  - It maintained that the future of the nation was dependent on maintaining an agrarian society.
  - Following Jefferson, a Francophile, the party favored support of France.

- The Hamiltonian Movement
  - The spirit of the movement was embodied in the Federalist Party, which represented the interests of the capitalist class.
  - It favored the expansion of the federal government's power and a loose interpretation of the Constitution.
  - It maintained that the future of the nation was dependent on developing manufacturing and industry.
  - Following Hamilton, an Anglophile, the party favored Great Britain.

The term "Revolution of 1800" is appropriate in many respects. The fact that, in a fledgling democracy pioneering the very idea of republicanism, our country's government (and citizenry) allowed for the peaceful transfer of power between two parties with polar views on the nature of government and authority is no small feat. Jefferson's assumption of power came without bloodshed and he proclaimed to the nation, "We are all Federalists...We are all Republicans."

Content Review Questions

1. Which one of the following did NOT serve in George Washington's administration?
   (A) Thomas Jefferson
   (B) Alexander Hamilton
   (C) John Adams
   (D) John Marshall

2. In the Report on Manufactures
   (A) Hamilton sought to promote the agrarian sector of the economy.
   (B) Hamilton and Jefferson promoted an excise tax.
   (C) Jefferson argued that the nation should develop its infrastructure.
   (D) Hamilton supported policies that would protect American industry from foreign competition.

3. The first chief justice of the U.S. Supreme Court was
   (A) John Marshall.
   (B) John Jay.
   (C) Thomas Paine.
   (D) Edmond Genet.

4. The compromise that led to the Assumption Bill involved southerners accepting Hamilton's economic program in return for
   (A) an end to the protective tariff.
   (B) legalizing the slave trade.
   (C) relocating the nation's capitol to the South.
   (D) purchasing the Louisiana Territory.

5. The Twelfth Amendment to the Constitution
   (A) abolished slavery.
   (B) led to the creation of the judicial branch.
   (C) gave to the federal government the authority to create a national bank.
   (D) changed the method used by the Electoral College to choose the president and vice president.

6. Which one of the following represents an improvement in French-American relations?
   (A) The Milan Decree
   (B) The Orders in Council
   (C) The XYZ affair
   (D) The Convention of 1800

7. Which of the following would have been opposed by a believer in the strict interpretation of the Constitution?
   (A) The raising of taxes by the national government
   (B) The use of military force to put down the Whiskey Rebellion
   (C) The opening of trade with the British
   (D) The creation of the national bank

8. Why did Alexander Hamilton and other Federalists refuse to support the French Revolution?
   (A) Because of the radicalism and mob-rule of the French Revolution
   (B) Because King Louis XVI of France had given the Americans favorable trade terms
   (C) Because the United States was too busy at war with the British
   (D) Because the French officials "X,Y, and Z" had requested bribes before meeting with American envoys

9. The Kentucky and Virginia Resolutions of 1798 focused on the widely debated question of
   (A) whether the Constitution was created licitly.
   (B) whether the legislature represented the states or the people.
   (C) whether the federal government is supreme over the state governments in all cases.
   (D) whether immigrants are valuable parts of the political society.

10. Pinckney's Treaty resulted in all of the following EXCEPT
    (A) it improved Spanish-American relations.
    (B) it gave the Americans the right of deposit in New Orleans.
    (C) it gave to the United States Spain's Caribbean islands in return for American aid.
    (D) it settled the Florida boundary dispute.

11. The Bill of Rights addresses all of the following EXCEPT
    (A) freedom of speech.
    (B) trial by jury.
    (C) right to privacy.
    (D) prohibition against cruel and unusual punishment.

12. Which of the following cabinet positions was NOT established in Washington's first term in 1789?
    (A) Secretary of labor
    (B) Secretary of state
    (C) Secretary of the treasury
    (D) Attorney general

13. The Judiciary Act of 1789 was significant in the creation of
    (A) the Justice Department.
    (B) habeas corpus rights.
    (C) the impeachment powers of the legislative branch.
    (D) the U.S. Supreme Court.

14. In his Farewell Address, Washington advised the nation to avoid entangling foreign alliances and to
    (A) avoid excise taxes.
    (B) limit the powers of the states in relation to the authority of the federal government.
    (C) limit westward expansion in order to prevent hostilities with Indian tribes.
    (D) avoid political party factionalism.

15. Which of the following was a feature of the Federalist Party's political ideology?
    (A) Rule by a well-informed electorate of the common people
    (B) A loose interpretation of the Constitution
    (C) Opposition to a national bank
    (D) No special treatment for manufacturing

Short-Answer Questions

1. The United States faced considerable difficulties in establishing itself after the ratification of the Constitution.
   (A) Give ONE example of a challenge faced by the new United States government in the period between 1789–1800.
   (B) Describe the response of the United States government to the challenge you explained in Part A.
   (C) Did the United States respond to the challenge effectively? Provide at least ONE piece of evidence to support your position.

Question 2 is based on the following passage.

> "As avenues to foreign influence in innumerable ways, such attachments are particularly alarming to the truly enlightened and independent patriot. How many opportunities do they afford to tamper with domestic factions, to practice the arts of seduction, to mislead public opinion, to influence or awe the public councils. Such an attachment of a small or weak towards a great and powerful nation dooms the former to be the satellite of the latter...Excessive partiality for one foreign nation and excessive dislike of another cause those whom they actuate to see danger only on one side, and serve to veil and even second the arts of influence on the other... Why quit our own to stand upon foreign ground? Why, by interweaving our destiny with

that of any part of Europe, entangle our peace and prosperity in the toils of European ambition, rivalship, interest, humor or caprice?"

George Washington, Farewell Address (1796)

2. Based on the message delivered by George Washington, complete the following tasks:
   A) Briefly explain the main point made by President Washington.
   B) Provide ONE piece of evidence from American history that supports his argument.
   C) Provide ONE piece of evidence from American history that refutes his assertions.

Long-Essay Questions

1. Evaluate the presidency of John Adams. Include in your answer discussion of
   - Adams's foreign affairs policies and actions
   - Adams's domestic policies and actions
2. Compare and contrast the Hamiltonian and Jeffersonian movements in regard to TWO of the following.
   - political philosophy
   - long-term social and economic outlook
   - interpretations of the Constitution
   - federal versus state power

Answers

Content Review Questions

1. **(D)** Jefferson was secretary of state, Hamilton, secretary of the treasury, Knox, secretary of war, and Adams was vice president. Marshall was first appointed to the Supreme Court by Adams (*The American Pageant*, 14th ed., pp. 230–231/15th ed., p. 181; Learning Objective POL-2).
2. **(D)** Hamilton wanted government to assist in the development of American industry and manufacturing. Jefferson was strongly opposed to Hamilton's economic agenda (*The American Pageant*, 14th ed., p. 203/15th ed., pp. 184–185; Learning Objective POL-2).
3. **(B)** Jay was the first, but it was only under John Marshall, who became chief justice in 1801, that the role and powers of the judicial branch were defined (*The American Pageant*, 14th ed., pp. 202–203/15th ed., p. 182; Learning Objective POL-2).
4. **(C)** The location of the capitol in the South was considered quite prestigious to that section (*The American Pageant*, 14th ed., pp. 202–203/15th ed., p. 183; Learning Objective ID-5).

5. **(D)** After the election of 1796 in which the Federalist John Adams was elected president and the Democratic-Republican Jefferson was elected vice president, the Twelfth Amendment was drafted. It was ratified in 1804 (*The American Pageant,* 14th ed., pp. 213–214/15th ed., p. 194; Learning Objective POL-2).

6. **(D)** The Convention of 1800 thawed hostile American-French relations. Answers A, B, and E were actions taken by France and Britain that violated American neutrality. The XYZ affair was a French demand for a bribe as a prerequisite to opening negotiations with American delegates (*The American Pageant,* 14th ed., pp. 216–217/15th ed., pp. 194–196; Learning Objective WOR-5).

7. **(D)** Believers in a strict interpretation of the Constitution, like Jefferson, were wary of claims that the "necessary and proper" (or elastic) clause allowed Congress the power to create a national bank because it had the power to coin money and pay debts (*The American Pageant,* 14th ed., p. 204/15th ed., p. 185; Learning Objective POL-5).

8. **(A)** Hamilton and other aristocratic Federalists feared the radicalism of the French Revolution—and its resulting anti-elite reign of terror (*The American Pageant,* 14th ed., p. 207/15th ed., p. 187; Learning Objective WOR-2).

9. **(C)** Advanced most clearly in the Virginia Resolution, the "compact" or states' rights theory of government challenged the idea that the national government could impose a law contrary to the interests of a particular state (*The American Pageant,* 14th ed., pp. 218–219/15th ed., pp. 197–198; Learning Objective POL-5).

10. **(C)** This was never an issue between the United States and Spain, which maintained its important colonial possessions in the Caribbean (*The American Pageant,* 14th ed., p. 213/15th ed., p. 193; Learning Objective WOR-5).

11. **(C)** The right to privacy is not specified in the Bill of Rights, though over time Americans have acquired rights protecting privacy (*The American Pageant,* 14th ed., p. 201/15th ed., p. 182; Learning Objective POL-5).

12. **(A)** The position of secretary of labor was not established until 1913, during the Wilson administration. The position of secretary of war was established in 1789 but was redefined and renamed in 1947 as secretary of defense (*The American Pageant,* 14th ed., p. 201/15th ed., p. 181; Learning Objective ID-1).

13. **(D)** The Judiciary Act of 1789 (later ruled unconstitutional by the Marshall Court) established the federal judiciary (allowing for the creation of lower courts under the Supreme Court) as well as the cabinet office of attorney general (*The American Pageant,* 14th ed., p. 202/15th ed., p. 182; Learning Objective POL-5).

14. **(D)** Many historians claim that Washington feared the nation would dissolve into political party bickering and therefore warned against such factionalism. Some believe he was being critical of the Democratic-Republicans and was hoping Americans would align themselves with the Federalists (*The American Pageant,* 14th ed., p. 213/15th ed., p. 193; Learning Objective POL-2).

15. **(B)** The Federalists favored a loose construction of the Constitution and therefore viewed the elastic clause as necessary to create, for example, the Bank of the United States (*The American Pageant,* 14th ed., p. 219/15th ed., pp. 198–199; Learning Objective POL-2).

SHORT-ANSWER QUESTIONS

1. In identifying a challenge, consider the new nation's divisions along varying interpretations of the Constitution, its weakness in the face of British refusals to abide by the Treaty of Paris, or the enormous economic difficulties facing the infant country. As you explain the government's response, consider its effectiveness. Was it able to present a unified face before the nations of the world? Was it able to govern effectively and force naysayers into accepting the rule of law? Was it able to establish economic security to allow for future growth?

2. This section of the Farewell Address warns the nation against foreign entanglements. Considering that the Federalists wanted to cast their lot with the industrial British, and that the Jeffersonians wanted to stand by the revolutionary French, this advice wasn't taken to heart well. In which case(s) has our involvement with other nations hurt our own national interests? Though this will likely require you to go beyond the scope of the chapter, there are also examples of times when America's best interest required us to establish lasting relationships with other countries (think about the imperial age, or the Cold War).

LONG-ESSAY QUESTIONS

1. You should incorporate in your essay Adams's struggles with maintaining relations with the French, including his attempts to avoid war despite domestic pressure from his fellow Federalists. Also important is his handling of anti-government sentiments at home, most notably the Alien and Sedition Acts. (Historical Thinking Skill IV-8: Interpretation)

2. Your essay should compare Hamilton's support for an extensive role for the federal government and his loose-constructionist view—for example, the Bank of the United States—with Jefferson's strict-constructionist view. Also include a description of Hamilton's economic program and compare it to Jefferson's support for the yeoman farmer. (Historical Thinking Skill II-4: Comparison)

7

THE GROWTH OF THE NATION FROM 1800 TO THE 1850S

After the successful transfer of power in the "Revolution of 1800," the United States continued to experience growing pains, literally and figuratively. While domestically, the early nineteenth century was fairly quiet, the Supreme Court—led by John Marshall—was busy solidifying the powers and responsibilities of the federal government. Meanwhile, Congress, the presidents, and indeed, the nation, had expansion fever. In fact, the United States has been consistent in its foreign policy in that it has always had expansionist tendencies, or, as one historian has phrased it, "Empire as a way of life."

KEY CONCEPTS

- The Marshall Court defined the role and powers of the judicial branch.
- Territorial expansion was an objective of the U.S. government from its inception, as witnessed by the Louisiana Purchase, the removal of Native Americans and by the Mexican-American War.
- Various groups and ideologies supported territorial expansion for economic, political, and cultural reasons.
- Controversial British actions and American policies aggravated relations between the two nations, leading to the War of 1812.
- New England and the Federalists strongly opposed the war and floated the idea of secession.
- Under the Monroe Doctrine, the United States established a policy of hegemony—dominance—in the Western Hemisphere.

Early nineteenth-century nation-building is discussed in depth in *The American Pageant,* 14th and 15th eds., Chapters 11–14, 17.

THE MARSHALL COURT

When Federalist John Marshall—a distant cousin of President Jefferson—was appointed to the Supreme Court in 1801, his party was already in decline. Nevertheless, his position as chief justice would ensure that as the nation grew in territory, so would the powers of the central government grow as well. Though a political chasm opened between Marshall and Jefferson, as Marshall forged a role for the judicial branch that expanded the powers of the federal government, Marshall's vision of a government strong enough to rule over its ever-expanding borders in many ways made possible the survival of the United States.

When he assumed his duties, the Supreme Court lacked both power and prestige. The Court met only six weeks each year—the first Supreme Court justice, John Jay, resigned due to inactivity! Although he was not a legal scholar, in his thirty-five years on the bench, Marshall wrote nearly half of its decisions and in the process transformed the Court. The Marshall Court became strongly identified with

- vested rights in contract clauses
- expanding the Court's jurisdiction
- judicial nationalism over states' rights
- blocking state regulations that limited property rights
- freeing American commerce from restraints placed on it by the states

The most significant decisions made by the Marshall Court include the following:

- ***Marbury* v. *Madison* (1803)** This decision established the concept of judicial review—that is, the implied power of the judicial branch to determine the constitutionality of state and federal legislation.
- ***Fletcher* v. *Peck* (1810)** The Court ruled that a state could not pass laws that invalidated a contract.
- ***Martin* v. *Hunter's Lessee* (1816)** Established the supremacy of federal courts over state courts.
- ***Dartmouth College* v. *Woodward* (1819)** Reaffirming the *Fletcher* decision, the Court ruled that a state cannot alter or invalidate a contract.
- ***McCulloch* v. *Maryland* (1819)** The Court ruled that the government possessed the implied power to create a national bank; that the bank could not be taxed by a state because this would give the "power to destroy" to the bank; and that federal law is absolute over state law.
- ***Gibbons* v. *Ogden* (1821)** The Court recognized the federal government's authority over interstate trade.
- ***Cohens* v. *Virginia* (1821)** Much to the dismay of states' rightists, the Court asserted the right of the Supreme Court to review the decisions of state supreme courts in issues dealing with the authority of the federal government.

Key Events in Jefferson's Presidency

In his first term, Jefferson generally carried out the domestic and foreign policies of his predecessors. He maintained the Bank of the United States and continued Hamilton's debt repayment plan. Following Washington's advice, he sought to steer clear of international alliances and maintain the nation's neutrality. The latter allowed him to reaffirm his party's philosophy by reducing the size of the government. In this case, the military saw its funding reduced. Also, the hated excise tax was eliminated while the government's budget was simultaneously cut. However, for all of his conservatism, the Louisiana Purchase (1803) was the most notable achievement of Jefferson's first term—one that set the country on the path of Manifest Destiny long before anyone had coined that phrase.

The French emperor, Napoleon, strapped for cash, needed more money to fight Britain. His decision to sell France's last major territorial possession in North America was made more palatable by a successful slave revolt against the French on the Caribbean island of Santo Domingo. Napoleon reasoned that if he could not hold on to a small island in the Caribbean, there was little chance he would be able to control an enormous swath of land west of the Mississippi River. France's quandary was America's gain. In return for the enormous Louisiana Territory including New Orleans (which France had reacquired from Spain at the turn of the century), the United States paid only $15 million. Despite reservations about the constitutionality of the president's treaty, the purchase of this land was too good to reject. Almost overnight, the territory of the United States doubled in size.

Having purchased the land from France, Jefferson decided it was time to find out more about the vast territory. Jefferson organized an expedition led by Meriwether Lewis and William Clark, instructing the men to find out as much as possible about the territory's topographical features and resources as well as to gain scientific evidence about the climate and flora and fauna of this western land. Two years after departing, Lewis and Clark reached the Pacific Ocean. Upon returning east their journals were published. Extremely helpful to the U.S. government, their work also caught the imagination of the American public and consequently paved the way for future westward exploration and development.

If Jefferson's first term had been comparatively smooth; the second was anything but. Far away in North Africa, coastal nations collectively known as the Barbary States were seizing international ships and holding their crews for ransom. Because the United States had no navy to speak of, its merchant ships were vulnerable. The U.S. government decided to pay tribute to protect its ships, but not until the United States defeated the Barbary pirates, in 1815, did the depredations cease.

Tensions with France and Britain also worsened. Near the end of Jefferson's first term, the two European powers had intensified their conflict, which in turn again threatened to interrupt American shipping. By 1805 Napoleon's forces had gained control of much of the European continent, though the British navy continued to dominate the seas. Supplying both sides of the conflict was initially beneficial for

American merchants and shippers. But when Britain sought to stop the lucrative trade between the United States and France, the situation quickly spiraled out of control, as is obvious from the following sequence of events:

- **Essex decision (1805)** The British ruled that trade closed during peacetime could not be opened during wartime. For U.S. shippers, this meant that they would be prohibited from trading with the French West Indies.
- ***Leopard-Chesapeake* Incident (1807)** Although it was powerful, the British navy was short on sailors. To remedy this problem it began the highly questionable tactic of stopping American ships on the high seas and impressing—forcing—its sailors, whether they were British or not, into their navy. In one egregious case, the British warship *Leopard* fired on an American warship, the *Chesapeake,* and removed several sailors, a few of whom were deserters from the British navy.
- **Orders in Council (1806 and 1807)** Britain blockaded the ports of France and its allies, thereby preventing neutral nations from trading with these nations.
- **Berlin Decree (1806)** France responded in kind to the Orders in Council.
- **Milan Decree (1807)** France announced it would seize any ships that had obeyed Britain's Orders in Council.

As a result of these decrees, Britain and France frequently seized American ships. Rather than go to war with one or both powerful European nations, Jefferson—and his successor, James Madison—sought to punish British and French commercial interests through a series of trade acts:

- **Nonintercourse Act (1806)** This halted the importation of many British commodities but failed to influence the British.
- **Embargo Act (1807)** This prohibited all foreign trade in hopes of protecting American shipping interests. It had a devastating effect on the New England economy and ultimately hurt more than helped the United States. Many New Englanders (traditionally Federalist territory anyhow) denounced Jefferson and Madison and gave their support to Charles Pinckney, the Federalist candidate in the 1808 election. The Embargo Act severely tarnished Jefferson's reputation among the people, many of whom resorted to smuggling.
- **Nonintercourse Act (1809)** Trade was opened with all nations except the belligerents, Britain and France. Jefferson agreed to trade with either nation as soon as it repealed its trade restrictions against American shipping.
- **Macon's Bill No. 2 (1810)** Madison replaced the Nonintercourse Act with his own plan to open trade with both Britain and France. He promised to suspend trade with the enemy of the nation that first agreed to cease its violations of American shipping rights. Napoleon deceived the American president by claiming to revoke the Berlin and Milan decrees so long as Britain repealed its Orders in Council. Madison accepted France's terms and agreed to a policy of nonintercourse with Britain. In the meantime, pressured by its own merchants and traders, the British had every intention of

ending their trade dispute with the United States. Unfortunately, by the time Britain's concession had reached the United States it had declared war on Great Britain.

THE WAR OF 1812

As the United States entered the second decade of the nineteenth century, tensions with Britain were exacerbated by the Napoleonic Wars in Europe. As you know, both Britain and France had violated America's neutral shipping and commercial rights. The British were no more or less at fault than the French, but Americans were already blaming them and British Canadians for inciting Native American uprisings in the West. (In truth, Americans, in their hunger for more land, incited the unrest.) A famous example of conflict between white Americans and Native Americans that was blamed on the British was Shawnee Chief Tecumseh's raids on settlements in the Indiana Territory. Tecumseh's attempt to unite all the tribes in the Mississippi Valley ended when future president William Henry Harrison's force defeated him at the Battle of Tippecanoe in 1811.

THE WAR HAWKS

The defeat of Tecumseh coincided with the convening of Congress. Many of those who came to Washington for the 1811–1812 session were newly elected, mostly western and southern Democratic-Republican congressmen who also happened to be highly nationalistic. They were soon labeled "war hawks" and their hostility to Britain was a large reason why they were given this moniker. Led by Henry Clay of Kentucky and John C. Calhoun of South Carolina, the war hawks favored punishing Britain militarily for seizing merchant ships and impressing American sailors, violations of American neutrality. But they also wanted to seize land from the Native Americans in the West, drive the British from Canada, and even annex Spanish Florida. Opposition to such endeavors came from the Federalists and their region of influence, New England; they tended to be Anglophiles, and they also believed—correctly—that war with Britain would damage their commercial interests. Nevertheless, an unprepared United States declared war on Britain on June 18, 1812.

THE WAR: MILITARY OPERATIONS

Unfortunately for the United States, it declared war with an army numbering fewer than ten thousand soldiers and a navy numbering fewer than twenty ships—this when it was challenging the mightiest fleet in the world and a formidable British army as well. But fortunately for the Americans, Great Britain was yet again involved in another phase of its ongoing conflict with France and so could not apply the full weight of its military might against the United States. This did little to alter the results on the battlefield, however, as three separate American invasions of Canada failed. Surprisingly the Americans experienced considerably more success against the British navy in the Great Lakes and as far south as Bolivian waters. Two of the most famous and successful naval engagements in U.S. history took place between the American warship *Constitution* and HMS *Guerriere,* in 1812, and at the Battle of Lake Erie, in 1813. Although the United States experienced initial success using privateers to attack British shipping and sustain American commerce, by the second year of the war the British had effectively paralyzed American trade and commerce. The region most affected was of course New England.

The Federalists, New England, and the War: The Hartford Convention

The Federalists and those they represented, mainly in the New England states, deeply opposed the war against Britain for personal as well as commercial reasons. From their perspective, the Jefferson and Madison administrations (both Democratic-Republicans) were to blame for unwisely forcing a war against the British. Rest assured, New England Federalists were vocal in their opposition. However, some of their actions were highly questionable, and others were clearly treasonous. For example, while many New Englanders refused to buy war bonds, others actually sold provisions to enemy forces in Canada. Some states even refused to send their militias to fight in Canada. Federalist hostility to the war peaked in 1814 when New England delegates were sent by their states to a convention in Hartford, Connecticut, to organize resistance to what they perceived were highly questionable measures by the Democratic-Republicans. Using the compact theory of government as their guide, they proceeded to draft resolutions that would reduce the influence of the South and of the Democratic-Republicans. Their proposals included

- eliminating the three-fifths clause because it inflated the South's representation in the House
- requiring a two-thirds vote in Congress to admit new states, impose embargoes, and declare war
- limiting a president to one term so as to prevent two consecutive terms from the same state (four of the first five presidents were referred to as the "Virginia Dynasty")
- holding a future conference to discuss the possibility of secession (not convened because the war ended first)

On land U.S. forces fared better against the Native Americans than they did against the British. William Henry Harrison's troops were victorious against Tecumseh's force at the Battle of the Thames, killing the tribal leader in the process. To the south, another future president, Andrew Jackson, and his militia troops defeated the Creeks at the Battle of Horseshoe Bend (then proceeded to slaughter Creek women and children as retribution for Native American attacks). The two defeats, for all intents and purposes, neutralized the Native Americans as British allies. The British, however, continued on with their own military strategy. Utilizing a three-pronged attack, they invaded the United States, marched on Washington, D.C., in the summer of 1814, and burned the White House and other public buildings. They then turned north and marched on Baltimore, but they were unable to capture the strategically placed Fort McHenry—this was the battle that inspired Francis Scott Key to write "The Star Spangled Banner." At the same time, the British were decisively defeated in upstate New York.

By winter 1814 both sides had had enough. In December they signed a peace treaty in Ghent, Belgium, ending all hostilities, except one. Because of the slowness of travel in the early nineteenth century, the peace terms had not reached the United States before the most famous engagement of the war had taken place, the Battle of New Orleans. Although the war had already ended, the lopsided U.S. victory added luster to the military reputation of the Americans and their commanding general, Andrew Jackson.

Effects of the War

The Treaty of Ghent brought about no significant concessions. For the most part, relations and conditions between the two warring nations returned to their prewar status. In fact, none of the issues that caused the war were resolved, though both sides returned conquered territory to its original owner. The consequences of the war for the United States were mixed:

- The U.S. economy was devastated.
- Large areas of the nation's capitol were destroyed.
- American nationalism intensified.
- The nation won foreign respect for its military capabilities, which allowed the United States to hold its own against the mighty British Empire.
- The Federalists and New England were discredited by their antipathy to the war and the actions they took to impede the war effort. This temporarily reduced the importance of sectionalism as the nation prepared to enter the "Era of Good Feelings," a newspaper term used to describe the two terms of President James Monroe. During this period, there was only one major political party, the Democratic-Republicans; it was therefore assumed that political discord had evaporated.
- Military careers were launched or enhanced by the war, most noticeably those of Jackson and Harrison, who would use their new-won popularity to propel them into the Oval Office.

Two years after the treaty was signed the United States and Britain agreed to demilitarize the Great Lakes in the Rush-Bagot Treaty. As for the attempt to annex Florida, Secretary of State John Quincy Adams and Spanish Minister Luis de Onís concluded an agreement, the Adams-Onís Treaty (1819), which revealed the weakened state of Spain in the early nineteenth century; for $5 million the United States received Florida. The southwestern boundary now extended as far as the Mexican territory of Tejas (Texas). Seizing on Spain's obvious weakness, all of Spain's South American colonies gained their independence by the early 1820s. It was not long, however, before the United States would become the hegemonic power in both North America and South America.

The Impulse for Expansion

In the two centuries since the ratification of the Constitution, the size of the United States has more than quadrupled. As historian Arthur Schlesinger, Jr., has pointed out, "The drive across the continent does not call for complicated analysis. An energetic, acquisitive people were propelled by their traits and technologies to push restlessly into contiguous spaces sparsely inhabited by wandering aborigines." But there may be more to it than that. Even before independence was won, Americans lusted after the lands west of the Appalachian Mountains—so much so that the British imposed the Proclamation of 1763 to keep the colonists closer to the Eastern Seaboard. Our first four presidents gave voice to this expansionist impulse:

- Washington called the new nation a "rising empire."
- John Adams remarked that the United States was "destined to occupy all of the northern part of this quarter of the globe and that when accomplished, would be a significant achievement for mankind."
- Jefferson referred to a "vast territory that would provide room enough for the descendants to the thousandth and ten thousandth generation."
- Madison urged that the United States "extend the sphere, extend the republic as one great respectable and flourishing empire."

The purchase of the Louisiana Territory, in 1803 and the War of 1812 both reflect the driving force—territorial expansion—behind U.S. foreign policy in this period. As in the previous century, Americans continued their drive westward, acquiring new territories and conquering indigenous Native American tribes. By the 1840s the United States would again be at war, this time with Mexico, ultimately taking by conquest that nation's northern territory. By the eve of the Civil War, the United States had expanded well beyond the Mississippi River. As the nation continued to enlarge, Americans would cite a number of economic, political, cultural, and historical arguments to justify U.S. territorial expansion. Politicians, literary figures, educators, newspapermen, and religious leaders, all contributed to a set of ideas that collectively became known as Manifest Destiny. The term was coined by a newspaper editor, John O'Sullivan, in the 1840s as Americans began rapidly crossing the Mississippi River and beyond the Rocky Mountains to reach California and Oregon. Manifest Destiny implied that it was a God-given right and inevitability for the United States to spread its Protestant religion, capitalist economy, and democratic-republican political system across the continental United States. Religious leaders claimed that God wanted Americans—"God's chosen people"—to expand and dominate other peoples in order to convert these "heathens" to the Christian religion. More sophisticated proponents of empire provided a more comprehensive argument by integrating the economic, political, and cultural rationalizations. The ideology of Manifest Destiny was useful in its own right, serving

- to rationalize U.S. foreign policy—it was often cited to ease what may have been guilty consciences at taking someone else's land
- to create national unity and to inspire citizens to rally around the government
- to counter criticisms raised by other nations

Interest in territorial expansion and the quest for empire cut across many segments of the American population:

- farmers and those wishing to become landowners

- manufacturers seeking a source of abundant and inexpensive natural resources
- investors and industrialists seeking profitable investment opportunities in the areas of mining, agriculture, land speculation, and the like
- those who believed that American civilization was biologically and culturally superior
- politicians and military men searching for ways to enhance the nation's political and geographic situation relative to other nations

AP Tip

Take note that internal political factors sometimes inhibited territorial aggrandizement—for example, the internal debate that ensued over Cuba and the Ostend Manifesto.

Major Territorial Acquisitions: 1783–1853

Territory (Date Acquired)	Circumstances of Acquisition
Original Thirteen States (1783)	Treaty of Paris—all land east of the Mississippi River
Louisiana Purchase (1803)	Purchased from France for $15 million—825,000 square miles
Florida (1819)	Adams-Onís Treaty; United States pays $5 million
Texas (1845)	Initially declared itself independent from Mexico; eventually enters the Union as a slave state
Oregon Country (1846)	Forty-ninth parallel established by the United States and Britain as the boundary for Oregon
Mexican Cession (1848)	Treaty of Guadalupe Hidalgo—Mexican defeat leads to the loss of its northern territory, for which United States pays $15 million
Gadsden Purchase (1853)	U.S. purchase of a strip of land from Mexico for $10 million to complete a southern transcontinental railroad

THE MONROE DOCTRINE

Following the end of the Napoleonic Wars in 1815, the victorious nations met in Vienna to discuss postwar goals. One of the decisions made by the European powers was to restore monarchies and governments that had collapsed or had been overthrown by Napoleon's Grand Army. This concerned the United States because it suspected that the reactionary powers would attempt to restore Spain's control over South America. For their own reasons, the British were opposed to such a development, though they and the Russians sought to control the Pacific coast of North America. Secretary of State John Quincy Adams informed both nations not to interfere in territory that he claimed belonged naturally to the United States. Leery of Europeans' intentions of acquiring territory in the Americas or even colonizing South America, the Monroe administration decided to act. At the behest of his cabinet, President Monroe issued a stern foreign policy statement that became known as the Monroe Doctrine. Monroe admonished the Europeans from colonizing the Western Hemisphere. To do so, warned the president, would be deemed a threat to U.S. national security. In short, Europe should stay out of the Western Hemisphere and the United States would stay out of Europe.

Traditionally, historians have viewed the Monroe Doctrine as a defensive strategic policy. It has often been cited as an example of American altruism and anti-imperialist tradition. Recently, historians have questioned this perspective. They argue that the Monroe Doctrine was an expression of Manifest Destiny: in order for the United States to dominate the Western Hemisphere, it would have to prevent European nations from doing so. Subsequent presidents have added to the Monroe Doctrine, and it even played a role in U.S. foreign policy following World War II.

THE TRAIL OF TEARS: THE PLIGHT OF THE CHEROKEE

As the nation kept a wary eye on Europe, it focused the other eye on the one major Native American tribe in the area southeast of the Mississippi, the Cherokees. Having earlier pacified the Cherokees, the next objective was to move them to the West. The Cherokees inhabited several states—Alabama, Tennessee, Georgia, and Mississippi. In 1827 a tribal council established a constitutional representative government, not unlike the U.S. political system, and proceeded to declare independence. The Georgia legislature maintained that to declare a separate government and nation within its borders was unconstitutional. Georgia then requested assistance from the federal government in removing the Cherokees from its borders. The discovery of gold in the Cherokees' land certainly played a role in the state legislature's wish to relocate them. Later, the Cherokees, insulted by President Andrew Jackson's lack of sympathy for Native Americans and by the passage in 1830 of the Indian Removal Act, sued to stop their resettlement. The Marshall Supreme Court, while sympathetic to their plight, ruled in *Cherokee Nation* v. *Georgia* (1831) that because they were not a foreign nation, the Cherokees could not bring suit in federal court. The following year, however, the Court ruled in *Worcester* v. *Georgia* that state law had no authority within Cherokee territory. An advocate of states' rights when it was expedient and an opponent of Native American rights, Jackson exclaimed, "John Marshall has made his decision, now let him enforce it." The chief executive would not use his constitutional authority to enforce federal law when it came to Native Americans. Before the decade was out, most of the Cherokees were driven west in a grueling trek known as the "Trail of Tears."

Texan Independence

In 1821 Mexico had gained its independence from Spain. Hoping to draw settlers to its sparsely inhabited northern province, the Mexican government enticed large numbers of immigrants by introducing a system of landownership that was considerably more favorable than what was available in the United States. Before long, southerners by the thousands began streaming into Texas in northern Mexico. Stephen Austin, for example, brought hundreds of families to settle in the area, starting a migration that soon found the Mexican inhabitants far outnumbered by the American settlers and their slaves. Americans continued to resettle in northern Mexico despite the Mexican government's new stipulations: in 1829 it required all settlers to convert to Catholicism, and it abolished slavery. Most settlers were not willing to obey these laws so the Mexican government halted immigration. Unfazed, the Americans ignored Mexican law and poured in, many from the South. In 1834 the dispute came to a head when General Antonio de Santa Anna proclaimed himself dictator of Mexico. Santa Anna was determined to enforce the laws of his nation as it applied to the American settlers in the northern province. In response, the settlers declared their independence from Mexico in 1836, created a government, and selected Sam Houston as commander of the Texas military. Santa Anna moved in to stop the Texans. Initial conflicts between the two sides favored the Mexican army, despite money, supplies, and volunteers from American citizens. The most famous Texan defeat occurred in 1836 at the Alamo, a fortified mission held by the Texans. Despite holding out against enormous odds, the Texas garrison was annihilated by Santa Anna's forces. Shortly thereafter, another Texas army surrendered to Santa Anna. On orders from the Mexican general, they were massacred. But the Texans soon had their revenge. Sam Houston's small army inflicted a mortal blow on the Mexicans at the Battle of San Jacinto, in the process capturing Santa Anna. This battle effectively ended hostilities and guaranteed Texas independence. Most Texans supported U.S. statehood, but they would have to wait; for more than a decade, Texas was to remain an independent republic.

President James K. Polk and Territorial Expansion

When James K. Polk was inaugurated president in March 1845, he had several foreign policy objectives in mind: the settlement of the Oregon boundary dispute with Britain, which had almost led to military hostilities in the 1839 Aroostook War; the acquisition of California; and the incorporation of Texas into the Union. He achieved all of these goals. John Tyler had already paved the way for Texas statehood, and despite strong opposition from antislavery forces, Texas was admitted on December 29, 1845. As for the Oregon question, it was resolved at the same time relations with Mexico were unraveling. In the Webster-Ashburton Treaty (1842), the United States and Britain had settled the boundary dispute between Maine and Canada and also agreed to suppress the slave trade. Soon, however, they were again bickering over the Oregon Territory's northern border. Initially the Americans offered the 49th parallel as the dividing line; that was rejected by the British. Despite bellicose outbursts by the Americans such as "Fifty-four forty or fight," Britain was in no mood for another war with the United States. In the Oregon Treaty (1846), the nations agreed to settle the dispute peacefully by extending the Oregon Territory–Canadian border along the 49th parallel.

THE MEXICAN-AMERICAN WAR

The fragile relationship between the United States and Mexico deteriorated even further when the United States formally annexed Texas in 1845. Not satisfied with acquiring this enormous territory, Polk also wanted to acquire the California–New Mexico region as well. After the failure of the Slidell mission, an attempt to purchase the territory from Mexico, Polk resorted to a decidedly more aggressive and controversial posture; he sent troops into the disputed area near the Nueces River and the Rio Grande. Many Americans and their political representatives believed the area belonged to the Mexicans, but when hostilities erupted, the United States declared war on Mexico. Polk claimed that Mexican forces had crossed the border to attack Americans, but this was never verified. Regardless, Polk had his war. Although the U.S. Army was supported by poorly trained and ill-disciplined volunteer troops, some of whom committed atrocities in the course of the war, U.S. forces had taken control of the entire Southwest by 1847. Several other American military successes followed before General Zachary Taylor's army defeated Santa Anna's force near Buena Vista. Taylor then proceeded to take Monterrey but was replaced by President Polk for disobeying orders. (Taylor returned home a hero and later became president.) The new U.S. commander, General Winfield Scott, captured Vera Cruz followed a short time later with a victory in the Battle of Cerro Gordo. More victories followed before the Americans launched their final attack on Mexico City. After first taking the mountain fortress of Chapultepec, the Americans captured the Mexican capital. Santa Anna fled and the war ended. The Treaty of Guadalupe Hidalgo (1848) included the following provisions:

- Mexico recognized the American claims to the area north of the Rio Grande.
- Mexico ceded California and New Mexico to the United States in return for $15 million.
- The United States agreed to assume approximately $3 million in debts Mexico owed to American citizens.

President Polk was not satisfied with the terms of the treaty. He believed the United States should have received even more territory from the defeated Mexicans. But he would have to settle for the one-half million square miles of territory (one million if Texas is included in the tally) taken from the Mexicans. In his one term as president, Polk had given meaning to Washington's reference to the United States as a "rising empire."

Content Review Questions

1. In his more than thirty years as a Supreme Court justice, John Marshall
   (A) strengthened the powers of the states in relation to the federal government.
   (B) ruled time and again in support of the compact theory of government.
   (C) ruled that the Supreme Court could not overturn a decision handed down by a state supreme court.
   (D) blocked state regulations that limited property rights.

2. The concept of judicial review means that
   (A) the executive branch can veto legislation.
   (B) the president has the final say in all decisions of the judicial branch.
   (C) the courts have the power to determine the constitutionality of laws.
   (D) the Supreme Court is required to review all bills passed by Congress.

3. Which of the following is true of the Embargo Act (1807)?
   (A) It was designed to open trade with one of the belligerents (British or French) if it repealed its own trade restrictions.
   (B) It caused devastating shortages of food in France.
   (C) It nearly destroyed the New England economy.
   (D) The Supreme Court ruled that it was an unconstitutional overstretch of national authority.

4. All of the following are complaints of the United States against the British in the period before the War of 1812 EXCEPT
   (A) the British were conspiring with the French to cripple the infant American industry.
   (B) the *Leopard-Chesapeake* incident.
   (C) many believed the British were inciting Native Americans to attack American settlers in the West.
   (D) the practice of impressments and ship seizures violated American sovereignty.

5. Which of the following was NOT in favor of U.S. territorial expansion in the first half of the nineteenth century?
   (A) Farmers
   (B) Manufacturers
   (C) Investors
   (D) Abolitionists

6. The term Manifest Destiny implies
   (A) a desire to limit the territorial expansion of the United States.
   (B) that the cost of expansion is greater than its benefits.
   (C) that it was America's God-given right to expand.
   (D) that nations should share newly discovered resources rather than fight over them.

7. The Gadsden Purchase
   (A) allowed the United States to build a southern transcontinental railroad.
   (B) was territory in the West where the Cherokee were relocated.
   (C) allowed the United States to extend its northern border with Canada to the Pacific Ocean.
   (D) was vetoed by President Polk.

8. The war hawks
   (A) were opponents of territorial expansion.
   (B) were U.S. congressmen who represented the New England states.
   (C) supported going to war against Britain in the early nineteenth century.
   (D) was a Native American tribe who fought against U.S. territorial expansion.

9. The Hartford Convention
   (A) ended the War of 1812.
   (B) was organized by the Federalist opposition to the war with Britain.
   (C) included some of the most important leaders of the Democratic-Republican Party.
   (D) was organized to oppose territorial expansion.

10. "Fifty-four forty or fight" refers to
    (A) the Federalists' opposition to the war with Britain.
    (B) the amount of money Mexico demanded from the United States in return for allowing it to annex Texas.
    (C) the boundary dispute between the United States and Mexico.
    (D) the dispute between Britain and the United States over the Oregon Territory.

11. Which of the following decisions by the Mexican government angered Americans who settled in Texas?
    (A) The Americans were required to pay enormous taxes to the Mexican government.
    (B) The Mexicans forbade the American settlers from trading with the United States.
    (C) The American settlers were prohibited from becoming citizens of Mexico.
    (D) The Mexicans abolished slavery.

12. The Supreme Court ruled in *Worcester* v. *Georgia* that
    (A) Native American tribal land could not be purchased by the state of Georgia.
    (B) Georgia must grant citizenship rights to the Cherokees living within its borders.
    (C) the Cherokees could not sue the state of Georgia in federal court.
    (D) Georgia's state laws had no authority within Cherokee territory.

13. In the Treaty of Guadalupe Hidalgo (1848),
    (A) Mexico did not lose territory to the United States, but was compelled to grant independence to Texas.
    (B) Mexico lost approximately half its territory to the United States.
    (C) the United States was obliged to pay millions of dollars to convince the Mexicans to end the war.
    (D) California won its independence from Mexico.

14. "Conscience Whigs"
    (A) supported the Texas independence movement.
    (B) advocated the purchase of Mexican territory in order to avert war.
    (C) were antislavery congressmen who generally opposed the war with Mexico.
    (D) condemned the U.S. government's treatment of Indians.

15. All of the following encouraged American expansion between 1800 and 1848 EXCEPT
    (A) the growth of American industrial power, in search of new markets.
    (B) the rise of American nationalism.
    (C) notions of racial and cultural supremacy over the Native Americans and Mexicans.
    (D) an interest in competing with threats of the expansion of British, Mexican, or Spanish influence in North America.

Short-Answer Questions

Question 1 is based on the following image.

Bettmann/Corbis

1. Use the image of President Monroe and his cabinet and your knowledge of United States history to answer Parts A and B.
    A) Briefly describe the point of view reflected in the image about American expansion.

B) Describe ONE specific action taken by the United States in line with the viewpoint portrayed in this image.

2. United States historians generally agree that John Marshall expanded the power of the federal government during his term as Supreme Court chief justice.
   A) Describe Marshall's philosophy as related to ONE of the questions below.
      The jurisdiction of the Supreme Court
      The issue of states' rights with respect to the national government
      The status of American commerce and business
   B) Explain and name ONE decision of the Marshall Court that reflects the philosophy you described in Part A.

Long-Essay Questions

1. To what extent did nationalism play a role in the formulation and application of U.S. foreign policy in the early nineteenth century?
2. Evaluate the decision of President James K. Polk to lead the United States into war with Mexico.

Answers

Content Review Questions

1. **(D)** Marshall strengthened the federal judiciary, especially in relation to the states and the legislative branch (*The American Pageant,* 14th ed., pp. 231–232/15th ed., pp. 208–209, 238; Learning Objective POL-5).

2. **(C)** This is an essential power of the federal court system in that it provides a check against unconstitutional legislation (*The American Pageant,* 14th ed., p. 232/15th ed., p. 209; Learning Objective POL-5).

3. **(C)** By eliminating all trade in hopes of protecting American ships and exerting pressure on the British and French, the Embargo Act—which was barely noticed economically by the warring nations—devastated New England, which relied on trade (*The American Pageant,* 14th ed., pp. 240–241/15th ed., p. 217; Learning Objective WOR-3).

4. **(A)** The British, in the midst of their own wars with France—again—had failed to abide by their promises in the Treaty of Paris and had repeatedly made affronts to American neutrality (*The American Pageant,* 14th ed., pp. 238–239/15th ed., pp. 215–216; Learning Objective WOR-5).

5. **(D)** Abolitionists feared that with the expansion of U.S. territory, slavery would spread (*The American Pageant,* 14th ed., pp. 383–390/15th ed., p. 357; Learning Objective WOR-6).

6. **(C)** Manifest Destiny implied that Americans were God's "chosen people" and therefore had a right to expand (*The American Pageant,* 14th ed., pp. 403–404/15th ed., p. 366; Learning Objective ID-2).

7. **(A)** The purchase of this thin strip of land south of the Rocky Mountains allowed the United States to build a southern transcontinental railroad (*The American Pageant,* 14th ed., pp. 431–432/15th ed., p. 392; Learning Objective ENV-4).

8. **(D)** Incensed by British violations of American neutrality and supportive of territorial expansion, war hawks strongly supported war against Britain (*The American Pageant,* 14th ed., p. 242/15th ed., pp. 219–220; Learning Objective POL-6).

9. **(B)** The Federalists were strongly opposed to the War of 1812. They met in Hartford, Connecticut, to discuss strategies for reducing the power of the southern and western Democratic-Republicans (*The American Pageant,* 14th ed., p. 253/15th ed., pp. 228–229; Learning Objective ID-5).

10. **(E)** Eventually the United States and Britain compromised on the 49th parallel (*The American Pageant,* 14th ed., pp. 404–405/15th ed., pp. 366–367; Learning Objective WOR-5).

11. **(E)** The Mexican government established two laws in 1829: settlers must convert to Catholicism, and slavery was prohibited. Both angered the settlers, who were mostly southern Protestant supporters of slavery (*The American Pageant,* 14th ed., p. 293/15th ed., pp. 265–266; Learning Objective ID-4).

12. **(D)** Though previously the Supreme Court ruled against the Cherokees, this decision provided them some autonomy (*The American Pageant,* 14th ed., pp. 283–284/15th ed., p. 257; Learning Objective PEO-5).

13. **(B)** The treaty ending the war was indeed punitive as the Mexicans lost half of their territory in return for $15 million (*The American Pageant,* 14th ed., p. 410/15th ed., p. 372; Learning Objective WOR-5).

14. **(C)** The "conscience Whigs" were deeply concerned that a successful war with Mexico would expand slavery and therefore the power of the "slavocracy" (*The American Pageant,* 14th ed., p. 411/15th ed., p. 372; Learning Objective WOR-6).

15. **(A)** Though America had not yet industrialized to any significant extent by 1848, its desire for economic and territorial gain, as well as its hopes of being master of the continent led the country to expand time and again (*The*

American Pageant, 14th and 15th eds., Chapters 11 and 17; Learning Objective WOR-6).

Short-Answer Questions

1. Overall, this image supports the idea of American expansionism and, one might say, Manifest Destiny. The map on the back wall offers several options for discussion, including the recent Louisiana Purchase, the territories of Mexico in North America, and the disputed Oregon Territory. Furthermore, Monroe's stance next to the globe, and his protective hand over the Americas offer insight into the Monroe Doctrine.

2. Marshall certainly expanded the power of the national government, but always a true Federalist, he also sought to protect the interests of commerce and business. As such, consider his use of the elastic (or necessary and proper) clause to expand the national government's responsibilities, but also his interpretation of the commerce clause to preclude state interference in contract law or business practice. Of course, where the Courts are concerned, *Marbury* v. *Madison* is the foremost example of his expansion of the Court's duties.

Long-Essay Questions

1. You should address the ideologies that supported territorial expansion—for example, the Mexican-American War—the goals and attitudes of the war hawks on the War of 1812, the significance of the Monroe Doctrine in extending U.S. influence to the entire Western Hemisphere, and the relocation of Native Americans so that their land could be used by white Americans. (Historical Thinking Skill I-2: Patterns of Continuity and Change over Time)

2. To support this statement, you can point out that Polk was an advocate of territorial expansion, shown by his work to settle the Oregon border question and the acquisition of California. Bringing Texas into the Union was a key part of his territorial ambitions. All of these acquisitions would benefit the United States economically.

   To oppose the statement, point out that by adding new southern territory, Polk had reopened the slave state/free state controversy. Would Texas's admission set off heated exchanges between the regions and their politicians? Also point out that there was no justification for the U.S. invasion of Mexico and that many Americans, especially in the north, were morally opposed to the war. Others were opposed to an imperialist policy. (Historical Thinking Skill III-6: Historical Argumentation)

8

JACKSONIAN DEMOCRACY AND THE AGE OF REFORM: 1820S–1850S

Paradoxically, at the same time the United States was acquiring land, often through conquest, it was engaged in democratizing its own institutions. This era, the 1820s to the 1850s, has been referred to as the Age of Reform. Some historians, however, choose to title the period after its most celebrated president, Andrew Jackson, and refer to it as Jacksonian democracy. It is important to note, however, that this designation is challenged by historians who maintain that Jackson was actually indifferent, opposed to, or unaware of some of the reforms. Those critical of the term see obvious contradictory impulses present during this period: slavery, expansion and imperialism, and the marginalization of blacks, women, Native Americans, and laborers. Yet over the years, the terms have come to mean the same thing—an unprecedented expansion of egalitarian ideas that transformed America socially, politically, and economically, if only for white men.

KEY CONCEPTS

- Social, economic, and political conditions and attitudes led to the reform spirit in the mid-nineteenth century.
- As the Federalist Party faded, an "Era of Good Feelings" set in.
- The second party system took shape as the National Republicans challenged the Democrats.
- Grassroots movements and government reforms attempted to address the social and economic problems confronting the nation.
- The intellectual roots of reform shaped perceptions of the individual's role in society.

- This period witnessed important economic and political reforms, but women, blacks, and Native Americans remained subordinated.

Jacksonian democracy and the Age of Reform are discussed in depth in *The American Pageant,* 14th and 15th eds., Chapters 13–15.

SETTING THE STAGE FOR REFORM

There are two sources of reform: the first is the government, which can draw up policies and legislation that further democratize society; the second is grassroots movements. In the case of the latter, individual citizens and private groups, classes, organizations, and movements take it upon themselves to address the maladies that plague their society. In the period following the end of the War of 1812 until the eve of the American Civil War, both the government and grassroots movements had a role in reforming American society, although, more often than not, grassroots movements have influenced the government to initiate programs and policies needed to address society's problems.

There are various origins of the Age of Reform:

- Democratic impulses were the basis of the American Revolution, which sought to address the inequalities inherent in colonial American society and to free Americans from their subordinate relationship with Britain.
- The Antifederalists of the 1780s and 1790s were determined not to sacrifice civil and democratic liberties in creating a new constitutional government.
- The Jeffersonian Democratic-Republicans professed to represent the ideals and aspirations of the common farmer.
- Profound social and economic changes occurred in the early nineteenth century—for example, the influence of what many historians refer to as the market revolution on the U.S. economy along with the social and cultural changes of the Second Great Awakening.

The Northeast and Old Northwest experienced rapid improvements in transportation (railroads; canals, such as the Erie Canal; and the National, or Cumberland, Road). Furthermore, the growth in industrial technologies like the steam engine and interchangeable parts (though America was far from an industrialized nation in the 1840s) set the nation on course for what is known as a Market Revolution. Concurrently, the nation was experiencing an immense wave of immigration. These factors hastened the collapse of the older yeoman and artisan economy and stimulated the further development of a cash-crop agrarian system and capitalist manufacturing. For instance, in the South, a cotton boom revived a flagging plantation slave economy, which then continued to expand.

Additional tensions developed as the economy expanded. Some farmers could not keep up with the changing economy and experienced farm foreclosures. In the Northeast, an emerging laboring class was dogged by abject working conditions and subsistence-level wages. In the South, strained relations existed between non-slaveholders and the planter class. In the West, tensions between would-be yeoman farmers and land speculators and banks prevailed. Farmers and laborers had every reason to believe that the free-market system would bring them not boundless opportunities but new forms of dependence. Jacksonianism grew directly from the tensions that these changes generated within white society. Even expectant capitalists (those with surplus capital searching for investment opportunities in this growing market economy) suspected that entrenched capitalists would block their way and shape the nation's economic development to suit only themselves.

Henry Clay's American System (a tariff to protect industry and manufacturing, a national bank to facilitate credit and provide sound currency, and federally funded infrastructural development), which became the center of his 1824 presidential campaign, confirmed the suspicions of the opponents of an ever-expanding central government that the powerful and wealthy would be best served by this design. Clay's program became the core of the National Republicans' platform, which explains why some Americans saw the Jacksonian Democrats as representing the masses, whereas the National Republicans represented the elites.

The Era of Good Feelings, the Second Party System, and Emergence of Jackson

Following the War of 1812, the Federalist Party for all intents and purposes imploded. Its unpopular position on the war as well as a number of questionable actions by the Federalists, not least of which was the Hartford Convention, destroyed the party. Since ostensibly only one party, the Democratic-Republicans, was left standing, the decade or so following the war is often referred to as the "Era of Good Feelings"; the assumption being that because there was no political party strife, most Americans tended to have a common outlook. In other words, the term suggests that social relations in the United States were characterized by consensus and relative social harmony. True or not, sectionalism and the slavery issue were always under the surface, ready to disturb the tranquility. It was not long before these differences manifested themselves in opposing political parties—the second American political party system. For the time being, however, the nation had only one party.

In 1824 all four candidates—John Quincy Adams, Andrew Jackson, Henry Clay, and William Crawford—ran as Democratic-Republicans. In the election Adams defeated his fellow party member in what Jackson's supporters claimed was the result of a "corrupt bargain" between Adams and Clay, who was also the Speaker of the House. Jackson had received more popular votes as well as more electoral votes, but he had not won a majority and it was not enough to give him the presidency. The Twelfth Amendment required that the issue be resolved in the House of Representatives, with each state having one vote. When the vote was tallied, Adams had won. Jackson's backers accused Clay of manipulating the voting to benefit Adams. Although this was obviously denied by Clay, eyebrows were raised when President Adams made Clay his secretary of state, a position viewed at the time as heir to the presidency. In the next election, 1828,

Jackson, running as the Democratic candidate (the Republican suffix was dropped) had his revenge, defeating Adams (who ran on the new National Republican ticket) handily in both the popular and electoral votes. In a sense, the National Republicans, who were strong in the Northeast, rose out of the ashes of the old Federalist Party in that they advocated for the Bank of the United States and the tariff (especially after the Panic of 1819 damaged the Northeast's economy). The National Republicans ran Clay for the presidency in 1832, but he too was defeated by Jackson. (The National Republicans would, over the next couple of decades, become the Whig Party, and eventually the Republican Party.) For our purposes, the man at the center of this reform period, Jackson, would be elected to two terms. His eight years in office and those of his successor, Martin Van Buren, are considered the heart of the Age of Reform.

Dorr's Rebellion

In Rhode Island voting was restricted to those who held property worth at least $150. Consequently, unequal representation prevailed within the state. For example, although Providence had a larger population than Newport, the latter had more representatives in the state legislature because it had more landowners. In the 1842 gubernatorial election, the reform candidate, Thomas Dorr, was elected; however, the opposition refused to recognize his victory. The two sides then armed themselves and prepared to settle the dispute violently, if necessary. Dorr's arrest defused the situation, but several years later his reform party was reelected. Sentiments outside the state were mixed. Some Americans viewed it as a threat to law and order while others viewed Dorr's rebellion as an effort to correct an undemocratic system.

In analyzing American society in the antebellum period it is important to identify those problems—political, economic, and social—that reformers sought to address:

- Unfavorable Political Conditions
  - In general, many American citizens were excluded from the political process. They had little impact, if any, on how and what decisions were made.
  - Women were disenfranchised (denied the right to vote and participate in the political process).
  - Free black Americans were disenfranchised as well. Of course, slaves had no citizenship rights.
  - In some states, property ownership was a requirement for voting.
  - The process associated with how political parties chose their presidential candidates, called "King Caucus," was exclusive and closed to most. There was no primary system to provide rank-and-file party members the opportunity to select candidates. Instead, political party leaders selected candidates.
  - Disproportionate representation still existed.
- Unfavorable Economic Conditions
  - There were no stay laws (which prevented a person from going to prison for indebtedness).

  - Oppressed urban workers were attempting to protect themselves by forming unions.
  - The existence of unfair tax laws discriminated against small farmers and members of the urban working class, many of whom were mired in debt.
  - Land was not attainable for many inhabitants of the United States.
  - Many farmers could not afford to own their own farm. Instead, they hired themselves out or rented land.
  - The market economy was susceptible to the fluctuations and problems inherent in the business cycle (recession, depression, inflation, and deflation).
  - There were limited opportunities for small and expectant capitalists because of monopolies and the political and economic power and influence of the entrenched capitalists.
- Unfavorable Social Conditions
  - Because of discrimination, women were second-class citizens.
  - Racial discrimination was pervasive.
  - Slavery was becoming intolerable. There were a number of slave revolts during this period, such as Denmark Vesey's plot for rebellion in 1822 and Nat Turner's rebellion in 1831.
  - Treatment of the mentally ill was inhumane, as were the conditions prevalent in prisons.
  - Urban decay and problems such as poor housing and sanitation, crime, and disease were rampant.
  - Working conditions were both unsafe and unhealthy.
  - Because there was no public education system, learning was available only to those who could afford it.
  - The Native American population was being systematically decimated by the Indian Removal Act and other actions and policies of the states and the federal government.

The Anti-Renters Movement

In upstate New York, property ownership resembled that of a feudal society. Wealthy and powerful landowners held old leases to enormous tracts of land. Their tenants were often compelled to provide feudal obligations, such as working on the landlord's manor for a set number of days per year. Following the American Revolution, many tenants were convinced that the terms of the leases had long since expired, that the leases were highly exploitative, and that, at the very least, feudal relationships had been swept away by the American Revolution. By 1839 a grassroots organization of tenant farmers was organized to prevent the collection of rents. Sure enough, when authorities attempted to collect the rents, violence erupted. It was not until the early 1850s that new legislation was passed to limit leases of farmland to twelve years. Still the farmers refused to pay "back rents," and they formed the Anti-Renters Association.

Cures for these maladies were proposed. The first, put simply, was to expand democratic rights, beginning with the abolition of property qualifications for voting in those states that retained this prerequisite. Also, the economy could be redirected to include the interests of the non-entrenched capitalist class. And by making available more and cheaper land in the West, those seeking relief from creditors, speculators, and bankers (especially the despised Second Bank of the United States) would be helped.

Why then did disenchanted, alienated, and exploited white males coalesce behind Jackson, a one-time land speculator and opponent of debtor relief, and the Democrats? Born into poverty, Jackson entered business at a relatively young age. By the 1820s, his own ill-fated business experiences soured him on speculation and paper money and left him permanently suspicious of the credit system in particular, and banks in general. To many, then, Jackson represented a healthy contempt for the old hierarchical, preferential system. His position on a number of key issues reflects this perspective:

- **The spoils system** For decades, individuals holding positions in the federal government were not replaced when their presidential appointee left office. Jackson changed this tradition. For him and the Democratic Party, the expression "To the victor belong the spoils" described the way federal jobs were distributed. Jackson replaced those loyal to the previous administration with supporters of his own party. Critics referred to this method as the spoils system. (Defenders had a more democratic-sounding term: rotation in office.) Like Jackson, they detested experts and deemed the common man more than capable to fill any government post.
- **The Indian Removal Act** Discussed in the previous chapter, Jackson's attitudes regarding Native Americans often reflected those of the average citizen. When he spoke of the common man, Jackson was simply not referring to Native Americans.
- **Veto power** Claiming he was the representative of the people, protecting them against governmental abuses and policies that enhanced the standing of the politically and economically entrenched, Jackson vetoed more bills than all of his predecessors combined.
- **Unofficial advisers** Rather than limit himself to the views of professional politicians, such as cabinet members—who, with the exception of Martin Van Buren, were mediocre men selected to appease sectional interests and the Democratic Party—Jackson came to rely on a group of informal advisers (mostly newspaper editors) known as the "kitchen cabinet."
- **The bank war** Although it was successful in regulating interest rates and adopting policies conducive to economic stability and growth, the Bank of the United States was not rechartered by Congress in 1811 because of the resentment of smaller state chartered banks. Five years later Congress chose to recharter the (Second) Bank of the United States despite continued opposition by state banks. And again, the bank was successful. It provided credit, which allowed for economic development in the East and West. Despite the Supreme Court's ruling in *McCulloch* v. *Maryland*, in 1819, which made the bank paramount in relation to state banks, Jackson strongly opposed it. To him, the bank represented

preference and monopoly; it violated states' rights and was partially controlled by foreigners. Besides, he reasoned, as did Jefferson, that the bank was unconstitutional because the Constitution did not explicitly provide for such an institution. Jackson's personality clash with the president of the bank, Nicholas Biddle, only increased his contempt for the institution. (At one point Jackson told Biddle, "I do not like your Bank any more than all banks.") Jackson's opponents, foremost among them Senator Henry Clay, were able to convince Congress to pass a bill to again recharter the bank in hopes of making the bank a major campaign issue in 1832. Jackson vetoed the bill. If the election of 1832 was any indication of the public's position on the Bank of the United States, which the president made the central issue of his campaign, Jackson's landslide defeat of Clay put any doubts to rest. During the campaign, Jackson had declared, "The Bank is trying to kill me, but I will kill it." And he did. But the impact on the economy was devastating. His vetoing of the bank set off a chain of events that ultimately intensified the downward spiral the economy would experience. Unfortunately for Martin Van Buren, Jackson's demolition of the bank would have dire consequences when Van Buren became president.

After vetoing the rechartering of the Second Bank, Jackson withdrew federal funds from the bank and distributed it to state banks, referred to as "pet banks." This action had the long-range effect of contributing to wild speculation:

The additional money the pet banks possessed made it possible for them to expand and extend credit.

This had the effect of increasing demand for land. Prices for land skyrocketed.

Many banks found that they were overextended.

Because the one force that could have controlled wild speculation and overextension—the Bank of the United States—had been destroyed by Jackson, he was thus forced to issue the Specie Circular:

Banks and all types of lenders were forced to call in their loans and specie.

This resulted in panic selling.

Consequently, prices plummeted, and many borrowers defaulted on their debts.

As a result, many banks went bankrupt.

From 1837 to 1843 the economy spiraled downward. The Specie Circular served only to aggravate the economic decline the nation was soon to experience when a depression hit during Van Buren's term. The following are causes of that depression:

- the domestic and international decline in the demand for cotton
- uncontrolled land and financial speculation
- the withdrawal of capital by British investors
- the normal workings of the business cycle—expansions and contractions common in the capitalist system

Jackson's Position on Federal Versus States' Rights

There has been considerable debate among historians as to whether Jackson was an advocate of states' rights or a firm believer in the supremacy of the federal government.

Others maintain that constitutional questions had little to do with his support or opposition to specific issues. Below are a number of events in Jackson's presidency that correlate to this debate:

- **The Maysville Road veto** In 1830 Congress passed a bill that would authorize the government to invest in the construction of a road from Maysville, Kentucky, to Lexington, the hometown of Henry Clay. Jackson's veto of the bill provided him the opportunity to weigh in on federal funding for internal improvements and strike a blow at Clay, his political enemy. Jackson argued that since the road lay within one state (regardless that the road was to become a section of the National Road), the bill was unconstitutional. His veto of the Maysville Road Bill established a precedent that would go unchanged until the twentieth century. Until then, individual states and private capital, not the federal government, would be responsible for the construction of roads.
- **Cherokee Nation** Jackson refused to intervene on behalf of the Cherokees after John Marshall's favorable ruling toward them in the *Worcester* v. *Georgia* Supreme Court case. As chief executive it was his constitutional responsibility to uphold federal laws.
- **Nullification** In 1828 Congress passed what became known in the South as the "Tariff of Abominations," a very protective tax that was very high on some imports and lower on others. The bill was actually a political ploy by Jackson supporters to embroil President Adams in a political controversy. Never one to tolerate legislation that he believed violated states' rights (especially those of his home state, South Carolina), Senator John C. Calhoun cited the argument (known as *interposition*) that if a state believed the federal government had exceeded its authority, it could object to the government's acts and actions. Although at one time Jackson's vice president, Calhoun and Jackson were soon at odds over the tariff and other issues relating to states' rights. At an 1832 dinner celebrating the anniversary of the birth of President Jefferson and attended by leaders of the Democratic Party, including Jackson and Calhoun, President Jackson toasted, "Our Federal Union—it must be preserved." To which Calhoun responded, "The Union—next to our liberty the most dear. . . ." One of Calhoun's more radical solutions to the prevailing political animosities between the North and South was the antiquated notion of a *concurrent majority* to secure and maintain a balance between the political rights of the less populated (and therefore minority) South with those of the more populated North, even going so far as to consider a dual

presidency. As if this was not enough, Calhoun declared in his *South Carolina Exposition* (1828) that state legislatures had the right to rule federal laws unconstitutional and to nullify those laws, which is exactly how the South Carolina legislature responded to the Tariff of 1828 and the only slightly lower tariff of 1832. In the eyes of Calhoun—and many others in the South—the Tariff gave too much preference to the budding northern industries and discriminated against the export-reliant South. Calhoun further reasoned that, if necessary, a state had the right to secede from a government that did not protect its interests. When Jackson became president, the tariff and nullification were still hot issues. Faced with South Carolina's refusal to abide by federal law and threatened secession, Jackson warned that he would use the U.S. Army to invade the state. Not until Henry Clay worked out a compromise tariff, in 1833, did South Carolina rescind its nullification, thus preventing a showdown between Calhoun and the federal government. Jackson had shown that he would use all means at his disposal to enforce national law.

While President Jackson was redefining the role of the presidency, individuals in the North and West took it upon themselves to address the ills of the nation and reconstruct society according to their principles and ideas. Because of the rigid nature of southern society in the antebellum period, most of the reform movements that sprung up between the 1820s and 1850s did not find fertile ground in the South.

Grassroots Movements in the Age of Reform

One of the ideological inspirations behind this desire to reform was the religious revivals that became popular at the turn of the century. Often women were at the center of these revivals, which were among the few opportunities they had to operate outside their clearly defined roles as wives and mothers. This was not the first time religious fervor of this magnitude erupted on the national scene. In the 1730s and 1740s, a New England reverend named Jonathan Edwards had preached that personal repentance and faith in Christ could lead to salvation. George Whitefield, an English preacher, traveled extensively throughout the colonies advocating personal repentance. In powerful and dramatic religious meetings throughout the colonies, "sinners" confessed their guilty ways and then repented in emotional outpourings of devotion. The impact of this, called the First Great Awakening, was a reduction in the influence of church leaders, for the individual could find salvation on his own, and it led to a schism within the Protestant Church. Newer sects such as Baptists and Methodists (the "New Lights") emerged, only to be challenged by the older, more established ("Old Light") churches such as the Anglicans.

The Second Great Awakening represented an individualistic and emotional reaction to the Enlightenment's reliance on reason over faith, a decline in church attendance, and what many perceived as a decline in piety. Unlike its predecessor in the eighteenth century, religious camp meetings did not take firm hold in the South because the revivals included many women, and even some blacks, and because individualism was being promoted in a section of the country that had no tolerance for such ideas. Beginning around the turn of the century and peaking in the 1830s and 1840s, ministers preached "hellfire and brimstone" sermons (in areas that became known as "burned over districts"). Participants were swept into powerful and emotional states in which they hoped to find repentance and salvation. Leading the way in this religious revival was Charles Grandison Finney. An abolitionist, Finney preached that through good works and deeds, individuals could find salvation, not only for themselves, but also for the nation. In this way then there is a connection between the influence of the Second Great Awakening and the fervency of reform in the antebellum period.

The secular intellectual foundation of the reform spirit had its origins in large part in the ideas of Immanuel Kant. In his *Critique of Pure Reason* (1781), the German scholar raised doubts about the power of reason. Those who accepted this view, the romanticists, believed that while science can test hypotheses, individuals know their own reality through faith. The most significant expression of romanticism was the transcendentalist movement of New England. Advocates believed that one could "transcend" the limits of the intellect and strive for emotional understanding and unity with God without the assistance of organized religion. The transcendentalist movement provided intellectuals with a secular ideology that compelled individuals to scrutinize their own views and then to follow one's conscience.

AP Tip

In constructing an essay, how does one make connections between events, movements, and effects and the intellectual origins that shaped them? Often students will write about the philosophical or ideological influences of a period separate from what was actually happening at that time. A more effective and analytical approach is to use the ideas to explain motivations and causation. For example, in making a connection between the Second Great Awakening, transcendentalism, and romanticism, and the reform spirit of the antebellum period, you might assert that these movements asked individuals to get in touch with their own emotions rather than their sense of reason. Thus, while an individual in the antebellum era might present a reasonable economic and social justification for the existence of slavery, one responding to emotional visions of enslavement and degradation might very well come to the conclusion that the institution of slavery was simply barbaric.

Around the same time, American artists who were popularizing landscape painting, known as the Hudson River School, sought to evoke emotional responses to the beauty of the United States as a "chosen nation." Literary figures also spread the transcendentalist message across the nation in such important works as Henry David Thoreau's *Walden* and Ralph Waldo Emerson's *Nature*. Speaking for those attempting to better their society, Emerson asked: "What is man born for but to be a reformer, a remaker of what man has made?"

The following were major reform movements:

- **Women's rights** The women's rights movement emerged as a result of shared discontent by those who no longer tolerated subjugation—their own and that of the slave. Led by Elizabeth Cady Stanton and Lucretia Mott, among others, women's rights advocates met at Seneca Falls, New York, in 1848. There they expressed in the "Declaration of Rights Sentiments" their demand to be enfranchised. Later their agenda included attaining women's property rights. Throughout the antebellum period women's rights activists were also intimately involved in the abolitionist movement. Unfortunately, women would have to wait until 1919 to vote in federal elections. Even the Fourteenth Amendment provided only for universal male suffrage.
- **Abolitionist movement** Though the international slave trade had been abolished in 1808—the earliest possible date allowed by the Constitution—the institution of slavery had only become more entrenched in the economic, political, and social make-up of the South. Hoping to bring an end to the horrors of enslavement, major abolitionist leaders included Theodore Weld, Frederick Douglass, Harriet Tubman, John Brown, and William Lloyd Garrison. The latter's newspaper, *The Liberator*, was influential in abolitionist circles. The movement itself was divided in many ways, however, weakening its effectiveness. Some cried for the transport of freed slaves back to Africa, others opposed slavery but embraced the racist idea that blacks should not be leaders, even in the abolitionist movement itself. As this movement gained steam, albeit slowly, in the North, southerners reacted strongly, calling for the federal government to strengthen its support of the institution that, they claimed, the Constitution protected.
- **Education reform** One of the most outspoken advocates of education reform was Horace Mann. His Massachusetts model was the basis of a tax-supported public school system.
- **Mental health** Outraged at the barbaric treatment of patients in mental health facilities, Dorothea Dix led the way to better treatment of those afflicted with mental illnesses.
- **Prison reform** Humiliation, physical abuse, and neglect were common practices used to maintain order and discipline in prisons (as they were in mental health institutions). Reformers sought more humane measures through discipline and the moral improvement of inmates, a sort of nineteenth-century attempt at rehabilitation.
- **Social welfare** These reformers attempted to confront the adverse effects of urbanization and industrialization on the working class.
- **Trade unionism** Supporters attempted to organize workers in order to combat exploitative conditions and wages.
- **Reform of the U.S. policy toward Native Americans** Some favored assimilation, others supported autonomy for Native American tribes, most notably former president John Quincy Adams.
- **Utopian societies** By establishing experimental societies, supporters of utopianism believed they could further their own moral and spiritual development through cooperative communities. Some utopian societies were religious and economic in nature (The Harmonists, Amana Colony, and Brook Farm). Others followed a

particular leader (Robert Owens's New Harmony). A third type was based purely on a religious model (Shakers, Oneida Community).

- **The temperance movement** This movement was led by those who believed that alcohol was interfering with the political and social development of the nation.
- **Anti-immigration movements** While reformers were finding ways to expand democracy for the citizens of the United States, the nativist movement was organized to keep foreigners out. Nativists believed that the customs, traditions, and values of American society were being compromised by the arrival in large numbers of Irish and German immigrants. The nativists reached their political zenith in the 1850s when they formed the Know-Nothing, or American, Party. It was able to gain control in several states but died out by the late 1850s. Nativist sentiment towards immigrants, however, would continue to be an ongoing feature of U.S. history.

Political and Economic Accomplishments in the Age of Reform

The political accomplishments in this period were significant. In many states, especially in the new western states, property qualifications for voting and holding office were abolished. The method of selecting presidential candidates was democratized in various states; the people were given the power to select the candidates, effectively doing away with "King Caucus," which was a major issue in the 1828 campaign. Many more public offices were elective rather than appointive, making public officials more accountable to the electorate. The spoils system and rotation in office were adopted.

There were economic accomplishments too. One of the primary economic objectives was to break the bonds between entrenched capitalists and certain members of the political hierarchy, thereby putting an end to privilege and monopoly. In other words, there was an effort to create a competitive economy based on equal opportunity. These ideas especially represented the wishes of expectant and small capitalists. One way to accomplish this was to enact incorporation laws. In the past, a corporation charter had to be granted before one could start a business. If the business posed a threat to entrenched capitalists, the charter application was often refused. With incorporation laws, a person needed only to fulfill the criteria for a charter to be granted. One case in particular expresses the change in governmental attitude in this period. The Charles River Bridge case shows the change in governmental attitude in this period. In the late eighteenth century, Massachusetts chartered the Charles River Bridge Company to construct a bridge connecting Boston and Charlestown. The state gave permission to the bridge company to collect tolls for seventy years. In 1828 the state legislature chartered a second company to build a bridge adjacent to the original one. The use of this second bridge was free. The Charles River Bridge Company sued on the grounds that the construction of the new bridge was a contract violation the company had with the state. Earlier, in the *Dartmouth College* case, the Marshall Court had ruled in favor of the sanctity of contracts. In the *Charles River Bridge* case, Chief Justice Taney ruled against the Charles River Bridge Company for two reasons: the old charter stunted future infrastructural development, and it represented a monopoly. Yet another accomplishment was the enactment in many states of stay laws.

In some areas, accomplishments were more limited. For example, low-priced federal land was not always available. A national bankruptcy law was not enacted; it would be realized at a later date. And while trade unions were formed, raising the consciousness of laborers to their plight, real gains would not occur until much later in the nation's history.

REFORM DEEPENS SECTIONAL DIVISIONS

As the Age of Reform shaped the West and North, the South remained for the most part traditional and unindustrialized. After visiting the United States, Alexis de Tocqueville contrasted the North and South in his major work, *Democracy in America*. One was vibrant with business and activity, the other, considerably less so. In some ways, the period of reform that shaped the nation in the antebellum years served to widen the chasm between the South and the rest of the nation. Cracks in the sense of nationalism that had pervaded the Era of Good Feelings emerged in 1820. When the slave-owning inhabitants of Missouri Territory petitioned for statehood, the North—increasingly sympathetic to abolitionist appeals—balked at the upset in the balance between the number of free and slave states. The Missouri Compromise, hammered out by Henry Clay and others in Congress, seemed to establish a truce that would last, but only 40 years later the nation would become embroiled in conflict. Though few would have predicted it in the 1820s, the chasm that had developed between the North and South—owing to growing disparities in their cultural, political, and economic interests—would lead to the bloodiest war the nation has ever fought. Brought to a head by clashes over the role of the national government and the expansion of the United States (bringing with it questions about the expansion of slavery), armed conflict seems today to have been almost inevitable.

Content Review Questions

1. The spoils system
   (A) was condemned by Jackson and his supporters for being undemocratic.
   (B) prevented women, Native Americans, and blacks from voting.
   (C) was a derisive term used by opponents of the Tariff of 1828.
   (D) is a term that is synonymous with rotation in office.

2. The origins of the Age of Reform can be found in all of the following EXCEPT
   (A) the defeat of the South and slavery in the Civil War.
   (B) the democratic influences of the American Revolution.
   (C) the Jeffersonian Democratic-Republicans.
   (D) the Antifederalists of the 1780s and 1790s.

3. The "kitchen cabinet"
   (A) was the name given to Jackson's political opponents.
   (B) was a derisive term for men who advocated for women's rights.
   (C) was a term used to attack critics of Jackson's position on the Bank.
   (D) was the nickname of Jackson's unofficial advisers.

4. Jackson's Maysville Road veto was an opportunity for him to
   (A) challenge federal infrastructural development.
   (B) attack opponents of his policy to relocate Native Americans.
   (C) disregard John Marshall's ruling on contracts.
   (D) advocate for the construction of a National Road.

5. The leader of South Carolina's opposition to the "Tariff of Abominations" was
   (A) Martin Van Buren.
   (B) Henry Clay.
   (C) William Lloyd Garrison.
   (D) John C. Calhoun.

6. Jackson was embroiled in a controversy with Nicholas Biddle over the
   (A) construction of the Maysville Road.
   (B) construction of the Charles River Bridge.
   (C) resettlement of Native Americans.
   (E) Bank of the United States.

7. The Specie Circular
   (A) sought to address the problems associated with the Panic of 1819.
   (B) was a primary factor in the development of the New Market economy.
   (C) was nullified by the South Carolina legislature.
   (D) was an attempt by Jackson to remedy the problems associated with the destruction of the bank.

8. William Lloyd Garrison is most associated with which of the following reform movements?
   (A) Prison reform
   (B) Reforming mental health facilities
   (C) Abolition of slavery
   (D) Education reform

9. The Seneca Falls Convention is associated with which of the following reform movements?
   (A) Women's rights
   (B) Abolition
   (C) Education reform
   (D) Opposition to Jackson's policies toward Native Americans

10. Which of the following is FALSE regarding the Second Great Awakening?
    (A) It promoted individualism.
    (B) It was not experienced by southerners.
    (C) It placed reason over faith.
    (D) It challenged the Enlightenment's reliance on reason.

11. The Anti-Masonic Party
    (A) strongly supported the protective tariff as essential in protecting the nation's industries.
    (B) embraced those who sought to promote religious and moral reforms in government and society.
    (C) nominated Andrew Jackson because he was a strong opponent of the Masons.
    (D) was the only third party in U.S. history to win a presidential election.

12. A primary cause of the panic of 1837 was
    (A) considerable overseas competition.
    (B) a depression in Europe that soon spread to the United States.
    (C) rampant financial speculation.
    (D) the hard money policy adopted by the Bank of the United States.

13. The two major political parties in the 1840s, the Whigs and the Democrats, found common ground in their
    (A) support for a high protective tariff.
    (B) support for federally funded internal improvements.
    (C) support for a strong central government and limited powers to the states.
    (D) historical roots in Jeffersonian republicanism.

14. The so-called corrupt bargain of the 1824 presidential election was a factor in the election of
    (A) John Quincy Adams.
    (B) Andrew Jackson.
    (C) Henry Clay.
    (D) John C. Calhoun.

15. In response to the passage of the 1824 tariff, referred to by opponents as the Tariff of Abominations,
    (A) South Carolina seceded from the Union.
    (B) every southern state refused to abide by it; consequently, it was repealed.
    (C) New Englanders stated it was detrimental to their business interests.
    (D) John C. Calhoun wrote *The South Carolina Exposition* in order to articulate the right of nullification.

Short-Answer Questions

Question 1 is based on the following two images.

William L. Clements Library, University of Michigan

Granger Collection

1. Use the images above and your knowledge of history to answer Parts A, B, and C.
   A) Briefly explain the point of view of the cartoonist in Image 1.
   B) Briefly describe the efforts to remove Native Americans from their homelands during the first half of the nineteenth century.
   C) Give ONE piece of evidence justifying or condemning the actions of Andrew Jackson and others who supported Indian Removal in the first half of the nineteenth century.

Question 2 is based on the following passage.

> "The decision on the system of policy embraced in this debate, involves the future destiny of this growing country. One way...it would lead to deep and general distress; general bankruptcy and national ruin; the other, the existing prosperity will be preserved and augmented, and the nation will continue rapidly to advance in wealth, power and greatness."
>
> Henry Clay, Speech on the American System, 1832

2. Based on the passage above and your knowledge of U.S. history, complete the following tasks:
   A) Briefly summarize the American System.
   B) Explain Henry Clay's point of view in reference to the American System.
   C) Describe how Americans reacted to the proposition of the American System in ONE of the following regions:
      The Northeast
      The West
      The South

Long-Essay Questions

1. To what extent can the period from the 1820 to 1850 be characterized as an expansion of democratic ideals?
2. Were the grassroots movements in the Age of Reform successful in achieving their goals? Evaluate TWO of the following:
   women's rights
   abolition
   public education
   prison reform

Answers

Content Review Questions

1. **(D)** Jackson saw the spoils system as a way of increasing participation in government and rewarding party loyalists (*The American Pageant*, 14th ed., p. 280/15th ed., p. 251; Learning Objective POL-2).

2. **(A)** The Civil War occurred after the Age of Reform (*The American Pageant*, 14th ed., p. 272/15th ed., p. 307; Learning Objective CUL-5).

3. **(D)** Jackson was suspicious of "experts" and professionals and relied on editors of pro-Democratic newspapers for political advice (this material does not appear in the text; Learning Objective POL-2).

4. **(A)** Jackson claimed that since the Maysville Road lay within one state, the federal government should not be responsible for the cost of its construction. This provided him an opportunity to challenge federally funded infrastructural development (this material does not appear in the text; Learning Objective POL-5).

5. **(D)** Calhoun, a gifted politician, protested the "Tariff of Abominations" in *The South Carolina Exposition* (*The American Pageant,* 14th ed., pp. 280–281/15th ed., p. 255; Learning Objective ID-5).

6. **(D)** Biddle was the president of the bank, the institution that Jackson destroyed (*The American Pageant,* 14th ed., p. 286/15th ed., p. 259; Learning Objective WXT-2).

7. **(D)** Jackson's Specie Circular attempted to address the economic problems caused by his destruction of the bank, but it only aggravated the situation (*The American Pageant,* 14th ed., p. 290/15th ed., p. 262; Learning objective WXT-2).

8. **(C)** Garrison was the publisher of *The Liberator,* an abolitionist newspaper and one of the leading proponents of the abolition of slavery (*The American Pageant,* 14th ed., p. 386/15th ed., pp. 350–353; Learning Objective CUL-5).

9. **(A)** At the Seneca Falls Convention in 1848, the delegates issued the "Declaration of Sentiments," a call for enfranchisement and other rights accorded to white men (*The American Pageant,* 14th ed., pp. 352, 1022/15th ed., pp. 317–320; Learning Objective POL-3).

10. **(C)** The Second Great Awakening placed faith over reason, which was the cornerstone of Enlightenment ideas (*The American Pageant,* 14th ed., p. 341/15th ed., p. 308; Learning Objective CUL-5).

11. **(B)** Believing elitism in government (and secret societies such as the Masons) to be anti-American, the Anti-Masons also attracted evangelicals who viewed politics as a means to incorporate religious and moral principles into U.S. culture and government (*The American Pageant,* 14th ed., p. 288/15th ed., p. 261; Learning Objective POL-2).

12. **(C)** Stimulated by the infusion of money into the nation's economy through "wildcat banks," rampant speculation, especially in land, led to a downturn in the economy that in turn precipitated a financial panic (*The American Pageant,* 14th ed., p. 292/15th ed., p. 264; Learning Objective WXT-2).

13. **(D)** Though both parties identified with various aspects of Jeffersonian republicanism, they strongly differed on key political issues such as the Bank of the United States and the protective tariff (*The American Pageant,* 14th ed., p. 301/15th ed., p. 262; Learning Objective POL-2).

14. **(A)** Clay threw his support to Adams, who was elected president and subsequently appointed Clay secretary of state. Jackson supporters claimed the two had a corrupt bargain (*The American Pageant,* 14th ed., p. 274/15th ed., pp. 246–248; Learning Objective POL-2).

15. **(D)** Claiming that a state had the authority to nullify a federal law, Calhoun wrote *The South Carolina Exposition* to articulate this principle of states' rights (*The American Pageant,* 14th ed., pp. 281–282/15th ed., p. 255; Learning Objective POL-5).

Short-Answer Questions

1. The cartoonist believes that Jackson's claim to have compassion for the Native Americans is hypocritical, given his actions. You might reference the legal battles between the Cherokee Nation and the State of Georgia, or the eventual Trail of Tears (pictured in image 2). Key to a strong answer to Part C is an understanding of the interests of the South in the Cherokee's land, and Jackson's claim to represent the "people." Who did Americans mean when they talked about "the people" in the 1830s? What might have happened to the Native Americans if they had not been removed from Georgia?

2. The 3-pronged American System sought to strengthen and unify the nation's economy through the creation of a stronger tariff, the use of the national bank, and the development of a national network of transportation infrastructure. Clay believed that without this system, the nation's economy would ultimately fail because the three major regions of the nation could not stand alone economically. Each region of the nation, however, had its own interests. The South, in particular, would have benefited very little from the system Clay proposed.

Long-Essay Questions

1. You should address the nature of reform that emanated from both the federal government and grassroots movements. To support the claim that Jackson was the inspiration for this reform period, point out that he represented the common man, favored states' rights over the power of the federal government, and freed up Native American land to be used by whites.

   To refute the claim, you can point out that Jackson was a member of the planter-slaveholding class whose interests were not with the common man at all. He was not supportive of some reforms, such as the women's rights movement; opposed others, such as abolition; or was unaware of a number of reforms. His spoils system/rotation in office approach to government had its supporters and detractors. (Historical Thinking Skill I-3: Periodization)

2. Your essay should first take up the objective conditions—how things were—that existed in the antebellum period, such as

abolition and women's rights, then explain the accomplishments or failures of the three reform movements you have selected. For example, while women organized at the Seneca Falls Conference to create a list of demands and expectations, the Cult of Domesticity was merely replaced with Republican Motherhood in this period. Women were still relegated to second-class status. (Historical Thinking Skill IV-8: Interpretation)

Period 5: 1844-1877

Manifest Destiny, Civil War, and Reconstruction

Between 1844 and 1877 the United States experienced significant and formative changes that shaped the future of the nation. Beginning with the election of President Polk in 1844 the United States focused on completing its territorial and cultural expansion to the Pacific Ocean. While this brought glory and enhanced status to the nation, the unintended consequences and deepening sectional tensions incurred by this expansion set the nation on the path towards civil war.

Some historians refer to the Civil War as the "Second Revolution," as it was this war that brought meaningful political, economic, and social change to the United States. Understanding the impact of this conflict is crucial to comprehending the course of the nation both before and after the war.

Although the Civil War ultimately became a war about slavery, there were no easy solutions for the newly freed African Americans when the war ended. The African American freedom struggle is, in fact, as old as the nation. Beginning in the middle of the Civil War and ending in the late 1870s, the Reconstruction era remains a controversial topic in U.S. history with different schools of thought characterizing the era in radically different ways. Whatever one's view, it is important to understand that Reconstruction was more than a civil rights movement. It also redefined and re-created the South, expanded capitalism, and temporarily led to the rise and division of one political party, the breakdown of another, and set in motion forces that would have long-term consequences for the nation. What is more, it helped determine the nature of the American nation-state.

Key Concepts from the College Board

5.1 The United States became more connected with the world as it pursued an expansionist foreign policy in the Western Hemisphere and emerged as the destination for many migrants from other countries.

5.2 Intensified by expansion and deepening regional divisions, debates over slavery and other economic, cultural, and political issues led the nation into civil war.

5.3 The Union victory in the Civil War and the contested Reconstruction of the South settled the issues of slavery and secession, but left unresolved many questions about the power of the federal government and citizenship rights.

9

THE AMERICAN CIVIL WAR: 1860–1865

To understand this nation's history, you must understand the causes and effects of the American Civil War (1861–1865). History writer Shelby Foote even referred to the Civil War as the "crossroads of our being." The Civil War radically altered economic, political, and social life throughout the country, with no one, regardless of regional or political affiliation, untouched by the deadliest war the nation has ever seen.

KEY CONCEPTS

- As the nation expanded, sectional tensions and the slavery issue intensified.
- Various tensions within and between regions came together to cause the Civil War.
- A fundamental disagreement between Northerners and Southerners about the Constitution contributed to the Civil War.
- Slavery became a crisis in the context of western expansion.
- Compromise on slavery, dating from the writing of the Constitution, became harder and eventually impossible by 1860.

The Civil War is discussed in depth in *The American Pageant*, 14th ed., Chapters 16, 18, and 19; 15th ed., Chapters 16, 18–21.

Many social scientists view the Civil War as a watershed in American historical development, for it shaped the future of the nation in a number of ways:

- The war was a catalyst in the industrialization of the United States, and the industrial capitalist class became dominant.

- The federal government was deemed paramount in relation to the states.
- Race and class relations were profoundly affected by the war.
- The war further stimulated and accelerated industrialization.
- The war forever ended the institution of slavery.
- Asked about the causes of the Civil War, everyone talks about slavery. Of course, slavery was the fundamental cause, but there were other causes too. A deeper understanding of the Civil War reveals other tensions in this nation prior to the war, though all were in one way or another affected by the slavery issue. Some of these tensions came from regional differences, some from political differences.

AP Tip

There are usually numerous causes that explain why an event happened. Some are more important than others, but an understanding of the many causes will allow you to write a fuller free-response or DBQ essay, in addition to scoring well on the multiple-choice section of the AP exam. If you are explaining why the Civil War occurred, a response such as "To free the slaves" would be seriously inadequate.

MANIFEST DESTINY FULFILLED: PRESIDENT JAMES K. POLK AND TERRITORIAL EXPANSION

When James K. Polk was inaugurated president in March 1845, he had several foreign policy objectives in mind: the settlement of the Oregon boundary dispute with Britain, which had almost led to military hostilities in the 1839 Aroostook War; the acquisition of California; and the incorporation of Texas into the Union. He achieved all of these goals. John Tyler had already paved the way for Texas statehood, and despite strong opposition from antislavery forces, Texas was admitted on December 29, 1845. As for the Oregon question, it was resolved at the same time relations with Mexico were unraveling. In the Webster-Ashburton Treaty (1842), the United States and Britain had settled the boundary dispute between Maine and Canada and also agreed to suppress the slave trade. Soon, however, they were again bickering over the Oregon Territory's northern border. Initially the Americans offered the 49th parallel as the dividing line; that was rejected by the British. Despite bellicose outbursts by the Americans such as "Fifty-four forty or fight," Britain was in no mood for another war with the United States. In the Oregon Treaty (1846), the nations agreed to settle the dispute peacefully by extending the Oregon Territory–Canadian border along the 49th parallel.

THE MEXICAN-AMERICAN WAR

The fragile relationship between the United States and Mexico deteriorated even further when the United States formally annexed Texas in 1845. Not satisfied with acquiring this enormous territory, Polk also wanted to acquire the California–New Mexico region as well. After the failure of the Slidell mission, an attempt to purchase the territory from Mexico, Polk resorted to a decidedly more aggressive and controversial posture; he sent troops into the disputed area near the Nueces River and the Rio Grande. Many Americans and their political representatives believed the area belonged to the Mexicans, but when hostilities erupted, the United States declared war on Mexico. Polk claimed that Mexican forces had crossed the border to attack Americans, but this was never verified. Regardless, Polk had his war. Although the U.S. Army was supported by poorly trained and ill-disciplined volunteer troops, some of whom committed atrocities in the course of the war, U.S. forces had taken control of the entire Southwest by 1847. Several other American military successes followed before General Zachary Taylor's army defeated Santa Anna's force near Buena Vista. Taylor then proceeded to take Monterrey but was replaced by President Polk for disobeying orders. (Taylor returned home a hero and later became president.) The new U.S. commander, General Winfield Scott, captured Vera Cruz followed a short time later with a victory in the Battle of Cerro Gordo. More victories followed before the Americans launched their final attack on Mexico City. After first taking the mountain fortress of Chapultepec, the Americans captured the Mexican capital. Santa Anna fled and the war ended. The Treaty of Guadalupe Hidalgo (1848) included the following provisions:

- Mexico recognized the American claims to the area north of the Rio Grande.
- Mexico ceded California and New Mexico to the United States in return for $15 million.
- The United States agreed to assume approximately $3 million in debts Mexico owed to American citizens.

President Polk was not satisfied with the terms of the treaty. He believed the United States should have received even more territory from the defeated Mexicans. But he would have to settle for the one-half million square miles of territory (one million if Texas is included in the tally) taken from the Mexicans. In his one term as president, Polk had given meaning to Washington's reference to the United States as a "rising empire."

THE EFFECTS OF EXPANSION

As the United States gained territory and expanded westward, debates over who would control the new land intensified in Congress and among the people. The debate over slavery in the new territory flared with the introduction of the Wilmot Proviso which, if passed, would have prohibited slavery in all territory acquired after 1846—though it was passed by the House of Representatives, it never got out of the more sectionally-balanced Senate. The new land, though beneficial to the nation in many ways, exacerbated already existing tensions that leaders spent years attempting to eradicate through compromise.

Regional Economic Differences

The types of economies that developed in the three regions of the United States in the first half of the nineteenth century had a powerful impact on political goals and decisions. The South grew important cash crops such as cotton, tobacco, sugar, and rice. The North was far more industrialized than the South or West, having shifted from mercantile capitalism. At the same time the West shifted from subsistence farming to commercial agriculture and produced more foodstuffs, such as corn and wheat, than the other two regions. The North came to rely more and more on western foodstuffs. In return, westerners became consumers of northern industrial and commercial products. By the 1850s the North and West were economically joined, and the North's economy was rapidly evolving into a modern-day industrial and commercial system.

- Characteristics of the North's Economy
  - banking
  - shipping
  - insurance
  - small and large business ownership—creating a middle, or bourgeois, class
  - some agriculture—both commercial and subsistence farming
  - availability of wage laborers
- Political Objectives of the North
  - a tariff, a tax on imports to protect the North's growing industries
  - federal aid in the development of infrastructure—those things necessary for business to flourish, such as roads, canals, bridges, and railroads
  - a loose immigration policy, which would provide cheap labor
  - availability of free or cheap land in the West for settlement and investment opportunities, creating new markets for Northern manufactured goods
  - the containment of slavery

In the South, cash crops such as rice and tobacco were grown extensively. Yet no commodity was more important to the South than cotton. One southern political leader was so certain that the rest of the nation depended on the South's cotton production that he declared, "Cotton is King!"

Cotton was one of the most important commodities in the world in the nineteenth century. Factories in the Northern states as well as European countries such as Britain and France needed cotton for their important textile industries. The most powerful producers of cotton in the South were the planter-slaveholders (owners of a hundred slaves or more, sometimes thousands). This class, a fraction of the entire Southern population, was politically, economically, and socially important. Some slaveholders owned only a few slaves. The majority of the Southern population was either subsistence farmers, who grew just enough food to sustain themselves, or yeoman farmers, who grew and sold surplus crops. As much as 25 percent of the South's white population owned slaves on the eve of the Civil War.

Many of the whites who owned no slaves resented the planter-slaveholding class. However, their fear of economic loss if slavery was abolished as well as their belief that whites are superior to blacks were powerful forces in maintaining the status quo. The planters made all of the political and economic decisions. Many nonslaveholders, with dreams of improving their lot and owning slaves, supported what many began calling the "peculiar institution." For most, however, preserving the planter-slaveholder's dominance of the South was not a reason to wage war.

- Characteristics of the South's Economy
  - dependent on the plantation system, the center of economic, political, cultural, and social life in the South
  - slave labor, the dominant labor force in the South producing the greatest value in the region
  - a majority of the white population engaged in subsistence farming
  - yeoman farmers, who owned small- or medium-sized commercial farms, a small proportion of the white population
  - a small urban bourgeois (or middle) class
- Political Objectives of the South
  - low tariffs because of the planter class's dependence on trade with Britain—cotton in return for consumer goods
  - the expansion of slavery for political, economic, and ideological reasons
  - opposition to a cheap public land policy, which would force the planter-slaveholder to compete politically, economically, and ideologically with the independent farmer in the West
  - make it far more difficult for the planter-slaveholder class to exert control over new territories
  - expose poor whites and even slaves to the capitalist and democratic views expressed by Northern emigrants to the new territories

Tensions over Political Theories

Northerners believed in the *contract theory* of government, whereas Southerners believed in the *compact theory*. This explains why Southerners believed they had the right to secede from the Union and why Northerners were willing to prevent them from doing so. Here are the basic features of each theory:

The Compact Theory

- The states, not the people, created the national government.
- The laws of the states are supreme when in conflict with the laws and actions of the federal government. For example, in the antebellum North, personal liberty laws were passed to counteract federal fugitive slave laws.
- The states can declare the laws of the federal government null and void if they deem it necessary and appropriate.
- The logical conclusion of this theory if taken to its extreme is secession.

Examples of the compact theory include

- the Virginia and Kentucky Resolutions (1798)
- the Hartford Convention (1815)
- the *South Carolina Exposition and Protest* (1828)
- the Ordinance of Nullification (1832)

The Contract Theory

- The people, not the states, created the Union.
- The federal government is supreme.
- Thus, federal laws and actions take precedence over state laws and actions.

Examples of the contract theory include

- the various decisions made by the Marshall Court
- John Locke's *Second Treatise on Government*
- *Texas* v. *White* (1869)

Attitudes in the North and South

In the first half of the nineteenth century, many Northerners were content to allow slavery to reside in the Southern states. Only when Southern leaders sought to expand slavery did many Northerners become concerned. Most Northerners, however, were not necessarily morally opposed to slavery. After all, the ancient Greeks and Romans owned slaves. Even the Bible seemed to justify its existence. Politically and economically, however, the expansion of slavery worried many Northern citizens and their political leaders. Did it matter if it spread to Kansas, Oregon, or California? Absolutely! Slavery was at the root of a social, economic, political, and cultural system that many Northerners disdained, partly because it was antithetical to the values of a vibrant, expanding capitalist system. Many Northerners tended to see the South as static. There was little social or economic mobility, little industry, and therefore few opportunities for wage laborers. For these reasons and because land was available out West, many immigrants avoided the South and settled in one of the other two regions.

Southern political leaders, on the other hand, ironically referred to Northern wage earners as "wage slaves." To them, the North was a mess. Northern cities were congested, and workers earned poverty wages and worked and lived in dismal conditions. Southerners saw slavery as a paternalistic system that provided slaves with the basic needs of life. Furthermore, they argued, a slave was an investment; a Northern wage earner could be replaced. Although their owners often horribly mistreated slaves, Southern apologists claimed the opposite was true. Slaves, they maintained, were too valuable to mistreat. On the eve of the Civil War, a prime field slave could cost upward of $2,000, a substantial sum of money in the mid-nineteenth century.

Containing slavery became important to Northerners, who believed that as slavery expanded, Northern industrial capitalism would be limited. In fact, a new political party emerged in the 1850s, the Republicans, whose political goals were "free labor, free soil, free men." The industrial capitalists, owners of the North's factories and workshops, had the most to gain by containing the spread of slavery and expanding capitalism. For example, as capitalism expanded, they hoped to expand the labor pool (by supporting a loose immigration policy), which in turn would drive down the wages they would have to pay to workers. Just as the planters dominated the South, the industrial capitalists profoundly influenced the North's political, economic, and cultural system. What is more, their political and economic objectives often clashed with those of the South's planter class. In the South, militant political leaders, referred to as fire-eaters, chafed at the notion of containing slavery, let alone abolishing it entirely.

Helping to shape the debate on the containment of slavery were the abolitionists, whose ranks were made up of whites and blacks. Unlike many who supported the containment of slavery—some of them racists—abolitionists sought to eliminate slavery. Some would simply free the slaves. Others, like Abraham Lincoln in the 1850s, sought to send freed slaves to Africa (the American Colonization Society). Whereas some abolitionists sought the gradual abolition of slavery, others (among them Frederick Douglass, William Lloyd Garrison, Harriet Tubman, John Brown, and Sojourner Truth) favored an immediate end—peaceful or violent—to the institution.

AP Tip

A good way to organize your understanding of the causes of the war is to consider if the war was reconcilable or irreconcilable. In other words, could it have been prevented? The fact that it did happen does not mean that it had to happen. For example, some historians claim that a generation of bumbling politicians in the 1850s could not match the compromises reached by Clay, Calhoun, and Webster prior to 1850. Other historians contend that fire-eaters in the South and radical abolitionists in the North exacerbated the relationship between more moderate politicians, making compromise impossible. Still others argue that a dual civilization—the South based on a culture of slavery, the North on a culture of wage labor—could no longer be sustained under the same government. Lincoln may have had something like this in mind when he declared, "A house divided against itself cannot stand. I believe this government cannot endure permanently half slave and half free. It will become all one thing or all the other."

THE BREAKDOWN OF COMPROMISE

Throughout the first half of the nineteenth century, various differences between the North and South were resolved. But the relationship deteriorated over the issue of territorial expansion. By 1860 all attempts at compromise failed, and within a year the nation was in the midst of the bloody Civil War that would cost over 600,000 Americans their lives. You need to understand the important decisions that shaped the political debate over such issues as the tariff and the expansion and containment of slavery. These include

- **The compromises at the Constitutional Convention** (See *The American Pageant*, 14th and 15th eds., Chapter 9.)
- **The Missouri Compromise (1820)** This compromise was an attempt to maintain the balance in the Senate between slave and free states. In a compromise worked out by Senator Henry Clay, Maine entered the Union as a free state while Missouri came in as a slave state. Slavery north of latitude 36°30′ was prohibited. War was averted for forty years and thus for a later generation to fight, but the damage to American nationalism helped to erode the so-called Era of Good Feelings.
- **The Nullification Crisis and the Compromise of 1833** In 1828 Congress passed a tariff that protected Northern industries but consequently drove up domestic prices. This new bill outraged Southerners, who began calling it the Tariff of Abominations. In particular, South Carolina, citing the doctrine of nullification, sought to challenge the new bill. The issue of nullification was eventually taken up in the Senate in the famous Webster-Hayne debate. When a new protective tariff was added in 1832, South Carolina, under the leadership of John C. Calhoun, its primary spokesperson and, at the time, vice president, voted to nullify the new tariff. President Jackson, though an advocate of states' rights, threatened to invade South Carolina if its leaders refused to participate in the collection of tariff duties. He even threatened to "hang the first man of them I can get my hands on to the first tree I can find." (Jackson just may have done it.) After Calhoun's resignation, the crisis ended when Congress passed a bill that reduced the protective tariff the following year. No one was hanged, but South Carolina became the hotbed of southern dissent.
- **The Compromise of 1850** This crisis might never have occurred had, say, coal and not gold been discovered in California. By 1850 over 100,000 hoping-to-get-rich-quick settlers had poured into California, and it was not long before they asked that California be admitted into the Union as a free state. Though he was a slaveholder, President Taylor supported California's admission. Not surprisingly, southern fire-eaters threatened to pull their states out of the Union. Enter Henry Clay. His compromise, which was eventually signed into law by the new president, Millard Fillmore, included the following features:
  - California would enter the Union as a free state.
  - The more stringent Fugitive Slave Act of 1850 had guarantees that the law would be rigidly enforced.

  - The slave trade, but not the ownership of slaves, was banned in Washington, D.C.
  - The land taken from Mexico (Mexican Cession) would be divided into two new territories, New Mexico and Utah. Both territories would determine the status of slavery in their areas by *popular sovereignty*.
- **The Kansas-Nebraska Act (1854)** Senator Stephen A. Douglas (Illinois's "Little Giant") favored the passage of a bill that would route a major railroad line through Illinois (and consequently drive up the value of his own landholdings in the region). Even though this would stimulate the further settlement of the West, not everyone was convinced that the plan had merit. In order to get the bill passed, Douglas sought out Southern allies in Congress, and a deal was struck. Little did they know that their compromise, the Kansas-Nebraska Act, would touch off intense sectional hostilities. The features of the bill included the following:
  - The Nebraska Territory would be divided into the Kansas and Nebraska territories.
  - Settlers in those areas would determine the status of slavery—popular sovereignty.

Although the bill sounded reasonable to Southerners, it was the North's turn to be outraged. Both territories were located north of the 36°30' line, which the Missouri Compromise had closed to slavery. Still, the bill passed both houses of Congress and was signed by President Pierce. So angered were Northerners and Westerners by the passage of the Kansas-Nebraska Act that they began forming a political party that they hoped would take a stronger stand against the South's "slavocracy." Before long the Republican Party was a major player in American politics.

- **The *Dred Scott* decision (1857)** The U.S. Supreme Court did not play a significant role in the conflict over slavery until Dred Scott compelled it to act. Scott was a slave who had been taken from Missouri, a slave state, to Wisconsin, a free territory, by his owner. He resided there for two years until he was returned to Missouri. Scott sued for his freedom, contending that his residence in a free state made him a free citizen. Unfortunately for Scott, the chief justice of the Supreme Court was Roger Taney, a pro-Southern Democrat. Under Taney, the Court's ruling went well beyond the underlying principle of the case:
  - Because Congress did not have the power to deny a citizen the right to his or her property without due process—and Scott, as a slave, was considered property—Congress could not prevent a slaveholder from taking his property to a free state. Thus the Missouri Compromise was invalid. There were now no limits to the potential expansion of slavery. Not satisfied with this decision, the Court went further.
  - The Constitution had not provided citizenship rights for blacks. Therefore, Scott had no constitutional right to sue his master in federal court.

The South was overjoyed by the Supreme Court's ruling. The North was outraged, again. Northern Democrats like Stephen Douglas found it increasingly difficult to reconcile their support of popular sovereignty with the *Dred Scott* decision. To more and more Northerners, the Republican Party seemed to represent their views best. The Republicans were a coalition of:

- Free-Soilers, a political party formed in 1848 to represent western farmers by advocating a Homestead Law (cheap federal land for sale out West), internal improvements, and the containment of slavery
- Northern capitalists, who favored a high protective tariff, internal improvements, liberal immigration laws, and a sound money and banking system
- social reformers
- abolitionists
- Northern Democrats who felt betrayed by their party's support for the Kansas-Nebraska Act
- members of the Whig Party who sought the containment of slavery
- various labor groups in the North

Democrat James Buchanan defeated the first Republican presidential candidate, John C. Frémont, in the 1856 election. In the 1860 presidential race, the Republican candidate, a tall, lanky former Illinois congressman called Abe by his friends, would fare much better, though his election would convince the South to secede.

THE ROAD TO WAR

A series of events in the late-1850s seemed to propel the nation to war:

- **Ostend Manifesto**: Southern-supported plan to take Cuba from Spain by force after Spain refused to sell the island to the United States due to fears of slave rebellion there. Northerners viewed the plan as an attempt to expand slavery beyond the U.S.'s borders.

- **"Bleeding Kansas"** This hostility in 1856 was a prelude to the full-scale war that would begin five years later. The conflict arose over whether Kansas would enter the Union as a free or slave state. (Keep in mind that the majority of antislavery forces in Kansas wanted to contain the spread of slavery, not end it.) Since popular sovereignty would decide the issue, it seemed that the majority of Kansas's antislavery farmers would align Kansas with free states. Proslavery sympathizers in neighboring Missouri were not about to stand by while their neighbor cast its lot with the free states. Soon "border ruffians" crossed into Kansas with the intention of making it a slave state. In response, Northern opponents of slavery like the New England Emigrant Society began sending supporters to Kansas. Fighting soon erupted as advocates of slavery created a government in Lecompton, Kansas, and their opponents established an antislavery government in Topeka. Shortly thereafter, proslavery forces massacred citizens of the antislavery town of Lawrence. In retaliation, a violent abolitionist named John Brown organized his own massacre of proslavery advocates at Pottawatomie Creek. Democratic President Pierce's decision to remain aloof from the events in Kansas further damaged what was left of his party's cohesion. In the ensuing months it seemed as if Kansas would enter as a free state—that is, until the new president, James Buchanan, accepted the proslavery Lecompton Constitution, which would admit Kansas as a slave state. Some Democrats, Stephen Douglas among them, joined forces with Republicans in 1858 to oppose the Lecompton Constitution, and Kansas ultimately became a free state.

- **Lincoln-Douglas Debates (1858)** Having served only one term in the House, Lincoln challenged the nationally recognized Illinois senator Stephen Douglas in his campaign for reelection. Despite the fact that Lincoln lost the election, the debates thrust him into the national spotlight, for Lincoln had found a responsive chord with opponents of slavery. Although no abolitionist himself, Lincoln's rhetoric matched the sentiments of those who were opposed to the expansion of slavery as well as those who morally condemned it.
- **John Brown's Harpers Ferry Raid (1859)** John Brown's crusade to eradicate slavery was indeed noble, but his methods were violent. He believed that the planter-slaveholders who maintained a violent system of human ownership could be compelled to end slavery only through violent means. In what many consider a misguided attempt to start a slave rebellion, Brown and his supporters seized the federal arsenal at Harpers Ferry, Virginia (now West Virginia). Hoping that slaves would flock to his cause and take up arms, Brown was instead met by U.S. Army troops under the command of Colonel Robert E. Lee. Captured and ultimately hanged, Brown became a martyr to many Northerners, which in turn made Southerners suspect that Northerners were involved in or at least supportive of violent slave rebellions.

Though many did not know it then, one more significant event would shatter the Union. A slave revolt? Another bloody conflict like the one in Kansas? No. It was a presidential election that led to secession and civil war. The election of 1860 showed just how divided the nation was. Four candidates sought the presidency:

- The Republican candidate was Abraham Lincoln, whose major political platform was the containment of slavery.
- The Democrats split between a Northern candidate and a Southern candidate. The former, Stephen A. Douglas, continued to advocate popular sovereignty. The latter, John C. Breckinridge, opposed the containment of slavery.
- The Constitutional Unionists ran John Bell. His position was generally ambiguous, though preserving the Union seemed to be his primary goal.

Lincoln was elected despite the fact the he received only about 39 percent of the popular vote. In most Southern states his name did not even appear on the ballot. Because Lincoln was determined to stop the spread of slavery, South Carolina believed its future in the federal Union was threatened: more and more new free states would dramatically tip the balance in Congress in the North's favor. Shortly after Lincoln's election, South Carolina seceded from the United States, followed by six other Deep South states.

The new Southern government, called the Confederate States of America, elected Jefferson Davis, a former secretary of war and U.S. senator, as its president, with former U.S. senator Alexander Stephens as vice president. The other Southern states waited to see if Lincoln would use force against South Carolina when he entered the White House in March 1861. In the meantime, the incumbent, James Buchanan, fretted and frowned, and did nothing.

Lincoln had to wait nearly half a year after his election to become president. During that time, Kentucky senator John Crittenden proposed a compromise that would essentially return the nation to 1820 and the Missouri Compromise. This last-ditch attempt to prevent war failed as many Republicans, including Lincoln, believed the proposal would allow slavery to spread to the territories.

The War

- The opening shots occurred on April 12, 1861, when Confederate shore batteries fired on Fort Sumter off the coast of Charleston, South Carolina, compelling the fort's commander to surrender. Although seen as a military victory in the South, it was a political victory for the Lincoln administration because the South had opened hostilities.
- Lincoln immediately called for 75,000 volunteers to suppress the rebellion, whereby four more Southern states seceded. The capital of the Confederacy was moved from Montgomery, Alabama to Richmond, Virginia.
- In what became known as the Trent Affair, a Union warship stopped and seized a British ship carrying Mason and Slidell, Confederate diplomats to Britain and France, and arrested the two. Lincoln was forced to release them for fear that Britain would declare war on the United States.

Comparison of Union and Confederate Strengths and *Weaknesses*

Union	**Confederate**
Population: 22 million	*Population: 6 million whites*
Had to conquer the South (offensive war)	Defensive war
Considerably more factories, wealth; a much more diverse economy than the South's	*Economy is backward and underdeveloped; relies on overseas demand for cotton*
Strong central government (including A. Lincoln)	*New and weak central government*
Generals who understood the nature of "total war," such as Grant and Sherman	Initially better generals, such as Lee and Jackson

At the outbreak of hostilities, Lincoln had Confederate sympathizers arrested and in the process suspended the writ of habeas corpus, a fundamental legal right that requires the government to bring specific charges against the accused and prevents it from jailing an individual indefinitely. Justice Taney ruled that Lincoln had violated their civil rights and ordered them released.

Initially the South was successful in waging war against the Union, in part because of the type of war—defensive—that the South was fighting. The Union military had the considerably more difficult task of capturing and holding major strategic areas. It had to conquer the South, whereas the Confederacy hoped that if the war dragged on, the Northern public would soon grow tired of "Lincoln's war" and sue for peace. The result of the war, however, was in large part ordained by the enormous population and industrial and transportation advantages of the North. To be sure, historians refer to other important factors such as better political leadership (Lincoln versus Davis). But as one Civil War historian put it, the North fought the war "with one hand tied behind its back." Below is a list of major military engagements. In general, the Union named battles after the nearest body of water (in italics) and the Confederates named them after the nearest town (roman).

- *First Bull Run*, 1861 (Manassas): Confederate victory; led the North to realize this would not be a "Ninety Day War"
- Peninsula Campaign, 1862 (Seven Days): Confederate victory made possible by the brilliant leadership of Robert E. Lee
- *Second Bull Run*, 1862 (Manassas): Confederate victory
- *Antietam, 1862* (Sharpsburg): Union victory. After a string of Union defeats, this victory, which turned back a Confederate invasion of the North, allowed Lincoln to issue the Emancipation Proclamation several months after the battle. This decreed that slaves living in those states that were in open rebellion against the United States would be forever free. The Emancipation Proclamation did not apply to the four Border States (Maryland, Missouri, Kentucky, and Delaware); for though they were slave states, they had not seceded. Lincoln had enough on his hands without inviting more states to take up arms against his government. This battle therefore changed the nature of the war from a war to preserve the union to a battle over slavery.
- Fredericksburg, 1862: Confederate victory
- *Monitor* and *Merrimac*, 1862: In order to break the Union blockade of Southern ports, which was designed to prevent the South from exporting cotton and importing needed supplies (the Anaconda Plan), the Confederacy launched the *Merrimac*, an ironclad ship. The *Merrimac* proceeded to wreak havoc on the wooden Union blockade ships. But the North had not been idle in its development of an ironclad vessel. The North's ironclad, the *Monitor,* fought the *Merrimac* to a draw. The consequences of this famous naval battle were twofold: it rendered wooden fleets obsolete, and the Union, given its vast resources, began to build a fleet of ironclad warships, which it used to gain control of important waterways and defeat Confederate forts that guarded such important rivers as the Mississippi.

- Gettysburg, 1863: Union victory. Considered the most famous battle fought on North American soil, the defeat of the second and last major Confederate invasion of the North was the turning point of the war. The Confederates had reached their high-water mark, a point from which their fortunes steadily declined.
- Vicksburg, 1863: Union victory. This gave control of the Mississippi River to the North, effectively cutting the Confederacy in half.
- Sherman's "March to the Sea," 1864: Union victory. The Confederacy was again cut in half.
- Petersburg Campaign, 1864–1865: Union victory. Grant closed in on the Confederate capital.
- Appomattox Court House, 1865: Confederate General Lee surrendered to General Grant, effectively ending the war. Five days later, Lincoln was assassinated by a Confederate sympathizer, John Wilkes Booth.

IMPACT OF THE WAR

Both the North and the South were transformed dramatically by the war. Slavery was of course abolished (Thirteenth Amendment), the planter class was defeated, and the South quickly came under military rule. The war also marked the emergence of the United States as a nation-state. It was no longer a confederation of states—when his state seceded in 1861, Robert E. Lee resigned his commission in the U.S. Army because he could not take up arms against his "country," Virginia. The United States had become a federal union.

Even as it fought a major civil war, the North was changing. During the war it had passed a number of important acts, such as

- the Morrill Tariff of 1861, a high protective tariff
- the Homestead Act of 1862, leading to further development of the West
- the Morrill Land Grant Act of 1862, stimulating the growth and development of higher education
- a banking act that created (in 1863) the National Banking System
- a loose immigration law

The U.S. government also continued to develop the transcontinental railroad, further linking East and West, and it provided black Americans the opportunity to fight for their freedom as soldiers in the Union Army, which they did in considerable numbers—180,000.

Because of the application of industry and technology to warfare in the period 1861–1865, the Civil War is sometimes seen as the first modern war. The use of submarines, aerial reconnaissance, repeating rifles (an early form of machine gun), and ironclad ships is a short list of new technologies applied to waging that war. Moreover, the Napoleonic tactics, rampant disease, and amputations together with modern warfare led to astronomical death tolls. War also became considerably more personal and shocking with the extensive use of early photography in the Civil War. (The Crimean War, 1854–1856, was the first military conflict to be photographed, but it produced nowhere near the volume and graphic nature of pictures taken during the American Civil War.)

Extraordinarily, the North also held a democratic presidential election in the midst of the Civil War, despite the fact that the incumbent, Lincoln, seemed certain to lose. But he didn't. By late spring 1865, the American Civil War was over. But a new battle was looming, one that would attempt to combat racial injustice and shape the way Americans viewed their newly reunited nation.

Content Review Questions

1. Which of the following is NOT an accurate statement regarding the North in the antebellum period?
   (A) Its industrial development was greater than the other two regions.
   (B) The textile industry was important to several of the states in this region.
   (C) The planter class was dominant in most of the states in the region.
   (D) Northerners favored a high protective tariff.

2. The turning point of the American Civil War occurred at the battle of
   (A) First Bull Run.
   (B) Gettysburg.
   (C) *Monitor* and *Merrimac.*
   (D) Antietam.

3. Which of the following is consistent with the contract theory?
   (A) *South Carolina Exposition*
   (B) The political views of John C. Calhoun
   (C) The states, not the federal government, are supreme
   (D) The decisions handed down by the Marshall Court

4. The Compromise of 1850
   (A) allowed California to enter as a free state.
   (B) ended the Fugitive Slave law.
   (C) gave all of the land taken from Mexico to Texas.
   (D) banned slavery in Washington, D.C.

5. Popular sovereignty was the idea that
   (A) the government of each new territory should be elected by the people.
   (B) the American public should vote on whether to admit states with or without slavery.
   (C) it was for the citizens of a territory to decide if their territory would enter the Union as a slave state or a free state.
   (D) the United States should assume popular control of the territory acquired from Mexico.

6. In the *Dred Scott* decision, the Supreme Court
   (A) avoided controversy by ruling that Dred Scott had no right to sue in federal court.
   (B) ruled that Congress could not prohibit slavery in the territories because slaves were private property.
   (C) ruled that slaves could sue in federal court only if their masters allowed them to do so.
   (D) ruled that a slave that had been transported to a free state or territory was a free citizen of the United States.
7. The Crittenden Proposal
   (A) forbade slavery west of the Mississippi River.
   (B) would have granted the Southern states their independence if they abolished slavery.
   (C) would have lowered the protective tariff in return for abolishing the Fugitive Slave Act.
   (D) would have guaranteed slaveholders the right to own slaves south of the 36°30′ line.
8. In the election of 1860
   (A) most Southerners refused to vote in protest against Lincoln's candidacy.
   (B) the Republicans gained control of the executive branch for the first time.
   (C) the tariff was the most controversial issue.
   (D) the vast majority of southerners voted for the compromise candidate, John Bell.
9. The Emancipation Proclamation
   (A) abolished slavery in all states that were in open rebellion.
   (B) abolished slavery in the Border States.
   (C) ended the slave trade but not slavery.
   (D) was ruled unconstitutional by the Taney Supreme Court.
10. Which of the following is NOT associated with the North during the war?
   (A) Continued industrialization
   (B) The Homestead Act of 1862
   (C) The use of blacks in the Union military
   (D) The ratification of the Fifteenth Amendment guaranteeing voting rights to male U.S. citizens
11. In *American Slavery as It Is* (1839), Theodore Weld articulated the view that
   (A) abolitionists were to blame for fanning the flames of sectional discord.
   (B) nullification was a constitutional obligation needed to sustain the institution of slavery.
   (C) American slavery could be reformed by placing a time limit on how long one could legally be a slave.
   (D) slavery was an immoral institution that brought misery to millions of people.

12. Which state entered the Union as a result of the Compromise of 1850?
    (A) California
    (B) Texas
    (C) Missouri
    (D) Maine

13. Which Confederate state broke apart when one of its regions seceded from the Union to form a new state?
    (A) Virginia
    (B) Tennessee
    (C) Arkansas
    (D) Kansas

14. The Morrill Tariff Act of 1861
    (A) is the lowest protective tariff in U.S. history.
    (B) was warmly embraced by the South as a compromise of goodwill by the North.
    (C) ultimately led to the most devastating depression in U.S. history until the financial collapse in the Great Depression.
    (D) raised tariff rates to levels established by the Walker Tariff in 1845.

15. Which of the following was a major achievement in the settling and development of the West during the Civil War?
    (A) Missouri Compromise
    (B) Wilmot Proviso
    (C) Homestead Act
    (D) Clayton-Bulwer Treaty

Short-Answer Questions

1. The Civil War was the result of multiple factors. Historians debate which factor is the most significant in bringing about the war.
    A. Choose one of the causes of the Civil War listed below and explain why this factor was the most significant cause of the war. Provide at least ONE piece of evidence to support your explanation.
       Slavery
       States' rights
       Ineffective leadership
       Sectionalism
    B. Contrast your choice against ONE of the other options, demonstrating why that cause of the war was not as significant a factor as the one you chose.

Question 2 is based on the following passages.

> "You say you will not fight to free Negroes. Some of them seem willing to fight for you; but, no matter. Fight you, then, exclusively to save the Union. I issued the proclamation on purpose to aid you in saving the union."
>
> --Abraham Lincoln, Open Letter to Democrats, August 26, 1863

> "The hundreds of thousands, if not millions of slaves [the act] will emancipate will come North and West and will either be competitors with our white mechanics and laborers, degrading them by competition, or they will have to be supported as paupers and criminals at the public expense."
>
> —*Cincinnati Enquirer*

2. Based on these two views on the Emancipation Proclamation, complete the following tasks:
   A) Briefly explain the main point made by Abraham Lincoln in the first passage.
   B) Briefly explain the main point in the *Cincinnati Enquirer* in the second passage.
   C) Choose ONE event during the Civil War that illustrates the main idea in one of the passages, and explain how that event reflects the passage you chose.

Long-Essay Questions

1. Compare and contrast the industrial capitalist class and the Southern planter-slaveholding class. Discuss the following topics in your essay:
   economic priorities
   the expansion of slavery

2. Analyze the following statement:
   The Civil War was the result of irreconcilable differences between the North and West on the one hand and the South on the other.

   To what extent is this statement true?

Answers

Content Review Questions

1. **(C)** The planter class was the dominant social, economic, and political class in the antebellum South (*The American Pageant*, 14th ed., pp. 319–324, 373/15th ed., pp. 288–293, 339; Learning Objective ENV-3).

2. **(B)** Gettysburg. From this point on, though the South did win several important battles, it was greatly weakened (*The American Pageant*, 14th ed., p. 492/15th ed., pp. 445–446; Learning Objective ENV-3).

3. **(D)** Answers A–D all support the alternative contract theory. In a number of important decisions, the Marshall Court strengthened the role of the federal government in relation to the states (*The American Pageant*, 14th ed., pp. 231–232/15th ed., p. 238; Learning Objective POL-5).

4. **(A)** California's entrance into the Union as a free state was a major concession of the South. The slave trade, not slavery, was banned in Washington, D.C. The Fugitive Slave Act was strengthened, not ended. The territory acquired from Mexico was divided into two territories, Utah and New Mexico (*The American Pageant*, 14th ed., pp. 423–437/15th ed., pp. 384–387; Learning Objective POL-6).

5. **(C)** Popular sovereignty, an idea put forth by Lewis Cass as a means to compromise, gave citizens of a territory the right to decide on the status of slavery when joining the Union (*The American Pageant*, 14th ed., pp. 416–417/15th ed., p. 378; Learning Objective POL-6).

6. **(B)** The Taney Supreme Court ruled that Scott, as a slave, was property that could be transported wherever his master decided to take him. The decision, highly controversial, invalidated the Missouri Compromise, not the Kansas-Nebraska Act (*The American Pageant*, 14th ed., pp. 445–446/15th ed., pp. 403–404; Learning Objective POL-5).

7. **(D)** This last-ditch attempt to forestall civil war would have, for all intents and purposes, returned the United States to 1820 and the Missouri Compromise (*The American Pageant*, 14th ed., pp. 456–457/15th ed., pp. 413–414; Learning Objective POL-6).

8. **(B)** Lincoln, the first Republican to win the presidency, was elected with only 39 percent of the popular vote. Southerners did indeed vote, but primarily for Breckinridge. The tariff was not the most controversial issue in 1860, though it was still a point of tension between the North and South (*The American*

Pageant, 14th ed., pp. 456–457/15th ed., pp. 409–412; Learning Objective POL-2).

9. **(A)** Although controversial, the proclamation added another important moral and legal dimension to the Union cause by undermining slavery in those states that had seceded. It also made it morally difficult for France and Britain to provide aid to the Confederacy (*The American Pageant*, 14th ed., pp. 488–489/15th ed., pp. 440–441; Learning Objective CUL-5).

10. **(D)** The Fifteenth Amendment was not ratified until 1870, fully five years after the end of the Civil War (*The American Pageant*, 14th ed., pp. 476–479, 525–527/15th ed., pp. 431–433, 475; Learning Objective ENV-3).

11. **(D)** A moral indictment of chattel slavery, *Slavery as It Is* was considered propaganda by Southerners (and even some historians today) (*The American Pageant*, 14th ed., p. 386/15th ed., pp. 349–350; Learning Objective CUL-5).

12. **(A)** In the Compromise of 1850 the North benefited by having a new free state (California) enter the Union, thus tipping the balance in the Senate to the North (*The American Pageant*, 14th ed., p. 423/15th ed., p. 385; Learning Objective POL-6).

13. **(A)** As early as the American Revolution era, Virginians in the western part of the state felt underrepresented and compelled to pay high taxes. The outbreak of the Civil War provided them with an opportunity to separate from the rest of Virginia, which they did on June 11, 1861 (*The American Pageant*, 14th ed., p. 464/15th ed., p. 420; Learning Objective ID-5).

14. **(D)** When the South seceded from the Union, it gave Congress an opportunity to supersede the low tariff that had been established in 1857. The Morrill Tariff raised duties by 5 to 10 percent on many commodities (*The American Pageant*, 14th ed., p. 476/15th ed., p. 431; Learning Objective WXT-6).

15. **(C)** The Homestead Act of 1862 authorized Congress to sell 160 acres of western land to a settler who agreed to live on that property for at least five years. It was an integral feature of western settlement (*The American Pageant*, 14th ed., p. 479/15th ed., p. 433; Learning Objective PEO-5).

Short-Answer Questions

1. There are effective arguments to be made for all four of the options listed. Slavery caused tension in the country dating back to colonial times, and its possible expansion exacerbated those hostilities. Similarly, the battle over states' rights versus federal power lingered from the creation of the Constitution, with southern states persistently believing that their needs were ignored by the national government and a Congress ruled by the more populous northern states. Any of the four factors can also be contrasted with another. Ineffective

leadership, for example, might be seen as less important than the issues that abounded from slavery and sectionalism because the issues were bigger than any one person.

2. Abraham Lincoln claims that even if Northerners aren't willing to fight to end slavery in the wake of the Emancipation Proclamation, the order would still strengthen the North's forces and enable them to win the war. The *Cincinnati Enquirer*, meanwhile, asserts that freeing the slaves will harm Northern workers by creating increased competition for jobs or harm the economy by draining its resources. You could cite the 1863 draft riots as an example of an event that echoes the sentiments made by the *Cincinnati Enquirer*.

Long-Essay Questions

1. When you are asked to compare and contrast two or more items it is important that you identify both their similarities and their differences. In this question, the topics are selected for you. Identify and discuss economic priorities—for example, both sides attitudes towards the tariff. A discussion of the political objectives—in favor of the expansion or containment of slavery—as it relates to the interests of the industrial and capitalist class of the North and the planter-slaveholder class of the South should be your focus for the second part of the essay. (Historical Thinking Skill II-4: Comparison and II-5: Contextualization)

2. In order to thoroughly answer this question, you need to decide how accurate you think the statement is and incorporate evidence that supports your conclusion. You may wish to discuss the divergent political and economic differences and disputes between the sections, as well as the ideological justifications each side utilized to defend its way of life. Another aspect of your discussion may include the view held by some historians that the North and the South had two incompatible civilizations that could not be sustained under one government, and thus they resorted to war to settle their economic and political differences. (Historical Thinking Skill III-6: Historical Argumentation and III-7: Appropriate Use of Relevant Historical Evidence)

10

Reconstruction: 1863–1877

A pivotal movement in recent U.S. history has been the struggle by blacks to achieve racial equality. Many remember or are at least aware of the leaders, organizations, and demonstrations that shaped the 1950s and 1960s over the question of the rights of African Americans. But the plight of black Americans did not begin thirty or forty years ago. In fact, it can be said that this struggle is as old as the nation. Yet, two decades in the nineteenth century, the 1860s and 1870s, stand out as much as any, including the 1950s and 1960s, as essential to the goal of redefining race relations in the United States. After four years of horrific warfare, the South needed to be rebuilt economically, politically, and socially. Though it remains an especially controversial period in American history, Reconstruction attempted to do just that.

Key Concepts

- Attitudes and economic and political forces influenced the dimensions of Reconstruction.
- Lincoln's and Johnson's lenient Reconstruction plans clashed with the radical Republicans' Reconstruction methods and objectives.
- The Republican Party sought to contain blacks in the South in order to establish the nucleus of their party in that section of the country.
- Southern "Redeemers" temporarily reinstated the South's prewar political and social system, leading to the more punitive radical Republican Reconstruction.
- Congress ratified three important civil rights amendments—the Thirteenth, Fourteenth, and Fifteenth Amendments.
- Reactionaries regained control of the South, and blacks were relegated to sharecropping and social and political subordination.

- A political deal between Southern Democrats and the Republican Party ended Reconstruction.

Reconstruction is discussed in depth in *The American Pageant,* 14th and 15th eds., Chapters 22 and 23.

AP Tip

As much as any period in U.S. history, historians hold widely divergent views about the causes, ramifications, successes, and failures of Reconstruction. You should attempt to read as widely as possible on the interpretive nature of the debate over this topic. Should the College Board offer a free-response question or a DBQ on Reconstruction, an understanding of various historians' interpretations will provide you with a broader grasp of its significance as well as relevant interpretations around which you can develop your own view. If your AP teacher does not infuse class discussions and notes as well as assigned readings with evaluative essays, ask for suggestions regarding analytical literature on the subject.

THE WAR, THE EXPANSION OF THE FEDERAL GOVERNMENT, AND THE IMPACT ON RECONSTRUCTION

Before we explore the dimensions and dynamics of Reconstruction, it is important to understand how the war transformed the U.S. government, for in the end, it was the government that was center stage in the debate over reconstructing the South and addressing the problems of integrating blacks into the nation's social, political, and economic fabric. In March 1865, just one month before the end of the war, Congress passed the Bureau of Refugees, Freedmen, and Abandoned Lands Act (more commonly known as the Freedmen's Bureau). Under the leadership of General O. O. Howard, it assisted both freed slaves and poor whites who were destitute and in need of food and medical care. It also provided them farmland that had earlier been owned by slaveholders; President Johnson undermined this effort when he returned most of the confiscated land to previous owners. But the most well known legacy of the Freedman's Bureau was its success in constructing schools that educated thousands of Southern blacks and poor whites, often under the tutelage of Northern whites, many of whom were women. Despite the achievements of the Northerners who worked for the Freedmen's Bureau, many Southerners referred to them derisively as "carpetbaggers," implying that they were opportunists who, for their own self-interest rather than altruistic reasons, rushed down South after the war. This transformation of governmental power was taking place as war was being waged, for the war expanded the role of the federal government in unprecedented ways. A short list would include the following:

- In an unprecedented decision, the government instituted conscription—the draft.

- For the first time in U.S. history, the national government assumed responsibility for guaranteeing and protecting the constitutional rights of a segment of U.S. society.
- The government had to raise millions of dollars to fight the war. To do this, the government issued greenbacks (paper currency) in record amounts.
- Lincoln used the power of the government to suspend basic constitutional rights such as habeas corpus.

AP Tip

Students sometimes ask whether they should incorporate contemporary ideas and issues into their free-response and DBQ essays. Believing that history is a continuum in which the forces that shape our contemporary world have their historical antecedents, you can make connections between past and present events. For example, Lincoln's suspension of habeas corpus rights is relevant to a discussion of the USA PATRIOT Act. *Make certain, however, that you maintain your focus on the specific question that is asked of you.* A question on Lincoln, the Civil War, and habeas corpus should not get lost in a political discussion on governmental powers in combating terrorism since 9/11. Also, *do not incorporate an issue into your discussion if you know little or nothing about it.* College Board readers can identify these. Ask what your teacher advises.

Reconstruction continued this trend of governmental intervention and influence in all regions of the United States. In the North a powerful relationship was fostered between government and capital. And in the South, the government was instrumental in creating a new mode of production, capitalism, to replace the collapsed slave-based economy. In short, the federal government took on the responsibility of reconstructing the South, which in the end required the application of laws, old and new, the use of federal troops to ensure order and stability, and significant amounts of money. One controversial extension of federal power serves nicely as an example of the application of the government's willingness to use its expanded political and military power to carry out domestic policy—namely, the division of the South into military districts and the stationing of U.S. troops in Southern states to carry out federal law and to prevent reactionary and violent responses to Reconstruction. The government played an important role in altering the South's social and political institutions, though in some cases only temporarily.

The Economic and Political Foundations of Reconstruction Policies

It can be argued that Reconstruction began even before the Civil War ended. When President Lincoln issued the Emancipation Proclamation, in 1863, he redefined the nature of the struggle by giving the Union cause a broader meaning. A significant development in U.S. race relations did come about with the end of the war and the abolition of slavery. But though laws can be changed, people's attitudes are often considerably more difficult to alter. As we will see, many whites in the South, and even numerous whites in the North, were not about to give freed blacks access to the major institutions, rights, and privileges of American citizenship. Tragically, many blacks were free in name only. In fact, many white Northerners favored a policy of containing blacks in the South for two key reasons:

- **Racism** Although Lincoln made abolition a cause of the Union war effort with the announcement of the Emancipation Proclamation, many Northerners preferred that blacks stay in the South.
- **Economic competition** Northern whites worried that blacks might migrate to the North, where there were more economic opportunities than could be found in the war-torn South. This in turn would drive down workers' wages. Consequently, while the wage-earning classes felt threatened by black migration north, the capitalist class desired an expanded labor pool, which would drive down wages.

There were political objectives as well. The Civil War indeed ended slavery and reestablished the Union, but it had two other desired consequences from the perspective of the North's political and economic leaders. The South's defeat had ended the reign of the planter aristocracy and decimated the Democrats (sneeringly referred to by Republicans as the "party of secession"). To ensure that neither the planters nor the Democrats would reemerge in the postwar South, Northern political and economic interests maintained that both of these objectives could be met if the Republican Party was firmly entrenched in the South. This would make the Republicans a national party and make the Democrats a nuisance at worst, but certainly not a threat to Republican hegemony. The Republicans attempted to realize their goals by implementing the following measures:

- They denied to the former Confederate leaders, many of them from the planter-slaveholding class, their political rights, which in turn would remove them as an obstacle to the Republicans' economic and political agenda.
- They provided blacks in the South with just enough political and economic rights and opportunities so that they would choose to stay in the South, thereby establishing a base for the Republican Party as well as obviating the racial and economic tensions that would occur if blacks began moving north.

PLANNING RECONSTRUCTION: CONFLICTING METHODS

Had Lincoln not been assassinated at the end of the war, Reconstruction and, in fact, the subsequent history of the nation might have been fundamentally different. Lincoln's plan for reconstructing the South was moderate in every sense of the word, especially in comparison with a wing of his party that became known as the radical Republicans. Lincoln's successor, Andrew Johnson, applied a plan that was quite similar but one that would bring him into direct confrontation with the radical Republicans. The stage would soon be set for a clash between the executive and legislative branches over how best to reconstruct the South and address the status of black Americans.

Lincoln wanted to quickly—and for the most part, painlessly—reincorporate the South back into the Union. His ideological rationale for this was his view that the people of the South did not secede; their economic and political leaders initiated secession and war. Lincoln argued that because the government was indivisible, secession was politically impossible. Instead, the Civil War represented a rebellion by a small minority who had brazenly violated the authority and laws of the national government. (Shortly after the war's end, in *Texas* v. *White*, the Supreme Court affirmed the contract theory of government.) This explains why he was opposed to the radical Republicans' plan (see below). Lincoln's design included the following features:

- Before a state could be readmitted into the Union, (only) 10 percent of voters needed to take a loyalty oath to the United States.
- The South had to repudiate the compact theory of government and accept the contract theory.
- Until the above requirements were met, military governors would oversee the conquered Southern states.

Initially, Johnson was accepted by many Republicans, for his contempt of the planter aristocracy in his home state of Tennessee was well known. But he quickly became an obstacle to those seeking a more radical and punitive solution to reconstructing the South. Johnson's plan was very similar to Lincoln's, though with a few additions, such as the disenfranchisement of very wealthy and politically powerful former Confederates. But one loophole that Johnson used frequently was the right to grant pardons to the same individuals that he claimed he sought to exclude from power. Given this approach, it was not long before most of the South's elites were back in power and every Southern state had been readmitted to the Union. In fact, the 1872 Amnesty Act lifted the last political restriction on former ex-Confederate leaders. Imagine the irritation of Northern senators at seeing the former vice president of the Confederacy, Alexander Stephens, reclaim his seat in the United States Senate. Although the readmitted states drew up constitutions that repudiated secession and abolished slavery, accepting the Thirteenth Amendment, nothing was done to enfranchise the South's black population. Enter the radical Republicans.

Not satisfied with disenfranchising blacks, the newly formed Southern state governments went even further by establishing what became known as Black Codes. The codes were designed to limit severely the movement of millions of dislocated blacks as well as to deny them the right to own property, including much-needed farms. Further, they were returned to a form of perpetual servitude by being compelled to sign work contracts that were little more than a thinly disguised attempt to make them dependent once again on their former owners. Legally, their rights were abridged as well; they still could not testify in a court of law against a white person (even if they had the courage to do so). For Southern reactionaries, the Thirteenth Amendment was irrelevant; they would, in the postwar years and following the end of Reconstruction, find other methods to subordinate and repress the newly freed slaves. Although steps were taken to address these abuses, in the decades following Reconstruction blacks were in fact returned to a state of subordination and degradation. Infuriated at how suddenly reactionaries reclaimed control of the South, Northern politicians openly challenged Southern elections that had returned the former Southern elite to power. The radical Republicans seemed to have anticipated these developments. Even before the war was over, they offered up their most decidedly punitive Reconstruction plan in 1864, referred to as the Wade-Davis Bill:

- Slavery was banned in the United States.
- All former high-ranking military, political, and economic (planter class) leaders of the former Confederacy, like Robert E. Lee and Jefferson Davis, were disenfranchised.
- Unlike Lincoln's modest 10 percent requirement for readmission, the radical Republicans required a more substantial commitment: 50 percent of a state's citizens must swear loyalty and allegiance to the United States.

A little over a year after becoming president, Johnson was in direct confrontation with the radical Republicans, led by Senator Charles Sumner (who before the war had been beaten to within an inch of his life by a South Carolina congressman, Preston Brooks, *in the Senate chamber*), and Representative Thaddeus Stevens. The conflict centered on a piece of legislation called the Civil Rights Act of 1866, which included the following features:

- Blacks were to be considered citizens of the United States, entitled to all the rights and privileges expressed in the U.S. Constitution.
- Attempts to restrict basic rights, such as owning property and testifying in a court of law, were illegal.
- The federal government, not the states, would enforce the act.

Johnson's veto of the bill was overridden by Congress; however, supporters of the legislation feared that the Supreme Court would rule the bill unconstitutional. Something more permanent was necessary.

THE FOURTEENTH AMENDMENT

Whereas the Thirteenth Amendment ended slavery, the Fourteenth defined citizenship rights, not only for freed slaves, but for all Americans. At least that was the implication. Women and minority groups would have to continue their battle for equal rights as citizens under the Constitution. Pointedly attacking the Black Codes, Congress's passage of the amendment established the following constitutional limitations on a state's power to modify or eliminate the rights of its citizens under the federal government. (Keep in mind that not until the 1950s would the federal government expand protection of Fourteenth Amendment rights to other civil rights groups, such as women, children, and those accused of a crime.) The most important provisions of the Fourteenth Amendment include the following:

- All persons who are born in or who are naturalized in the United States are citizens.
- A citizen of the United States cannot be denied *equal protection under the law* and must be provided *due process rights* under the law regardless of race, gender, class, religion, political views, or ethnicity.
- Any state that refuses a segment of its population protection and rights accorded them by this amendment would suffer a reduction in its congressional representation.

Knowing they had an ally in the White House, Southern states refused to ratify the Fourteenth Amendment, especially since one clause prohibited former Confederate leaders from holding state or federal offices. Again, battle lines were drawn. The radical Republicans mobilized their forces and sought to outmaneuver their opponents, whether they were in Southern state assemblies, the U.S. Congress, or even in the Oval Office.

The Radical Republicans Ascendant

In the summer of 1866 the radical Republicans acted after a joint committee of Congress recommended that those Southern politicians elected to Congress under Johnson's lenient requirements for readmission and representation be barred from taking their seats. Moreover, the committee placed the responsibility and authority for Reconstruction under the direction of the legislative branch, thus devaluing the chief executive's role. Consequently, from 1867 to 1870 the radical Republicans were at the height of their power. In that brief time they instituted sweeping policies, with the Fourteenth Amendment as their guide. First and foremost they replaced Johnson's Reconstruction plan with their own.

The former Confederate states would be divided into five military zones, each governed by a U.S. Army general entrusted with considerable powers.

In order for a state to be readmitted into the Union it had to ratify the Fourteenth Amendment and establish a state constitution that would guarantee black suffrage and disenfranchise ex-Confederate leaders. (In 1870, Hiram Revels of Mississippi became the nation's first black congressman when he was elected to the Senate seat previously occupied by the former president of the Confederacy, Jefferson Davis. Ironically, Davis, who had been captured at the end of the war, had recently been released from a federal prison.) These state constitutions had first to be ratified by Congress before readmission was possible.

The right of blacks to vote would be guaranteed by the federal government, which would oversee voting in the Southern states.

By the end of Reconstruction in the late 1870s, only three states had not been readmitted into the Union and were therefore still under the control of the military.

The Impeachment of President Johnson

Fully aware that their nemesis in the White House would continually attempt to thwart their plans, the radical Republicans passed the Tenure of Office Act over the president's veto. In retrospect, the act appears as a trap waiting to ensnare President Johnson, for it prohibited the president from removing civilian or military officials without the consent of the Senate. In essence, it profoundly reduced his authority as commander in chief. As expected, Johnson believed that the law encroached on the authority granted to the executive branch by the Constitution, and he set about to challenge the Tenure of Office Act. The obvious target was Secretary of State Edwin Stanton, who not only was allied with the radical Republicans, but also supervised the South's military districts. When Johnson fired Stanton, the radical Republicans impeached him. Charged with numerous counts of "high crimes and misdemeanors," Johnson avoided removal from office by merely one Senate vote. Retrospectively, the impeachment and trial seem purely politically motivated. Had Johnson been removed from office, a dangerous precedent would have been established. Not only would it have seriously damaged the system of checks and balances—not to mention the independence of the executive branch—it would encourage any subsequent majority political party in Congress to remove a sitting president for political reasons. Although he survived removal, Johnson was greatly weakened and posed no further serious threat to the radical Republican agenda.

Reactionaries and Racists Respond to Reconstruction

Most Southerners disdained the Republicans' reconstruction of the South. Over time they took the following steps to regain control:

- Many in the South's upper class believed it best to accept the Republicans' measures, gain the trust of the new black voters, and proceed to use this newfound relationship to entice them to become Democrats.
- They worked to gradually regain control of the state legislatures from, among others, "scalawags" (Southerners allied with radical Reconstruction). While some white politicians hoped to appeal to black voters, poor whites rejected this since the war had exacerbated their condition. The last thing they wanted was political and economic competition from poor blacks.
- Violence and intimidation were used against blacks to maintain their subordination. To this end, various antiblack, anti-Republican reactionary groups, such as the Ku Klux Klan (KKK) and the Knights of the White Camellia, were created. Utilizing violence and intimidation as their methods of control, such as burning homes,

whippings, and lynching, the Klan and the Knights were determined to keep blacks and sympathetic whites from voting. Garbed in white hoods and gowns, carrying torches, and firing weapons, the KKK would sweep down on unsuspecting victims, whether in their homes or at political meetings, and terrorize them. Although moderate whites condemned such actions, many terrified blacks and white Republicans stayed away from the polls. Not to be deterred, Congress passed the Force Act and the Ku Klux Klan Act, which made it illegal to use force or intimidation with the intention of disenfranchising citizens and denying them their Fourteenth and Fifteenth Amendment rights. The president was authorized to use military force to carry out these acts. Although membership in the Klan diminished, their use of fear and terror had panicked enough voters that by 1876 only three Southern states (South Carolina, Florida, and Louisiana) still had radical Republican state governments.

By the time the Force Act and the Ku Klux Klan Act were passed, the radical Republicans had already reached the zenith of their power and influence. Soon they would experience a precipitous decline, to be replaced by more conservative-minded political leaders. Yet they had at least one more significant bill left to pass: the Civil Rights Act of 1875. This far-reaching piece of legislation called for full equality in all public facilities—in other words, access to public accommodations and institutions could not be denied based on race. Unfortunately, the Supreme Court ruled the act unconstitutional in 1883. The nation would not see the likes of such legislation for over eighty years.

The End of Reconstruction: The Election of 1876 and the Compromise of 1877

Reconstruction's life span did not exceed two decades, leaving students of history to ponder the circumstances of its short existence and sudden demise. Just as paleontologists often reflect on why the dinosaurs died off after flourishing for millions of years, historians are compelled to ask the same of Reconstruction's very brief life. Of course, there are any number of plausible explanations, one of which has to do with the state of the nation in the mid-1870s, when the motivation for continuing Reconstruction was waning.

- Starting in 1873, the nation experienced a depression. Funding to sustain Reconstruction was drying up. At the same time, sympathetic whites in the North were more concerned with their own economic situation than with those in the South.
- The hegemonic upper classes in both the North and South were concerned that the masses would somehow unite and threaten their interests. And, at the end of Reconstruction, the railroad strike of 1877 did little to assuage their fears.
- Because they were no longer enemies, the ruling elites in the North and South were increasingly interdependent as a result of their mutual economic interests.

- Given its power in the North and ever-expanding West, the Republican Party no longer believed it had to dominate in all regions of the United States.
- Corruption and scandal were rampant.
  - The Grant administration was riddled with corrupt officials ("spoilsmen") and illegal deals—for example, the Crédit Mobilier scandal and the Whiskey Ring.
  - In some municipal governments, such as New York City's Tweed Ring, there were glaring abuses. Through the efforts of political cartoonist Thomas Nast, the extent of the Tweed Ring's corruption was conveyed to the public in persuasive images that influenced citizens to demand investigations into the abuses. As a result, some began to hold the view that Reconstruction programs were another way for corrupt and opportunistic politicians and businessmen to get rich at the public's expense.
  - Some Northerners were appalled by reports of corruption in Reconstruction governments.
  - There were abuses on Wall Street—for example, the attempt by financiers Gould and Fisk to corner the gold market in 1869.

Given these factors, many were tiring of the Grant administration and the Republican Party. Conditions were rife for a change. However, the election of 1876 showed just how politically divided the nation had become. The Republicans ran a Civil War veteran and governor of Ohio, Rutherford B. Hayes. His Democratic opponent was New York's reform governor, Samuel J. Tilden. Tilden initially won both the electoral and popular vote, but Republicans charged that several Southern states had denied many blacks their right to vote; they contended that these were votes lost to the Republican candidate. For a time, there seemed to be no clear winner. On the one hand, the Democrats were certain their candidate had won; on the other hand, the Republicans claimed the election results in the states where the alleged abuses occurred should be nullified. A special electoral committee was established to decide which candidate was entitled to the disputed votes. Given the makeup of the commission (eight Republicans, seven Democrats), a partisan decision was made to give all of the contested votes to the Republican Hayes. Outraged Democrats threatened to filibuster the decision in the House of Representatives. The nation was in political limbo. And then, a deal was struck. The Southern Democrats relinquished the contested votes and therefore the election to Hayes and the Republicans in return for

- the removal of the remaining federal troops from the South
- federally funded development of a Southern railroad network
- the appointment of a Democrat to Hayes's cabinet

With this agreement, Reconstruction came to a sudden and, some would argue, premature end.

THE LEGACY OF RECONSTRUCTION

In the short term, blacks in the South found themselves languishing in a form of agrarian servitude once more. They were relegated to sharecropping whereby, under contract, they often labored in the same fields they had worked as slaves. Even as tenant farmers (a slight improvement over sharecropping) who received tools and seed in return for usually half their crop, freedmen toiled their lives away once again in abject poverty and misery.

Decades later, at the turn of the twentieth century, blacks were still living a marginal existence. Following the Supreme Court's *Plessy* v. *Ferguson* ("separate but equal") decision in 1896, whatever hope they may have had about equal protection under the law and social acceptance had turned to dust. "What happens to a dream deferred?" asked the black poet Langston Hughes. "It dries up like a raisin in the sun." For many blacks who had lived through slavery, the Black Codes, and the terror of "night riders" such as the KKK, the end of Reconstruction bequeathed to them a new form of misery known by the name Jim Crow laws, which further subordinated blacks in the South in the following ways:

- Political restrictions were imposed to circumvent the Fifteenth Amendment:
  - Poll taxes, a fee for voting, disenfranchised the poor, blacks and whites alike.
  - Literacy tests worked because there were very few schools for blacks in the South.
  - The grandfather clause (if your grandfather had the right to vote, you did as well) excluded most blacks because their grandfathers had been slaves.
  - Gerrymandering, the redrawing of voting districts to alter a racial, ethnic, or political majority, was used to neutralize votes.
- Blacks were denied access to many public and municipal facilities such as parks, theaters, housing, and mass transit. When Jim Crow laws failed to intimidate recalcitrant blacks, they were often threatened, beaten, and lynched.
- Various economic sanctions were placed on blacks in order to maintain their subjugated status and keep them dependent on their fellow white Southerners.

Still, Reconstruction did set a precedent that would stand the test of time. Government can and often does intervene to redress grievances and address the social, economic, and political needs of those who have been exploited. Reconstruction was quite possibly a failure, especially for those who lived through its promise of hope and equality. Yet, as with all reform movements, it did at the very least attempt to raise the consciousness of Americans about their own definitions of democracy, and at times it succeeded. For blacks, some educational opportunities were now available, and as a race they had finally experienced the cherished right to vote and elect fellow blacks to important positions during Reconstruction.

Unfortunately, over one hundred years after the last federal troops were withdrawn from the South, black Americans were still fighting for their rights and hoping that, unlike their ancestors, their dream would not be deferred.

Content Review Questions

1. The original purpose of the Freedmen's Bureau was to
   (A) generate support among Southern whites to attempt to end federal military occupation.
   (B) organize blacks as sharecroppers.
   (C) provide freed blacks with food, clothing, and educational opportunities.
   (D) register blacks to vote.
2. Lincoln's plan for Reconstruction, developed in 1863, allowed for a state to be readmitted once
   (A) 50 percent of its voters took an oath of allegiance to the Union.
   (B) the state legislature ratified the Fourteenth and Fifteenth Amendments.
   (C) 10 percent of its voters repudiated the contract theory.
   (D) it abolished slavery.
3. The Fourteenth Amendment to the Constitution
   (A) abolished slavery.
   (B) gave to the federal government supreme authority over the states.
   (C) gave black males the right to vote.
   (D) defined citizenship rights.
4. Carpetbaggers were
   (A) Southerners who supported radical Republican governments in the South.
   (B) Northerners such as teachers and ministers who traveled South after the war to aid the freedmen.
   (C) freed blacks who fled the South after being emancipated.
   (D) Southern governments that refused to accept the Thirteenth Amendment.
5. Andrew Johnson was impeached because
   (A) Southerners were opposed to his radical Reconstruction policies.
   (B) he failed to enforce federal law in combating the KKK.
   (C) his administration was involved in a number of corrupt activities.
   (D) he was an obstacle to the radical Republicans' Reconstruction plan.

6. In the election of 1876
   (A) the contested election was decided by the Supreme Court.
   (B) Tilden received more electoral votes but far fewer popular votes than Hayes.
   (C) most white Southerners refused to vote.
   (D) Republicans claimed that blacks had been denied the right to vote in several Southern states.

7. Which of the following did NOT attempt to disenfranchise black voters?
   (A) Force Act
   (B) Literacy test
   (C) Grandfather clause
   (D) Poll tax

8. Jim Crow laws
   (A) were ruled unconstitutional by the U.S. Supreme Court immediately following the end of the war.
   (B) were designed to subordinate blacks.
   (C) allowed for the integration of all public facilities.
   (D) were designed to address the abuses of racist organizations such as the KKK and the Knights of the White Camellia.

9. Hiram Revels
   (A) was the leader of the radical Republicans in the House of Representatives.
   (B) was head of the Freedmen's Bureau.
   (C) was the first black American elected to Congress.
   (D) was instrumental in organizing the KKK.

10. In the compromise that was reached by Republicans and Democrats over the impasse in the presidential election between Hayes and Tilden,
    (A) Tilden was given the presidency in return for selecting Republicans for every cabinet position in his administration.
    (B) the radical Republicans agreed to disband if Hayes was given the presidency.
    (C) Southerners generally voted for a third-party candidate.
    (D) Hayes was given the presidency in return for the removal of federal troops from the South.

11. To reduce racial tensions that had erupted following the end of the Civil War, Congress passed the Reconstruction Act (1867), which
    (A) divided the South into five military districts.
    (B) denied citizenship rights to those who joined racist organizations such as the Ku Klux Klan.
    (C) granted to former Confederate states financial assistance to rebuild their economies.
    (D) compelled all former Confederate states to ratify the Thirteenth Amendment.

12. "Scalawag" was the insulting label given to
    (A) Southern blacks who had fought for the Confederacy.
    (B) Southern whites who cooperated with the Reconstruction efforts of the U.S. government.
    (C) white Northerners who violently opposed the Reconstruction policies of the U.S. government.
    (D) Northerners who went south after the war to participate in the reconstruction of the South.

13. The Tenure of Office Act (1867) was instrumental in
    (A) removing Union troops from the South, thereby ending Reconstruction.
    (B) placing term limits on the executive branch.
    (C) the impeachment of President Andrew Johnson.
    (D) the rise of Southern Redeemers.

14. In the Supreme Court case *Ex parte Milligen*, the court ruled that
    (A) the Fourteenth Amendment was unconstitutional.
    (B) freedmen were entitled to possess the land they worked as slaves.
    (C) Southern states were constitutionally required to ratify the Thirteenth Amendment as a prerequisite for readmission to the Union.
    (D) citizens could not be tried by a military court if a civilian court was in session.

15. One of the most enduring legacies of the Reconstruction era was the passage of the Fifteenth Amendment, which
    (A) granted voting rights to all male American citizens regardless of race or color.
    (B) made the appointment of cabinet members a duty of the legislative branch of government.
    (C) prevents the government from suspending the writ of habeas corpus during peacetime.
    (D) abolished the institution of chattel slavery.

Short-Answer Questions

Question 1 is based on the following image.

Granger Collection

1. Based on the picture, complete the following tasks:
   A. According to the picture, what was one major success of the Reconstruction era?
   B. Provide ONE example of how the federal government supported this extension of rights.
   C. How did later events in the South undermine this success? Provide at least ONE example as historical evidence.

2. Andrew Johnson was the first president in American history to be impeached. Some historians claim that his impeachment was politically motivated.
   A. Briefly describe the differences between Johnson and Congress.
   B. Briefly describe the Tenure of Office Act.
   C. Based on the evidence, did Andrew Johnson deserve to be removed from office? Provide ONE example to support your answer.

Long-Essay Questions

1. Compare and contrast the three major Reconstruction plans: Lincoln's, Johnson's, and the radical Republicans'.

2. To what extent can Reconstruction be considered both a success and a failure?

Answers

Content Review Questions

1. **(C)** The Freedmen's Bureau, which helped poor blacks and whites, is considered an important success of Reconstruction, despite various claims that some Bureau employees were corrupt (*The American Pageant,* 14th ed., p. 511/15th ed., p. 469; Learning Objective POL-6).

2. **(D)** Option A describes the radical Republicans' Reconstruction plan. Option B is incorrect since both amendments were passed after the war. Southern citizens were never asked to repudiate the contract theory—option C. If anything, they would be asked to repudiate the compact theory, which the Supreme Court nevertheless did in the *Texas* v. *White* decision. The South was never called on to pay war reparations—option D (*The American Pageant,* 14th ed., p. 519/15th ed., p. 470; Learning Objective POL-6).

3. **(D)** The Thirteenth, Fourteenth, and Fifteenth Amendments were all passed between 1865 and 1870. The Fourteenth Amendment entitled blacks to the same citizenship rights as other Americans (*The American Pageant,* 14th ed., p. 511/15th ed., pp. 473–474; Learning Objective POL-5).

4. **(B)** Though unwelcome by some Southerners as opportunists seeking to get rich off the South's misfortune, many sacrificed the comforts of home to help the freed slaves and poor whites of the South (*The American Pageant,* 14th ed., p. 528/15th ed., pp. 478–479; Learning Objective PEO-5).

5. **(D)** President Johnson's policies conflicted with the radical Republican agenda. When he challenged the Tenure of Office Act, he was impeached (*The American Pageant,* 14th ed., p. 523/15th ed., pp. 480–481; Learning Objective POL-5).

6. **(D)** This claim threw the election into turmoil. Whites in the South generally voted Democratic—options A and D; a special electoral commission, not the Supreme Court, decided in Hayes's favor (*The American Pageant,* 14th ed., pp. 544–545/15th ed., pp. 494–495; Learning Objective POL-2).

7. **(A)** The Force Act was passed to address the abuses of groups such as the KKK (*The American Pageant,* 14th ed., pp. 529–530/15th ed., p. 480; Learning Objective POL-5).

8. **(B)** Years after the end of Reconstruction, Jim Crow laws were passed to segregate and subordinate blacks in the South (*The American Pageant,* 14th ed., p. 547/15th ed., p. 496; Learning Objective POL-6).

9. **(C)** Elected to the Senate in 1870, Revels was the first of his race to serve in Congress (*The American Pageant*, 14th ed., pp. 527–528/15th ed., p. 478; Learning Objective POL-3).

10. **(D)** This agreement effectively ended Reconstruction (*The American Pageant*, 14th ed., p. 545/15th ed., pp. 494–495; Learning Objective POL-2).

11. **(A)** In order to end racial violence and implement Reconstruction programs, the South was divided into five military districts, each commanded by a Union general (*The American Pageant*, 14th ed., p. 525/15th ed., p. 475; Learning Objective ENV-3).

12. **(B)** Some white Southerners who had opposed secession and were generally considered supporters of Reconstruction programs were given the derisive name "scalawags" (*The American Pageant*, 14th ed., p. 528/15th ed., p. 478; Learning Objective ID-5).

13. **(C)** The act forbade the president from dismissing cabinet members without Senate consent. When President Johnson fired Secretary of State Stanton, the president was impeached. The bill was initiated by the radical Republicans, who were angered by President Johnson's opposition to their Reconstruction policies. The Senate, however, voted against the president's removal from office with a one-vote majority (*The American Pageant*, 14th ed., p. 531/15th ed., pp. 480–481; Learning Objective POL-5).

14. **(D)** The Supreme Court's decision applied to wartime as well as peacetime conditions (*The American Pageant*, 14th ed., p. 526/15th ed., pp. 475–476; Learning Objective POL-5).

15. **(A)** The amendment also included the phrase "or previous condition of servitude," obviously meaning freed slaves. The Fifteenth Amendment has become one of the cornerstones of American political democracy (*The American Pageant*, 14th ed., p. 526/15th ed., p. 475; Learning Objective POL-5).

Short-Answer Questions

1. The picture is clearly showing African Americans in the South voting during the Reconstruction period, thus gaining equal political rights (for men, at least) is the success of Reconstruction. There are several ways that the federal government supported this, the clearest being the Fifteenth Amendment. You could also discuss the Fourteenth Amendment, the Ku Klux Klan Act, or the military zones in the South after the war. There are a number of ways in which this regressed by the end of Reconstruction, including the use of poll taxes, literacy tests, and grandfather clauses. You can also discuss the violent tactics and lynchings used against African Americans in the South in the late nineteenth century.

2. Andrew Johnson's tensions with Congress stemmed from a variety of sources. Johnson was a Democrat while Congress was dominated by Republicans. Johnson's views on Reconstruction varied greatly from Congress's, especially the radical Republicans', leading to his vetoing several important bills that were swiftly overridden. The Tenure of Office Act mandated that the president attain the Senate's approval before removing any official confirmed by that body, including Cabinet officials. There are several ways to respond to whether Johnson deserved to be removed from office. Although he did undermine the legislative branch and attempt to stymie the progress of Reconstruction, the law that he was impeached for breaking was trumped up for that purpose.

LONG-ESSAY QUESTIONS

1. You should point out the similarities between Lincoln's and Johnson's plans. Both sought a quick readmission process. Lincoln maintained that the political leadership of the South, not the Southern people, had seceded. The radical Republicans believed in a punitive Reconstruction plan that would also guarantee the rights of blacks. Generally speaking, the Republicans in Congress sought to enfranchise blacks and provide economic aid in the South for two reasons: to keep blacks in the South so that they would not compete with Northern laborers for jobs, and to create the nucleus of a Southern Republican party. Thus it is important to discuss Reconstruction as a struggle between the executive and legislative branches. (Historical Thinking Skill II-4: Comparison)

2. As with all questions that begin with "To what extent," there can be a wide range of responses. Organize your information based on a list of the successes and failures—categorized as economic, political, or social—of Reconstruction. Remember that the question does not ask whether Reconstruction was a success *or* a failure but to what extent it was a success *and* a failure. Thus pointing out, say, the economic accomplishments of Reconstruction may include the work of the Freedmen's Bureau and the development of black educational institutions, as well as a negative economic effect: sharecropping and the crop-lien system. (Historical Thinking Skill III-6: Historical Argumentation and III-7: Appropriate Use of Relevant Historical Evidence)

Period 6: 1865-1898

The Gilded Age

The United States was a different nation after the Civil War. No longer a nation of farmers, the nation's cities experienced immense growth as immigrants came from abroad and Americans moved around the country in search of opportunity amid a changing landscape. With the support of pro-industry administrations in Washington, D.C., the United States rapidly industrialized and big businesses—beginning with railroads—gained prominence and influence in all aspects of life. Mark Twain famously referred to the second half of the nineteenth century in the United States as the "Gilded Age," indicating that the prosperity on the surface covered up the corruption that lay underneath. While many benefited from the emergence of business and industry, many more were forced to deal with the unintended, and sometimes harmful, consequences.

Key Concepts from the College Board

6.1 The rise of big business in the United States encouraged massive migrations and urbanization, sparked government and popular efforts to reshape the U.S. economy and environment, and renewed debates over U.S. national identity.

6.2 The emergence of an industrial culture in the United States led to both greater opportunities for, and restrictions on, immigrants, minorities, and women.

6.3 The "Gilded Age" witnessed new cultural and intellectual movements in tandem with political debates over economic and social policies.

11

THE INDUSTRIAL ERA: 1876–1900

When Reconstruction ended in 1877, the United States was still a mostly agricultural nation that contained some large commercial urban areas, such as New York and Philadelphia, yet also small towns, villages, and hamlets. In many places the economic landscape had been scarcely changed by the Civil War. After all, economic development never occurs evenly in a nation. Yet by the end of the century, new major metropolitan areas such as Chicago and Pittsburgh had sprung up where a few decades earlier there had been an "urban frontier." By 1885 Chicago boasted a ten-story skyscraper. By 1900 America's urban population was three times larger than it had been just thirty years earlier. By 1920 more Americans would live in cities than on farms or in small rural towns. Think of a person who was born around 1830. When he is in his seventies he leaves, say, rural Vermont for a visit to New York City. Amazed, he sees electric trolleys and buildings that dwarf anything in the towns nearest his home. He notices that many buildings have indoor plumbing, electricity, and even telephones. Large commercial areas dot the urban landscape. Department stores are many times larger than the stores in which he has ever shopped. Urban dwellers converse with one another in languages he has never heard before, for many are foreign-born. Looking across the East River toward Brooklyn, he sees the engineering marvel of his day, a massive steel structure, the Brooklyn Bridge. Yet behind the technology, the architectural wonders, and the excitement of city life, our traveler soon notices the darker side of modernization, industry, and urbanization: poverty, congestion, pollution, corruption, and crime.

Key Concepts

- The state and federal governments played significant roles in promoting business interests.
- This period witnessed the rise of the corporation.
- Proponents and opponents of the government in assisting laissez-faire capitalism offered numerous justifications for their positions.
- The U.S. economy expanded enormously during the late nineteenth century, easily surpassing European industrial nations.
- Representing different objectives and memberships, labor unions formed, and major strikes occurred in the period.
- The Supreme Court handed down decisions that for the most part favored business by controlling unions and undoing legislation that would interfere with capital accumulation.

Industrialization and the period of rapid capital accumulation are discussed in depth in *The American Pageant,* 14th and 15th eds., Chapters 23–25.

U.S. Policy Towards Native Americans Following the Civil War

In the years following the Civil War, thousands of settlers poured into areas that were home to Native American tribes such as the Cheyenne, Nez Perce, and Lakota Sioux. Both sides committed various atrocities as white Americans and Native Americans clashed over western lands. Treaties concentrated many tribes on small reservations, where in some cases they became dependent on federal agencies. Other tribes fought on, most famously the Comanche and the Sioux. The latter, in fact, wiped out General George Armstrong Custer's entire command at the Battle of Little Big Horn in 1876. Revenge was taken at the expense of Sioux women and children who were slaughtered alongside the male warriors by U.S. troops at the Battle of Wounded Knee in 1890. Before the Native Americans were completely destroyed or placed on reservations, reformers sought other options:

Assimilation Native American children were given a Christian education (for example, the Carlisle School in Pennsylvania) that eventually would allow them to be assimilated into white American society.

The Dawes-Severalty Act Congress persuaded Native Americans to relinquish their tribal ways by granting them plots of land and citizenship if they stayed on the land for twenty-five years and made a concerted effort to become "civilized." Unfortunately, the best land had been sold to speculators, railroad companies, and mining companies, so the policy failed. Not until the 1920s did the U.S. government grant citizenship rights to Native Americans.

The Rise and Development of Industrialism in America

At the end of the Civil War the United States ranked fourth in industrial output, behind Britain, France, and Germany. By the close of the century, in many industries, the United States produced more than the other three *combined*. So extensive was U.S. industrial growth in the late nineteenth and early twentieth centuries that one historian referred to this era as "the Second American Revolution." Consider some statistics:

- Between 1869 and 1913 the GNP rose by 56 percent.
- Between 1860 and 1900 wheat and corn production, spurred by the new technology in agricultural machinery, grew by 200 percent.
- Bituminous coal production increased 2,000 percent.
- Petroleum production increased over 9,000 percent.
- Steel production increased over 10,000 percent.
- Over 150,000 miles of new railroad track was laid between 1865 and 1895.
- By the first decade of the twentieth century, the United States accounted for one-third of the world's manufacturing capacity.

By 1900 the transition of the U.S. economy to an advanced, centralized, and government-supported industrial-capitalist system was complete in every region of the nation. (This is not to imply, however, that every region experienced industrialization and the impact of technology simultaneously.) As the United States entered the twentieth century it was well on its way to becoming a nation of industry, large urban areas, interconnected economies, and large-scale business enterprises. While much of this transformation was occurring in the nation's industrial hub, the Northeast, the West and the South were experiencing profound changes as well. The South, which had been devastated by the Civil War, experienced dramatic economic growth and diversification. Before the century was out, major southern cities such as Birmingham, Alabama, and Memphis, Tennessee, were producing enormous amounts of steel and lumber. In large part the availability of cheap labor (southern workers faced even more significant obstacles in organizing unions than their counterparts in the North), well-developed transportation and communication systems, and the acceptance of capitalist principles played central roles in the development of the New South. Out West, as the frontiers of the nation expanded, so too did industry and commerce. Stimulated by demand in the East and aided by the continuing construction of an integrated national railway system, western cattle and mining industries flourished. What accounts for this incredible transformation? Remember that every effect has numerous causes.

AP Tip

A College Board essay dealing with this period will most certainly require you to understand the causes and effects of the enormous expansion of the U.S. economy in the post–Civil War period.

Although less active than today, the federal government in the late nineteenth century played a decisive role in promoting business interests.

- The federal government imposed protective tariffs.
- The government encouraged a boom in railroad construction through, for instance, land grants (over 200 million acres were offered to railroad companies by states and the federal government). The Pacific Railroad Act not only provided enormous tracts of land to railroad companies but also granted them substantial loans as well. Unfortunately, the price of western land rose higher than what the government intended when railroad companies sold their surplus land at ever-higher prices.
- By aiding in the settlement of the West, a national market was created. When the Republican Congress passed the Homestead Act, in 1862, it freed up many acres of excellent land for settlers moving to the West.
- Mineral-rich land was sold by the Public Land Office for as little as $2.50 an acre.
- The federal government adopted a loose immigration policy that, by providing more laborers, increased production and demand in the domestic market. While the problem of labor shortages was effectively addressed by this policy, it also had the undesired effect of driving down wages for laborers.
- The government also encouraged capital investment by leaving large-scale businesses virtually untaxed.
- Foreign capital investments helped stimulate the creation of new industries and businesses in the United States.

The ascendancy of the corporation was the result of the capitalist class's success in controlling the free market system, thereby ensuring profitability and economic growth. This was accomplished by

- regulating production
- creating stable markets
- setting prices and wages

The following were factors that brought about the enormous production of industrial commodities, which in turn concentrated considerable wealth in the hands of the nation's most successful capitalists:

- new technological developments, such as the steam engine, conveyer belt, and better construction materials (steel)
- a huge labor force of men, women, and even children
- large-scale factories and production centers
- an enormous amount of capital

With abundant resources—technological, economic, and human—and little government restraint, some larger-than-life personalities emerged from the capitalist class.

- **Andrew Carnegie** A poor Scottish immigrant, he eventually came to dominate the steel industry. Using new technological innovations such as the Bessemer process, he was able to produce better steel at a lower price than his competitors. With considerable surplus capital at his disposal, he purchased everything necessary for the production of steel, such as land rich in iron-ore deposits (the Mesabi Range in Minnesota), and railroads and ships to transport the ore. This is called vertical integration—the control of all the steps necessary to turn raw materials into finished commodities. He retired in 1900 after selling his corporation to J. P. Morgan, but not before playing a major role in the development of the modern corporation. In his retirement he became a philanthropist and a living example to the defenders of the capitalist system that anyone could get rich in America.
- **John D. Rockefeller** Even at a young age he had his eyes set on accumulating great wealth. He paid a substitute to serve for him in the Civil War and set about amassing his fortune. His name was synonymous with the oil industry, which he came to control. He further concentrated his wealth through a variety of often extralegal methods such as the creation of trusts, horizontal and vertical integrations, and the holding company. Although oil prices decreased significantly (in early 1861 from $10 a barrel to merely 10 cents later that year), Rockefeller's Standard Oil controlled approximately 90 percent of the nation's oil market. Prices again rose, but to an acceptable level.
- **William H. Vanderbilt** Like his father, Cornelius (who once ranted at a competitor, "I won't sue you . . . I'll ruin you!"), William was a railroad magnate. For decades the family dominated the railroad industry.
- **J. P. Morgan** An investment banker, he was instrumental in funding corporations. By eliminating cutthroat competition in the railroad industry, whereby competing companies drove down prices and thus their own profits, he was able to consolidate rival railroad lines. He later went on to create U.S. Steel, the nation's first billion-dollar corporation. Due to a skin ailment, he had an enormously bulbous nose. His piercing eyes added to his persona. Morgan was also lucky. At the last minute he canceled a cruise on a luxury liner, the *Titanic*.

The Era of Rapid Capital Accumulation

For every Rockefeller or Carnegie success story, there were millions of citizens who lived in squalor and despair in America's industrial urban areas. Trade unions and social settlement houses as well as a few municipal aid societies tried to help the destitute worker and his family, but for most, life in industrial America was severe. Industrialists and their adherents continued to press for limited regulation of business and limited social spending to address poverty. After all, they argued, America was a land of opportunity for those willing to work hard, maintain self-discipline, and overcome whatever obstacles stood in the way of advancement and financial success. Few really believed that given these attributes you could become a Carnegie or a Morgan, but defenders of the status quo maintained that social mobility was available to all who sought it. Further, they contended, business functioned best when government limited its intervention. In 1776, the same year the American colonies declared their independence from Britain, economist Adam Smith had published *The Wealth of Nations,* a book that would become the economic bible for those later generations that favored limited government intervention (laissez-faire) in the affairs of business. Smith's thesis was that prices and wages and supply and demand were already regulated, not by government, but by the "invisible hand" (a self-seeking equilibrium) of the marketplace. A capitalist, Smith maintained, will not sell a commodity that is too costly for the consumer, nor will he offer wages that are unattractive to workers. Taking into account his costs to produce a commodity, the capitalist will naturally seek out a balance between costs and profit. The result is that supply will ultimately equal demand and the capitalist will realize a profit, all without government's "artificial" interference.

Yet most capitalists were not necessarily opposed to all government intervention—they were happy to see tariffs imposed—but they rejected any regulations that could reduce profits. Following the Civil War the U.S. government assisted industrial capitalism by protecting it from challenges by those who sought its regulation.

The relationship between government and big business took on two forms:

- State and federal court systems were used to prevent regulation of business by state legislatures. One critic has claimed that the Supreme Court became the "handmaiden" of private enterprise.
- Trade unions were suppressed. Again, the federal court system was enlisted to achieve this goal. The Supreme Court fortified its protection of private enterprise under the "due process" clause in a series of landmark cases. Police, state militias, and the U.S. Army were also used to suppress labor activities.

The outcome of this view was, in many industries, not fair and equal competition, but the rise of monopoly capitalism. Ironically, the same competition that would drive capitalism was marginalized by monopolies, which sought to reduce competition.

With this view in mind, justifications that reinforced this idea of laissez-faire capitalism were developed to complement Smith's thesis. While certainly not a homogeneous group, advocates of the views presented below all saw capitalism, especially laissez-faire capitalism, as a highly developed step in social evolution.

- **Social Darwinism** Possibly the most influential justification of laissez-faire capitalism, this philosophy was developed by British social philosopher Herbert Spencer and popularized in the United States by Yale University's William Graham Sumner. It applied Charles Darwin's theory of evolution and natural selection to government, the marketplace, and society. Social Darwinists argued that government should not provide assistance to those who were unable to make it on their own, businesses and private citizens alike. Rather, society's "fittest," the wealthy, should be protected because it was this class through its development of businesses and as financial contributors to educational and cultural institutions that was improving the species.

- **Horatio Alger** His rags-to-riches stories popularized the notion that self-sacrifice, determination, and hard work could overcome poverty and result in financial success and social status. His fictional characters, such as Mark the Matchstick Boy, became an inspiration to young men pursuing the American Dream.
- **Russell Conwell** For those who were poor and could see no way out of their predicament, Conwell's "Acres of Diamonds" sermon was deflating to say the least: "It is your duty to get rich. It is wrong to be poor." Now the poor were not only destitute, they were "wrong" as well. Yet this view mirrored nicely the Social Darwinist notion that, as Shakespeare put it, "The fault . . . is not in our stars, But in ourselves, that we are underlings."
- **Carnegie's "Gospel of Wealth"** Why Carnegie ultimately became a philanthropist was explained in his article "(Gospel of) Wealth": It is the duty of the wealthy to contribute to society the wealth they have accrued through philanthropic programs. In other words, the wealthy, not government, was society's benefactor.

People who were most directly affected by the social consequences of industrialization advocated for reforms that would alleviate much of the suffering they were enduring socially, economically, and politically. Unfortunately, their political influence paled in comparison with the entrenched capitalist class. Reformers were not without their allies, however, for citizens who were important politically, religiously, and economically viewed reform as a way to prevent the radicalization and potentially revolutionary tendencies of the working class. For them, capitalism could be democratized, and qualitative changes could be made to living and working conditions without jettisoning the free market system. Still others interpreted Darwinism noticeably differently from the way Social Darwinists did. These Reform Darwinists maintained that through planning and cooperation, human evolution could and should overcome many of the challenges and obstacles that confronted previous generations. The following groups raised concerns about the impact of unregulated capitalism on the economy and society:

- **Journalists** such as Edward Bellamy, Henry George, and Henry D. Lloyd wrote articles critical of big business's "unethical" practices and monopolistic tendencies. One of their goals was to compel the government to impose regulations that would maintain the competitive nature of capitalism. Bellamy's *Looking Backward,* for instance, envisions a future world in which government applies socialist principles to society and the economy, such as the nationalization of industry. George's *Progress and Poverty* proposed a tax on land value that he believed would prevent economic depression and reduce the gap between rich and poor.
- **Small producers** such as farmers complained of artificially inflated shipping rates that drove up their costs and increased commodity prices. Small businessmen complained that their powerful

competitors engaged in unfair labor practices, which drove them out of business.

- **Consumers** demanded probing investigations into the ways that corporations used their control of the market to charge exorbitant prices. Many opposed trade barriers, removal of which would permit the law of supply and demand to operate effectively.
- **Social reformers** such as those associated with the social gospel movement, a Christian liberal following, established social settlement houses.
- **Radicals and revolutionaries** such as anarchists, socialists (led by Eugene Debs), and Marxists maintained that capitalism was inherently exploitative and must be replaced by a more humane economic system.

LABOR UNIONS AND LABOR STRIKES

Disgusted by the poverty wages they were receiving while the owners of the means of production were reaping enormous profits, workers organized into trade unions that agitated for change. It is important to note that the methods and goals of trade unions were often quite disparate. The four major national trade unions in the late nineteenth century were

- **National Labor Union (NLU)** Formed right after the end of the Civil War, in many ways this union was years ahead of its time. It was the first trade union to organize workers regardless of their race and gender, whether they were skilled or unskilled. It was open to workers in both the agrarian and industrial sectors of the economy. Some of its goals were more modest (higher wages, the eight-hour workday) than others (gender and racial equality). At a time when the ten-hour workday was the norm and many workers toiled even longer hours, it was able to win the eight-hour workday for federal employees.
- **Knights of Labor** Organized in 1869 and led by Terence Powderly, its objectives were often radical though its methods were more modest. Like the NLU, which sought racial and gender equality, Powderly preferred arbitration to the strike. Its membership peaked at nearly three-quarters of a million members before its star faded in the wake of the Haymarket riots in 1886.
- **American Federation of Labor (AFL)** Very much a "bread and butter" union that was not out to change the world but to achieve what it considered were realistic and attainable goals, the AFL under its president, Samuel Gompers, was open exclusively to skilled workers. Far from being reform-minded, Gompers used the power of his membership (1 million by the turn of the century) to win concessions from management. By the standards of its time, it was more successful than the other major unions. Even so, it was not nearly as potent as it would become in the twentieth century.
- **Industrial Workers of the World (IWW)** If you were a radical imbued with a revolutionary spirit and willing to challenge the owners for control of the factories and businesses, the IWW was your ticket. The Wobblies, as they were called, were not content with merely increasing wages; ownership of the means of

production by the working class was the only solution to the exploitative nature of the wage labor system, they believed. Sometimes violent, sometimes victimized by the government, the IWW presented a perspective of labor and social agitation that few unions could match. Naturally, they were led by a colorful figure, "Big Bill" Haywood.

You should also know the causes and effects of the major labor strikes of the period.

- **Railroad Strike of 1877** This was the first major post–Civil War strike and was indicative of labor unrest following the war. Employees of the Baltimore and Ohio struck when the company lowered their wages. The strike soon turned violent, and ultimately President Hayes called out the U.S. Army to suppress the strike.
- **Haymarket Square (Chicago) Riot of 1886** A labor demonstration organized to protest the treatment of workers at the nearby McCormick Harvester factory as well as methods used by police in dealing with the protestors abruptly ended when an unknown assailant threw a bomb that killed a number of police officers who had been ordered to break up the demonstration. Although there was no proof that they had been involved, eight anarchists were arrested, four of whom were executed. The public blamed trade unions for the violence.
- **The Homestead (Pennsylvania) Strike of 1892** Despite higher profits, the Carnegie Steel Company cut workers' wages. Accordingly, the workers went on strike. This in turn provided the company an opportunity to crush the union by hiring a private security company, the Pinkerton Detective Agency, to engage the strikers. When the strikers opened fire on the Pinkertons, killing several, the state militia was called in. Out of funds and out of hope, the union itself ended the strike.
- **The Pullman Strike of 1894** To be sure, no one likes to have his or her wages cut. Having it done during a major depression, however, so that the company can maintain stockholders' dividends, is demoralizing, to say the least. But that's what happened to employees of the Pullman Palace Car Company. A number of workers were even laid off. Led by the American Railway Union and its president, the soon-to-be head of the Socialist party Eugene Debs, a boycott was established that greatly affected the railroad industry in the Midwest. Members of the Railway Managers Association responded by calling on the federal government to intervene; they argued that the strikers were in restraint of trade. An injunction by a federal court, citing the Sherman Antitrust Act, did little to stop the strikers. The boycott was ended when President Cleveland sent in troops to make certain that the strikers did not interfere with the train delivery of the U.S. mail and when Debs and other union leaders were jailed for violating the federal injunction.

The Supreme Court, Congress, and State Legislatures Weigh in

The executive branch was not the only ally of big business. The judicial and legislative branches were also fundamental to the expansion of monopoly capitalism. However, on the state level actions were taken to address the needs of the exploited and impoverished lower classes. Essential to this concern was the Fourteenth Amendment, which defines citizenship rights. Specifically, the due process clause of this amendment, which gave state governments an indispensable responsibility to protect the life, liberty, and property of its citizens, was taken to mean by more reform-minded state governments that they had the authority to enact legislation that would address issues such as work and living conditions. A short list of problems addressed by such legislation would include

- housing laws
- regulating safety and health conditions in the workplace
- regulating corporations when their behavior and actions contradicted the well-being of citizens and of the capitalist system
- sanitation laws
- minimum wage and maximum hour laws
- child labor laws

Reform governments were motivated to take such bold action for a variety of reasons:

- Many feared that the lower classes might demonstrate and riot if conditions deteriorated even further. In order to defuse this agitation, reforms to quell any potential revolutionary or radical spirit that might emanate from the masses were needed.
- Some individuals in positions of power were motivated by altruistic tendencies. For whatever personal and philosophical reasons, they could no longer maintain their neutrality given the abuses that swirled around them.
- The lower classes pressed the government to act on their behalf.

Paradoxically, many of these reforms were ruled unconstitutional by state and federal governments and the Supreme Court on the grounds that they violated corporations' due process rights! In other words, in *Wabash, St. Louis & Pacific Railway Company* v. *Illinois* (1886) the Court ruled that corporations had the same Fourteenth Amendment rights as citizens; they were entitled to due process rights. One major piece of legislation and one federal court case sum up the sentiments of the nation's political and legal vanguard in the late nineteenth century:

- **The Sherman Anti-Trust Act** The key clause of this law holds that "any combination or condition which is *in restraint of trade* is illegal." Many historians and political scientists have traditionally interpreted this to mean that the legislative branch was acting on behalf of the nation's economic system and its citizens by attacking monopolies (which, after all, seek to limit competition). Other historians claim the opposite is true. The act was passed in order to defuse public criticism of corporations, to restore the legitimacy of the government as the supporter of the public interest and not a mere appendage of business, and to attack trade unions. In the end, they argue, due to government undertakings such as the Sherman Anti-Trust Act, monopoly capitalism was preserved, and unions that went out on strike were promptly served with a court injunction for being in restraint of trade.

- ***United States*** **v.** ***E. C. Knight Company*** After purchasing a competitor, the American Sugar Refining Company, the E. C. Knight Company controlled approximately 98 percent of the sugar refining industry. Because of its economic power, E. C. Knight could prevent further challenges to its domination and determine market prices for its product. In retrospect, this appears to be a textbook example of a monopoly. But not so to the pro-business Supreme Court in the late nineteenth century. The Court ruling involved a rather creative rationale: because E. C. Knight was engaged in *manufacturing* sugar and not in interstate *commerce* (at least within the meaning of the law), it was regulated by state and not federal law. Therefore, it could not be dismantled by the federal government.

Maximizing Profits: The Rationale and Tactics of the Capitalist Class

To increase profits, a capitalist has to find a way to neutralize the competition. If you consider that capitalists are playing a game, albeit a very serious one, then understanding why they seek to concentrate as much capital as possible will help you comprehend the turn American businesses and the economy in general took in this period. The concentration of capital was accomplished in a number of ways, including

- using pools, gentlemen's agreements, mergers (horizontal and vertical), holding companies, and conglomerates
- cutting prices in the hope that the competition would not be able to sustain a loss of profits
- introducing labor-saving technology when the outlay of capital for new production technology is not so prohibitive as to be harmful
- expanding commodities into a competitor's marketplace
- engaging in industrial spying (for instance, the theft of research and development information)
- employing innovations in industrial and managerial organization and techniques

Because a major cost in the production process is labor, reducing this expense can not only lead to greater profits; it can allow the capitalist to use surplus funds to reinvest in the business, making it even more efficient and therefore more competitive. Naturally, trade unions, which seek higher wages and shorter hours, not to mention medical insurance, drive up the cost of production. Not surprisingly, unions were the bane of the capitalists' existence. Various tactics and methods were used by the capitalists to counteract trade union activities:

- The open shop gave workers a choice as to whether they must join a union if they work in a certain industry. Obviously, unions opposed the open shop because it undermined collective bargaining, the source of unions' effectiveness and strength; the potency of labor demands in a particular industry relates to the number of workers who are unionized.
- Replacement workers (derisively called "scabs" by union members) who are willing to take the jobs of those out on strike and often work for less pay were hired.
- Government was used to suppress trade union activities, such as strikes.
- Blacklists prevented union organizers and activists from employment opportunities.
- Workers were compelled to sign yellow-dog contracts in which they agreed not to join a union.
- Subsistence wages were offered while the workday was often lengthened.
- Labor was intensified—informally referred to as "speed up."
- Low-wage immigrants, women, and children were employed.
- Divisions were created within the working class by paying differentiated wages, often based on race.

Workers, however, had their own tactics in attempting to convince their employers to recognize their unions as the legitimate collective bargaining agent:

- Closed shop meant that union membership was required. The rationale behind this seemingly undemocratic policy is to counteract the tactics of the employees.
- Unions picketed noncompliant businesses in the hope that the public would ally itself with the workers on strike.
- They slowed down the production process, which naturally reduces profits.
- They used sabotage to destroy company property.
- Workers physically occupied the factory or workplace ("sit-down strike"), though this was more popular in the 1930s than in the late nineteenth century.

Despite these tactics, membership in U.S. trade unions never exceeded more than 3 percent by the turn of the century.

As the nineteenth century came to a close, the United States had reached new heights in its economic development. To be sure, it had taken its place among the other economic giants of the Western world. Its growth was testimony to the enormous productive capabilities of the capitalist system. What is more, enormous fortunes had been made and important companies were created, many of which continue to shape our lives. But a substantial price had been paid in terms of misery, poverty, and the despair of America's wage laborers. True, America's workers did experience an improvement in their standard of living, but the industrial process reduced them to mere cogs in the machine. Although the federal government had failed to address the plight of the nation's workers, it recognized their contribution in at least one way. In 1894 the U.S. Congress made Labor Day a national holiday.

Content Review Questions

1. Andrew Carnegie's use of the vertical integration was significant in that it
   (A) synthesized the various immigrant labor groups into one cohesive productive force.
   (B) led to substantial cooperation between industry and banking.
   (C) stimulated competition in the steel industry.
   (D) allowed a capitalist to control all aspects of the production process.
2. Which of the following statements accurately reflects the impact that industrialization had on the American worker?
   (A) The standard of living for most workers had declined by the late nineteenth century.
   (B) The standard of living for most workers improved by the late nineteenth century, but workers had become mere mechanisms in the production process.
   (C) Many wage laborers ultimately saved enough of their salaries to start their own small businesses.
   (D) Most workers experienced ever higher wages and even greater control over what they produced.
3. In his "Gospel of Wealth," Andrew Carnegie articulated the view that
   (A) the wealthy were entitled to their riches and had no responsibility to share it with others.
   (B) only those born into wealth were the real economic leaders of the nation.
   (C) religious leaders had a responsibility to convince their parishioners that success was attainable to those who worked hard.
   (D) the wealthy were morally obligated to use some of their wealth for the improvement of society.
4. By the late nineteenth century
   (A) the U.S. economy ranked fourth in the industrialized world.
   (B) the United States had bypassed France and Germany in industrial output, but still lagged behind Great Britain.
   (C) the U.S. economy was producing as much as Britain, France, and Germany combined in many sectors.
   (D) the U.S. economy had not grown significantly since the 1860s.
5. The Industrial Workers of the World differed from the other major trade unions in that
   (A) it sought to negotiate and mediate its differences with management.
   (B) unlike the other unions, it disdained using boycotts and strikes against capital.
   (C) its objective was to eliminate the private ownership of the means of production.
   (D) it was outlawed by the U.S. government.

6. Which of the following would NOT be used by a supporter of the capitalist system as it existed in the Gilded Age?
   (A) Reform Darwinism
   (B) Russell Conwell's, "Acres of Diamonds" sermon
   (C) The novels of Horatio Alger
   (D) The perspective held by Herbert Spencer
7. In order to promote the interests of labor, trade unions would support
   (A) collective bargaining.
   (B) subsistence wages.
   (C) yellow-dog contracts.
   (D) the closed shop.
8. The railroad strike of 1877
   (A) was the first time a president ordered U.S. troops to stop a strike.
   (B) led to significant wage increases for railroad workers.
   (C) was the first time that management recognized the legitimacy of a trade union.
   (D) led to significant improvements in worker safety laws but not wage increases.
9. This capitalist created U.S. Steel, the nation's first billion-dollar corporation.
   (A) Andrew Carnegie
   (B) J. P. Morgan
   (C) Cornelius Vanderbilt
   (D) John D. Rockefeller
10. In *United States* v. *E. C. Knight Company,* the Supreme Court ruled that
    (A) trade unions that were on strike were in restraint of trade.
    (B) monopolies such as the E. C. Knight Company were illegal combinations.
    (C) because the company was involved in production and not commerce, it fell under state jurisdiction.
    (D) vertical integration was not in restraint of trade.
11. Which initially secret labor organization formed after the Civil War sought to include all workers in "one big union" for skilled and unskilled workers regardless of race or gender?
    (A) Industrial Workers of the World
    (B) American Federation of Labor
    (C) Congress of Industrial Organization
    (D) Knights of Labor
12. The Union Pacific and Central Pacific railroad companies were instrumental in
    (A) hiring workers regardless of race or religion.
    (B) establishing the nation's first transcontinental railroad.
    (C) establishing the nation's first eight-hour workday.
    (D) connecting the Northeast with the upper Midwest for business and travel purposes.

13. What 1887 legislation forbade pools and rebates and compelled railroads to publish their rates?
    (A) Pendleton Act
    (B) Sherman Anti-Trust Act
    (C) Interstate Commerce Act
    (D) Mann-Elkins Act

14. Andrew Carnegie maintained that the wealthy had an obligation to use some of their riches justly and for the benefit of society as articulated in
    (A) the "Gospel of Wealth".
    (B) Social Darwinism.
    (C) The Octopus.
    (D) the *Acres of Diamonds* speech.

15. J. P. Morgan consolidated rival businesses and eliminated competitive discord by placing his bank officers on those businesses' boards of directors. This creates what is termed
    (A) horizontal integration.
    (B) vertical integration.
    (C) monopoly.
    (D) interlocking directorates.

Short-Answer Questions

1. Several unions were founded and grew in the second half of the nineteenth century in response to issues workers faced as the nation industrialized. The unions had different philosophies, goals, and memberships. Choose ONE of the following unions:
   - American Federation of Labor
   - Knights of Labor
   - Industrial Workers of the World (Wobblies)

   A. Describe the union's membership, philosophy, and tactics.
   B. Why might this union have a better chance of accomplishing its goals than other unions? Provide at least ONE example in comparison.

Question 2 is based on the following cartoon:

Library of Congress

2. Based on the cartoon, respond to the following:
   A. What is Rockefeller's relationship to the government during the "Gilded Age"?
   B. How might this relationship lead to efforts to reform big business and break up trusts later on?

Long-Essay Questions

1. To what extent did government assist in the rise of corporate capitalism following the Civil War?
2. The trade union movement in the post–Civil War era successfully organized workers and achieved its economic goals.

   To what extent is this statement true?

Answers

Content Review Questions

1. **(D)** Vertical integration allowed Carnegie, for example, to cut out the "middleman" by owning businesses necessary for the production of a commodity (*The American Pageant*, 14th ed., p. 575/15th ed., p. 521; Learning Objective WXT-3).

2. **(B)** While there was an increase in worker salaries, the laboring class had little control over the production process. In other words, they were dispensable (*The American Pageant*, 14th ed., p. 585/15th ed., p. 528; Learning Objective WXT-5).

3. **(D)** This helps to explain why Carnegie became a philanthropist after he retired from business. His contributions made Carnegie Hall and the Carnegie Endowment for Peace possible (*The American Pageant*, 14th ed., pp. 579–580/15th ed., p. 525; Learning Objective WXT-5).

4. **(C)** Incredibly, the United States ranked fourth after the Civil War and more than bypassed the other three major industrial nations by the turn of the century (this material does not appear in the text; Learning Objective WXT-6).

5. **(C)** Composed of radicals, the IWW wanted to eliminate private ownership of factories and major businesses (this material does not appear in the text; Learning Objective WXT-7).

6. **(A)** Options B–E justify, condone, or support the capitalist class's control of society, government, and business (this material does not appear in the text; Learning Objective CUL-5).

7. **(D)** Options A–D would harm the interests of workers, whereas the closed shop would increase union membership (*The American Pageant*, 14th ed., p. 589/15th ed., p. 536; Learning Objective WXT-7).

8. **(A)** President Hayes became the first U.S. president to use troops to quell a strike (*The American Pageant*, 14th ed., pp. 548–549/15th ed., p. 497; Learning Objective WXT-6).

9. **(B)** In 1900, Morgan bought Andrew Carnegie's steel business for more than $400 million and combined it with other holdings to create U.S. Steel (*The American Pageant*, 14th ed., p. 577/15th ed., p. 523; Learning Objective WXT-6).

10. **(C)** Ruling in the company's favor the Court interpreted the meanings of commerce and production in a literal and narrow sense (this material does not appear in the text; Learning Objective WXT-6).

11. **(D)** Whereas the National Labor Union included skilled and unskilled workers, as well as farmers and some blacks and women, the Knights of Labor welcomed all workers no matter their race, gender, or line of work. It was therefore extremely democratic, especially given that it was formed when racial and gender-based discrimination were rampant (*The American Pageant,* 14th ed., p. 588/15th ed., pp. 533–535; Learning Objective WXT-7).

12. **(B)** The two major railroad companies linked up at Promontory Point, Utah, in May 1869, establishing the nation's first transcontinental railroad (*The American Pageant,* 14th ed., p. 569/15th ed., pp. 514–515; Learning Objective WXT-3).

13. **(C)** The Act also established the Interstate Commerce Commission, to supervise the application of federal regulations (*The American Pageant,* 14th ed., p. 573/15th ed., p. 519; Learning Objective WXT-8).

14. **(A)** After selling U.S. Steel to J. P. Morgan, Carnegie spent the remainder of his life as a philanthropist. His financial contributions helped build libraries, pensions, and other institutions so that he would not die in "disgrace," given the enormous sum of money he accrued during his business career (*The American Pageant,* 14th ed., p. 579/15th ed., p. 525; Learning Objective CUL-5).

15. **(D)** Morgan's use of interlocking directorates concentrated wealth in the hands of a few corporations (and thus drove out competition), but did bring some stability to the marketplace (*The American Pageant,* 14th ed., p. 575/15th ed., p. 522; Learning Objective WXT-3).

Short-Answer Questions

1. Each union is distinct—the American Federation of Labor (AFL) only admitted skilled workers, and they only allowed white males to be members. Moreover, the union was anti-strike, preferring other methods of achieving their goals. The Knights of Labor was much more inclusive, allowing women and immigrants and catering to unskilled workers. The Knights of Labor participated in some of the more violent strikes of the late nineteenth century, although they also supported less extreme methods. The Industrial Workers of the World, or Wobblies (IWW), were socialists and therefore much maligned. In terms of effectiveness, you could start with the fact that the AFL is the only one that still exists, but it is also worthwhile to think about which union would incur the government's wrath the least.

2. The cartoon portrays Rockefeller's power and influence over federal government. This led to reform efforts in a number of ways, as groups that did not share in the wealth generated by corporations or were trampled by them mobilized to see these large businesses broken up. The strikes and rise of unions in

the Gilded Age are also examples of reform efforts in this arena.

Long-Essay Questions

1. You may want to begin your essay with a brief discussion of the expansion of the role of government during the Civil War and its continued expansion in the postwar era. Policies that the government used to assist corporations include a protective tariff and land grants to railroad companies. Keep in mind that the question is asking "to what extent" the government assisted. Also, discuss the role played in suppressing labor as well as the pro-business decisions handed down by state and federal courts. (Historical Thinking Skills I-3: Periodization, III-6: Historical Argumentation and IV-8: Interpretation)

2. You should indicate that the growth of industry and corporate capitalism during and after the Civil War led to tensions between the capitalists and their employees. Keeping in mind that the government and business were allied, you may want to briefly discuss the various strikes and the responses of the government and capitalists to them as well as the divisions within labor itself—some unions were more radical than others; some were exclusionary based on race or skill level. Thus a response may indicate that trade unions were generally successful in organizing workers but not particularly successful in achieving their goals. (Historical Thinking Skills II-5: Contextualization, III-7: Appropriate Use of Relevant Historical Evidence, and IV-9: Synthesis)

12

Postwar Politics and the Populists: 1870s–1896

Republican administrations, which dominated the federal government in the late nineteenth century, did much to support the rise of big business. The populists represented a wide coalition of groups that had a broad political platform. With the demise of the movement, many would find a home in the Democratic Party.

Key Concepts

- Republican presidents dominated the postwar era and tended to support big business.
- The Grange, Farmers' Alliances, and Populists emerged to contest big business's control over the marketplace.
- The Populists were a diverse coalition that sought to confront a wide variety of urban and rural problems.
- The Populists and Democratic Party fused in the late nineteenth century.

This period is discussed in depth in *The American Pageant*, 14th ed., Chapters 23–26 and 15th ed., Chapters 23–24, 26.

Politics in the Gilded Age

Despite his success as a military leader, Ulysses S. Grant's two terms in the White House (1869–1877) were anything but stellar. In fact, historians consistently rank Grant among the two or three worst presidents in the nation's history. Skilled on the battlefield, Grant obviously lost his edge upon becoming president. Although honest himself, he was surrounded by corrupt officials, friends, and appointees who did not know or care to know the meanings of honesty and responsibility. But with a diminished Democratic Party, at least in the North and West (it was very strong in the South), Americans ultimately were faced with a dubious task of selecting from different varieties of Republicans. This they did with great regularity. In fact, with the exception of Grover Cleveland's two nonconsecutive terms (1885–1889 and 1893–1897), the United States did not elect a Democrat to serve in the White House until Woodrow Wilson's victory in the 1912 election. Unfortunately for the American people, the vast majority of presidents who served the nation after the Civil War and until the turn of the century were mediocre political leaders. The administrations of Hayes, Garfield, Arthur, and Harrison reflected the political stalemate and patronage problems that shaped the Gilded Age as well as a desire by many Americans for a "do-little" government following the abuses that occurred in Grant's terms.

- **Hayes** Although his election (or, critics would say, selection) ended Reconstruction, he did try to restore honesty to government after the corruption that plagued the Grant administration. Towards that end, Hayes supported social movements advocating temperance. As industrialization progressed under his administration, he sought to limit Chinese immigration.
- **Garfield** Because of an assassin's bullet, he served only four months, but his election reflected the bitter division that existed within the Republican Party between the conservative "Stalwarts" (led by Senator Roscoe Conkling) and the more reform-minded "Halfbreeds" (led by James Blaine). The commonality between the two wings of the Republican Party was that they both vied for power in order to have access to treasured patronage positions. A third wing of the Republican Party, the Mugwumps, refused to join the patronage game. Eventually, the patronage problem was addressed in 1883 by the Pendleton Act, which established the Civil Service Commission.
- **Arthur** No reformer, he nonetheless distanced himself from the Stalwarts and supported civil service reform such as the Pendleton Act to address the problems of patronage and nepotism in government hiring practices. A supporter of a strong navy, his opposition to a high protective tariff cost him his party's renomination as president in 1884.
- **Harrison** In a long line of second-rate presidents, Harrison may very well be considered the most mediocre. More Americans voted for his opponent, Cleveland, but Harrison received more electoral votes, and therefore the presidency. In his one term in office, he played second fiddle to Congress—the legislative branch in this era was generally more influential. The emergence of the executive branch as the more dominant force coincided with the growing crises, both domestic and in foreign affairs, faced by the United States at the turn of the century.

The Tariff (Again) and the "Billion Dollar Congress"

The tariff issue, always lurking below the surface, yet again played a role in the politics of the nineteenth century. The combatants this time were western farmers and eastern capitalists. During the war, the United States had been able to adopt a high protective tariff (the Morrill Tariff of 1861) because the southern obstacle to such a bill was no longer present in Congress. Not long after the war's end, southern Democrats and some of their northern Democratic allies objected to a high protective tariff on the grounds that it would increase the price of consumer goods as well as perhaps provoke a retaliatory tariff by foreign producers affected by the tax. As the agrarian sector began producing more and more food, foreign markets were increasingly playing a larger role in their sales. In the election campaign of 1888, an important question shaped the debate: Was a (high) protective tariff necessary? It was a question that for the first time in many years truly differentiated the two major political parties. Republican candidate Harrison and his party were able to convince many voters that lowering the tariff would wreck business prosperity and lead to mass unemployment, an issue that resonated with the nation's laboring classes. Not only was a Republican returned to the White House, where Harrison safeguarded the tariff but the party also had majorities in both houses of Congress. The new Republican Congress was active over the next decade politically and fiscally. (It became known as the first "billion-dollar Congress" due to its enormous expenditures.) Key pieces of legislation passed by this Congress include

- the McKinley Tariff of 1890
- the Sherman Silver Purchase Act of 1890
- the Sherman Anti-Trust Act of 1890
- the Wilson-Gorman Act of 1894, which increased the tariff
- increased monthly pensions to Civil War veterans and their families (a transparent attempt, opponents claimed, for the Republican Party to retain the support of northern Civil War veterans and their families)

Although the tariff was a significant issue in the election, for many Americans it was not the only political issue. Possibly even more controversial was the debate over currency.

Debate over Expanding the Money Supply

Following the end of Reconstruction the nation engaged in an intense debate over whether to expand the amount of money in the economy. (Recall how this issue developed into a politically explosive controversy during the second Jackson term.) Too little money could have serious consequences for the financial system, not to mention those who would benefit or be hurt by one policy or the other.

Supporters of an expanded money supply included expectant capitalists, debtors, and farmers because this would enable them to

- borrow money at lower interest rates
- pay off their loans faster and easier with inflated dollars
- increase prices for the commodities they produced

After an economic depression called the Panic of 1873, many Americans suspected that the cause of the slump was the government's policy of backing its currency with gold, which restricted and therefore contracted the amount of money in the system. They favored a "soft" (or inflationary) currency (greenbacks) as well as unlimited minting of silver coins, which is also more inflationary than gold.

Opponents of an expanded money supply included bankers, entrenched capitalists (established businesses), creditors, and investors. They favored a "hard" (or deflationary) policy in which currency was backed by gold in U.S. government vaults. The benefits of this policy would be

- to allow currency to hold its value, since gold-backed money is less susceptible to inflationary instabilities
- to increase the value of gold as the population expanded (which it ultimately did, by as much as 300 percent in the thirty-year period following the end of the war)

In the short term the supporters of a hard money supply won out when Congress passed the Specie Resumption Act, in 1875, and thus withdrew the last of the greenbacks from circulation. Advocates of a soft money policy responded by creating the Greenback party to counteract the deflationary effects of the Specie Resumption Act. In the 1878 congressional elections, Greenback candidates received over 1 million votes, and fourteen of their candidates were elected. The most noteworthy of these was James B. Weaver, of Iowa, who would soon go on to form a broader party, the Populists. As for the Greenback party, it died out when the economic hard times of the 1870s ended, though the goal of expanding the supply of money was still very much alive. In the 1870s when Congress halted the coining of silver (referred to by critics as the "Crime of '73"), the debate intensified. When silver deposits were discovered in the West, demand for the use of silver to expand the money supply grew. Eventually a compromise was worked out in 1878, the Bland-Allison Act (which was passed over Hayes's veto). It allowed only a limited coining of silver ($2–4 million in silver each month at the standard silver to gold ratio, which was set at 16:1). Not satisfied with this deal, farmers, debtors, and western miners continued to press for unlimited coinage of silver.

Though certainly not limited to any two or three issues, farmers and their allies began to consider organizing to protest the government's adoption of what they viewed as injurious policies in regards to the railroads, the tariff, and hard money. At that very time, they were feeling most vulnerable because of changes in their sector of the economy.

THE GROWTH OF DISCONTENT: FARMERS ORGANIZE

Between the end of the Civil War and the turn of the century, the nation experienced enormous growth in terms of population, production, and demand for foodstuffs and commodities. In this thirty-five-year period the nation's population more than doubled and the number of farms tripled. As the nation urbanized, the demand for food increased significantly. Americans grew and consumed enormous amounts of food, leaving little for export. A number of factors (mostly having to do with technology and mechanization) led to this enormous burst of productivity in the agrarian sector of the economy:

- improvements in the cotton gin
- the introduction of harvesters, combines, and reapers
- improved plows made of stronger materials such as steel
- greater specialization in agricultural production—for example, wheat was grown mostly in the West

Consequently, the number of hours necessary to grow and harvest crops was more than halved in this period. But greater production doesn't always mean greater profits. Many forces and factors came together to harm farmers engaged in the free market economy of the late nineteenth century, among them the following:

- Grain elevator operators stored grain when it was not in transit, and often charged excessive rates.
- Manufacturers kept raising prices on their commodities, even as farmers found they had less disposable income.
- Banks increased interest on credit. Farmers in particular are reliant on credit and are therefore hurt by interest rate increases. Also, wealthy planters provided credit so that farmers could purchase seed and equipment. Known as the crop-lien system, it created a level of indebtedness that was difficult to pay off.
- Industries that farmers relied on for machinery kept raising the cost of harvesters and combines.
- The railroad industry became the symbol and focus of farmer discontent. It affected the profit levels farmers could earn from their labor because of shipping price increases. Furthermore, in many states the railroad industry was immune to regulations, especially the amounts they charged for long and short hauls, and set shipping rates arbitrarily. In addition, the industry was not beyond using nefarious measures to maximize profits.
- In some states regulations were nonexistent.

Within a twenty-year period, from about the end of Reconstruction to the mid-1890s, the market price of important crops such as wheat, corn, and cotton dwindled. Mary Elizabeth Lease, an attorney active in Farmers' Alliance affairs, provided farmers with a solution to their overproduction problems: "What you farmers have to do," she told them, "is to raise less corn and more hell!" This they indeed would do. In the last decade of the century, they would organize the Populist party.

As the United States continued its drive to industrial supremacy and as the capitalist class raked in enormous profits, the nation's growers experienced a downturn in their fortunes. There were a number of factors that help to explain the serious economic crisis that confronted the nation's farmers after the war, such as

- **The cost to introduce new time- and labor-saving technology** Although this would undoubtedly increase production, it required significant expenditures, which often had to be borrowed with interest charged by the banks.
- **A great increase in the value of land** The availability of land was limited because so much land had been granted to railroad companies or sold to land speculators.
- **High taxes** Because states often rewarded railroad and grain storage companies with reduced taxes, the remainder was paid by private citizens.
- **The cost to store and ship grains and crops** These costs were very high.

Most farmers were not prepared for a transformation of the American economy following the Civil War, one that made them even more susceptible to the fluctuations that often occur in a market economy and frequently dry up profits, as happened to many farmers. By the 1880s numerous farms had been foreclosed on by banks; others were no longer owned but rented. Farmers were not willing to stand idle, however, while their livelihood was undermined by the frequent instability in market prices and ruinous interest, freight, and storage costs. Rather than sink into powerlessness, they organized. Not long after the end of the war, the National Grange of the Patrons of Husbandry was formed both to educate its members about new developments in agriculture and to create a social and cultural bond among farmers. It was not long, however, before the Grange became actively involved in politics. As membership in the organization quickly rose to 1.5 million members by mid-1870, it became a force to be reckoned with, especially in the Midwest and the South.

Utilizing their political clout, the Grangers were able to enact a number of laws that sought to address the abuses that were so damaging to their businesses. To this end, several "Granger laws" were passed to regulate the railroads and the grain elevator operators. However, though they were a potent force in the rural areas of the nation, farmers were met with strong opposition. Confronted by the railroad industry and the operators of the grain elevator and storage facilities, the farmers and their opponents faced off in federal court. In a series of landmark Supreme Court decisions, the farmers generally experienced success.

- ***Munn* v. *Illinois* (1877)** In the same year that President Hayes called out federal troops to crush a strike by workers in the railroad industry, the Court handed down a pivotal decision. As in other states, the Grangers in Illinois had already obtained regulations for maximum rates that could be charged by grain elevator and storage facilities. These laws were often challenged by the owners of these businesses (who said the Granger cases were in violation of Fourteenth Amendment rights), and sometimes they ended up in federal court, such as the *Munn* case. So long as property was "devoted to public use," the Court ruled, the states could place regulations on the railroads for the good of the public. The decision was not a complete victory for the farmers, for the Court decided that states could not regulate rates for long hauls. To compensate for their loss in short-haul rates, the railroad companies responded by inflating the long-haul rates.

- ***Peik* v. *the Chicago and Northwestern Railway* (1876)** The Supreme Court's decision in this case held that the Granger laws were not in violation of the federal government's power to regulate interstate trade and commerce and that states could establish their own interstate regulations when federal law was not present.
- ***Wabash, St. Louis & Pacific Railway Company* v. *Illinois* (1886)** The Court reversed its earlier decision in the *Peik* case and ruled that commerce and trade that crossed state lines was directly under the authority of the federal government, not the states. Even Congress got into the act, passing the Interstate Commerce Act (which in turn created the Interstate Commerce Commission). Under the ICA's guidelines certain rules had to be obeyed, such as reasonable shipping rates and the elimination of abuses by the railway companies. It was given the authority to use the courts to compel recalcitrant railway companies to obey its policies.

In the early twentieth century, under the influence of the progressives (those who sought political and economic reforms), further legislation would regulate the railroad industry. Until then, the various Farmers' Alliances—such as the Southern Farmers' Alliance, the Northern Farmers' Alliance (successor to the Grange), the Louisiana Farmers' Union, the Texas Alliance, the Northwestern Farmers' Alliance, and the Colored Farmers' Alliance—represented agrarian interests. By the turn of the century the various alliances had merged into the National Farmers' Alliance and Industrial Union. In 1890 the Farmer's Alliance formulated a platform in Ocala, Florida, that enumerated their demands, which in 1892 would become the foundation of the Populist party's goals as expressed in the Omaha Platform:

- Government should own the major utilities such as the railroads.
- There should be free and unlimited coinage of silver.
- The fixed income tax should be replaced with a graduated income tax.
- All excess lands granted to the railroads should be returned to public ownership.
- Laborers should have an eight-hour day as well as the right to collective bargaining.
- A plan to establish federal offices near grain storage facilities into which farmers could deposit their nonperishable crops should be adopted. This would allow farmers to market their crops when their value was highest and store it when they were low.
- Immigration should be limited to control the expansion of the labor pool.
- Private detective and security agencies such as the Pinkerton and Baldwin-Felts agents should not be used to break up strikes.
- The U.S. political system should be democratized through the following measures:
    - direct election of U.S. senators (prior to the ratification of the Seventeenth Amendment in 1913, senators were commonly elected by state legislatures, a practice that often led to corruption)

- use of the secret ballot to end the intimidation associated with publicly announcing one's choice for office
- a single term for presidents
- use of the initiative, by which a proposed law can be voted on if the advocates of the bill submit a petition beforehand and with the required number of signatures—in this way, legislative bodies would not have a monopoly on initiating legislation
- use of the referendum to allow voters to vote on governmental legislation and programs

To be sure, the Alliance was effective in electing its members to offices in the state and federal governments. For example, in 1890, over fifty candidates allied with or sympathetic to the Farmers' Alliances were elected to Congress. But discontent was not limited to the nation's farmers. By the late 1880s many throughout the nation had become disconcerted by government corruption, the ever-expanding concentration of economic power, as well as the tariff, money supply issues, and the railroad industry's abuses. True, government had taken steps to address some of their concerns; however, it would take a third party and a major depression in 1893 to shake the Democrats and Republicans from their lethargy.

The depression of 1893 represented the worst collapse of the American economy up to that time. Twenty percent of the workforce was without jobs, and many Americans were living at or below the poverty level. Employers continued to cut wages, and unions went out on strike. In the spring of that year, Jacob S. Coxey, an Ohio businessman, led hundreds of unemployed and desperate men—Coxey's Army—on a march to Washington, D.C., to appeal to the government for assistance in the form of work-relief. They received none, but a few of Coxey's lieutenants were arrested, not for disturbing the peace or for starting a riot, but for walking on the grass! Police dispersed the rest of Coxey's Army.

THE POPULIST PARTY

Many economic, social, political, and cultural factors led to the dramatic rise and ultimate decline of the Populists. At the time the Populist movement seemed revolutionary, not only because of its attack on laissez-faire and monopoly capitalism, but also because of its attempt to form a political alliance between poor whites and blacks. The Populists were in every sense of the word a coalition of seemingly disparate groups, unions, and political parties: Grangers, Farmers' Alliances, former Greenback party members, Knights of Labor, socialists, Free Silver party members, prohibitionists, women's rights groups, anarchists. If the Populist movement suffered from internal divisiveness, its members were still deeply passionate about their organization's effort to address the problems that undermined their livelihood.

AP Tip

Because the heart of the Populist movement was centered in predominantly rural areas and more often than not focused on agrarian issues, it is easy to lose sight of the other forces that were drawn to the movement. Take note of the various components of the Populists when discussing them in a free-response essay.

In the election of 1892, Populist candidate James Weaver received 1 million votes. He even won electoral votes, rare for a third-party candidate. Although he lost the presidential race, the Populist party experienced some remarkable victories: almost 1,500 Populist candidates were elected to state legislatures, three won gubernatorial elections, five were elected U.S. senators, and ten were elected to the House of Representatives. Unfortunately for Weaver and his party, they fared poorly in the South primarily because conservative southern Democrats were fearful of the Populists uniting poor blacks and whites. Remember that at this point, blacks in the South were politically neutralized by Jim Crow laws, and many white southerners were in favor of maintaining this racial status quo. Surprisingly, the party failed to attract many northern urban workers, despite the fact that the Populists fought for labor's rights in the halls of Congress, in state legislatures, and in public forums. Additionally, they provided financial support to workers out on strike.

In the 1896 presidential election the Democrats were split between "Gold Bugs," who were loyal to Cleveland and his advocacy of the gold standard, and pro-silver advocates, who did not yet have their own candidate—that is, until William Jennings Bryan (only thirty-six at the time) gave a speech on the silver issue to the delegates at the Democratic Convention. His speech not only electrified the audience but remains one of the most memorable speeches in U.S. history: "You shall not press down upon the brow of labor this thorn of crowns," he exclaimed, "you shall not crucify mankind upon a cross of gold." The Democrats had their candidate for the presidency, except of course for the Gold Bugs, who ran their own contender. Because the Democrats had already incorporated into their platform much of the Populists' platform, such as outlawing injunctions in labor disputes, the free coining of silver, and a lower tariff, the Populist party also nominated Bryan as their candidate, though not without some difficulty. Many Populist delegates opposed a "fusion" ticket for fear that their goals would be neutralized by allying themselves with a Democratic candidate. In fact, Bryan's support was sectional. Southern and western delegates had earlier fused with the Democrats on the state and local levels; southern delegates opposed such an alliance. In order to satisfy the southerners, Tom Watson, a Populist, was selected as the vice presidential candidate instead of a Democratic candidate. Consensus had been reached. For their part, the Republicans had effective and potent campaign leadership. Under the campaign direction of Mark Hanna, the Republicans effectively cast blame on the Democrats for the depression in 1893. Further helped by the defection of the Democratic Gold Bugs, by increasing crop prices, especially for wheat, and by employers who frightened their workers into voting

Republican by claiming that a low protective tariff would lead to business closings, the Republican, William McKinley, decisively defeated the "fusion" Democrat-Populist candidate Bryan.

After the 1896 election, the Populists ceased to exist as a national political party. The power of the monopolies, combined with the shortcomings of its own membership—who, according to some historians, could not leap the hurdle of racism despite their common economic interests—led to the party's demise. But there was one consolation for its leaders and rank-and-file members: much of its platform was ultimately absorbed into those of the Democrats and the Republicans. In the early twentieth century, during the progressive era, issues that the Populists had fought so hard for, such as the direct election of U.S. senators and a graduated income tax, would become a reality.

The Populist party was indeed unique in the history of the nation's political evolution. While some historians claim its downfall came in part from its inability to resolve the racial divides that existed within the party, other historians take the opposite view. At a time when black Americans were, at best, second-class citizens, these historians argue that the party fought for black economic and political rights because exploitation had to be confronted, regardless of the victim's skin color. To this end Populists viewed government not as a force to be overthrown, but to be redefined, because government could, in the right hands, be a tool to bring about opportunities for all citizens, not just the politically and economically entrenched. Hand in hand with this outlook was a total rejection of Social Darwinism, which Populists maintained was an obstacle to humanity's efforts to triumph over its own shortcomings. But this is not the only legacy of the Populist party. At a time when the American family farm is rapidly being replaced by enormous agribusinesses, one can more easily sympathize with the plight of the nation's food producers as the country moves into the twenty-first century.

Content Review Questions

1. All of the following were political objectives of the Populists EXCEPT
   (A) government ownership of major industries such as the railroads and telegraphs.
   (B) the free and unlimited coining of silver.
   (C) direct election of U.S. senators.
   (D) creating a national system of unemployment insurance.

2. William Jennings Bryan became the presidential candidate of both the Democrats and Populists in 1896 because of his support for
   (A) high protective tariffs to protect domestic industries.
   (B) unlimited and free coinage of silver.
   (C) nationalizing the railroad industry.
   (D) policies that would unite poor black and white farmers.

3. A major reason why McKinley was able to defeat Bryan in 1896 was
   (A) the Populists ultimately withdrew their support for Bryan.
   (B) the Republicans were split between gold and silver advocates.
   (C) American farmers experienced an increase in farm prices during the campaign.
   (D) Bryan's repudiation of the silver cause during the campaign.

4. Coxey's Army
   (A) reflected discontent with the government's response to the depression in 1893.
   (B) was the military wing of the Populist party.
   (C) was the name given to supporters of Jacob Coxey's candidacy for president in 1896.
   (D) were strong advocates of the gold standard.

5. Which of the following did the nation's farmers advocate in the late nineteenth century?
   (A) Government should reduce farmers' costs by providing farmers with seed and farm implements
   (B) The government should privatize the railroads
   (C) A sub-Treasury system should be established that would allow farmers to sell their crops on the market when prices rose
   (D) A high protective tariff

6. Which of the following did NOT lead to greater productivity by farmers in the late nineteenth century?
   (A) Iron and steel plows
   (B) The use of new farm machinery, such as harvesters
   (C) Greater specialization of agricultural production
   (D) The rates charged by grain elevator owners

7. In which case did the Supreme Court rule that as long as property was "devoted to public use," states could place regulations on the railroads for the good of the public?
   (A) *Peik* v. *the Chicago and Northern Railway*
   (B) *Munn* v. *Illinois*
   (C) *Illinois* v. *Wabash*
   (D) *Pollock* v. *Farmers Loan and Trust*

8. Which industry, *more than any other,* became the symbol and source of agrarian discontent in the post–Civil War period?
   (A) The insurance industry
   (B) Companies that developed harvesters and combines
   (C) Railway companies
   (D) Banks

9. Which of the following groups was NOT identified with the Populist party?
   (A) Supporters of the gold standard
   (B) Knights of Labor
   (C) Grangers
   (D) Greenback party

10. The Specie Resumption Act of 1875
    (A) led to a dramatic increase in the amount of silver in the economy.
    (B) was a compromise bill that allowed for an equal amount of gold and silver to be introduced into the economy each month.
    (C) removed all of the greenbacks from circulation.
    (D) dramatically inflated currency, which led to a depression.

11. "Waving the bloody shirt" and "Vote as you shot" were admonitions made by
    (A) former Confederates opposed to the reconstruction of the South.
    (B) the Ku Klux Klan in an attempt to increase membership in its anti-Reconstruction, anti-black organization.
    (C) Democrats in an attempt to reorganize their political party after the Civil War.
    (D) Republican politicians appealing for votes from Union veterans.

12. The Crédit Mobilier scandal tarnished the reputation and presidential administration of
    (A) Ulysses S. Grant.
    (B) James Garfield.
    (C) Andrew Johnson.
    (D) Abraham Lincoln.

13. Which of the following statements regarding the Populists is accurate?
    (A) They supported term limits for state and federal legislatures.
    (B) They favored government ownership of utility companies.
    (C) They found their greatest support in the industrial Northeast.
    (D) They sought a loose immigration policy.

14. Which important Populist leader and presidential candidate ultimately came to be associated with the racist faction within his party?
    (A) William Jennings Bryan
    (B) James B. Weaver
    (C) Thomas Edward Watson
    (D) Jay Gould

15. Although the "Billion-Dollar" Congress passed bills that favored Civil War pensioners and "silverites," it also passed legislation that favored industrialists, in the form of the
    (A) Pendleton Act of 1893.
    (B) McKinley Tariff Act of 1890.
    (C) Resumption Act of 1875.
    (D) Civil Rights Act of 1875.

Short-Answer Questions

1. Government support for big business created discontent among workers and farmers in the late nineteenth century.
    A. Which of the following government actions did the most to counter the idea that the government existed to support and

promote big business? Provide at least ONE piece of historical evidence in your explanation.
Sherman Anti-Trust Act
Munn v. *Illinois*
Interstate Commerce Act

B. Choose one other action from the list. Why was the act/decision you chose more beneficial to those oppressed by big business? Support your answer with historical evidence.

Question 2 is based on the following cartoon.

Library of Congress

2. This cartoon satirizes William Jennings Bryan's 1896 "Cross of Gold" speech.
   A. Describe the imagery used in the cartoon.
   B. Does the cartoonist support Bryan's position on the gold v. silver issue? How does the image indicate this?
   C. Was Bryan's position ultimately beneficial for the country? Provide historical evidence to support your answer.

Long-Essay Questions

1. To what extent did the Populists and Farmers' Alliances effectively challenge the established Democratic and Republican Parties in the late nineteenth century? In your answer discuss TWO of the following:
   a. the economic agenda of the Populists and Farmers' Alliances
   b. the degree of political success experienced by the Populists and Farmers' Alliances
   c. the ability of the Populists and Farmers' Alliances to organize farmers and others into a cohesive political force

2. Government's response to the plight of America's farmers and laborers in the late nineteenth century was insufficient.

   To what extent is this statement true?

Answers

CONTENT REVIEW QUESTIONS

1. **(D)** Unemployment insurance would have to wait until the New Deal in the 1930s. Options A–D were important features of the Populists' platforms (*The American Pageant,* 14th ed., p. 557/15th ed., p. 598; Learning Objective WXT-7).

2. **(B)** The silver issue and the condemnation of the gold standard were at the heart of Bryan's appeal. His "Cross of Gold" speech catapulted him into the national spotlight (*The American Pageant,* 14th ed., p. 662/15th ed., pp. 601–602; Learning Objective WXT-7).

3. **(C)** An increase in farm prices was one of the key factors that helped McKinley win support from farmers. B is incorrect because the Democrats and not the Republicans were split over the silver/gold issue. Bryan would never repudiate his primary campaign issue—option D. True, Gold Bugs (who had more in common with Cleveland than Bryan) did desert the party in the 1896 election, but most Democrats supported Bryan's candidacy (this material does not appear in the text; Learning Objective POL-3).

4. **(A)** Coxey and his supporters marched to Washington, D.C., in 1894 to appeal for aid for those unemployed as a result of the economic collapse in 1893 (*The American Pageant,* 14th ed., p. 658/15th ed., p. 599; Learning Objective WXT-7)

5. **(C)** The sub-Treasury system would provide farmers some control over the prices they could receive for their crops (*The American Pageant,* 14th ed., pp. 656–657/15th ed., p. 598; Learning Objective WXT-7).

6. **(D)** Farmers maintained that the grain elevator operators charged exorbitant fees (*The American Pageant,* 14th ed., p. 655/15th ed., pp. 594–596; Learning Objective WXT-8).

7. **(B)** *Munn* v. *Illinois* (this material does not appear in the text; Learning Objective WXT-8).

8. **(C)** While farmers were often susceptible to rate changes in other businesses, it was the railroad industry that most noticeably cut into farmer's costs to get their crops to market and thus became a symbol for their exploitation (*The American Pageant,* 14th ed., p. 655/15th ed., p. 596; Learning Objective WXT-3).

9. **(A)** Populists were strong supporters of the free and unlimited coining of silver. They sought to devalue the currency, which is what silver, not gold, would achieve (*The American Pageant,* 14th ed., p. 662/15th ed., pp. 596–598; Learning Objective WXT-7).

10. **(C)** Passed by the Republican Congress, it called for redeeming all greenbacks and replacing them with gold certificates (*The American Pageant,* 14th ed., p. 542/15th ed., p. 492; Learning Objective WXT-8).

11. **(D)** Although somewhat graphic in nature (apparently some Republicans physically waved a bloodied Union soldier's tunic at political rallies), these exclamations appealed to Union war veterans, encouraging them not to throw their support behind what many Republicans considered to be the party of "disunion," the Democrats (*The American Pageant,* 14th ed., p. 539/15th ed., p. 489; Learning Objective POL-3).

12. **(A)** Although not himself implicated in the scandal (which involved bribing congressmen and the vice president to not report the illegal activities of Union Pacific Railroad operatives), Grant's reputation was tarnished by his personal and political association with the accused (*The American Pageant,* 14th ed., p. 541/15th ed., p. 490; Learning Objective POL-2).

13. **(B)** Disenchanted by the two major political parties and suffering from the effects of a postwar depression, the Populists (who grew out of the militant Farmer's Alliance, whose center of popularity was in the rural South and West), put forth a platform that included government ownership of major industries such as the railroads, telegraph, and telephone; they also supported a graduated income tax and immigration restrictions (*The American Pageant,* 14th ed., p. 557/15th ed., p. 598; Learning Objective WXT-7).

14. **(D)** Watson apparently came to racism later in his political career. He initially supported interracial cooperation in addressing political and economic problems confronting the nation's suffering farmers. Later, he condemned blacks, Jews, socialists, and Catholics, giving a decidedly racist hue to the Populist's democratic, grassroots crusade (*The American Pageant,* 14th ed., p. 560/15th ed., p. 508; Learning Objective CUL-3).

15. **(B)** The McKinley Tariff Act increased tariff rates to their highest peacetime level in the nation's history, a boon to corporate America but devastating to the nation's indebted farmers, who were then compelled to purchase American-made commodities at inflated prices (*The American Pageant,* 14th ed., p. 557/15th ed., p. 505; Learning Objective WXT-8).

SHORT-ANSWER QUESTIONS

1. Each of the acts/precedents on the list were conceived to counter the ill effects of big business with varying degrees of success. The Sherman Anti-Trust Act was designed to break up trusts but was used more against unions than the big businesses for which it was intended. *Munn* v. *Illinois* allowed states to regulate property devoted to public use, including railroads, but railroads found ways around the provisions. The Interstate Commerce Act, which established the Interstate Commerce Commission oversaw and regulated any business that operated between two or more states, including railroads. Of the three, the Interstate Commerce Commission was ultimately the most successful, but they were all landmark for their time.

2. Bryan was a major advocate for the 16:1 silver to gold ratio. This cartoon mocks his position and his devotion to it, portraying him as a demagogue with foolish notions. The United States did begin to coin silver eventually with disastrous results, leading to an economic panic.

LONG-ESSAY QUESTIONS

1. You should begin by explaining why the Populist movement and Farmers' Alliances were created in the first place. To this end, provide some of the economic and political factors that negatively affected those who joined these organizations. An explanation of their goals (such as public ownership of the railroads and inflated paper or silver currency) is also necessary. The second aspect, b, is similar to a question that begins with "To what extent." Responding to this question, you should identify which of the important objectives set forth by the Populists and Farmers' Alliances were actually achieved. (Historical Thinking Skills I-3: Periodization, II-5: Contextualization, and IV-9: Synthesis)

2. For this essay you should address the relationship between government and business and how this relationship affected laborers and farmers. Identify the response of government to strikes; are there any patterns you can see? Did government address the needs of farmers by alleviating the problem of overproduction and declining farm prices? Discuss the decisions of the Supreme Court—for example, *Munn* v. *Illinois*—in this period as they relate to the plight of workers and farmers. (Historical Thinking Skills I-3: Periodization, III-6: Historical Argumentation, and IV-8: Interpretation)

Period 7: 1890-1945

Changes at Home and Abroad

By the end of the nineteenth century the United States was far removed from the isolated, agrarian nation that it was prior to the Civil War and industrialization. Having expanded from coast to coast and needing new ports and markets for its increasing industrial output, the United States began to look beyond its borders, intervening and exerting its influence throughout the Western Hemisphere. Becoming a world power, however, led to entanglements and commitments abroad that would eventually draw the nation into two massively destructive world wars in the first half of the twentieth century. Moreover, the United States' enhanced role in foreign affairs did not prevent movements for change at home, as the beginning of the twentieth century witnessed calls for increased rights for the disenfranchised, greater restrictions on big business, and an end to economic and political corruption. Neither did the nation's new status protect it from the ravages of a worldwide depression that engulfed the majority of the country in extreme economic hardship throughout the 1930s, irrevocably changing the United States government, economy, and culture.

Key Concepts from the College Board

7.1 Governmental, political, and social organizations struggled to address the effects of large-scale industrialization, economic uncertainty, and related social changes such as urbanization and mass migration.

7.2 A revolution in communications and transportation technology helped to create a new mass culture and spread "modern" values and ideas, even as cultural conflicts between groups increased under the pressure of migration, world wars, and economic distress.

7.3 Global conflicts over resources, territories, and ideologies renewed debates over the nation's values and its role in the world, while simultaneously propelling the United States into a dominant international military, political, cultural, and economic position.

13

U.S. FOREIGN AFFAIRS FROM 1860 TO 1914

Prior to the American Civil War, the United States embarked on a systematic policy of territorial expansion across the continental United States. In the process, through wars, treaties, and conquests, it acquired land from Native Americans and Mexicans and settled territorial disputes with Britain and Spain. In the decades after the Civil War, the United States continued to expand across the continent, but by the late nineteenth century it turned its attention to noncontiguous territories—land beyond the continental United States. If the United States did not emerge from the Civil War with its sense of nationalism intact, it was nevertheless most certainly a rising power. By the end of the nineteenth century, the United States would be an economic giant and a military power with international colonial possessions. Less than two decades into the twentieth century, it would emerge from World War I an even stronger economic and military power. One of the driving forces behind this development was the same both before and after the Civil War: territorial expansion. Industry, immigration, the enormous expansion of the economy, all played a role in making the United States a major participant on the international scene.

KEY CONCEPTS

- The United States created an international empire as a result of its one-sided victory in the Spanish-American War.
- Those who supported or opposed U.S. imperialism provided theories and justifications for their views.
- The United States penetrated Asia, establishing the Open Door policy in China.

- Throughout this period, the United States intervened in Central and South American internal affairs.

U.S. foreign policy during this period is discussed in depth in *The American Pageant,* 14th and 15th eds., Chapters 27, 29–30.

THE PURCHASE OF ALASKA

In 1867 Secretary of State William Seward brokered a deal in which Russia agreed to sell Alaska to the United States for approximately $7.5 million. In acquiring Alaska, Seward, an expansionist, eliminated Russian influence in the Western Hemisphere. The American public and many in Congress thought the purchase was a waste of funds and dubbed the deal "Seward's Folly" and Alaska itself "Seward's Icebox." Seward was later vindicated when gold and coal were discovered.

THE NEW IMPERIALISM: THEORIES

To be sure, the United States was not alone in building an international empire. In fact, it came late to the race. The New Imperialism of the late nineteenth century differed from earlier imperialist rivalries in the number of competitors vying for empire. Great Britain, France, Germany, Japan, and Russia, among others, had created empires by the late nineteenth century. The impetus for this enormous burst of expansionist activity was the growing opinion that the opportunities for creating an empire were fading as more and more land was coming under the influence and control of rivals. Yet there are other theories to explain why nations adopted an imperialist foreign policy. Social scientists have for decades attempted to create an explanation as to why nations embark on a policy of imperialism. Many have been critical of the imperialist activity for different reasons. Below is a sampling of some of the more notable theorists:

- **John Hobson (1858–1940)** A liberal economist, Hobson contended that underconsumption (or overproduction) convinces governments to adopt an imperialist policy: the colony becomes a source of demand for commodities that go unsold in the imperialist nation. Hobson, who was critical of imperialism, maintained that increasing wages would allow workers to purchase the goods they produced, thereby resolving the problem of underconsumption and eliminating the need to adopt an imperialist policy.
- **V. I. Lenin (1870–1924)** The leader of the Bolshevik Revolution in 1917, Lenin argued that when the rates of profits fall the capitalist class seeks new markets to dominate and invest surplus capital. Because all capitalist nations take the same approach, dangerous inter-imperialist rivalries result.
- **Rosa Luxemburg (1870–1919)** A German Marxist revolutionary, Luxemburg claimed that when supply exceeds demand, capitalist nations must find new markets in noncapitalist areas. Eventually, however, capitalism would have nowhere left to expand and, she hoped, would collapse.
- **Joseph Schumpeter (1883–1950)** A German economist, Schumpeter held that underconsumption led to imperialism as the

center, the mother country, sought a larger market. He maintained that imperialism represented atavistic behavior—that it was a reflection of a more primitive state—and that capitalism represented a sophisticated system of supply and demand.

METHODS ADOPTED BY THE UNITED STATES TO ACHIEVE ITS IMPERIALIST GOALS

- **Formal imperialism** One of the most pervasive methods used by the United States and other imperial powers, formal, or direct, imperialism involves the physical presence of the center—the mother country—politically and often militarily. Examples of formal imperialism by the United States include the acquisition of
  - Hawaii
  - Guam
  - Puerto Rico
- **Informal imperialism** In this form of imperialism, formal control is not necessary. Instead, the imperial power can dominate a colony, nation, or region in several different ways. The imperial power can support those in power in the dominated area whose policies are beneficial to the center. It can draft treaties that subordinate the economic, social, and political interests of the dominated nation to the interests of the center. The Open Door policy, adopted by the United States at the turn of the century, would allow any area to be penetrated by the imperial nations. John Hay, President McKinley's secretary of state, was a strong advocate of the policy, which was initially applied to China, but eventually extended to other continents as well.

Despite the enormous productive capabilities of U.S. capitalism, the nation in the late nineteenth century was experiencing a period of economic stagnation and social and political instability, not unlike what was occurring in other capitalist nations. In order to combat these problems, the United States, like other capitalist nations, adopted a dual plan. Domestically, the government attempted to reform capitalism by addressing the problems that led to discontent. The progressive era was a period of intense interest in reform. Internationally, the government adopted an expansionist—imperialist—foreign policy.

Whether their expectations regarding the benefits of imperialism were realistic is still debated today. Nevertheless, the decision to adopt this foreign policy option was based on policymakers' perceptions of what an imperialist policy could achieve in the short and long term. Specifically, the United States and other world leaders believed an imperialist policy would have the following effects:

- An imperialist policy would bring the economy out of immediate financial crisis—a severe depression struck the United States in 1893.
- An imperialist policy would help create conditions that would allow for future investments.
- An imperialist policy would reduce domestic conflict—for example, between the working class and the capitalist class. (Remember,

industrialization and rapid capital accumulation brought on serious confrontations between labor and capital following the Civil War.) This could be achieved by:

- reducing the extent of unemployment because of the favorable conditions imperialism would bring, such as increased demand from overseas colonies
- passing on some of the economic benefits derived from imperialism to the working class
- appealing to the patriotism of the working class to mute class tensions

A primary reason why the United States embarked on a policy of creating an international empire was the closing of the frontier, as officially reported in the 1890 census. The significance of this report was that all of the areas within the continental United States had been settled by the late nineteenth century. There was only one direction left to expand—overseas.

AP Tip

According to the renowned historian Frederick Jackson Turner, the frontier helped shape the democratic attributes of the American character and culture. In his famous 1893 essay, "The Significance of the Frontier in American History," Turner put forth the thesis that as Americans moved to the West, they had consistently regenerated the societies and cultures they had previously created in the East. In the process, they had cultivated a unique American system based on democratic values and individualism. Turner's thesis has prompted considerable discussion between historians who support his view and those who challenge it. Keep this in mind should you be presented with a College Board free-response question that deals with topics such as Jacksonian Democracy, Manifest Destiny, and the New Imperialism of the late nineteenth century.

Ideological Justifications for an American Imperialist Policy

Because imperialism tends to be a highly controversial course of action, various justifications are utilized to explain the need for such a foreign policy and to mollify those who question its necessity. In the late nineteenth century, the following were important justifications for U.S. imperialism:

- **Captain Alfred T. Mahan's *The Influence of Sea Power upon History* (1890)** In one of the most influential books of the era, Mahan proposed that for the United States to become a world power it must develop a first-class navy. This would give the United States a global reach and considerably increase its military power. However, in order to have a great navy, coaling stations and naval bases were necessary—in other words, the acquisition of colonies. A staunch advocate of imperialism, Mahan's book had a profound influence on President Theodore Roosevelt, himself a supporter of a global U.S. empire.

- **Frederick Jackson Turner's "The Significance of the Frontier in American History" (1893)** This essay sums up Turner's belief that the possibilities associated with the frontier and territorial expansion promotes social, economic, and political stability. His essays, published in professional journals in the late nineteenth and early twentieth centuries, influenced President Woodrow Wilson, himself a historian.
- **Religious justifications** The notion that imperialism allowed "civilized" Christian cultures an opportunity to spread their way of life to "lesser" cultures was advocated by the nativist Reverend Josiah Strong in his 1885 book *Our Country*, among others. Often, in an attempt to mute criticism of the economic motives behind the adoption of an imperialist policy, noneconomic justifications such as the missionary rationale were used.
- **Social Darwinism** Advocates of imperialism maintained that the United States was simply biologically and morally superior to those cultures and peoples that were being dominated. Imperialism was merely a reflection of that superiority.

AP Tip

Some social scientists maintain that U.S. foreign policy should not be shaped by theoretical and ethical justifications, but by *Realpolitik*—the "politics of reality"—the practical and realistic needs and concerns of the nation. They hold that U.S. economic imperatives and political/military objectives helped shape the foreign policy adopted by the United States beginning in the late nineteenth century. The realization of a global empire was a realistic and necessary objective of U.S. policymakers, they contend. Others argue that morality should be a primary factor in adopting a particular or general course of action when adopting a foreign policy, for the implementation of a policy based on realpolitik has its limitations and unintended deleterious consequences. A brief discussion of realpolitik as it applies to U.S. foreign policy (in any period) may add a compelling dimension to a free-response question that asks you to address foreign affairs.

OPPONENTS OF AMERICAN IMPERIALISM

Not all Americans supported their government's foreign policy. Even President Cleveland opposed the annexation of Hawaii in 1894. In fact imperialism was so controversial that it became the key issue in the 1900 presidential campaign between William McKinley and William Jennings Bryan. By then, an influential association opposed to expansionism had been organized, the Anti-Imperialist League. Its members included politicians (for example, Bryan), literary figures (for example, Mark Twain), economic leaders (for example, Andrew

Carnegie), and scholars (for example, Charles Francis Adams and William Sumner). Their opposition to imperialism ran the gamut from distress over the costs necessary to maintain an empire to the immorality of denying others self-determination to the racial notion that incorporating "lesser" cultures into a U.S. empire would weaken American "purity."

U.S. Foreign Relations in East Asia and the Pacific

To U.S. political and economic leaders in the late nineteenth century, China was a region that offered infinite economic possibilities. The United States was not alone in this analysis. All imperial powers knew that gaining a foothold in China, and eventually in the rest of Asia, would enhance their power in relation to one another. While the United States looked to China for opportunities, a new force in East Asia was demonstrating its power—Japan. In the late nineteenth century, it became clear that the United States and Japan were emerging as the leading contestants for hegemony in Asia. Beginning with Japan's victory over China in the Sino-Japanese War in 1895 and over Russia in the Russo-Japanese War in 1905, U.S.-Japanese enmity grew as each sought to influence East Asia. This antagonism would ultimately take them down the path to war in 1941. Several examples show how the United States and Japan tried to address their strained diplomatic relations throughout the first half of the twentieth century:

- President Theodore Roosevelt organized the Treaty of Portsmouth ending the Russo-Japanese War in 1905. Japan was clearly the victor and thus received concessions from Russia; however, many in Japan blamed Roosevelt's treaty, and therefore the United States, for what the Japanese claimed were only modest gains.
- The Taft-Katsura Agreement (1905): Japan recognized U.S. control over the Philippines and the United States recognized Japan's control over Korea.
- In order to show the extent of the U.S. global reach, President Roosevelt sent the U.S. Navy on an international cruise in 1907, making certain it stopped in Japan. The fleet of warships duly impressed the Japanese. They welcomed the American navy, but they may have seen this Great White Fleet (so called because of the ships' distinctive coloring) as a possible threat to its plans to dominate East Asia.
- The Root-Takahira Agreement (1908): At the time, the Japanese and Americans desired to improve relations; by this agreement, they promised to preserve China's independence, support the Open Door policy, and recognize each other's possessions in the Pacific.

Although they were allies in World War I, from this point on, and despite efforts to forestall conflict, relations between the United States and Japan were never entirely amicable.

As for the other imperial powers in Asia, their grab for wealth and power in China in many ways resembled their scramble in Africa during the same period. This spurred the United States to formulate the Open Door policy. The goal of the policy was to prevent the total dissection of China, which would further weaken the country and allow the competing imperial powers to create spheres of influence in

China, and to ensure that the United States had the same opportunities to trade in China as did the other powers.

In 1900 a Chinese group called the Boxers attempted to drive out the foreign powers. The United States was in the vanguard in organizing an international military response that eventually put down this nationalist uprising. Later the United States worked out an agreement that attempted to preserve China's independence. However, the other nations involved—Britain, France, Russia, Italy, Germany, and Japan—compelled China to pay enormous indemnities, which weakened it considerably; the United States returned a majority of its share of the indemnities to an appreciative Chinese government.

Around the same time, the United States was acquiring territorial possessions east of China, in the Pacific:

- **Samoa** A trade relationship had developed between American merchants and Samoans even before the Civil War. In the decade following the Civil War the United States was permitted to establish a naval base on one of the Samoan islands. Soon Germany and Britain wanted what the Americans had in Samoa. When the American and Germany navies almost fought each other over the islands, a treaty was worked out. It gave Germany two of Samoa's islands; the other islands were given to the United States; Britain received other concessions.
- **Hawaii** As was the case in Samoa, American merchants had opened trade with the Hawaiians in the decades before the Civil War. The key commodity was sugar. The export of sugar benefited both American merchants and Hawaiian traders. Standing in the way of an even more lucrative trade relationship was the monarch of Hawaii, Queen Liliuokalani, who opposed foreign economic and political intervention in her country. In short order the queen was overthrown by Hawaii's white population under the leadership of Hawaiian Supreme Court justice Sanford Dole and assisted by U.S. Marines. The U.S. government quickly recognized the new government, one amenable to increased trade. On July 4, 1894, the Republic of Hawaii was proclaimed. Ostensibly Hawaii was an independent nation. However, many Hawaiians opposed a key provision in their new constitution that would allow the United States to annex the Hawaiian Islands.

While Samoa and Hawaii were indeed important acquisitions, it was not until the United States went to war against the Spanish Empire that it fully established itself as a major global power. Nevertheless, the U.S. interest in Cuba did not begin in the late nineteenth century. In the antebellum era, southern economic and political leaders wanted to annex Cuba, a Caribbean island that was certainly suitable for a southern-styled slave plantation system. President Polk attempted to purchase the island from Spain but was refused. Even independent proslavery military expeditions failed to wrest Cuba from Spain. Later President Pierce sent several proslavery U.S. representatives to Ostend, Belgium, to negotiate for the sale of Cuba; they implied that if Spain refused to give up Cuba, the United States would take it by force. When the negotiations were leaked to the press, angry antislavery forces in Congress saw to it that the Ostend Manifesto, as it was called, was repudiated.

THE SPANISH-AMERICAN WAR (1898)

The war that made the United States a global power in possession of an overseas empire came about because of a variety of causes:

- Spain's treatment of the Cubans under General Valeriano "The Butcher" Weyler was brutal.
- The United States supported the Cuban independence movement.
- Cuba's strategic location in the Caribbean was enticing to the United States.
- Financial interests in the United States were being hurt by the ongoing war between the Cuban rebels and the Spanish military.
- The influence of the "Yellow Press": William Randolph Hearst's and Joseph Pulitzer's newspapers unscrupulously sensationalized Spanish atrocities in Cuba in order to increase sales, correctly speculating that a war in Cuba would stimulate newspaper readership. Although some of their stories were outright fabrications, the reading public devoured the graphic and sometimes salacious stories.

Relations between Spain, whose glory days as Europe's first major empire in the Western Hemisphere were well behind it, and the United States, which was a newcomer to global empire-building, deteriorated even further as a result of two events:

- **The DeLôme letter** In 1898 a U.S. newspaper published private correspondence stolen from the Spanish minister in Washington, Dupuy DeLôme. In the letter the minister made derogatory comments about President McKinley, which, when made public, outraged the American people. Although DeLôme resigned, the damage had been done.
- **The sinking of the *Maine*** The U.S.S. *Maine* was sent to Havana Harbor to protect U.S. citizens and property. Just one week after the DeLôme incident, a massive explosion blew up the ship, killing over 250 American sailors. Given the mood of the American people at this point, they believed the obvious culprit was Spain. After the Hearst and Pulitzer papers sensationalized the story, the public was, for the most part, decidedly sympathetic to a war with Spain. To this day the cause of the sinking is a mystery, though many experts believe the explosion was a tragic accident.

Following the sinking of the *Maine,* President McKinley demanded a cease-fire in Cuba. Spain agreed. But in the minds of the American people and the U.S. Congress, a line had already been crossed. Under pressure, McKinley asked Congress for a declaration of war. Congress's affirmation came in the form of a congressional resolution, the Teller Amendment. In it the United States assured the Cuban people that they would be granted autonomy and self-determination once Spain was defeated. The United States prepared to engage Spain's forces in the Caribbean and in the Pacific.

The Spanish-American War lasted several months, cost more American lives from disease and spoiled food than from Spanish bullets, and in the end provided the United States with a global empire. Secretary of State John Hay knew it had been "a splendid little war." The following were major military events of the war:

- One Spanish fleet was destroyed by U.S. warships under the command of Commodore George Dewey in Manila Bay on June 1, 1898.
- Manila, capital of the Philippines, was captured two months later.
- In Cuba the U.S. military force was unprepared for tropical conditions. Despite the loss of thousands of soldiers to malaria and other diseases, Cuban rebels and American soldiers were able to wear down the Spanish forces. One of the most famous land battles occurred in the American attack on San Juan Hill, an event made popular by the rousing charge of the Rough Riders, led by Theodore Roosevelt, on Spanish forces.
- The destruction of the other Spanish fleet at Santiago Bay on July 3 convinced the Spanish to open negotiations to end the fighting. That month, the United States annexed Hawaii. It would soon add other territories as well.

These are the principal terms of the peace treaty signed in Paris in December 1898:

- Cuba received its independence from Spain. The United States would have liked to annex Cuba, but it could not because it had gone to war to win Cuban freedom.
- Spain relinquished control of Puerto Rico, in the Caribbean, and Guam, in the Pacific.
- In return for $20 million, the United States acquired the Philippines. Opponents claimed this violated America's basic principles as expressed in the U.S. Declaration of Independence, but the pro-imperialist forces in Congress won the day. Unfortunately for the United States, the Filipinos had other thoughts. Led by Emilio Aguinaldo, a former U.S. ally, Filipino rebels fought for three years against the U.S. military before the uprising was put down.

By then the United States had compelled the Cubans to agree to the Platt Amendment, which denied Cuban self-determination by allowing the United States to intervene in Cuban affairs when it believed its own interests were threatened and by allowing the United States to lease naval bases such as the one at Guantanamo, on the eastern tip of the island. In reality, while the United States claimed it had fought for Cuban freedom, the Platt Amendment effectively made Cuba an American protectorate.

Puerto Rico, on the other hand, had an unusual relationship with the United States. It was neither a U.S. territory nor an independent nation. Under the Foraker Act (1900), Congress provided the Puerto Ricans with substantial political autonomy, although the United States continued to exert heavy political and economic influence on the island's government. The Puerto Ricans had a civil government and an American governor. But were they entitled to the same constitutional rights as American citizens? In the early twentieth century the Supreme Court ruled on this question about constitutional rights in a series of cases called the *Insular Cases*: in a controversial decision, the Court ruled that the Constitution does not follow the flag—all the rights, privileges, and provisions accorded U.S. citizens under the Constitution do not apply to those living under the U.S. flag in overseas territories and possessions.

The war was a windfall for McKinley and the Republican Party. Late in the century, the United States experienced domestic prosperity and prestige overseas. To many Americans the rise in economic prosperity was well worth the financial and military burdens of empire. The depression of 1893, the worst in the nation's history to that time, seemed like a memory. Not surprisingly, the 1900 presidential race was a particularly difficult one for the Democrats, who tended to oppose overseas imperialism. The Republican President McKinley rode a wave of popular support for the war and the public's general acceptance of U.S. imperialism. He received nearly twice the number of electoral votes as the Democratic candidate, William Jennings Bryan.

U.S. FOREIGN RELATIONS IN LATIN AMERICA AND THE CARIBBEAN

Since the 1890s, U.S. intervention in the domestic affairs of many Latin American nations has been extensive. In 1904 President Roosevelt extended the authority of the United States in the Western Hemisphere as articulated in the Monroe Doctrine. Responding in part to the bellicose actions of several European nations in 1902 regarding money owed to them by Venezuela, Roosevelt believed the Monroe Doctrine had to be strengthened. In the Roosevelt Corollary, the president recognized the principle of self-determination, but only for nations that acted "with reasonable efficiency and decency in social and political matters," adding that "chronic wrongdoing" would result in the United States acting as an "international police power." In other words, the United States would intervene when it thought it was necessary to do so. This firm approach became known as the "Big Stick" policy, in reference to an African proverb: "Speak softly and carry a big stick, [and] you will go far." Citing the Corollary, the United States opposed nationalist and reform governments and those movements that sought greater autonomy as a threat to U.S. political, military, and economic interests. Roosevelt's successor, William Howard Taft, added a new ripple to the Roosevelt Corollary in the form of "Dollar Diplomacy." Taft believed that economic and political instabilities in Latin America required U.S. intervention to protect American financial interests. (Following World War I, the most intense U.S. responses have been reserved for leftist and communist movements.) Not surprisingly, many Latin Americans resented the policy. Below is a sampling of U.S. interventions in Latin America:

- **Cuba** The United States occupied Cuba from 1898 to 1902 and intervened again militarily in 1906, 1909, 1917, and 1961.
- **Dominican Republic** The United States militarily occupied the island nation from 1916 to 1924. It was a U.S. protectorate from 1905 to 1940. The United States last sent troops to the Dominican Republic in 1965.
- **Haiti** A U.S. protectorate from 1915 to 1941, it was militarily occupied by the United States between 1915 and 1934. U.S. troops were sent to Haiti in the late twentieth and early twenty-first centuries.

- **Nicaragua** The United States militarily and politically intervened in 1909, 1912–1925, 1927–1933, and again in the 1970s and 1980s.
- **Mexico** The United States militarily intervened in 1916 during the Mexican Civil War.
- **Colombia** In 1903 the United States helped establish a secessionist movement in northwestern Colombia (Panama), which soon came under U.S. control. It would later be the site of the Panama Canal.

The next American president, Woodrow Wilson, claimed he was an opponent of imperialism and repudiated the policies of his predecessors, Roosevelt and Taft. During his administration the United States took the following actions:

- **Panama Canal Tolls Act of 1912** The act allowed U.S. ships to use the Panama Canal toll-free. Wilson convinced Congress to repeal the act, which angered strong nationalists like Roosevelt but was appreciated by the British, who had earlier challenged the exemption.
- **Jones Act of 1916** The act provided for eventual Filipino independence, made the Philippines a full-fledged U.S. territory, and granted universal male suffrage.
- **Jones Act of 1917** The act conferred citizenship rights on all Puerto Ricans and made democratic improvements to their legislative system.

In just over fifty years, from the end of the American Civil War to the eve of World War I, the United States had taken its place as an economic leviathan and international world power. Coincidentally, the first phase of U.S. territorial expansion, the period of Manifest Destiny, coincided with the advent of a major reform movement, Jacksonian Democracy. Likewise, the U.S. role in the New Imperialism coincided with two domestic reform movements: the Populists in the late nineteenth century and the progressives in the early twentieth century. As the United States looked outward beyond its borders, many began to take stock of the domestic conditions shaping the nation. Again, the government and grassroots movements would take steps to democratize the institutions of American life.

Content Review Questions

1. Which of the following is an example of informal imperialism?
   (A) The mother country takes political and military control of the colony.
   (B) The stronger country signs trade agreements with the weaker country.
   (C) The imperial power exerts influence over the weaker land but does not formally take power at the local level.
   (D) Multiple countries work together to dominate a colony.

2. This theorist claimed that underconsumption in the center, or mother country, is the primary reason why nations adopt an imperialist policy.
   (A) Joseph Schumpeter
   (B) V. I. Lenin
   (C) Rosa Luxemburg
   (D) John Hobson

3. The Open Door policy was initially applied to
   (A) Korea.
   (B) Japan.
   (C) China.
   (D) Latin America.

4. Alfred T. Mahan was influential during the era of New Imperialism because of his
   (A) support for self-determination for conquered peoples.
   (B) advocacy for a large U.S. Navy in order to extend the nation's power internationally.
   (C) opposition to the U.S. adoption of an imperialist policy.
   (D) candidacy for the U.S. presidency as an advocate of imperialism.

5. Which of the following was NOT an opponent of U.S. imperialism?
   (A) Theodore Roosevelt
   (B) Mark Twain
   (C) William Jennings Bryan
   (D) Andrew Carnegie

6. In the Taft-Katsura Agreement, Japan recognized the U.S. control over the Philippines and the United States recognized Japan's control of
   (A) China.
   (B) Korea.
   (C) Guam.
   (D) Hawaii.

7. Which of the following held that those living in U.S. territories are not accorded the same constitutional rights as U.S. citizens?
   (A) Foraker Act
   (B) Root-Takahira Agreement
   (C) Insular Cases
   (D) Platt Amendment

8. The Teller Amendment
   (A) granted independence to the Philippines.
   (B) convinced the Filipino rebels to lay down their arms in return for financial concessions.
   (C) recognized Japan's influence in East Asia.
   (D) was a U.S. guarantee of self-determination to the Cubans once Spain was defeated.

9. Which U.S. president repudiated the imperialist policies of his predecessors?
   (A) Roosevelt
   (B) McKinley
   (C) Taft
   (D) Wilson

10. Which one of the following was NOT a cause of the Spanish-American War?
   (A) The yellow press
   (B) The U.S. desire to prevent European nations from controlling the Caribbean
   (C) The U.S. desire to control Cuba for its strategic location in the Caribbean
   (D) The sinking of the *Maine*

11. William Randolph Hearst and Joseph Pulitzer convinced Americans to go to war against Spain by
   (A) promising that the war would revive the economy.
   (B) printing graphic and salacious stories about events in Cuba in their newspapers.
   (C) preparing the military for battle in a foreign land.
   (D) supporting Spanish atrocities in Cuba.

12. In his controversial corollary to the Monroe Doctrine, President Theodore Roosevelt maintained that
   (A) the United States would not form any permanent alliances with Latin American countries.
   (B) no nation had the right to intervene in the internal affairs of another.
   (C) the United States reserved the right to construct military bases in its sphere of influence.
   (D) the United States would intervene if its Latin American neighbors were unable to maintain order.

13. In the 1907–1908 "Gentleman's Agreement," Japan agreed to suspend the flow of immigrants to the United States in return for
   (A) California's repeal of its school order segregating Asian students.
   (B) minor U.S. naval bases in the Pacific.
   (C) assistance from the U.S. government in bringing an end to the Russo-Japanese War.
   (D) U.S. funding to enhance the modernization of Japan's industries.

14. The Hay-Paunceforte Treaty overturned which earlier Anglo-American agreement prohibiting the United States from exclusively controlling an isthmian route through Central America?
   (A) Rush-Bagot agreement
   (B) Pinckney's Treaty
   (C) Milan Decrees
   (D) Clayton-Bulwer Treaty

15. Which of the following would most likely adhere to the principles and goals of the Anti-Imperialist League?
    (A) Theodore Roosevelt and speaker of the House Thomas Reed
    (B) Mark Twain and Theodore Roosevelt
    (C) William Jennings Bryan and Theodore Roosevelt
    (D) Mark Twain and Andrew Carnegie

Short-Answer Questions

Question 1 refers to the following two passages.

> "The Philippines are ours forever.... And just beyond the Philippines are China's illimitable markets. We will not retreat from either. We will not abandon our opportunity in the Orient. We will not renounce our part in the mission of our race: trustee, under God, or the civilization of the world."
>
> —Senator Albert J. Beveridge, 1900

> "You cannot maintain despotism in Asia and a republic in America. If you try to deprive even a savage or a barbarian of his just rights you can never do it without becoming a savage or a barbarian yourself."
>
> —Senator George F. Hoar, 1902

1. As the United States began to expand beyond its borders, several schools of thought emerged on whether or not these actions were justified.
   A. How do Beveridge's and Hoar's opinions on overseas expansion differ?
   B. Whose ideas on expansion did the United States act on? Provide historical evidence to support your answer.
2. How did United States policies and actions in the late nineteenth and early twentieth centuries adhere to or contradict the ideals expressed in the Monroe Doctrine? Support your answer with historical evidence.

Long-Essay Questions

1. The primary factor in the United States adopting a policy of imperialism was economic.

   To what extent is this statement correct?
2. To what extent was the United States justified in going to war against Spain in 1898? In your response, take into account political, economic, moral, and diplomatic factors.

Answers

CONTENT REVIEW QUESTIONS

1. **(C)** In informal imperialism, the imperial power supports those in power and has the power to draft treaties for that nation, but it is not the central ruling party in the new land (this material does not appear in the text; Learning Objective WOR-7).

2. **(A)** Schumpeter, a German economist, later taught at Harvard (this material does not appear in the text; Learning Objective WOR-5).

3. **(C)** Secretary of State John Hay designed the Open Door policy to make certain the United States had continued access to the China market (*The American Pageant,* 14th ed., p. 688/15th ed., pp. 623, 626; Learning Objective WOR-3).

4. **(B)** Mahan's *The Influence of Sea Power upon History* convinced the government to expand its naval fleet as a prerequisite to expanding its global power (*The American Pageant,* 14th ed., p. 670/15th ed., p. 609; Learning Objective WOR-6).

5. **(A)** Roosevelt vigorously supported U.S. imperialism (*The American Pageant,* 14th ed., pp. 698–699/15th ed., p. 620; Learning Objective WOR-6).

6. **(B)** The 1905 agreement was one of several demonstrations of the rivalry between Japan and the United States for hegemony in Asia (this material does not appear in the text; Learning Objective WOR-3).

7. **(C)** This was the conclusion of a badly split Supreme Court. The decision concerned constitutional questions raised by the Foraker Act (*The American Pageant,* 14th ed., p. 683/15th ed., pp. 620–621; Learning Objective POL-6).

8. **(D)** Unfortunately for the Cubans, the lure of economic incentives convinced the United States to rethink its promise (*The American Pageant,* 14th ed., pp. 675–676/15th ed., pp. 613–614; Learning Objective WOR-7).

9. **(D)** Wilson loathed imperialism (*The American Pageant,* 14th ed., p. 734/15th ed., pp. 667–668; Learning Objective WOR-6).

10. **(B)** A European nation, Spain, already controlled Cuba (*The American Pageant,* 14th ed., pp. 673–674/15th ed., p. 612; Learning Objective WOR-7).

11. **(B)** Hearst and Pulitzer were two of the major purveyors of yellow journalism, a style of reporting that sensationalized the

news to stimulate newspaper sales. Both men believed that a war in Cuba would lead to increased circulation and greater profits. Hearst allegedly told an artist he sent to Cuba, "You give me the pictures. I'll give you the war." (*The American Pageant*, 14th ed., p. 674 /15th ed., p. 612; Learning Objective WOR-6).

12. **(D)** As a result of various international events, Roosevelt concluded that warning European nations against recolonizing nations in the New World (the Monroe Doctrine) was not enough, and that internal instability (for example, Latin American indebtedness to European nations) could lead to foreign intervention. Thus he issued his corollary to the Monroe Doctrine, authorizing the United States to act as a hemispheric "policeman" (*The American Pageant*, 14th ed., p. 692/15th ed., pp. 629–630; Learning Objective WOR-6).

13. **(A)** San Francisco segregated Asian students, thereby freeing up more educational opportunities for white children. The Japanese were outraged by this order, and not until Theodore Roosevelt worked out the Gentleman's Agreement did the conflict subside (*The American Pageant*, 14th ed., p. 696/15th ed., p. 631; Learning Objective PEO-5).

14. **(D)** The United States was given the right to build a canal across the isthmus and, in addition, to fortify it (*The American Pageant*, 14th ed., p. 691/15th ed., pp. 627–628; Learning Objective WOR-7).

15. **(D)** Those opposed to the nation's desire to acquire noncontiguous territories at the turn of the twentieth century included an eclectic assortment of influential Americans including Gompers, Carnegie, Bryan, Twain, and Reed. The latter resigned as Speaker of the House in part because of the nation's new expansionist foreign policy (*The American Pageant*, 14th ed., p. 682/15th ed., p. 620; Learning Objective WOR-6).

Short-Answer Questions

1. Beveridge clearly supports overseas expansion while Hoar sees it as immoral. The United States' wholehearted commitment to overseas expansion from the 1890s on—including the Spanish-American War, military action in the Philippines, Open Door policy, and forays into Latin America—indicates that its policies aligned with Beveridge's thinking more so than Hoar's.

2. The Monroe Doctrine declared the Western Hemisphere closed to European colonization and committed the United States to protecting Latin America in case of European incursion in the region. In the late nineteenth and early twentieth centuries, U.S. leaders asserted police powers over Latin America in case of instability, which technically didn't stray from the Monroe Doctrine but also took it to an unforeseen level.

LONG-ESSAY QUESTIONS

1. You can discuss the limitations of this view while addressing the importance of economic factors. To this end, discuss the economic imperative to expand and find new markets for investments, surplus commodities, and raw materials. Point out that there were socio-political and cultural objectives and imperatives as well: Social Darwinism as a justification for expansion, the desire to develop a hegemonic relationship with, for example, South America, and the desire to create a world empire. (Historical Thinking Skills: I-1: Historical Causation, III-6: Historical Argumentation, and IV-8: Interpretation)

2. To support this view, you should discuss the terrible treatment of the Cubans under Spanish rule, U.S. support for Cuban independence, the sinking of the *Maine,* and the DeLôme letter. To refute this view, you should address the influence of the Yellow Press; the desire on the part of the United States to create a global empire at the expense of Spain, a waning European power; and the demand for war on the part of U.S. business interests because the war between Spain and the Cuban rebels was hurting U.S. economic interests. (Historical Thinking Skills: III-6: Historical Argumentation and IV-8: Interpretation)

14

THE PROGRESSIVE ERA: 1900–1920

By 1900 the United States was a world power; its aggressive foreign policy and dynamic domestic growth were powered by enormous industrial production and the federal government's more assertive domestic and international policies. At the turn of the century, the United States had unprecedented prestige and power. Its seemingly ever-expanding economic opportunities and basic democratic rights were a magnet for millions around the world who had few of these things. For America's large businesses, corporations, and the upper class, life was good. For the most part, they operated with little government interference other than measures that facilitated the concentration of capital. Approximately half of the nation's wealth was in the hands of 1 percent of the population.

Yet under the surface were serious problems. In some cases, not much had changed since the Gilded Age in the 1870s and 1880s when a small percentage of the nation's population was enormously wealthy while millions suffered in abject poverty, scratching out an existence in America's bustling, overcrowded, and filthy cities. Industrialization made the American worker simply a cog in the production process. Some laborers were mere children, compelled to work so that their families did not sink deeper into poverty. Throughout most of the late nineteenth century, America's farmers also experienced hardship, as farm prices fluctuated and farmers in increasing numbers lost their property and their livelihood. As for black Americans, decades earlier they had been relegated to a second-class status. Women were still disenfranchised; they could not vote or run for political office. What is more, they continued to languish as subordinates to men economically and socially.

While industrialization brought despair to millions of urban workers, it was the impetus for the emergence of a middle class of professionals, office workers, social workers, educators, and government employees. As in the antebellum period, the middle class was willing and had the time to take up the challenge of addressing America's social ills. Their motives were sometimes altruistic but often simply personal, as these problems affected their class as well. Because of reform-minded public officials and private citizens and organizations, a concerted effort was made to address the maladies that undermined American democracy. This period in U.S. history, 1900–1920, is referred to as the progressive era, and it was the first manifestation of liberalism in the twentieth century.

KEY CONCEPTS

- The progressive movement was one major phase of liberalism in the twentieth century.
- Grassroots and government reformers attempted to address the abuses and deficiencies in American life at the local, state, and federal levels.
- Important reforms were enacted by Congress to address abuses in business, the economy, and the environment.
- Women and African Americans organized to improve their condition and status, but despite major economic and political reforms, they continued to experience hard times.

The progressive era is discussed in depth in *The American Pageant,* 14th and 15th eds., Chapters 28–29.

LIBERALISM IN THE TWENTIETH CENTURY: HISTORIANS' PERSPECTIVE

To place the progressive era in perspective, it is important to view it as one phase in the ongoing struggle to reform American society, the economy, and government. In the twentieth century alone, there have been five major reform periods:

1900–1920 Progressive Era	**1933–1945 New Deal**	**1945–1953 Fair Deal**	**1961–1963 New Frontier**	**1963–69 Great Society**
T. Roosevelt, Taft, and Wilson	Franklin D. Roosevelt	Harry S Truman	John F. Kennedy	Lyndon B. Johnson

Before exploring the details and dimensions of the progressive movement, you will need a working knowledge of the term "liberalism"—it is often considered synonymous with reform and progressivism, but it is not. On this topic there is little consensus among social and political scientists. Some historians, for example, view liberalism this way:

- Liberalism is the true expression of American democracy and represents the traditions established by Jefferson and Jackson and further developed by twentieth-century presidents (see above).

- Liberalism represents an alliance between the public and the government to guard against and correct the abuses of capital. In the process, equilibrium is established between the interests of the public and the interests of corporations.
- Reforms and reform movements have two fundamental objectives:
  - to alleviate immediate short-term economic, political, and social problems
  - to bring about significant fundamental change within existing economic, political, and social relationships and institutions

Reforms

Economic	Political	Social
reforms that seek to control corporate behavior and check the abuses practiced by large corporations	reforms that 1) extend or protect the political rights of previously disenfranchised groups, 2) are intended to make public officials more accountable to the public, 3) attack corruption and abuses of power by political officials	reforms that seek to protect and promote the human and social rights of deprived groups in society

Other historians do not agree that liberalism is an expression of American democracy. They hold that liberalism represents an alliance between the government and corporations designed to preserve and enhance the following conditions and relationships:

- maintaining power in the hands of a small elite class
- maintaining this class's hegemony over other classes in American society
- preserving the status quo, a goal of both the liberal elite and the conservative elite, who differ only in their methods

The Early Twentieth-Century Progressives

The progressives were a composite of a variety of groups, individuals, and movements. Like reformers before and since, they held to the view that humanity and the institutions created by humans could be improved. To this end, progress and advancement of U.S. society and culture were the foundations of progressive thought and actions. In the vanguard were professionals, both men and women, who represented the middle class. Rather than rely exclusively on traditional sources of reform—the church, private benefactors, and municipal government—they approached societal problems systematically and pragmatically. Progressives rejected both laissez-faire capitalism and a radical approach to the crises—recessions and depressions, for example—inherent in the capitalist system:

- They viewed government as a potentially positive force for change and reform, one that could be used to combat monopolies and corruption in government.
- They maintained that government could neutralize special-interest groups that had long been a drain on the nation's governmental resources.
- A long-term objective of the progressives was to instill order and stability to the institutions and relations of American life.
- Some progressives combined the Protestant religion and humanitarian work, a synthesis that became known as the social gospel movement. Operating predominantly in urban areas, those belonging to this movement believed it was their Christian duty to be concerned about the plight of the poor and the immigrant and to take steps to improve their lives.
    - The Salvation Army is an excellent example of the social gospel movement at work. It provided material and spiritual assistance to the urban poor.
    - One of the leaders of the movement, Walter Rauschenbusch, distinctively combined socialist thought with religious principles to bring salvation through Christianity and reform ideals.
    - Settlement houses served as centers for the urban poor and immigrants; they provided the needy with educational services, child care, technical skills, and recreational activities. The most famous American social settlement house was Jane Addams's Hull House, situated in one of Chicago's most distressed wards.
- The muckrakers were investigative reporters and journalists who wrote about the abuses that were prevalent in American society. (They received this unflattering label from President Theodore Roosevelt, who believed they were sensationalizing their stories to attract readership.) The graphic and hard-biting exposés inspired a public uproar against those causing the abuses. Examples include
    - Jacob Riis's *How the Other Half Lives* (1890) is one of the earliest examples of muckraking. Riis's photos of urban poverty evoked an emotional response from the public, especially his photographs of forlorn young street orphans.
    - Upton Sinclair's *The Jungle* (1906) exposed gruesome working conditions and the tainted meat that emerged from Chicago's meatpacking plants. Although it did not generate support for socialism, which was Sinclair's intention, it did lead to legislation to correct the abuses: the Pure Food and Drug Act and the Meat Inspection Act.
    - Ida Tarbell's *History of the Standard Oil Company* (1904) targeted the company's abuses so effectively that it was successfully prosecuted in 1911.
    - Frank Norris's novel *The Octopus* (1901) exposed corrupt politicians conspiring with the powerful Southern Pacific Railroad to exploit California farmers.

- Lincoln Steffens's *The Shame of the Cities* (1904) exposed municipal corruption.
- David Graham Phillips' *The Treason of the Senate* (1906) targeted the undue influence corporations held over the national legislature.

Reforming Local and State Political Systems

Political machines are organizations that manage, sometimes illegally, the administration of local and state governments. Favoritism, sordid dealings, and nepotism are features of the political machines. They often work in conjunction with municipal governments but have often come to dominate the city in which they operate. Most machines have been corrupt, financially and politically. After the Civil War and well into the twentieth century, in return for performing favors for residents, especially new immigrants, the recipient was expected to be politically loyal to the machine. The most famous machine was "Boss" Tweed's "Ring," which dominated New York City's government during and after the Civil War. As boss of Tammany Hall, the nickname of New York's political machine, the Tweed Ring essentially ran the city, in the process bilking it of millions of dollars. The famous cartoonist Thomas Nast (who also introduced the elephant and donkey as symbols for the Republicans and Democrats) exposed the corruption and abuses of the Tweed machine in a series of startling political cartoons. Tweed went to prison, but other cities had their machines as well. Years later, in Kansas City, Tom Pendergast ran a powerful Democratic Party machine. One of his protégés—Harry S Truman—eventually became president.

To many progressives, political corruption, disenfranchisement, and unequal political influence prevented substantial changes in all realms of American society. To this end, a number of initiatives were taken at all levels of government. Reforms at the local and city levels of government include the following:

- Home-rule charters gave cities greater flexibility and autonomy by taking away many powers from the state governments and allowing local governments to draw up their own plan of government. In the process, local areas were freed from corruption on the state level that affected their communities.
- The National Municipal League was formed to carry out fact-finding investigations related to government's role in urban problems and to make recommendations in the hope of producing a model government.
- The city-manager system and the commission system placed executive and legislative powers in the hands of a small elected commission that would manage a city much like a business enterprise—with great emphasis on efficiency. Thus, the management of local municipalities would be taken out of politics and operated on a nonpartisan basis.
- In some urban areas reformers pressed for public ownership of utilities. Referred to as "gas and water socialism," it was an idea that came to fruition. Today, most municipalities own their utilities.

- Minimum wage and maximum working hours were established for city employees in various municipalities.
- Some municipalities funded recreational and day-care facilities.

In order to correct urban problems, it was first necessary to correct the abuses at the state level. Various reform-minded governors focused on the abuses that weakened their state. For example, in New Jersey, Governor Woodrow Wilson brought about reforms to regulate public utilities and address corrupt business practices. California's Hiram Johnson sought railroad regulations, and New York's Theodore Roosevelt addressed urban living conditions. Other major state reforms adopted in some states in the period include the following:

- Attempts were made to ban child labor.
- Minimum wage and maximum hour laws to protect women laborers were established.
- Workers' compensation was set up to protect workers against on-the-job accidents.
- Pensions were provided for widows and children when the husband/father was killed on the job.
- Building codes and state inspections acts were passed. Designed to protect workers against hazardous working conditions, the catalyst for this reform was the Triangle Shirtwaist Company Fire in New York (1911), which killed almost 150 young women textile workers.
- Businesses such as railroads and insurance companies and the food industry were regulated. A graduated income tax was imposed on businesses, replacing the inequitable fixed income tax.

The most far-reaching state reforms, however, occurred under the tutelage of Wisconsin's Senator Robert La Follette. In what became known as the "Wisconsin Idea," La Follette brought about a series of reforms geared to address a variety of problems and abuses. So extensive was his program in bringing about social and political reforms that Wisconsin became the model of a progressive state. They included the following:

- A direct primary system was adopted to nominate presidential candidates, in the process removing this power from the hands of political machines, which were a phenomenon of city politics.
- La Follette was instrumental in the passage of the Corrupt Practices Act, which made political figures liable to prosecution for wrongdoing.
- The state of Wisconsin passed laws limiting campaign expenditures (a precursor to today's campaign finance reforms) and lobbying activities.
- Utilizing professionals, intellectuals, and experts, La Follette created special commissions and agencies to investigate problems in conservation, taxes, education, highway construction, and politics.
- Progressives also advocated for political reforms including referendum, initiative, and recall, giving the voters a greater say in state and local governments and taking power away from political machines.

Reform under Progressive Presidents

Piecemeal state and city reforms, while important, did not solve the problems of society and the increasing complexity of the economy. Federal policies and legislation were needed to address the problems associated with industrialization and urbanization. Three presidents are associated with the progressive era: Theodore Roosevelt (1901–1908), William Howard Taft (1909–1912), and Woodrow Wilson (1913–1920). All three supported progressive reform.

Theodore Roosevelt, a Republican, had campaigned on the promise of a square, or fair, deal for citizens while reconciling this with the needs of business. This promise resonated with many Americans. As president, he was amenable to legislation that monitored and regulated big business. Unlike his predecessors, he believed a president should take an active role as an arbiter between the demands of laborers and profit-driven businesses.

In 1902 the United Mine Workers (UMW) in Pennsylvania, led by John Mitchell, went out on strike. They demanded 20 percent higher wages, a reduction from a ten- to nine-hour workday, and recognition for their union by the coal companies. The mine operators had raised wages a few years earlier but now refused to budge on any of the union's demands. Since most homes and businesses were heated by coal, Roosevelt was so concerned that the strike would last into the winter that he invited the coal operators and UMW representatives to the White House to negotiate an end to the strike. When the mine company heads stubbornly refused to negotiate with the UMW, a frustrated Roosevelt threatened to send the U.S. Army to occupy and run the mines. Frightened that he might actually seize their property, the operators agreed to have an arbitration committee settle the dispute. The strike ended in the fall; the workers received a 10 percent wage increase, their workday was shortened to nine hours, but the operators refused to recognize the union as a legitimate bargaining agent of the workers. Some historians are quick to point out that Roosevelt's actions were driven less by his support for labor than by his concerns about the effect of the strike on the economy and, indeed, capitalism itself. He challenged individual corporate giants when their actions endangered the interests and viability of capitalism as a whole. To them, Roosevelt was adamantly opposed to recognizing unions as a collective bargaining agent for labor, and his antipathy prevailed in this conflict. It remains significant, though, that this was the first time in American history that the government supported the workers over the owners.

Often viewed as an opponent of monopolies and other unfair business practices, Roosevelt was considered a "trust buster." However, his successor, William Howard Taft, actually dismantled more trusts than he did. During Roosevelt's time in office, Congress passed key legislation integral to regulating business. Many of these reforms had Roosevelt's support.

- In 1903 the Department of Commerce and Labor was created.
- Passage of the Elkins Act (1903) strengthened the Interstate Commerce Act of 1887 by requiring railroad companies to charge only the published rate and made illegal secret rebates. The railroad

companies generally favored the act because it minimized the effects of a rate war between railroad companies that was driving down profits.

- Also in 1903 the Bureau of Corporations was created to investigate antitrust violations. By this time, 1 percent of corporations produced nearly 40 percent of the nation's manufactured goods. A key example in attacking monopolies that were clearly in restraint of trade was the Northern Securities Company, a railroad holding company that controlled nearly all long-distance railroads west of Chicago. In *Northern Securities* v. *United States* (1904), the Court ordered the company to be dissolved.
- The Hepburn Act (1906) further empowered the Interstate Commerce Commission (ICC) to set maximum railroad rates and established other standards and regulations. The large railroad companies did not welcome government intervention, but they did welcome the establishment of fair rules of competition.
- In 1906 the Pure Food and Drug Act and the Meat Inspection Act barred the sale of adulterated foods involved in interstate commerce. All meatpacking facilities engaged in interstate commerce were to be federally inspected.
- An avid sportsman, Roosevelt took an active role in conservation policies. In so doing, he confronted the business sector, which wanted unfettered opportunities to harvest natural resources wherever they could be found. Over time, many corporate leaders did come to recognize the need for a rational policy for the nation's resources. By no means was Roosevelt antibusiness, but his administration sought a balance between the needs of America's environment and the needs of America's businesses. To preserve the environment, Roosevelt's administration was active in the following:
  - enactment of the Newlands Reclamation Act Bill, by which a further 150 million acres were added to the national forest reserve
  - establishment of the Conservation Congress to address national conservation efforts
  - appointment of Gifford Pinchot, a strong conservationist, to head the Department of Agriculture's Division of Forestry

When Roosevelt's second term ended, he designated his confidant William Howard Taft as his successor. In Taft's four years in the White House, the following initiatives were taken:

- Passage of the Mann-Elkins Act (1910) strengthened the Interstate Commerce Commission (as had the Elkins Act and the Hepburn Act) by giving to it the power to regulate the new communications industry. In addition, the ICC was given more authority to regulate railroad companies' short- and long-haul rates. (Often railroad companies charged more for transportation of passengers and commodities between two points on a railway line than for a longer journey on the same line.)
- Taft "busted" twice as many trusts in four years as Roosevelt did in eight, including one, U.S. Steel, that had been approved by Roosevelt. This was one factor in a split between Roosevelt and Taft

that eventually divided the Republican Party. During Taft's one term, the Supreme Court dissolved two major corporations: American Tobacco Company and the Standard Oil Company.

THE REPUBLICAN PARTY SPLITS

As Roosevelt's handpicked successor, Taft proved to be a disappointment, both to Roosevelt and to progressives in general. During his presidency, Taft moved closer to the conservative wing of his party, alienating his political base in the process. Four major issues eventually divided the Republican Party:

- **The Payne-Aldrich Tariff (1909)** was a high protective tariff (up to 40 percent tax on imports) that was supported by conservatives but opposed by progressives. Taft decided to support the conservative wing on this issue.
- **The Ballinger-Pinchot controversy (1910)** grew out of western opposition to conservation measures because they inhibited the development of the West. Ballinger, secretary of the interior, was identified with those westerners and conservatives who opposed conservation measures. Pinchot represented the progressive (and eastern) wing that favored conservation measures. Once again, Taft threw his weight behind the conservatives and sided with Ballinger, who proceeded to open over 1 million acres of land that Roosevelt had reserved. (Taft did, however, set aside some of that reserved land for public use.)
- **The Speaker of the House controversy** erupted over Joseph Cannon. Few Speakers of the House of Representatives have been as powerful as Cannon, nor as conservative. Cannon opposed nearly all social-welfare programs. As chairman of the Rules Committee, he decided which bills would be discussed in the House. The progressives wished to curtail the Speaker's power by, for instance, making membership on the Rules Committee an elected rather than appointed position. The conservatives opposed any erosion of the Speaker's power. Taft further alienated the progressive wing by supporting the conservatives.
- **Taft's antitrust suit against U.S. Steel (1911)** dated back to 1908, when U.S. Steel purchased the bankrupt Tennessee Coal and Iron Company. The combination seemed to be in violation of the Sherman Anti-Trust Act. Roosevelt's position had been that U.S. Steel had provided a public service to the nation by acquiring a company that, if it defaulted on its loans, could have dire consequences for the economy. Roosevelt assured U.S. Steel that the Justice Department would not prosecute the company, but under Taft that is exactly what happened. Roosevelt felt as if Taft had undermined his integrity. The enmity that had developed between the two former friends split the party.

At the Republican Party Convention in 1912, the progressive wing, led by "Battling Bob" La Follette, attempted to replace Taft as the party's candidate. Roosevelt refused to support either Taft's renomination or La Follette's attempt to unseat Taft. Instead, he chose to run as a candidate on a third-party ticket, the progressive party (more commonly referred to as the "Bull Moose party," named for an animal that Roosevelt had admired for its strength and vigor). Roosevelt's campaign program (the "New Nationalism") advocated use of the federal government as a positive interventionist tool to advance democracy. The Democratic candidate, Woodrow Wilson, argued in his campaign program (the "New Freedom") that government should intervene only when democracy was threatened by social, economic, and political privilege and unfair business practices.

There was yet another candidate in the race, Eugene Debs, of the Socialist party. Debs promoted public ownership of the nation's natural resources and those industries vital to the nation's economic health. Amazingly, he received nearly 1 million votes. As for the Republicans, the party's division was a major factor in the election of Woodrow Wilson, only the second Democrat to win the presidency in over fifty years.

Reform under Woodrow Wilson

Before becoming president, Democrat Wilson had been a popular reform governor of New Jersey. He took this reform spirit with him to the White House, where he was bent on tackling the "triple wall of privilege": the tariff, the trusts, and banking. Whereas Roosevelt regulated monopolies, Wilson regulated competition. His support for certain policies and his rejection of others were shaped by his general support for big business. In his two terms in office, he took an active role in seeing that the following domestic measures were taken:

- **The Underwood Tariff (1913)** was the first significant reduction in the tariff in fifty years. Wilson sided with consumers, who he believed were paying inflated prices because of the protection accorded businesses. Yet he believed that lowering tariffs and thereby increasing foreign competition would compel U.S. businesses to become more efficient, lower their prices, and make better products. The nation's corporate leaders agreed, though the idea of lowering tariffs is often a hard pill for business to swallow.
- **The Clayton Anti-Trust Act (1914)** was the response to Wilson's call for steps to be taken to break up monopolies. The new law modified the Sherman Anti-Trust Act (1890) by now exempting unions from restraint of trade provisions, but only when pursuing legitimate aims. This provided the government an opportunity to limit labor's power. For example, the Supreme Court, in *Duplex Printing Press Company* v. *Deering* (1921) upheld an injunction against a secondary boycott. The Clayton Act supplemented the Sherman Act by including new provisions prohibiting unfair and illegal business practices such as price fixing.
- **The Federal Trade Commission** was created in 1914 to regulate business by controlling trusts and monopolies, investigate misconduct, and issue cease and desist orders to intractable businesses.
- **The Federal Reserve Act (1913)** addressed glaring currency problems: the inability of the federal government to regulate the amount of money in the economy and to regulate banking practices. All national banks were required to join the Federal Reserve System.

  - The nation was divided into twelve regional Federal Reserve Banks.
  - The Federal Reserve System served banks, not private citizens.
  - The district banks extended credit and accepted deposits from member banks based on the needs of the specific district. The Federal Reserve regulated credit by either raising or lowering interest rates.
  - The district banks issued national currency in the form of Federal Reserve notes. This currency could be expanded (more money in the system) or contracted (less money in the system) depending on the status of the economy.
  - A board of directors composed of financial experts was to oversee the Federal Reserve System.
- **The Adamson Eight-Hour Act (1916),** growing out of concern that a railroad strike would severely damage the economy, had Wilson's support. The act also provided compensation for overtime work.
- **The Keating-Owen Child Labor Act (1916)** prohibited interstate trade involving commodities produced by children under the age of fourteen. It was subsequently ruled unconstitutional in the 1918 Supreme Court case *Hammer* v. *Dagenhart*. In 1924 a constitutional amendment to abolish child labor failed to receive the approval of the required three-fourths of the states for ratification.

AP Tip

During the progressive era four constitutional amendments were adopted. Keep them in mind for AP free-response essays.

- The Sixteenth Amendment (1913) provided for an income tax. As you recall, the Supreme Court had ruled in *Pollock* v. *Farmers Loan and Trust Company* (1895) that the Income Tax Act of 1893 was unconstitutional.
- The Seventeenth Amendment (1913) replaced the method of selecting U.S. senators as prescribed in the Constitution—by state legislatures—with direct election of senators by popular vote.
- The Eighteenth Amendment (1919) (repealed in 1933 by the Twenty-first Amendment) prohibited the "manufacture, sale, or transportation of intoxicating liquors" within the United States. Some reformers blamed alcohol for many of society's problems.
- The Nineteenth Amendment (1920) granted women the right to vote. No state could deny or abridge this right.

Progressives had mixed success with the Supreme Court. Some of the court's key cases in the progressive era are the following:

- ***Lochner* v. *New York* (1905)** invalidated a New York State law that had limited night work hours in bakeries. The court contended that the law was a violation of the work contract between employer and employee.
- ***Muller* v. *Oregon* (1908)** upheld a law that limited work hours for women laundry workers only. It did not apply to other workers (see

the *Adkins* case below) and did not overturn the *Lochner* decision. In the *Muller* case, the Court decided that the inherent "weakness" of females required their protection by the government.

- ***Adkins*** **v.** ***Children's Hospital*** **(1923)** held that a maximum ten-hour workday for women workers in Washington, D.C., was unconstitutional, overturning *Muller* v. *Oregon*.

The Women's Rights Movement

While a milestone in the women's rights effort had been reached with ratification of the Nineteenth Amendment, women continued to be relegated to a second-class status, both economically—in the workplace—and socially. More and more women entered clerical and factory work, and some entered the professions, but their pay was considerably lower than men's pay, and they were denied access to certain professions and jobs. Roosevelt and Wilson, while progressive-minded in other ways, were certainly not strong advocates of the federal government's involvement in the women's rights cause. Some progressive women sought alternatives. For example, Charlotte Perkins Gilman's *Women and Economics* advocated for female financial independence. Another reformer, Margaret Sanger, observed the ill effects that unwanted pregnancies had on women, especially the poor, and thus advocated for the legalization of birth control. Even though she was arrested for disseminating contraceptive literature through the U.S. Mail, the indomitable Sanger set up the nation's first birth-control clinic in 1916. Alice Paul, a militant suffragist, engaged in acts of civil disobedience to draw attention to the need for a constitutional amendment guaranteeing women the right to vote. In addition, Jeannette Rankin became the first woman elected to Congress (1917). She promptly involved herself in the peace movement and would vote against U.S. intervention in World War I and World War II.

The Socialist Challenge

Formed in 1901 by Eugene Debs and V. L. Berger as a radical alternative to the two dominant political parties, the Socialist party of the United States was dedicated to the welfare of the laboring class. Socialists called for policies and programs that went beyond the aspirations of the progressives, such as public ownership of utilities, railroads, and major industries such as oil and steel. On issues such as workers' compensation and minimum-wage laws, however, progressives and socialists cooperated. Over time, state, local, and federal governments embraced some Socialist ideas: public ownership of utilities, the eight-hour workday, and pensions for employees. During World War I, the party's supporters were persecuted, and following the war, the party was decimated in the first red scare. Yet the Socialist party offered Americans a viable alternative to the platforms of the Democrats and Republicans.

Debs was the party's presidential candidate five times. He embraced socialism while imprisoned for participating in the Pullman Strike in 1894. Debs did best in 1920 while in prison for violating the

Espionage Act by opposing America's entry into World War I; in that election he garnered 6 percent of the popular vote.

The Wobblies

While most unions, such as the American Federation of Labor (AFL), sought to compromise and coexist with big business, the Industrial Workers of the World (IWW, founded in 1905 by revolutionary socialists and nicknamed the Wobblies) took a radically different approach. To them, capitalism was a tool of oppression that extended beyond the workplace into every aspect of one's social, economic, cultural, and political life. Led by "Big Bill" Haywood, the Wobblies dreamed of "one big union" of skilled and unskilled workers as the only way to challenge the enormous clout of America's corporations. When the United States entered World War I, the Wilson administration began to prosecute the Wobblies for treasonous acts; they had engaged in strikes and supported others to do so, which the administration claimed was undermining the war effort. At its height, it had enrolled 100,000 members, but its power waned after World War I.

Black Americans and the Progressive Movement

While Roosevelt and Wilson were catalysts for numerous reforms in the early twentieth century, the status and rights of black Americans were not priorities for them. Wilson, born in Virginia during the Civil War, did not appear to have much sympathy for the plight of black Americans. (Some historians maintain Wilson was a blatant racist.) Roosevelt concurred. He saw no political solution to the problem despite his outcries against the lawless acts perpetrated against blacks. Most progressives were frankly indifferent to the discrimination that was so very much a part of the black experience in the United States at this time. The most reform-minded politician could also be a racist. In most cases, black Americans had to look to their own leaders to develop a response to the political, economic, and social barriers that confronted them daily. Three gifted leaders emerged in this period:

- **Booker T. Washington** gained national attention in 1895 when he spoke at the Cotton States and International Exposition in Atlanta. In his speech, known as the Atlanta Compromise, Washington advised blacks to "put down your bucket where you are" and work for individual self-improvement. Once blacks were economically independent, he maintained, social change would follow. To this end, he started the Tuskegee Institute, a vocational school for blacks. For many white Americans, Washington's advice to his fellow blacks was sound. Washington (who was born a slave) was not advocating a radical or militant solution to the condition of blacks in America, but one that was moderate and therefore generally acceptable to white America. When President Roosevelt invited Washington to dine at the White House, it caused a national furor.
- **W. E. B. Du Bois**, like many other blacks, had serious reservations about Washington's approach. Born after the Civil War, he had been educated at Harvard University. His views were more

expansive than Washington's in that he looked to white Americans to eliminate racism and segregation. In 1903 he published *The Souls of Black Folk,* in which he attacked Washington's patient approach to racial acceptance and equality. Instead, talented blacks should go beyond developing a trade or skill and seek a university education. This "talented tenth" would be the vanguard in the effort to have black rights restored without delay and would become the nucleus of an organization called the Niagara Movement, forerunner to the National Association for the Advancement of Colored People (NAACP). Started in 1909, the NAACP soon went to work challenging Jim Crow laws. In *Buchanan* v. *Worley* (1915) the Court struck down a Louisville, Kentucky, law that required segregated communities. In *Guinn* v. *United States* (1919), the Supreme Court ruled unconstitutional Oklahoma's use of the grandfather clause. To this day, the NAACP is active in promoting the rights of black Americans.

- **Marcus Garvey** embraced nationalism as the solution to the black struggle. Believing that blacks would never gain acceptance and equality in the United States, he created the Universal Negro Improvement Association (UNIA), which had as its goal the creation of an independent nation in Africa. Although other civil rights leaders such as Du Bois repudiated him, thousands of blacks, mostly in poor urban areas, purchased stock in the Black Star Line, whose fleet would ostensibly transport them to Africa. Garvey's scheme failed, and many lost what little money they had in their investment. Ironically, Garvey's desire for a segregated black nation was exactly what reactionary and racist organizations like the Ku Klux Klan supported.

THE END OF THE PROGRESSIVE ERA

By the early 1920s the progressive movement had run its course. However, many progressive organizations' supporters were imbued with a spirit of reform that would continue to thrive. As war loomed, the foreign threat siphoned off the attention that domestic conditions had received. The devastation of World War I dampened the enthusiasm of many who believed that through government a more democratic society could be realized. Others embraced the notion that the material growth the nation was experiencing following the war was an indication that life in America had indeed improved. Still others believed that, given the tribulations of war and the social, economic, and political struggles of the previous twenty years, a "return to normalcy" was needed.

Content Review Questions

1. Which of the following took the lead in reforming the United States in the early twentieth century?
   (A) Corporate leaders
   (B) The lower classes
   (C) The middle class
   (D) The conservative wing of the Republican Party
2. Which one of the following presidents is NOT associated with a major reform movement in the twentieth century?
   (A) Warren Harding
   (B) Woodrow Wilson
   (C) Lyndon Johnson
   (D) Theodore Roosevelt
3. This muckraking novel addressed the abuses that occurred in Chicago's meatpacking industry.
   (A) *The Octopus*
   (B) *How the Other Half Lives*
   (C) *Shame of the Cities*
   (D) *The Jungle*
4. Which one of the following did NOT divide the Republican Party on the eve of the 1912 election?
   (A) The Ballinger-Pinchot controversy
   (B) Taft's antitrust suit against U.S. Steel
   (C) The progressive wing's advocacy for black rights
   (D) The Speaker of the House controversy
5. Which Supreme Court case decision made the Keating-Owen Child Labor Act unconstitutional?
   (A) *Lochner* v. *New York*
   (B) *Hammer* v. *Dagenhart*
   (C) *Muller* v. *Oregon*
   (D) *Adkins* v. *Children's Hospital*
6. This constitutional amendment provided for a federal income tax.
   (A) Fourteenth
   (B) Fifteenth
   (C) Sixteenth
   (D) Seventeenth
7. Marcus Garvey
   (A) was a powerful Speaker of the House in the early twentieth century.
   (B) advocated for equal rights for women, including the right to vote.
   (C) was a reform-minded senator from Wisconsin who made his state a model of reform.
   (D) was a black leader whose nationalist movement advocated a return to Africa for the nation's exploited black population.

8. Which one of the following did NOT occur during Woodrow Wilson's presidency?
   (A) The formation of the Federal Trade Commission
   (B) The passing of the Federal Reserve Act
   (C) The passing of the Clayton Anti-Trust Act
   (D) The formation of the Department of Commerce and Labor

9. The Socialist party of America
   (A) opposed civil rights legislation.
   (B) supported government ownership of utility companies.
   (C) was eventually absorbed into the conservative wing of the Republican Party.
   (D) advocated for the creation of the Federal Reserve System.

10. The Salvation Army is identified with
   (A) the women's rights crusade.
   (B) the black civil rights movement.
   (C) the social gospel movement.
   (D) the conservation movement.

11. What progressive-era legislation was designed to address a variety of corporate abuses including monopolies, false advertising, bribery, and food adulteration?
   (A) Clayton Anti-Trust Act
   (B) Federal Trade Commission Act
   (C) Pure Food and Drug Act
   (D) Federal Reserve Act

12. Woodrow Wilson was elected the twenty-eighth president of the United States in 1912 in large part because
   (A) he favored a loose immigration policy at a time when most Americans sought to significantly reduce immigration.
   (B) he received support from opponents of social reform programs.
   (C) the Republicans were divided over two presidential candidates.
   (D) the Republican Party had been associated with political corruption and scandal.

13. The Bull Moose (or progressive) party objectives included all of the following EXCEPT
   (A) government intervention to improve the condition of and opportunities for black Americans.
   (B) greater governmental role in economic affairs.
   (C) continued consolidation of trusts.
   (D) women's suffrage.

14. Woodrow Wilson won reelection in 1916 by defeating the Republican candidate,
   (A) William McKinley.
   (B) Charles Evans Hughes.
   (C) William Jennings Bryan.
   (D) Calvin Coolidge.

15. What progressive-era legislation provided for an eight-hour workday for railroad employees engaged in interstate commerce?
    (A) Jones Act
    (B) Hepburn Act
    (C) Mann-Elkins Act
    (D) Adamson Act

Short-Answer Questions

1. The progressive era featured several different reform movements advocating for a variety of changes in the United States.
    A. Which reform movement had the greatest impact on the nation? Why?
    B. Cite one government action to support your claim.

Question 2 is based on the following passage:

> "Now, it is very necessary that we should not flinch from seeing what is vile and debasing. There is filth on the floor and it must be scraped up with the muck-rake; and there are times and places where this service is the most needed of all services that can be performed. But the man who never does anything else, who never thinks or speaks or writes, save of his feats with the muck-rake, speedily becomes, not a help to society, not an incitement to do good, but one of the most potent forces of evil."
>
> —Theodore Roosevelt, 1906

2. Based on the passage and the opinion Roosevelt expresses on muckrakers, respond to the following tasks:
    A. How does Theodore Roosevelt describe muckrakers?
    B. Do the major reformers of the progressive era conform to or contradict Roosevelt's description? Use at least ONE example to support your answer.

Long-Essay Questions

1. To what extent did the government play a role in reforming American social, economic, and political life in the early twentieth century? In your response include TWO of the following:
    A. reforms at the federal level
    B. reforms at the state level
    C. reforms at the local/city level

2. To what extent can the Roosevelt, Taft, and Wilson administrations be considered progressive?

Answers

Content Review Questions

1. **(C)** The middle class was interested in reform because it felt pressure from big business and from labor and the poor (*The American Pageant,* 14th ed., p. 708/15th ed., p. 641; Learning Objective CUL-5).

2. **(A)** Harding was a conservative who wanted to return the nation to "normalcy" after the changes that occurred because of the progressive movement and the impact of World War I (*The American Pageant,* 14th ed., p. 799/15th ed., p. 637; Learning Objective POL-6).

3. **(D)** Upton Sinclair's novel caused a national uproar over working conditions and the unsafe foods that emerged from meatpacking plants (*The American Pageant,* 14th ed., p. 715/15th ed., p. 650; Learning Objective WXT-7).

4. **(C)** Most progressives were indifferent to the plight of black Americans (*The American Pageant,* 14th ed., p. 725/15th ed., pp. 658–659; Learning Objective POL-7).

5. **(B)** The 1918 ruling concerned the Keating-Owen Child Labor Act (1916). (This material does not appear in the text; Learning Objective WXT-7)

6. **(C)** The Sixteenth Amendment provided for a graduated income tax (*The American Pageant,* 14th ed., p. 732/15th ed., p. 665; Learning Objective POL-5).

7. **(D)** Garvey's Universal Negro Improvement Association maintained that blacks would never gain acceptance in a white-dominated United States and should instead develop their own nation in Africa (*The American Pageant,* 14th ed., p. 791/15th ed., pp. 719–720; Learning Objective POL-7).

8. **(D)** The Department of Commerce and Labor was created in 1903, nine years before Wilson became president (*The American Pageant,* 14th ed., pp. 712–714/15th ed., pp. 664–666; Learning Objective WXT-7).

9. **(B)** The Socialist party, led by Eugene Debs, maintained that industries vital to the health of the nation's economy should not be owned by individuals whose only objective is to make a profit (*The American Pageant,* 14th ed., pp. 658–659/15th ed., pp. 599–600, 663; Learning Objective WXT-7).

10. **(C)** The social gospel movement combined Christian ethics and social responsibility (*The American Pageant,* 14th ed., pp. 610–611/15th ed., p. 639; Learning Objective CUL-5).

11. **(B)** Passed in 1914, the Federal Trade Commission Act authorized the president to establish an oversight commission that would identify and eliminate corporate abuses (*The American Pageant*, 14th ed., p. 733/15th ed., p. 666; Learning Objective WXT-8).

12. **(C)** The fissure that erupted in Republican ranks ultimately cost the party the 1912 election because Republicans were divided over William Howard Taft, the party's nominee, and former Republican president Theodore Roosevelt, who ran as a third-party candidate (*The American Pageant*, 14th ed., p. 729/15th ed., pp. 662–663; Learning Objective POL-6).

13. **(A)** Although roundly criticized for inviting black activist Booker T. Washington to lunch at the White House, Roosevelt and his "bull moosers" did not actively promote black rights in their 1912 presidential campaign (*The American Pageant*, 14th ed., p. 729/15th ed., pp. 661–662; Learning Objective POL-6).

14. **(B)** Many Republicans favored another run for the presidency by Theodore Roosevelt, but in large part because he had bolted from the party in 1912, the Republican Party selected the bland Supreme Court justice Charles Evans Hughes to challenge Wilson (*The American Pageant*, 14th ed., p. 742/15th ed., p. 674; Learning Objective POL-2).

15. **(D)** The Adamson Act of 1916 also provided for overtime pay (*The American Pageant*, 14th ed., p. 734/15th ed., p. 666; Learning Objective WXT-8).

Short-Answer Questions

1. There are several examples that you might want to use here. You could discuss the movements for women's suffrage, which results in the Nineteenth Amendment and women attaining the right to vote. You could also discuss movements against child labor, including the role of settlement houses in these efforts, and laws that limited or outlawed child labor in this time period. You could also discuss the political reforms of the time period and the efforts of Robert La Follette, which led to the direct primary, referendum, initiative, and recall.

2. Roosevelt, who defined the term "muckraker" here, is clearly describing such a person negatively as one who focuses on the worst of society without doing anything about it. Surely there were many who affirmed this definition, but the figures that we commonly refer to as muckrakers today tend to contradict that definition, including Upton Sinclair, who revealed the conditions in the meatpacking plants in *The Jungle*; Jacob Riis who exposed tenement life in *How the Other Half Lives*; and Ida Tarbell's condemnation of big business in *The History of the Standard Oil Company*.

LONG-ESSAY QUESTIONS

1. You want to keep in mind that reforms emanate from both the government and from grassroots movements. The question asks you to address only government-related reforms, but this does not preclude you from discussing reforms that resulted from the work of nongovernment activists. This is a straightforward question in which you identify those reforms that you deem significant and discuss what abuses they were intended to correct. You may want to mention the creation of the Food and Drug Act, the Nineteenth Amendment, legislation that targeted big businesses, and political reforms like referendum, initiative, and recall. (Historical Thinking Skills: I-2: Patterns of Continuity and Change Over Time, III-7: Appropriate Use of Historical Evidence, and IV-9 Synthesis)

2. Again, this is a straightforward question. It nonetheless requires a high-level thinking skill: the ability to evaluate a president's record on reform. Identify the reform measures taken by each, evaluate the success of the reforms, and discuss whether there is a pattern of social, economic, and political reforms initiated by these presidents. (Historical Thinking Skills: II-4: Comparison, II-5: Contextualization, IV-8: Interpretation, and IV-9: Synthesis)

15

World War I: 1914–1918

By the early twentieth century the United States had established an international empire that stretched from the Caribbean to the Pacific. Ironically, while acquiring the land of others, the government and various grassroots movements were engaged in democratizing the nation's social, economic, and political systems, in a reforming spirit known as the progressive movement. As the United States entered the second decade of the century, storm clouds were appearing on the horizon in faraway Europe. Before long, a considerable part of the globe was engaged in what would become the most destructive war in history up to that time. When World War I broke out in 1914, Americans looked warily from across the Atlantic Ocean at the political machinations of Europe's powers, and they were determined to follow the advice given by President Washington over a century earlier: maintain the nation's neutrality in foreign disputes. Despite this sentiment, in 1917 American troops were fighting in France and Belgium in a war that would ultimately elevate the United States to world-power status.

Key Concepts

- German violations of American neutrality, strong economic and political ties to Britain, and effective British propaganda helped shape American public opinion about the combatants.
- Despite a strong desire on the part of the American public to remain neutral, the United States entered the conflict in 1917.
- World War I affected American civil liberties as the government suppressed dissent.
- The punitive nature of the Treaty of Versailles laid the foundation for resentment in Germany.
- Woodrow Wilson's idealism, as articulated in the Fourteen Points, including the establishment of a League of Nations, was challenged at home.

World War I is discussed in depth in *The American Pageant,* 14th and 15th eds., Chapters 29, 30, and 32.

Causes of World War I

While the United States entered the war fully three years after it began, it is important for the student to identify the major factors that brought the European powers into conflict. All historical events involve a multiplicity of short- and long-term causes, but four primary factors led to the onset of World War I in 1914.

- **The rise of nationalism** Those ethnic groups that had earlier been absorbed into large European empires sought self-determination and desired freely elected governments that would best represent their interests. The Austro-Hungarian Empire is a prime example of a patchwork nation comprising a variety of ethnic and religious groups held together by an autocratic monarchy.
- **The growth of imperialism** In the late nineteenth and early twentieth centuries, European powers raced to acquire colonies—in some cases simply to prevent their rivals from obtaining land that often had dubious benefits, as expressed in the term, the "scramble for Africa." This in turn led to increased tensions and threatened military conflicts among the European imperial powers. For example, the French and Germans nearly came to blows over control of Morocco, and German-British competition for markets in Africa and the Middle East increased tensions between the two. To make matters worse, there was no permanent international organization to settle disputes between nations.
- **The formation of sometimes-secret military alliances** Distrust among rival imperialist European nations led to the creation of antagonistic alliances. The two most important were the Triple Alliance (later known as the Central Powers and comprising Germany, Austria-Hungary, and the Ottoman Empire) and the Triple Entente (later known as the Allies and comprising Great Britain, France, and Russia). The United States, Italy, and Japan would later side with the Allies.
- **Increased militarism** The major European powers had been stockpiling military arms and expanding the size of their armies and navies. For example, the naval arms race between Britain and Germany exacerbated relations between the two. Further, in France a strong sense of revenge against the Germans for the French defeat in the Franco-Prussian War over thirty years earlier was still strong. In that conflict, the French had suffered a humiliating defeat and the loss of two of its key provinces, Alsace and Lorraine.

The stage was set for war. The spark that started it was the assassination of the heir to the Austro-Hungarian throne, Francis Ferdinand, by a Serb nationalist in June 1914. Tensions rose to a fever pitch when the Austrian government blamed Serbian authorities for the assassination. Reeling from the murder, Austrians nonetheless saw it as an opportunity to crush Serb nationalism once and for all and quell Serb dissent within the Austro-Hungarian Empire. A harsh ultimatum was given to the Serbs, who failed to meet the Austrian demands. On July 28 Austria-Hungary declared war on Serbia. Two days later Serbia's ally, Russia, entered the war, followed in short order by the other European powers—and ultimately non-European nations as well.

AMERICAN NEUTRALITY

When war broke out, President Woodrow Wilson was determined to keep the United States out of the conflict. He was deeply concerned that the war would seriously interrupt international trade and, worse, that the United States might be drawn into the maelstrom. Somewhat unrealistically Wilson believed that a neutral United States could somehow mediate an end to the dispute. But as we will see, if Wilson's hope of mediating an end to the war in 1914 or 1915 was nearly impossible, working out the peace terms proved equally challenging.

For both the Allies and Central Powers the demands of war required that they interrupt each other's expansive trade relationships, which included, of course, the United States. To this end, the British blockaded Germany in hopes of cutting off supplies to the Central Powers. In violation of international maritime law, the British deemed a wide range of goods contraband that could be seized by the Royal Navy. When the United States complained that the British were in fact in violation of international law, the British government claimed it was seizing contraband obviously intended for Germany and that it was not interfering with trade destined for neutral ports.

To the delight of the British, German violations of neutrality soon overshadowed their own transgressions. Early in 1915 the Germans declared that British waters would be deemed a war zone and that all shipping in that area could be attacked by German U-boats (submarines). From Germany's perspective, the loss of civilian lives could be avoided if neutrals stayed outside this zone and refrained from sailing on Allied ships. The very nature of submarine warfare—namely, stealth—often required U-boat captains to attack ships without first stopping and searching them for contraband. Not surprisingly, this led to the sinking of neutral ships and the loss of civilian lives. For the United States, the policies of both warring sides seriously interfered with freedom of the seas and placed American citizens in harm's way. The same year the British instituted their blockade, the inevitable happened. A British passenger liner, the *Lusitania,* was sunk by a German U-boat, resulting in the loss of over a thousand passengers, including 128 Americans.

In 1916 Wilson threatened to cut off diplomatic relations with Germany if unrestricted submarine warfare continued to cost the lives of Americans and jeopardize American shipping. Secretary of State William Jennings Bryan resigned in protest, believing that Wilson's rhetoric would bring the United States into the war. But when two Americans were injured after a French ship, the *Sussex,* was torpedoed, Wilson threatened to break off diplomatic relations with Germany. The Germans were at the time fighting the war on two fronts, against the British and French in the west and the Russians in the east. Keeping the United States out of the war was a German priority, and so the Germans promised not to sink passenger ships carrying noncombatants without warning and without care for the lives of the passengers (the "*Sussex* pledge"). For the better part of 1916, the Germans held true to their word.

U.S. Relations with Britain and France, Public Opinion, and War Propaganda

Prior to the war the United States had experienced a recession, but French and British military contracts helped stimulate a recovery. By 1915 the economy had rebounded in terms of production and business profits. Of course, U.S. manufacturers wanted to ship supplies to the Germans as well as to the Allies, but the British blockade of Germany prevented this. Whereas between 1914 and 1917 U.S. trade with the Allies quadrupled, trade with Germany all but dried up. U.S. economic interests and the Allied war effort became even closer when U.S. financiers such as J. P. Morgan were given permission by the U.S. government to extend $3 billion in credit to Britain and France. To be sure, had the Allies lost the war, that money would be lost to U.S. bankers, a factor that probably played a role in the eventual decision by the U.S. government to intervene in the war.

Most Americans supported the Allied war effort for noneconomic reasons, a perspective that was shaped in part by the effectiveness of British propaganda, which depicted the Germans as modern-day Huns brutalizing Belgians and anyone else who stood in their way. Yet support for one side or the other depended in large part on one's ethnicity. For example, German Americans supported the Central Powers, whereas Italian Americans supported the Allies after Italy entered the war in 1915. Many Irish Americans supported the Central Powers because of their hatred for the British government. Some Americans identified with the French because of their perceptions of a shared revolutionary past and French help during the American Revolution. Still, even by early 1917, most Americans, especially in the Midwest and West, were opposed to U.S. involvement in what they perceived as an entirely European affair. National leaders such as former Secretary of State Bryan, social activist Jane Addams, and Jeanette Rankin, the first woman elected to Congress, gave voice to sentiment for American neutrality, though once the United States entered the war most opposition dwindled. However, American socialists, unlike European socialists, maintained their opposition to the war from beginning to end and were often imprisoned for expressing their views or refusing to serve in the military.

U.S. Intervention

In early 1917 the Germans decided to resume unrestricted submarine warfare. While probably a necessary military measure, it was one of the primary reasons the United States entered the war in November of that year. The immediate response of the United States was "armed neutrality"—that is, U.S. merchant ships would be armed in order to protect themselves from the stealthy U-boats. The Germans fully realized that their resumption of unrestricted U-boat warfare would probably draw the United States into the war, but they gambled that American intervention would come too late to effect a change in the course of the war. In February 1917 the British intercepted a diplomatic telegram written by Germany's foreign minister, Alfred Zimmerman, to Mexico. When the telegram, referred to as the Zimmerman note, was published, Americans were shocked by the offer made by Zimmerman to Mexico: in return for Mexico's military assistance in the event the United States entered the war, Mexico would receive most of the land it had lost in the Mexican-American War if the Central Powers were victorious.

In March 1917 the Romanov Tsar Nicholas II of Russia was overthrown by revolutionary democratic forces. The provisional government kept Russia in the war until Lenin's Bolsheviks took power and signed a peace treaty with Germany, the Treaty of Brest-Litovsk, in 1917. But the overthrow of the tsar convinced Wilson that repressive regimes like Tsar Nicholas's and Kaiser Wilhelm II's represented a threat to democracy and economic liberalism. Wilson inched ever closer to the idea that the war, and specifically U.S. involvement in it, was a struggle "to make the world safe for democracy." On April 2, 1917, President Wilson called for a special session of Congress at which he asked for a declaration of war in order to stop Germany's "warfare against mankind." On April 4 Congress concurred; the United States was at war with Germany and its allies.

AP Tip

In explaining any historical effect, you should distinguish between short- and long-term causes. U.S. intervention in World War I did not suddenly occur. For example, German violations of American neutrality had long been a source of tension between the two nations. However, there were important short-term causes of President Wilson's decision to declare war on the Central Powers:

- Germany's decision to renew U-boat attacks on neutral shipping
- the Zimmerman note, which had a profound impact on American public opinion
- the Russian Revolution, which overthrew the Romanov dynasty—and satisfied Wilson's concerns regarding a U.S. alliance with an autocratic Russia and allowed him to claim the war was being fought to make the world safe for democracy

WORLD WAR I AND SUPPRESSION OF CIVIL LIBERTIES AND DISSENT

Given the nearly unanimous support in Congress for the war, one would think that the entire nation embraced U.S. intervention. But the actions of the government in 1917 and 1918 indicate that it was deeply concerned with domestic dissent. For example, the following legislation was passed to address this "problem":

- **Espionage Act of 1917** This called for fines and imprisonment for anyone "aiding the enemy" by obstructing the war effort. The postmaster-general was authorized to ban the dissemination of "treasonable literature." Socialist leader and 1912 presidential candidate Eugene Debs was convicted and imprisoned for violating the act. In 1919 the Supreme Court upheld the constitutionality of the Espionage Act in its decision in *Schenck* v. *United States,* a case involving an individual who used the U.S. mail to attempt to dissuade draftees from reporting for induction in the military. Justice Oliver Wendell Holmes argued that such actions presented a "clear and present danger" to national interests and therefore First Amendment free-speech rights could be limited by the government.

- **Sedition Act of 1918** This law made it a criminal act punishable by fine or imprisonment to attempt to persuade or discourage the sale of war bonds or to in any way disparage the military, the Constitution, or the government.

To complement its attack on dissenters, the government created the Committee of Public Information (run by George Creel, who, interestingly enough, was a progressive). In the process of equating the government's case for war and patriotism, the committee's work set off a groundswell of distrust. Immigrants and those with foreign-sounding names were considered "un-American."

The Economics of War

The federal government's intervention in the economy increased profoundly during the war as more and more agencies and resources were centralized under the government's control. This would serve as a foundation and precedent for later governmental interventions (the New Deal, for instance) and as a way to resolve economic problems and organize the expansive nature of American capitalism. The following are representative of this centralization:

- **War Industries Board (1917)** Led by Bernard Baruch, the board was created to coordinate all aspects of industrial production and distribution.
- **Lever Act (1917)** Led by Herbert Hoover as food administrator, this act aimed to mobilize agriculture and establish prices to encourage production.
- **War Labor Board (1918)** This board arbitrated management-labor disputes, prevented labor strikes, and regulated wages and work hours.

To be sure, U.S. economic and military intervention (over 1 million troops) in the war helped break the stalemate that had shaped warfare on the Western Front, where the Allies and Central Powers battered each other month after month, with neither side able to gain a decisive advantage. For Germany, the war was sapping its resources and public support for continuing the fight. After the Allies launched a major offensive in the fall of 1918, it became abundantly clear to the Germans that their nation would ultimately be invaded. The kaiser abdicated and was replaced by a representative government, which agreed to an armistice in November 1918. The "war to end all wars" had ended, but not before claiming millions of lives, of which over fifty thousand were American. The war had cost over $300 billion. Four great empires—Russian, German, Ottoman, and Austro-Hungarian—collapsed in the process.

Treaty of Versailles and the League of Nations

The "Big Four" (Wilson, France's Clemenceau, Britain's Lloyd George, and Italy's Orlando), representing the victorious Allied Powers, met in Paris and Versailles, France, in 1919 to work out the details of the peace treaty that would be imposed on the defeated Central Powers. Having suffered enormous losses, the European Allies sought a punitive peace treaty. Despite Wilson's misgivings about the harsh punishment meted out to Germany in the Treaty of Versailles, the following provisions were adopted:

- The provinces of Alsace and Lorraine (lost by the French in the Franco-Prussian War) were returned to France.
- Germany was prevented from placing troops on the western side of the Rhine River.
- The German military was dramatically reduced in size and strength.
- Germany was to ship coal from the occupied Saar region to France for a period of fifteen years.
- Germany lost all of its colonies.
- New nations were created: Estonia, Latvia, Yugoslavia, Czechoslovakia, and Poland.
- Austria-Hungary lost three-fifths of its land and three-fifths of its population.
- The Central Powers were to pay crushing war reparations.
- Germany was branded with "war guilt" as the primary perpetrator of the war.

For his part, Wilson was greatly disturbed by the harshness of the treaty, even threatening at one point to negotiate a separate treaty with Germany. Instead, he outlined his vision for the postwar world in a list of political and economic objectives referred to as The Fourteen Points. They included

- the elimination of secret treaties, the stimulus for which was the Bolshevik revelation that Britain and France had engaged in this diplomatic practice prior to the war
- open access to the seas in times of war and peace, which was important for economic expansion and trade
- reduction of military stockpiles
- adjustment of colonial claims
- self-determination for Europeans, but not for those under colonial control
- the creation of an international assembly (the fourteenth point) that would "afford mutual guarantees of political independence and territorial integrity"

Wilson believed that the fourteenth point—his call for the creation of what ultimately became the League of Nations— could be the basis for resolving the problems associated with the first thirteen points. Open to all nations, this international body would be the forum for resolving international disputes and making military confrontations obsolete.

Wilson worked tirelessly to convince the American people and Congress to support the Versailles Treaty. Unfortunately, the commissioners he selected to represent the United States at the peace conference were all Democrats, which angered and antagonized the Republican Party and key Republican political leaders, especially the most influential member of the Senate, Henry Cabot Lodge. Wilson's second political blunder was to travel to France for the peace talks rather than mobilize support for the treaty at home. Wilson's emphasis on the treaty made it the most important issue of the 1918 Senate elections. He took his appeal for its ratification directly to the American people in an exhausting national speaking tour, which ultimately broke his health. A stroke, in September 1919, paralyzed not only his body, but his personal crusade to see the treaty ratified. Senator Lodge, for his part, offered certain important reservations to the treaty that would have diminished the role and commitment of the United States to the League of Nations. With Senator Lodge and the "irreconcilables" (those staunchly opposed to the treaty) in the vanguard, the opponents of ratification won the day. Although the issue of admission to the League was taken up after Wilson left the White House, the United States never became a member of that body.

THE INTERWAR YEARS

Shocked by the enormous loss of life in the war, world leaders grasped at ways to prevent such a thing from happening again. The League of Nations was seen as one method, but without U.S. and Soviet involvement, its potential for solving international disputes was limited. Nevertheless, various international agreements were made in the interwar years to limit the size of militaries and resolve potential political disputes. Some were practical, others, rested on naïve optimism.

- **The Five-Power Naval Treaty** At the Washington "Disarmament" Conference (1921–1922), convened by President Harding, the United States, Britain, Japan, France, and Italy agreed to limit their capital ships to the following ratio respectively: 5:5:3:1.7:1.7. The participants also agreed to ban the use of certain insidious weaponry such as poison gas and restricted submarine warfare.
- **The Four-Power Treaty** At the same conference, the United States, Britain, Japan, and France agreed to respect one another's Pacific territorial possessions by, in part, not creating forward military bases in the Pacific.
- **The Nine-Power Treaty** Yet another product of the same conference, this treaty reaffirmed the Open Door policy in China.
- **Kellogg-Briand Pact (1928)** This international agreement outlawed war. However, it made no provision for enforcement, nor did it provide for defensive wars.

Economic Imperatives: Intervention, World War I Debts, and Reparations

The interwar years were dominated by Republican presidents whose domestic and foreign policies were designed to advance American business interests. To this end the Coolidge administration saw to it that a new constitution passed by Mexico in 1917, which called for nationalizing Mexico's important industries, would not jeopardize American investments in those businesses. Throughout the 1920s U.S. troops were sent to South America and the Caribbean to reinforce U.S.-backed regimes and to protect U.S. financial interests. Of equal concern to U.S. policymakers and financial institutions were the billions of dollars in loans extended to the Allies during the war. President Coolidge wanted the debts repaid, but the Europeans balked, claiming that they were unable to collect the billions in war reparations owed to them by a bankrupt Germany and adding that U.S. losses paled in comparison to their losses. Equally troubling was the U.S. passage of the Fordney-McCumber Tariff. The tariff made it exceedingly difficult for Europeans to sell their products in the United States and make the money that could be used to pay back the war loans. In response to this problem, the United States offered the following solutions:

- **The Dawes Plan** This plan significantly reduced Germany's reparations and provided loans to Germany in a roundabout way: the United States loaned money to Germany, Germany used this to pay its reparations to the Allies, who in turn used these funds to pay off the interest on its war debts to the United States.
- **The Young Plan** This plan further reduced Germany's payments and established the Bank for International Settlements to assist in the process of reparations payments.

Nevertheless, the collapse of national economies brought on by the Great Depression caused most nations to default on their debt payments to the United States.

Throughout the 1920s and well into the 1930s, the United States continued to influence the affairs of its own hemisphere as well. Time after time it intervened in Central and Latin America in order to protect U.S. economic and political interests while simultaneously it attempted to draw those nations closer to the United States, especially in light of the rise of antagonistic governments in Japan, Germany, and Italy. At the Pan-American Conferences of 1923 and 1928, the United States agreed to treat all nations on an "equal footing." The Clark Memorandum of 1928 took this rapprochement one step further by repudiating the Roosevelt Corollary to the Monroe Doctrine. Later, in the 1930s, President Franklin Roosevelt would replace Dollar Diplomacy with the Good Neighbor policy, which stated that no nation would interfere in another's internal affairs. For the time being, this new, less hegemonic policy satisfied most South Americans. Even in the far reaches of the American empire, the Philippines, the United States, partially recognizing the costs of maintaining an international empire, promised Filipino independence by 1946 (Tydings-McDuffie Act). Post–World War II international affairs, however, would convince U.S. administrations to pull back from these prewar agreements and statements.

In the two decades following the war, as the horrors of World War I battlefields faded from public consciousness, the United States experienced an economic boom, highlighted by the "Roaring Twenties." But the harshness of the Versailles Treaty, the onset of the Great Depression, and the rise of militarism and imperialism in Europe and Asia would guarantee that the peace would not be maintained for long. By 1939 the world was again at war. Two years later, the United States, which had emerged from World War I as a major economic and military power, would for the second time in less than twenty-five years send its young men to fight and die on foreign battlefields. But this time, the stakes seemed so much higher.

Content Review Questions

1. Which of the following was NOT a cause of World War I?
   (A) Imperialism
   (B) Militarism
   (C) Secret military alliances
   (D) The Russian Revolution
2. Which of the following was a member of the Central Powers?
   (A) Germany
   (B) France
   (C) Britain
   (D) United States
3. The spark that ignited World War I was
   (A) the Zimmerman note.
   (B) the assassination of the Austrian heir to the throne by a Serb nationalist.
   (C) Germany's ultimatum to Serbia.
   (D) the sinking of the *Lusitania*.
4. In the Zimmerman note
   (A) Germany offered to compensate the United States for the American lives lost in the *Lusitania* sinking.
   (B) the United States agreed not to intervene in the war if Germany halted its sinking of neutral shipping.
   (C) the United States secretly agreed to supply the Allies with war supplies in return for concessions following the war.
   (D) the Germans promised to restore to Mexico the land it lost in the Mexican-American War in return for a military alliance with Germany.
5. In the *Sussex* pledge
   (A) Germany promised to cease sinking passenger ships without warning or care for the passengers.
   (B) Germany promised to resume U-boat attacks on neutral shipping if the United States continued to supply the Allies.
   (C) the Germans promised to stop using U-boats to attack Allied warships and merchant ships.
   (D) the United States agreed not to arm its merchant fleet.

6. In the U.S. Supreme Court case *Schenck* v. *United States,* the Court ruled that
   (A) the government could prohibit U.S. citizens from traveling on ships of nations at war.
   (B) conscientious objectors could not be forced to serve in the U.S. military.
   (C) the Espionage Act of 1917 was constitutional.
   (D) the American Socialist party represented a clear and present danger to the United States.

7. Which of the following was NOT a feature of the Treaty of Versailles?
   (A) Germany would be occupied by France and Britain for twenty years.
   (B) Germany would provide France with coal for fifteen years.
   (C) Germany would pay reparations to the Allies.
   (D) Alsace and Lorraine were returned to France.

8. Which of the following was an international agreement designed to outlaw war?
   (A) The Five-Power Naval Treaty
   (B) The Kellogg-Briand Pact
   (C) The Four-Power Treaty
   (D) The *Sussex* pledge

9. The same year (1917) that the United States entered World War I on the Allied side, this Allied power dropped out of the war:
   (A) Britain
   (B) France
   (C) Italy
   (D) Russia

10. The Dawes Plan and the Young Plan
    (A) increased U.S. financial aid to South America.
    (B) repudiated the Roosevelt Corollary to the Monroe Doctrine.
    (C) assisted Germany with its reparations payments.
    (D) placed significant limitations on the role the United States would play in the League of Nations.

11. Which of the following was NOT one of President Wilson's Fourteen Points?
    (A) The establishment of a Jewish homeland in Palestine
    (B) The abolition of secret treaties
    (C) Readjustment of colonial claims to benefit both the imperialist powers and the colonists
    (D) Freedom of the seas

12. In *Schenck* v. *United States* (1919), the Supreme Court ruled that freedom of speech could be revoked if
    (A) a clear and present danger to the nation exists.
    (B) the individual is not a citizen of the United States.
    (C) Congress passes legislation that would necessitate such a curtailment of First Amendment rights.
    (D) the president issues an executive order that necessitates the suspension of the freedom of speech.

13. George Creel played an important government role during World War I by
    (A) organizing and overseeing the nation's munitions industries.
    (B) drawing up U.S. negotiating positions in preparation for the Paris Peace Conference.
    (C) heading the Committee on Public Information, which was designed in part to promote the war to the American public.
    (D) heading the War Industries Board, which sought to reconvert the nation's industries from producing consumer items to war-related materiel.

14. The National War Labor Board
    (A) was headed by former president Theodore Roosevelt.
    (B) sought to reinstate the ten-hour workday.
    (C) pressed employers to grant concessions to labor in the form of higher wages and a shorter workday.
    (D) was ruled unconstitutional by the U.S. Supreme Court on the grounds that it interfered in employer-employee relations.

15. Those American political leaders who were militant isolationists and therefore opposed to the League of Nations were referred to as
    (A) doughboys.
    (B) irreconcilables.
    (C) Huns.
    (D) wobblies.

Short-Answer Questions

Question 1 is based on the following images:

Library of Congress

1. Before the United States entered the war there were several threats to the nation's neutrality.
   A. What are the goals of these posters?
   B. Besides war-related propaganda, there were several other threats to neutrality. Choose one of the following and discuss whether this was a greater or lesser threat to the nation's neutrality than propaganda. Support your answer with historical evidence.
   Unrestricted submarine warfare
   The immigrant population of the United States
   German threats to America's safety

2. There were several significant changes on the homefront during World War I.
   A. Choose one of the following and describe how it created change in the United States during the war. Use historical evidence to support your answer.
   Food conservation
   Economic reforms
   Schenck v. *United States*
   B. Choose one other change from the list, and discuss why it was more or less significant than your first choice. Provide at least ONE concrete historical example to support your answer.

Long-Essay Questions

1. President Wilson had no choice but to enter World War I on the side of the Allies.

   To what extent is the above statement true?

2. Woodrow Wilson's vision for the postwar world and the methods he used to achieve these goals was riddled with naïve thinking and political miscalculations.

   To what extent is the above statement true?

Answers

Content Review Questions

1. **(D)** The Russian Revolution took place during the war (*The American Pageant,* 14th ed., pp. 746–747/15th ed., p. 687; Learning Objective WOR-7).

2. **(A)** The others were members of the Allied Powers (*The American Pageant,* 14th ed., p. 747/15th ed., p. 670; Learning Objective WOR-7).

3. **(B)** Austria-Hungary declared war on Serbia, and the other nations quickly followed by declaring war on each other (*The American Pageant,* 14th ed., p. 738/15th ed., p. 670; Learning Objective WOR-3).

4. **(D)** The Zimmerman note played a significant role in aggravating U.S.-German relations (*The American Pageant,* 14th ed., p. 746/15th ed., p. 678; Learning Objective POL-6).

5. **(A)** The *Sussex* pledge did not hold throughout the war (*The American Pageant,* 14th ed., pp. 742, 746/15th ed., pp. 673–674; Learning Objective ENV-5).

6. **(C)** The *Schenck* decision was a serious attack on civil liberties (*The American Pageant,* 14th ed., p. 750/15th ed., p. 681; Learning Objective POL-5).

7. **(A)** Parts of Germany were indeed occupied, but not the entire nation. The other features were indicative of the punitive nature of the treaty (*The American Pageant,* 14th ed., pp. 763–764/15th ed., p. 694; Learning Objective WOR-7).

8. **(B)** The Kellogg-Briand Pact failed because it did not include provisions for enforcement (*The American Pageant,* 14th ed., p. 803/15th ed., p. 732; Learning Objective WOR-7).

9. **(D)** The Bolsheviks, under the leadership of V. I. Lenin, signed a peace agreement, the Treaty of Brest-Litovsk, with the Central Powers (*The American Pageant,* 14th ed., pp. 756–757/15th ed., p. 687; Learning Objective WOR-3).

10. **(C)** The plans were designed to help Germany pay back its loans to the U.S., from which it had borrowed to pay war reparations to the European Allies (*The American Pageant,* 14th ed., p. 809/15th ed., p. 737; Learning Objective WOR-7).

11. **(A)** Zionism, or the movement to establish a Jewish homeland, was not one of Wilson's Fourteen Points, though self-determination for subjugated minorities was. Israel was established after World War II (*The American Pageant,* 14th ed., p. 748/15th ed., p. 680; Learning Objective WOR-7).

12. **(A)** During World War I a number of prominent Americans opposed the war in general and America's involvement specifically. For example, labor leaders Eugene V. Debs and William "Big Bill" Haywood were convicted under the Espionage Act of 1917 for speaking out against the war. The Supreme Court maintained that the government had the right to limit their First Amendment rights if their rhetoric posed a "clear and present danger" to the nation (*The American Pageant,* 14th ed., p. 750/15th ed., p. 681; Learning Objective POL-5).

13. **(C)** Employing 150,000 workers internationally, the Creel Committee propagandized America's role in the war, as well as President Wilson's vision for the future as laid out in his Fourteen Points (*The American Pageant,* 14th ed., p. 748/15th ed., p. 680; Learning Objective WOR-4).

14. **(C)** The government viewed strikes as an obstacle to the nation's war effort. To stave off interruptions to the nation's industrial production, the National War Labor Board, headed by former president Taft, tried to convince employers to grant concessions (not least of which was to recognize unions as legal and legitimate collective bargaining agents) to their workers (*The American Pageant,* 14th ed., p. 751/15th ed., pp. 682–683; Learning Objective WXT-7).

15. **(B)** Led by Republican senators Henry Cabot Lodge, Hiram Johnson, and William Borah, the "irreconcilables" maintained that U.S. membership in the League of Nations would be detrimental to U.S. interests. Believing the United States would continue to be drawn into European affairs if it joined the League, these senators favored a more isolationist foreign policy (*The American Pageant,* 14th ed., p. 763/15th ed., p. 693; Learning Objective POL-6).

Short-Answer Questions

1. The goals of the posters is to convince the British and the Americans of the evil of the Germans and the need to fight against them. These are two of several such posters, and there were many other forms of propaganda as well. Wilson, in fact, established the Committee on Public Information during the war. You can compare propaganda with some of the military actions that eventually draw the United States into war. Many historians would argue that it was unrestricted submarine warfare and the sinking of U.S. ships that really brought the United Sates into war and propaganda supported that. You could also discuss tactics like the Zimmerman telegram, and

discuss its impact on the government's decision making as well as public opinion on the war.

2. Each of these had an impact on the country. Under Herbert Hoover's Food Administration people conserved meat, wheat, and other foodstuffs for the soldiers. Moreover, people invested in Liberty Bonds and conserved money and resources in other ways, as well. The *Schenck* case ruled that First Amendment rights could be restricted where a "clear and present danger" existed. Your answer, and your point of comparison, will likely depend on whether you believe things that affect daily life or issues impacting larger swaths of the nation represent greater change.

Long-Essay Questions

1. To agree with the statement, you can begin with a discussion of American neutrality, the Zimmerman note, and Germany's use of unrestricted U-boat warfare. To refute it, you should discuss Britain's violations of U.S. neutrality, the effectiveness of British propaganda, the economic investment U.S. capitalists made to the Allied war effort, and the suppression of domestic dissent. (Historical Thinking Skills: I-1: Historical Causation, III-6: Historical Argumentation, III-7: Appropriate Use of Relevant Historical Evidence, IV-8: Interpretation)

2. To agree with the statement, you should discuss the resistance of the European Allies to a peaceful settlement with Germany, favoring instead a punitive peace treaty, much to Wilson's chagrin. Further, you can address the shortsighted approach the president took in not making his mission to the peace talks a bipartisan one—he took only Democrats to Paris with him. Wilson may have also miscalculated the strong neutral and isolationist sentiments among Americans after the war. To refute the statement, point out that Wilson's idealism was expressed in the expectation that an international body, the League of Nations, would resolve future problems and therefore prevent military conflicts. His Fourteen Points were an attempt to address some of the abuses and problems that led to World War I. (Historical Thinking Skills: II-5: Contextualization, III-6: Historical Argumentation, III-7: Appropriate Use of Relevant Historical Evidence, IV-8: Interpretation, IV-9: Synthesis)

16

CONSERVATISM AND CULTURAL DIVERSITY IN THE 1920S

The period between the end of World War I and the collapse of the nation's economy in 1929 is often referred to as the "Roaring Twenties." Indeed, in many ways that characterization is appropriate, for the 1920s witnessed an explosive cultural transformation that affected the lives of the nation's youth, its African American population, and women. In some ways, the decade has a counterpart in the civil rights and women's rights movements and with youth rebellion associated with American life in the 1960s. Yet in the 1920s there were contradictions: women and black Americans were still subordinated, and despite the burst of cultural development that took place, the nation was led by conservative presidents who represented the social, cultural, economic, and political status quo. Political radicalism and trade unionism would challenge the economic and political relations that prevailed, bringing radicals and trade unions into direct confrontation with a government that would not tolerate deviations from the accepted political ideology.

What then made the Twenties "roar"? Following the war, the nation experienced an economic boom. Many Americans, especially in the nation's urban areas, helped the expansion of the economy by increasingly participating in America's growing consumer culture, from the automobile to the phonograph. New cultural forms such as jazz and modern art revolutionized American civilization, and the Harlem Renaissance offered black poets, artists, and authors an opportunity to make valuable contributions to American cultural life. Still, under the surface there were pressures, contradictions, and the same racial and ethnic maladies that had always plagued the nation. Increasingly, the nation was divided demographically, as rapidly changing, dynamic urban life stood in stark contrast with the more static, traditional, and—to a certain sense—more Protestant rural areas. Also, while the economy boomed, not all benefited. Many who were poor after the war remained that way through the 1920s and beyond. Millions of immigrants entered the nation during this period, alarming indigenous Americans that the United States would soon be overwhelmed by foreign cultures, especially from southern and eastern Europe. An investigation of the features, tensions, and passions of the 1920s offers an opportunity to view the nation at a pivotal point in its history, when many sought to leave the past behind and others yearned for a "return to normalcy."

KEY CONCEPTS

- The 1920s were dominated by conservative Republican presidents.
- Americans experienced an unprecedented burst of consumer activity as new mass-produced commodities were made available.
- Tensions prevailed between rural and urban America.
- The decade witnessed a rise in nativism and racism.
- The period was culturally vibrant as new forms of music and art became popular.
- The U.S. government persecuted radicals in the red scare.

The decade of the 1920s is discussed in depth in *The American Pageant,* 14th and 15th eds., Chapters 31 and 32.

POLITICAL DEVELOPMENTS

The presidential election of 1920 focused on whether to accept President Wilson's idealism (for example, to enter the League of Nations) or to, as the Republican candidate Warren G. Harding stated, "Return to normalcy"—in other words, return to an earlier time when Republicans occupied the Oval Office and the nation was not embroiled in foreign problems. The Democratic ticket was composed of presidential candidate James M. Cox and his running mate, Franklin D. Roosevelt. The election, the first in which women nationally had the right to vote, was a landslide for Harding and his running mate, Calvin Coolidge. It appeared the Republicans were given a mandate from the American people, who rejected the policies and philosophy of Wilson's administration by returning a Republican to the White House in such a convincing way. In the meantime a reconversion of the nation's economy had taken place as wartime government regulations on business were relaxed. Two pieces of legislation serve as significant examples of this reconversion:

- **The Jones Merchant Marine Act (1920)** The act authorized the sale of ships built by the government to private bidders.
- **The Esch-Cummins Act (1920)** Control of the railroad industry was returned to private companies. Unions had offered the Plumb Plan (named after a railway union's legal counsel), which would have allowed the government to purchase the railroads; management of the industry would comprise government officials,

railway employees, and railway operators. Congress rejected the plan, however.

The Harding administration sought to cut taxes, especially for the wealthy—as could be seen in the Mellon tax plan—reduce government spending, and to protect American industries from the demands of labor and from foreign competition. In the case of the latter, Congress passed the Fordney-McCumber Tariff, which placed high taxes on imports, a policy that the nation's trade partners would adopt in retaliation.

Harding had never really wanted to be president. Content as an Ohio newspaper owner and U.S. senator, he found the role of chief executive more stressful than his mind and body could endure. Three years into his term, in 1923, he died suddenly, catapulting Calvin Coolidge into the Oval Office. Had Harding lived, he would have endured the humiliation of congressional investigations that revealed widespread corruption on the part of Harding's associates and advisers. The most infamous case involved the sale of U.S. naval oil reserves at Teapot Dome, Wyoming, to private businesses. Harding's secretary of the interior, Albert Fall, was convicted of bribery and sent to prison, the first cabinet member in U.S. history to suffer such a disgraceful fate. Other political associates, such as Attorney General Henry Daugherty and Secretary of the Navy Edwin Denby, barely escaped conviction. However, one of Harding's closest friends, Jesse Smith, who had arranged the payoffs, committed suicide.

"Silent Cal" Coolidge and the "Do-Nothing" Herbert Hoover

The new president, Calvin Coolidge, the former governor of Massachusetts, rose to national prominence by putting down a police strike in Boston. A man of very few words, Coolidge believed the best thing a president could do for the nation was to do very little, especially when it came to government control or regulation of the economy. Under his conservative stewardship the business sector flourished, though his critics claimed he maintained the status quo by failing to address important social and economic concerns. Farmers, for one, could find little support from the administration, especially after farm prices slumped in the postwar years. Even though Congress passed the McNary-Haugen Bill (in 1927 and 1928), which provided for the government to purchase crops in order to maintain price levels comparable to what they were before the war, both times Coolidge vetoed the legislation as being an economic burden on the government.

Because he had not been tainted by the scandals of the previous few years, Coolidge ran for election in his own right in 1924. He easily defeated his Democratic opponent, John W. Davis, and a third-party candidate, the progressive senator from Wisconsin, Robert La Follette, who nevertheless received 5 million votes. Coolidge's election, then, served as an indicator that Americans were more concerned with economic progress than progressivism. Throughout the nation, women were elected to serve in local, state, and federal positions. The nation's first two women governors, for example, were elected in 1924.

When it came time for Coolidge to seek reelection in 1928, the taciturn president told reporters, "I choose not to run for president in 1928," and kept to his word. In the '28 election another Republican, Herbert Hoover, was elected over New York's Governor Al Smith. Smith's religion (he was a Catholic) probably cost him significant support among Protestants. (It would be another thirty-two years before the nation would elect its first Catholic president, John F. Kennedy.) Sadly for Hoover, the Great Depression struck less than two years into his one and only term. Unfortunately for the American people, Hoover, who had done so much as an administrator for Belgian war relief in 1917, did so little to provide aid to Americans suffering from the effects of the economic collapse. His detractors called him a "do-nothing" president. His successor, Democrat Franklin D. Roosevelt, would oversee the nation as it made its way through the perilous waters of the worst economic collapse in the nation's history.

MASS CONSUMERISM

After a brief recession in the first two years of the decade, the economy quickly rebounded. It would soon reach unprecedented heights as the nation engaged in a torrent of consumer spending stimulated in part by the stock-market "bubble" and available surplus capital that often comes with periods of economic recovery. Purchasing on credit (installment buying) allowed Americans to "buy now and pay later." Consequently, those items that had earlier been considered out of reach for millions of Americans, such as home appliances, could now be purchased and paid off over time. Unfortunately, this spending spree led many to fall into debt. The advent of department-store catalogs, such as those offered by Sears Roebuck and Montgomery Ward, made it easier to purchase commodities, especially for people who did not have access to large urban department stores. And mass advertising convinced the consumer of the need to purchase new and improved commodities. The advent of the radio provided Americans a new form of entertainment and faster access to national and international news, as well as a venue for the nation's advertisers.

The period's most notable consumer item was the automobile. Although there were very few cars in the United States prior to World War I, by the end of the 1920s over 25 million autos would be registered; 20 percent of Americans owned cars by 1930. Of course not everyone could afford to purchase such an expensive commodity, but Henry Ford's revolutionary use of the assembly line made the Model T accessible to many, including his own workers, who were paid an unprecedented $5 per eight-hour day! The expansion of the auto industry spurred associated developments, such as highway construction, increased suburbanization, and the growth of the rubber, oil, insurance, and advertising industries. By the mid-1920s, many in the middle class came to associate their status with automobile ownership. Yet the expansion of one form of transportation spelled the decline of another—namely the railroad industry.

Entertainment: The Motion Picture Industry and Professional Sports

Like the birth of radio and the recording industry in the 1920s, of television in the post–World War II years, or of the Internet today, the motion picture industry provided Americans with a revolutionary new source of entertainment and information. The first one-reel movie (*The Great Train Robbery*) had been produced in 1913, followed by the first feature-length film, *Birth of a Nation* (1915). Utilizing editing techniques, *Birth of a Nation* captivated the American public despite its politically charged representation of racist stereotypes and glorification of the KKK. The 1920s movie industry built on the successes of the previous decade as silent motion pictures became enormously popular. The first movie documentary, *Nanook of the North,* was released in 1922. Animated films also became very popular in the 1920s as the American public was drawn to such cartoon characters as "Krazy Kat" and Walt Disney's "Steamboat Willie" (later known as Mickey Mouse). It was not until 1927 that Americans had the opportunity to hear their first "talkie," *The Jazz Singer.*

Although baseball had suffered a serious black eye as a result of the Black Sox scandal of 1919 when members of the Chicago White Sox threw the World Series, the sport rebounded in the 1920s as athletes such as Babe Ruth became national icons. Boxing and football also grew as popular diversions in the 1920s.

While the economy boomed, there were social and cultural undercurrents that indicated that all was indeed not well domestically. In fact, prominent American writers known by the collective moniker the "Lost Generation" wrote of American ills and excesses in works like Sinclair Lewis's *Babbitt* (1922), F. Scott Fitzgerald's *The Great Gatsby* (1925), and Ernest Hemingway's *The Sun Also Rises* (1926). By 1930 many Americans who had spent enormous sums on consumer items in the 1920s would find it difficult to purchase even the most basic needs of life.

Divisions on the Domestic Scene

Many social scientists see the 1920s as a time when the ideals of modernism clashed with the stability of tradition, secular and religious. These tensions manifested themselves in a variety of political, social, and cultural ways:

- **Urban versus rural** To those living in rural America, the nation's cities represented vice and sin. Ironically, as the nation was prepared to enter into the decade known as the Roaring Twenties, the sale, distribution, and consumption of alcoholic beverages was outlawed in the United States by the Eighteenth Amendment and enforced by the Volstead Act. The campaign to outlaw alcohol, launched by Protestant fundamentalists—the "drys"—was based on the assumptions that liquor caused crime, poverty, poor health, and broken families. With prohibition, speakeasies popped up in cities large and small. There, "wets" would dance—for example, the frenetic Charleston played by jazz musicians like Louis Armstrong—and drink illegal alcohol. Rural Americans viewed it as an exceedingly provocative lifestyle. (Prohibition ultimately led to the rise of urban gangs, such as the one led by Chicago's Al Capone. It also cost millions to enforce, and it failed to resonate on a moral level with the American people. Having outlived its welcome, the Eighteenth Amendment was repealed in 1933 by the Twenty-first Amendment.) The attitude of urban women as represented in their clothing and behavior (in part shaped by advertising) seemed equally disturbing to small-town Americans. Each year, it seemed, women's hemlines inched ever higher, and some women were wearing cosmetics and smoking cigarettes. Known as "flappers," these women flaunted their disdain for traditional women's roles in a manner that angered those who favored a more Victorian comportment for women.

- **Moderate versus radical unionism** Major moderate unions such as the American Federation of Labor (AFL) experienced a decline in their membership due to their limited successes in achieving real gains for workers when the nation's economy was booming. Radical unions such as the Industrial Workers of the World (the "Wobblies") had been effectively neutralized by the government during the war. The 1920s witnessed the growth of industrial unions whose members identified with radical political and economic solutions to their plight.
- **Science versus religion: the Scopes Monkey Trial** In 1925 a Tennessee teacher was arrested for teaching Darwin's theory of evolution in defiance of state law. The case provided fundamentalist Christians an opportunity to silence those who questioned the theory of creation as described in the Book of Genesis. Moreover, the case pitted the ideals and ideas of urban modernism against the religious fundamentalism of rural Protestant America. Three-time presidential candidate William Jennings Bryan was the prosecutor in the case; the famous attorney Clarence Darrow represented John Scopes. The jury ruled against the teacher, but the verdict was eventually overturned. To this day, the role of religion in education is debated in the halls of Congress and across the nation.
- **Modern versus traditional art forms** The emergence of abstract art forms such as impressionism and cubism provoked controversy. At the infamous Armory Show, held in New York City in 1913, the highly controversial works of Pablo Picasso and other modern artists were exhibited. Picasso's use of geometric abstract shapes in his paintings outraged traditionalists, as did Marcel Duchamp's "Nude Descending a Staircase," which seemed suggestive and provocative to those with more modest sensibilities. Ultimately the modernists won out. In 1929 the Museum of Modern Art opened in New York City. By that time many had come to accept and even appreciate the new art form, whose case was prejudiced by the nativist sentiment that consumed the nation in this decade. Following World War I, New York's Harlem became the center of black American cultural and intellectual life. Black artists, poets, authors, musicians, and painters flocked to this cultural mecca, where they produced some of the finest literary, musical, and artistic works in the 1920s—or in any decade, for that matter. James

Weldon Johnson, Jean Toomer, Countee Cullen, Langston Hughes, and other authors and poets touched a chord in white and black Americans alike. The musical arrangements that emerged from this movement tended to be a synthesis of gospel music, jazz, and African rhythms. Known as the Harlem Renaissance, the movement also provided an opportunity to protest racial attitudes and promote black pride.

AP Tip

What was it about the 1920s that seems so important and unique that it deserves a separate chapter? As with all historical questions, the answer is very much interpretive. Some historians see the period as essentially one in which Americans became increasingly identified with consumerism and materialism, repudiating the reforms associated with the pre–World War I era and embracing conservatism and even racist and reactionary politics, in part as a response to the progressive era. Other historians see the reaction by more traditional and conservative citizens as a legitimate attempt to preserve the values they associated with being an American, which was expressed, for example, in nativism and anti-modernism. What is more, many Americans were responding to what they viewed as an unhealthy expansion of federal power that they attributed, in part, to the progressive era and World War I. Other historians view this expansion of federal power as a not unexpected consequence of the development and expansion of the American economy. To be sure, this is a sampling of interpretations, but you should be conscious of divergent perspectives, as well as how many of the issues that shaped an earlier historical period are contemporary concerns as well.

NATIVIST ANXIETY

The success of the Bolshevik Revolution in Russia in 1917 gave rise to the first red scare (1919–1920). Americans and their government believed that communism was on the rise and could someday spread to the United States. When bombs exploded outside the home of Attorney General A. Mitchell Palmer in 1919 and on Wall Street the following year, killing thirty-eight people, the attacks were blamed on communists. Paranoia swept the nation in what became known as the "red scare," a period when the government reacted against domestic radicals, many of whom, though opponents of capitalism, were law-abiding citizens who should have been protected by the First Amendment. Under Palmer, deportations soon followed, as did attacks on trade union members, socialists, and immigrants.

After the red scare died down, the 1920s were characterized by a conservative reaction to immigration and political radicalism. Foreigners were perceived as somehow posing a radical challenge to the American way of life. Nativist sentiment consumed the nation in this decade. It can be seen on a number of fronts:

- **The reemergence of the Ku Klux Klan** The KKK had fallen on hard times in the late nineteenth and early twentieth centuries as membership declined. By 1915, however, it had returned with a vengeance. Its targets were now Jews, eastern Europeans, Catholics, radicals, and unions, as well as black Americans. By 1924 the organization's membership peaked at 5 million, and it had expanded into northern states. The Klan was even successful in electing its members to important political positions in the 1920s.
- **The Sacco and Vanzetti Trial** In some ways this legal case was a microcosm of the political and ethnic problems and tensions that existed in the 1920s. Accused of murder, the two Italian anarchists were convicted and executed in 1927, despite claims that there was insufficient evidence to convict them. Many of their contemporaries argued that the men's ethnicity and political views, not their complicity in the crime, convicted them. Historians are still divided over the nature of the case.
- **The "Hundred Percenters"** Considering themselves 100 percent American, not foreign-born, this group attempted to limit foreign cultural and political influences on the United States and sought a foreign policy that would isolate the United States from foreign entanglements and relations.

Anxiety about foreigners inevitably gave rise to immigration restrictions. Despite the growing need for cheap labor, intense anti-immigration sentiment for cultural and racial reasons again took hold, as expressed in the following legislation:

- **Literacy Test Act (1917)** Passed over Wilson's veto, it required immigrants to pass a literacy test in English or their own native tongue.
- **Emergency Quota Act (1921)** This act reduced southern and eastern European immigration.
- **Immigration Act (1924)** Based on the belief that immigrants from eastern and southern Europe were more difficult to assimilate, this legislation provided a national origins plan that dramatically restricted immigration to 2 percent for each nationality represented in the 1890 census.
- **Chinese Exclusion Act (1882)** This act limited Asian immigration, which was not significantly changed until 1965.

In 1929 the Roaring Twenties came to an abrupt and unexpected end when the stock market crashed, bringing down with it the nation's economy. To be sure, the lives of millions of Americans, black and white, rural and urban, had been untouched by either the prosperity or cultural achievements that defined the 1920s. As the nation entered one of its darkest hours, the Great Depression, the lives of those already marginalized would deteriorate even further. For those who had flourished in the 1920s, their lives in the next decade would be in stark contrast to the excitement and sense of newness of the 1920s.

Content Review Questions

1. Politically the decade of the 1920s
   (A) was dominated by conservative presidents.
   (B) experienced one of the major reform periods in the nation's history.
   (C) was dominated by Democratic presidents.
   (D) was favorable to unions as government passed collective bargaining laws.

2. The Eighteenth Amendment
   (A) gave women the right to vote.
   (B) made it illegal to belong to a radical organization.
   (C) made it illegal to purchase, distribute, or consume liquor.
   (D) made it legal to teach evolution in public schools.

3. The Volstead Act
   (A) allowed the government to purchase railroad companies from private companies.
   (B) provided a tax cut to wealthy Americans.
   (C) restricted immigration.
   (D) provided for the enforcement of the Eighteenth Amendment.

4. Which of the following is NOT associated with the Harlem Renaissance?
   (A) Countee Cullen
   (B) Langston Hughes
   (C) James Weldon Johnson
   (D) Booker T. Washington

5. A. Mitchell Palmer is associated with
   (A) the Harlem Renaissance.
   (B) prohibition.
   (C) the motion picture industry.
   (D) the red scare.

6. Sacco and Vanzetti were
   (A) leaders of the prohibition movement.
   (B) arrested and convicted for placing bombs on Wall Street.
   (C) trade union leaders arrested by the government for organizing illegal strikes.
   (D) anarchists who were controversially convicted and executed for murder.

7. The Teapot Dome scandal occurred during which president's administration?
   (A) Coolidge
   (B) Hoover
   (C) Harding
   (D) Wilson

8. A major reason why Al Smith was defeated in the 1928 presidential race was because
   (A) of his vocal support for radical movements.
   (B) he had been involved in the Teapot Dome scandal.
   (C) he was associated with Wilson's idealism.
   (D) he was a Catholic.

9. Which of the following was considered to be the symbol of post–World War I consumerism?
   (A) Television
   (B) Automobile
   (C) Refrigerator
   (D) Radio

10. The "Hundred Percenters"
   (A) advocated for the repeal of the Volstead Act.
   (B) favored a loose immigration policy.
   (C) were rural Americans who condemned urban life.
   (D) opposed the teaching of Darwin's theory of evolution in public schools.

11. Following World War I, the "red scare" was fueled by
   (A) Russia's decision not to enter World War I.
   (B) the claim that many members of the U.S. government were communist sympathizers.
   (C) the success of the Bolsheviks during the Russian Revolution.
   (D) the influence of isolationists in Congress following World War I.

12. Al Capone is most associated with which of the following post–World War I activities?
   (A) Evangelism
   (B) Organized crime
   (C) Major League Baseball
   (D) Jazz

13. The Emergency Quota Act of 1921
   (A) temporarily stopped immigration from Asia.
   (B) drastically limited immigration from Latin America.
   (C) ultimately benefited eastern and southern Europeans.
   (D) was ruled unconstitutional by the Supreme Court because it favored certain nationalities at the expense of others.

14. Though considered a film classic, D. W. Griffith's *Birth of a Nation* is highly controversial because of its
   (A) portrayal of women seeking greater political rights.
   (B) glorification of the Ku Klux Klan.
   (C) depiction of urban life as degrading to its inhabitants.
   (D) critique of the Founding Fathers.

15. Margaret Sanger championed
   (A) prohibition.
   (B) pacifism.
   (C) immigration reform.
   (D) birth control.

Short-Answer Questions

1. Two technological advances of the 1920s created great social and cultural change.
   A) For both of the following, discuss at least one example of how it affected people's daily lives in the 1920s.
   Cars
   Radios
   B) Discuss ONE example of how the changes brought about by these items led to backlash during the decade.

Question 2 refers to the following passage.

> "Strange,
> That in this nigger place
> I should meet life face to face;
> When, for years, I had been seeking
> Life in places gentler-speaking.
> Until I came to this vile street
> And found Life stepping on my feet!"
>
> —Langston Hughes, "Esthete in Harlem," 1930

2. Langston Hughes was a major figure and prolific poet in the Harlem Renaissance.
   A) How does Hughes describe Harlem in this poem?
   B) Why were the 1920s the right time for a movement like the Harlem Renaissance? Include at least ONE historical example in your answer.

Long-Essay Questions

1. Despite the popular image of the 1920s as a time of rampant leisure and prosperity, the decade was also significantly marked by social, economic, and cultural discord among Americans.

   In your essay discuss THREE of the following to support the above statement:
   A. urban versus rural attitudes
   B. nativism versus immigration
   C. science versus religion
   D. the red scare

2. To what extent did the United States undergo a cultural transformation in the 1920s?

Answers

CONTENT REVIEW QUESTIONS

1. **(A)** Harding, Coolidge, and Hoover were all Republican conservatives (*The American Pageant,* 14th ed., p. 798/15th ed., p. 728; Learning Objective POL-2).

2. **(C)** For the text, see *The American Pageant,* 14th ed., pp. A17–A18/15th ed., pp. A17-A18; Learning Objective POL-5.

3. **(D)** The Volstead Act provided for the enforcement of the Eighteenth Amendment (*The American Pageant,* 14th ed., p. 775/15th ed., pp. 704–705; Learning Objective POL-5).

4. **(D)** Booker T. Washington was an educator, not an artist (*The American Pageant,* 14th ed., pp. 612–613/15th ed., pp. 554–555; Learning Objective CUL-6).

5. **(D)** Palmer led the mass arrests of suspected "subversives" in the red scare (*The American Pageant,* 14th ed., pp. 770–771/15th ed., p. 700; Learning Objective POL-6).

6. **(D)** Italian immigrants Sacco and Vanzetti were convicted of the murder of a paymaster and his guard. Many believed they were victims of nativist fear (*The American Pageant,* 14th ed., p. 771/15th ed., p. 701; Learning Objective POL-6).

7. **(C)** The Teapot Dome scandal was the most infamous of the scandals for which the Harding administration was famous (*The American Pageant,* 14th ed., pp. 803–804/15th ed., p. 733; Learning Objective POL-2).

8. **(D)** Many historians believe Smith's Catholicism was a factor in his defeat (*The American Pageant,* 14th ed., p. 810/15th ed., p. 739; Learning Objective CUL-5).

9. **(B)** The automobile defined American consumerism and had a profound impact on other industries as well (*The American Pageant,* 14th ed., p. 782/15th ed., pp. 711–712; Learning Objective WXT-3).

10. **(D)** The Hundred Percenters sought to reduce foreign influence on American culture and favored an isolationist foreign policy (this material does not appear in the text; Learning Objective POL-6).

11. **(C)** Many Americans were not only critical of Russia's decision to pull out of World War I but also fearful of the rise of communism in the world's largest nation, especially given Soviet president Lenin's desire to spread communism to other nations (*The American Pageant,* 14th ed., p. 770/15th ed., p. 700; Learning Objective POL-6).

12. **(B)** Capone, a racketeer, was the leader of Chicago's most notorious organized crime gang. Taking advantage of prohibition, Capone's gangsters distributed illegal liquor and profited from other unlawful vices such as gambling and prostitution. He was eventually convicted of falsifying his income tax returns and sent to prison (*The American Pageant,* 14th ed., p. 779/15th ed., p. 708; Learning Objective ID-7).

13. **(C)** The act set immigration quotas at 3 percent of the people of a particular nationality already in the United States. Since there were already many eastern and southern Europeans living in the United States at the time the act was passed, they benefited the most from it (*The American Pageant,* 14th ed., p. 773/15th ed., p. 703; Learning Objective PEO-7).

14. **(B)** *Birth of a Nation* is considered a cinematic masterpiece although it has long been criticized for its racist treatment of blacks during the Civil War and Reconstruction eras (*The American Pageant,* 14th ed., p. 787/15th ed., p. 716; Learning Objective CUL-6).

15. **(D)** Sanger was determined to address unplanned pregnancy, which she considered to be a national crisis that affected the quality of life for thousands of American women. Highly controversial at a time when disseminating contraceptives was illegal in many places, Sanger persevered in her birth-control crusade (*The American Pageant,* 14th ed., p. 788/15th ed., pp. 716–717; Learning Objective POL-7).

Short-Answer Questions

1. The car and the radio both led to multiple changes in society. The increased popularity of the car led to physical changes as roads needed to be created; it also led to social changes by allowing people to move farther away from their jobs and giving women and younger people more freedom to move around. The radio brought new access to information and entertainment, as well as popularizing forms of music that could only be heard at live performances prior to its invention. You could discuss multiple forms of backlash here, including the rise of fundamentalism and Harding's declaration of a return to normalcy amid a backdrop of jazz and flappers.

2. This poem celebrates Harlem and the opportunities it provided for black artists like Langston Hughes. You could discuss several reasons for the 1920s providing the space for the Harlem Renaissance to happen, including the work of prior activists like Washington, DuBois, and Garvey; the effects of the Great Migration and creation of enclaves of African Americans in the North; the greater acceptance of new forms and expressions of culture in the 1920s; or one of several other reasons.

LONG-ESSAY QUESTIONS

1. Although in some ways a lively decade that witnessed important cultural innovations, the 1920s also represented an era of conformity, repression, and bigotry. Significant tensions developed during this period that you should discuss. As the nation's cosmopolitan urban areas reflected modernism and consumerism, rural America continued to represent tradition and stability. Urban areas were ethnically and culturally heterogeneous, whereas rural America was homogeneous culturally and religiously as well; this is an appropriate opportunity for you to discuss the tensions that prevailed between "Bible Belt" areas and those areas that were exposed to scientific literature and ideas. This is indicated in the tensions that existed between U.S.-born Americans and the millions of immigrants who were arriving in the United States in this decade. Even events outside of the United States had an impact on the discord and intolerance that prevailed in the 1920s. For example, the red scare was in large part caused by the success of the Bolshevik Revolution in Russia. (Historical Thinking Skills: I-3: Periodization, II-4: Comparison, IV-8: Interpretation)

2. In responding to this question, you should take into account the profound effect consumerism had on American culture. New consumer items shaped the way Americans lived in many unprecedented ways. Radio, motion pictures, the automobile, and modern art were both causes and effects of a cultural transformation that helped to shape the Roaring Twenties. Further, you can incorporate into your essay a discussion of the causes of prohibition and its effects, such as the cultural phenomenon known as the speakeasy. You might discuss changing gender roles as well. Keep in mind that the question asks you to "discuss the extent" of this cultural transformation; therefore, you should also identify its limitations. For instance, much of the Roaring Twenties was an urban experience; the rural areas of the nation did not experience the 1920s in the same way as those living in major cities did. (Historical Thinking Skills: I-2: Patterns of Continuity and Change Over Time, II-4: Comparison, II-5: Contextualization, IV-8: Interpretation, IV-9: Synthesis)

17

The Great Depression and the New Deal: 1929–1941

In 1929, a little over a decade after the most devastating war in modern times up to that point, the United States and the rest of the world endured the worst economic crisis in history in terms of intensity and duration. The economic, political, and social crises that resulted from the Great Depression required massive intervention by the government on an unprecedented scale in order to preserve the capitalist system and recover from the ruinous effects of the depression. During the 1920s there were many weaknesses in the economy that were ignored by both politicians and economists and that were symptomatic of deep-seated problems that became more apparent over the next ten years. The election of Franklin Delano Roosevelt in 1932 marked the end of twelve years of Republican rule and the emergence of Roosevelt's New Deal, which represented the second manifestation of liberalism in the twentieth century. (The first was the progressive movement in the early twentieth century.) Ultimately the New Deal preserved capitalism by balancing the needs of the capitalist class with the demands of the working classes. Equally important was that the New Deal represented the federal government's expansion and implementation of its authority to tax, borrow, and spend in order to help find solutions for both short- and long-term problems in the economy. In short, Roosevelt and the New Deal took great strides in ending the depression, but it was not until World War II that the United States recovered from the despair of the Great Depression.

KEY CONCEPTS

- A number of major factors caused the Great Depression, among them underconsumption and high protective tariffs.
- The extent of the economic collapse for the United States and the world was unprecedented.
- President Hoover failed to stem the decline of the economy.
- Upon becoming president, FDR instituted a vast array of relief, recovery, and reform policies and agencies to address the collapse of the economy.
- Several New Deal programs were ruled unconstitutional by the conservative Supreme Court.

The Great Depression and the New Deal are discussed in depth in *The American Pageant,* 14th and 15th eds., Chapters 32–33.

CAUSES OF THE GREAT DEPRESSION

Politically conservative Republican administrations dominated the 1920s: Warren G. Harding (1921–1923), Calvin Coolidge (1923–1929), and Herbert Hoover (1929–1933). Each of these administrations was in some way accountable for creating and/or intensifying the maladies that led to the collapse of U.S. capitalism in 1929. Collectively, the following economic factors played a role in the worst depression in U.S. history:

- **Unequal distribution of wealth** Differences in income and wealth are inherent in the capitalist system; however, the extent of the concentration of wealth in the United States prior to the Great Depression was enormous. In 1929 the top 5 percent of income earners averaged $13,960 and controlled 30 percent of the nation's total wealth; the bottom 40 percent of income earners controlled 12.5 percent of the income. What is more, the median income in the nation at the time was $2,335, yet nearly 16 percent of the income-earning population received under $1,000 per year. Repressive labor policies used by the government and business in the previous decades had prevented the working class from making substantial financial gains. This in turn affected the purchasing power of millions of Americans. The tax policies of the Republican administrations—most famously the Mellon tax plan—aggravated the problem by concentrating even more wealth in the hands of a small percentage of the population, thus lowering aggregate demand and consumption.
- **Underconsumption** As the per capita income of the working class declined, so too did its ability to consume the products it was producing. The absence of adequate credit also reduced demand. There simply was not enough stimulation of the economy by the federal government to address effectively the problem of underconsumption. (A study by the prestigious Brookings Institution in 1929 revealed that 42 percent of all consumers lived at or below the subsistence/poverty level, while another 36 percent were at the minimum-comfort level.) The short-term effect of underconsumption was overproduction, leading to surpluses. Capitalists then cut back on production, which affected

The Mellon Tax Plan: An Early Version of Supply-Side Economics

Andrew Mellon, Harding's secretary of the Treasury, dominated his administration despite the presence of other capable and strong-minded cabinet secretaries, such as Herbert Hoover (secretary of commerce) and Charles Evans Hughes (secretary of state). Mellon was an experienced financier and a highly seasoned presidential adviser, having served three administrations. Extremely pro-business like his former superiors, Presidents Harding and Coolidge, Mellon believed U.S. industry must be protected from overseas competition, and so advocated a high protective tariff. He also maintained that taxes on the wealthy were too high, thus limiting the expansion of the economy. His position on tax cuts for the wealthy rested on the assumption that if the wealthy had more money, they would invest it in new business enterprises or expand already established businesses. Consequently more workers would be employed, they would spend more money, and demand would again increase, necessitating more investments and even more employment. In other words, he believed that tax breaks for the wealthy would invariably "trickle down" to the rest of society so long as the wealthy invested their money in new enterprises. In the 1920s Congress passed Mellon's tax plan and other new tax laws. Critics maintain that Mellon's tax policies provided the wealthy even more surplus capital, much of which was invested in the stock market, thus dramatically inflating the price of stocks.

employment levels, and the downward spiral continued. Added to this were the problems of deflation and falling prices, which in turn led to more layoffs as profits dwindled in many sectors of the economy.

- **The rise of protectionism** On Mellon's recommendation, the Fordney-McCumber Tariff was introduced in 1922. This tariff raised taxes on agricultural, chemical, and metal imports to an unprecedented level. While ostensibly protecting domestic production, this tax had serious ramifications on Europe and the United States. Before the war, overseas capital had played a significant role in expanding the U.S. economy through foreign investments. World War I had transformed the United States from a debtor to a creditor nation because of U.S. financial aid given to the Allies during the war. In the 1920s the United States demanded repayment. The trade barrier established by the Fordney-McCumber Tariff prevented the former Allies from selling their commodities in the United States, which would have allowed them to pay off their debts. Yet, throughout the 1920s, U.S. loans and investments continued. Once the depression hit, Congress made another ill-fated attempt to protect American industry and manufacturing from foreign competition. In 1930 it passed the highest protective tariff in the nation's history, the Hawley-Smoot Tariff, which only aggravated the problems created by the Fordney-McCumber Tariff.
- **Inadequate capital investment** Profitability is the major reason why a capitalist invests in a business. However, there was little incentive to invest given the decline in the overall rate of profit that occurred with increasing frequency in the late 1920s and continuing into the 1930s.

- **The fragility of the banking system** Banks overextended themselves to individuals and corporations whose financial situation was precarious. In other words, they made numerous bad loans. The fragility of the banking industry in the United States was revealed by the collapse of the European banking system. Because economic systems had become increasingly interdependent in regards to trade, finance, and production, a problem in one part of the world affected other markets.
- **Borrowing on margin: the speculation bubble bursts!** A substantial amount of the money invested in stocks prior to the collapse of the market in 1929 was borrowed on margin—the amount a buyer uses as a down payment to purchase stock. In the 1920s, the down payment was often substantially lower than the actual price of the stock. Technically, the stockbroker who handled the transaction loaned the balance of the investment to the buyer. In reality, the banks often provided the difference between the margin and the actual cost because the interest rates on such loans were uniformly high. Consequently stock prices became highly inflated. For example, the price per share of AT&T stock on the New York Stock Exchange in March 1928 was $179.50. Within six months, the price had nearly doubled. RCA's stock price went from $94.50 to $505.00 in the same period. There was obviously a substantial risk in all of this, for as long as the original price of the stock remained stable or increased, the buyer was safe. If the price fell, however, the stockbroker could legally demand immediate payment of part or all of the money loaned. This is exactly what happened in the autumn of 1929 as many loans were called in. On Thursday, October 24, panic swept the stock market. Nearly 13 million shares were traded. Five days later, a record 16.5 million shares were dumped on the stock exchange, shattering the market. Banks went under, and hundreds of thousands of investors, many of whom had invested whatever surplus funds they had on hand, were ruined. The collapse of the stock market in specific and the state of the economy in general had a profound effect on the nation's most vulnerable citizens: the elderly, the poor, blacks, women, and the working class, despite the efforts of reformers on the local and state levels to alleviate their condition.
- **Technology** In order for capitalists to remain competitive, they often utilize laborsaving methods. The consequences for the worker are obvious: machines turn out more commodities using fewer workers, resulting in higher unemployment, overproduction (because machinery increases production), and underconsumption.

THE EXTENT OF THE COLLAPSE (1929–1933)

The entire capitalist world experienced the collapse. The crisis was most devastating in the most highly industrialized countries—the United States, Germany, and Great Britain. In the United States alone eighty-five thousand businesses closed. Listed below are the other major effects and symptoms of the economic crisis:

- The gross national product (the total net value of goods and services produced nationally within a given time, usually one year) fell from $104 billion in 1929 to $56 billion in 1933.
- Per capita disposable income (the money available after taxes, inflation, and other necessary expenses are taken out) fell from $678 in 1929 to $369 in 1933.
- Farmers' income declined from $5.7 billion in 1929 to $1.7 billion in 1933. Four hundred thousand farmers lost their land through foreclosures; many became tenant farmers. By 1932 farmers began destroying their own crops to drive up prices.
- Unemployment increased from 1.5 million in 1929 to 12.8 million (or 25 percent of the working population) in 1933. In 1931 three-quarters of the nation's cities banned married women from holding jobs as teachers while at the same time children were forced to look for work.
- New investments declined from $10 billion in 1929 to $1 billion in 1933.
- Exports fell from $5.2 billion in 1929 to $1.7 billion in 1933.
- Building construction decreased from $300 billion in 1929 to $500 million in 1933.
- In 1928 and 1929, bank failures averaged 550 per year. Between 1930 and 1933, there were 1,700 bank failures per year.
- Hunger, homelessness, and mental depression and other social maladies increased dramatically.
- Capacity utilization (the percentage of functional factories and mines in use) fell from a high of 91 percent in 1925 to 42 percent in 1932.

Hoover and the Collapse of the Economy

When the depression intensified, Hoover argued that direct federal assistance to the victims of the crisis should not occur. Believing that the marketplace was resilient and would soon recover from the effects of the depression, he reasoned that government intervention would establish an unhealthy precedent that would undermine the very character of hardworking, independent Americans with a state-supported welfare system. Instead, Hoover preached about the virtues of:

- **Localism** Addressing the needs of the unemployed and impoverished was the responsibility of local and state governments, not the federal government.
- **Voluntarism** Charitable organizations would see people through the difficult times, providing them with basic needs.
- **Rugged individualism** Only through hard work, sacrifice, and determination have Americans found success. These attributes would allow them to weather the depression; they should not rely on government, but themselves, to recover.

Given Hoover's laissez-faire philosophy and policies, his critics—both historians and his contemporaries alike—have labeled him as a "do-nothing" president who was a prisoner of ideologies (laissez-faire capitalism and Social Darwinism) that were destined to fail. To suggest that he did absolutely nothing, however, is incorrect.

- On June 20, 1931, Hoover proposed an international moratorium on war reparations and debts.
- The following year he established the Reconstruction Finance Corporation (RFC). This agency had more than $2 billion at its disposal to loan to failing banks, farm mortgage associations, building and loan societies, railroads, and insurance companies. Regrettably, Hoover did not go far enough. As with his predecessor, Calvin Coolidge, the idea of an unbalanced budget so worried him that he declined to pump enough money into the system. Hoover believed that the depression was an overseas phenomenon and that a strong U.S. economy would convince foreigners to invest in the U.S. economy. To this end, he attempted simultaneously to balance the budget and raise taxes. A bill passed the same year allowed the RFC to loan millions of dollars to state and local governments.
- At Hoover's request, Congress passed the Federal Home Loan Bank Act. This legislation was designed to increase funds to banks, which would then be able to finance loans for home mortgages.

Despite these and many other efforts, the depression deepened. Throughout the nation, homeless families lived in makeshift shacks and tents on the outskirts of America's towns and cities. These "communities" were derisively called "Hoovervilles." As the depression intensified, citizens began to take action into their own hands. Often their conduct stemmed from frustration and despair. Two dramatic developments during the Hoover years demonstrate the growing anger and disenchantment of large parts of the population:

- **The Bonus Army** Over fifteen thousand World War I veterans camped in the nation's capital, hoping to persuade Congress to allow them to cash in the bonus certificates given them in 1924 as recognition of their military service, which were to come due in 1945. On orders from Hoover, the U.S. Army, under the command of General Douglas MacArthur, destroyed the primary encampment at Anacostia Flats.
- **The Farmers' Holiday Association** Congress had taken some steps in the 1920s that were favorable to farmers. For example, the McNary-Haugen Farm Relief Bill proposed that the government become a purchaser of surplus farm crops. The government, in turn, would sell the surplus overseas. Nevertheless, declining farm prices and foreclosures after 1929 led farmers to organize the Farmers' Holiday Association. This group clamored for an end to bank foreclosures and in favor of government-regulated price controls for farm commodities.

It seemed to some, even the owners of the means of production, that capitalism was collapsing, and the government, under Hoover, had no idea how to save it. The nation's laborers, at the very least, were becoming disenchanted with the free-market system, and they were now mobilizing. To be sure, thoughts of riotous workers destroying private property, overthrowing the government, and even initiating a reign of terror must have crossed the minds of even the most resolute patricians. By this time, the majority of Americans were more than ready for a political change. It came in the form of the Democratic governor of New York, Franklin Delano Roosevelt (FDR).

FDR

Upon assuming office, FDR recruited intellectuals and university professors—many from Columbia University—to play major roles in his administration. The press dubbed them the "Brain Trust." Some were unofficial advisers; others held cabinet-level positions. New Dealers came from a variety of backgrounds and political shades, including progressive Republicans, agrarian and urban interest groups, Democrats who had earlier supported Wilson's reforms, and labor leaders. With the assistance of his Brain Trust and other advisers, Roosevelt adopted a reform program he called the New Deal. It had two primary objectives:

- **Maintain Americans' loyalty to the government and to the capitalist system as a whole** Given the staggering unemployment rate, rural discontent, and the growing attraction of communist and fascist alternatives, discontent with capitalism and the government was a real concern.
- **Create conditions favorable to capital accumulation** Roosevelt had to jump-start the sluggish economy and convince capitalists and investors to reopen closed businesses and invest in new businesses.

To achieve these goals, the president and his advisers established a wide range of federal programs and agencies to attack the various trouble areas of the economy. FDR's approach tended to be pragmatic and methodical. His handling of the Great Depression can be divided into three major phases:

- spring of 1933 to summer 1933: the "Hundred Days"
- summer of 1933 to 1935: the First New Deal
- 1935 to 1938: the Second New Deal

The New Deal articulated three major efforts to address short- and long-term goals:

- relief, to provide immediate assistance to businesses and individuals
- recovery, to make recovery of the economy permanent
- reform, to address those abuses that had helped cause the depression

FDR's First Hundred Days to the First New Deal

On March 4, 1933, Democrat Franklin Roosevelt took over the reins of government from a tired, demoralized, and exceedingly unpopular Herbert Hoover. In his inaugural address the new president declared how he would attack the economic collapse and disillusionment of the American people: "I shall ask Congress for the one remaining instrument to meet the crisis—broad executive power to wage a war against the emergency as great as the power that would be given me if we were in fact invaded by a foreign foe." Over the next three months (the first hundred days) the new chief executive initiated in rapid succession a series of measures designed to alleviate the effects of the Great Depression. In this so-called honeymoon period, enhanced by his party's congressional majority, Roosevelt initiated the following measures to promote economic recovery and relief for the millions of unemployed:

- **National Bank Holiday (Emergency Banking Relief Act)** More banks closed in 1933 than in the previous four years combined. Confidence had to be restored in America's banking system, so FDR closed all banks for four days. Only those banks that were solvent were allowed to reopen. The nation was also taken off the gold standard. This was intended to give the government more flexibility in determining the amount of money in the system and to inflate prices and stocks. Paper currency was no longer redeemable in gold.
- **Glass-Steagall Act** Also known as the Banking Act of 1933, this forbade commercial banks from engaging in excessive speculation, added $1 billion in gold to the economy, and established the Federal Deposit Insurance Corporation (FDIC), which guaranteed bank deposits up to $5,000.
- **Agricultural Adjustment Act (AAA)** To control the wild fluctuations in farm prices, the government paid farmers to reduce their crop yield, thereby—it was hoped—increasing prices. After the Supreme Court ruled the 1933 AAA unconstitutional, a second AAA, designed to circumvent the Supreme Court's wording in outlawing the first act, was passed in 1938.
- **Federal Emergency Relief Act (FERA)** This provided funds to states to aid in unemployment relief and to subsidize public works projects.
- **Home Owners' Refinancing Act** This created the Home Owners' Loan Corporation (HOLC), which made funds available to refinance mortgages.
- **Tennessee Valley Authority (TVA)** The brainchild of Nebraska Senator Frank Norris, the TVA constructed hydroelectric dams in the Tennessee River Valley to control flooding and bring electricity to rural communities.
- **Civilian Conservation Corps (CCC)** The federal government's first public works project, the CCC employed thousands of young men in conservation work. It provided employment and as a result injected much-needed money into the economy.
- **National Industrial Recovery Act (NIRA)** This created the National Recovery Administration (NRA), which allowed industry to establish voluntarily its own regulations such as price and production guidelines and fair competition codes. The NRA supervised business policies and agreements and had the authority to approve or reject these agreements. It recognized the right of workers to establish unions and engage in collective bargaining. The act also established the Public Works Administration (PWA), which employed hundreds of thousands of men to build roads, bridges, and public buildings. Like other work relief programs, the PWA is an example of "pump priming"—stimulating both capital investment and consumer demand. The latter would grow as a result of increased employment.

There were other programs in the First New Deal:

- **The Civil Works Administration (CWA)** Through this agency, the federal government employed workers for construction jobs.
- **The Securities and Exchange Commission (SEC)** This commission was established to regulate the stock market and reduce wild speculation.
- **The Federal Housing Administration (FHA)** This agency was created to stimulate the construction of new homes.

Many of the reforms of the First New Deal focused on relief, recovery, and reform, a focus that was carried over into the next phase. To understand better why this second phase of the New Deal was launched, keep the following factors in mind:

- Throughout the 1930s, there was growing disillusionment among segments of the population, not only with the capitalist system, but also with New Deal programs that were considered ineffective or did not address specific needs. Farmers and laborers, for example, were quite vocal in their discontent, and this resonated with the government.
- Conservative business leaders were becoming increasingly antagonistic to the New Deal. The economy still seemed to be stagnant, and some were opposed to FDR's attack on laissez-faire capitalism.
- Vocal critics such as Francis Townsend, the Reverend Charles Coughlin, and Huey Long offered what to many seemed viable alternatives to the New Deal, which threatened to siphon off support for FDR's reelection bid in 1936.
    - **Francis Townsend** Townsend's Old Age Revolving Pension Plan called for a monthly stipend of $200 to citizens over the age of sixty; the recipients, however, would be required to spend the money, which would stimulate the economy.
    - **Charles Coughlin** A Catholic priest, Coughlin established the National Union for Social Justice. Appealing to the public in his weekly radio addresses, he garnered millions of supporters. A harsh critic of the New Deal, his increasingly anti-Semitic remarks convinced the Catholic Church to take him off the radio.
    - **Huey Long** The governor of Louisiana, Long organized the "Share Our Wealth" program, which called for the federal government to provide each American family a home and an annual $2,000 income. Nationally, Long's popularity might have posed a serious challenge to Roosevelt's reelection bid, but in 1935 Long was assassinated.

THE SECOND NEW DEAL

With a Democratic victory in the 1934 congressional midterm elections, FDR believed his New Deal had been given a mandate from the public. Though his three goals—relief, recovery, and reform—overlapped throughout his administrations, the Second New Deal concentrated on relief and reform:

Labor Strikes

Workers—especially factory employees—who had earlier been exempt from joining craft, or skilled, unions now had their own collective bargaining agent, the Congress of Industrial Organizations (CIO). One consequence of labor's right to collective bargaining as protected by the federal government was the frequency of strikes. Many of the major strikes, however, predated the creation of the National Labor Relations Act. Some historians contend that even after its creation, the NLRA was often lax in carrying out its mandate and that it was the workers themselves who played a decisive role in ushering in a period of industrial democracy. Major industries such as steel, textiles, and automobiles experienced strikes in the 1930s. The response of businesses to unions was mixed; some accepted them while others opposed them violently. By 1938 the rights of workers and unions were bolstered by the passage of the Fair Labor Standards Act, which set the maximum workweek at forty hours, established a minimum wage, and limited child labor. Several measures were adopted to limit the power and right to strike. In several southern states, right-to-work legislation that banned the closed shop and outlawed picketing was passed.

- **Works Progress Administration (WPA)** A massive work relief program, the WPA employed millions who had been receiving assistance from state and local governments. The WPA built roads, airports, public buildings, and other major construction projects. It also employed actors, musicians, artists, and writers. Wages were higher than state relief rates, but so as not to compete with the free-market system, they were lower than what businesses offered.
- **Resettlement Administration (RA)** This provided assistance to the agrarian sector of the economy, especially small farmers, those renting farmland, and sharecroppers.
- **Rural Electrification Administration (REA)** This brought electricity to rural areas not served by private utility companies.
- **National Labor Relations Act (NLRA)** Also known as the Wagner-Connery Act, this superseded the NIRA, which the Supreme Court ruled unconstitutional in 1935. The act created the National Labor Relations Board to address unfair labor practices and confirmed workers' rights to collective bargaining and to form and join unions.
- **Tax restructuring** A higher income tax was placed on the wealthy as well as on capital gains (income generated from investments such as stocks).
- **Social Security Act** One of the longest lasting New Deal programs, it established a trust fund to which workers and employers contributed. At age sixty-five, individuals could retire and collect monthly payments. The act also applied to those who suffered from a disability, were unemployed, or were dependent mothers and children. Social Security remains an important government program.

AP Tip

When studying this period, students are frequently overwhelmed or confused by the vast assortment of New Deal alphabet programs. You will find that organizing the agencies according to the three phases (for example, work relief programs or farm assistance programs), by dates, or by category (relief, recovery, or reform) is helpful.

Obviously, these programs had large budgets requiring the federal government to engage in an enormous outlay of capital intended to stimulate capital accumulation in hopes of expanding the economy through new investments. Despite their concerns about an unbalanced budget, the president and his advisers maintained that through deficit spending, the economy would recover. They were echoing the ideas of the influential economist John Maynard Keynes.

KEYNESIAN ECONOMICS

Roosevelt had always been apprehensive about pouring too much money into the system. He was never comfortable with the principle and practice of deficit spending, despite the fact that two of the leading advocates of Keynesian economic policy, Harry Hopkins and Harold Ickes (head of the Public Works Administration), were two of his most valuable advisers.

According to Keynes, the private sector was unable to prevent severe cyclical downturns in the economy. Consequently Keynes asserted that it was imperative for the government to play a major role in the economy.

- Government should create additional demand by becoming a major purchaser/consumer of goods and services.
- Government should encourage investments by the private sector through tax policies that lower the corporate tax rate.
- Government should facilitate the growth of exports.
- Government should make use of deficit spending. If the primary emphasis of government spending policy during an economic downturn is on balancing the budget, the economic crisis will continue. Therefore, the government must spend more than it takes in during periods of economic stagnation.

When the economy did pick up in the 1930s, FDR made the ill-fated decision to balance the federal budget in 1937. A recession ensued: capacity utilization fell from 83 percent to 60 percent; unemployment rose from 14.3 percent to 19 percent. The attempt to balance the budget in the midst of an economic recovery was quickly abandoned. On the advice of his advisers, FDR returned to the idea of deficit spending as articulated by Keynes. However, because of Roosevelt's inhibitions and reservations on Keynesian policy, the federal government never spent enough money to lift the United States out of the Great Depression. In fact, not until the United States became involved in World War II did FDR adopt the kind of spending programs prescribed by Keynes.

By 1939 the economy began to recover, but those who had lost their jobs—again, in some cases—saw their faith in the New Deal begin to erode.

THE COURT-PACKING SCHEME

In the first two phases of the New Deal, the Supreme Court revealed its aversion to some of FDR's most important programs such as the NIRA and the AAA:

- ***Schechter Poultry Corporation* v. *United States* (1935)** In this case, called the Sick Chicken Case, the Court invalidated the NIRA on several grounds—for example, that the federal government could not constitutionally regulate wholly intrastate commerce.
- ***Butler* v. *United States* (1936)** The Court invalidated the AAA on the grounds that Congress did not have the power to create a tax that would benefit one sector of society and that agriculture was a responsibility of the states, not the federal government.

FDR called the Court's decisions "horse and buggy thinking" and looked for a way around the intransigent justices.

Support for FDR declined because of his attempt to "pack" the Supreme Court. A majority of the justices had been appointed by FDR's conservative predecessors. Discouraged by the Court's rulings against a number of key New Deal programs such as the AAA and the NIRA, FDR aimed to solve the problem by reorganizing the Court: he proposed a bill to increase the number of Supreme Court justices from nine to fifteen (giving FDR an opportunity to appoint six justices of his choosing). Even his supporters had misgivings about this scheme because it posed a threat to the principle of checks and balances. Fortunately, the bill never saw the light of day, but from that point on the Supreme Court upheld the constitutionality of a number of key New Deal programs. Before he died in office (in his fourth term!), FDR would go on to appoint seven new justices, among them three of the Supreme Court's greatest judges—Felix Frankfurter, William O. Douglas, and Hugo Black.

Despite efforts to address ongoing problems in the agricultural and industrial sectors and to supplement the relief programs of the earlier phases of the New Deal, by the end of the decade no new policy goals or measures were offered by the president. Although FDR and the New Deal were still very popular, opposition continued to grow. Southern Democrats were increasingly nervous about the New Deal's social agenda, conservatives were organizing to oppose FDR's bid for a fourth term, and the Republicans increased their membership in both houses of Congress in the 1938 congressional elections.

BLACK AMERICANS, WOMEN, FDR, AND THE NEW DEAL

Ironically, many black Americans came to revere FDR. In fact his election in 1932 signaled the end of black support for the Republican Party that had begun during Reconstruction. Unfortunately FDR's record does not necessarily reflect a great concern for the condition and future of the nation's black population. As bad as the national unemployment rate got, it was worse for blacks, who tended to be the last hired and the first fired. Few Americans suffered more than black farmers, who were already at the bottom of the socioeconomic scale when the depression struck. Some New Deal agencies segregated blacks, some excluded them entirely, and some were clearly discriminatory. Black tenants and sharecroppers lost their property when they were forced from their land by the AAA in order to reduce crop yields and drive up prices. Nevertheless, some gains were made, as blacks were able to find employment opportunities in the PWA and the WPA. FDR himself took some steps to address the abuses. He appointed the first black federal judge in the nation's history and created a Civil Rights Division in the Department of Justice. Mary McLeod Bethune, an African American educator and activist, advised Roosevelt on race issues and served in his "Black Cabinet." In addition, black Americans sat for the first time as delegates to the Democratic National Convention in 1936.

Historians and the New Deal

Many historians consider FDR one of the few great presidents in the nation's history. They praise him for the substantial transformation that occurred under the New Deal, such as minimum wage/maximum hour laws, extensive energy programs like the TVA, expanded rights for workers and unions, and assistance programs such as Social Security. Addressing the problems that caused the Great Depression, they argue, is also part of FDR's legacy. But critics are not so enamored with FDR. Some claim the New Deal was in fact conservative in nature, that it did not fundamentally change social conditions and left the same class of people in power. While filled with great expectations, the New Deal did not go far enough in addressing the inequality that prevailed in American life. For their part, conservative critics contend that the New Deal established a precedent for enormous government spending and the creation of the welfare state.

If the president was often indifferent to the plight of the nation's black population, his wife, Eleanor, was not. Blacks had no greater ally in the White House than the First Lady, who advocated for increased rights for blacks and raised funds for the NAACP. Although black Americans made limited gains in the 1930s, those gains were enough for most blacks to switch from the party of Lincoln to the Democrats.

The New Deal's record regarding women is equally mixed. More and more women entered the workplace in order to keep their families from sinking into or below poverty levels, but they received lower wages than did men, they were laid off first, and they rarely received promotions. In some cases they were denied access to certain jobs so that they would not compete with men. Yet women did benefit from employment in various New Deal agencies, as well as from the employment protection accorded them by NRA. Some women found opportunities in government. In fact, the first woman to hold a cabinet position, Frances Perkins, was appointed secretary of labor by FDR.

THE LEGACY OF THE NEW DEAL

Unquestionably, FDR's expansionist fiscal and monetary policies stimulated the nation's moribund economy, as witnessed in the 1930s by increases in prices, production, and investment. By the end of the decade, wages had returned to pre-depression 1929 levels in many industries, and real wages had increased as well. Confidence in the economy and the government had also improved. Yet on the eve of America's entry into World War II, the effects of the depression continued to plague the nation. In 1940 unemployment continued to hover at approximately 10 percent. World War II helped remedy the vestiges of despair and economic malaise that continued to linger. By 1942 approximately one-third of the economy was devoted to the war effort. Consequently industrial and agricultural demand grew and unemployment shrank, especially because millions of young men and women were by then employed by the military. Corporate profits and real wages reached high levels. Even the earning power of the bottom one-fifth of the nation's population increased dramatically. Finally, the gross national product doubled during the war.

World War II and the New Deal changed the size and scope of the government as well as how Americans viewed the role of the federal government. Many came to accept its expanded role as indispensable in confronting economic problems and, in general, the problems of industrial society. Prior to the Great Depression, the federal government did not play a large role in people's lives, but the New Deal changed that. Government programs, from education to infrastructural development to relief, in one way or another affected every aspect of life. To this day, some view the New Deal and subsequent reform programs as undermining states' rights, the free-market system, and social and cultural traditions. Others contend that this is not the case, and furthermore, they argue, the alternative to government intervention is far worse, as witnessed by the collapse of the nation's economy and the resulting despair that traumatized the nation in the 1930s.

Content Review Questions

1. Which of the following was NOT an underlying cause of the Great Depression?
   (A) Underconsumption
   (B) The effects of World War I
   (C) The fragility of the banking system
   (D) The vastly unequal distribution of wealth

2. The Mellon tax plan
   (A) helped lift the nation out of the Great Depression.
   (B) was adopted by FDR as a remedy for underconsumption.
   (C) distributed wealth evenly between the nation's social classes.
   (D) led to underconsumption and wild speculation in the stock market.

3. The Hawley-Smoot Tariff
   (A) facilitated improved trade relations between the United States and its trade partners.
   (B) reduced the tax on imported industrial goods, thus hurting American industry.
   (C) was the highest tariff in the nation's history, and an underlying cause of the Great Depression.
   (D) was ruled unconstitutional by the Supreme Court.

4. Which of the following is NOT associated with Hoover's ideology in regards to addressing the problems created by the collapse of the economy in 1929?
   (A) Deficit spending
   (B) Voluntarism
   (C) Laissez-faire
   (D) Rugged individualism

5. Which opponent of FDR introduced an alternative to the New Deal in the form of an Old Age Revolving Pension Plan?
   (A) Herbert Hoover
   (B) Huey Long
   (C) Father Coughlin
   (D) Francis Townsend

6. Which of the following programs was instituted by President Hoover?
   (A) Federal Deposit Insurance Corporation
   (B) Home Owners' Loan Corporation
   (C) Going off the gold standard
   (D) Reconstruction Finance Corporation

7. The U.S. Supreme Court ruled this New Deal agency unconstitutional in the 1930s.
   (A) Tennessee Valley Authority
   (B) Federal Deposit Insurance Corporation
   (C) National Industrial Recovery Act
   (D) Federal Housing Administration

8. In order to address the problem of rampant speculation in the stock market, FDR
   (A) closed the stock exchange for four days.
   (B) placed a limit on how much money an individual or company could invest in the stock market.
   (C) established the Securities and Exchange Commission.
   (D) set a ceiling on how high the price of a stock could go.

9. FDR's goal to reorganize the federal judiciary
   (A) provided him the opportunity to replace conservative judges who had been appointed by the previous administration.
   (B) was achieved, but it was ruled unconstitutional by the Supreme Court.
   (C) allowed him to bypass the judiciary when considering new programs and agencies.
   (D) was described by angry critics as "court packing."

10. The Social Security Act
    (A) was designed to provide assistance to the agrarian sector of the economy.
    (B) employed musicians, artists, actors, and writers.
    (C) provided assistance to the elderly and handicapped and to dependent women and children.
    (D) allowed workers to form unions and engage in collective bargaining.

11. Which New Deal program established the Federal Deposit Insurance Corporation (FDIC), which protects individual bank deposits?
    (A) Wagner Act
    (B) Securities and Exchange Commission
    (C) Glass-Steagall Banking Reform Act
    (D) Reorganization Act

12. Which of the following was NOT a critic of FDR's New Deal?
    (A) Frances Perkins
    (B) Huey Long
    (C) Charles Coughlin
    (D) Henry Ford

13. The National Recovery Administration (NRA) sought to address which of the following economic concerns with relief, recovery, and reform?
    (A) Banking, industry, and trade
    (B) Unemployment, labor, and industry
    (C) Labor, trade, and banking
    (D) Farming, banking, and unemployment

14. President Hoover's rationale in vetoing the Muscle Shoals Bill, which would have dammed the Tennessee River, was based on his view that
    (A) there was no need for the project because the Tennessee Valley was rural and its residents would not benefit from electricity.
    (B) the bill would benefit only one region rather than the entire nation.
    (C) the government was adopting socialist methods to resolve concerns of utilities.
    (D) the bill would promote internal improvements within Tennessee and therefore was not the responsibility of the federal government.

15. Opposition to the Fair Labor Standards Act came primarily from
    (A) labor unions.
    (B) the agrarian sector.
    (C) black Americans.
    (D) southern states.

Short-Answer Questions

1. Franklin Roosevelt divided his New Deal into three phases: relief, recovery, and reform.
   A) Briefly describe the goal of each phase.
   B) Which phase was most important for the American people? Use historical evidence to support your answer.
   C) Which phase was most important for the economy? Use historical evidence to support your answer.

Question 2 is based on the following images.

© Bettmann/Corbis

FDR Library

2. In the 1932 presidential election Herbert Hoover, who was president at the onset of the Great Depression, lost the presidency to Franklin Delano Roosevelt.
   A) Briefly describe the first image.
   B) Briefly describe the second image.
   C) How did the first image play a role in the events that led to the second image? Use historical evidence to support your answer.

Long-Essay Questions

1. A key feature of the New Deal was that it gave too much authority to the federal government and specifically the executive branch.

   To what extent is the above statement true?

2. To what extent is it accurate to characterize the New Deal as a conservative effort to maintain the social, economic, and political status quo?

Answers

CONTENT REVIEW QUESTIONS

1. **(B)** Many Americans experienced economic prosperity following the war (*The American Pageant,* 14th ed., p. 770/15th ed., p. 730; Learning Objective WXT-6).

2. **(D)** The Mellon tax plan concentrated even more capital in the hands of the relatively small wealthy class. This in turn gave them an opportunity to invest in the stock market, in some cases inflating stock value, and left less money in the hands of the rest of the population, which exacerbated the problem of underconsumption (*The American Pageant,* 14th ed., pp. 794–795/15th ed., p. 710; Learning Objective WXT-8).

3. **(C)** The Hawley-Smoot Tariff set import tax rates so high in order to protect American industries that it led to other nations enacting their own trade barriers (*The American Pageant,* 14th ed., p. 812/15th ed., p. 740; Learning Objective WXT-8).

4. **(A)** Deficit spending is associated with FDR, not Hoover (*The American Pageant,* 14th ed., pp. 815–816/15th ed., pp. 743–744; Learning Objective POL-4).

5. **(D)** A retired physician who had lost his savings, Townsend proposed the pension plan (*The American Pageant,* 14th ed., p. 832/15th ed., p. 759; Learning Objective CUL-5).

6. **(D)** The RFC was a source of government lending (*The American Pageant,* 14th ed., p. 818/15th ed., p. 746; Learning Objective WXT-8).

7. **(C)** The Court invalidated the NIRA in the *Schechter Poultry Corporation* v. *United States* case (*The American Pageant,* 14th ed., p. 836/15th ed., p. 762; Learning Objective POL-5).

8. **(C)** The SEC is still the "watchdog" of the stock exchange (*The American Pageant,* 14th ed., p. 839/15th ed., p. 765; Learning Objective POL-4).

9. **(D)** Many Americans met FDR's court-packing scheme with considerable derision, and he therefore dropped the plan (*The American Pageant,* 14th ed., pp. 844–845/15th ed., pp. 770–771; Learning Objective POL-5).

10. **(C)** The Social Security Act addressed the needs of the unemployed and the elderly (*The American Pageant,* 14th ed., p. 841/15th ed., p. 767; Learning Objective POL-4).

11. **(C)** The Glass-Steagall Act established the Federal Deposit Insurance Corporation, which insures bank deposits—originally up to $5,000, today up to $250,000 (*The American*

Pageant, 14th ed., p. 829/15th ed., p. 756; Learning Objective POL-4).

12. **(A)** Perkins, the first female cabinet member in U.S. history, became FDR's secretary of labor (*The American Pageant*, 14th ed., p. 832/15th ed., p. 760; Learning Objective POL-6).

13. **(B)** The NRA was a farsighted and comprehensive program that focused on the needs of three economic sectors: the unemployed (approximately 25 percent of the workforce), labor, and industry. It did so in part by establishing business codes, maximum work hours, and collective bargaining (*The American Pageant*, 14th ed., p. 835/15th ed., p. 761; Learning Objective POL-4).

14. **(C)** Hoover contended that the Muscle Shoals Bill was socialistic in that it would empower the federal government to sell electricity, putting it in direct competition with private utilities (*The American Pageant*, 14th ed., p. 839/15th ed., p. 746; Learning Objective WXT-8).

15. **(D)** Most industrialists opposed the act, but the most potent opposition came from southern textile manufacturers, who historically had prospered by offering low-paying jobs, which the act would ostensibly address (*The American Pageant*, 14th ed., p. 842/15th ed., pp. 768–769; Learning Objective WXT-8).

Short-Answer Questions

1. Relief efforts immediately stemmed the effects of the Great Depression, like the Bank Holiday. Recovery efforts aimed to get people back on their feet and create jobs to get the economy running again. Reform programs were put in place to protect the economy from another Great Depression in the future. For the people, you might argue that curing their immediate problems and putting them to work was most meaningful, in which case you might cite recovery programs like the PWA or the CCC. For the government and the economy, though, protections like the SEC and the Glass-Steagall Act (reform) were essential to the future economic health of the nation.

2. The first image shows the Bonus Army, a group of veterans who protested in Washington, D.C. in 1932 to receive the pensions they were owed for service in World War I. Hoover sent troops in to break up the protest. The second image is a cartoon depiction of Franklin Roosevelt's inauguration, showing FDR all smiles and ready to take on the nation and its problems while Hoover sits bitterly and watches. There are several reasons that you can say the first image leads to the second. Many people were dissatisfied with Hoover's response and many blamed him for their plight, leading to names like Hoovervilles and Hoover blankets. The government's reaction to the Bonus Army was for many the final straw as Hoover appeared to turn against men who fought and risked their lives

for the United States The fact that it happened during an election year was even worse.

LONG-ESSAY QUESTIONS

1. For many conservatives and proponents of laissez-faire capitalism, the New Deal is seen as an overexpansion of the federal government in regulating the economy and business. You can support this claim by discussing legislation promoted by FDR that overstepped his authority—for example, by establishing New Deal programs that were in competition with private businesses or adopted various aspects of a socialist economy such as the Tennessee Valley Authority. To support the idea that FDR used his authority properly, you can point out that he took extraordinary steps because the economic collapse was so extensive. As a contrast, discuss the policies of the conservative Hoover—laissez-faire economics, volunteerism, and localism—that were insufficient to lift the nation out of its economic woes. (Historical Thinking Skills: III-6: Historical Argumentation and IV-8: Interpretation)

2. Few would initially associate the New Deal with conservatism, instead viewing it as a major manifestation of liberalism. However, critics on the left believe the New Deal was not particularly liberal. You can support this position by pointing out that the New Deal did not go far in addressing the socioeconomic problems confronting women and minorities and that the goal of the New Deal was to preserve capitalism. To this end, the New Deal did not fundamentally change class, gender, and racial relations in the United States To support the view that the New Deal was profoundly liberal, discuss the legislation that displayed an unprecedented expansion of government power and authority in establishing social programs for the aged, the unemployed, and those ordinarily marginalized such as black Americans. Furthermore, you can write on ways the New Deal leveled the playing field for labor and business, not to mention engaging in deficit spending to fund New Deal programs and agencies. (Historical Thinking Skills: II-4: Comparison, II-5: Contextualization, III-6: Historical Argumentation, IV-8: Interpretation, and IV-9: Synthesis)

18

World War II: 1939–1945

As nations struggled to survive the ordeal of the Great Depression, they would soon be confronted with malevolence greater than the horrors of World War I or the desperation associated with the collapse of the world's economy. For in Europe and Asia imperialism, militarism, and fascism were taking hold and would soon envelope the world in a catastrophe that made other modern wars pale in comparison.

Germany's capitulation in World War I combined with devastating war reparations and the collapse of its economy in the 1930s provided fertile ground for various extremist organizations to flourish, most infamously the Nationalist Socialist party, the Nazis. But Germany's defeat in the war did not have only economic ramifications. Saddled with "war guilt" by the victors in the Treaty of Versailles, its national psyche was damaged by the extremely punitive nature of the Treaty of Versailles. Adolf Hitler exploited Germany's shame and humiliation to elevate himself and the Nazi party to the nation's political leadership. Using powerful and passionate oratory, along with intimidation, arrests, and violence, Hitler convinced the German people that their defeat in the war, the humiliating peace terms, and the collapse of the German economy were the result of poor political leadership, defeatism on the home front, and the economic machinations of Germany's Jewish population. Hitler's Nazi party synthesized nationalism with populist rhetoric, while simultaneously rejecting liberal values, communism, and republicanism. Utilizing coercion and violence, his regime promoted the "cult of personality," in which the leader—Hitler in this case—was portrayed as being larger than the nation itself. Tapping into the average German's nationalistic sentiments, in little more than a decade Hitler rose from being an obscure World War I veteran and third-rate artist to become chancellor of Germany in 1933. Without pause, he began to rebuild Germany's military in order to restore its commanding presence in Europe.

The story was not profoundly different in Italy. There, another would-be demagogue named Benito Mussolini took advantage of his nation's postwar crises—labor strikes, the breakdown of law and order, and ongoing battles between right- and left-wing groups—to catapult himself and his Fascist party to the leadership of Italy. Like his fascist comrade in Germany, Mussolini would assume dictatorial powers. Likewise in Japan, there were those who believed that only through extreme nationalism and militarism could Japan take its place in the sun.

Although these events increasingly concerned American political leaders, the developments in Europe and Asia could not shift the American public away from the belief that these were uniquely European and Asian problems, and that the United States should most certainly avoid involvement in yet another war that, like World War I, had dubious benefits for the United States. Thus, throughout the interwar years, the United States maintained an increasingly fragile policy of neutrality.

KEY CONCEPTS

- The rise of fascism, militarism, and imperialism were significant developments that ultimately led to World War II when Germany, Italy, and Japan embarked on policies of territorial expansion and conquest.
- The 1930s Neutrality Acts limited but did not entirely prevent FDR from providing assistance to Great Britain.
- Deteriorating relations between Japan and the United States ended in war.
- The United States adopted a discriminatory policy towards Japanese Americans.
- The Holocaust brought unprecedented suffering to millions of European Jews and others the Nazis found objectionable.
- The dropping of the atomic bombs on Japan ended the war, but some later questioned whether the attacks were necessary.
- The roots of the Cold War lay in the tensions that developed between the Soviet Union and the Western Allies.

World War II is discussed in depth in *The American Pageant,* 14th and 15th eds., Chapters 34 and 35.

GERMAN AND ITALIAN MILITARISM AND TERRITORIAL EXPANSION

After assuming control of their respective nations, Hitler and Mussolini embarked on a massive rearmament program that was a prerequisite for them to carry out their foreign-policy objective: territorial expansion through conquest. For Hitler the buildup of Germany's military was in direct violation of the Treaty of Versailles. No matter, Hitler simply withdrew Germany from the League of Nations when that body forbade his request to rearm his nation. Hitler

Neutrality or Isolationism?

Some textbooks refer to American foreign policy in the interwar years as one based on isolationism. True, following World War I many Americans believed that the United States should curtail or, in extreme cases, end its involvement in international affairs, especially in Europe. This sentiment was given added weight in 1934 when a Senate investigation headed by Senator Gerald P. Nye concluded that political pressure exerted on American policymakers by U.S. bankers, financiers, and munitions corporations had been a determining factor in the U.S. government's decision to enter World War I. In order to maintain a neutral stance, a bill authored by Senator Hiram Johnson and passed into law in 1934 (the Johnson Act) forbade foreign nations that had defaulted on their debt payments to the United States from receiving further loans. In 1935, 1936, and 1937 the U.S. Congress passed Neutrality Acts designed to keep the United States out of foreign conflicts. The acts ran the gamut from preventing exports to nations at war, to warning Americans that they traveled on ships of warring nations at their own risk, to preventing loans to belligerents. The president was even authorized to deny the ships of belligerent nations access to American ports. After the outbreak of World War II in 1939, the American isolationist movement found its voice in the America First Committee, which maintained that isolationism was in the nation's best interest. However, given the U.S. intervention in Latin America in the postwar decades, the presence of its military in Asia, the strong economic relationship between the United States and many European and Asian nations, and the military assistance given to Britain once war broke out, some historians question whether the United States was even neutral by 1940, let alone isolationist. A close investigation of U.S. policies and objectives in the interwar years is therefore necessary in order for you to develop your own interpretation of the nature of American foreign affairs in this period.

continued to defy the League by occupying the demilitarized Rhine Valley in 1936. He next set his sights on repatriating the over 1.5 million German-speaking citizens who were then living outside of Germany and Austria because of the collapse of Austria-Hungary and the creation of new states following World War I. To this end, his forces occupied the Rhineland and annexed Austria. In the Munich Conference of 1938, Hitler secured an agreement from the French and British that gave him the German-speaking area of Czechoslovakia known as the Rhineland. Hitler promised that his thirst for territorial expansion had been quenched. British Prime Minister Neville Chamberlain, and his French counterpart, Edouard Daladier, believed him, mistakenly thinking they had prevented another European war. "Peace in our time," Chamberlain naively declared upon his return to Britain.

But this was wishful thinking, given what we now know of Hitler's ambitions. Not long after the Munich Agreement, Germany occupied all of Czechoslovakia. Paralyzed by the thought of another world war, Britain and France assumed that a policy of appeasement would satisfy the German dictator. The occupation of Czechoslovakia convinced them of the folly of such a policy. On September 1, 1939, Germany invaded Poland. Negotiations, appeasement, and agreements having run their course, France and Britain declared war on Germany. A few years before the German expansion into Czechoslovakia, their ally Italy invaded Ethiopia. The League of Nations imposed an embargo on war-related items but did little else to assist the overmatched Ethiopians, despite a personal appeal to the delegates by Emperor Haile Selassie. The Soviet Union would not engage German troops until 1940, for, to the shock and surprise of the world, the two ideological antagonists—one communist, the other fascist—had signed a nonaggression pact in 1939.

AP Tip

In order to comprehend the conflict in ideologies that shaped the economic and political structures of the combatants, the following definitions may be helpful:

- **Fascism** An authoritarian, antidemocratic economic and political system that subordinates the individual to the needs of the state and party. For example, trade unions are outlawed because they promote the interests of laborers, not of the nation. Obedience to the nation's leader is required. Italy and Germany in the 1930s are examples of fascist countries.
- **Totalitarianism** Similar in several respects to a fascist society, a totalitarian system requires obedience to the leader and the needs of the state. Consequently, the government controls most aspects of society, such as education and the legal system. Germany and the Soviet Union in the 1930s were totalitarian.
- **Democratic-Republicanism** A political system in which certain basic rights and privileges are guaranteed to all citizens, who in turn have the right to elect representatives to serve their interests and those of the nation at various levels of government. Great Britain and the United States are examples of democratic-republics.
- **Communism** A social, political, and economic system in which private ownership of the means of production is controlled by the state. A key objective of communism is to rid society of class-based interests and the exploitation of the working class by those who own the means of production. The Soviet Union from 1917 to 1989 was a communist nation.

THE SPANISH CIVIL WAR

The Spanish Civil War is considered a prelude to World War II in that it pitted forces representing divergent ideologies—fascism and republicanism—against each other in a war to determine Spain's political future. Both sides in the conflict were assisted by outside forces. Supplementing the Republican government (the Loyalists) were 52,000 volunteers from around the world, including the most famous American unit, the Abraham Lincoln Brigade. Soviet dictator Stalin sent war materiel and military personnel to assist the government's forces as well. Hitler and Mussolini, on the other hand, sent air and ground units to assist fascist general Francisco Franco overthrow the Spanish government. Although President Roosevelt supported the Loyalists, his hands were tied by the Neutrality Act of 1937, which forbade arms shipments to the belligerents in the Spanish Civil War.

He recommended that the United States join with the other powers to "quarantine" aggressor nations. But by 1939, the same year World War II broke out, Franco's fascist forces prevailed.

Japanese Imperialism

Once Japan entered the modern age in the late nineteenth century, it had embarked on an intensive program of industrialization, westernization, militarism, and territorial expansion. In the late nineteenth century Japan had defeated China, and to the surprise and chagrin of westerners, it had decisively defeated Russia in 1905. Its success continued. In World War I it had fortuitously joined the Allied side. Although its troops saw limited combat in the war, Japan received China's Shandong Peninsula and Germany's colonies in the Pacific. Yet Japan still believed that it was not given the respect it deserved as a major world power by the other victorious nations. It would therefore create its own Asian empire (the Co-Prosperity Sphere), a decision that would culminate in a war with the United States over which nation would be the hegemonic power in the Pacific.

The first step in its imperialist objective was to occupy the Chinese province of Manchuria in 1931, in complete defiance of the League of Nations, establishing a puppet government called Manchukuo. Despite refusing to take steps to join other nations in economically punishing Japan, the United States did take umbrage with its invasion of China, seeing it as a violation of the Open Door, and a host of other interwar agreements. But the Hoover administration's response was tepid and sanctimonious at best: Secretary of War Henry Stimson declared in the Stimson Doctrine that the United States would not recognize the pseudo-government established in China by the Japanese and would adhere to the Nine-Power Treaty by condemning the acquisition of territory taken by force. The League of Nations endorsed the doctrine but did little else. In 1937 a full-scale war erupted between the Japanese and Chinese. In the course of events a U.S. gunboat, the *Panay,* was sunk by Japanese planes. Not wanting the incident to escalate any further, a Japanese apology was quickly accepted by the U.S. government. Four years later, however, Japan would intentionally attack U.S. warships at Pearl Harbor, Hawaii, a decision that could only be met by a declaration of war by the United States.

Roosevelt and the Allies

By the late 1930s, despite the continued public support for the Neutrality Acts, the militarist actions of Japan, Germany, and Italy (who eventually formed the Rome-Berlin-Tokyo alliance and were known thereafter as the Axis Powers) made Congress more amenable to President Roosevelt's request for increased military expenditures. After the German conquest of Denmark and Norway, and the fall of France in 1940, Great Britain stood alone against Nazi domination of Europe. Still, the American public was wary of U.S. military involvement despite growing concerns that the Nazis might soon conquer all of Europe.

From Roosevelt's perspective the defeat of Great Britain would pose dire consequences for U.S. national security. Thus FDR worked around the Neutrality Acts, finding ways to aid Britain and, in the process, U.S. self-interest. In a series of policies designed to aid Britain the president methodically eroded the Neutrality Acts:

- **"Cash and Carry"** A belligerent could purchase arms from the United States if it paid in cash and transported the supplies in its own vessels. FDR reasoned that this policy was in line with the Neutrality Acts because it allowed access to U.S. materiel for any nation at war. But inasmuch as the British Royal Navy dominated the seas, it obviously benefited the British.
- **Lend-lease** In order to help a financially strapped Britain, Roosevelt ended cash and carry and instead provided credit to the British so that they could continue to purchase much-needed military supplies. Roosevelt justified this action by telling the American people that "we must be an arsenal of democracy" and that the policy was designed to defend the "four freedoms" that Americans valued: freedom of religion, freedom of speech, freedom from want, freedom from fear. Despite the strong opposition to assisting Britain in this manner from isolationists and those advocating a policy of neutrality, the Lend-Lease Act became law in early 1941 and was further expanded when Roosevelt ordered that U.S. warships escort British ships carrying lend-lease items for part of their journey. When a German submarine attacked one of the warships, Roosevelt ordered that all German ships should be attacked on sight. For all intents and purposes, the United States was fighting an undeclared war with Germany. Little did the American public know that before the year was out the United States would formally be at war with the Axis Powers.
- **Destroyers for bases** Even though Britain's surface ships "ruled the seas," German submarines were wreaking havoc on British shipping. Although resolute in their defiance of Hitler's attempt to pummel them into submission, by late 1940 Britain's ability to sustain itself was in dire straits. Roosevelt desperately wanted to provide direct military assistance to Britain, but he could not openly violate the Neutrality Acts. Instead, he came up with a creative way to circumvent the acts and in the process augment the British Royal Navy. In return for fifty dated U.S. Navy destroyers, the British allowed the United States to construct military bases on Britain's Caribbean islands.
- **The draft** In order to prepare the nation in the event it was drawn into the war, Roosevelt took the momentous step of convincing Congress to institute a peacetime draft, the Selective Training and Service Act of 1940. Predictably, those who wanted to keep the United States out of the war at all costs interpreted the act as a prerequisite to U.S. military involvement. The legal bulwark that kept the United States from participating in the war—the Neutrality Acts—by now seemed like a guiding principle in name only. In the summer of 1941 Roosevelt met with British Prime Minister Churchill in a secret meeting held on a warship off the coast of Newfoundland and declared in the Atlantic Charter that both nations stood for the four basic freedoms, self-determination for all nations, opposition to territorial expansion, freedom of the seas, a

repudiation of any territorial gains made as a result of the war, and arms control. In other words, their declaration avowed all the beliefs that were inconsistent with the behavior of the militarist Axis Powers: Germany, Italy, and Japan.

DETERIORATING RELATIONS WITH JAPAN

The antecedents of the war between Japan and the United States can be found in the escalating tensions between the two nations in the 1930s, which culminated in the Japanese attack on Pearl Harbor in 1941. As the Japanese sought to extend their hegemony in Asia, the United States became increasingly concerned with Japan's aggressive foreign policy. The invasion of China confirmed American fears that the Japanese would not be satisfied until they dominated Eastern Asia and the Pacific. The creation of the Rome-Berlin-Tokyo military alliance only confirmed Japan's bellicose intentions, which were realized when the Japanese military occupied French Indochina in the summer of 1941. The British and Americans responded by imposing a trade embargo on Japan, cutting off resources it needed to sustain its industries and military, such as rubber and oil. It was made clear to the Japanese government that further expansionist acts would provoke a military response. In the months leading up to Japan's attack on the United States, both nations engaged in what were fruitless attempts to forestall war, as neither country was prepared to do battle with the other. From the Japanese perspective, however, war with the United States seemed inevitable if Japan was to successfully carry out its foreign-policy objectives.

In order to neutralize the most potent U.S. obstacle to Japanese control of the Pacific—the U.S. Seventh Fleet stationed at Pearl Harbor, Hawaii—a surprise attack was launched on December 7, 1941. Although the attack killed thousands of U.S. servicemen and destroyed approximately twenty U.S. ships and hundreds of airplanes, the United States was fortunate that its aircraft carriers were out to sea at the time of the attack. Simultaneously, Japanese forces conquered the Philippines, Guam, and Hong Kong. December 7 was "a day which will live in infamy," according to Roosevelt; it propelled the United States into a war against Japan as well as Germany and Italy. Though some Americans still hoped for a peaceful solution, whatever doubts most had about their nation's involvement in the war were now put to rest as the U.S. government and the American people mobilized their resources for the war effort.

Unfortunately the U.S. government and the military remained segregated. Although black Americans served the nation at home and in the armed forces, they continued to suffer discrimination in the workplace even after the nation's economy expanded as a result of the demands of the war. Some gains were made, largely through the work of Eleanor Roosevelt and A. Philip Randolph, such as the creation of the Fair Employment Practices Committee, a federal agency that attempted to address discrimination in the economy. Due to the federal government's less discriminatory hiring practices, the number of blacks employed by the government increased profoundly. But it was not until 1948 (as a result of an executive order by President Truman) that the military was desegregated.

JAPANESE AMERICAN INTERNMENT

One tragic consequence of the Pearl Harbor attack was a virulent anti-Japanese sentiment that culminated in the persecution of Japanese Americans. President Roosevelt exacerbated this racism by issuing Executive Order 9066, which resulted in the resettlement of over 125,000 Japanese Americans to miserable internment camps in the western United States for fear that they would undermine the American war effort against Japan. While this travesty of justice was taking place, Japanese American servicemen were serving honorably in the U.S. military. What is more, the U.S. government did not expand this program to include Italian Americans or German Americans. Moreover, in 1944 the Supreme Court affirmed the constitutionality of Japanese internment as a national security measure in *Korematsu* v. *US*. The message was clear: Asians could not be trusted. Though the U.S. war against Germany, Italy, and Japan was noble, the legacy of the unjust treatment of U.S. citizens of Japanese descent is an unfortunate legacy of a war that was fought to stop racism and fascism.

THE HOLOCAUST

One nefarious aspect of the Nazi regime was its treatment of political opponents, dissidents, homosexuals, and most especially Jews. Hitler had a long-standing hatred of Europe's Jews, whom he blamed for a variety of German and European problems. Tragically, they became scapegoats for all that the dictator claimed was wrong in the world. During his twelve-year reign his government systematically destroyed approximately 6 million German Jews and those who lived in nations overrun by the German army. Initially Jews were terrorized, as in the infamous 1938 "Night of Broken Glass"—*Kristallnacht*—in which synagogues and Jewish homes and businesses were destroyed. Next, Jews were rounded up and sent to concentration camps or restricted to ghettos, where they starved to death or fell victims to diseases. Finally, in what the Nazis referred to as the Final Solution, millions of Jews, as well as millions of Russians, homosexuals, and political opponents, were killed in death camps designed to eliminate the victims in large numbers.

It was not until the middle of the war that the Allies became aware of the extent of the atrocities. Some critics argue the United States should have taken steps to stop the attempted genocide, whereas others claim that the best way the Allies could have ended the Holocaust was to defeat the German military. Only when the death camps—most notably Auschwitz— were liberated by U.S. soldiers was the full extent of the horror made known. Entire families had been destroyed, millions had been gassed, and others worked and starved to death. Horrifically, the Germans had conducted "scientific experiments" on live subjects. It was later revealed that the Japanese had also committed atrocities. After the war, at the Nuremberg War Crimes Trial and similar legal proceedings against Japanese military and political leaders, the defendants were charged with crimes against humanity. Important German and Japanese leaders were executed and others given prison sentences as punishment for their actions.

WARTIME CONFERENCES AND THE COLD WAR

In the last two years of the war the Allied leaders met with one another in a series of conferences designed to discuss strategies and objectives, as well as to discuss the post-war world. Often the Allied leaders seemed unified in their thinking; at other times there appeared to be tensions and suspicions between the Americans and British on one hand and the Soviet dictator Josef Stalin on the other.

- **Casablanca Conference (January 1943)** President Roosevelt and Prime Minister Churchill agreed that Allied forces would invade Sicily and end Italy's participation in the war. A strategy was discussed to defeat the Japanese as well. Most important, the two leaders announced that they would accept nothing less than the unconditional surrender of Japan and Germany.
- **Teheran Conference (November–December 1943)** This was the first conference of the "Big Three" (Stalin, Roosevelt, and Churchill), and though it ended amicably, it was not without its tense moments. The leaders discussed strategies for ending the war, including an invasion of Nazi-held France. Stalin agreed to enter the war against Japan upon the defeat of Germany. Roosevelt and Stalin supported the idea of a postwar international body that would settle disputes between nations, though Churchill had some misgivings about the effectiveness of such an organization. For the time being, the leaders decided that Germany would be severely punished for its role in causing the war.
- **Yalta Conference (February 1945)** By the time the Big Three met at Yalta, it was obvious that the defeat of Germany was imminent. Once again Stalin agreed to enter the war against Japan in return for the restoration of its pre-1905 status in East Asia. The leaders also began working out the details of the organization that would soon become the United Nations. The most controversial issue, the status of postwar East European countries, especially Poland, was vaguely defined. Some historians believe the origins of the Cold War can be found in this meeting, when a gravely ill Roosevelt was outmaneuvered by a wily and deceitful Stalin, who promised free elections in Soviet-controlled Eastern Europe. To these historians, Yalta laid the groundwork for Soviet domination of Eastern Europe in the postwar period. Others argue that Russia, which had been invaded twice in less than twenty-five years, required a buffer zone between it and its potential future enemies to the west.
- **Potsdam Conference (July–August 1945)** By the time this conference was convened, Roosevelt had died and Churchill had been succeeded by Clement Attlee as Britain's prime minister. The fissures that appeared in the Allied relationship at Yalta had widened by the time the leaders met at Potsdam (Berlin). All agreed that Germany must be demilitarized and the Nazi influence purged from German culture. But reparations and the occupation of Germany were left unresolved, thereby intensifying the uneasiness

that now seemed to define the relationship between the Western Allies and the Soviet Union.

THE WAR

In the early stages of the war the Axis Powers experienced considerable success. The Japanese overran much of East Asia and islands in the Pacific. Germany conquered its neighbors, until Britain stood alone. The Battle of Britain, in which the Royal Air Force defeated the German Luftwaffe (air force), put an end to Hitler's aim of invading Britain. Stymied, he turned east and invaded the Soviet Union, his troops reaching Stalingrad in 1941; they then laid siege to the city. By 1942, however, the Germans were cut off, exhausted, and demoralized. Over 300,000 of Germany's best troops surrendered. The Russians then launched a massive counteroffensive, which ultimately took them to the outskirts of Berlin.

In the meantime the United States had entered the war and, with their British allies, was successful in establishing a foothold in Europe as a result of the successful, though costly, D-Day landing (June 6, 1944). Over the next ten months the Germans were driven from France and Italy. Mussolini was killed and Italy sued for peace. Finally Berlin itself was under siege. By early 1945 the Americans and British were also on the outskirts of Berlin, where Hitler had taken refuge in his underground bunker. Rather than be captured alive, he chose to commit suicide. On May 8, 1945, the Germans surrendered (V-E Day).

The war against Japan continued on for three more months. In a series of bloody battles Japanese military units holding strategically important islands such as Iwo Jima and Okinawa were eventually defeated, until the Japanese mainland itself was open to attack. Before an invasion could take place, President Truman, who had ascended to the presidency upon FDR's death in April, ordered that atomic bombs be dropped on Hiroshima and Nagasaki. U.S. scientists had for several years been working on an atomic weapon in a secret program known as the Manhattan Project. Five days after the second bomb was dropped on Nagasaki, the Japanese unconditionally surrendered.

When the atomic bombs were first dropped on Japan, few questioned the military necessity of such a decision. After all, the Truman administration's convincing argument that the bombs, though devastating, would save the lives of one million Allied servicemen if Japan itself was invaded was proof enough that the dropping of the atomic weapons was necessary. The bloody battles on Iwo Jima and Okinawa, in which the Japanese fought almost to the last man, convinced many that an invasion of the Japanese mainland would be even more bitterly contested. Thus President Truman was forced to sacrifice the lives of thousands of Japanese civilians in order to convince the emperor and the Imperial War Cabinet that capitulation was Japan's only option.

In the past few decades historians have questioned whether Truman's decision was intended to end the war with Japan or to send a clear message to the Soviet Union that the United States had the military capability to challenge the Soviets if necessary in the postwar period. Furthermore, the United States may have been concerned that the Soviet Union's imminent entry into the war against Japan would provide it an opportunity, along with the United States, to occupy that nation after the war, possibly leading to the type of territorial division that had occurred in Korea. In fact, it seems that by 1945 the once-formidable Japanese military was but a shell of its past power. For example, the Japanese Navy had essentially been neutralized, Japan's merchant fleet was nearly destroyed, millions of Japanese soldiers were isolated in China and elsewhere and could not be returned to Japan to defend the homeland, and the Japanese Air Force was reduced to using kamikaze pilots. Moreover, every major military target in Japan had already been bombed at least once. Even the projected estimate of 1 million casualties is also questioned. To this day, the decision whether the United States should have used atomic weapons on Japan triggers passions on both sides of the issue. It is important for you to understand that every controversial issue or decision has its supporters and detractors.

World War II cost approximately 50 million lives, hundreds of billions of dollars, and untold suffering and despair for millions of others. Although the international price was massive, the defeat of Germany, Japan, and Italy ended the horrors perpetrated by those nations against humanity. Importantly, the year the war ended, the United Nations was established in the hopes of preventing such barbarity from ever happening again. As for the United States, it had endured over 1 million casualties, killed and wounded, but had emerged from the war a superpower. For the time being it had a nuclear-weapons monopoly that gave it an advantage over the Soviets in the first few years of the Cold War. Yet, as the nation entered into a postwar period of consumerism and economic reconversion, foreign and domestic concerns would profoundly shape the quality of life for the American people.

Content Review Questions

1. Which of the following is NOT associated with the Axis Powers?
   (A) Hitler
   (B) Mussolini
   (C) Japan
   (D) Franco

2. In the Munich Conference
   (A) Hitler agreed to form an alliance with Italy and Japan.
   (B) the Big Three agreed to demand unconditional surrender from the Germans and Japanese.
   (C) Britain and France gave in to Hitler's territorial demands.
   (D) the United States promised Germany that it would remain neutral in the war.

3. Which future Allied nation provided support to the Loyalists in the Spanish Civil War?
   (A) United States
   (B) Britain
   (C) France
   (D) Soviet Union

4. The America First Committee
   (A) was strongly in favor of providing economic assistance to Britain, but opposed military aid.
   (B) was strongly in favor of the assistance President Roosevelt gave to the British.
   (C) believed "cash and carry" would not jeopardize American neutrality.
   (D) strongly opposed U.S. intervention in the war.

5. At which conference did the Big Three first meet?
   (A) Casablanca
   (B) Potsdam
   (C) Yalta
   (D) Teheran

6. In the *Panay* incident
   (A) the Japanese sank a U.S. gunboat on patrol in China.
   (B) the Japanese launched a surprise attack on the Seventh Fleet at Pearl Harbor, Hawaii.
   (C) Japan invaded China.
   (D) the Japanese government agreed not to invade China in return for territorial concessions in Southeast Asia.

7. The Stimson Doctrine
   (A) was widely condemned by the America First Committee.
   (B) stated that the United States would not recognize Japan's puppet government in China.
   (C) implied that the United States would not challenge Soviet influence in Eastern Europe.
   (D) stated that the United States would seek unconditional surrender terms from Japan and Germany.

8. When President Roosevelt stated that this event was "a date which will live in infamy," he was referring to
   (A) the D-Day landing.
   (B) the dropping of the atomic bombs on Japan.
   (C) the surprise attack on Pearl Harbor.
   (D) Germany's invasion of Poland.

9. In order to establish a new Italian empire, Mussolini ordered his military to invade
   (A) Poland.
   (B) France.
   (C) Belgium.
   (D) Ethiopia.

10. The Manhattan Project was a top-secret plan
   (A) to prevent Japan from acquiring raw materials necessary for the expansion of its military.
   (B) devised by the Nazis to eliminate Europe's Jews.
   (C) by the United States to develop the atom bomb.
   (D) that culminated in the Allies' D-Day landing.

11. During World War II, President Roosevelt issued Executive Order No. 9066, which
    (A) authorized the use of atomic weapons against Japan.
    (B) integrated the U.S. military for the first time in the nation's history.
    (C) forcibly interned Japanese Americans because they were considered a security risk.
    (D) established noncombat duties for women in the army, navy, and coast guard.

12. In 1942, the *bracero* program was set up to improve which key economic sector?
    (A) Agricultural sector
    (B) Automotive industry
    (C) Oil and electricity industries
    (D) Industrial sector

13. The U.S. national debt skyrocketed between 1930 and the end of World War II because of
    (A) the cost of New Deal programs.
    (B) the cost of fighting the war.
    (C) increased labor costs as a result of collective bargaining.
    (D) interruptions in international trade because of German submarine attacks on shipping.

14. The success of the D-Day invasion was pivotal in the destruction of Germany's war machine in that
    (A) it gave the Allies a foothold in Europe that they used to invade Germany.
    (B) it interrupted German-Italian plans to invade France.
    (C) it compelled the Germans and the Japanese to use their depleted financial and military resources to fend off the invasion.
    (D) Germany could no longer coordinate its military activities with Italy and Japan.

15. The Allies' demand that Japan surrender or face annihilation was made at which wartime meeting?
    (A) Teheran Conference
    (B) Yalta Conference
    (C) Cairo Conference
    (D) Potsdam Conference

Short-Answer Questions

1. The United States attempted to remain neutral in the 1930s as it became apparent that Europe would once again enter a massive war. In the late 1930s and early 1940s, though there were signs that this thinking was beginning to change.
   A) Choose one of the following government acts and discuss why this is the clearest indication of a change in government thinking about involvement in World War II. Make sure to include historical evidence to support your answer.
      - Lend Lease
      - Cash and Carry

- Destroyers for Bases
- The draft

B) How did U.S. actions at the beginning of World War II differ from the beginning of World War I? Include at least one comparison.

Question 2 is based on the following images.

Bettmann/Corbis

Archie Miyatake/Picture Research Consultants & Archives

2. Anti-Japanese sentiment was strong after the attack on Pearl Harbor, as Japanese Americans were suspected of spying for the Japanese government.
   A. Describe these images.
   B. How did the sentiments in the first image lead to the situations in the second and third images?
   C. Does this violate Japanese citizens constitutional rights? Support your answer with historical evidence.

Long-Essay Questions

1. President Roosevelt's foreign policy before the United States entered World War II encountered and was influenced by the considerable opposition and obstacles he faced in helping Great Britain.

   Discuss the extent to which each of the following affirms or contradicts the above statement:

   Neutrality Acts
   America First Committee
   Assistance provided to the British

2. The United States was justified in using the atomic bombs against Japan in 1945.

   To what extent is the above statement true?

Answers

Content Review Questions

1. **(D)** While Germany and Italy assisted Franco's fascists, Spain remained neutral in the war (*The American Pageant,* 14th ed., pp. 905–906/15th ed., p. 781; Learning Objective WOR-7).

2. **(C)** Hitler promised an end to his territorial ambitions if Czechoslovakia was compelled to relinquish control of the Sudetenland to Germany (*The American Pageant,* 14th ed., p. 860/15th ed., p. 784; Learning Objective WOR-7).

3. **(D)** The Soviet Union provided aid, though not as much as Germany and Italy provided (*The American Pageant,* 14th ed., pp. 858–859/15th ed., p. 783; Learning Objective POL-6).

4. **(D)** The America First Committee favored isolationism (*The American Pageant,* 14th ed., pp. 865–866/15th ed., p. 789; Learning Objective WOR-7).

5. **(D)** An earlier conference, the Casablanca Conference, was between Roosevelt and Churchill (*The American Pageant,* 14th ed., p. 891/15th ed., p. 817 Learning Objective WOR-7).

6. **(A)** Japan apologized for the sinking of the U.S. gunboat rather than risk escalating tensions between the two nations (*The American Pageant,* 14th ed., p. 859/15th ed., p. 784; Learning Objective WOR-7).

7. **(B)** The Stimson Doctrine is widely viewed as a tepid response to Japan's aggression in China (*The American Pageant,* 14th ed., pp. 819–820/15th ed., p. 747; Learning Objective WOR-7).

8. **(C)** This attack was the basis of the U.S. entry into World War II (*The American Pageant,* 14th ed., p. 871/15th ed., p. 794; Learning Objective WOR-7).

9. **(D)** The defeat of the Ethiopians and Italian occupation of portions of the Adriatic and Balkans was the extent of Mussolini's empire (*The American Pageant,* 14th ed., pp. 856–857/15th ed., p. 781; Learning Objective ENV-5).

10. **(C)** Albert Einstein convinced Roosevelt to start the project (*The American Pageant,* 14th ed., pp. 864–865/15th ed., p. 820; Learning Objective WXT-3).

11. **(C)** Cruel and unnecessary, the internment of Japanese American citizens was viewed as essential to American national security. It was racist in that German Americans and Italian Americans were not interned. The U.S. government later compensated the families who were persecuted under this

executive order (*The American Pageant,* 14th ed., p. 876/15th ed., p. 799; Learning Objective WOR-4).

12. **(A)** War demands created significant shortages, not least of which were in agriculture and food production. To address this problem the United States and Mexico established the *bracero* program, which allowed thousands of Mexicans to harvest American crops (*The American Pageant,* 14th ed., p. 881/15th ed., p. 803; Learning Objective WOR-4).

13. **(B)** One misconception about the dramatic increase in the national debt during this period is that it was caused by costly New Deal programs. However, the enormous cost of the war ($330 billion), much of which was borrowed in order to sustain the nation's war effort, drove up the national debt (*The American Pageant,* 14th ed., p. 885/15th ed., p. 807; Learning Objective WXT-8).

14. **(A)** Once the Allies gained a beachhead in France, they poured in troops and war materiel to drive the Germans back across the Rhine River into Germany (*The American Pageant,* 14th ed., p. 891/15th ed., pp. 813–814; Learning Objective WOR-7).

15. **(D)** At the seventeen-day Potsdam Conference, which opened on July 16, 1945, President Truman, Joseph Stalin, Winston Churchill, and Clement Attlee discussed first the status and future of defeated Nazi Germany, then the issue of unconditional Japanese surrender. By this time the United States had successfully developed atomic weapons, which made the threat of annihilation a distinct possibility (*The American Pageant,* 14th ed., p. 899/15th ed., p. 820; Learning Objective WOR-7).

Short-Answer Questions

1. You can discuss any of these as indications of changes in government thinking. Lend Lease puts the United Sates in the war because it helps one side, so any claims of neutrality were eradicated. The same can be said of Destroyers for Bases. Cash and carry was a firm step away from neutrality because the United States was arming the warring parties. The draft indicates that the United States is preparing for war because it is forming a corps of people to fight. Before WWI the United States believed that, as a neutral nation, it could continue its trade unabated. The United States also remained out of the actual fighting for far longer. This directly contrasts with policy as Europe built up to war in the 1930s.

2. The images show white Americans' sentiment toward Japanese Americans as well as the conditions in the camps. You can discuss the fear and irrational thought that led to internment, in which more than two-thirds of those in camps were American citizens. In terms of constitutionality, you can mention the *Korematsu* decision, but you can also talk about

property rights, habeas corpus, and rights accorded to citizens in the Bill of Rights.

Long-Essay Questions

1. In this essay you should indicate that President Roosevelt wanted to assist Britain in its war against Germany but was prohibited from directly providing aid by the Neutrality Acts. You should discuss the specific restraints placed on the president by the acts as well as the efforts of those individuals and groups who sought to keep the United States neutral in what they viewed as a European war, such as the America First Committee and Charles Lindbergh. Over time, however, Roosevelt was able to assist Britain. You should therefore discuss "Cash and Carry," lend-lease, and the "bases for destroyers" agreement. (Historical Thinking Skills: I-1: Historical Causation, II-5: Contextualization, III-7: Appropriate Use of Relevant Historical Evidence, IV-8: Interpretation, and IV-9: Synthesis)

2. If defending the use of the atomic bombs on Japan in 1945, you should address the enormous cost of the battles that led up to Truman's decision, such as the Battles of Iwo Jima and Okinawa. Include in your essay the reasoning that if the Japanese military had fought almost to the last man in those battles, and in the process inflicted staggering casualties on the Americans, the cost in lives for conquering Japan itself would make the other battles pale in comparison. To refute the statement you should discuss the condition of the Japanese military and Japan itself in 1945: its air force and navy had been decimated, its merchant fleet had been reduced to insignificance, and every major military target in Japan had already been bombed at least once. Added to this is the willingness of the Japanese to surrender weeks before the bombs were dropped. Another major argument that supports this perspective is the view that the United States attacked Japan with atomic weapons in order to defeat that nation before the Soviets could enter the Pacific war. (Historical Thinking Skills: I-1: Historical Causation, III-6: Historical Argumentation, III-7: Appropriate Use of Relevant Historical Evidence, and IV-8: Interpretation)

Period 8: 1945-1980

Domestic and International Challenges in Cold War America

When World War II ended in 1945 Europe was economically and physically destroyed. Out of the ashes of war emerged two superpowers, diametrically opposed to each other: the United States and the Soviet Union. Though historians debate the starting point of the Cold War, the fact remains that the next forty-five years were marked by tension between these superpowers and the nations aligned with them. The Cold War—and the ominous specter of nuclear war that accompanied it— dictated American foreign policy from the end of World War II until the collapse of the Soviet Union in 1991. Though the United Sates and the Soviet Union never entered into the dreaded World War III that some saw coming, the U.S. military did engage in fights to contain and/or eradicate communism all over the world.

Domestically, the United States experienced great highs and alarming lows in the second half of the twentieth century, with postwar prosperity reaching new heights and technology revolutionizing the way that people lived and communicated. Amidst this boon, minorities fought for civil rights with their accomplishments mixed in with some tragic results, and protests against the Vietnam War threatened the social fabric of the nation. By the 1980s, the social and cultural makeup of the United States was significantly different than when the nation entered World War II forty years earlier.

Key Concepts from the College Board

8.1 The United States responded to an uncertain and unstable postwar world by asserting and attempting to defend a position of global leadership, with far-reaching domestic and international consequences.

8.2 Liberalism, based on anticommunism abroad and a firm belief in the efficacy of governmental and especially federal power to achieve social goals at home, reached its apex in the mid-1960s and generated a variety of political and cultural responses.

8.3 Postwar economic, demographic, and technological changes had a far-reaching impact on American society, politics, and the environment.

19

U.S. DOMESTIC AFFAIRS FROM 1945 TO THE 1980S

In 1945 much of Europe lay in ruins with their economies and political systems shattered and millions displaced. In Asia, the United States occupied Japan, China was poised to revert to civil war, and Southeast Asia and the Korean peninsula would soon be divided between communist and anticommunist groups and governments. The war had taken approximately 50 million lives, and cost hundreds of billions of dollars. It had taken its toll on the United States as well, which suffered over 1 million casualties, of which 300,000 were killed in action. In monetary terms, it had cost well over $300 billion. In many ways, however, the United States emerged from the war more powerful in political and economic terms than the other combatants. To be sure, the number of Americans killed was staggering, but it paled in comparison with the Soviet Union's losses—approximately 8 million civilians and 14 million soldiers. Many nations in Europe and Asia had experienced invasion as well; the continental United States was untouched by such an experience during the war. The United States entered the war as an international power and emerged a superpower, the only nation in the world at that time with a nuclear arsenal.

Numerous problems lay ahead for the United States despite its success in the war and its healthy condition relative to other nations. President Roosevelt died in April 1945, just weeks before the surrender of Germany's Third Reich. The vice president was the untested and seemingly inexperienced Harry Truman. His task was daunting. The United States and its allies would first have to defeat Japan and then decide how to integrate millions of service members back into the economy. Demobilization was not the only economic concern; reconversion from a war to a consumer economy would also present a considerable challenge. As Americans adjusted their lives to the new realities of the postwar years, they would soon find that relations with their former ally, the Soviet Union, would rapidly deteriorate, leading to decades of tension, conflict, and enormous military expenditures. The Cold War—the adversarial relationship between the United States and its allies and the Soviet Union and its allies—defined in many ways the quality of life in the postwar era, made worse by the knowledge that there were more than enough nuclear weapons to destroy the planet.

KEY CONCEPTS

- In the postwar period, the U.S. economy reconverted from one geared to the production of military supplies to one that was consumer-oriented.
- The postwar years witnessed an enormous expansion of the economy, highlighted by the baby boom, suburbanization, and massive consumer spending.
- The civil rights movements helped black Americans, but they were still relegated to a second-class status economically, politically, and socially.
- The presidential administrations in the postwar decades expanded the size and scope of government.
- Some administrations addressed the demands of labor, whereas others had an adversarial relationship.
- Liberalism reshaped social, economic, gender, racial, and political relations.
- A conservative backlash evolved in response to the liberal policies of the 1960s.
- The Watergate scandal undermined the American people's trust in their political system.

This period is discussed in depth in *The American Pageant,* 14th and 15th eds., Chapters 36–40.

THE ECONOMIC "BOOM"

Of course it is easy to see the United States after World War II as a nation overwhelmed by the Cold War and the arms race that developed between the two powerful adversaries, the United States and the Soviet Union. Yet conditions were still dreadful for millions of Americans at the end of the war, and they would stay that way. Poor whites, blacks, Latinos, and others lived desperate lives, struggling to stay above the poverty line, as postwar prosperity did not touch their lives. For example:

- Twenty percent of the population lived in poverty.
- Parts of rural America had been untouched by modern developments in sanitation, housing, education, and health care. For example, as late as 1952 some parts of rural America still did not have access to electric power.

Yet for many Americans the postwar years represented a new level of national and personal prosperity few had ever known. The generations that had fought the war had not only experienced the unparalleled devastation of World War II but also endured the Great Depression. The decade following the war, when the nation achieved unprecedented and sustained economic growth, must have seemed like an illusion to some. Citizens and the government embarked on a massive spending spree, stimulated by the carefree spending habits of many Americans, who had saved millions of dollars during the war, and government spending. The government had stimulated the economy out of necessity during the war, but it continued to do so when the conflict ended. Billions of dollars were budgeted for public education and welfare programs. The Interstate Highway Act of 1956 allotted over $30 billion to highway development. The primary beneficiaries of this infrastructural development were the trucking and automobile industries (the auto became the symbol of postwar prosperity), and the integrated highway network, a major conduit between urban central business districts and the "bedroom communities" of suburbia, altered the national landscape forever. Government spending for former service members covered a variety of areas: the Veterans Administration and the Federal Housing Administration provided low-interest loans for purchasing homes and for low-cost public housing. The Servicemen's Readjustment Act, commonly known as the GI Bill, provided veterans low-interest loans to start businesses and enroll in technical schools and universities.

The vitality of the economy was remarkable:

- Production of goods and services doubled as Americans engaged in unprecedented consumerism.
- Unemployment and inflation stayed below 5 percent.
- The gross national product had increased fivefold during the war.

Demobilization and Economic Reconversion

Shortly after becoming president, Harry Truman changed the paperweight on his desk; one modeled after a gun was replaced by one modeled after a plow. The message was clear: reconvert the economy from a war footing to a consumer one. As more and more service people returned home—approximately 7 million servicemen and servicewomen had returned to civilian status just one year after V-J Day—economic reconversion was a high priority for the administration.

Another concern soon surfaced: postwar inflation. Some feared inflation could spark a recession and widespread unemployment. The Office of Price Administration (OPA), created during the war, had imposed price controls—and therefore controlled inflation. But what would happen after the war, when it was anticipated that consumer demand would drive up prices and the general cost of living? Fortunately, the OPA, rapid reconversion to producing consumer goods, and considerable demand offset a temporary increase in inflation. By late 1947 most concerns had dissipated. The growth of the economy was further sustained by the military demands of the Cold War; the government continued to be a major purchaser of goods and services. With so much money in the system, combined with ever-growing consumer demand, businesses introduced a new phenomenon in consumer spending, an early form of the credit card, in order to further stimulate consumer demand.

THE BABY BOOM AND SUBURBANIZATION

Between 1945 and 1960 the total U.S. population increased by 40 million. In the 1950s alone the population increased by 28 million. This expansion represented an almost 20 percent population increase, the largest since the height of immigration earlier in the century. Americans who were born in the decade and a half after the war and came of age in the midst of the Cold War are known as "baby boomers."

The population explosion created a demand for affordable family housing in the late 1940s and 1950s, which precipitated dramatic demographic changes:

- The need for housing immediately following the war spurred the remarkable growth of the suburbs. However, almost the entire population increase in this period was an urban experience, as millions settled in the nation's bustling cities.
- Much of the demographic shift that took place led to substantial growth in what became the "sunbelt" states, an arc that stretches from the Carolinas to Florida, Texas, and California. Millions of Americans relocated, lured by lower taxes, a more temperate climate (aided by the introduction of air conditioning in businesses and homes), and economic opportunities in defense-related industries. The industrial areas of the Northeast, which became known as the "rustbelt," experienced economic hard times and a reduction in representation in the House.
- The Northeast, however, remained the most densely populated section of the nation. Twenty years after the end of the war, one in five Americans lived in the narrow corridor that stretched from Massachusetts to Virginia.
- By the early 1960s population growth was mostly a suburban phenomenon, so that by the 1970s many more Americans were living in suburban neighborhoods than in cities.
- With military spending increasing employment opportunities in the North from 1941 to 1945, black Americans had migrated to the North in significant numbers; this trend would continue well after the end of the war.
- The growth of suburbia was the consequence of numerous factors: the automobile, the highway system, consumer demand to live outside congested urban areas, and the efforts of development contractors such as William Levitt. Levitt mass-produced low-priced family homes (the prototype was Long Island, New York's Levittown). This massive construction project, offering low-interest rates on mortgages that were government insured and tax deductible, paved the way for millions to own their own suburban homes. Unfortunately, Levitt homes were not made available to black Americans. The effect of this demographic shift and racial discrimination was "white flight" from urban to suburban areas. Consequently, inner cities became increasingly poorer and racially segregated.
    - Advocates of suburbanization claim that it represents the American dream of home ownership, a cleaner environment, and less crime.

- Critics contend that it despoils the environment, leads to conformity, promotes racial segregation, and weakens the economic and cultural qualities of urban areas.

Domestic Developments During the Truman Administration (1945–1953)

Harry Truman had been vice president of the United States only three months when President Roosevelt died in April 1945. Many skeptics were convinced that he lacked the experience and leadership skills necessary to run the nation at such a pivotal moment. It did not take him long, however, to form his own identity independent of the long shadow cast by his predecessor. As president Truman wanted to adopt many of the features of the New Deal into his reform program, called the Fair Deal. One critic implied that he came up with so many programs and policies that resembled the New Deal that not even the Brain Trust had thought of them. Political consequences would doom many of his programs to failure. The short postwar recession convinced enough Americans to vote for Republicans, who proceeded to take over both houses of Congress in 1946. Consequently, Republican conservatives in Congress blocked most of Truman's domestic programs, such as a comprehensive civil rights program, a national health insurance program, agricultural reforms, and aid to education. Actually, the last had bipartisan support, but the issue floundered on whether to fund religious parochial schools as well.

Labor's relationship with Truman was rocky at times. Postwar wages had not kept up with inflation, and by 1946 nearly 2 million workers went out on strike. When railroad workers struck, Truman threatened to seize and operate the railroads, thus ending the work stoppage. When the United Mine Workers union went out on strike and refused to heed the same warning, the government took over the mines until a compromise contract was worked out.

Labor's fortunes took a turn for the worse when Congress changed hands. Dismayed at the frequency of strikes and intensity of labor unrest, the pro-business Republican Party acted quickly to stop the strikes, passing the controversial Taft-Hartley Act in 1947 over Truman's veto. The bill defined "unfair labor practices" as boycotts, sympathy strikes, and the closed shop, and required unions to adhere to a sixty-day cooling-off period before workers could strike. Union leaders were required to swear that they were not communists.

Undaunted, Truman pushed ahead with his own domestic agenda. In his two terms, the following measures were taken:

- **Housing Act of 1949** This act budgeted $3 billion for slum clearance and new low-rent housing.
- **Minimum Wage Act of 1949** The Fair Labor Standards Act of 1938 was amended to increase the minimum wage.
- **Social Security Act of 1950** Coverage to individuals who were self-employed was added, and retirees were given increased benefits.
- **Civil rights** Truman's policies alienated the southern wing of the Democratic party, or Dixiecrats, who in turn created their own States' Rights party and ran South Carolina Governor Strom

Thurmond against Truman in the 1948 election. Truman took the following steps despite the anticipated opposition from southern Democrats and Republican conservatives:

- created the Committee on Civil Rights, which proposed, for instance, that public institutions engaging in racial discrimination be denied federal funds, segregation in interstate transportation be prohibited, and lynching made a federal offense—all matters for which Congress refused to enact legislation
- desegregated the federal government and the armed forces
- appointed black federal judges

Despite strong opposition from the progressive wing of his own party (which ran Henry A. Wallace) and the Dixiecrats, not to mention his popular Republican opponent, Thomas E. Dewey, Truman surprised pollsters and political pundits by receiving over one hundred more electoral votes than did Dewey in the 1948 election. Prevented from seeking a third term when the Twenty-second Amendment was ratified in 1951, and with his popularity waning, Truman retired from public office.

DOMESTIC DEVELOPMENTS DURING THE EISENHOWER ADMINISTRATION (1953–1961)

Dwight Eisenhower emerged from World War II a national hero. As supreme allied commander, he was enormously popular. In 1952 he ran as a Republican and easily defeated Illinois's Adlai Stevenson. His campaign slogan, "Time for a Change," resonated with the public after two decades of Democratic leadership. He would repeat his victory over Stevenson again in 1956. The cabinet he selected comprised wealthy advocates of business. Despite this, labor did better in the 1950s compared with other sectors of the economy. In 1955 the AFL and the CIO merged, forming a powerful union. That year the government raised the minimum wage from seventy-five cents to one dollar an hour. In Eisenhower's two terms in office, the following steps were taken:

- The Department of Health, Education, and Welfare (initially recommended by Truman) was organized as a cabinet-level position in 1953. Its first secretary was Oveta Culp Hobby.
- Social Security was amended in 1954 to include new groups: state and local government employees and farmers. Retirees received cost-of-living increases. Two years later it was amended again to cover physicians. The eligibility requirement was lowered to age sixty-two for women and to age fifty for the disabled.
- The National Defense Education Act (1958) appropriated $1 billion for education, in large part because of concerns about Soviet advances in aeronautics. The act provided financial aid to college students, and provided matching federal funds for state education to improve courses in science, math, and language arts.

Civil rights claimed much of the country's attention. Blacks had experienced some important gains under Truman and some assistance from the Eisenhower administration when they took bold steps to challenge segregation and discrimination in the 1950s. With the *Brown* v. *Board of Education of Topeka, Kansas* decision (1954), the Warren Court shattered the eighty-year history of Jim Crow laws in the South and forever transformed black rights in relation to the Fourteenth Amendment. In overturning the 1896 *Plessy* v. *Ferguson* decision, the court ruled that separate but equal is unconstitutional because facilities for the races were inherently unequal.

Some southern communities refused to abide by the new law. When Arkansas's Governor Orval Faubus sent the National Guard to turn away black students from Little Rock's Central High School, Eisenhower sent the U.S. Army to the school to guarantee the safety of its newly registered black students. When the Little Rock School Board challenged the president's authority to integrate Little Rock's schools, the court decision in *Cooper* v. *Aaron* (1958) reiterated its rationale in the *Brown* case as a fundamental right of citizens under the Fourteenth Amendment. Legalized segregation was dead, though the struggle for integration continues to this day.

As segregation lingered on in the South, blacks took it upon themselves to challenge municipal and state laws that sustained inequality and segregation. In late 1955 Rosa Parks, a black resident of Montgomery, Alabama, refused to relinquish her seat on a city bus to a white person in accordance with the city's segregation statute. Parks's arrest galvanized Montgomery's black community. Led by a twenty-six-year-old Baptist minister, the Reverend Dr. Martin Luther King, Jr., a successful, nonviolent boycott of Montgomery's buses was organized. The following year the Supreme Court ruled that segregated seating in municipal buses was unconstitutional. The boycott, Dr. King, and his philosophy of nonviolent resistance received international attention.

One year after the Montgomery bus boycott, Congress passed the Civil Rights Act of 1957, the first civil rights legislation since Reconstruction. It was designed to enforce voting rights that had been systematically denied to blacks throughout the South. A bipartisan Civil Rights Commission was established to oversee and prosecute (through the Justice Department) those interfering with a citizen's Fifteenth Amendment rights. In 1960 the act was strengthened to make such abuses a federal crime. Further, in response to a wave of bomb attacks on mostly southern black churches and homes in the 1950s, the act made transporting explosives across state lines a federal crime.

Domestic Developments During the Kennedy Administration: "The New Frontier" (1961–1963)

John F. Kennedy (JFK) narrowly defeated the Republican candidate, Richard M. Nixon, in a campaign notable for the first nationally televised presidential debates. An assassin's bullet ended his life less than three years into his term in office, but in that brief time, JFK sought to expand on FDR's New Deal and Truman's Fair Deal programs. Like FDR he sought out the advice of intellectuals and university professors. As in Truman's presidency, Congress rejected most of Kennedy's most progressive programs. The following are representative of the programs and measures enacted during his short term in office:

- The Housing Act of 1961 budgeted $5 billion for slum clearance.
- The Minimum Wage Act of 1961 increased minimum hourly wages to $1.25.
- Amendments to Social Security extended coverage to children of unemployed workers and increased payments to retirees; however, a penalty was imposed on retirement before age sixty-five.
- Congress approved a Federal Water Pollution Control Act.

Civil rights still dominated the domestic scene. Kennedy was at first hesitant to use all of the federal government's power to tackle civil rights problems, but events compelled him to act. He eventually took important steps to guarantee black Americans their constitutional rights. Under the direction of his brother, Attorney General Robert F. Kennedy, the Justice Department sued in federal court to protect voting rights for black Americans. In 1961 he dispatched federal marshals to protect the Freedom Riders, who had been brutally attacked when they attempted to integrate interstate bus facilities. After announcing his support for the Voter Education Project, which was designed to register southern blacks to vote, JFK told Dr. King, "I may lose the next election, but I don't care." When a black Korean War veteran named James Meredith attempted to enroll in the all-white University of Mississippi in 1962, the governor of the state ordered that Meredith be rejected despite having met the academic requirements for admission. President Kennedy ordered federal marshals to Mississippi to compel the school to enroll Meredith. Violence erupted and two people were killed. It eventually took over five thousand federal marshals to register Meredith at the university. The following year Medgar Evers, the head of Mississippi's NAACP, was assassinated by a white racist in front of his home. Ironically, that very evening Kennedy had appeared on television to persuade the nation that stronger civil rights legislation was needed.

In 1963 another southern governor, George Wallace of Alabama, attempted to accomplish what his fellow governors in Arkansas and Mississippi had failed to do: stop the enrollment of qualified black students in a state university. Again, the result was the same. Wallace symbolically and ceremoniously stood in the doorway of the registrar's office at the University of Alabama, preventing the black students from registering. Careful not to send the U.S. military into the state for fear it would result in rioting, Kennedy outmaneuvered Wallace: he nationalized the Alabama National Guard and commanded its senior general to order Wallace away. His act of bravado complete, Wallace left the university and it was soon integrated. That same year, under the leadership of Dr. King and his organization, the Southern Christian Leadership Conference (SCLC), the "cradle of the Confederacy," Birmingham, Alabama, was integrated.

Inspired by these gains, but not satisfied that almost ten years had passed since segregation was outlawed in the *Brown* decision, over 200,000 black and white demonstrators participated in the March on Washington, demanding an end to segregation and racial discrimination. Three months later Kennedy was dead, and it was left to a progressive southerner, Vice President Lyndon B. Johnson, to continue the series of reforms started by his predecessors.

Domestic Developments During the Johnson Administration: "The Great Society" (1963–1969)

A great admirer of Franklin Roosevelt, Lyndon Johnson sought to emulate him as a political leader. Like FDR, Johnson came to the White House during a traumatic moment in U.S. history, but fortunately he had had considerable experience in government. Domestically Johnson sought to combat poverty, disease, inadequate education, racial injustices, and generally improve the quality of life for millions who knew little more than hardship and discrimination. His approach appealed to the voting public. When he ran for election in 1964 he received over 61 percent of the popular vote, even more than FDR had received in his four successful bids for the presidency. Johnson's Great Society reform program brought about or inspired the following:

- **The Economic Opportunity Act of 1964** The act authorized $1 billion for the War on Poverty. In addition, it created the Job Corps to provide vocational training and educational opportunities for underprivileged youth.
- **Appalachian Regional Development Act of 1965** The act set aside $1 billion for aid to the poverty-stricken Appalachian mountain regions.
- **Elementary and Secondary Education Act of 1965** The act provided extensive financial aid to public and parochial schools.
- **Medicare Act of 1965** The act provided nursing and hospital care, funded by the Social Security system, to the elderly.

Johnson also oversaw the creation of two cabinet-level agencies: the Department of Housing and Urban Development (HUD) 1965, which was led by Robert Weaver, the nation's first black cabinet secretary; and the Department of Transportation in 1966, which oversees and coordinates national transportation policies. In addition two constitutional amendments were ratified: the Twenty-fourth Amendment (1964) prohibited the use of a poll tax as a prerequisite for voting; and the Twenty-fifth Amendment (1967) provided for the vice president to assume the duties of the president if the chief executive is incapacitated.

Two crucial civil rights acts were passed in the mid-1960s:

- **Civil Rights Act of 1964** This act strengthened antisegregation policies by withholding federal funding to states that did not comply with federal laws regarding voting rights, education, and public facilities.
- **Voting Rights Act of 1965** The act forbade literacy tests under certain circumstances and authorized the president to enforce the Fifteenth Amendment.

To Martin Luther King, these two civil rights acts gave crucial federal protection for blacks seeking to exercise their constitutional rights. More radical and militant black leaders and groups such as Malcolm X and the Black Panthers challenged this view. Malcolm X, who had converted to Islam while in prison in the 1950s, advocated racial separation and Black Nationalism, but eventually modified his position somewhat before he was assassinated in 1964. The Black Panthers, led by Bobby Seale, Huey Newton, and Eldridge Cleaver, advocated a militant response to police harassment, inequality, and systematic racial subordination. The police regularly arrested Black Panther members until the early 1970s, when the organization decided to redirect its energies from armed defense of black rights to community development programs. In fact, in 1973, Bobby Seale was a mayoral candidate in Oakland, California. Other groups that had experienced discrimination and were mired in poverty, such as Puerto Ricans and Mexican Americans, also organized. Labor leader César Chávez, for instance, organized Mexican American farm workers in a bid for higher wages. He appealed to the public to boycott certain crops such as grapes in order to force employers to raise wages.

Even though he had been elected in a landslide in 1964, the war in Vietnam eroded much of Lyndon Johnson's initial support. In 1968, weary and overwhelmed by the quagmire in Vietnam, he surprised the nation by deciding not to run for reelection.

AP Tip

The postwar decades were filled with turmoil, especially the 1960s. In order to understand this decade better, you need a working understanding of the countercultural movements that shaped American domestic life. The decade was characterized by the rebelliousness of America's youth in response to what many perceived as the socially stifling mores and lifestyles of the previous decades.

- Many of the nation's "baby boomers" sought to combat the social ills they saw as fundamentally undemocratic: racism, poverty, inequality, and American foreign policy, especially in Vietnam. In the early 1960s, for example, Students for a Democratic Society (SDS) was formed with the intention of democratizing the institutions that shaped American life, such as universities and government.
- A new generation of feminists re-energized the women's movement, which worked to raise the consciousness of women themselves and society as a whole and pressed for profound changes in both social and economic life.
- Sexual mores were under attack as earlier changes in sexual attitudes inspired even more criticisms of traditional sexual values. The advent of birth control ("the pill") as well as increasingly risqué advertising and sexuality in movies and television loosened certain stereotypes about sexuality. The 1980s would witness a backlash to the revolution in sexuality that took place in the previous decades.
- The music of the 1960s, as well as the dress of many young people ("hippies"), was seen as an expression of a frustrated, sometimes angry, but politically conscious American youth.

THE PRESIDENCY OF RICHARD M. NIXON (1969–1974)

Richard Nixon's unfortunate legacy is that he is the only chief executive to resign the office of president. Nixon ran for election as the Republican candidate on the promise that he could end the war in Vietnam honorably. Although foreign affairs often dominated his presidency, a number of key domestic events and policies shaped his administration as well. Nixon appealed to the "silent majority," middle-class Americans, some of whom were Democrats, who had not participated in one or another sort of demonstration, were opposed to "big government," and rejected the nation's cultural and social direction. His cabinet secretaries, reflecting Nixon's pro-business, conservative constituency, were initially white Christian males, hardly a reflection of the social crusades sweeping the nation at the time.

Nixon entered the White House in January 1969 and immediately faced significant economic problems. The cost of Johnson's Great Society programs and the war in Vietnam had led to inflation, increasing unemployment, and a moribund gross national product. Nixon tried to cut government spending while reducing personal income taxes to encourage consumer spending, but the economy worsened. Even a ninety-day wage and price freeze did not have the desired effect. Surprisingly, the fiscally conservative Nixon turned to a Keynesian solution: deficit spending. In order to address the nation's huge trade deficit, Nixon devalued U.S. currency by taking the dollar off the gold standard, thereby making products manufactured in the United States more affordable to foreign consumers. By 1972 the economy was showing signs of recovery.

At that same time, Nixon was exploring his reelection bid. Having received only 43.3 percent of the popular vote in the 1968 election, Nixon and his advisers formulated a strategy to appeal to the disaffected "silent majority" and southern voters discontented with the Democrats' domestic and foreign affairs policies. When he attempted to slow integration and nominated two conservative southerners to the Supreme Court, Congress rejected both maneuvers. He even took steps to "reform" welfare, but was again thwarted by Congress. In response to growing concerns about the environment since the publication of Rachel Carson's *Silent Spring* in 1962, Nixon did create the Environmental Protection Agency, a move that seemingly contradicts the more conservative aspects of his agenda. Yet Nixon, with his abrasive vice president Spiro Agnew in the vanguard attacking liberals and antiwar protestors, won over many southerners. In the 1972 election he defeated his Democratic opponent, George McGovern, in a landslide.

Nixon's administration coincided with two important developments, one constitutional, the other scientific. In response to the cry "Old enough to fight, too young to vote," the Twenty-sixth Amendment, lowering the voting age to eighteen, was ratified in 1971. In 1969 Apollo 11 landed on the moon, profoundly boosting American morale in the midst of domestic turmoil and the quandary in Vietnam. By 1973, however, the economy worsened again, in large part because of the Organization of Petroleum Exporting Countries' (OPEC) oil embargo against the United States for its support of Israel in the Six-Day War.

It was Watergate, however, that unraveled the Nixon presidency. The unfortunate acronym for Nixon's reelection organization was CREEP (Committee to Re-Elect the President). Having won the popular vote by a slim majority in 1968, Nixon's advisers were prepared to do everything possible to guarantee victory, even if that meant breaking the law and engaging in a vast array of "dirty tricks." When burglars (called "plumbers" by the White House because they plugged political leaks) were caught breaking into the Democratic Party headquarters in Washington, D.C.'s Watergate complex, suspicions were raised that the plot had been formulated in the White House. CREEP officials and Nixon's administration, led by White House Chief of Staff H. R. Haldeman and domestic adviser John Ehrlichman, vehemently denied a connection to the "plumbers." Two determined reporters for the *Washington Post*, Carl Bernstein and Bob Woodward, dug deeper into the affair, ultimately exposing criminal acts and cover-ups at the highest levels of government. What is more, the administration had even used independent government agencies to do some of its dirty work and had created an "enemies list," which included politicians, actors, newspaper and television reporters, and opponents of the administration who could be harassed by the White House in a variety of ways (for example, with income tax audits).

Nixon and his aides attempted to cover up their activities, but unfortunately for the president, it was revealed that he habitually tape-recorded all of his Oval Office conversations. The Justice Department and the Senate demanded that Nixon release the tapes to them. Nixon's response was to appoint a special prosecutor, Archibald Cox, to investigate. Cox then demanded Nixon turn over the tapes. On October 20, 1973, Nixon ordered Attorney General Elliot Richardson to fire Cox, but Richardson and his assistant both resigned in protest. Solicitor General Robert Bork (a future unsuccessful candidate to the Supreme Court) finally agreed to fire Cox in what became known as the "Saturday Night Massacre." Nixon's popularity plummeted. The House Judiciary Committee began to consider impeachment proceedings. At last, Nixon turned over what were obviously extensively edited tapes that conclusively proved that Nixon had been lying and had attempted to cover up a crime. The tapes also revealed that Vice President Spiro Agnew had engaged in criminal activities when he was governor of Maryland. Agnew resigned and was replaced by Congressman Gerald Ford. By this point even members of his own party considered Nixon a liability. When the House Judiciary Committee reported that it was prepared to impeach the president, and with his own advisers admitting that he lacked the support to survive such a proceeding, Nixon resigned the office of the president on August 9, 1974.

FORD AND CARTER (1974–1981)

Gerald R. Ford is the only vice president to become chief executive under the Twenty-fifth Amendment. In order to maintain continuity as the nation experienced a transfer of power because of Nixon's resignation, Ford kept most of Nixon's policies and even his cabinet secretaries. His first controversial act came one month into his presidency when he pardoned Nixon. Ford's domestic policy involved limiting government expenditures on social programs, such as welfare and education; high taxes on imported oil; and tax cuts to stimulate consumer demand. Ford spent much of his term unsuccessfully fighting the effects of inflation and the Democratic-controlled Congress. In an act of futility, he endeavored to get the American people and U.S. businesses behind his economic policies by distributing WIN (Whip Inflation Now) buttons. Nevertheless, inflation was not whipped, and as it worsened, unemployment began to creep ever higher. As was the case during the Nixon years, the federal budget increased appreciably in Ford's term.

Social Concerns in the 1970s and 1980s

Politics played a significant role in American life in the two decades following Nixon's resignation, but no more than social changes.

- By the early 1980s, Asian Americans became the nation's fastest growing ethnic minority.
- Illegal immigration reached record proportions, possibly as high as 12 million in the late 1970s.
- Latino Americans began entering politics and winning elected offices throughout the nation.
- Native Americans began organizing to preserve the vestiges of their culture from the effects of assimilation and to call attention to the terrible standard of living they were experiencing. The American Indian Movement (AIM), a militant organization, seized government property to generate awareness for the plight of the nation's original inhabitants.
- Inspired by the publication of Rachel Carson's *Silent Spring* (1962), a dire warning about the use of insecticides on plant and animal life, the American environmental movement came into its own in the 1960s and 1970s. The nation grew increasingly conscious of and concerned about the frequency and extent of industrial disasters: oil spills, a near-catastrophic accident at the Three Mile Island nuclear power plant in Pennsylvania, and the spoliation of the nation's land by companies that irresponsibly dumped toxic waste material. In New York an entire community, Love Canal, was built on a toxic waste dumpsite; over time, residents began experiencing serious health problems. Concerned citizens across the nation demanded that the federal government take action. In 1970 the government created the Environmental Protection Agency (EPA), and two years later, the Clean Water Act passed Congress.
- Many women sought a constitutional amendment (an equal rights amendment) to address gender abuses and discrimination in the workplace.
- Reproductive rights became a hotly contested issue, especially when the Supreme Court ruled in *Roe* v. *Wade* (1973) that states could not prohibit abortion in the first trimester of a woman's pregnancy.

In 1976 the nation celebrated its bicentennial and the election of a new president, Georgia governor Jimmy Carter, who defeated Ford in a close race. Carter's popularity rested largely on his claim to be a populist and an outsider—meaning that his political career had not been shaped by the machinations of Washington politics. His one term in office was marred by runaway inflation and a foreign policy that seemed at times amateurish. Domestically, President Carter pardoned thousands of Vietnam War draft evaders to illustrate to the American people that it was time to move on and not dwell on the turmoil and divisiveness of the late 1960s and early 1970s. During his presidency the following policies and legislation were enacted:

- The minimum wage was increased.
- The Social Security payroll tax was increased.
- Two cabinet-level departments were created: the Department of Energy (1977) and the Department of Education (1979).

Carter's budget, like the rest of the economy, was highly inflationary. The inability to harness runaway inflation ravaged the economy while unemployment, the deficit, and interest rates rose. But the nation's confidence in Carter declined. In his bid for re-election, Republican Ronald Reagan defeated Carter in a landslide.

THE REAGAN "REVOLUTION" (1981–1989)

Not since Hoover had an unambiguously conservative president like Ronald Reagan been elected to lead the nation. On the campaign trail and in the Oval Office he openly criticized the New Deal and the Great Society.

He fulfilled his campaign pledge to redefine the Supreme Court by nominating conservative justices. Three of his appointees, Antonin Scalia, Anthony Kennedy, and Sandra Day O'Connor (the first female Supreme Court justice), were confirmed by the Senate. However, the Senate rejected the outspoken conservative judge Robert Bork. Reagan's appointments shifted the balance away from a more progressive to a decidedly conservative Supreme Court, as evidenced by the limitations it placed on abortion rights and affirmative action.

His economic record is an indication of the direction he took the nation in his eight years as president. President Reagan's administration is associated with deep cuts in government spending and considerable business deregulation. For example:

- A freeze was placed on the number of workers on the federal government's payroll.
- Tax cuts for citizens and corporations were passed.
- Government funding for a range of social programs, such as student education loans and mass transportation, was significantly reduced. Welfare-related programs such as food stamps also suffered budget cuts. Medicare was not touched, but the age for Social Security recipients was raised.
- An attempt was made to reorganize the federal government by eliminating the Departments of Energy and Education.
- Previous restrictions on certain types of mergers and takeovers were removed, as were certain environmental protection standards that businesses contended were driving up their costs. Restrictions on the savings-and-loan industry were reduced while the government simultaneously increased the federal government's depositors' insurance from $20,000 to $100,000. Bad loans, opportunists, and crooks precipitated a flood of bankruptcies,

leaving the American taxpayer to pay for the $200 billion bailout of the savings-and-loan industry.

President Reagan is the only former union president (of the Screen Actors Guild) to serve as president of the United States, so it is ironic that his presidency is associated with a strongly pro-business outlook (as indicated by his view that federal regulations inhibited business growth) and an adversarial relationship with unions. Nineteen months into his first term he eviscerated the air traffic controllers union (PATCO) by firing strikers who refused to return to work. As with his predecessors, Reagan had to confront looming economic problems. The federal budget deficit was growing in part because of his tax cuts, which reduced the government's revenue. Reagan's solution was supply-side economics: massive tax cuts through the Tax Reform Act which would, it was believed, stimulate the economy by starting new businesses and expanding others. Admirers called his plan "Reaganomics," but critics, reminded of Treasury Secretary Mellon's justification for tax cuts in the 1920s, called it "trickle down." Certainly the wealthiest citizens benefited from supply-side economics, but so did some middle-class investors, who could now invest some of their money in tax-free Individual Retirement Accounts (IRAs). Unfortunately the middle class's real wages (surplus capital after all other cost-of-living expenses have been paid for) did not increase in the 1980s. Offsetting the enormous budget cuts was unprecedented spending on the military, in part to undermine the Soviet Union's ability to keep pace with the United States in military expenditures.

When President Reagan entered the White House, the United States was the world's number one creditor nation. Eight years later it had a $200 billion a year federal deficit and an almost equally large trade deficit. Congress's response to the bloated deficit was to pass the Gramm-Rudman-Hollings Balanced Budget Act in 1985, which succeeded in reducing the deficit by approximately $60 billion in just one year. Despite the economic problems facing the nation, many Americans admired Reagan for instilling a sense of patriotism and pride in the United States that had seemed to dissipate over the previous decade. Critics blame him for a host of domestic and foreign policy debacles, but undeniably, his stature is greater than of any American president since Franklin Roosevelt.

Content Review Questions

1. President Reagan's nominations of Justices Scalia, O'Connor, and Kennedy to the Supreme Court
   (A) were warmly supported by Democrats in Congress.
   (B) failed to win the approval of the Senate.
   (C) reveal his attempt to make the Supreme Court more conservative.
   (D) indicated to many Americans his moderate stance on constitutional issues.

2. A stimulus to postwar prosperity was
   (A) the spending habits of Americans as more consumer items became available.
   (B) the significant cuts in the military budget made by Presidents Truman, Eisenhower, and Kennedy.
   (C) the purchasing power of millions of women who entered the workforce at war's end.
   (D) the elimination of the income tax.

3. Which U.S. president is associated with the Fair Deal?
   (A) Franklin Roosevelt
   (B) Harry Truman
   (C) John Kennedy
   (D) Lyndon Johnson

4. The Supreme Court case *Roe* v. *Wade* dealt with
   (A) voting rights.
   (B) environmental protection laws.
   (C) reproductive rights.
   (D) federal funding for welfare programs.

5. In the Supreme Court case *Brown* v. *Board of Education*
   (A) the Court reaffirmed the *Plessy* v. *Ferguson* decision of 1896.
   (B) the Court affirmed voting rights of all citizens in accordance with the Fifteenth Amendment.
   (C) segregation was ruled unconstitutional.
   (D) the Court ruled that the federal government was not responsible for integrating facilities and institutions.

6. The National Defense Education Act
   (A) was passed during the administration of Lyndon Johnson.
   (B) was designed in response to Soviet advancements in aeronautics.
   (C) significantly increased the federal aid to military research programs.
   (D) appropriated billions of dollars for developing peaceful uses for nuclear energy.

7. The Taft-Hartley Act
   (A) helped fund the construction of schools and hospitals in economically depressed areas.
   (B) provided billions in federal aid to communities faced with serious environmental problems.
   (C) was ruled unconstitutional by the Supreme Court on the grounds that the federal government could withhold funds from states that refused to integrate.
   (D) placed serious restrictions on the rights and powers of labor unions.

8. The Reverend Dr. Martin Luther King, Jr., played a significant role in
   (A) the integration of the University of Alabama.
   (B) the integration of the University of Mississippi.
   (C) the Montgomery, Alabama, bus boycott.
   (D) the formation of the Black Panthers.

9. Which postwar president is most associated with business deregulation?
   (A) Dwight Eisenhower
   (B) Gerald Ford
   (C) Jimmy Carter
   (D) Ronald Reagan

10. Which of the following challenged President Truman in his bid for election in 1948?
    (A) Northern Democrats who believed his integration of the military had been premature
    (B) Corporate interests who believed Truman was pro-union and anti-business
    (C) Northern liberals who opposed his Fair Deal
    (D) Southerners who were opposed to his civil rights policies

11. Which of the following is NOT associated with Lyndon Johnson's presidency?
    (A) The Medicare Act
    (B) Appalachian Regional Development Act
    (C) Voting Rights Act
    (D) Supply-side economics

12. Published in 1963, author Betty Friedan's landmark work on women's rights is titled
    (A) *The Vindication of the Rights of Women.*
    (B) *Revolution from Within.*
    (C) *The Feminine Mystique.*
    (D) *Women and the New Race.*

13. The televised "Checkers Speech" saved which candidate's political career and position as vice presidential candidate?
    (A) Richard Nixon
    (B) Dwight Eisenhower
    (C) Harry Truman
    (D) Joseph McCarthy

14. President Lyndon Johnson chose not to run for reelection in 1968 because he
    (A) had been implicated in the Watergate affair.
    (B) was under indictment for tax evasion.
    (C) had been involved in the Whitewater affair.
    (D) believed his policy in Vietnam had divided the nation.

15. Key to Democratic presidential candidate Jimmy Carter's 1976 victory was the enormous support he received from
    (A) blue-collar workers.
    (B) African Americans.
    (C) suburban women.
    (D) military servicemen and servicewomen.

Short-Answer Questions

1. The second half of the twentieth century was marked by social movements, many of which were influenced by the civil rights movement of the 1950s and 1960s.
   A) Choose one of the following social movements and discuss how its goals and/or tactics were influenced by the civil rights movement:
      - Women's movement
      - Student movement
      - Anti-war movement

   B) Did the movement you chose achieve its goals? Provide historical evidence to support your answer.

Question 2 is based on the following cartoon.

Smoking Pistol Exhibit A, cartoon by Pat Oliphant. Reprinted with permission of Universal Press Syndicate. All rights reserved.

2. The Watergate scandal during Richard Nixon's presidency led to the only presidential resignation in American history.
   A) What is the main idea of the cartoon?
   B) How did this event affect Americans' faith in their leaders? Provide historical evidence to support your answer.

Long-Essay Questions

1. To what extent did New Deal liberalism continue to shape the United Sates domestically in the decades after World War II? In your answer include relevant information from
   Truman's "Fair Deal"
   Johnson's "Great Society"
   Kennedy's "New Frontier"

2. Compare and contrast the conservative ideologies of Presidents Nixon and Reagan with the liberal views of Presidents Truman, Kennedy, and Johnson.

Answers

Content Review Questions

1. **(C)** The three justices reflected Reagan's conservative ideology (*The American Pageant,* 14th ed., pp. 1041–1043/15th ed., pp. 953–954; Learning Objective POL-4).

2. **(A)** Many consumer items were unavailable during the war. As more goods became available and wages rose, consumers happily spent (*The American Pageant,* 14th ed., p. 912/15th ed., pp. 831–832; Learning Objective ID-7).

3. **(B)** The Fair Deal was the name given to Truman's domestic reform program (*The American Pageant,* 14th ed., p. 937/15th ed., p. 854; POL-4).

4. **(C)** The Court prohibited states from interfering with a woman's abortion rights during the first trimester of pregnancy (*The American Pageant,* 14th ed., p. 1044/15th ed., p. 932; Learning Objective POL-5).

5. **(C)** The Court overturned the *Plessy* decision, opening the way for integration in all public facilities and institutions (*The American Pageant,* 14th ed., p. 953/15th ed., pp. 868–869; Learning Objective POL-5).

6. **(B)** One billion dollars was appropriated for improving science, math, and language arts courses in order to keep pace with the Soviet Union's advances (*The American Pageant,* 14th ed., p. 962/15th ed., p. 877; Learning Objective WOR-4).

7. **(D)** The act forbade the closed shop, restricted boycotts and sympathy strikes, and required a sixty-day cooling off period before workers could strike (*The American Pageant,* 14th ed., p. 911/15th ed., p. 830; Learning Objective WXT-8).

8. **(C)** His work on the bus boycott brought King to national attention (*The American Pageant,* 14th ed., p. 953/15th ed., p. 868; Learning Objective ID-8).

9. **(D)** Reagan's pursuit of deregulation freed businesses from costly and restrictive federal requirements but led to mergers, takeovers, and the savings-and-loan fiasco (*The American Pageant,* 14th ed., pp. 1041, 1045–1046/15th ed., p. 951; Learning Objective WXT-8).

10. **(D)** Southern Democratic states' rights Dixiecrats nominated their own candidate, Strom Thurmond, to challenge Truman (*The American Pageant,* 14th ed., pp. 935–936/15th ed., p. 853; Learning Objective POL-7).

11. **(D)** Johnson was inspired by the New Deal and engaged in deficit spending, not supply-side economics, to stimulate the economy. Supply-side economics is associated with Reagan's presidency (*The American Pageant,* 14th ed., pp. 1041–1042/15th ed., pp. 945–946; Learning Objective POL-4).

12. **(C)** *The Feminine Mystique* critiqued the essentially dreary existence of modern housewives, the contemporary variant of the nineteenth-century "cult of domesticity." The book was widely read and proved influential in inspiring women in the 1960s to challenge the status quo (*The American Pageant,* 14th ed., p. 945/15th ed., pp. 861–862; Learning Objective ID-8).

13. **(A)** As Eisenhower's running mate, Nixon nearly saw his career derailed when he was accused of accepting illegal donations (including a dog the Nixons named Checkers). In an attempt to appeal to the American people, he appeared on television to repudiate the claims made against him; the appeal worked, and he was kept on the ticket (*The American Pageant,* 14th ed., p. 948/15th ed., p. 864; Learning Objective POL-6).

14. **(D)** Antiwar protests had been a regular feature of the Johnson presidency. The president came to believe that in order for the nation to reunify, heal, and move forward, he must step aside. His televised speech to the nation in March 1968 greatly surprised even his closest advisers (*The American Pageant,* 14th ed., p. 994/15th ed., p. 908; Learning Objective WOR-4).

15. **(B)** Ninety-seven percent of African Americans who voted cast their ballot for Carter, who also nearly swept the South (*The American Pageant,* 14th ed., p. 1021/15th ed., p. 933; Learning Objective POL-7).

SHORT-ANSWER QUESTIONS

1. Each of the movements borrows from the civil rights movement. You can discuss the tactics each movement used, including civil disobedience and protests as well as demands for workplace equality and equality in the public sphere. You might also want to address the idea that the successes of the civil rights movement convinced other groups that the time was right to fight for their own goals. Each of the movements had varying success. The student movement secured some rights but eventually devolved into radicalism and violence. The anti-war movement ultimately toppled a president and led to the withdrawal of American troops. The women's movement succeeded in gaining greater status for women and entry into professions, but failed to see the ERA ratified which was a major goal.

2. The cartoon is showing that Nixon was ultimately caught red-handed with evidence of his involvement in Watergate. His long nose is reminiscent of Pinocchio, showing him to be a liar, and his clothes look like a 1920s gangster. The Watergate scandal affirmed people's thoughts about government abuses

and corruption that began to come to the fore in a widespread way during Vietnam. The way that we question our leaders today is the result of events like Vietnam and Watergate in the second half of the twentieth century.

Long-Essay Questions

1. You should discuss how the New Deal redefined the role of government by adopting a Keynesian approach to the economy and by budgeting millions of dollars to establish various social programs. Truman, Kennedy, and Johnson all in one way or another expanded on the ideology and policies of Roosevelt liberalism. You should identify those programs, like the War on Poverty, that have a correlation to similar programs of the New Deal. (Historical Thinking Skills: I-2: Patterns of Continuity and Change Over Time, II-4: Comparison, II-5: Contextualization, IV-8: Interpretation, and IV-9: Synthesis)

2. You should discuss how Reagan's election was in part a conservative response to the liberal programs under Roosevelt, Truman, Kennedy, and Johnson. Include a discussion as to why this occurred, such as the view that government bureaucracy and government spending had become too extensive. Point out that while Reagan's budget was enormous, much of his budget was used for military spending, whereas the liberal presidents—Truman, Kennedy, and Johnson—also sought to establish social programs as well as engage in enormous military spending. Another relevant contrast is the relationship Reagan had with labor as opposed to the lack of such relationship for Truman, Kennedy, and Johnson. Finally, a discussion of Reagan's supply-side ("trickle-down") economics versus the demand-side approach of the liberal presidents should be included in your response. (Historical Thinking Skills: II-4: Comparison, II-5: Contextualization, IV-8: Interpretation, and IV-9: Synthesis)

20

U.S. Foreign Affairs from 1945 to the 1980s

When Japan surrendered on September 2, 1945, ebullient Americans spontaneously broke into wild celebrations. Their sense of relief was universal. As people around the world took stock of the war's effects, they were appalled by the devastation in terms of lives, property, and money lost. In the major theaters of the war—Europe, Asia, and the Pacific—survivors had already begun to dig out of the wreckage caused by the war and rebuild their shattered lives; they could only imagine what the future held in store. They had lived through the worst economic disaster the world had ever seen; they had survived the worst military conflict, including attempted genocide, in modern times. They longed for a respite from suffering and despair.

Even before atomic bombs destroyed Hiroshima and Nagasaki, however, new storm clouds had appeared on the horizon in the form of a world divided into two armed camps, each ready to use whatever means were at its disposal to achieve its political objectives. As it turned out, there would be no reprieve from the anxiety and uncertainties millions had experienced since the Great Depression. Almost without pause, the world would shift from total war to what became known as "Cold War."

The two Cold War adversaries, the United States and the Soviet Union, had experienced World War II differently. The United States had suffered 1 million casualties; the Soviets, at least twenty times that number. For the second time in twenty-five years, Germany had invaded the Soviet Union. Millions of Soviet citizens had been killed, and its western agrarian and urban areas had been devastated by the Nazi invasion in 1941. The Soviet government, led by Josef Stalin, would make certain that no European nation ever invaded again. For Americans, the war had been fought from afar, and they were comforted by the protection accorded by the vast Atlantic and Pacific Oceans.

When the war ended, the United States and Soviet Union were the world's two most powerful nations—superpowers—and they were suspicious of each other's political and economic systems, not to mention foreign policy objectives. Despite tensions that had existed between the two nations ever since the communists overthrew Russia's czarist regime in the 1917 Bolshevik Revolution, the two had been wartime allies. One promising indicator that cooperation, rather than conflict, could guide postwar international affairs was the creation of the United Nations in 1945. The most powerful organ of the United Nations, the Security Council, comprised fifteen nations. The major allied powers in the war—the United States, the USSR, Britain, France, and China—each possessed veto power. Nevertheless, the Americans and Soviets remained wary of each other's intentions.

KEY CONCEPTS

- Conflicting U.S. and Soviet postwar objectives played a significant role in creating the tensions between the two superpowers that led to the Cold War.
- The United States sought to contain the spread of communism in Europe, Asia, South America, and Africa.
- The second red scare (McCarthyism) affected the United States domestically as the public was led to believe that there were communists seeking to undermine American institutions.
- The United States succeeded in containing communism in Europe.
- The United States was unable to contain the spread of communism to China but did so in South Korea.
- The Vietnam War seriously divided the American people and showed the limitations of the containment policy.
- The collapse of the Soviet Union transformed international affairs.

U.S. foreign affairs after World War II are discussed in depth in *The American Pageant,* 14th and 15th eds., Chapters 36–40.

SOVIET AND AMERICAN POSTWAR OBJECTIVES AND PRIORITIES

The end of the war found the Soviets in possession of much of Eastern Europe. After the failure of Hitler's Operation Barbarossa—the invasion of the Soviet Union—the Soviets had counterattacked, driving the German invaders west and out of the East European nations that had been under their control. Germany itself was invaded and finally capitulated to the Allies in May 1945. It soon became abundantly clear that there were deep tensions between the wartime allies. The war ravaged the Soviet Union in human, military, and financial terms. The immediate Soviet priorities, then, were economic rehabilitation and military defense:

- **Reconstruction of the economy** The Soviets demanded that Germany pay it $20 billion in war reparations. Initially, the United States promised large loans to the Soviets.
- **Military competition** The Soviets sought to remain on par with the

United States militarily. This resulted in the nuclear arms race.

- **Self-defense** The Soviets wanted to make certain that they no longer would be surrounded by countries hostile to the USSR. They therefore created a buffer zone, referred to as the Soviet-bloc nations, in Eastern Europe, contradicting promises Stalin made to the Allies during World War II.

The United States was deeply concerned that nations devastated by the war might be susceptible to Soviet-backed communism. Furthermore, if the United States itself were to grow its economy, it would need trading partners, which meant helping to rebuild Europe's destroyed infrastructure and manufacturing centers. Essential to the expansion of the U.S. economy was cheap energy sources. To this end the United States in 1953 helped overthrow Iran's government, which had promised to nationalize foreign-controlled oil companies, and replaced it with Shah Reza Pahlavi, who then proceeded to supply the West with inexpensive oil. In the immediate postwar period, the United States sought to achieve the following:

- **Reconstruction of Europe** This became a major goal of the United States. It set out to help rebuild the economies of West European nations such as France, Great Britain, Norway, the Netherlands, Denmark, Greece, and Germany for the following reasons:
  - These nations would be able to repay their war debts.
  - An economically stable Western Europe would eventually benefit the U.S. economy by importing U.S. goods.
  - For the United States to reap the economic benefits of a stable and reconstructed Western Europe, it was imperative that the Europeans eschew policies and political systems antithetical to U.S. postwar economic needs, including, but not limited to, socialist and communist systems. This policy was also applied to Asia, South America, and Africa during the Cold War.
- **Military superiority** This would be achieved through nuclear monopoly, later through nuclear superiority.
- **Containment of Soviet-backed communism** Ultimately containment became the focus of U.S. foreign policy in the decades after the war's end.

THE COLD WAR IN EUROPE

According to one school of thought, the Cold War began even before World War II ended. This view postulates that at the Yalta Conference—the final meeting in February 1945 between the Big Three: Churchill, Roosevelt, and Stalin—the Soviet premier deceived a gravely ill President Roosevelt. Stalin pledged to declare war on Japan in return for its pre-Russo-Japanese War status in the Far East. It was decided that the United States, the USSR, and Britain, with French participation, would divide and administer Germany and its capital, Berlin, following the German surrender. Several important issues dealing with Europe were left unresolved, with the expectation that post-war commissions and agreements would settle them. The most

AP Tip

Who started the Cold War? The responsibility for starting the Cold War has been an enduring topic of discussion among historians for over half a century. Predictably, a simple answer is not the case here. For the most part historians are seriously divided in their analysis of the causes of the Cold War.

- One perspective claims that ideology was at the center of the conflict. That is, there existed an ideological incompatibility between the United States, which stood for freedom and democracy, and the tyrannical, imperialist Soviet Union. Thus the United States adopted a policy that at the very least would contain this "evil" or, possibly, even assist in its demise.
- Another viewpoint is that the Cold War was less an expression of ideology than an objective by which each power could enhance its national interests. As for the Soviet Union, it was behaving as it had always done, whether under the tsars or under the communists—namely, expansion and mistrust of the outside world. For example, the U.S.-sponsored Baruch Plan to regulate nuclear energy and nuclear disarmament was rejected by the Soviets, who may have mistrusted American intentions, believing the plan was an attempt to thwart their goal of nuclear parity with the United States.
- For other historians, the onus for starting the Cold War rests with both the United States and the USSR. The Cold War could have been prevented had it not been for misperceptions, misguided idealism, and unfounded suspicions.
- A fourth view places the responsibility for starting the Cold War with the United States. While not condoning the brutal aspects of the Soviet regime, tension between the two nations had its origins in the early twentieth century when the United States revealed its counterrevolutionary tendencies during the Russian Civil War. The Cold War was simply another expression of that predisposition. What is more, they argue, given the need for capitalism to expand, the United States itself had engaged in imperialism. The Cold War then is viewed as just another example of aggressive and exploitative U.S. foreign policy, which seeks to extend its hegemony worldwide. Whereas some historians view, say, the Soviet refusal to participate in the development of the International Bank for Reconstruction and Development (also known as the World Bank) as symptomatic of Soviet power politics, others acknowledge Soviet suspicions that the World Bank might become a tool of American capitalist hegemony.

troublesome issue involved the establishment of a Polish government, not to mention the other East European nations liberated by the Soviets. Military necessity may have convinced Roosevelt that Soviet support for the war against Japan required granting concessions to the Soviets in the Far East and an acceptance of Stalin's promise to hold elections in Eastern Europe. Nevertheless, the elections promised by Stalin exacerbated relations with the West when Soviet-supported communists took over the governments of what became known as the Soviet bloc: East Germany, Czechoslovakia, Hungary, Bulgaria, Poland, Albania, and Romania. Yugoslavia, a communist nation, remained independent of the USSR because of the efforts of its president, Tito. To the Americans the wartime conference had divided Europe into East European communist and totalitarian governments and Western capitalist democracies. The Soviets, from their perspective, had merely addressed a long-standing military necessity: protection of its vulnerable western border from invasions by creating a buffer zone between it and potentially hostile West European nations.

Later, Soviet refusal to remove its troops from oil-rich northern Iran further convinced Western leaders that the Soviets were bent on being the hegemonic power in more than Eastern Europe. A strident rebuke from Truman convinced Stalin to remove his troops from Iran, but suspicions remained. Former British Prime Minister Winston Churchill echoed the concern about Soviet expansionism when he warned that an "iron curtain" had "descended across the continent" as the Soviets attempted to extend "their power and doctrine." Churchill's recommendation was for the Western democracies to stop this expansion. President Truman concurred. "I'm tired of babying the Soviets," he fumed in response to what he perceived as Soviet intransigence in controlling Eastern Europe. For their part, the Soviets seemed equally resistant to thawing relations with the United States. When George Kennan, an American diplomat and specialist on Russian and Soviet affairs, warned that the Soviets would spread their ideology if given the opportunity but could be stopped if challenged, Truman took to heart his counsel. Just as A. T. Mahan's *The Influence of Sea Power upon History* had profoundly influenced U.S. policymakers at the turn of the twentieth century, Kennan's analysis became the foundation of an American foreign policy. In effect legitimizing the U.S. government's vigorous anti-Soviet position, Kennan's major observations included the following:

- The United States can exploit the frailty of the Soviet economy, the lassitude of its people, and the brutal nature of the Soviet leadership if it adopts policies that would discourage Soviet expansion.
- It is unrealistic to expect a thaw in U.S.-Soviet relations in the near future.
- Soviet mistrust of the outside world borders on paranoia.

Kennan recommended that the United States adopt a policy of containment, although he later opposed the way in which his observations were interpreted and implemented, especially when NATO was created. What follows are important examples of the containment policy as applied by the United States to Europe. Keep in mind that for over forty years this policy was applied to other continents as well.

- **Truman Doctrine (1947)** Just two years after the war's end, Truman came before Congress to request a $400 million aid package to Greece and Turkey in order to prevent communist rebels from overthrowing their governments. Soviet pressure on Turkey to relinquish control over the strategic Dardanelles was another incentive for Truman to act. Neither country became communist.

- **Marshall Plan (1947)** The United States was acutely concerned that Europe's depressed economic condition, common to those nations that had experienced the war firsthand, was susceptible to communist influences. In Italy, for instance, there was considerable popular support for leftist movements. In response, Secretary of State George Marshall recommended a program called the European Recovery Plan to rehabilitate over twenty nations, including the Soviet Union (which rejected the funds). Over $12 billion was distributed in four years, helping to restore the economies of important U.S. trade partners such as Britain, West Germany, and France and preventing the spread of communism to Western Europe.
- **Berlin Blockade and Airlift (1948–1949)** At war's end the former capital of Nazi Germany, Berlin, lay deep inside communist East Germany. As with the rest of Germany, Berlin had been divided into four zones, each administered by the United States, Britain, France, and the USSR. In an attempt to consolidate their control of East Germany, the Soviets ordered the access roads into West Berlin closed. Without needed supplies, the West Berliners would have nowhere to turn and would be absorbed into the rest of communist Berlin—or so the Soviets hoped. What they did not anticipate was a yearlong airlift that numbered one thousand planes per day and successfully provided 2 million West Berliners with basic necessities. Realizing the blockade was fruitless, the Soviets lifted it in May 1949. Although West Berlin did not become communist, tensions mounted between the two superpowers.
- **North Atlantic Treaty Organization (NATO)** Buoyed by the success of the Berlin airlift, but acutely concerned about the Soviet bloc's military power and suspicious of its intentions, the Western allies believed that a coordinated military alliance could thwart a potential communist invasion of Western Europe. In fact, a number of European nations, France and Britain among them, had already organized a mutual defense pact called the Brussels Treaty. The United States had never entered into a peacetime European alliance; however, the mounting friction with the Soviet Union convinced U.S. leaders to do just that. The U.S. rationale for the creation of NATO was deterrence—that is, an attack on one member nation would be considered an attack on all. By 1955 NATO had fifteen members, the largest permanent peacetime military coalition in history. That year the Soviets responded to NATO's expansion with its own military alliance of Soviet-bloc East European nations called the Warsaw Pact. Europe was now divided between two hostile and heavily armed camps, each possessing nuclear weapons—despite the U.S. government's contention that the Soviets were years away from developing and successfully testing an atomic weapon, its monopoly ended in the spring of 1949 when President Truman announced to the nation that the Soviets had in fact successfully tested such a weapon. The Cold War immediately entered into an even more potentially catastrophic phase, the nuclear arms race.

- **The Division of Germany** In 1955 French, American, and British occupation of West Germany ended. Many hoped that this would be a prelude to German reunification. Although discussions with the Soviets about reunification went nowhere, four years later a summit was organized that brought together President Eisenhower and Premier Khrushchev of the Soviet Union. The two agreed to continue their discussion in Paris but the meeting was never held. In 1960 a U.S. spy plane piloted by Francis Gary Powers was shot down over the Soviet Union. The Eisenhower administration acknowledged responsibility for the surveillance mission, and an angry Khrushchev cancelled not only the Paris summit but also a personal invitation for Eisenhower to visit the USSR. In the meantime, Germany remained divided.

ROLLBACK, BRINKMANSHIP, AND RISING TENSIONS

Upon becoming president, Dwight Eisenhower selected John Foster Dulles, a Republican expert on foreign affairs, to be his secretary of state. Dulles saw serious limitations in the containment policy. He believed that communism was a moral evil that should be rolled back if possible, not merely contained. To achieve this aim, he based his diplomatic strategy on "brinkmanship" and "massive retaliation." Dulles maintained that the Soviets could be taken to the brink in disputes, at which point they would inevitably back down. Further, it would be in the best interest of the United States to build such a massive nuclear weapons stockpile that the Soviets would be deterred from ever challenging the United States. Given this approach, and the presence of hard-liners in the Kremlin (the center of Soviet administrative and political affairs), U.S.-Soviet relations continued to be tense.

Despite this mistrust, both nations still seemed determined to reduce the tensions that prevailed between the two nuclear superpowers. A summit meeting in 1956 between Khrushchev and Eisenhower failed to produce an "open skies" policy that would allow each nation to fly over the other's territory, thus preventing a "first strike" attack, but it did indicate that both sides were willing at least to negotiate. When the Soviet premier repudiated the actions and policies of his predecessor, Josef Stalin, a thaw in relations seemed possible. To some in the Soviet-bloc nations of Poland, East Germany, and Hungary, this was taken to mean that reforms could be instituted, giving them greater autonomy and expanded freedoms. In 1956 the Hungarians actually took the momentous step of overthrowing their Soviet-backed government, but the Soviets immediately crushed the rebellion; they would do the same in Czechoslovakia in 1968. The U.S. response, which was to do nothing for fear of sparking a nuclear confrontation, revealed the limitations of Dulles's policies. Essentially, Eastern Europe was in the Soviet sphere of influence, and the United States would not challenge that reality.

The Second Red Scare: McCarthyism

The Cold War was obviously at the center of U.S. foreign policy; however, it also influenced the nation domestically, sometimes in ways not foreseen. In 1947 Republicans pressured President Truman to establish a Loyalty Review Board to investigate current and prospective federal employees for possible affiliations with radical groups. Thousands consequently lost their jobs. Four years later the federal government prosecuted American Communist party leaders under the Smith Act (1940), which made it illegal to promote the overthrow of the U.S. government or belong to an organization that advocated this intention. In 1951 the Supreme Court upheld the constitutionality of the act in *Dennis* v. *United States*. Earlier, in 1938, the House Un-American Activities Committee (HUAC) had been formed to investigate political "subversives." It was resuscitated during the Cold War, in part because of the exposure of Soviet sympathizers such Ethel and Julius Rosenberg. The Rosenbergs were accused of providing atomic bomb information to the Soviets during World War II when the USSR was America's ally, thereby, according to federal prosecutors, accelerating the Soviet A-bomb program. Although it was peacetime, the nation was in the grips of the red scare, and the "loss" of China to Mao Zedong's communists and the Korean War all weighed heavily in the government's decision to electrocute the two convicted spies on June 19, 1953.

The most famous case to come before HUAC involved a former State Department official and adviser to President Roosevelt at the Yalta Conference named Alger Hiss. Hiss's accuser, Whittaker Chambers, claimed that Hiss had not only been a communist sympathizer in the 1930s; he had also transmitted secret information to the Soviets. Hiss was convicted of perjury in 1950, in large measure because of the efforts of a young California congressman named Richard M. Nixon. The case led some to question whether there were other Soviet "sympathizers" in public and private life.

HUAC ultimately became a postwar tool whereby anyone who had been even sympathetic to radical causes (and there were quite a few given the disenchantment with capitalism during the Great Depression) could be called to Washington to recant their suspected political allegiance and inform on neighbors, friends, and colleagues. Some refused and suffered dearly. Numerous politicians took advantage of the anticommunist hysteria that swept the nation after the war, but no one did it as effectively and reprehensibly as Wisconsin's junior Republican senator, Joseph R. McCarthy. Searching for a campaign issue on which to run for reelection, McCarthy found that making unsubstantiated claims and accusations about communist infiltration into every segment of American life generated for him considerable publicity. One week he would claim there were 250 communist sympathizers in the U.S. State Department; the following week the number would arbitrarily change. Before long McCarthy was one of the most powerful and popular political figures in the nation. Few in or out of government would challenge him, for to do so would invariably invite the charge that that person was "soft" on communism. McCarthy even accused George Marshall, the former U.S. Army chief of staff and Truman's secretary of state and defense, of taking part in a communist conspiracy. Not even President Eisenhower, Marshall's former comrade in the war, would defend him. Some Republicans personally rejected McCarthy's tactics, but as his victims tended to be Democrats, they said nothing—with the exception of senators Margaret Chase Smith and Ralph Flanders, both of whom publicly repudiated their colleague.

Over the course of McCarthy's crusade, many lives and careers were ruined, among them entertainers, screenwriters, teachers, and government employees. Not until Senator McCarthy's "witch hunt" was televised (during the Senate's 1954 investigation into possible communist infiltration of the U.S. Army; there was none) did the American people see firsthand the abusive and arbitrary verbal tactics McCarthy used to assault his victims. Many did not like what they saw. The American public, at one time supportive of the showy senator, turned against him. Later that year the Senate censured McCarthy, finally ending the demagogue's crusade. McCarthy died three years later, leaving in his wake thousands of shattered lives and a legacy of unfounded hysteria.

The following year, 1957, the Soviets launched the world's first satellite, *Sputnik*. Similar U.S. efforts continually failed, raising suspicions that U.S. technological superiority may have been exaggerated. Emboldened by the successful orbiting of *Sputnik* and subsequent satellites, Khrushchev employed his own policy of brinkmanship when he demanded that the West vacate West Berlin. Eisenhower of course refused but invited the Soviet leader to a summit in Paris. The meeting was never held because of the downing of the American spy plane over the Soviet Union in 1960. Khrushchev persisted in his demand; the American response was to strengthen NATO. The following year the Soviets walled off East Berlin in an attempt to halt the flow of refugees to West Berlin.

To the West the Berlin Wall became a symbol of Soviet repression. Despite the increased tensions, the United States, Britain, and the Soviet Union (and eventually over one hundred other nations) signed the Limited Test Ban Treaty in 1963, which banned nuclear weapons tests in the oceans, atmosphere, and outer space. Beginning with Richard Nixon and Henry Kissinger's policy of détente, or cooling of tensions, over the years other arms agreements followed:

- **Nuclear Nonproliferation Treaty (1968)** The treaty banned the transfer of nuclear weapons to nonnuclear nations.
- **Strategic Arms Limitation Talks (1969–1972)** Known as SALT I, this aimed to prevent the expansion of U.S. and Soviet nuclear arsenals. SALT II sought further reductions, but when the Soviets invaded Afghanistan, the Senate refused to ratify the treaty.
- **Anti-Ballistic Missile Treaty (1972)** ABM restricted the development of defense systems that could be used against strategic ballistic missiles.
- **Strategic Arms Reduction Talks (initiated in 1982)** START aimed to reduce long-range nuclear missiles. President Reagan's Strategic Defense Initiative (SDI), or "Star Wars," a satellite defensive system that would ostensibly destroy incoming missiles, was an impediment to START.
- **Intermediate-Range Nuclear Forces (INF) Agreement (1987)** The United States and the Soviet Union agreed to eliminate all intermediate-range nuclear weapons from their arsenals.

THE CONTAINMENT POLICY AND LATIN AMERICA: FROM EISENHOWER TO REAGAN

Ever since the early nineteenth century, the United States had warned European nations not to intervene in the internal affairs of nations in the Western Hemisphere. Every U.S. president in the twentieth century had taken steps to prevent this, but after World War II, grassroots movements were often associated with Soviet infiltration into economically and politically vulnerable South American and Caribbean nations. Relations between the United States and South America had generally improved in the decades before World War II, but following the war resentment increased because of U.S. support for dictatorial governments that did little to address the poverty and despair many South Americans were experiencing. Years later the anger had still not subsided. When Vice President Nixon visited South

The Korean War

Korea had been occupied during World War II by the Japanese. At the end of the war, Korea was divided along the 38th parallel, the Soviets occupying the area north of the dividing line, the United States south of it. Both nations left after North Korea and South Korea developed their military strength, though North Korea had a more formidable army. Elections were held; North Koreans voted for a communist government under Kim Il Sung, while South Koreans elected an anticommunist government led by Syngman Rhee. Both leaders were strong nationalists who wanted reunification. The Korean War broke out in June 1950, when North Korea invaded South Korea to unify the nation.

Just two months earlier, a U.S. National Security Council memorandum (NSC-68) had recommended to President Truman that the United States engage in a massive development of its conventional and nuclear capabilities in order to send a clear message to the Kremlin. Consequently the U.S. military budget skyrocketed from $13 to $50 billion. Some of that money would be used to supply U.S. troops in the ensuing Korean conflict. To counter North Korea's invasion, Truman, who mistakenly believed the attack had been planned in Moscow, ordered U.S. troops stationed in occupied Japan to Korea. In the meantime Truman asked the U.N. Security Council to pass a resolution condemning the invasion and to send troops immediately to assist South Korea. The resolution passed only because of the absence of the Soviets—they would have vetoed it, but they had been boycotting the U.N. over the U.S. veto of communist China's admission into the U.N. Troops were rushed to Korea from many nations, though the bulk of the force was American.

They were almost too late. The invasion was so sudden and overpowering that South Korean and U.S. forces had been driven into the southwestern corner of the Korean peninsula around the city of Pusan. General Douglas MacArthur, commander of U.N. troops in Korea, devised an audacious maneuver that outflanked the North Korean army at Inchon and drove it back across the 38th parallel. Not content with that, Truman sought to roll back communism by overthrowing Kim Il Sung; he therefore ordered MacArthur's forces to cross the 38th parallel into North Korea. China threatened to enter the conflict if MacArthur's troops continued their invasion of North Korea. MacArthur, an advocate of rollback as well, believed the Chinese would do no such thing, and he pressed on north to the Chinese-Korean border at the Yalu River. To his surprise, in November 1950 nearly a half million Chinese soldiers, dressed as North Korean soldiers, poured across the border and drove the U.N. forces back across the 38th parallel. MacArthur was insistent that China itself should be attacked, but Truman, now having second thoughts about invading North Korea, favored a political solution. Outraged, MacArthur publicly criticized the commander in chief's handling of the war and disobeyed his orders. Truman fired him. MacArthur returned to the United States a national hero, despite his insubordination.

By the summer of 1951, the war had settled into a stalemate. Negotiations for an armistice began that summer and dragged on for two more years. Finally, in 1953 at Panmunjom, on the 38th parallel, a cease-fire was agreed to. The United States had successfully contained communism in South Korea, but it had been compelled to use its military to do so. To this day, Korea is still divided, and thousands of U.S. troops continue to be stationed there.

THE VIETNAM WAR

The Vietnam War grew out of France's effort to reclaim its colonial possession, Indochina, which had been conquered by the Japanese during the war. Ho Chi Minh, the leader of the Vietnamese independence movement, appealed to the United States and the United Nations for assistance and recognition. Neither was forthcoming. Ho was more warmly received, however, by China and the USSR. When the French tried to crush the insurgents, the United States provided France with economic and military assistance. The French were nevertheless defeated by Ho's nationalist guerrilla force, the Viet Minh. Concern swept Washington that the rest of Southeast Asia would in turn fall like dominoes (the "domino theory").

At the 1954 Geneva conference, Cambodia, Laos, and Vietnam—the three had comprised the French colony of Indochina—received their independence. Vietnam, however, was temporarily divided along the 17th parallel. Ho became the leader of North Vietnam, and the U.S.-backed Ngo Dinh Diem took control in the South, with elections scheduled for 1956. Within South Vietnam, a guerrilla force comprising mostly communists known as the Vietcong were determined to reunite Vietnam under Ho's leadership. Almost immediately, civil war erupted between North Vietnam and South Vietnam. The United States sent more and more military advisers to help the South Vietnamese turn back the Vietcong. For his part Diem refused to participate in the election scheduled for 1956, and his brutal measures lost him whatever support he had from the citizens of South Vietnam. Diem's generals told American officials in Saigon of their plans for a coup and asked for assurances that the United States would not thwart the coup and that U.S. financial assistance would continue after it. The assurances were given. Diem was assassinated in the coup. Three weeks later, Kennedy was assassinated in Dallas, Texas.

In 1962 Soviet Premier Khrushchev prophetically remarked: "In South Vietnam, the United States has stumbled into a bog. It will be mired down there a long time." American presidents Kennedy, Johnson, and Nixon all sought one way or another to either win the war or, at the very least, to extricate the United States from the conflict. Johnson intensified U.S. involvement in 1964 after alleging that the North Vietnamese attacked two of its warships in the Gulf of Tonkin. In a near unanimous vote, Congress gave the president a "blank check" to wage war in Vietnam (Gulf of Tonkin Resolution). By 1965 the United States had nearly 200,000 troops in Vietnam. The war continued to escalate until by 1968 a half million U.S. troops were involved. They were bolstering what seemed to many to be an unpopular government under Nguyen Van Thieu, whose forces, along with American troops, were battling the Army of North Vietnam and the Vietcong. Until this point, most Americans had supported the war, but by 1968, with no end to the conflict in sight and the American people now badly divided over Johnson's foreign policy, the president chose not to run for reelection. Richard Nixon, who claimed to have a secret plan to bring "peace with honor," was elected president. Nixon's plan was known as Vietnamization: the United States would train and equip the South Vietnamese army while American forces were gradually withdrawn.

Throughout the United States demonstrations in favor of and opposed to the war broke out. Some turned deadly—for example, Ohio National Guard troops opened fire on antiwar demonstrators at Kent State University, killing four students, and police used machine guns and armor-piercing bullets to control demonstrators at Jackson State, killing two students. Now Americans were dying in the Vietnam War at home.

Television, which had considerably changed American culture in the postwar years, dramatically brought the Vietnam War into American living rooms. Search and destroy missions, the use of napalm and defoliants such as Agent Orange, and the massive bombing raids on North Vietnam such as Operation Rolling Thunder convinced many Americans that the war had become one of brutal attrition. Antiwar demonstrations increased and, ultimately, over one-half million American men resisted the military draft. Still, the government repeatedly attempted to convince the public that the end of the war was in sight.

However, doubts intensified when the North Vietnamese and Vietcong launched a major offensive on the Vietnamese New Year (Tet) in 1968 against every major city in South Vietnam, even breaching the grounds of the U.S. embassy in Saigon. Although the attackers suffered huge casualties, the Tet offensive was a political defeat for the U.S. government; it convinced even more Americans that the end of the war was not in sight and that it was time to withdraw from Vietnam. This position was given added weight when in 1971 the *New York Times* published the Pentagon Papers, a top-secret study of the war commissioned by the Johnson administration. It revealed that the government had misled the public and Congress about the reasons the United States entered the conflict and had escalated U.S. involvement.

From the end of Johnson's presidency through Nixon's, the United States sought a negotiated settlement to the war in peace talks that were convened in Paris in 1968. When talks broke down at one point, Nixon ordered a massive bombardment of Hanoi, the capital of North Vietnam. Finally, on January 23, 1973, an agreement was announced, followed shortly thereafter by the withdrawal of all U.S. troops. Two years later North Vietnamese troops overran Saigon, the capital of South Vietnam, and unified the nation, but not before an estimated 2 million Vietnamese and 56,000 Americans had been killed.

Foreign Affairs in the Post-Vietnam Era

In the late 1970s President Carter initiated a shift in the U.S. approach to foreign policy. In an attempt to rebuild America's image, especially in the Third World, he infused morality and human rights into his policies. To Carter, U.S. support of anticommunist totalitarian governments had serious limitations. Conservatives were deeply opposed to this approach, as they believed it would ultimately weaken U.S. power and influence worldwide. However, Carter proved to be inconsistent in his application of human rights to foreign policy:

- He negotiated the Panama Canal Treaty, which returned the Canal Zone to the Panamanians in 2000, angering many conservatives.
- In Central America after the Marxist Sandinistas took over Nicaragua, Carter thought it best to provide aid to the government of El Salvador, which itself was engaged in a civil war. Despite the Salvadoran government's tolerance of right-wing death squads, turning a blind eye to those abuses, Carter obviously preferred this regime to another leftist government in the region.
- Carter's greatest success came in the Middle East, when he negotiated a peace treaty between Egypt and Israel. It did not bring peace to the region, however.
- Despite his rhetoric to end the Cold War, and the Strategic Arms Limitation Treaty (SALT) he signed with his Soviet counterpart in 1979, Carter's actions often proved that he was as much a cold warrior as his predecessors. When the Soviets invaded Afghanistan in 1979 to support a faltering Marxist government, Carter refused to send American athletes to participate in the 1980 Moscow Olympics and supplied the Afghan guerrillas with weapons and supplies. Both actions obviously infuriated the Soviets.
- The overthrow of the U.S.-backed shah of Iran in 1979 reverberated through the White House. Angered that the United States had maintained the corrupt and repressive shah's government in power for so long, as well as U.S. support for Israel, Islamic fundamentalists led a successful popular revolution against their leader. They proceeded to take U.S. embassy officials hostage after Carter allowed the shah to seek medical treatment in the United States. Carter's futile attempts at a negotiated settlement, an attempted military solution, and neutral intervention all failed. His contradictory foreign policy, the inability to resolve the Iranian crisis, and the slumping U.S. economy were factors in his failed bid for reelection.

If Carter intended to infuse foreign affairs with morality, President Reagan represented the alternative view. In Reagan's view, the Carter administration had failed to protect the nation's self-interests, its prestige, and the morale of its people. For Reagan the enemy of the United States was still the "evil empire," the Soviet Union. It was the Soviet Union, not political repression and poverty, that was behind the instability in the Third World. With this view in mind, Reagan did not hesitate to intervene in all parts of the world when he believed it was in the best interests of the United States to do so. The 1980s saw the United States involved in one way or another in Central America and the Caribbean, Lebanon, the Persian Gulf, Libya, Angola, Afghanistan, and Cambodia.

The events in Lebanon revealed a weakness in the United States role as the world's policeman. When a civil war ripped that nation apart, the president sent Marines to restore order. In 1983, in a precursor of what would become an increasingly common tactic, a truck packed with explosives blew up the U.S. barracks, killing 241 Marines. The Reagan administration then ordered a "strategic deployment" of its forces out of the area.

The end of the Cold War was a watershed event in the 1980s. When Reagan denounced SALT II and proceeded to take a hard-line approach to the Soviet Union, the Soviets reacted by deploying more nuclear missiles. It seemed as if the Cold War would continue indefinitely. In the meantime a new Soviet government, led by Mikhail Gorbachev, came to power in 1985. Gorbachev took over a country whose economy could not maintain both an arms race and a consumer economy. He was tired of the economic burden of sustaining the Cold War, especially given the expansion of the U.S. arms buildup under Reagan. Moreover, he wanted to introduce greater democratic freedoms into the Soviet system. To achieve this goal he initiated two important reforms:

- ***Perestroika*** This restructured the Soviet economy by introducing features of a free-market system.
- ***Glasnost*** This expanded citizens' democratic and political freedoms.

Then, in an historic decision, Gorbachev redefined his nation's relationship with its East European allies by removing Soviet troops from those countries. Beginning with Poland, one after another Soviet-backed governments fell from power in Eastern Europe. Finally, in 1989, the Berlin Wall was torn down, and the two Germanys were reunited. It was not long before the USSR itself was dismantled, as nine of its republics broke away and formed the Commonwealth of Independent States.

The end of the Cold War did not make the United States and the world as safe as most had hoped. Now the Persian Gulf Wars; the terrorist attacks on the World Trade Center, the Pentagon, and other international targets; and the enduring Middle East crisis have come to define post–Cold War anxieties.

Content Review Questions

1. An objective of the Marshall Plan was to
   (A) provide military assistance to the Chinese Nationalists.
   (B) limit the nuclear stockpiles of the United States and Soviet Union.
   (C) rebuild West European nations that had been devastated during the war.
   (D) roll back communism in Eastern Europe.

2. Joseph McCarthy
   (A) was commander of U.N. forces in Korea.
   (B) was successful in exposing thousands of communist sympathizers in the U.S. government.
   (C) was a congressman who strongly opposed U.S. intervention in Vietnam.
   (D) is associated with the second red scare in the 1940s and 1950s.

3. Which of the following is NOT a permanent member of the U.N. Security Council?
   (A) Germany
   (B) France
   (C) Britain
   (D) China

4. In order to prevent the Soviets from placing nuclear missiles in Cuba, President Kennedy
   (A) threatened to strike Moscow with U.S. intercontinental ballistic missiles.
   (B) imposed a trade embargo on Cuba.
   (C) placed a naval quarantine around Cuba.
   (D) agreed to remove U.S. missiles from Europe.

5. The Korean War
   (A) ended in a stalemate.
   (B) resulted in the first successful attempt by the United States to contain communism in Asia.
   (C) was a direct cause of the Chinese Civil War.
   (D) ended when the U.N. sent peacekeeping forces to the Korean peninsula.

6. Which U.S. president advocated the development of a satellite-based defensive system known as Strategic Defense Initiative?
   (A) Eisenhower
   (B) Kennedy
   (C) Johnson
   (D) Reagan

7. The Tonkin Gulf Resolution
   (A) was passed by the U.N. authorizing the United States to send combat troops to Vietnam.
   (B) was passed by Congress giving President Johnson unlimited powers to wage war in Vietnam.
   (C) ended hostilities in Korea.
   (D) recognized the Viet Minh as the legitimate government in Vietnam.

8. President Nixon authorized a military coup that toppled the popularly elected government of Salvador Allende in
   (A) Guatemala.
   (B) El Salvador.
   (C) Chile.
   (D) Mexico.

9. President Reagan's administration illegally circumvented Congress's Boland Amendment in order to
   (A) secretly fund Nicaragua's Contras.
   (B) increase the U.S. nuclear stockpile.
   (C) undermine Mikhail Gorbachev's reformist government.
   (D) purchase arms for the Chinese Nationalists.

10. In order to prevent communist forces from toppling the governments of Greece and Turkey, the United States
   (A) sent combat troops to both nations at the end of World War II.
   (B) initiated the Truman Doctrine.
   (C) initiated the Marshall Plan.
   (D) established NATO.

11. Jimmy Carter's presidency was tarnished by which of the following events?
    (A) The outbreak of the Iran-Iraq war
    (B) The Soviet invasion of Afghanistan
    (C) The Iranian hostage crisis
    (D) The OPEC oil embargo

12. The limitations of the policy of "massive retaliation" were revealed in which Cold War event?
    (A) The construction of the Berlin Wall
    (B) The Berlin airlift
    (C) The Iranian hostage crisis
    (D) The Hungarian uprising

13. The Camp David Agreement, mediated by President Carter, resulted in
    (A) a peace accord between Israel and Egypt.
    (B) a nuclear arms limitation agreement with the Soviet Union.
    (C) a multinational agreement to reduce global warming.
    (D) U.S. recognition of the Palestine Liberation Organization.

14. The policy whereby the United States would honor its current military agreements but in the future would limit its use of combat troops in its allies' wars is known as
    (A) mutually assured destruction.
    (B) containment.
    (C) Vietnamization.
    (D) the Nixon Doctrine.

15. Relations between the United States and the Soviet Union warmed in 1972 as a result of an agreement by the former to sell the latter
    (A) nonnuclear military supplies.
    (B) much-needed foodstuffs.
    (C) computers.
    (D) oil and other petroleum products.

Short-Answer Questions

1. The United States fought two prolonged "hot wars" during the course of the Cold War in Korea and Vietnam.
   A) Briefly describe the U.S. goals in Korea.
   B) Briefly describe the U.S. goals in Vietnam.
   C) How do both wars reflect the U.S. larger goals during the Cold War?
   D) Describe one way in which the wars differed.

Question 2 is based on the following cartoon.

Granger Collection

2. President Carter differed from some of his predecessors by advocating for morality in foreign policy. Some of his policies were, therefore, criticized by the establishment.
   A. What is the main idea of the cartoon?
   B. How does this cartoon reflect the shift in foreign policy from earlier in the century?
   C. Did Carter's act of good faith regarding the Panama Canal have the intended result for U.S.-Latin America relations? Use historical evidence to support your answer.

Long-Essay Questions

1. Compare and contrast the success of the containment policy during the Cold War. Select TWO of the following case studies:
   a. containment in Europe
   b. containment in Asia
   c. containment in South America
2. It is reasonable to assume that the actions, behavior, and policies of the Soviet Union following World War II caused and prolonged the Cold War.

   To what extent is the above statement true?

Answers

Content Review Questions

1. **(C)** The Marshall Plan provided billions in aid to rebuild Europe's war-torn economies (*The American Pageant,* 14th ed., p. 929/15th ed., pp. 847–848; Learning Objective WOR-8).

2. **(D)** McCarthy was at the center of the red scare that profoundly affected American life in the 1940s and 1950s (*The American Pageant,* 14th ed., pp. 950–951/15th ed., pp. 866–867; Learning Objective POL-7).

3. **(A)** Germany is not a permanent member of the U.N. Security Council (*The American Pageant,* 14th ed., p. 923/15th ed., p. 844; Learning Objective WOR-8).

4. **(C)** In an act of brinkmanship, Kennedy blockaded Cuba (*The American Pageant,* 14th ed., p. 979/15th ed., p. 895; Learning Objective WOR-7).

5. **(A)** After three years of fighting, the war essentially ended where it began, with the two Koreas divided along the 38th parallel (*The American Pageant,* 14th ed., pp. 948–949/15th ed., p. 865; Learning Objective WOR-8).

6. **(D)** It was popularly referred to as Star Wars (*The American Pageant,* 14th ed., p. 1036/15th ed., pp. 946–947; Learning Objective WOR-8).

7. **(B)** Congress gave Johnson a blank check to wage war in Vietnam (*The American Pageant,* 14th ed., p. 986/15th ed., p. 901; Learning Objective WOR-7).

8. **(C)** Allende was a democratically elected leader (this material does not appear in the text; Learning Objective WOR-8).

9. **(A)** Reagan claimed he was not aware of the actions of his subordinates whose support for the Contras was designed to topple Nicaragua's Sandinista government, despite the Boland Amendment's prohibition of such activities (*The American Pageant,* 14th ed., pp. 1040–1041/15th ed., pp. 950–951; Learning Objective WOR-8).

10. **(B)** The Truman administration sent millions in economic and military aid to Greece and Turkey to assist them in their fight against communist rebels (*The American Pageant,* 14th ed., pp. 928–929/15th ed., pp. 846–847; Learning Objective WOR-8).

11. **(C)** When an Islamic fundamentalist government took power in Iran in 1979, the U.S. embassy came under attack, and members of the staff were held hostage for 444 days. The Carter administration initiated what turned out to be a disastrous rescue mission that severely hurt his public image (*The American Pageant,* 14th ed., p. 1028/15th ed., p. 939; Learning Objective WOR-4).

12. **(D)** In 1956 Hungarians rose up in open revolt against Soviet domination. The revolutionaries appealed for U.S. assistance, but there was little the United States could do short of confronting the Soviets militarily. The use of nuclear weapons was never considered suitable for such a relatively minor crisis, thus exposing the limitations of nuclear power (*The American Pageant,* 14th ed., p. 959/15th ed., p. 875; Learning Objective WOR-7).

13. **(A)** The historic agreement was reached by Prime Minister Menachem Begin of Israel and President Anwar Sadat of Egypt. Sadat was later assassinated because of his participation in the Camp David Agreement (*The American Pageant,* 14th ed., p. 1024/15th ed., pp. 933–934; Learning Objective WOR-8).

14. **(D)** With the U.S. military bogged down in the quagmire of Vietnam, Nixon adopted a policy of limiting the number of combat troops in future wars involving allies (*The American Pageant,* 14th ed., p. 1004/15th ed., p. 917; Learning Objective WOR-8).

15. **(B)** The Soviet Union was suffering from a succession of poor harvests and President Nixon worked out an arrangement with the Soviets to sell $750 million in much-needed grains and cereal products (*The American Pageant,* 14th ed., p. 1007/15th ed., p. 920; Learning Objective ENV-5).

SHORT-ANSWER QUESTIONS

1. Although the Vietnam and Korean Wars are extremely different they are often confused. Korea was meant to be a limited war in which democracy was preserved in South Korea and the communist forces were repelled. The Vietnam War was also meant to keep northern forces out of the South, although the fighting escalated beyond that. Both wars reflect a military application of the containment policy. The wars differ in several ways, including the role of television, the length and effects of the war on the public, and the eventual outcomes, among other disparities.

2. The cartoon expresses some of the outrage among critics of Carter's deal to return the Panama Canal to Panama in 2000. Theodore Roosevelt, whose tactics secured the canal zone in 1902, believed in taking the land that he wanted for the country while Carter voluntarily gave it back. In some ways, this represents a reversal of U.S. policy for years prior, which was

much more assertive than defensive. Carter's show of good faith failed to temper later hostilities between the United States and Latin American nations, especially considering his successor's policies regarding Latin America.

LONG-ESSAY QUESTIONS

1. When asked to *compare*, you should identify commonalities; when asked to *contrast*, identify differences. In discussing containment in Europe, you may wish to first describe the containment policy and then incorporate economic and military programs such as the Truman Doctrine, the Marshall Plan, and the creation of NATO that sought to achieve this objective. In discussing containment in Asia, you should address the three major case studies of U.S. containment on that continent: Chinese Civil War, Korean War, and the Vietnam War. For South America discuss U.S. interventions, the reasons for these interventions, and their outcomes. Three case studies should suffice. (Historical Thinking Skills: II-4: Comparison, III-6: Historical Argumentation, III-7: Appropriate Use of Relevant Historical Evidence, IV-8: Interpretation)

2. In your essay, you can identify major actions taken by the Soviets in the Cold War and evaluate whether they were reasonable reactions on their part. For example, the development by the Soviets of nuclear weapons, the creation of the Warsaw Pact, the decision to place nuclear missiles in Cuba, and Soviet interventions in Hungary and Czechoslovakia are some of the events that can be used to support or refute the statement, given your interpretation of the Cold War. Keep in mind that there are three basic interpretations around which a thesis can be constructed: the Soviets caused and prolonged the Cold War, the United States caused and prolonged the Cold War, or both are responsible. (Historical Thinking Skills: I-1: Causation, III-6: Historical Argumentation, IV-8: Interpretation, and IV-9: Synthesis)

Period 9: 1980–Present

The United States in the Global Community

As the twenty-first century approached change was afoot in the United States. The conservative tide that swept in with the "Reagan revolution" changed both the power structure and social mores of the nation in the 1980s in enduring ways. New groups emerged to advocate for equality and, in 2008, the United States elected its first African American president. New, ever-changing technology made former innovations obsolete. The twenty-first-century world is interconnected in ways no one could have dreamed as little as fifty years prior, changing the United States position in the world as well as the way decisions are made and issues arise within the country.

Key Concepts from the College Board

9.1 A new conservatism grew to prominence in U.S. culture and politics, defending traditional social values and rejecting liberal views about the role of government.

9.2 The end of the Cold War and new challenges to U.S. leadership in the world forced the nation to redefine its foreign policy and global role.

9.3 Moving into the twentyfirst century, the nation continued to experience challenges stemming from social, economic, and demographic changes.

21

THE POST–COLD WAR ERA: 1980–2013

The collapse of the Soviet Union put a sudden end to the Cold War, which had cost billions of dollars and millions of lives and had created insecurity and anxiety for more than fifty years. Yet the decades following the dissolution of the Soviet empire did not bring peace to the United States and the world. In fact, every American president since Ronald Reagan has used the military and economic resources of the United States to resolve foreign-affairs problems. Around the world, from Nicaragua to Lebanon, Afghanistan, Iraq, and elsewhere, the United States has engaged new adversaries. The United States has itself been attacked. Even now, years after 9/11, the extent of the devastation is hard to comprehend.

Domestically, the past twenty-five years have been tumultuous as well, including an attempted assassination of one president and the impeachment of another; one popular war in the Mideast and an increasingly unpopular one in the same region a decade later. At home, many Americans have embraced evangelical religious fundamentalism as the essence of their personal and political lives, and they played an important role in the rise to the presidency of a born-again Christian. The cultural and political influence of Christian fundamentalism went hand in hand with the reemergence of conservatism as a political force. With the nation divided into so-called red and blue states, these forces are at the foundation of contemporary American social, political, economic, and cultural life for now and the foreseeable future.

KEY CONCEPTS

- With the election of Ronald Reagan, conservatism reemerged as a rejection of the liberal social and economic policies of previous administrations. Under Reagan, military spending ballooned, while spending for domestic programs was significantly slashed.

- The Cold War ended during the administration of George H. W. Bush. In the post–Cold War era, the United States often intervened militarily in the affairs of foreign nations.
- The United States experienced a period of sustained economic growth under President Clinton. During his term in office, the federal budget was balanced for the first time since the 1960s, but the Republicans gained control of Congress for the first time in forty years.
- China and Russia began to play an increasingly important economic and political role in world affairs.
- The post–Cold War era was fraught with domestic and international terrorism. Less than a year after the inauguration of President George W. Bush, the United States experienced the worst domestic attack in the nation's history.
- George W. Bush led the United States into the Iraq War to search for weapons of mass destruction and, with the hope of changing the dynamic in the Middle East, to liberate and democratize Iraq.
- President Bush's domestic and foreign policies polarized the nation, allowing the Democratic Party to recapture both houses of Congress in 2006 and, with the election of Barack Obama, the White House in 2008.
- In late 2008, the United States and the world faced a dire financial crisis as the U.S. housing market and key banking and lending firms collapsed.

The United States since 1980 is discussed in depth in *The American Pageant,* 14th and 15th eds., Chapters 40–42.

THE PRESIDENCY OF RONALD REAGAN

When he entered the White House as the nation's fortieth president, Ronald Reagan was already a household name. A famous movie actor in the 1940s and 1950s, Reagan entered politics in the early 1960s and won the California governorship as a conservative Republican in 1966. Less than two decades later, he routed the Democratic incumbent, Jimmy Carter, in the 1980 presidential election. As president, Reagan would steer the nation through the final stages of the Cold War and redefine the federal government's role in the economy. Ultimately he would become the inspiration and guiding light for political conservatives and the nemesis of liberals, who viewed his domestic policies as a threat to hard-won reforms dating back to the New Deal. Not surprisingly, foreign affairs and domestic policies under Reagan had both ardent supporters and vehement detractors, but most would agree that his two terms as president had amounted to a political revolution.

For his supporters, Reagan's conservatism fortuitously came just when many citizens—in both major political parties—were beginning to question the cultural, economic, and political transformations that had occurred in the post–World War II years. Two streams fed into the rise of conservatism:

- The religious right was made up of evangelical Christians disenchanted with what they considered damaging social and cultural trends, such as feminism, gay rights, affirmative action, and abortion rights, and they were deeply concerned about what they considered a too-powerful federal government.
- The New Right had coalesced in the 1964 presidential campaign as a challenge to the more liberal wing of the Republican Party and began to play an increasing role in the intellectual debate on the nation's direction. Some who joined the New Right were former liberals alarmed by the growing power and authority of the federal government; they are now called neoconservatives.

Conservative religious groups such as the Moral Majority, organized by the charismatic and combative Reverend Jerry Falwell, became politically active. In establishing grassroots political movements, they helped enlarge the nation's political arena and bring new topics to political debate. The New Right got support from corporate America, which embraced the New Right as allies in the struggle to develop a more pro-business environment in Washington. Claiming to represent traditional values and family relationships, conservatives swept into the White House, Ronald Reagan in the vanguard. Soon the religious right's priorities, peripheral to previous administrations, became cultural and political focal points. A central priority was abortion. In 1973, the Supreme Court had ruled in *Roe* v. *Wade* that abortion is legal, a decision that outraged many Americans, including Ronald Reagan. Anti-abortion rights activists saw a true ally in President Reagan, and over time, the federal government and individual states enacted policies and prohibitions that modified *Roe*—for example, by limiting Medicaid funding for abortions. Abortion today continues to be a fiercely controversial topic.

Reaganomics

Using economic policy to shrink the federal government, President Reagan persuaded Congress to pass smaller federal budgets, with cuts mostly in social programs. Tax reform bills passed in 1981 and 1986 reduced government regulation, long an aspiration of conservatives. And Reagan cut taxes. At the heart of his domestic economic agenda was supply-side economics (so-called Reaganomics), which the president hoped would stimulate the moribund U.S. economy. Theoretically, a supply-side approach provides wealthy individuals and corporations even more money, through tax cuts, which then goes back into the economy in the form of new investments and new businesses. That results in greater consumerism and lower unemployment. Critics contended that the tax cuts reduced government revenues, which financed domestic programs such as welfare, federal aid to the arts, urban renewal and development, and education. Furthermore, there was no guarantee that the wealthy would in fact stimulate the economy; rather, they might keep the money and just become wealthier.

At the same time, Reagan pushed for the development of an enormously expensive missile defense system: the Strategic Defense Initiative (SDI), nicknamed Star Wars. Advocates claimed that SDI was essential for the future defense of the nation. Most scientists doubted that the system would work, and other critics claimed the expense was prohibitive given the economic needs of millions of Americans.

Also at the heart of Reagan's domestic agenda was the desire to increase the power and influence of the states at the expense of the federal government. This approach, referred to as New Federalism, would mean that the budgets of certain federal programs would be slashed and the money turned over to the individual states, to be used at their discretion. While New Federalism resonated with those Americans who considered the federal budget to be bloated, critics held that a steep price would be paid as the government deregulated businesses and cut funding for programs that, for example, protected the environment. The administration's response was that deregulation would lower prices, which would stimulate consumerism and expand employment opportunities. In this corporate-friendly environment, labor unions were marginalized.

Always comfortable in front of a camera, President Reagan's charisma and straightforward dialogue convinced many Americans that his hard-line views on the Cold War were correct, and he was able to splinter even diehard Democrats from their party. These "Reagan Democrats" helped him win handily in the 1984 presidential race—a campaign noteworthy, in part, because of the Democratic candidate Walter Mondale's running mate, Geraldine Ferraro, the first female in the nation's history to run for such a high office.

In his first campaign for the presidency, Reagan had promised to reduce the federal deficit, but as president he actually enlarged it. The huge federal budget included significant military spending, but the substantial tax cuts initiated by his administration meant reduced federal revenues and caused the federal debt to soar. However, the president was more successful in tackling other economic maladies, such as unemployment and inflation. Critics acknowledged that unemployment did indeed decrease, but they pointed out that more and more Americans were relegated to low-paying jobs in the service sector. Nevertheless, the economy of the nation was healthy enough to contribute to Reagan's bid for reelection.

REAGAN'S FOREIGN POLICY

When it came to the Soviet Union (and communism in general), President Reagan had nothing but contempt for what he referred to as the "evil empire." To end the Cold War on his terms, Reagan decided to negotiate with the Soviets from a position of military strength. He launched a massive military arms buildup, thereby challenging the Soviet leadership to keep pace while somehow simultaneously satisfying the consumer sector of their economy. The Strategic Defense Initiative was one facet of this strategy; economic sanctions, another. When the Soviets or their proxy governments in Eastern Europe acted in an antagonistic or undemocratic way—for example, when Poland was placed under martial law after Polish workers organized a labor movement known as Solidarity—Reagan imposed sanctions. By the mid-1980s, U.S.-Soviet relations had hit rock bottom.

It was not long, however, before events in the Soviet Union took a dramatic turn. In 1985, a reform-minded and engaging leader, Mikhail Gorbachev, took over as chairman of the Soviet Communist party. Just as Reagan was determined to transform the U.S. government and economy, Gorbachev was resolved to move the Soviet Union away from what he viewed as the economic waste of the Cold War and to end his nation's long history of domestic repression. Gorbachev set out two new policies:

- *Perestroika,* or restructuring, was the incorporation of capitalist features into the Soviet economy.
- *Glasnost,* or openness, referred to the introduction of democracy into Soviet life and politics.

These policies endeared many Americans to the new Soviet leader. If Reagan was hesitant to trust the new Soviet leader, Gorbachev reassured him by reducing the Soviet nuclear presence in Europe. In a series of summits, the two political leaders warmed to each other and reached an accord that went a long way to ending the Cold War.

AP Tip

Note some of the comparisons that can be drawn between different periods in U.S. history. For example, historians have drawn some parallels between the 1920s and the 1980s. Both decades were dominated by conservatives: in the 1920s, three Republican conservatives occupied the White House (Harding, Coolidge, and Hoover), and in the 1980s, two Republican conservatives (Reagan and Bush) served as president. The economic approach taken in the two decades is also similar: the Mellon tax plan (a series of tax reductions on the wealthy and corporations) in the 1920s and the Reagan administration's supply-side approach in the 1980s. Be careful not to overanalyze these comparisons; despite the parallels, each period is unique.

As a diehard anticommunist, Reagan based his foreign policy on the containment policy, the approach taken by U.S. presidents toward communism since the end of World War II. (Some contend that given his record of interventions in various parts of the world, Reagan identified more with a policy of rolling back, rather than containing, communism.) Accordingly, Reagan applied economic and military pressure on leftist nations and leaders worldwide, but most especially in the Western Hemisphere. Intent on supporting governments that were anticommunist, even if they were authoritarian and repressive (such as those in the Philippines, El Salvador, and Mozambique), Reagan had no qualms about destabilizing or overthrowing leftist governments. In 1983, the president sent U.S. troops to the tiny Caribbean island nation of Grenada when a Cuban-backed coup toppled the government and installed a communist as president. The invasion was a successful display of U.S. authority in the Western Hemisphere. Less successful was Reagan's foray into the turmoil of the Middle East. U.S. Marines were dispatched to Lebanon as part of an international peacekeeping force, an exercise that ended abruptly when a suicide bomber killed hundreds of U.S. servicemen, which precipitated a U.S. withdrawal from Lebanon.

The Reagan administration also made every effort to subvert the newly ensconced (1979) Marxist Sandinista government in Nicaragua by supporting an anti-Sandinista guerrilla force known as the Contras. To provide weapons to the Contras—expressly forbidden by Congress because of atrocities committed by the guerrillas—the administration attempted to address two concerns simultaneously: to win the release of American hostages in Lebanon with the help of Iran and to provide military aid to the Contras. Despite strong American public and official outrage against the new government of Iran, especially given its refusal to immediately release U.S. embassy workers taken hostage after that nation's 1979 revolution, the Reagan administration secretly sold weapons to Iran; the proceeds of the sale were then sent to the Contras. In what became known as the Iran-Contra affair, Congress launched a televised investigation into the administration's activities, and several White House officials were convicted on criminal charges.

Despite uncertainties about his involvement in the scandal, President Reagan's popularity with the American people remained high, in large measure because of his role in thawing U.S.-Soviet relations. His vice president, George H. W. Bush, would benefit from his association with the Reagan administration when he ran for the presidency in 1988.

THE PRESIDENCY OF GEORGE H. W. BUSH

President Bush defeated the Democratic candidate, Massachusetts governor Michael Dukakis, in a campaign noted for its intense and sometimes objectionable negative ads, such as the infamous Willie Horton television commercial. Bush had considerable foreign-affairs experience, which he put to good use in confronting a threat to the world's oil supplies when Iraqi dictator Saddam Hussein invaded neighboring oil-rich Kuwait. Skillfully organizing a United Nations military coalition, Bush ordered an invasion of Kuwait. Operation Desert Storm successfully drove the Iraqis out of Kuwait in what is referred to as the Persian Gulf War. Questions remained, however, about the limitations of the U.N. mandate and U.S. hegemony in the region, for it left Saddam in power—a condition that would be resolved by the president's son, George W. Bush, the forty-third president.

As president, Bush witnessed the final collapse of the Soviet empire and an end to the enormously costly Cold War. A friendly relationship soon developed between Bush and the new Russian president, Boris Yeltsin. Unfortunately, the hard-line government in China had not warmed to the democratic ideas that had helped transform the Soviet Union and its Eastern European allies; when a peaceful prodemocracy demonstration took place in China's Tiananmen Square in 1989, it was mercilessly crushed. Like Reagan, Bush did not hesitate to influence affairs in the Western Hemisphere. For instance, he ordered an invasion of Panama to topple Panamanian strongman Manuel Noriega, whom the U.S. government claimed was involved in the international drug trade.

Domestically, Bush was less successful. Campaigning for the presidency, he had promised not to raise taxes: "Read my lips—no new taxes," he had said. It was a promise he would regret making. A skyrocketing deficit and a weak economy compelled him to increase taxes, a reversal the Democrats would not let the voting public forget when Bush ran for reelection in 1992. Unlike Ronald Reagan, Bush was not the "Great Communicator." He had difficulty articulating his conservative domestic agenda, such as school prayer. The problems of his presidency were further aggravated by the collapse of the savings-and-loan industry. In part a result of the Reagan administration's deregulation of savings-and-loan associations, bailing them out would cost American taxpayers $250–$350 billion. Then, as the president began his bid for reelection, the United States experienced a recession, which did not bode well for Bush.

The Presidency of Bill Clinton

When Bill Clinton, governor of Arkansas, ran for the presidency on the Democratic ticket in 1992, his party had controlled the White House for only four of the past twenty-four years. Fortunately for Clinton, many voters had become disenchanted with President Bush's inability to resolve key national problems, especially the faltering economy. Further, at a time when conservatism was gaining popularity—a boost to the Republicans because it was an ideological perspective associated with their party—Clinton offered a new outlook on what it meant to be a Democrat. That outlook was in some ways consistent with the Republicans'. Clinton believed that Democrats could no longer hope to attract voters unless the party supported policies that addressed crime, a strong national defense, and the establishment of a friendlier relationship with the business sector.

In the 1992 presidential campaign, Clinton's appeal was not limited to traditional Democratic bastions such as the Northeast and the Far West. In fact, he performed well in nearly every region, including a number of southern states, defeating not only the incumbent, George H. W. Bush, but also a third-party candidate, Texas billionaire H. Ross Perot (who ultimately captured nearly 20 percent of the popular vote). Clinton was the first person born after World War II to become chief executive.

Clinton initiated his presidency with an effort to address a controversial issue: gays in the military. However, his goal of eliminating a ban on gays serving in the military was met with a firestorm of indignation, and he had to settle for a considerably modified approach, a "don't ask, don't tell" policy. The president then tackled a long-standing social problem, the nation's inadequate health-care system. He appointed his wife, Hillary Rodham Clinton, director of a task force charged with designing a comprehensive health-care reform. The plan was offered to Congress, but it fared no better than the attempt to lift the ban on gays in the military. Clinton had apparently mistaken his presidential campaign victory as a mandate from the American people. He did, however, sign into law the Family and Medical Leave Act (1993), which requires employers to grant unpaid medical leaves in cases of family emergency.

Clinton's Economic Policies

Clinton had greater leverage in tackling other national problems, especially the massive federal deficit. His administration worked hard at reducing the deficit. That effort and a booming economy produced a significant surplus in 1998, an impressive achievement. Clinton, with the help of a Republican-controlled Congress, balanced the federal budget for the first time in nearly thirty years.

Another major accomplishment was the passage of the North American Free Trade Agreement (NAFTA). The president strongly supported NAFTA, insisting that it would improve the economies of the United States, Mexico, and Canada. Supporters of NAFTA point out that increasing imports has stimulated employment. Critics claim that U.S. businesses have relocated plants to Mexico, where labor is considerably cheaper. Another free-trade proposal supported by Clinton, creation of the World Trade Organization (WTO), provoked large-scale demonstrations at a WTO meeting held in Seattle in 1999. Although globalization was long an objective of free-trade advocates, opponents raised serious questions about its negative impact: environmental degradation and poverty wages. The issue of trade with China, a nation Clinton had excoriated before he became president, was addressed near the end of his second term with passage of a trade bill that made China a vital trade partner.

OTHER DOMESTIC ISSUES

Gun control was another concern of the president. Gun control had powerful opponents, especially the National Rifle Association. But gun control made sense to many Americans who remembered the assassinations of President Kennedy, Martin Luther King, Jr., and Robert Kennedy in the 1960s and, more recently, the attempted assassination of President Reagan in 1981. Further, a nationwide rise in gun violence seemed nothing less than a pandemic. In 1994, Congress signed into law the Brady Bill (named for one of the victims in the assassination attempt on Reagan), which banned certain assault weapons.

Still, violence shook the nation, often in ways that Americans had never experienced. A 1993 standoff between federal agents and a religious sect known as the Branch Davidians in Waco, Texas, ended in the fiery destruction of the sect's compound and the death of many of its members, including children. In 1995, American-born terrorists destroyed a federal building in Oklahoma City, killing 168 people—again, including children. And in 1999, a murderous attack carried out by two heavily armed students killed twelve other students and a teacher at Columbine High School in Colorado. Demand for stricter gun-control legislation crescendoed. Opponents argue that instead of enacting more gun-control laws, the government should enforce those laws already on the books, while protecting the Second Amendment rights of law-abiding citizens. So far, the opponents have carried the day.

A long-festering cynicism about the federal government dating back to the 1960s had convinced many Americans that the conservatives' message of limited federal government made sense. Led by the confrontational House minority whip, Newt Gingrich, the Republicans overwhelmed the Democrats in the 1994 midterm elections and took control of Congress. Under pressure from this new potent political force (whose agenda was encapsulated in the Contract with America), Clinton was compelled to sign into law a decidedly conservative Welfare Reform Bill, which critics claimed would eviscerate federal aid to those in need. Believing that they now had a mandate to eliminate long-standing federally funded social programs, the Republicans alienated some Americans by failing to compromise with the president over the federal budget, a standoff that shut down the federal government for a short time. Although politically wounded by his political foes in both parties—some Democrats believed he had neutralized the Republicans only by moving to the right—Clinton recovered from these political battles in time to win reelection against the Republican candidate, Bob Dole, the Senate majority leader, in 1996.

For liberals who had welcomed a Clinton presidency, Clinton's political rhetoric seemed just that and nothing more. But his generally middle-of-the-road approach and the buoyant economy resonated with the American people and provided him some political clout. He did little to stem the Republican tide against affirmative-action programs, however, much to the dismay of liberals.

Clinton's Foreign Policy

President Clinton's initial forays into foreign affairs often reflected his inexperience. At times it seemed that his administration went from one crisis to another without any real focus. Unlike his post–World War II predecessors, Clinton could not build on Cold War thinking and policies, for the Cold War was over.

Upon his inauguration, Clinton inherited a problem that seemed to have been resolved by the previous Bush administration—namely, a humanitarian mission in Somalia. A devastating civil war between rival warlords had devastated that African nation, and the people of Somalia faced dire conditions, most ominously starvation. Although many U.S. troops were removed from Somalia after aid had been given, Clinton unilaterally decided to keep thousands of troops there to engage the warlords. When a detachment of U.S. Army Rangers was killed in October 1993, pressure mounted to remove the troops, which Clinton did. In Haiti, after international economic pressure failed, the president again used combat troops to restore the elected Haitian president, Jean-Bertrand Aristide, who had been deposed by a military coup. In the Balkans, Clinton deployed U.S. troops as part of a combined NATO military force. The Serbian-controlled Yugoslavian government had begun ethnic cleansing in Bosnia-Herzegovina, Slovenia, and Croatia shortly after the fragmenting of Yugoslavia in 1991—some estimated that as many as 175,000 Croats and Muslims had been killed by 1992. Three years later, after intensive NATO bombing of Serb positions, the belligerents met at the negotiating table and ultimately ended hostilities, though U.S. troops remain as part of the NATO peacekeeping force.

Like his predecessor, President Bush, President Clinton paid attention to the intrigues of Iraqi dictator Saddam Hussein. Under Clinton, U.S. forces mobilized periodically—for instance, in response to Saddam's threatening remarks regarding Kuwait or to neutralize Iraqi troop movements in northern Iraq. But when Saddam refused to cooperate with U.N. weapons inspectors searching for suspected Iraqi weapons of mass destruction, the United States, along with Great Britain, launched a massive air attack on Iraq. It did significant damage; still, the dictator remained firmly in power.

IMPEACHMENT

Clinton's hold on power was tenuous at best in 1999 when the U.S. House of Representatives impeached him. A lengthy investigation by Kenneth Starr, a special prosecutor, revealed that the president had perjured himself while testifying about an affair with a young White House intern, Monica Lewinsky. The president's defenders were quick to point out that the investigation by a partisan special prosecutor and impeachment by a Republican-controlled House was tantamount to a kangaroo court. But the president survived the impeachment trial in the Senate. Although Clinton's reputation was tarnished, his popularity with the American people remained high. Ironically, the Republicans experienced fallout from the investigation and trial; many Americans viewed the impeachment proceedings as nothing more than partisan politics, especially when it was revealed that several Republican leaders had themselves committed acts of marital indiscretion.

As President Clinton's term in office expired, foreign-affairs problems lingered. Tension between the Israelis and the Palestinians was high, despite Clinton's best efforts to broker a settlement to end their long-standing dispute. The unpredictable actions and rhetoric of North Korea's regime were also worrisome. In the end, assessment of Clinton's presidency is caught between charges that he despoiled the office of president and conducted an amateurish foreign policy and credit for his New Democrat policies that invigorated the economy and balanced the federal budget.

THE PRESIDENCY OF GEORGE W. BUSH

Texas's governor, George W. Bush, claimed to represent a new approach to right-wing ideology. He called himself a compassionate conservative, by which he meant that he would, for example, transform welfare programs so that recipients would have opportunities to work for the government assistance they received; in the process, they would gain both new skills and a new outlook on the value of hard work, thrift, and self-sacrifice. Liberals saw compassionate conservatism as a contradiction in terms. But Bush believed that when it was applied to the formulation of both domestic and foreign policy, compassionate conservatism offered Americans and people in nations around the world a materially and spiritually richer life.

THE CONTESTED ELECTION

In 2000 President Bush came to the White House after one of the most controversial elections in U.S. history. Bush received fewer popular votes than his opponent, Al Gore, and Florida's contested election would determine who received enough electoral votes. The design of the Florida ballot confused many voters, and voting machines did not work well. Eventually, after political wrangling at the state level, the Bush campaign took its case to the U.S. Supreme Court. In a highly partisan decision, the five conservative justices ruled for the Republican candidate, despite harsh criticisms by the other justices that the Court's decision would damage the judicial branch's reputation as a neutral political arbiter.

While in his forties, Bush had become a born-again Christian, and as president, he relied on his religious faith to guide his conservative agenda. Having pledged to work with the political opposition and to represent all Americans, the president was soon seen as a divisive force whose Christian fundamentalism and so-called compassionate conservatism alienated many. He took strong stands on moral and ethical issues such as stem-cell research, federal funding for faith-based charitable organizations, and abortion rights. His support of big business, critics claimed, often hurt workers, and it came at the expense of the environment and concerns about global warming. The intellectual inspiration behind many of Bush's domestic and foreign policies was Karl Rove. Noted for his political acumen and hardnosed approach to politics, Rove was not beyond using Machiavellian methods to achieve his conservative objectives.

Yet the president's popularity rating was high during his first term, especially in the so-called red states—those that tend to vote Republican. A massive tax cut had been enacted in 2001 to stimulate consumerism, investments, and economic expansion—whether it did so remains in doubt—and even though deficits reappeared and the economy was weak, Americans felt optimistic.

Bush and Terrorism

The defining event of Bush's first term was the September 11, 2001, attack on the United States by members of Al Qaeda, a Muslim terrorist group headed by Osama bin Laden. Hijacking four passenger planes and using them as guided missiles, the attackers destroyed the two World Trade Center towers in New York City and significantly damaged the Pentagon in Washington. The fourth plane crashed in Pennsylvania, brought down by passengers who overwhelmed the terrorists. Nearly three thousand people died in the attacks, and both the nation and the world were stunned by the magnitude of the destruction.

Later Bush would be criticized for having ignored warnings that the nation's enemies were planning an attack on American soil, but at the time his popularity ratings soared as Americans rallied to the side of their government and president. Not long after, President Bush ordered an attack on Afghanistan. Controlled by the Taliban, reactionary Islamic fundamentalists, Afghanistan had provided bin Laden and Al Qaeda refuge before and after the attacks. Making no distinction between terrorists and those who harbored them, Bush authorized Operation Enduring Freedom; U.S. forces, along with Afghans opposed to the Taliban, defeated the Taliban in short order and rolled back the policies of its oppressive regime. Although Osama bin Laden's influence and that of Al Qaeda were significantly neutralized, he and his key aides managed to escape into the mountainous border between Afghanistan and Pakistan.

Iraq

Seeing the war on terrorism as a global concern, in 2002 the Bush administration shifted its attention to a long-time nemesis, Iraq's Saddam Hussein. Relations between the United States and Iraq had been tense following the first Gulf War, when Iraqi troops were forced out of Kuwait but Hussein had been left in place. Hussein's violence against his own citizens and concern that he was developing weapons of mass destruction (WMD) spurred the Clinton administration to adopt a policy favoring regime change in Iraq. George W. Bush was determined to end Hussein's regime, which his father could not do given the objectives of the U.N. mandate in the First Gulf War.

Claiming that democracy could help developing countries achieve stability and prosperity, the president laid out a new foreign relations policy known as the Bush Doctrine: the United States would engage in international nation-building in order to promote the spread of democracy, and it would attack its enemies before they had an opportunity to attack the United States and American interests. Unlike his father, who had assembled a broad international coalition for the first Gulf War, the younger President Bush soon realized that even NATO member nations opposed a military solution and instead favored a resumption of United Nations weapons inspections. U.N. Resolution 1441, passed in November 2002, authorized that. It was accepted by Hussein, and weapons inspectors returned to Iraq in early 2003.

No evidence was found that Iraq had resumed development of WMD, but the Bush administration, playing on the public's doubts and anxieties, campaigned to convince Americans and the world that a military solution was necessary and ultimately inevitable; further, the administration maintained that Iraq had intimate ties with Al Qaeda. Unable to win United Nations approval for a military operation in Iraq, the United States and Britain, its one major ally, gave Hussein and his notorious sons an ultimatum: leave Iraq or be invaded. Despite unprecedented worldwide protests, the United States and its allies attacked Iraq in March 2003. The military phase of the war went well for the United States and coalition forces. The capitulation of Iraqi armed forces ended the major combat operations, as Bush claimed "Mission Accomplished."

But in a real sense, the conflict was just beginning. Over the next few years, as American and coalition casualties mounted and Iraq was on the brink of civil war, critics increasingly challenged not only the reasons for going to war but also its planning and execution. There were many questions about the administration's integrity and competence:

- To justify deposing Hussein, the administration had claimed that Iraq had purchased yellowcake uranium from Niger in order to develop its nuclear capabilities. U.S. intelligence documents later proved false.
- The so-called Downing Street memo made reference to a 2002 meeting of British and American officials to discuss ways to alter intelligence reports in order to legitimize military intervention.
- With the support of both parties, Congress passed the Authorization for Use of Military Force Against Iraq Resolution in 2002. Critics claim that in the absence of U.N. authorization, the invasion of Iraq was illegal.
- While the Iraqi army was easily routed, the occupation seemed to be a planning afterthought, and the coalition was unprepared when Iraq was overwhelmed by an insurgency and approached civil war.

- Secretary of Defense Donald Rumsfeld underestimated the troops and equipment that would be needed for the occupation of Iraq.

Convinced that traditional sources and means of gathering intelligence were woefully inadequate, the administration controversially embraced so-called asymmetrical warfare, the use of controversial techniques and tactics to gain information and destroy the nation's enemies, such as assassination and torture of suspected terrorists. This was a major departure from past governmental practices. However, even supporters of the administration's new policies could not justify a series of scandals that disturbed many Americans and tarnished the reputation of the United States worldwide. Photographs from Abu Ghraib prison near Baghdad of Iraqi prisoners being terrorized, humiliated, and abused traveled around the world and brought shame to the United States. Al Qaeda and Taliban prisoners at the U.S. naval base at Guantanamo, Cuba, were also harshly treated, and their legal status became a source of controversy. The Bush administration, claiming the prisoners were illegal combatants and therefore not entitled to legal rights under the Geneva Conventions, put them in legal limbo, incarcerated but not charged with criminal or terrorist behavior.

The very premise for the invasion of Iraq was destroyed when no weapons of mass destruction were found. The administration argued that establishing a new Iraqi state without Saddam was in the best interest of Iraq, the Middle East, and the world, but as American casualties inexorably rose, calls for ending the war increased.

Globalization

If the events in Afghanistan and Iraq are mostly U.S. concerns, the integration of the world's economies and societies, commonly referred to as "globalization," affects people and states worldwide. According to one observer, globalization has "flattened" the world—meaning that all nations have a shot at economic competitiveness in the global marketplace. Using various international organizations including the World Bank and the International Money Fund (IMF), as well as the General Agreement on Tariffs and Trade (GATT), advocates of globalization have sought to reduce obstacles to international trade such as protective tariffs. The North American Free Trade Agreement (NAFTA), among the United States, Mexico, and Canada, is another example of a free-trade initiative. Globalization has undoubtedly helped many developing economies such as India and China, but critics argue that it has exacerbated already acute environmental conditions, widened the gap between wealthy and poor nations, and stimulated a clash of cultures. While there is a noticeable increase in the flow of commodities worldwide, the demand for inexpensive products has caused a proliferation of sweatshops.

One consequence of expanded industrialization is the impact it has had on the environment. Global warming has certainly caught the attention of world leaders and grassroots organizations. Claiming that Earth's temperature is increasing primarily because of human activities, politicians and environmentalists have sought international cooperation in combating this global concern. However, believing that international agreements unfairly punish American industries, Bush refused to sign the Kyoto Protocol, established in 1997 to reduce global warming. The United States is the only developed nation that has not ratified the agreement.

HOMELAND SECURITY

The events of 9/11 took the U.S. military to Afghanistan and Iraq. They also affected civilians at home. In October 2001, soon after the attacks, Congress passed the USA PATRIOT Act (an acronym for Uniting and Strengthening America by Providing Appropriate Tools Required to Intercept and Obstruct Terrorism) by a nearly unanimous vote. The act is designed to enhance the ability of law enforcement agencies to investigate, apprehend, and deport suspected terrorists. Almost immediately, however, the Bush administration was assailed for giving to law enforcement expanded surveillance powers and access to citizens' medical records and communication such as letters and e-mails. Subsequent additions to the Patriot Act have permitted "roving wiretaps" and access to personal voicemails. Critics increasingly charge that some measures in the act come at the expense of personal freedoms and civil rights that are the essence of what it means to be an American.

KATRINA

As if 9/11 and the wars in Afghanistan and Iraq were not enough, a natural disaster of immense proportions befell New Orleans and the Mississippi Gulf Coast. Sitting at the bottom of a crescent-shaped bowl, well below sea level, New Orleans is susceptible to the effects of hurricanes, which are common in the nearby Gulf of Mexico. Over the years, the city, together with the U.S. Army Corps of Engineers, has invested large sums of money to construct levees to protect New Orleans in the event of exceedingly high tides. On August 29, 2005, the enormously powerful category-3 hurricane Katrina made landfall in New Orleans, and before long, giant ocean swells overwhelmed the levees, deluging most of the city. The tragic effects of the hurricane on the city and its inhabitants were compounded by the incompetence of the federal government. Charged with dealing with disaster relief, the Federal Emergency Management Agency (FEMA) was headed by Michael Brown, a political appointee with no experience in disaster management. FEMA's inability to help those in need shocked not only Americans but people around the world, who observed that many of the city's poor and black residents were left to fend for themselves. Nearly 2,000 Americans died in the hurricane and in the days after it made landfall, and more than six years later, many remained homeless.

BUSH'S LEGISLATION

George W. Bush was successful in putting many of his plans into effect. But he also suffered setbacks. At the beginning of his presidency, both parties knew that mounting medical insurance and prescription drug costs were of concern to the American public. The Democrats wanted to find a way to cover the approximately 45 million Americans who had little or no medical health care insurance. Republicans wanted to shrink the government's role in providing not just health care, but all social services, and privatizing some of these functions was always the mantra of the Bush administration. To compensate for cuts in government social programs, the administration controversially channeled federal funds to faith-based organizations that provided services. Republicans were leery of big government-run health care programs such as Medicare, which they charged were inefficient and provided substandard health care. A better solution, they contended, was to allow individuals to manage their own health care with special savings accounts, which could be used to fund and customize their health care insurance needs. Today health care remains a problem that eludes resolution.

In an effort to address legitimate concerns about the viability of Social Security and shrink the federal government, President Bush sought to partially privatize the enormously expensive program, which was established during the New Deal. His plan called for allowing individuals to direct a portion of their Social Security contributions to their own private accounts invested in stocks and bonds. Some 90 percent of Americans over the age of 65 rely on Social Security payments—for many it is their only retirement income—so it came as no surprise that a concerted attempt to change the program unnerved many Americans; Bush was stymied. With the collapse of so many financial institutions in the fall of 2008, it is hard to imagine this idea gaining much support in the near future.

Another hot-button issue, one as old as the nation itself, is immigration. Ironically, although Americans take pride in being a land of immigrants, we have built up a lot of legislation limiting or blocking immigration from certain regions and nations. Contemporary concerns, however, relate to illegal immigrants, many from Latin America and Mexico, who fill many low-paying jobs in the United States. Just how many there are is unknown, but the number is certainly in the millions. Critics claim that illegal immigrants both drive down wages and strain communities' social services, while those who favor a lenient policy argue that illegal immigrants are already an integral part of the nation's economy, filling jobs U.S. citizens refuse, and that deportation would be costly for the country and punitive toward hard-working people. Bush favored a lenient policy toward immigrants and had the support of many Democrats, but Republicans in Congress balked and would not back his legislation.

Bush was encountering substantial criticism in 2004, but he was able to win reelection in a close contest with Senator John Kerry. But the war in Iraq, national security controversies, and the impotent federal response to Katrina were growing sources of controversy in 2006, and Americans had come to think that the country was on the wrong track. The impact on the 2006 congressional elections was profound; the Democrats won back both houses of Congress. At the same time, the nation was gearing up for the 2008 election. For the first time in many years, neither the president nor the vice president would be running, making the contest truly "open."

The 2008 Election

Many candidates vied for the nomination in both parties. The Democratic field was quickly reduced to senators Hillary Clinton and Barack Obama, who struggled for the nomination to the bitter end of the primaries, when Obama eked out a narrow victory. In a campaign characterized by nearly flawless organization, a sophisticated use of the Internet, funding raised from a vast number of citizens giving small amounts of money, and avoidance of negative campaigning, Obama presented himself as the candidate of change.

Senator John McCain won the Republican nomination. A prisoner of war in Vietnam for more than five years, McCain was admired for his service to the country and liked for his wit. However, he was burdened by being in the same party as George W. Bush and by Americans' anxiety that the country had been seriously damaged in the past eight years. He chose as his running mate Governor Sarah Palin of Alaska, who proved to be a divisive figure.

The vitality and resilience of the economy became a key issue for voters. Enormous sums of money had been diverted to rebuilding Iraq's infrastructure, while Bush's huge tax cuts had reduced the government's revenue. Dramatic increases in oil prices exacerbated the nation's economic woes and destabilized the already shaky automobile industry, and robust economic competition from emerged economic giants such as China and India was unsettling. Suddenly, Wall Street investment banks were in deep trouble; greed, financial instruments that were both poorly understood and risky, a lack of transparency, and in some cases fraud brought a number of firms to their knees. The collapse of the subprime mortgage industry precipitated failures throughout the financial sector and led to a credit crunch.

The economic collapse was the most important factor in Barack Obama's victory, with 53 percent of the vote to John McCain's 46 percent. (The electoral vote was 365–173.) In Congress, the Democrats, who had taken back both houses in the 2006 midterm elections, strengthened their majorities. In the House of Representatives, Democrats picked up twenty-one seats, giving them 257 of the 435 seats; in the Senate, the Democrats gained eight seats, giving them, including the two Independents who caucus with them, 59 out of 100 seats.

THE GREAT RECESSION

President Obama's first priority when he came into office was to confront the economic crisis in which the nation was mired. Unemployment rates were escalating, large and small businesses were failing, and people continued to lose their homes. President Obama, under pressure to respond similarly to FDR in the 1930s, pushed his "stimulus package," the American Relief and Recovery Act, through Congress. The act included improvements to national infrastructure, loans and tax breaks to small businesses, new spending for jobs, and government assistance for big banks and major American automakers. As the 2012 presidential campaign began, the United States still had significant economic woes, complicated by those in Europe and Standard & Poor's downgrading of the U.S. credit rating. Rebuilding the economy, and disagreements between the executive and legislative branches on how to do so, became central features of President Obama's second term in office.

Health Care

One of the issues on which President Obama campaigned was improving health care and providing access to health care for all Americans. Despite resistance from Congress that led to significant revisions, the Patient Protection and Affordable Care Act passed in March 2010, marking the first time since 1965 that the government successfully instituted health-care reform. The Act mandated all Americans to purchase health insurance, required states to establish "exchanges" to facilitate insurance purchases at competitive rates, prohibited insurers from denying coverage to anyone with a preexisting medical condition, and allowed children up to the age of twenty-six to remain covered by their parent's health plans. There was a great deal of opposition to the act, largely from "small government" advocates who believed the national government was overstepping its boundaries and those who believed the plan placed an undue burden on the government's limited resources. Fourteen states sued to block the act, challenging its constitutionality in federal court with mixed results.

Domestic and Foreign Policy Issues Impacting the 2012 Election

The United States faced many questions as the 2012 presidential campaign began. While the Obama administration successfully removed most American troops from Iraq, with the exception of a small peacekeeping force, American troops remained in Afghanistan. Immigration became entrenched as a major national issue when Arizona passed harsh laws attempting to prevent illegal immigration and provide for the deportation of undocumented immigrants already in the country; other states followed Arizona's lead. The federal government challenged these laws; portions of the legislation have been declared unconstitutional. The emergence of the Tea Party—a conservative faction of the Republican Party—in response to Barack Obama's election changed the political landscape as Tea Party members insisted on a renewed emphasis on states' rights and strict adherence to the Constitution. The continued economic crisis combined with effective campaigns by some "Tea Partiers" contributed to the Republican Party's regaining their majority in the House of Representatives in the 2010 midterm elections. Republicans retained this majority in the 2012 elections, while the Democrats held onto their majority in the Senate. Gay marriage became a national issue as several states, through legislation and court decisions, legalized same-sex marriages. This led to challenges to established federal laws like the Defense of Marriage Act (DOMA) and the military's "Don't Ask, Don't Tell" policy. The uprisings in the Middle East, called the "Arab Spring," resulted in new regimes in Egypt, Libya, and Tunisia, while Syria devolved into a deadly and protracted civil war. These changes left the United States with questions about its relationships with long-standing allies as well as its responsibility to intervene in war-torn regions. Moreover, on May 2, 2011, Navy SEALS found and killed Osama bin Laden at a compound in Abbottabad, Pakistan, ending a nearly ten-year manhunt for the Al Qaeda leader. In the midst of all of this, Barack Obama sought and won a second term, defeating Mitt Romney, a former governor of Massachusetts, in the 2012 presidential election.

THE UNITED STATES IN PRESIDENT OBAMA'S SECOND TERM

Many of the issues that the United States faced after the 2008 election remained significant to the American people and the government as President Obama's second term began. Despite small improvements, the economy has yet to completely rebound from the recession that began in 2008. Questions about the implementation of the Affordable Care Act abound despite the Supreme Court ruling key parts of the legislation constitutional. Troop levels in Afghanistan are decreasing as the United States plans to withdraw from the region. Major issues facing the nation during Obama's second term include:

- The standstill between Congress and the president on the nation's budget led to the invocation of the sequester, $1.2 trillion in cuts in domestic and military expenditures affecting everything from air traffic control to unemployment benefits. The sequester is the ultimate result of tension between the branches on economic issues including raising the federal debt ceiling and budget allocations to domestic programs, the military, and foreign aid.
- In 2013, the Supreme Court handed down important decisions striking down part of the 1965 Voting Rights Act, a seminal accomplishment of the civil rights movement, as well as ruling DOMA unconstitutional, allowing states to decide their own policies on same-sex marriage and extending federal benefits to these couples.
- Environmental issues—and the debate over global warming—remain a significant concern, as major storms and natural disasters affect large swaths of the country and prove tragic and deadly.
- Gun control, a long time issue with both sides firmly entrenched in their positions, came to the forefront as instances of massive gun violence escalated including the deaths of twenty-six elementary schools students and staff members at Sandy Hook Elementary School in Connecticut in December 2012.
- The nuclear threat from hostile nations like North Korea and Iran remains a major foreign policy concern as the international community debates the best course of action.

Content Review Questions

1. Which of the following presidents reflected a comprehensive conservative approach to government in the post–World War II era?
   (A) Harry S Truman
   (B) John F. Kennedy
   (C) Ronald Reagan
   (D) Lyndon Johnson

2. In *Roe* v. *Wade,* the Supreme Court ruled that
   (A) the government cannot provide economic or military aid to groups that were in open rebellion against their government.
   (B) abortion is legal.
   (C) the president and Congress are required to balance the federal budget.
   (D) Florida's electoral votes were won by George W. Bush in the 2000 election.

3. The Iran-Contra affair is associated with the presidency of
   (A) Ronald Reagan.
   (B) George W. Bush.
   (C) Bill Clinton.
   (D) George H. W. Bush.

4. The Tea Party supports
   (A) Obama's stimulus plan.
   (B) increased presidential powers.
   (C) strict interpretation of the Constitution.
   (D) the same ideas as the Republican Party.

5. Which of the following did NOT occur during the presidency of Bill Clinton?
   (A) North American Free Trade Agreement
   (B) The passage of the Brady Bill
   (C) The federal attack on the Branch Davidian compound in Waco, Texas
   (D) The U.S. military invasion of Afghanistan

6. Jerry Falwell is associated with
   (A) pro-abortion rights.
   (B) the Oklahoma City bombing.
   (C) opposition to the Family and Medical Leave Act.
   (D) the Christian fundamentalist movement.

7. Geraldine Ferraro
   (A) is the first female to run for the vice presidency for a major political party.
   (B) is associated with the Reagan Democrats.
   (C) was President Reagan's secretary of state.
   (D) was a White House intern implicated in an affair that ultimately led to Bill Clinton's impeachment.

8. The controversy over the 2000 presidential election revolved around contested ballots in which state?
   (A) Georgia
   (B) Michigan
   (C) Ohio
   (D) Florida

9. President George W. Bush ordered a U.S. invasion of Afghanistan to
   (A) secure that nation's oil fields during a civil war.
   (B) topple the Taliban government, which had aided and abetted Al Qaeda terrorists.
   (C) restore to power a U.S.-backed government that had been overthrown by the Taliban.
   (D) topple the regime of Saddam Hussein.

10. Operation Desert Storm refers to
   (A) the U.S.-backed military operations in Kuwait.
   (B) the U.S. military operation in Somalia.
   (C) the overthrow of Saddam Hussein.
   (D) the U.S. effort to capture Al Qaeda leader Osama bin Laden.

11. Many conservatives oppose the Patient Protection and Affordable Care Act because they
   (A) believe the national government is taking too much power.
   (B) don't see any problems in the current health-care system.
   (C) support building up entitlement programs like Medicare and Medicaid.
   (D) proposed a less expensive plan that President Obama vetoed.

12. The economic recession that began in the United States in 2007 was caused in large part by
   (A) increased social spending by the Bush administration.
   (B) a failure to initiate tax cuts.
   (C) enormous taxes placed on corporations and the wealthy by the Bush administration.
   (D) the collapse of the housing market and banks that provide home mortgages.

13. Those responsible for the Oklahoma City bombing in 1995
   (A) carried out the attack in response to the federal government's assault on the Branch Davidian religious sect in 1993.
   (B) were members of Al Qaeda.
   (C) were members of a racist organization who blamed the federal government for passing civil rights legislation.
   (D) carried out the attack in preparation for a larger attack on the White House and the Pentagon.

14. The attacks on the United States on September 11, 2001, were perpetrated by
   (A) the Taliban.
   (B) Saddam Hussein.
   (C) the nations referred to by President Bush as the "Axis of Evil."
   (D) Al Qaeda.

15. The 2008 presidential election was unique in the nation's history because
   (A) for the first time since 1980 a presidential incumbent failed to be reelected.
   (B) a woman was selected as a presidential candidate.
   (C) a third-party candidate received more electoral votes than one of the major-party candidates.
   (D) an African American was the presidential candidate of a major party.

Short-Answer Questions

1. In the late twentieth and twenty-first centuries U.S. foreign policy became increasingly concerned with the Middle East. Though the Cold War ended, U.S. military presence abroad remains strong.
   A) Choose one of the following presidents and identify and discuss one major action his administration took in or regarding the Middle East.
   Ronald Reagan
   George H.W. Bush
   Bill Clinton
   Barack Obama
   B) How are the U.S. hostilities with the Middle East today an extension of events from the 1970s on? Provide at least one historical example to support your answer.

Question 2 is based on the following passage.

> "I think that we are at an extraordinary moment that is full of peril but full of possibility and I think that's the time you want to be president....[T]here's something about this country where hard times, big challenges bring out the best in us. This is when the political system starts to move effectively. This is when people start getting out of the petty and the trivial debates. This is when the public starts paying attention.... [W]hen things are going well...they've got better things to do than to think about public policy."
>
> —Barack Obama, 2009

2. Barack Obama came into office amid two wars and a major economic crisis. The policies he advanced and enacted in his first term were designed to address these issues, among others.
   A. Choose one of the following and discuss how the Obama administration addressed that issue.
   The Great Recession
   Health-care
   Environmental issues
   B. Did the solution to the issue you chose live up to the optimism that Obama expressed in his quote? Support your answer with historical evidence.

Long-Essay Questions

1. The period between 1980 and 2008 was marked by an increased conservative presence and influence in the U.S. government. Discuss the extent to which TWO of the following contributed to the growth of conservative ideology and policies during this time:
   - the presidency of Ronald Reagan
   - the Contract with America
   - the presidency of George H. W. Bush
   - the presidency of George W. Bush

2. President Obama's administration failed to deliver the significant changes in domestic and foreign policy that he promised during the 2008 presidential campaign.

   To what extent is the above statement true?

Answers

Content Review Questions

1. **(C)** Ronald Reagan is considered one of the most conservative presidents in the past sixty years (*The American Pageant,* 14th ed., pp. 1031–1032/15th ed., pp. 944–945; Learning Objective POL-4).

2. **(B)** The Supreme Court's decision in 1973 made abortion legal in the United States (*The American Pageant,* 14th ed., p. 1008/15th ed., p. 932; Learning Objective POL-5).

3. **(A)** The Iran-Contra affair was a scandal that broke when the Reagan administration engaged in a highly controversial—and probably illegal—effort to transfer weapons to the Contra guerrillas in Nicaragua (*The American Pageant,* 14th ed., pp. 1040–1041/15th ed., pp. 950–951; Learning Objective POL-6).

4. **(C)** The Tea Party formed in opposition to President Obama and his policies. Although Tea Party members were embraced by the Republicans, not all of their goals are the same. Tea partiers believe in a strict adherence to the powers established by the Constitution (*The American Pageant,* this material does not appear in the 14th ed./15th ed., p. 986; Learning Objective POL-4).

5. **(D)** In 2001, President George W. Bush ordered an invasion of Afghanistan to overthrow the Taliban government, which had given refuge to members of Al Qaeda (*The American Pageant,* 14th ed., p. 1068/15th ed., p. 975; Learning Objective WOR-8).

6. **(D)** Jerry Falwell was leader of the Moral Majority, a conservative Christian fundamentalist organization that has played a significant role in helping to elect candidates that reflect the views of its members (*The American Pageant,* 14th ed., p. 1043/15th ed., p. 951; Learning Objective CUL-7).

7. **(A)** Ferraro was Walter Mondale's running mate in 1984 (*The American Pageant,* 14th ed., p. 1037/15th ed., p. 947; Learning Objective ID-7).

8. **(D)** Florida experienced thousands of voting irregularities (*The American Pageant,* 14th ed., p. 1065/15th ed., p. 972; Learning Objective POL-3).

9. **(B)** The Taliban, a fundamentalist Muslim group, controlled Afghanistan and had provided refuge and assistance to Al Qaeda terrorists (*The American Pageant,* 14th ed., p. 1068/15th ed., p. 975; Learning Objective WOR-8).

10. **(A)** Operation Desert Storm was a U.S.-backed international military coalition that succeeded in driving Iraq's military from

Kuwait (*The American Pageant,* 14th ed., pp. 1049–1051/15th ed., p. 959; Learning Objective WOR-8).

11. **(A)** Social Security was a key program in Franklin Roosevelt's New Deal. Although costly, it provides retirement pensions, unemployment insurance, insurance for the disabled, and public assistance. President Bush's plan to privatize part of the program was met with suspicion and concern by many Americans (*The American Pageant,* 14th ed., p. 1077/15th ed., p. 979; Learning Objective WXT-8).

12. **(D)** There is no one reason why the U.S. economy has experienced such a significant downturn, but among the leading causes is the collapse of the subprime mortgage industry (this material does not appear in the text; Learning Objective WXT-8).

13. **(A)** Perpetrated by Gulf War veteran Timothy McVeigh, the attack on a federal office building in Oklahoma City in 1995 claimed the lives of 168 Americans. It was in direct response to what McVeigh believed was the ever-encroaching power of the federal government, as exemplified by its attack on the compound of the Branch Davidians, a fundamentalist religious sect, killing many (*The American Pageant,* 14th ed., p. 1058/15th ed., p. 967; Learning Objective WOR-4).

14. **(D)** Led by their virulently anti-Western leader Osama bin Laden, Al Qaeda terrorists used hijacked airplanes to destroy the World Trade Center and seriously damage the Pentagon. One hijacked airplane crashed in a Pennsylvania field, brought down by its passengers (*The American Pageant,* 14th ed., p. 1067/15th ed., pp. 974–975; Learning Objective WOR-8).

15. **(D)** U.S. Senator Barack Obama was the first African American to be nominated as the candidate of one of the two major parties. In November 2008 he became the first African American to be elected president of the United States (*The American Pageant,* 14th ed., p. 1079/15th ed., pp. 983–985; Learning Objective POL-7).

SHORT-ANSWER QUESTIONS

1. You can choose any of these presidents and discuss significant interaction in the Middle East. For Reagan, you should discuss the Iran-Contra scandal and the issue of negotiating with terrorists. For Bush you should discuss Operation Desert Storm. For Clinton you should discuss the bombing of Iraq. For Obama, you can discuss the wars in Iraq or Afghanistan or the capture and killing of Osama bin Laden. These events are the latest chapters in a saga that includes the OPEC embargoes of the 1970s and the Iran hostage crisis, as well as issues between the United States and Middle Eastern countries like Lebanon and Libya in the 1980s.

2. The Obama administration signed into law acts to counter all of these issues. The American Relief and Recovery Act, as well

as acts that targeted Wall Street practices, were designed to alleviate the effects of the economic crisis. The Patient Protection and Affordable Care Act became the first comprehensive bill to deal with health care since the Great Society. During Obama's first term Congress repealed Don't Ask, Don't Tell. The Obama administration also dealt with the oil spill in the Gulf of Mexico and climate change resulting in major storms like Hurricane Sandy. There is a great deal of tension between the executive and legislative branches and the two political parties, which detracts from the effectiveness of many laws. Thus, the optimism that Obama described is not as potent as it might be.

Long-Essay Questions

1. As with any assignment that asks you to evaluate, you need to use all other levels of thinking before you can judge the quality of, in this case, a political ideology. To that end, brainstorm factual information, then proceed to organize and analyze the information you've brainstormed, being sure to explain the significance of the information you're presenting in the body paragraphs of your essay. Next, synthesize this information—give some coherent organization to your information while possibly presenting a new meaning as it relates to the assigned question or topic. Finally, you will then be ready to apply your own judgment or perspective to the topic in the form of a thesis statement.

   In developing an essay that responds to the assignment above, be prepared to discuss conservatism as an ideology and method of governing. Then take into account the reasons for the reemergence of conservatism at the federal level with the landslide victory of Ronald Reagan and the success of Republicans in recapturing Congress. Be sure to discuss not only the reasons for Reagan's victory, but also the factions that identified with his presidential campaign and two terms in the White House, such as religious fundamentalists and the New Right. Key to Reagan's economic agenda was Reaganomics, or supply-side economics. Evaluate the success of this economic approach in the 1980s. Reagan also promised to reduce the role of, power of, and funding for the federal government substantially. To that end, he sought to deregulate the savings-and-loan industry, in keeping with his conservative ideology. Take note of the consequences of this action by analyzing and evaluating whether he was successful in this regard. In foreign policy, Reagan took a hard line against the Soviet Union and engaged in massive military expenditures to compel the Soviets to end the Cold War. This fact may also play a role in your essay.

   As for the Contract with America, once this became the nucleus of the Republican Party's agenda after it reclaimed Congress in 1994 under the leadership of Speaker of the House Newt Gingrich, the Republicans proceeded to dismantle some of the reform programs associated with previous, liberal administrations. Be prepared to discuss the Republican "reforms" in your essay.

The one-term presidency of George H. W. Bush is often associated with, though not limited to, the first Gulf War and his promise not to raise taxes—a consistent conservative theme in post–World War II American politics—though raise taxes is exactly what he was ultimately compelled to do.

President George W. Bush's two terms reflect his strong conservative ideology. In fact, the president was not content simply to establish a conservative agenda and programs; he attempted to roll back key reforms of the twentieth century, such as welfare, and privatize a part of Social Security. To reduce the role of the federal government, Bush further deregulated business and relied on, for example, federally funded faith-based organizations to address societal needs that had been the responsibility of local, state, and federal governments. His tax cuts were seen as an essential component of conservative fiscal policy. The role that neoconservatives played in his administration is seen most visibly in the U.S. invasion of Iraq and the subsequent process of nation-building. (Historical Thinking Skills: I-2: Patterns of Continuity and Change Over Time, I-3: Periodization, III-7: Appropriate Use of Relevant Historical Evidence, IV-8: Interpretation, and IV-9: Synthesis)

2. To thoroughly answer this question you must include information on President Obama's policies as well as compare these policies to those that were in place during President George W. Bush's administration. Domestically, President Obama increased the government's influence on people's daily lives with the passage of the Affordable Care Act and reversed a nearly two-decade-old policy with the repeal of Don't Ask, Don't Tell. The Obama administration also enacted tighter restrictions on banks and large businesses. The Obama administration has not boosted the economy to the extent promised or expected nor has the nation seen significant change in policies related to the environment or gun control. In terms of foreign policy, President Obama has withdrawn many troops from Iraq and continues to promise an end to U.S. presence in Afghanistan by 2014. Despite appeals to many Middle Eastern nations at the beginning of his presidency, Arab Spring and the ongoing crises and civil wars in the Middle East have resulted in unstable relationships and questions about the U.S. role in that region. Thus, one can argue for either side of this "to what extent" question. (Historical Thinking Skills: II-4: Comparison, III-6: Historical Argumentation, III-7: Appropriate Use of Relevant Historical Evidence, IV-8: Interpretation, and IV-9: Synthesis)

Part III

Practice Tests

Practice Test 1

AP UNITED STATES HISTORY EXAMINATION
Section I
Part A: Multiple-Choice Questions
Time—55 minutes
Number of Questions—55

Directions Each question below is part of a set of 2–5 questions that focus on a primary source, secondary source, or other historical issue. Each individual question has four possible answers. For each question, select the best response.

Questions 1–4 refer to the following quotation.

"The State governments will have the advantage of the Federal government, whether we compare them in respect to the immediate dependence of the one on the other; to the weight of personal influence which each side will possess; to the powers respectively vested in them; to the predilection and probable support of the people; to the disposition and faculty of resisting and frustrating the measures of each other. The State governments may be regarded as constituent and essential parts of the federal government; whilst the latter is nowise essential to the operation or organization of the former. Without the intervention of the State legislatures, the President of the United States cannot be elected at all. They must in all cases have a great share in his appointment, and will, perhaps, in most cases, of themselves determine it. The Senate will be elected absolutely and exclusively by the State legislatures. Even the House of Representatives, though drawn immediately from the people, will be chosen very much under the influence of that class of men, whose influence over the people obtains for themselves an election into the State legislatures. Thus, each of the principal branches of the federal government will owe its existence more or less to the favor of the State governments, and must consequently feel a dependence, which is much more likely to beget a disposition too obsequious than too overbearing towards them. On the other side, the component parts of the State governments will in no instance be indebted for their appointment to the direct agency of the federal government, and very little, if at all, to the local influence of its members.

—James Madison, *Federalist* No. 45, 1787

1. Based on the above passage, how did the government created by the Constitution differ from the one that existed under the Articles of Confederation?
   (A) Under the Constitution the state governments would dominate the national government, reversing what was established by the Articles of Confederation.
   (B) The Constitution created an all-encompassing national government that would have the power to determine daily life in the states.
   (C) The government under the Constitution would be run by elite members of society, who had little power under the Articles of Confederation.
   (D) The Constitution established a system of federalism wherein the national and state governments would share power, as opposed to the weak, ineffective national government under the Articles of Confederation.

2. What conclusion can be drawn about the government in the United States after the ratification of the Constitution based on James Madison's description in this passage?
   (A) The creation of a more effective government strengthened the

GO ON TO NEXT PAGE

nation internally and in its dealings with other nations.
(B) The state and national governments remained in balance, with neither overpowering the other under any circumstances.
(C) The idea of the elite holding power proved to be a misconception in the largely agrarian United States.
(D) Larger states found themselves overpowered by smaller states because of the equal distribution of power between them.

3. Based on the quote, what was one significant result of the government created by the Constitution?
(A) The United States prevented another war with Great Britain.
(B) Sectional tensions decreased.
(C) George Washington became the first leader of the nation.
(D) Political parties developed in the United States.

4. Based on the passage above, why was maintaining state power a major concern for many Americans in the eighteenth century?
(A) States had their own identities, laws, and cultures and did not want to see them abridged.
(B) Northerners feared the power of the state could bring an end to slavery.
(C) Smaller states worried that equal representation would curtail their say in national matters.
(D) State leaders were concerned about maintaining individual rights for all people.

Questions 5–8 refer to the following quotation.

"Black representation in Congress grew from five to seven in 1873 and reached a Reconstruction peak of eight (representing six different states) in 1875.... The number of black legislators rose dramatically in several states, and even where it did not, more blacks acquired committee chairmanships and seats in state senates.... This rising presence in office did not always translate into augmented power at the highest echelons of state government. Sixteen prominent black politicians in 1874 publicly complained of being excluded from 'any knowledge of the confidential workings of the party and government'...Accused by white Republicans of drawing a political 'color line,' black leaders responded that race, historically the 'cause of exclusion,' must now become a 'ground of recognition until scales are once more balanced.'...Blacks political role [grew], moreover, precisely as the Northern outcry against corruption and 'extravagance' reached its height. The depression, which devastated the Southern states...added further urgency to demands for retrenchment."

—Eric Foner, *Reconstruction: America's Unfinished Revolution 1863–1877*, pp. 538–539

5. How does Foner's description of Reconstruction indicate the fulfillment of one of the goals of the Civil War?
(A) The North and South were reunited and the states that seceded were brought back to the Union.
(B) The sectional issues that caused the war gave way to cooperation between different parts of the country.
(C) Former slaves in the South received the rights and opportunities they previously lacked.
(D) The rebellion's leaders were stripped of their rights as citizens.

6. What conclusions can be drawn about the success of Reconstruction for black Americans based on this quote?
(A) The early promise of Reconstruction eventually faded as a confluence of events conspired against their political advancement.
(B) Reconstruction policies cemented black Americans' equal access to government positions.
(C) The antebellum hierarchy in the South persisted even after the Civil War was over.
(D) If not for the economic depression, black Americans would have continued to thrive after the war.

7. Which Reconstruction Amendment was likely most essential to the black electoral success of which Foner writes?
   (A) Thirteenth Amendment
   (B) Fourteenth Amendment
   (C) Fifteenth Amendment
   (D) Sixteenth Amendment

8. How did life under Congressional Reconstruction differ from life in the South after the election of President Hayes?
   (A) Black Americans confronted Black Codes under Congressional Reconstruction that were removed when Hayes came into office.
   (B) As a result of the Compromise of 1877 the northern military left the South leading to reversals of many gains for black Americans.
   (C) Confederates who lost their citizenship as a result of the war were offered financial restitution by the Hayes administration.
   (D) Black politicians were reassured of the security of their elected positions when Hayes came into office.

Questions 9–11 refer to the following quotation.

"In the future days, which we seek to make secure, we look forward to a world founded upon four essential human freedoms.

The first is freedom of speech and expression—everywhere in the world.

The second is freedom of every person to worship God in his own way—everywhere in the world.

The third is freedom from want—which, translated into world terms, means economic understandings which will secure to every nation a healthy peacetime life for its inhabitants—everywhere in the world.

The fourth is freedom from fear—which, translated into world terms, means a world-wide reduction of armaments to such a point and in such a thorough fashion that no nation will be in a position to commit an act of physical aggression against any neighbor—anywhere in the world.

That is no vision of a distant millennium. It is a definite basis for a kind of world attainable in our own time and generation. That kind of world is the very antithesis of the so-called new order of tyranny which the dictators seek to create with the crash of a bomb."

—Franklin Delano Roosevelt, January 6, 1941
(From http://www.wwnorton.com/college/history/ralph/workbook/ralprs36b.htm)

9. Why did Franklin Roosevelt use these ideas to justify lend-ease aid?
   (A) The United States was directly threatened by Germany in early 1941, thereby threatening essential aspects of the American way of life.
   (B) Principles that Americans held dear were threatened by Nazi actions and victory in Europe.
   (C) The United States was the sole superpower and had to protect the values in which it believed all over the world.
   (D) The American people supported the Nazi regime and FDR needed to convince them to change their minds.

10. How did the Four Freedoms encompass multiple struggles facing Americans in the early 1940s?
   (A) First Amendment rights were severely restricted, creating anger among the people.
   (B) Many Americans were dismayed that they were unable to join the Spanish Civil War.
   (C) The Four Freedoms address the specter of World War and the struggles of the Great Depression.
   (D) Americans were afraid of being the victims of an atomic bomb.

11. How did lend-lease aid bring the United States closer, and eventually into, World War II?
   (A) U.S. ships were attacked by Germany, forcing the United States to retaliate.
   (B) Providing aid to one side established the U.S.'s allegiance to the Allies and trumped declarations of neutrality.
   (C) The United States poured too much money into the war effort

GO ON TO NEXT PAGE

and had to enter the war to receive reparations.

(D) Unanimous consent for lend-lease convinced the government that entering the war was a logical next step.

Questions 12–13 refer to the following quotation.

"Many of the Anasazi may have left the relatively cold and dry central San Juan Basin during the middle-12th century and they abandoned the entire Four Corners region [in the North American Southwest] in the late-13th century. . . . Great-house construction and renovation at Chaco and at Aztec which had accelerated during wet periods terminated near the beginning of the middle-12th century drought. . . . The loss of summer moisture is hypothesized to have resulted in reduced yields of maize, the dietary staple of the Anasazi, forcing them to abandon areas that were marginal for dry-land farming and migrate to better- watered areas."

—Larry Benson, Kenneth Petersen, and John Stein, "Anasazi (Pre-Columbian Native American) Migrations," 2006
Source from http://faculty.bennington.edu/

12. Which of the following conclusions may best be drawn from the information provided by Bensen, Petersen, and Stein?
    (A) The environment throughout North America was hostile to the development of permanent civilizations.
    (B) Native Americans adapted their lifestyle and settlement patterns around the dictates of local climate and available resources.
    (C) The arrival of European settlers created population pressure on the resources of the regions inhabited by Native Americans, causing conflict over territory.
    (D) Although Native Americans established settlements, their lack of technology and dependence on staple crops prevented them from extensive urbanization.

13. Which of the following most accurately explains the differences between settlements in the American Southwest and Native American cultures in the American Northeast?
    (A) Tribes in the Northeast did not rely on the cultivation of crops for their livelihood, focusing on hunting and gathering instead.
    (B) Unlike the Anasazi, the Native Americans in the Northeast lived largely as nomads, following game animals' migratory patterns.
    (C) The diverse natural resources of the Northeast provided Native Americans in that region with more options for cultivation, along with hunting and gathering.
    (D) Native Americans in the Northeast created larger, urban centers that made them much more vulnerable to climate variations.

Questions 14–17 refer to the following images.

Bettmann/Corbis

Charles Moore/Black Star/Stockphoto.com

14. How did the violent reaction to the civil rights movement lead to changes in American thinking on this issue?
    (A) Southerners were embarrassed by their actions and vowed to change their policies.
    (B) De facto segregation in the North decreased in response to the crisis in the South.
    (C) Key government figures began listening to civil rights leaders after witnessing the violence used against them.
    (D) Law enforcement agents began to side with civil rights protestors rather than organizations that opposed them.

15. In which of the following ways did the civil rights movement influence other twentieth-century efforts for reform?
    (A) Several groups adopted similar ideas on civil disobedience.
    (B) Other groups focused on the church as the central meeting place for their movement.
    (C) Civil rights leaders had close ties to important government figures.
    (D) The civil rights movement relied on Supreme Court decisions for all of its major accomplishments.

16. Why were these images and others like them a powerful tool of the civil rights movement?
    (A) The images showed the weakened state of African Americans.
    (B) Reports of southern brutality spread through the world making the movement a global phenomenon.
    (C) African Americans' conditions persuaded people that they should act violently in the face of oppression.
    (D) These images led to anti-civil rights movement propaganda.

17. How did Black Power advocates criticize the method of protest pictured here?
    (A) Black Power advocates believed that nonviolence was a weak form of protest.
    (B) Black Power sought integration in the future, but not the present.
    (C) Black Power advocates believed that civil rights protests needed to be more integrated.
    (D) Black Power advocates preferred to protest near halls of power in Washington, D.C., than in the South.

Questions 18–19 refer to the following quotation.

"There is a saying, that we should do all men like as we will be done ourselves.... But to bring men hither, or to rob and sell them against their will, we stand against.... Pray, what thing in the world can be done worse towards us, than if men should rob or steal us away, and sell us for slaves to strange countries, separating husbands from their wives and children?"

—Mennonites of Germantown, PA, 1688

18. How does the above quote indicate the sectional difficulties that will increasingly plague the colonies and the country for two centuries?
    (A) Disagreement on the slavery issue was already percolating in the seventeenth century.
    (B) There was dissention among religious groups seeking freedom in America.
    (C) Northerners began to question the morality of indentured servitude.
    (D) Colonists questioned the tactics used against Native Americans in the South.

19. Which of the following arguments was frequently used to contradict the claims made in the quote?
    (A) There were no other groups able to do the work that slaves did.
    (B) Slaves were given the same rights as white men in places where slavery existed.
    (C) Slavery was an economic necessity for the entire nation.
    (D) Slavery would eventually die out so it needed to be exploited while it existed.

GO ON TO NEXT PAGE

Questions 20–23 refer to the following quotation.

"All men recognize the right of revolution; the right to refuse allegiance to and to resist the government, when its tyranny or its inefficiency are great and unendurable. But almost all say that such is not the case now.... I say, when a sixth of the population of a nation which has undertaken to be the refuge of liberty are slaves, and a whole country is unjustly overrun and conquered by a foreign army, and subjected to military law, I think that is not too soon for honest men to rebel and revolutionize. What makes this duty more urgent is the fact, that the country so overrun is not our own, but ours is the invading army."

—Henry David Thoreau, 1849

20. On which era's ideas does Thoreau base his argument about the right to revolution?
(A) Renaissance
(B) Scientific Revolution
(C) Enlightenment
(D) Manifest Destiny

21. Which of the following explanations for the Mexican War corresponds with Thoreau's views of the war?
(A) The war was an unjustified land grab entered into to acquire desired territory.
(B) The United States was justified in fighting Mexico to defend its borders and soldiers.
(C) The war would enable the United States to prevent the spread of slavery.
(D) The Mexican Army's cruelty compelled the United States to fight for its honor and to defend Americans in Texas.

22. Which group in the United States would most likely agree with Thoreau's stance on the Mexican War?
(A) Southerners looking for arable land to found new plantations
(B) Politicians aiming to raise the United States' status in the world
(C) Northerners who believed that the war was an excuse to create more slave states
(D) Mexicans who hoped to become American citizens

23. Which of the following proposals echoed Thoreau's concerns about slavery in the newly acquired territory from Mexico?
(A) Fugitive Slave Act of 1850
(B) Wilmot Proviso
(C) Morrill Land Act
(D) Compromise of 1850

Questions 24–26 refer to the following quotation.

"I think that we are at an extraordinary moment that is full of peril but full of possibility and I think that's the time you want to be president...[T]here's something about this country where the hard times, big challenges bring out the best in us. This is when the political system starts to move effectively. This is when people start to get out of the petty and trivial debates. This is when the public starts paying attention...."

—Barack Obama, February 2009

24. Which of the following challenges might President Obama be referring to in the quote?
(A) The battle over a national health-care system
(B) The "Great Recession"
(C) Controversy over same-sex marriage
(D) The hunt for Saddam Hussein

25. Which of the following trends contradicts Obama's argument in this statement?
(A) Congress and the American people remain unfailingly divided along party lines.
(B) The Obama administration failed to take any action aimed at solving the nation's problems during his first term.
(C) President Obama was not elected by a wide enough margin to have the mandate of the people.
(D) The United States succumbs to challenges more often than it faces and defeats them.

26. Based on this quote, why do some politicians and journalists compare presidents Obama and Franklin Roosevelt?
(A) Both men were elected in war time.

(B) Both men failed to revive the economy despite their best efforts.
(C) Both men had the support of Congress and the Supreme Court in all of their endeavors.
(D) Both men faced harsh economic and international crises with optimism and belief in the American people.

Questions 27–29 refer to the following image.

Granger Collection

27. What conclusion can you accurately draw from this image?
(A) The United States sided with the Allies from the beginning of World War I.
(B) The United States government had reason to rely on the concept of freedom of the seas during war.
(C) Germany was willing to allow non-military passengers off ships before sinking them in 1915.
(D) American citizens should have been aware of the danger in traveling on belligerent ships in wartime.

28. Which of the following statements accurately identifies the *Lusitania's* significance to America's decision to enter World War I?
(A) The sinking of the *Lusitania* convinced Americans of the need to go to war against Germany.
(B) Americans blamed the *Lusitania's* passengers for failing to heed the warning and resolved to remain neutral.
(C) Germany's use of unrestricted submarine warfare set off years of negotiations and pledges between Germany and the United States before pulling the United States into war.
(D) The *Lusitania* had no significance to the United States because it was a British ship.

29. How did U.S. actions leading up to World War II reflect the lessons learned from this experience?
(A) The United States cut off all relations with Great Britain when war became imminent.
(B) The Neutrality Acts acknowledged the danger of sea travel during wartime.
(C) British ships were unable to dock in U.S. ports until after the United States officially declared war in 1941.

GO ON TO NEXT PAGE

(D) The war in Europe became a media sensation even before the United States joined the war effort.

Questions 30–32 refer to the following quotations.

"So at last I was going to America! Really, really going at last! The boundaries burst. The arch of heaven soared. A million suns shone out for every star. The winds rushed in from outer space roaring in my ears, 'America! America!'"

—Mary Antin, *The Promised Land,* 1912

"America is God's crucible, the great melting pot, where all the races of Europe are melting and re-forming!... Germans and Frenchmen, Irishmen and Englishmen, Jews and the Russians—into the Crucible with you all! God is making the American."

—Israel Zangwill

"It is said...that the quality of recent immigration is undesirable. The time is quite within recent memory when the same thing was said of immigrants who, with their descendants, are now numbered among our best citizens."

—President Grover Cleveland, 1897

30. What changes in the United States led to the influx of immigrants referenced by Antin, Zangwill, and Cleveland?
   (A) As the nation began to emphasize business and industry there were more opportunities to start a successful small business in the United States.
   (B) The growing labor union movement convinced immigrants that their jobs and livelihood would be better protected in the United States than their home countries.
   (C) The United States government attempted to integrate immigrants into the national community quickly to give them a sense of belonging.
   (D) Rapid industrialization created an enormous need for unskilled labor that immigrants could provide.

31. How was northern workers' reaction to immigration at the end of the nineteenth century similar to their reaction to the Great Migration in the twentieth century?
   (A) Northerners welcomed the assistance in understaffed factories.
   (B) Workers resented the arrival of people whom they believed would steal their jobs.
   (C) White northerners believed that an influx of minorities would raise their social standing.
   (D) Northerners hoped their urban population would grow, giving them more electoral power.

32. How did increased immigration lead to a change in government policy by the end of the nineteenth and early twentieth centuries?
   (A) The government eased citizenship requirements to encourage even more immigrants to enter the country.
   (B) Legislation began to restrict or prevent immigrants from certain countries from coming to the United States.
   (C) The government mandated that factories hire only immigrants.
   (D) Immigrants were restricted to living in neighborhoods with others from their home country.

Questions 33–36 refer to the following political cartoon.

National Archives

33. Which of the following conclusions can most definitively be drawn from the cartoon?
    (A) There are several different sources to blame for U.S. failures in Vietnam.
    (B) The Gulf of Tonkin Resolution was the sole reason the situation in Vietnam got out of control.
    (C) The anti-war movement placed the United States at more of a disadvantage than leaders' decisions.
    (D) American presidents recognized the role they played in the Vietnam quagmire.

34. In which of the following ways was the Vietnam War different than the wars that preceded it?
    (A) American soldiers were drafted into the military and sent overseas.
    (B) U.S. military forces in Vietnam were racially segregated.
    (C) Much of the war was fought in the air.
    (D) The public was able to watch the war on television.

35. How did the Vietnam War lead to changes in the way that Americans perceive of their leaders?
    (A) Americans began to believe that the government was lying to the people and omitting information.
    (B) The public was convinced that the nation's leaders were unaware of the magnitude of the situation.
    (C) People began to see their leaders as unwilling to compromise.
    (D) Americans saw their leaders as mistakenly concerned with the Cold War at the expense of other issues.

36. How did the Vietnam War reflect the United States' goals throughout the Cold War?
    (A) The United States aimed to defeat all communist nations in order to weaken the Soviet Union.
    (B) The United States believed it needed to show its military strength to avoid attack.
    (C) The United States took advantage of any opportunity to show off its nuclear arsenal.
    (D) The United States concerned itself with not allowing communism to spread outside its borders.

Questions 37–39 refer to the following quotation.

"The question before the court and you, gentlemen of the jury, is not of small nor private concern. It is not the cause of a poor printer, nor of New York alone, which you are now trying. No! It may, in its consequence, affect every freeman that lives under a British government on the main [land] of America. It is the best cause. It is the cause of liberty."

—Andrew Hamilton,
Closing Statement in the Zenger Trial, 1735

37. Which of the following most accurately connects Hamilton's statement with a prevailing reason that many colonists came to America?
 (A) Colonists were looking for greater freedom than they had in Britain.
 (B) Great Britain did not offer accused criminals a trial by jury.
 (C) Englishmen believed that all of the British colonies should enjoy the same rights.
 (D) Hamilton, like many colonists, differentiated between rights of freemen and slaves.

38. How did the issues expressed in this statement contribute towards the sentiments that led to the Revolutionary War?
 (A) Britain began exerting less control over the colonies in a time of crisis.
 (B) The British stripped American colonists of their liberties during the French and Indian War.
 (C) Colonists grew tired of demanding their rights throughout the eighteenth century and rebelled.
 (D) Accustomed to salutary neglect, the colonists fought British encroachments on their liberties.

39. How did the result of the Zenger trial set a precedent for future legal decisions in the United States?
 (A) Americans came to believe in the primacy of freedom of speech.
 (B) Freedom of the press was recognized as a fundamental right.
 (C) American citizens understood that it was dangerous to criticize their leaders.
 (D) Congress refused to make laws limiting First Amendment rights.

Questions 40–42 refer to the following political cartoon.

Library of Congress

40. According to the cartoon, how did the government's priorities change between the early 1960s and the 1980s?
 (A) The Reagan administration attempted to pay equal attention to domestic and foreign policy issues as opposed to the domestic focus of the Great Society.
 (B) Reagan was less willing to devote resources to defense than Kennedy and Johnson.
 (C) The emphasis on social programs that was a hallmark of the New Frontier and Great Society took a backseat to military spending under Reagan.
 (D) Reagan cut spending across the board to balance the budget, while the Great Society put the nation in debt.

41. Which of the following ideas is most closely associated with Reagan's focus on cutting social programs?
 (A) Mutually assured destruction
 (B) Supply-side economics

(C) Conservatism
(D) Small government

42. How do the policies of the Reagan administration impact the United States in the twenty-first century?
    (A) The Obama administration similarly emphasizes small government.
    (B) The Religious Right remains a major force in American politics.
    (C) The federal government focuses on foreign policy to the exclusion of domestic issues.
    (D) Reagan-era economic policies contributed to the crisis that began in 2007.

Questions 43–45 refer to the following image.

SOUTHERN CHIVALRY — ARGUMENT VERSUS CLUB'S.

Library of Congress

43. How does this image reflect the sectional tensions that existed in the United States leading up to the Civil War?
    (A) Upper-class Americans continued to rely on duels to settle disagreements.
    (B) Compromises legislated by Congress failed to settle the slavery question
    (C) The tension between the two sides led to violence even on the floor of Congress.
    (D) Southerners condemned their representative's actions and began to side with the North.

44. Which of the following events reflects the congressional tensions on a much larger scale?
    (A) John Brown's Raid
    (B) Bleeding Kansas
    (C) The Lincoln-Douglas debates
    (D) Boycotts of *Uncle Tom's Cabin*

45. How did the political tension represented here eventually lead directly to the Civil War?
    (A) Political parties disunited, evolving into northern and southern branches of a single party.
    (B) The Know Nothing Party threatened the values on which the nation was founded.
    (C) Congress was unable to pass laws due to disagreement, leading the people to react violently towards the government
    (D) The 1860 election of Abraham Lincoln caused southern states to secede from the Union.

Questions 46–48 refer to the following quotation.

"Everybody is talkin' these days about Tammany men growin' rich on graft, but nobody thinks of drawin' the distinction between honest graft and dishonest graft. There's all the difference in the world between the two. Yes, many of our men have grown rich in politics. I have myself. I've made a big fortune out of the game, and I'm gettin' richer every day, but I've not gone in for dishonest graft—blackmailin' gamblers, saloonkeepers, disorderly people, etc.—and neither has any of the men who have made big fortunes in politics.

There's an honest graft, and I'm an example of how it works. I might sum up the whole thing by sayin': "I seen my opportunities and I took 'em."

GO ON TO NEXT PAGE

Just let me explain by examples. My party's in power in the city, and it's goin' to undertake a lot of public improvements. Well, I'm tipped off, say, that they're going to lay out a new park at a certain place.

I see my opportunity and I take it. I go to that place and I buy up all the land I can in the neighborhood. Then the board of this or that makes its plan public, and there is a rush to get my land, which nobody cared particular for before.

Ain't it perfectly honest to charge a good price and make a profit on my investment and foresight? Of course, it is. Well, that's honest graft."

—George Washington Plunkitt, 1905

46. Why might progressive reformers like Lincoln Steffens believe that the situation described by Plunkitt needed to be remedied?
    (A) It provides one example of the long-standing corruption typical to political machines.
    (B) It shows how the people were exploited by the government.
    (C) He discusses the connection between big business and government.
    (D) He reveals plans for political machines to illegally control city government.

47. Why were the late nineteenth and early twentieth centuries ideal times for administrations like the one described by Plunkitt to rise to power?
    (A) More people moved out of overcrowded cities and into farming communities.
    (B) The growth of industry brought immigrants who could be easily manipulated to American cities.
    (C) Corrupt politicians were careful to hide their actions from the press and the public.
    (D) The tactics that Plunkitt described benefited large groups of people.

48. Which of the following progressive era accomplishments were designed to counter government corruption?
    (A) Anti-trust legislation
    (B) The Nineteenth Amendment
    (C) Direct election of senators
    (D) Referendum and recall

Questions 49–52 refer to the following quotation.

"During the whole '33 one-hundred days' Congress, people didn't know what was going on, the public. Couldn't understand these things that were being passed so fast. They knew something was happening, something good for them. They began investing and hoping and working again.

People don't realize that Roosevelt chose a conservative banker as Secretary of Treasury and a conservative from Tennessee as Secretary of State. Most of the reforms that were put through might have been agreeable to Hoover, if he had the political power to put them over. They were all latent in Hoover's thinking, especially the bank rescue. The rescue was not done by Roosevelt—he signed the papers—but by Hoover leftovers in the administration....

The bank rescue of 1933 was probably the turning point of the Depressions. When people were able to survive the shock of having all the banks close, and then see the banks open up, with their money protected, there began to be confidence. Good times were coming. Most of the legislation that came after didn't help the public. The public helped itself after it got confidence."

—Raymond Moley, Oral History interview in Studs Terkel, *Hard Times*, July 2005, pp. 250–251

49. According to Raymond Moley, in what way were Hoover and Roosevelt alike?
    (A) Both supported creating jobs for the unemployed during the Great Depression.
    (B) Both had conservative advisers helping to formulate policy during the Great Depression.
    (C) Both believed in closing the banks for the duration of the economic crisis.
    (D) Both advocated for local solutions to the crisis.

50. Which conclusion is best supported by the document?
    (A) Roosevelt's most important contribution was the reform acts that placed safeguards on the economy,
    (B) Hoover could have solved the nation's problems if he'd had more time in office.
    (C) Roosevelt's most significant act during the Depression was instilling confidence in the people.
    (D) The New Deal failed to alleviate suffering during the Great Depression.

51. How did FDR establish a model for the "first hundred days" of a presidency?
   (A) He passed many laws and immediately began creating programs to counter the effects of the Great Depression.
   (B) He was able to reach agreement with Congress on the necessary points of action and act on those agreements.
   (C) By the end of that time, most Americans were back to work.
   (D) He devised all his plans for the duration of his term from the outset in the first hundred days.

52. Based on the excerpt above, how does Moley's statement contradict public perceptions of Hoover's response to the Great Depression?
   (A) People believed that Hoover was too concerned with foreign policy to attend to the economic crisis.
   (B) Hoover's statements on rugged individualism convinced people that he had no interest in helping struggling individuals.
   (C) Newspapers portrayed Hoover as unable to push support measures through Congress.
   (D) Many Americans saw several similarities between Hoover and FDR.

Questions 53–55 refer to the following quotation.

"Despite Jefferson's philosophy and opposition to the views of his predecessors, he made remarkably few changes in the policies of the government during his two terms as President of the United States. Although he later referred to his election as the 'revolution of 1800,' there was little in his inaugural address to substantiate such a view. Stating that "we are all Republicans, we are all Federalists," he pledged his Administration to the "honest payment of our debts and the sacred preservation of the public faith; encouragement of agriculture and of commerce its handmaid." The inaugural was so conciliatory in tone that Hamilton thought it "virtually a candid retraction of past misapprehensions, and a pledge to the community that the new President will not lend himself to dangerous innovations, but in essential points tread in the steps" of the Federalists."

—Harry J. Carman and Harold C. Syretta, *A History of the American People* (1952), pp. 282–283

53. Why might Jefferson believe it necessary to claim, "we are all Republicans, we are all Federalists," in his inaugural address?
   (A) The division between political parties in the United States was growing too big for compromise.
   (B) He wanted to guarantee a smooth transition from one party to the other.
   (C) His vice president was a Federalist though he was a Republican.
   (D) He hoped to mask his moderate policies.

54. Which of the following examples illustrates Jefferson's willingness to place the country over his own political beliefs?
   (A) Allowing the Sedition Act to expire
   (B) Purchasing the Louisiana Territory from France
   (C) Enacting a trade embargo against European nations
   (D) Creating peace with France

55. How did the differences between Hamilton and Jefferson impact the future of American politics?
   (A) Their unity regarding Jefferson's inaugural address lessened political tensions in the nation.
   (B) Their inability to agree led to the duel in which Hamilton died, leading to the end of the Federalist Party.
   (C) Political parties, not mentioned in the Constitution, became a permanent part of American electoral politics.
   (D) Federalists and Democratic-Republicans remained the dominant political parties in the United States.

STOP
END OF SECTION I, PART A

IF YOU FINISH BEFORE TIME IS CALLED, YOU MAY CHECK YOUR WORK ON THIS SECTION. DO NOT GO ON TO SECTION I, PART B UNTIL YOU ARE TOLD TO DO SO.

AP UNITED STATES HISTORY EXAMINATION
Section I
Part B: Short-Answer Questions
Writing Time—45 minutes

Directions: Part B of the examination contains 4 questions. You will have 45 minutes to respond to all questions. You are not required to develop and support a thesis statement in your response. Rather, focus on directly answering each question using evidence from your study of history.

"The only question is, whether it has a right to incorporate this company, in order to enable it the more effectually to accomplish ends which are in themselves lawful. To establish such a right, it remains to show the relation of such an institution, to one or more of the specified powers of the Government. Accordingly, it is affirmed, that it has a relation, more or less direct, to the power of collecting taxes; to that of borrowing money; to that of regulating trade between the States; and to those of raising and maintaining fleets and armies. To the two former, the relation may be said to be immediate. And in the last place, it will be argued, that it is clearly within the provision which authorizes the making of all needful rules and regulations concerning the property of the United States, as the same has been practised upon by the Government."

—Alexander Hamilton, Statement on the Constitutionality of the National Bank (1791)

"The incorporation of a bank, and other powers assumed by this bill, have not, in my opinion, been delegated to the United States by the constitution…

[The Constitution gives Congress the power] "to make all laws necessary and proper for carrying into execution the enumerated powers." But they can all be carried into execution without a bank. A bank, therefore, is not necessary, and, consequently, not authorized by this phrase.

…the Constitution allows only the means which are "necessary," not those which are merely "convenient" for effecting the enumerated powers. If such a latitude of construction be allowed to this phrase as to give any non enumerated power, it will go to every one… Therefore it was that the constitution restrained them to the necessary means; that is to say, to those means, without which the grant of the power would be nugatory."

—Thomas Jefferson, Statement on the Constitutionality of the National Bank (1791)

1. Based on the two opinions offered by the members of President Washington's cabinet in the passage above, complete the following three tasks:
   a) Briefly explain the argument made by Alexander Hamilton.
   b) Briefly explain the argument made by Thomas Jefferson.
   c) Describe the development of the first political parties, explaining how the debate represented here contributed to that development. Provide at least ONE other example of the partisan divide among supporters of these two men.

2. United States historians disagree about the effectiveness of Reconstruction following the American Civil War.
   a) Choose ONE of the following and provide ONE piece of evidence demonstrating the success of Reconstruction in that area.

      Economic reconstruction of the South

      Rights for former slaves

      Political reconstruction and unity

   b) Provide ONE additional piece of evidence demonstrating the limitations or failures of Reconstruction in the area you chose in Part a.

© Bettmann/Corbis

3. Use the image above and your knowledge of United States history to answer Parts a, b, and c.
   a) Explain the point of view reflected in this postcard regarding ONE of the following:
      American territorial expansion
      Theories of race and responsibility
      America's role in the world
   b) Explain how ONE aspect of the postcard expresses the viewpoint you identified in Part a.
   c) Explain how the viewpoint you have identified shaped ONE specific American foreign policy between 1898 and 1905.

"Just as the period of American history from 1933 to the late 1960s...was chiefly one of liberal reform, so the past thirty-five years have been an era of conservatism...Without Reagan, the conservative movement would never have been as successful as it was. In his political persona, as well as his policies, Reagan embodied a new fusion of deeply conservative politics with some of the rhetoric and even a bit of the spirit of Franklin D. Roosevelt's New Deal and of John F. Kennedy's New Frontier...The impact of the age of Reagan is indicated even more strongly by the guiding assumptions and possibilities of American politics and government, and the hold they have on public opinion. Thirty years ago, the proposition that reducing taxes on the rich was the best solution for all economic problems inspired only a few on the right-wing fringe. Today, it drives the national domestic agenda and is so commonplace that it sometimes appears to have become the conventional wisdom."

—Sean Wilentz, *The Age of Reagan: A History, 1974–2008*–(HarperCollins, 2008)

4. Based on Sean Wilentz' argument about the impact of President Reagan in the passage above, complete the following two tasks.
   a) Provide ONE piece of evidence of the rise of conservatism from the time after 1980 that is not included in the passage.
   b) Provide ONE piece of evidence either supporting or refuting Wilentz' claim that "Reagan embodied a new fusion of deeply conservative politics with some of the rhetoric and even a bit of spirit of Franklin D. Roosevelt's New Deal and of John F. Kennedy's New Frontier."

STOP
END OF SECTION I

IF YOU FINISH BEFORE TIME IS CALLED, YOU MAY CHECK YOUR WORK ON THIS SECTION. DO NOT GO ON TO SECTION II UNTIL YOU ARE TOLD TO DO SO.

Section II: Free-Response Essays

Section II of the examination has two kinds of questions. Part A is the Document-Based Question, which includes a series of primary source documents organized around a central question. Part B will present a pair of long-essay questions, both focusing on the same historical thinking skill. Each of the two long-essay prompts will apply the skill to a different time period and you will choose ONE of the two prompts to answer. You will have a total of 95 minutes to complete the document-based essay and the long essay.

Part A: Document-Based Question (DBQ)
Time—60 minutes

Directions: Question 1 is based on the accompanying documents. The documents have been edited for the purpose of this exercise. You are advised to spend 15 minutes planning and 45 minutes writing your answer.

In your response you should do the following.

- State a relevant thesis that directly answers all parts of the question.
- Support the thesis or a relevant argument with evidence from all, or all but one, of the documents.
- Incorporate analysis of all, or all but one, of the documents into your argument.
- Focus your analysis of each document on at least one of the following: intended audience, purpose, historical context, and/or point of view.
- Support your argument with analysis of historical examples outside the documents.
- Connect historical phenomena relevant to your argument to broader events or processes.
- Synthesize the elements above into a persuasive essay.

Question 1. Analyze the evolution of race relations from the period between 1914 and 1965.

Document 1: Black Migrants' Reasons for Relocation (1917)

Sir: I am writing you to let you know that there is 15 or 20 familys wants to come up there at once but cant come on account of money to come with and we cant phone you here we will be killed they dont want us to leave here & say if we dont go to war and fight for our country they are going to kill us and wants to get away if we can if you send 20 passes there is no doubt that every one of us will com at once. we are not doing any thing here we cant get a living out of what we do now some of these people are farmers and som are cooks barbers and black smiths but the greater part are farmers & good worker & honest people & up to date the trash pile dont want to go no where These are nice people and respectable find a place like that & send passes & we all will come at once we all wants to leave here out of this hard luck place if you cant use us find some place that does need this kind of people we are called Negroes here. I am a reader of the Defender and am delighted to know how times are there & was to glad to, know if we could get some one to pass us away from here to a better land. We work but cant get scarcely any thing for it & they dont want us to go away & there is not much of anything here to do & nothing for it Please find some one that need this kind of a people & send at once for us. We dont want anything but our wareing and bed clothes & have not got no money to get away from here with & beging to get away before we are killed and hope to here from you at once. We cant talk to you over the phone here we are afraid to they dont want to hear one say that he or she wants to leave here if we do we are apt to be killed. They say if we dont go to war they are not going to let us stay here with their folks and it is not any thing that we have done to them.

Source: Letter Daphne, Alabama, 4120/17, Emmet Scott, ed., "Letters of Negro Migrants of 1916–1918," Journal of Negro History, *4 (July 1, 1919), pp. 290–340.*

GO ON TO NEXT PAGE

Document 2: Percentage of Black Voting-Age Population Registered

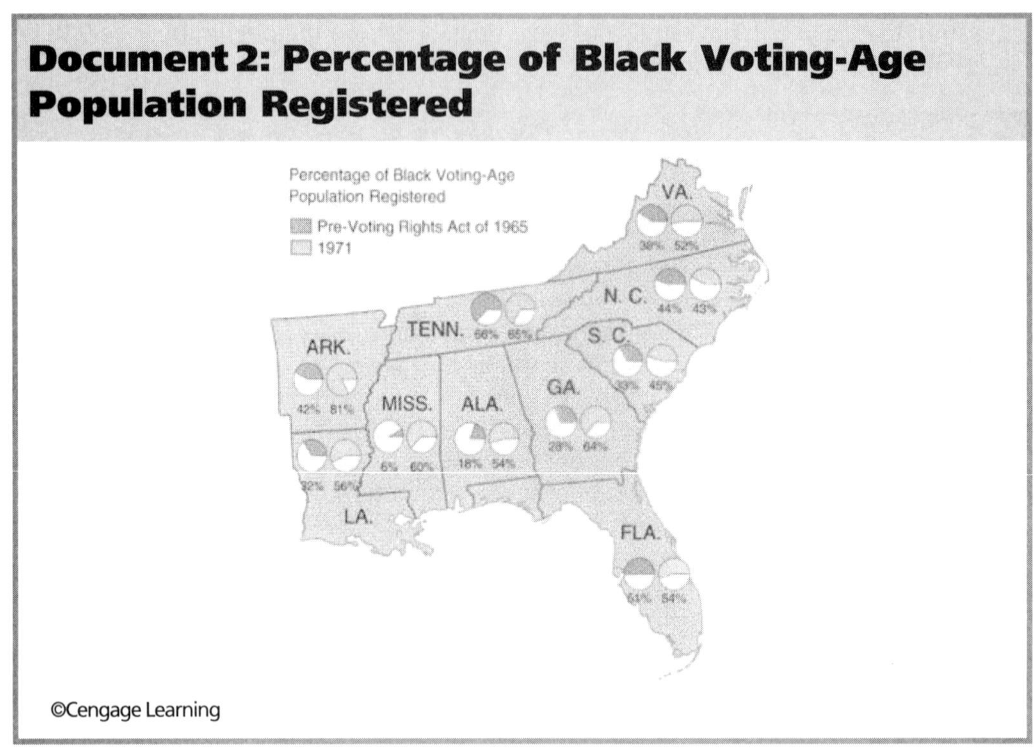

©Cengage Learning

Document 3: Freedom Ride, 1961

© Bettmann/Corbis

Document 4: Chicago Race Riot (1919)

The refusal of Policeman Daniel Callahan (white) . . . to arrest George Stauber (white) . . . last Sunday afternoon after the latter had knocked Eugene Williams, age 13 . . . from a raft as he was floating down Lake Michigan at Twenty-ninth street, fanned into action one of the worst race riots in the history of Illinois. Officer Callahan, it is charged, not only refused to make an arrest, but kept expert swimmers from reaching Williams. The news of Callahan's negligence reached the bathers at the Twenty-sixth street beach and a mob of fifty men marched to Twenty-ninth street to avenge the death of the boy. The patrolman's action so enraged the bathers that they pounced upon Callahan and commenced to pommel him. Callahan was chased to a drug store, where he summoned help. . . .

Source: Chicago Defender, *August 2, 1919, front page.*

Document 5: French Directive: "Concerning Black American Troops" (1918)

1. We must prevent the rise of any pronounced degree of intimacy between French officers and black officers. We may be courteous and amiable with these last, but we cannot deal with them on the same plane as with the white American officers without deeply wounding the latter. We must not eat with them, must not shake hands or seek to talk or meet with them outside of the requirements of military service.

2. We must not commend too highly the black American troops, particularly in the presence of [white] Americans. It is all right to recognize their good qualities and their services, but only in moderate terms, strictly in keeping with the truth.

3. Make a point of keeping the native cantonment population from "spoiling" the Negroes. [White] Americans become greatly incensed at any public expression of intimacy between white women with black men. They have recently uttered violent protests against a picture in the "Vie Parisienne" entitled "The Child of the Desert" which shows a [white] woman in a "cabinet particulier" with a Negro. Familiarity on the part of white women with black men is furthermore a source of profound regret to our experienced colonials who see in it an over-weening menace to the prestige of the white race.

Source: W.E.B. Du Bois, ed. "Documents of the War," The Crisis *28 (May 1919) Vol. 18: 1, pp. 16–18.*

GO ON TO NEXT PAGE

Document 6: Protest in Birmingham, Alabama (1963)

Charles Moore/Black Star/Stockphoto.com

AP Photo/Jackson Daily News/Fred Blackwell

Document 7: Onlookers with the Burned Body of Jesse Washington, Waco, Texas (1916)

Library of Congress

Document 8: School Segregation

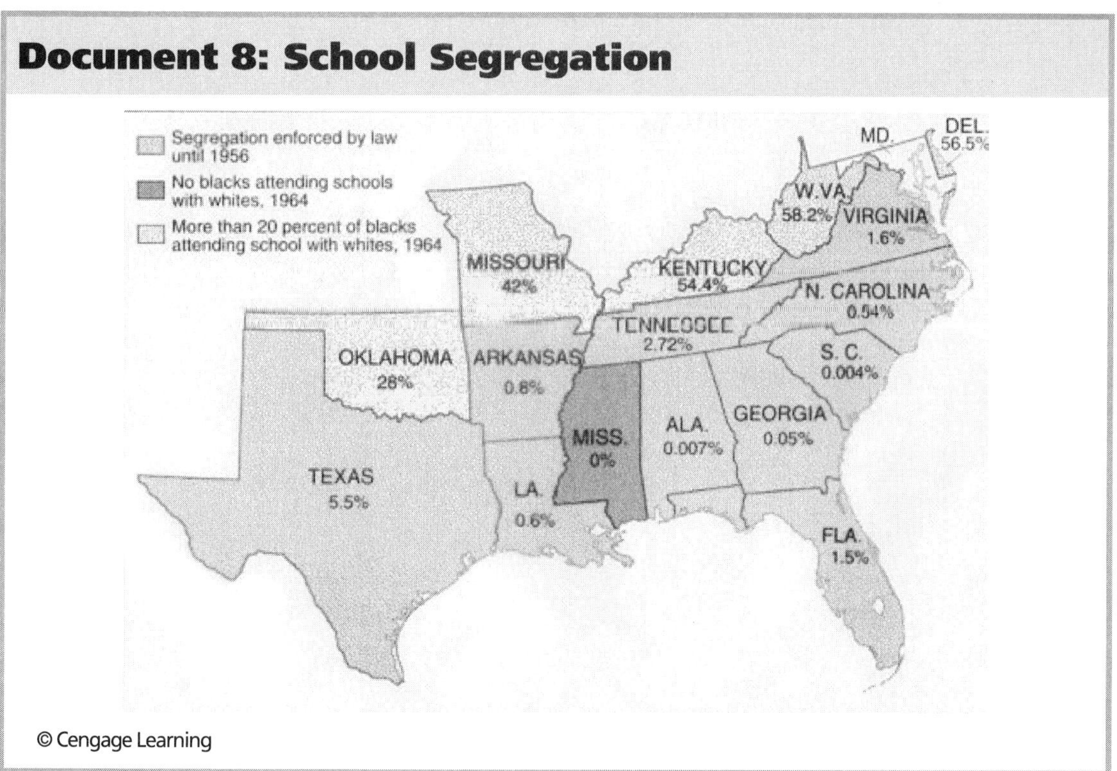

© Cengage Learning

End of documents for Question 1.
Go on to the next page.

GO ON TO NEXT PAGE

Part B: Long-Essay Questions
Writing Time—35 minutes

Directions Answer ONE of the following questions. It is recommended that you spend 5 minutes planning your essay and 30 minutes for writing. Write a well-structured, clearly written essay that provides sufficient evidence to support your thesis. Make certain to identify in the test booklet which essay question you have selected.

Question 1. Compare the relationship between Great Britain and its American colonies in the years prior to 1763 and that in the years after 1763.

Question 2. Compare the relationship between the United States and the Soviet Union in the years prior to 1945 and that in the years after 1945.

END OF EXAMINATION

ANSWERS FOR SECTION I

ANSWER KEY FOR MULTIPLE-CHOICE QUESTIONS

1. D	12. B	23. B	34. D	45. D
2. A	13. C	24. B	35. A	46. A
3. C	14. C	25. A	36. D	47. B
4. A	15. A	26. D	37. A	48. D
5. C	16. B	27. D	38. D	49. B
6. A	17. A	28. C	39. B	50. C
7. C	18. A	29. B	40. C	51. A
8. B	19. C	30. D	41. D	52. B
9. B	20. C	31. B	42. D	53. B
10. C	21. A	32. B	43. C	54. B
11. B	22. B	33. A	44. B	55. C

PART A: EXPLANATIONS FOR THE MULTIPLE-CHOICE ANSWERS

1. **(D)** One of the greatest weaknesses of the Articles of Confederation was that the national government had no power and no ability to tax, rendering it completely ineffective and unable to carry out even its meager duties. Under the Constitution, power was split between the states and the national government in order to remedy this (*The American Pageant* 14th ed., pp. 187–190/15th ed., pp. 170–172; Learning Objective POL-5).

2. **(A)** The stronger national government meant that other nations would respect and enter into trade agreements and treaties with the United States. It also ensured the smooth functioning of one nation working together as opposed to thirteen states working solely in their own interest (*The American Pageant* 14th ed., pp. 183–186/15th ed., pp. 166–167; Learning Objective ID-1).

3. **(C)** George Washington, one of the few nationally known figures at the time, was a natural choice as the first leader of the newly created executive branch (*The American Pageant* 14th ed., p. 200/15th ed., p. 181; Learning Objective POL-5).

4. **(A)** Distinct regional identities existed in the colonies and persisted even after independence. These identities were connected to economic activity, religion, family structure, and education. Moreover, smaller states worried that their power would be usurped by larger states that would impose their traditions and policies on them (*The American Pageant* 14th ed., pp. 192–195/15th ed., pp. 172–176; Learning Objective ID-1).

5. **(C)** In the beginning of Congressional Reconstruction African Americans in the South voted, held office, and participated in society, as the radical Republicans hoped (*The American Pageant* 14th ed., 515–518/15th ed., pp. 466–469; Learning Objective ENV-4).

6. **(A)** Despite early advances, as white southerners began to reclaim positions of power in the South the advances made by African Americans disappeared. By the end of Reconstruction the first Jim Crow laws began to appear (*The American Pageant* 14th ed., p. 533/15th ed., pp. 482–483; Learning Objective PEO-5).

7. **(C)** Foner discusses black males' participation in electoral politics in the early 1870s. This most closely links to the Fifteenth Amendment, which guaranteed black males' voting rights after the Civil War (*The American Pageant* 14th ed., p. 526/15th ed., p. 475; Learning Objective POL-5).

8. **(B)** Hayes won a bitter election after promising to withdraw federal troops from the South in a deal known as the Compromise of 1877. With the troops gone, white southerners felt free to rule the South as they wished (*The American Pageant* 14th ed., pp. 545–546/15th ed., pp. 494–495; Learning Objective POL-2).

9. **(B)** After years of declaring the United States neutral and refusing to trade with warring powers, the United States first amended this stance with cash and carry and later removed all barriers—except transportation-- to the Allies receiving military aid with lend-lease as they began to fall to German armies. The people, skeptical of involving the nation in another major war, needed to be convinced that providing weapons and war munitions was justifiable (*The American Pageant* 14th ed., pp. 868–869/15th ed., pp. 791–792; Learning Objective WOR-7).

10. **(C)** The Four Freedoms addressed what FDR saw happening in Europe as the Nazis spread their power and influence. With Freedom from Want, Roosevelt mentions the poverty and desperation that come with economic hardship associated with events like the Great Depression (*The American Pageant* 14th ed., p. 880 /15th ed., p. 803; Learning Objective WOR-4).

11. **(B)** The Axis powers saw the United States providing aid first to Britain, then to the USSR and eventually to China. This resulted in a target on the United States as it clearly chose one side over the other (The American Pageant 14th ed., pp. 870–871/15th ed., pp. 793–794; Learning Objective WOR-7).

12. **(B)** While the environment posed great challenges to the Anasazi, as evidenced by the passage, their ability to adapt combined with their use of technology enabled them to create urban settlements (*The American Pageant* 14th ed., pp. 8–11/15th ed., pp. 6–8; Learning Objective PEO-1).

13. **(C)** Though there was significant diversity among Native groups in the Northeast, most (like the Iroquois) took advantage of the abundance of available food resources to establish fixed settlements and villages (*The American Pageant* 14th ed., pp. 8–11/15th ed., pp. 6–8; Learning Objective PEO-1).

14. **(C)** Seeing these images in newspapers—they were on front pages around the world—and watching police attack children in

Birmingham on the evening news showed Americans the brutal actions of those opposing the civil rights movement. This changed public perception in some parts of the country as well as convincing leaders like John F. Kennedy that it was time to take action to protect African Americans and guarantee equal rights (*The American Pageant* 14th ed., pp. 980–982/15th ed., pp. 895–898; Learning Objective POL-7).

15. **(A)** The women's movement of the 1960s and 1970s, the anti-war movement, and the student movement all relied on the civil disobedience modeled by civil rights workers in the South. There was also a great deal of participant overlap in these movements (*The American Pageant* 14th ed., pp. 996–998/15th ed., pp. 910–913; Learning Objective ID-8).

16. **(B)** Nations worldwide published pictures of the atrocities committed against African American protestors, with many published on the front page of foreign language newspapers. This information also harmed the U.S.'s reputation as the land of the free, diminishing its bargaining power with the USSR and other nations whose behaviors the U.S. government condemned (*The American Pageant* 14th ed., pp. 979–982, 988–989/15th ed., pp. 895–898, 903–904; Learning Objective ID-8).

17. **(A)** After years of little progress, as well as violence against African Americans in the civil rights movement, Black Power advocates criticized nonviolence as too slow and continuing to allow whites physical, emotional, and legal power over African Americans. Disagreeing with the idea that nonviolence made civil rights protesters morally and ethically right and that this would, in fact, gain them the respect and equality they sought, Black Power advocates began to argue against integration in white society and in favor of reacting when confronted with violence (*The American Pageant* 14th ed., pp. 989–991/15th ed., pp. 904–905; Learning Objective POL-7)

18. **(A)** This is the first protest against slavery levied by a religious group in Pennsylvania, a northern colony at the same time as southern states like Virginia codified slave codes. This predicts the growing sectionalist tension that will revolve around slavery leading to the Civil War (*The American Pageant* 14th ed., p. 74/15th ed., p. 66; Learning Objective CUL-1).

19. **(C)** Slave holders relied on several arguments in defense of the "peculiar institution." One of the most common was the need throughout the country for slave labor, which indirectly benefited all sectors of the economy, including manufacturing (*The American Pageant* 14th ed., pp. 259, 262/15th ed., p. 234; Learning Objective WXT-1).

20. **(C)** Thoreau mentions overthrowing rulers who abuse their power and act tyrannically. These ideas derive from such Enlightenment thinkers as John Locke (*The American Pageant* 14th ed., pp. 362–363/15th ed., p. 329; Learning Objective CUL-4).

21. **(A)** Many people opposed the Mexican War, especially in the North where the need for land was not as pressing as it was for those in the South and the West. Critics who did not believe President Polk's reports that U.S. soldiers were attacked at the border asserted that there were ulterior motives for going to war with Mexico and that the entire thing was a hoax to ensure that the United States was able to fulfill its Manifest Destiny (*The American Pageant* 14th ed., pp. 407–408/15th ed., pp. 369–370; Learning Objective WOR-6).

22. **(B)** The disagreement about the war fell along sectional lines. Thus, much of the opposition to the war came from Northern Whigs who opposed the spread of slavery (*The American Pageant* 14th ed., p. 408/15th ed., p. 370; Learning Objective WOR-6).

23. **(B)** The Wilmot Proviso, which passed in the House of Representatives twice but never in the Senate, stated that slavery would be banned in any territory acquired as a result of the Mexican War (*The American Pageant* 14th ed., p. 414/15th ed., pp. 373, 376; Learning Objective POL-6).

24. **(B)** While President Obama faced many of the issues on this list the most pressing national problem in his first term was the massive economic crisis known as the Great Recession. Bringing the nation out of the recession was a major priority of the Obama administration in the first term and the focus of many laws and executive orders issued during those four years (*The American Pageant* 14th ed., pp. 1080–1081/15th ed., pp. 983–986; Learning Objective WXT-8).

25. **(A)** President Obama claims that Americans unify and work together during times of great crisis, but the "red and blue" mentality that exists in the country and the extreme congressional gridlock meant that neither the people nor the government could find common ground from which to build consensus on issues (Not in the text; Learning Objective POL-5).

26. **(D)** Obama and Roosevelt both faced massive economic crises and, eventually war. Both did so with an optimism meant to buoy the country in times of crisis in the hope of raising morale and reinvigorating the production and service sectors (*The American Pageant* 14th ed., pp. 825, 871–872, 1081/15th ed., pp. 754–755, 794–795, 983–986; Learning Objective POL-6).

27. **(D)** In addition to the fact that everyone knew about the blockades that existed and the tactics employed by the German navy, all passengers were clearly warned of the dangers of sailing on a ship under the flag of a belligerent nation (*The American Pageant* 14th ed., pp. 740–741/15th ed., pp. 672–673; Learning Objective WOR-7).

28. **(C)** The sinking of the Lusitania and death of over 100 Americans enraged the American people and forced the government to insist upon its freedom of the seas as a neutral nation, but it would take

two years and additional loss of life and cargo before America officially entered the war (*The American Pageant* 14th ed., pp. 741–742/15th ed., pp. 673–674; Learning Objective WOR-7).

29. **(B)** The Neutrality Acts specifically mandated that Americans and American ships avoid using waterways that served as war zones, having learned prior to entering World War I that freedom of the seas does not apply in wartime (*The American Pageant* 14th ed., p. 858/15th ed., pp. 782–783; Learning Objective WOR-7).

30. **(D)** America offered the promise of opportunity and advancement. Industries needed large numbers of unskilled workers for an ever increasing number of factories built in cities as industrialization progressed (*The American Pageant* 14th ed., pp. 599–606/15th ed., pp. 542–545; Learning Objective PEO-2).

31. **(B)** In both instances white northerners feared for their jobs, leading to tension between people who lived and worked in a place for most of their lives and newcomers whom they perceived as a threat to their livelihood and way of life (*The American Pageant* 14th ed., p. 608/15th ed., pp. 545–551; Learning Objective PEO-6).

32. **(B)** Native workers' fears coupled with the changes brought about by the massive influx of immigration led to legislation intended to restrict the number of immigrants coming to the country from nations outside of northern and western Europe. This began with the Chinese Exclusion Act and escalated to include the quotas passed in the 1920s (*The American Pageant* 14th ed., pp. 551, 773–774/15th ed., pp. 498, 703–704; Learning Objective ID-6).

33. **(A)** Although Johnson is most often connected with American involvement in Vietnam, presidents before and after him contributed to the quagmire as well. Though Johnson escalated the war, American presence there began before his time in office and extended beyond the 1968 election (*The American Pageant* 14th ed., 991–993, 1004–1005/15th ed. pp. 893, 906–908, 917–918; Learning Objective WOR-8).

34. **(D)** Vietnam was the first televised war. Americans could see coffins returning home and watch American soldiers under attack. In addition, trusted reporters like Walter Cronkite had a huge impact on American public opinion (Not in the text; Learning Objective CUL-7).

35. **(A)** The refusal to take responsibility and revelations of deceitful practices led many, especially among the younger generation, to question their faith in their leaders. This change in sentiment was, of course, condemned by those in power (*The American Pageant* 14th ed., p. 993/15th ed., pp. 906–908; Learning Objective ID-3).

36. **(D)** Vietnam, at the theoretical level, was about keeping communism out of South Vietnam and maintaining two distinct nations in Vietnam, one of which aligned with the United States.

U.S. actions, then, at the start of the war, reflect the policy of containment (*The American Pageant* 14th ed., p. 991/15th ed., p. 906; Learning Objective WOR-7).

37. **(A)** Many British colonists came to America seeking freedoms and rights that they did not have in Britain. These included religious freedom for some, especially in New England and Maryland. For others, the right to own land was a priority, since America, unlike Britain, did not have primogeniture laws (*The American Pageant* 14th ed., pp. 103–104/15th ed., p. 92; Learning Objective CUL-1).

38. **(D)** Until the end of the French and Indian War Britain operated under a policy of salutary neglect, allowing the colonies to govern themselves as long as the mother country continued to reap economic benefits. After the war, Britain began to levy taxes and other laws the colonists found oppressive, especially because the laws were passed without any colonial representation in Parliament (*The American Pageant* 14th ed., pp. 129–136/15th ed., pp. 116–122; Learning Objective WOR-2).

39. **(B)** In ruling that the press could not be punished for printing critical information so long as it was true, the Zenger trial established the broad freedom of the press that continues to exist in the United States. This was codified in the First Amendment and continues to be upheld by legislation and court decision (*The American Pageant* 14th ed., pp. 103–104/15th ed., p. 92; Learning Objective CUL-4).

40. **(C)** The Great Society emphasized domestic improvements and extending a variety of benefits and opportunities to the American people. Following his small government philosophy, Reagan believed that many of these programs were the province of the state, not the federal government. He increased the resources devoted to military spending in order to best the USSR in the Cold War, including the development of a satellite-based missile defense system known as the Strategic Defense Initiative (*The American Pageant* 14th ed., pp. 1033–1035/15th ed., pp. 944–946; Learning Objective POL-3).

41. **(D)** Reagan believed that the federal government should be responsible for the well-being of the nation, but not all of the needs of the individuals in it. Thus, while Reagan believed in stimulating the economy, he believed social services like Medicare and environmental policy were best left to the states (*The American Pageant* 14th ed., pp. 1033–1035/15th ed., pp. 944–945; Learning Objective POL-4).

42. **(D)** Among Reagan's economic policies was the deregulation of businesses and banks, leading to risky investments. In addition to myriad other factors, this is one reason for the so-called Great Recession (*The American Pageant* 14th ed., pp. 1035, 1080–1081/15th ed., pp., 951, 983–986; Learning Objective WXT-8).

43. **(C)** The caning of Charles Sumner by Preston Brooks became one of the most famous incidents leading up to the Civil War, as Brooks, in an effort to defend his family and his state, attacked Sumner for his anti-slavery views after Sumner made an especially inflammatory speech. This was indicative of the escalating tensions throughout the nation as the slavery issue flared (*The American Pageant* 14th ed., pp. 442–443/15th ed., pp. 400–401; Learning Objective POL-6).

44. **(B)** In 1856 the two sides of the slavery issue clashed in Kansas as both flooded in to cast their vote for a free or slave state as provided for by the Kansas-Nebraska Act. When violence broke out it was similar to a civil war on a smaller level, a microcosm of what was to come (*The American Pageant* 14th ed., pp. 440–442/15th ed., pp. 398–400; Learning Objective ID-6).

45. **(D)** Lincoln's election was the last straw for states that claimed they were willing to secede. Misinformed notions about Lincoln's desire to end slavery everywhere and the fact that he was elected without a single southern electoral vote justified the states' decisions (*The American Pageant* 14th ed., pp. 453–456/15th ed., pp. 410–413; Learning Objective POL-6).

46. **(A)** Plunkitt's description of "honest graft" details the way that city officials used their position to grow wealthy at the city's expense, long a target of those who targeted political machines (*The American Pageant* 14th ed., p. 540/15th ed., p. 489; Learning Objective POL-2).

47. **(B)** Political machines, for all of their faults, could be extremely beneficial for immigrants, providing them with homes, jobs, and paths to citizenship. As large numbers of immigrants arrived in America, they sustained these organizations (*The American Pageant* 14th ed., p. 606/15th ed., pp. 546–547; Learning Objective ID-5).

48. **(D)** Political reforms like referendum, initiative, and recall were designed to give voters more of a say in government and make the process more democratic (*The American Pageant* 14th ed., pp. 708–709/15th ed., p. 641; Learning Objective POL-3).

49. **(B)** Despite the perception that Roosevelt and his policies were overwhelmingly liberal, he did surround himself with conservatives—including holdovers from the Hoover administration—in planning the New Deal and the acts and agencies that would become part of it (Not in the text; Learning Objective POL-4).

50. **(C)** Moley discusses rising public confidence as a significant effect of the bank holiday and "first hundred days" legislation. The New Deal, as a whole, inspired people who spent four years living in despair. Ultimately it was production related to World War II, not the New Deal, that brought America out of the Depression (*The American Pageant* 14th ed., p. 849/15th ed., pp. 774–775; Learning Objective WXT-8).

51. **(A)** Since FDR presidents who come into office during times of crisis are watched by politicians and the media to see what they will accomplish in the "first hundred days." Most recently this was one way the media evaluated Barack Obama's presidency (*The American Pageant* 14th ed., pp. 826–827/15th ed., pp. 754–755; Learning Objective POL-4).

52. **(B)** Americans suffering during the Great Depression felt that they'd been abandoned by their president, dubbing shantytowns "Hoovervilles" and the newspapers that kept them warm "Hoover blankets." Hoover's stance that the national government was not responsible for individual economic relief and that people should "pull themselves up by their bootstraps" are his Depression-related legacy. In fact, by the time he left office Hoover and his advisors had several economic plans in the works. His administration did not last to see their fruition, and FDR receives credit for many of these ideas (*The American Pageant* 14th ed., pp. 816–818/15th ed., pp. 744, 746; Learning Objective WXT-8).

53. **(B)** The first two presidents of the United States were Federalists and Jefferson was a Democratic-Republican. People were unsure if the transition of power from one party to another would happen peacefully and if the Constitution could withstand this change in government. In addition, Jefferson's election had been especially contentious, ultimately decided in the House of Representatives. Hence, Jefferson's attempt to assuage the people's concerns (*The American Pageant* 14th ed., pp. 226–228/15th ed., pp. 203–204; Learning Objective POL-2).

54. **(B)** Jefferson believed in a strict interpretation of the Constitution. Although there is nothing in the Constitution that gives the president permission to buy land from foreign countries, Jefferson acted on the offer to buy Louisiana from Napoleon understanding the numerous benefits for the United States (*The American Pageant* 14th ed., pp. 234–235/15th ed., pp. 210–212; Learning Objective WOR-5).

55. **(C)** Political parties evolved from the differences between these two camps in the young United States. The Constitution doesn't mention political parties as an element of the electoral system. Since Washington's presidency, though, the nation has never been without at least one. Over the course of time, the relationship between the parties has grown more contentious (*The American Pageant* 14th ed., pp. 205–206/15th ed., p. 186; Learning Objective POL-2).

SECTION I, PART B: SHORT-ANSWER QUESTIONS

QUESTION 1

While Hamilton argues that the elastic (or necessary and proper) clause allows for the creation of the national bank, Jefferson asserts that this interpretation is not valid. Explaining the development of the first political parties requires an examination of these two men's opposing views on the nature of the Constitution. Hamilton supported a loose interpretation of the Constitution, arguing that whatever it did not forbid should be allowed in the interest of strengthening the nation. Jefferson, on the other hand, feared tyranny above all and supported a strict interpretation of the Constitution. He believed that any power not explicitly given to the national government must therefore be prohibited to it. You might discuss the difference in opinions over the relative status of the state governments or their clash over the economic future of the nation.

QUESTION 2

The question here asks you to choose an area—social, economic, or political—and give one piece of evidence demonstrating the success of Reconstruction followed by a piece of evidence refuting that success.

In rebuilding the economy of the South, advances were made in industrializing the region and in rebuilding the agricultural foundation. Nevertheless, consider who profited from that reconstruction—especially so-called carpetbaggers—and evaluate the relative success of the new system of sharecropping.

In relation to the former slaves, great strides were made in establishing their constitutional rights. Nevertheless, consider the shortcomings of the Freedman's Bureau, the rise of the KKK, and the growth of Black Codes following the establishment of Redeemer governments by 1877.

In regard to political reconstruction, evaluate the partisan divide between Republicans and Democrats and its persistence through the end of (and beyond) the nineteenth century. Discuss the rise of Republican governments in the South under military reconstruction and their subsequent replacement by Redeemer Democrats.

QUESTION 3

This image shows elements of paternalism and an unmistakable sense of pride in American accomplishments by 1900. The depiction of the "happy" people of the new American colonies and the smiling Uncle Sam indicates that America's claim over these people is just and benevolent. On the map—and represented among the people at the front of the image—are shown the American territories of Puerto Rico, Hawaii, the Philippines, and Guam.

A discussion of this image must include some reference to the debate over the acquisition of the Philippines—and perhaps to President McKinley's decision to "uplift, civilize, and Christianize" the Filipinos. The so-called "white man's burden" was heavily debated in this country, as was the decision by a nation that had overthrown colonial tyranny to take a colony of its own.

Policies you might discuss include the decision to retain the Philippines following the Spanish-American War (and the subsequent Philippine-American War), or the decision to get involved in the Spanish-American War at all. The Platt Amendment and the refusal to grant American citizenship to territorial possessions similarly supports these ideas.

Question 4

Essentially, this question asks you to examine Reagan's role in the rise of conservatism since 1980. Besides the fiscal policy goal listed in the passage, other evidence of conservatism in American government includes the influence of the Moral Majority and other evangelicals on American policies (related to issues like HIV/AIDS, gay marriage, and abortion) or the increasing power of corporations in national politics.

Discussions of Reagan's role ought to reference his political appeal, and might mention his nickname as the "Great Communicator." Furthermore, the apparent (at least, to conservatives) success of "Reaganomics" served to cement Reagan's role as hero even as did FDR's supposed salvation of the nation's economy. On the other hand, Reagan himself could be argued to have been ambivalent and uninvolved in most major governmental actions.

Section II, Part A: Document-Based Question (DBQ)

Below are short analyses of the documents. The italicized words suggest what your margin notes might include.

Document 1 In this letter to a northerner, *a desperate black Alabaman* pleads to be given the means to come to the North *to escape the discrimination, intimidation, and threats of violence* that defined the lives of black Americans in the South *around the time the United States entered World War I,* a conflict in which black soldiers fought nobly.

Document 2 This map and pie chart show that the *Voting Rights Act of 1965 enfranchised considerably more black southerners* than before the legislation was passed. Take note of *Mississippi as a stunning example of this change.*

Document 3 This photograph of the Freedom Riders' bus burning near Anniston, Alabama, demonstrates *white southerners' hatred of civil rights activists and their cause.* Rather than tolerate this peaceful protest, in which both black and white activists challenged segregation inside bus stations, *white southerners set fire to their buses and severely beat protestors, who were forced to flee.*

Document 4 This document discusses the *reaction of black Chicagoans* to the *murder of a young black swimmer* who had inadvertently drifted into a *segregated white bathing area* on Lake Michigan. The event *touched off one of the worst race riots in the nation's history.* The time and place of the riot indicate that even as late as the *post–World War I period northern blacks faced discrimination and segregation* like that found in the South, and they were *angered by their treatment* to the point where they *struck back at their oppressors.* In other words, *migration north was not synonymous with equality.*

Document 5 In this document the *French military* provides its troops with *advice regarding the complexities and nuances of American racism* so that they *would not antagonize or alienate the white American troops fighting in France.* Take note of the comment regarding *black officers, who were also relegated to a second-class status.*

DOCUMENT 6 This photograph shows what happened to black demonstrators in Birmingham, Alabama, *one of the nation's most segregated cities,* in 1963. Civil rights leaders organized a protest known as the Children's Crusade, in which *teenagers, rather than their parents, took to the streets to fight for equal rights.* Bull Connor and the city's police force responded by *spraying protestors with fire hoses strong enough to strip bark from trees and setting police dogs on peaceful teenagers.* Television coverage of this event spread throughout the world and convinced President Kennedy to act.

DOCUMENT 7 Taken in the early 1900s, this *photograph of the lynching and burning of a black man* has taken on an *atmosphere of amusement* judging from the facial expressions of the onlookers. You are left to draw your own conclusion about the *extent of "justice" meted out to black Americans* during this period in U.S. history.

DOCUMENT 8 While this *map shows some improvement in integrating public schools,* with the exception of Missouri, Oklahoma, Kentucky, and West Virginia, the *extent of improvement is negligible in the South. Contrast this map with Document B* (Black Registration in the South, 1964). *While Mississippi has registered a considerable number of black voters by 1965, schools in the state were still not integrated.*

One way to designate each document is by its basis—political, social, or economic. Keep in mind that some have more than one designation. This form of categorization can be seen below:

Political	**Social**	**Economic**
A	A	A
B		
C	C	
	D	
	E	
F	F	
G		G
	H	

In developing your essay, you should incorporate the following historical information:

- The legitimization of racial segregation was articulated in the *Plessy* v. *Ferguson* decision in 1896, in which the Supreme Court ruled that as long as facilities were equal for the races, segregation was constitutional.
- A number of significant groups formed early in the twentieth century, among them the Niagara Movement in 1905, the NAACP in 1908, the National Urban League in 1911, and the United Negro Improvement Association in 1916.
- The rise in popularity of the KKK in the 1920s was profound.
- The Committee on Civil Rights was formed in 1946.
- The federal government and the military were desegregated in 1948.

- The Supreme Court decision in *Brown* v. *Board of Education of Topeka, Kansas* in 1954 was a watershed.
- Demographics changed as more and more blacks migrated north.
- Important black political leaders such as Dr. Martin Luther King, Jr., and Malcolm X emerged. In addition, after World War II more civil rights organizations such as the Southern Christian Leadership Conference (SCLC), the Black Muslim movement, and, in the 1960s, the Student Non-Violent Coordinating Committee (SNCC) formed.
- The Montgomery bus boycott focused national attention on the plight of blacks.
- Nonviolent protests were aimed at segregated lunch counters, bus terminals, hotels, and other public facilities.
- Freedom Summer (1964) was an effort to register southern blacks to vote and provide educational support for the underfunded black communities in the South.
- Congress passed important legislation such as the Civil Rights Act of 1964 and the Voting Rights Act of 1965.

A Sample Essay

If you take the view that racism remained prevalent from World War I to the 1960s, your essay might look something like this:

While some substantial gains were made in combating racism in the period from World War I to the 1960s, a legacy of racism and discrimination lingered in the United States in the 1960s. Despite the fact that President Wilson had claimed that the United States was fighting in World War I to "make the world safe for democracy," this obviously did not include black Americans, quite a few of whom actually were doing the fighting in Europe. In 1916, the year before the United States entered World War I, President Wilson won passage of the Jones Act, which gave Filipinos basic democratic rights, including universal male suffrage. The same cannot be said of Wilson's attitudes towards black Americans. As a Virginian he was steeped in the racial ideology of the South. To avoid offending those Americans, in both the North and the South, who opposed racial equality, the French military advised its troops not to treat black American soldiers as equal to white American soldiers. "We cannot deal with them [black officers] on the same plane as with white American officers without deeply wounding the latter" (Document E).

So poor were conditions for black southerners that they were relegated to living out their lives in quiet desperation as sharecroppers and tenant farmers. The material demands of the war provided some opportunities for blacks to migrate north if they could, as expressed in Document A, in which a desperate black migrant appeals for assistance to move his family to the North in order to escape the persecution, intimidation, and violence associated with the South in this period. For those blacks who challenged the status quo or who broke the law, a different kind of "justice" was meted out, as shown in Document G, a photograph of a black man who has been lynched and his body burned as a warning to other blacks. In fact, so frequent were cases of lynching during the World War I era that the NAACP would hang a banner outside one of its northern offices that read: "Today a black man was lynched in the South." Not surprisingly, the Ku Klux Klan experienced a massive rebirth during the postwar years. Yet this period witnessed the emergence of important black civil rights organizations such as the Niagara Movement, led by W. E. B. Du Bois.

Unfortunately, by World War II attitudes had not dramatically changed in the United States in regards to its black citizens. The nation, including the military, continued to be segregated (a condition legitimized by the *Plessy* v. *Ferguson* Supreme Court decision in 1896). It was not until after the war that the military and the federal government were desegregated. In 1954 the Supreme Court overturned *Plessy* in its landmark decision in *Brown* v. *Board of Education.* Yet, in 1964, Mississippi schools were still not integrated (Document H). Although it was now unconstitutional to segregate the races, racist attitudes take a longer time to die.

To be sure, there were successes along the way, such as the Montgomery bus boycott, led by Dr. Martin Luther King, Jr. Also various southern universities such as the University of Alabama were integrated. Added to this was the passage of the Civil Rights Act in 1964 and the Voting Rights Act the following year, which went a long way in integrating public schools in the South. As more and more blacks and whites began to protest against racial injustice, discrimination, and segregation, many in the South responded shamefully and at times violently, as expressed in the southern response to the Freedom Rides in 1961 (Document C) and the Freedom Summer (1964), which sought to register blacks to vote and provide educational assistance. We see this clearly in Document F, showing the Birmingham, Alabama police and fire departments opening fire hoses on peaceful young protestors. Thus by the middle of the 1960s the government and civil rights activists had taken significant steps to address racial discrimination, but the attitudes of the World War I era continued unabated well into the 1960s.

COMMENT: This essay effectively synthesized document information—six of the nine documents—with appropriate comments and analysis of important outside information relating to the topic. The view that racial attitudes were maintained throughout the period from World War I to the 1960s despite some important civil rights gains is sustained throughout the essay.

SCORING: Based on the AP U.S. History Document-Based Question Rubric as established by the College Board, you should score your essay as follows (with a maximum possible score of 7).

A. Thesis: 0–1 point

Give 1 point for a stated thesis that directly answers all parts of the question. It must do more than simply restate the question.

B. Analysis of historical evidence and support of argument: 0–4 points

Give 1 point for an essay that offers plausible analysis of the content of a majority of the document, explicitly using that analysis to support the stated thesis or a relevant argument, OR

Give 2 points for an essay that offers plausible analysis of BOTH the content of a majority of the documents, explicitly using this analysis to support the stated thesis or a relevant argument; AND at least one of the following for the majority of the documents: intended audience, purpose, historical context, and/or the author's point of view, OR

Give 3 points for an essay that offers plausible analysis of BOTH the content of all or all but one of the documents, explicitly using this analysis to support the stated thesis or a relevant argument; AND at least one of the following for all or all but one of the documents: intended audience, purpose, historical context, and/or the author's point of view.

PLUS: **Add 1 additional point** for an essay that offers plausible analysis of historical examples beyond or outside of the documents to support the stated thesis or a relevant argument.

C. Contextualization: 0–1 point

Give 1 point for an essay that accurately and explicitly connects historical phenomena relevant to the argument to broader historical events and/or processes.

D. Synthesis: 0–1 point

Give 1 point for an essay that appropriately extends or modifies the stated thesis or argument, OR

Give 1 point for an essay that effectively accounts for disparate, sometimes contradictory evidence from primary sources and/or secondary works in crafting a coherent argument, OR

Give 1 point for an essay that appropriately connects the topic of the question to other historical periods, geographical areas, contexts, or circumstances.

SECTION II, PART B: LONG-ESSAY QUESTIONS

QUESTION 1

Some would argue that the relationship between Great Britain and the American colonies prior to 1763 was based on salutary neglect. That is, Britain at this point had not placed restrictions on the colonists that were either exploitative or hard to avoid. Prior to 1763 the British had not yet imposed revenue-raising taxes on the colonies, although the British did seek to control and subordinate American trade and the American economy to its own needs. The Navigation Laws were a series of British laws that attempted to expand Britain's economy, often at the expense of the American colonies.

After 1763—the end of the French and Indian War—however, Britain's need to pay off war debts led it to levy a series of increasingly severe taxes on the colonists. Furthermore, the British began to crack down on the smuggling that was rampant in the colonies before the war. This interference in the colonial economy led to a rise in radicalism among colonists and, eventually, to calls for independence.

In order to develop a strong thesis, you should focus on the role that the French and Indian War (which concluded in 1763) had in altering the relationship between the British and Americans. You might choose to argue that the relationship between the two was benign and perhaps cordial before the Seven Years War, discussing the freedom given to the colonies and the lack of enforcement of existing laws. Alternatively, one might argue that the British had always sought to subordinate American capitalism to British capitalism and simply explain the shift occurring in 1763 as an increase by way of scale—discussing the pre-existing Hat, Iron, and Wool Acts along with the hated Navigation Acts.

QUESTION 2

Though tensions clearly existed between the Americans and the Soviets in the years before 1945, the relationship between the two nations during the war years was one of friendship. Some would argue that this relationship was one of expediency, but the extension of lend-lease dollars and the frequent diplomatic initiatives clearly indicate a strong level of cooperation in the mutual fight to defeat the Nazis.

After WW II, however, friendship and cooperation turned almost immediately into hostility and distrust. From the refusal to disclose the potential of the nuclear bomb to the 1948 showdown over Berlin (not to mention the rising red scare within the United States), the relationship had broken down to the point of near war.

Again, to develop a strong thesis, you must focus on the year offered (1945) as a point of transition. Why did things change after this year? You might argue that Russian aggression in Eastern Europe, combined with American fears of Communism, led to the breakdown in relationships—citing changes that occurred following Yalta and Potsdam. On the other hand, you might argue that hostilities always existed and that the cooperation that the two nations enjoyed during the war was simply evidence of their desperation in trying to meet the challenge posed by fascism.

SCORING: Based on the AP U.S. History Long Essay Question Rubric as established by the College Board, you should score your essay as follows (with a maximum possible score of 6).

A. Thesis: 0–1 point

Give 1 point for a stated thesis that directly answers all parts of the question. It must do more than simply restate the question.

B. Support for argument: 0–2 points

Give 1 point for an essay that supports a stated thesis or makes a relevant argument using specific evidence, OR

Give 2 points for an essay that supports the stated thesis or makes a relevant argument using specific evidence, clearly and consistently stating how the evidence supports the thesis or argument, and establishing clear linkages between the evidence and the thesis or argument.

C. Application of targeted historical thinking skill: 0–2 points

This is a COMPARISON Essay, therefore:

Give 1 point for an essay that describes similarities AND differences among historical developments, OR

Give 2 points for an essay that describes similarities AND differences among historical developments, providing specific examples AND analyzes the reasons for their similarities AND/OR differences OR evaluates the relative significance of the historical developments.

D. Synthesis: 0–1 point

Give 1 point for an essay that appropriately extends or modifies the stated thesis or argument, OR

Give 1 point for an essay that explicitly employs an additional appropriate category of analysis (e.g., political, economic, social, cultural, geographical, race/ethnicity, gender) beyond that called for by the prompt, OR

Give 1 point for an essay that appropriately connects the topic of the question to other historical periods, geographical areas, contexts, or circumstances.

It is important that you be as objective as possible when evaluating your essays. You might ask a teacher, parent, fellow student, or friend to evaluate your essays for you and to offer advice on areas for improvement.

PRACTICE TEST 2

AP UNITED STATES HISTORY EXAMINATION
Section I
Part A: Multiple-Choice Questions
Time—55 minutes
Number of Questions—55

Directions Each question below is part of a set of 2–5 questions that focus on a primary source, secondary source, or other historical issue. Each individual question has four possible answers. For each question, select the best response.

Questions 1–3 refer to the following quotations.

"Now we ask, whether any man can coolly contemplate the idea of recalling our troops from the [Mexican] territory we at present occupy…and…resign this beautiful country to the custody of the ignorant cowards and profligate ruffians who have ruled it for the last twenty five years? Why, humanity cries out against it. Civilization and Christianity protest against this reflux of the tide of barbarism and anarchy."

—*New York Evening Post,* 1848

"The act of sending an armed force among the Mexicans was unnecessary, in as much as Mexico was in no way molesting or menacing the United States or the people thereof; and…it was unconstitutional, because the power of levying war is vested in Congress, and not in the President."

—Abraham Lincoln, June 1, 1860

1. Based on the above quotes, how did the Mexican War cause a high level of controversy in the United States?
   (A) Government officials could not agree on the size of Mexican territory they hoped to win at the end of the war.
   (B) The strength of the Mexican army causes massive casualties that horrified most Americans.
   (C) The similarities between the Mexican and American people led people to disagree with the war.
   (D) The role of the executive branch in encouraging war was debated in the government, in the press, and among the people.

2. Which of the following statements most accurately portrays the effect of the Mexican War on the national political climate?
   (A) The American public put aside their political and sectional differences to focus on the war effort.
   (B) The idea of fulfilling the nation's Manifest Destiny trumped other political issues and became the central focus of national attention.
   (C) The possibility of slavery expanding with the country exacerbated long existing tensions and hostilities within the country.
   (D) A new political party emerged in opposition to the war.

3. How do the above quotes set a precedent for the debate over imperialism fifty years later?
   (A) Mexico remained the focus of imperialists' goals after winning only a portion of the nation's land in the 1840s.
   (B) The role of leadership in a nation became a deciding factor in whether or not it became a

GO ON TO NEXT PAGE

target of American expansionists.
(C) Similar ideas about civilizing and Christianizing people as well as the presidential power to do so abound in imperialists' writing.
(D) The power of the U.S. military decreased after the Civil War, placing more attention on theory moving forward.

Questions 4–6 refer to the following quotation.

"[Dr. Martin Luther] King's stress on love and nonviolence was powerfully effective in building a sympathetic following throughout the nation, among whites as well as blacks. But there were blacks who thought the message naïve, that while there were misguided people who might be won over by love, there were others who would have to be bitterly fought, and not always with nonviolence."

—Howard Zinn, excerpt from *The People's History of the United States* (1980)

4. Which of the following groups of reformers laid out the promises that Dr. Martin Luther King and his fellow activists would seek to fulfill in the 1950s and 1960s?
(A) Progressive-era muckrakers
(B) Jacksonian-era Democrats
(C) Antebellum compromisers
(D) Reconstruction-era Radical Republicans

5. Which of the following statements most accurately describes the response of the federal government to the activism of King and others?
(A) By channeling the group's frustrations into anti-Communist rhetoric, the government managed to avoid taking action until after the turbulent Vietnam years.
(B) As public support mounted for the reformers, each branch of the federal government sought in its own way to promote measures of desegregation and enfranchisement.
(C) Out of fears of racial violence, the national government federalized many state institutions to ensure their rapid compliance with new national mandates.
(D) Acting on the belief that activists were seeking to initiate class conflict, the national government utilized its resources to crush large-scale protests and avoid changes that would upset the delicate balance in the Democratic Party.

6. The debate among activists about tactics for reform, as reflected in these passages, was most directly brought about by
(A) the refusal of the federal government to enforce integration mandates in southern schools.
(B) a widespread economic downturn in the mid-1960s, which hurt minorities disproportionately.
(C) strong white resistance in the South, including a string of violence directed toward activists.
(D) the failure of most nonviolent protests to achieve change, particularly in the realm of desegregation attempts.

Questions 7–8 refer to the following quotation.

"Who of those in future centuries will believe this? I myself who am writing this and saw it and know the most about it can hardly believe that such was possible."

—Bartolome de Las Casas, 1542

7. Based on the above quote, what conclusion can be drawn about European treatment of the natives in America?
(A) Europeans were especially kind to the natives they found when they landed in America.
(B) Europeans ignored the natives, preferring to explore on their own.

(C) Europeans demolished native populations through hard work and disease.
(D) Europeans attempted to replicate native cultures and traditions.

8. In which of the following ways did early treatment of natives affect the relations between Europeans and Native Americans later?
(A) Native Americans learned to resist European colonization and often drove away later groups that arrived in the Americas.
(B) The relationship between conqueror and conquered set a precedent for future enslavement and subjugation of the Europeans over the natives.
(C) Both groups were able to peacefully coexist after de Las Casas revealed the way in which Spanish explorers decimated the Arawaks.
(D) Native Americans learned to respect and fear Europeans, preventing future violent clashes between the two groups.

Questions 9–11 refer to the following quotation.

"American B-52 bombers dropped about 104,000 tons of explosives on Communist sanctuaries in neutralist Cambodia during a series of raids in 1969 and 1970.... The secret bombing was acknowledged by the Pentagon the Monday after a former Air Force major...described how he falsified reports on Cambodian air operations and destroyed records on the bombing missions actually flown."

—*The Washington Post,* July 17, 1973

9. Considering the atmosphere in the country in the 1960s, what effect might these revelations have on the American public?
(A) The American people supported the bombing of Cambodia as a necessary part of the war effort in Indochina.
(B) The American people began to understand the tactics used by the Johnson administration leading to a post-presidency increase in his approval.
(C) Americans blamed the army for following orders that led to crimes against civilians.
(D) The people protested against the Cambodian raids and faith in the government once again decreased despite the election of a new president.

10. Which Cold War policy did U.S. military action in Korea, Vietnam, and Cambodia hope to achieve?
(A) Brinkmanship
(B) Mutually assured destruction
(C) Containment
(D) Détente

11. How does the above report contradict the majority of Nixon's foreign policy goals?
(A) Nixon's foreign policy focused on nations in the Western Hemisphere rather than those farther from home.
(B) Nixon emphasized a theory of détente, taking major steps to cool—rather than to escalate—tensions with long-standing enemies.
(C) The Nixon administration preferred an isolationist foreign policy to work on domestic issues.
(D) Nixon focused solely on large powerful nations and ignored smaller nations all over the globe.

Questions 12–14 refer to the following quotations.

"For having protected, favored, and emboldened the Indians against His Majesty's loyal subjects, never contriving, requiring, or appointing any due or proper means of satisfaction for their many invasions, robberies, and murders committed upon us."

—Nathaniel Bacon accusing Governor William Berkeley, 1676

GO ON TO NEXT PAGE

"I have lived thirty four years amongst you [Virginians], as uncorrupt and diligent as ever [a] governor was, [while] Bacon is a man of two years amongst you, his person and qualities unknown to most of you, and to all men else, by any virtuous act that ever I heard of... I will take counsel of wiser men than myself, but Mr. Bacon has none about him but the lowest of the people."

—Governor William Berkeley responds to Nathaniel Bacon, 1676

12. What do these quotes suggest about the relationship between white settlers, Native Americans, and colonial government in seventeenth-century Virginia?
    (A) White settlers believed the government prioritized the interests of Native Americans over their own, to white settlers' detriment.
    (B) Colonial governors established a colony where all three groups lived and worked together for the good of the colony.
    (C) Native Americans were given independence and control in Virginia that they didn't experience elsewhere.
    (D) The three groups existed separately on the same land with little interaction.

13. What conclusions can be drawn about the social hierarchy in the southern colonies based on this exchange?
    (A) Native Americans and Africans achieved greater social position than small farmers and other poor whites.
    (B) White farmers rose to the highest levels of society.
    (C) White farmers felt threatened by Native Americans, whom they believed should have lower social standing.
    (D) Governors in different colonies decided who had social standing in each community.

14. How did the effects of Bacon's Rebellion go beyond Virginia?
    (A) Violence spilled into neighboring colonies like Maryland and Delaware.
    (B) Several colonies began to extend greater freedoms to Native Americans.
    (C) Wealthy whites realized that they needed a more subservient labor force than indentured servants.
    (D) Farmers in many colonies rebelled against their colonial governors.

Questions 15–17 refer to the following political cartoon.

THE BIG STICK IN THE CARIBBEAN SEA

Granger Collection

15. Based on the above political cartoon, what conclusions can you draw about the U.S.'s relationship with Latin America at the beginning of the twentieth century?
    (A) The United States played the role of the benevolent neighbor anxious to help Latin America when called upon.
    (B) The United States exerted its influence over the region regardless of the needs or desires of the Latin American nations themselves.
    (C) The United States conquered and colonized several Latin American nations in the interest of protecting them from European investors.
    (D) The United States remained isolationist and stayed out of Latin American affairs except to trade.

16. Which of the following acts best exemplifies the main idea of the cartoon?
    (A) The Platt Amendment
    (B) The Teller Amendment
    (C) The Monroe Doctrine
    (D) Freedom of the seas

17. How did U.S. dominance in Latin America change the region's geography?
    (A) The U.S. adjusted the borders of nations over which it exerted influence.
    (B) The U.S. destroyed rainforests to acquire natural resources.
    (C) The U.S. closed rivers to prevent European trade.
    (D) The U.S. constructed the Panama Canal through the Isthmus of Panama.

Questions 18–20 refer to the following quotation.

"Iraq continues to flaunt its hostility toward America and to support terror. The Iraqi regime has plotted to develop anthrax, and nerve gas, and nuclear weapons for over a decade. This is a regime that has already used poison gas to murder thousands of its own citizens—leaving the bodies of mothers huddled over their dead children. This is a regime that agreed to international inspections—then kicked out the inspectors. This is a regime that has something to hide from the civilized world.

States like these, and their terrorist allies, constitute an axis of evil, arming to threaten the peace of the world. By seeking weapons of mass destruction, these regimes pose a grave and growing danger. They could provide these arms to terrorists, giving them the means to match their hatred. They could attack our allies or attempt to blackmail the United States. In any of these cases, the price of indifference could be catastrophic."

—George W. Bush, *State of the Union,* 2002

18. Which of the following actions might be justified by George W. Bush's 2002 State of the Union?
    (A) Increasing troops deployed to Afghanistan
    (B) Military tribunals in Guantanamo Bay
    (C) Air strikes on Pakistan
    (D) The capture of Saddam Hussein

19. Which of the following statements best explains the U.S.'s role in the world in the twenty first century?
    (A) The post–Cold War United States is heavily involved in the Middle East and its foreign policy is devoted to taking action against terrorists in many parts of the world.
    (B) The United States suffered a significant decrease in power after the Cold War and has given up its position as a political, military, and cultural leader in the world.
    (C) Resistance to globalization in the United States under the guise of American exceptionalism damaged its position in world markets.
    (D) The Great Recession that began in 2008 damaged other countries significantly enough to make the United States the only remaining superpower.

GO ON TO NEXT PAGE

20. In what way did Operation Desert Storm lead to the U.S.'s military action in Iraq in the twenty-first century?
   (A) The U.S. wanted to avenge the massive casualties of the first conflict.
   (B) The UN sanctions that Iraq violated were a result of Desert Storm.
   (C) Iraq invaded Kuwait again, reigniting the conflict.
   (D) The U.S. military sought resources it could not find during the first war.

Questions 21–23 refer to the following map.

Cengage Learning

21. Based on the map, how had the U.S. economy changed by 1900?
   (A) The Southeast transitioned from being primarily agricultural to focusing on its industrial output in the years after the Civil War.
   (B) The United States was forced to deal with foreign nations to import the oil that it needed.
   (C) Different regions of the country began to specialize in various raw materials or industrial outputs.
   (D) The Northeast was the primary region of manufacturing.

22. Based on the map, why was the Northeast a more popular destination for immigrants than other regions?
   (A) The Northeast offered more opportunities for unskilled laborers than regions with fewer factories or more specialized labor needs.
   (B) Segregation in the South prevented immigrants from northern and western Europe from seeking opportunities there.
   (C) By 1900 few immigrants chose to enter the nation through ports in California due to the

decreased opportunity to find gold.

(D) Few immigrants were employed in the meatpacking and food production plants in the Midwest.

23. Which of the following is an effect of the changes illustrated on the map?
    (A) The government started offering subsidies to farmers as agriculture waned in the United States.
    (B) The United States invested in a federal highway system to move products from one part of the country to another.
    (C) The government began to look for overseas markets as more goods were produced.
    (D) Discrimination decreased as all people worked in similar positions to bolster industry in the country.

Questions 24–27 refer to the following quote.

"The object of recovery is to increase the national output and put more men to work. In the economic system of the modern world, output is primarily produced for sale; and the volume of output depends on the amount of purchasing power... Broadly speaking, therefore, an increase of output cannot occur unless by the operation of one or other of three factors. Individuals must be induced to spend more out of their existing incomes; or the business world must be induced, either by increased confidence in the prospects or by a lower rate of interest, to create additional current incomes in the hands of their employees... or public authority must be called in aid to create additional current incomes through the expenditure of borrowed or printed money. In bad times the first factor cannot be expected to work on a sufficient scale. The second factor will come in as the second wave of attack on the slump after the tide has been turned by the expenditures of public authority. It is, therefore, only from the third factor that we can expect the initial major impulse."

—John Maynard Keynes, "An Open Letter to President Roosevelt," *New York Times* (December 31, 1933)

24. The call for action issued here by John Maynard Keynes in many ways echoed the aspirations of
    (A) the Progressives.
    (B) the Jacksonian Democrats.
    (C) the Jeffersonian Republicans.
    (D) the Federalists.

25. Though John Maynard Keynes here lists the primary problem facing the nation in the 1930s as one of a lack of purchasing power, the root cause of this issue was
    (A) agricultural overproduction.
    (B) overregulation of major industries.
    (C) wild boom-bust cycles in the financial markets.
    (D) environmental degradation.

26. The lasting legacy of President Franklin D. Roosevelt's ultimate response to the Great Depression was
    (A) a decline in public trust of national economic policy.
    (B) an increase in the role of the federal government at providing social and economic security to the nation's citizens.
    (C) an unsustainable tax structure that placed too high a burden on the nation's working class.
    (D) a long-term decline in partisanship in light of the unified support for the New Deal among members of both parties.

27. Based on this description, which president's policies after the Great Depression followed Keynesian philosophy?
    (A) Barack Obama
    (B) Ronald Reagan
    (C) Harry Truman
    (D) Gerald Ford

GO ON TO NEXT PAGE

Questions 28–30 refer to the following quotation.

"The nearer any government approaches to a republic the less business there is for a king. It is somewhat difficult to find a proper name for the government of England. Sir William Meredith calls it a republic; but in its present state it is unworthy of the name, because the corrupt influence of the crown, by having all the places in its disposal, hath so effectively swallowed up the power, and eaten out the virtue of the house of commons (the republican part of the constitution) that the government of England is nearly as monarchical as that of France or Spain."

Thomas Paine, *Common Sense*, 1776

28. Why would this characterization of England's government serve Thomas Paine's higher purpose?
    (A) Paine advocated for colonists to reach an agreement with England, and a strong government would assist in that process.
    (B) Paine wanted to overthrow the king and portraying him as all powerful would rally support for that cause.
    (C) Paine wanted American colonists to fear and hate their mother country, but colonists resisted feelings of hostility.
    (D) Paine presented a case for independence and portraying King George as all-powerful provided colonists with an identifiable enemy.

29. Which of the following political trends in the American colonies reflect Paine's depiction of the struggle for power in England?
    (A) Salutary neglect
    (B) Taxation without representation
    (C) Colonial self-government
    (D) Virtual representation

30. Which of the following documents reflects Americans' fear of the government Paine describes?
    (A) U.S. Constitution
    (B) Northwest Ordinance
    (C) Mayflower Compact
    (D) Articles of Confederation

Questions 31–32 refer to the following quotation.

...We owe it, therefore, to candor and to the amicable relations existing between the United States and those powers to declare that we should consider any attempt on their part to extend their system to any portion of this hemisphere as dangerous to our peace and safety. With the existing colonies or dependencies of any European power we have not interfered and shall not interfere. But with the Governments who have declared their independence and maintain it, and whose independence we have, on great consideration and on just principles, acknowledged, we could not view any interposition for the purpose of oppressing them, or controlling in any other manner their destiny, by any European power in any other light than as the manifestation of an unfriendly disposition toward the United States. In the war between those new Governments and Spain we declared our neutrality at the time of their recognition, and to this we have adhered, and shall continue to adhere, provided no change shall occur which, in the judgement of the competent authorities of this Government, shall make a corresponding change on the part of the United States indispensable to their security.... It is impossible that the allied powers should extend their political system to any portion of either continent without endangering our peace and happiness; nor can anyone believe that our southern brethren, if left to themselves, would adopt it of their own accord. It is equally impossible, therefore, that we should behold such interposition in any form with indifference. If we look to the comparative strength and resources of Spain and those new Governments, and their distance from each other, it must be obvious that she can never subdue them. It is still the true policy of the United States to leave the parties to themselves, in hope that other powers will pursue the same course. . . .

—James Monroe, Monroe Doctrine
December 2, 1823

31. How did the Monroe Doctrine differ from previous U.S. foreign policies?
    (A) The United States fulfilled its alliance by fighting with France during the Napoleonic Wars.
    (B) As per Washington's Farewell Address, the United States avoided inserting itself into other nations' affairs.

(C) The United States previously supported European colonization in the Western Hemisphere to avoid instability.
(D) The United States preferred financial over military incentives to maintain peace in Latin America.

32. Which of the following statements accurately describes the Monroe Doctrine's enduring significance in U.S. history?
(A) The United States was forced to enter several military conflicts to defend the independence of Latin American nations.
(B) The Monroe Doctrine became a tool of expansionists in the United States hoping to exert greater influence in Latin America at the turn of the century.
(C) The Monroe Doctrine served as a model for subsequent edicts aimed at other regions of the globe.
(D) Issuing the doctrine made the United States a significant world power in 1823, a status it has never relinquished.

Questions 33–34 refer to the following cartoon.

Library of Congress

33. Which constitutional issue was crucial to Congress's hostility to the League of Nations?
(A) Article X shifted the power to declare war from Congress to the League of Nations.
(B) After World War I many congressmen wanted to return to isolationism.
(C) Several senators didn't believe the president had the power to deviate from a proposed peace plan.
(D) Congress was concerned about diverting too many government funds to the League of Nations.

34. Which of the following accurately expresses an impact of the Senate's refusal to join the League of Nations?
(A) The League thrived as a Europe-centric organization.
(B) The United States remained completely isolated from world affairs until entering World War II in 1941.
(C) Without the United States the League was ineffective and fell apart as Europe neared the Second World War.
(D) The United States' status as a world power decreased in the eyes of other powerful nations.

GO ON TO NEXT PAGE

Questions 35–37 refer to the following quotation.

"The movement of the Constitution of the United States was originated and carried through principally by four groups of personal interests…money, public securities, manufactures, and trade/shipping… A large propertyless mass was…excluded at the outset from participation in the working of the framing of the Constitution.

The members of the Convention which drafted the Constitution were, with a few exceptions, immediately, directly, and personally interested in, and derived economic advantages from the establishment of the new system…. The Constitution was essentially an economic document based on the concept that the fundamental private rights of property are anterior to government and morally beyond the reach of popular majorities."

—Charles Beard, *An Economic Interpretation of the Constitution of the United States,* 1956, pp. 324–325

35. Based on Beard's quote, how did the delegates to the Constitutional Convention create a document that benefited themselves?
    (A) The majority of the Framers were wealthy professionals and landowners, and the Constitution therefore protected their personal interests.
    (B) Most of the delegates were bankers and industrialists who needed their stake in the national economy protected.
    (C) The Framers were concerned that the new government would seize their property and took steps to prevent that.
    (D) The Constitution created a caste system led by a powerful and wealthy aristocracy.

36. Which aspect of the Constitution might one cite to contradict Beard's argument?
    (A) The Electoral College
    (B) Congress's power to tax
    (C) The supremacy clause
    (D) The Bill of Rights

37. Why might abolitionists have agreed with Beard's ideas on the Constitution?
    (A) Many were not among the elite and were therefore left out of the convention and ratification process.
    (B) Abolitionists believed that the national government would be too dominated by northern financial interests.
    (C) Several provisions of the Constitution, according to many abolitionists, favored the property rights of slave owners over the individual rights of men.
    (D) The Constitution was written with westward expansion in mind, which included the expansion of slavery.

Questions 38–39 refer to the following image.

Bettmann/Corbis

38. In which of the following ways does the above image express backlash to the changes in the 1920s?
    (A) The rise of the KKK discouraged people from believing in organized religion.
    (B) Greater freedom and individuality for some minority groups led to a fundamentalist resurgence.
    (C) Educational reforms led to a state-by-state re-evaluation of curriculum at every level of schooling.
    (D) The massive casualties of World War I forced a nationwide examination of the country's ethics and values.

39. Which of the following ongoing battles is depicted in the above image?
    (A) Public v. private education
    (B) National v. state power
    (C) Separation of church and state
    (D) Minority rights in the South

Questions 40–42 refer to the following quotation.

"The Constitution is either a superior paramount law, unchangeable by ordinary means, or it is on a level with ordinary legislative acts, and like other acts, is alterable when the legislature shall please to alter it. If the former part of the alternative be true, then a legislative act contrary to the Constitution is not law; if the latter part be true, then written constitutions are absurd attempts, on the part of the people, to limit a power in its own nature illimitable.... It is emphatically the province and duty of the judicial department to say what the law is.... If, then, the courts are to regard the Constitution, and the Constitution is superior to any act of the legislature, the Constitution, and not such ordinary act, must govern the case to which they are both applicable."

—John Marshall, Decision in *Marbury* v. *Madison*, 1803

40. How did the Supreme Court later apply the precedent set in *Marbury* v. *Madison*?
    (A) In the 1930s, the Supreme Court declared two major New Deal acts, the AAA and the NIRA, unconstitutional.
    (B) In 1955 the Court ruled that schools needed to desegregate with "all deliberate speed."
    (C) In 1965, the Court ruled that suspects must be informed of their rights before they are questioned in connection with a crime.
    (D) In 2000, the Court ruled in favor of George W. Bush, leading to his victory in that year's presidential election.

41. Which constitutional principle is affirmed by this decision?
    (A) Federalism
    (B) The supremacy clause
    (C) Popular sovereignty
    (D) Limited government

42. Which of the following examples describes an adverse effect of the Court's power to "say what the law is"?
    (A) The Warren Court expanded the rights of the accused in the 1960s.
    (B) Controversial decisions touch off protests and attempts to reverse the Court's judgment.
    (C) The *Dred Scott* decision overturned key slavery compromises.
    (D) The Marshall Court upheld the constitutionality of the national bank.

GO ON TO NEXT PAGE

Questions 43–45 refer to the following quotation.

"I ascribe the success of the Standard [Oil Company] to its consistent policy to make the volume of business large through the merits and cheapness of its products. It has spared no expense in finding, securing, and utilizing the best and cheapest methods of manufacturing. It has sought for the best superintendents and workmen and paid the best wages... It has not only sought markets for its principal products but for all possible byproducts. It has not hesitated to invest millions of dollars in methods of cheapening the gathering and distribution of oil by pipelines, special cars, tank steamers, and tank wagons... It is too late to argue about advantages of industrial combinations. They are a necessity."

—John D. Rockefeller, Testimony to the United States Industrial Commission before the House of Representatives (1899). *Annals of America*, vol. 12, 314–315

43. Beyond the economic justification advanced here by John D. Rockefeller, which of the following philosophical arguments would justify the power of large-scale industries?
    (A) The Social Gospel
    (B) Social Darwinism
    (C) Socialism
    (D) Industrial

44. Which of the following changes most strongly supported the growth of "industrial combinations" (or trusts) in the Gilded Age?
    (A) The expansion of the industrial workforce as a result of waves of immigration
    (B) The addition to the United States of vast new territories and a wealth of resources
    (C) The rise of the "New South" and an end to Southern reliance on sharecropping
    (D) The influence of wealthy businessmen in U.S. politics and the resulting governmental support of industry

45. Despite Rockefeller's confidence, the rise of "industrial combinations" (or trusts) led to significant controversy over
    (A) the role of states in regulating commerce.
    (B) immigration, especially from Eastern and Southern Europe.
    (C) the wealth gap and the responsibilities of industrial giants to the working class.
    (D) the decline in skilled jobs as mechanization of industry increased.

Questions 46–47 refer to the following image.

National Archives

46. Based on the above images, how did World War II lead to lasting changes in the United States?
    (A) Women's increased role in society and the workforce contributed to the feminist movement in the 1960s and 1970s.
    (B) Women were able to keep the jobs that they moved into during the war when men returned home.

(C) Women began to receive equal pay for equal work in several key industries.
(D) Women became more involved in military operations in the immediate aftermath of World War II.

47. Which of the following statements accurately describes the impact of the war on the nation's industry?
(A) The government devoted all of its financial resources to the war, leaving little available to counter the lingering effects of the Great Depression.
(B) War mobilization revived the nation's factories leading to a huge spike in output and hiring.
(C) Women were not able to work to men's capacity, slowing down the industrial process.
(D) Factories were unable to convert to peace time manufacturing at the end of the war and fell into debt again.

Questions 48–50 refer to the following quotation.

"Let the churches of all denominations speak out on the subject of temperance, let them close their doors against all who have anything to do with the death dealing abomination, and the cause of temperance is triumphant. A few years would annihilate the traffic. Just so with slavery.... It is a great national sin. It is a sin of the church. The churches by their silence, and by permitting slaveholders to belong to their communion, have been consenting to it.... The church cannot turn away from this question. It is a question for the church and for the nation to decide, and God will push it to a decision."

—Charles Grandison Finney, "Hindrances to Revivals," 1830s

48. Based on the above quote, what was one way in which alcohol consumpution and slavery were related?
(A) Both were acceptable because they existed in Biblical times.
(B) Both should be considered sinful and those who practice either of them should be removed from the church.
(C) Both were controversial subjects that led to dissent among congregations.
(D) The church refused to get involved with either cause, leaving both to be decided by local governments.

49. How were the Second Great Awakening and the civil rights movement of the 1960s similar?
(A) The church was an important fixture in both reform movements.
(B) Both believed that African Americans should have equal rights.
(C) Both encompassed social, economic, and medical causes.
(D) Both movements were supported by the majority of Americans.

50. How does the Second Great Awakening reflect a difference in religious thought in America?
(A) The church was formerly pro-slavery.
(B) Alcohol was a part of church ceremonies dating back to the establishment of Plymouth colony.
(C) Preachers previously avoided discussing how people lived their private lives.
(D) The church moved from being opposed to significant change to advocating in favor of it.

GO ON TO NEXT PAGE

Questions 51–53 refer to the following quotation.

"The Declaration of Independence mentions the Supreme Being no less than four times. 'In God We Trust' is engraved on our coinage. The Supreme Court opens its proceedings with a religious invocation. And the Members of Congress open their sessions with a prayer. I just happen to believe the schoolchildren of the United States are entitled to the same privileges as Supreme Court Justices and Congressmen."

—Ronald Reagan, March 8, 1983

51. Which constitutional principle did critics of Reagan's stance on school prayer claim that it violated?
    (A) Freedom of speech
    (B) Freedom of assembly
    (C) Separation of church and state
    (D) Right to privacy

52. Which of the following groups would support Reagan's stance on school prayer?
    (A) The Moral Majority
    (B) The American Civil Liberties Union
    (C) The National Organization for Women
    (D) The Strategic Defense Initiative

53. Based on this quote, why should schoolchildren engage in regular prayer?
    (A) It will help them focus on their studies for the day.
    (B) Prayer is a traditional part of American history and government.
    (C) Schools should be conducted similarly to political institutions.
    (D) The United States was founded as a Christian country and must continue to remind students of this heritage.

Questions 54–55 refer to the following documents.

Al Hirschfielargo Feiden Galleries LTD., New York. www.alhirschfield.com

"Until this moment, Senator, I think I never really gauged your cruelty or your recklessness. Little did I dream you could be so cruel as to do an injury to that lad.... If it were in my power to forgive you for your reckless cruelty, I would do so. I like to think that I am a gentleman, but your forgiveness will have to come from someone other than me.... Have you no decency, sir, at long last? Have you left no sense of decency?"

—Joseph Welch, 1954

54. Which of the following statements most accurately explains the effect of McCarthyism on the United States?
    (A) The government focused on detecting and eliminating significant communist threats to the nation.
    (B) The fear associated with the McCarthy era led people to insist on their civil liberties as Americans.
    (C) Freedom of speech and the press suffered as accusations increased and larger swaths of the population were targeted.
    (D) The arts thrived as a forum to oppose threats to democratic values in the nation.

55. Which of the following statements accurately expresses the similarities between the McCarthy era and the Salem Witch Trials?
   (A) Little evidence was needed to try, convict, and sentence someone once they were accused.
   (B) The majority of those accused were people in positions of influence.
   (C) Accusations were often the product of an unrelated disagreement.
   (D) The trials were connected to ideas that flourished in other places.

STOP
END OF SECTION I, PART A

IF YOU FINISH BEFORE TIME IS CALLED, YOU MAY CHECK YOUR WORK ON THIS SECTION. DO NOT GO ON TO SECTION I, PART B UNTIL YOU ARE TOLD TO DO SO.

AP UNITED STATES HISTORY EXAMINATION
Section I
Part B: Short-Answer Questions
Writing Time—45 minutes

Directions: Part B of the examination contains 4 questions. You will have 45 minutes to respond to all questions. You are not required to develop and support a thesis statement in your response. Rather, focus on directly answering each question using evidence from your study of history.

1. Slavery emerged in the colonies that would become the United States because of a combination of demographic, economic, and geographic conditions.
   a) Explain ONE demographic reason for the rise of slavery in any part of the North American British colonies.
   b) Explain ONE economic reason for the rise of slavery in any part of the North American British colonies.
   c) Explain ONE geographic reason for the rise of slavery in any part of the North American British colonies.

"Nineteenth-century evangelicals like Finney, or Lyman Beecher, or Francis Asbury ... unrelenting in their emphasis on the terrible sinfulness of humans. But they focused on sin as human action. For all they preached hellfire and damnation, they nonetheless harbored an unshakable practical belief in the capacity of humans for moral action, in the ability of humans to turn away from sinful behavior and embrace moral action... The label [of the Second Great Awakening] sought to describe a broad religious phenomenon that transcended sectarian and denominational boundaries...Nineteenth-century evangelicals consider[ed] themselves participants in a much broader spiritual movement to evangelize the nation and world."

Donald Scott, "Evangelicalism, Revivalism, and the Second Great Awakening," National Humanities Center (October 2000)

2. Based on the description of the Second Great Awakening offered by Donald Scott in the passage above, complete the following two tasks:
   a) Explain the impact of the Second Great Awakening's "belief in the...ability of humans to turn away from sinful behavior and embrace moral action."
   b) Provide ONE piece of evidence that supports the impact you described in Part a.

"Looking Backward" by Joseph Keppler, 1893 Library of Congress

3. Use the cartoon above that was published in 1893 and your knowledge of United States history to answer Parts a, b, and c.
   a) Briefly explain the message intended by the cartoonist who created this image.
   b) Provide ONE piece of evidence from American history that would have motivated the cartoonist to create this image.
   c) Explain ONE reason for the increase in immigration in the 1890s.

4. United States historians debate the effectiveness of Franklin D. Roosevelt's New Deal programs.
   a) Choose ONE of the following areas and explain the problems faced by the nation in the years leading up to the New Deal.
      Agriculture
      Unemployment
      Banking
   b) Name and explain ONE New Deal policy or program that addressed the problems in the area you chose in Part a.
   c) Explain at least ONE criticism of the New Deal policies or programs in the area you chose in Part a.

STOP
END OF SECTION I

IF YOU FINISH BEFORE TIME IS CALLED, YOU MAY CHECK YOUR WORK ON THIS SECTION. DO NOT GO ON TO SECTION II UNTIL YOU ARE TOLD TO DO SO.

Section II: Free-Response Essays

Section II of the examination has two kinds of questions. Part A is the Document-Based Question, which includes a series of primary source documents organized around a central question. Part B will present a pair of long-essay questions, both focusing on the same historical thinking skill. Each of the two long-essay prompts will apply the skill to a different time period and you will choose ONE of the two prompts to answer. You will have a total of 95 minutes to complete the document-based essay and the long essay.

Part A: Document-Based Question (DBQ)
Time—60 minutes

Directions: Question 1 is based on the accompanying documents. The documents have been edited for the purpose of this exercise. You are advised to spend 15 minutes planning and 45 minutes writing your answer.

In your response you should do the following.

- State a relevant thesis that directly answers all parts of the question.
- Support the thesis or a relevant argument with evidence from all, or all but one, of the documents.
- Incorporate analysis of all, or all but one, of the documents into your argument.
- Focus your analysis of each document on at least one of the following: intended audience, purpose, historical context, and/or point of view.
- Support your argument with analysis of historical examples outside the documents.
- Connect historical phenomena relevant to your argument to broader events or processes.
- Synthesize the elements above into a persuasive essay.

Question 1. To what extent did American society's views of women change from the World War I era to the mid-1970s?

Document 1: World War II Poster

National Archives

GO ON TO NEXT PAGE

Document 2: Women in the Workforce (1950s)

© Bettmann/Corbis

Culver Pictures, Inc.

Document 3: Betty Friedan, *The Feminine Mystique* (1963)

The suburban housewife—she was the dream image of the young American woman and the envy, it was said, of women all over the world. The American housewife—freed by science and labor-saving appliances from the drudgery, the dangers of childbirth and the illnesses of her grandmother. She was healthy, beautiful, educated, concerned only about her husband, her children, her home. She had found true feminine fulfillment. As a housewife and mother, she was respected as a full and equal partner to man in his world. She was free to choose automobiles, clothes, appliances, supermarkets; she had everything that women ever dreamed of.

In the fifteen years after World War II, this mystique of feminine fulfillment became the cherished and self-perpetuating one of contemporary American culture. Millions of women lived their lives in the image of those pretty pictures of the American suburban housewife, kissing their husbands goodbye in front of the picture window, depositing their stationwagonsful of children at school, and smiling as they ran the new electric waxer over the spotless kitchen floor. They bake their own bread, sewed their own and their children's clothes, kept their new washing machines and dryers running all day. They changed the sheets on the beds twice a week instead once, took the rug-hooking class at adult education, and pitied their poor frustrated mothers who had dreamed of having a career. Their only dream was to be perfect wives and mothers; their highest ambition to have five children and a beautiful house, their only fight to get and keep their husbands. They had no thought for the unfeminine problems of the world outside the home; they wanted the men to make the major decisions. They gloried in their role as women, and wrote proudly on the census blank "Occupation: housewife." . . .

Document 4: Suffrage Poster, Pre-1919

Poster Collection, Hoover Institution Archives

GO ON TO NEXT PAGE

Document 5: National Organization for Women Statement of Purpose (1966)

The purpose of NOW is to take action to bring women into full participation in the mainstream of American society now, exercising all the privileges and responsibilities thereof in truly equal partnership with men.

NOW is dedicated to the proposition that women, first and foremost, are human beings, who, like all other people in our society, must have the chance to develop their fullest human potential. We believe that women can achieve such equality only by accepting to the full the challenges and responsibilities they share with all other people in our society, as part of the decision-making mainstream of American political, economic and social life.

We organize to initiate or support action, nationally, or in any part of this nation, by individuals or organizations, to break through the silken curtain of prejudice and discrimination against women in government, industry, the professions, the churches, the political parties, the judiciary, the labor unions, in education, science, medicine, law, religion and every other field of importance in American society.

Enormous changes taking place in our society make it both possible and urgently necessary to advance the unfinished revolution of women toward true equality, now. With a life span lengthened to nearly 75 years it is no longer either necessary or possible for women to devote the greater part of their lives to child-rearing; yet childbearing and rearing—which continues to be a most important part of most women's lives—still is used to justify barring women from equal professional and economic participation and advance.

Document 6: Women Depicted in Various Occupations (1915)

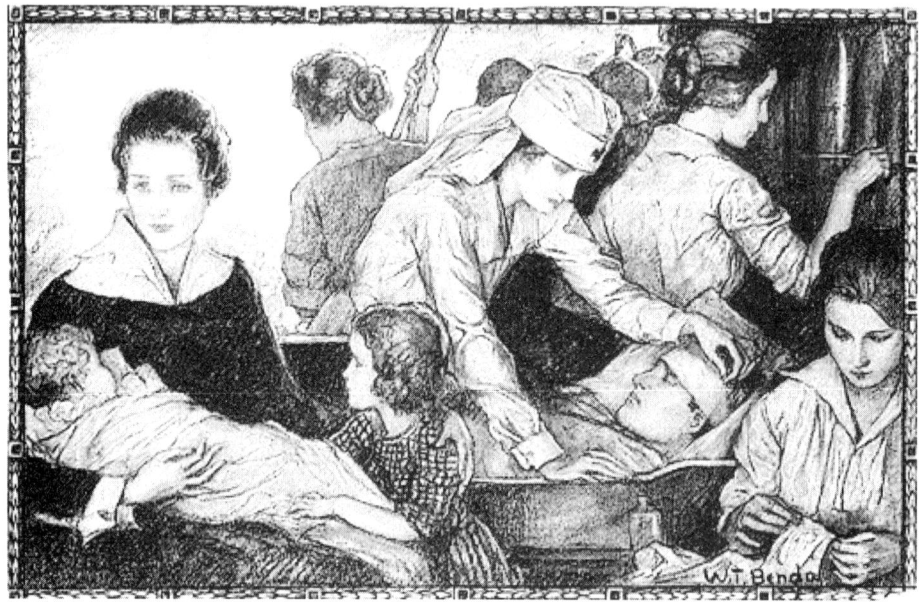

Library of Congress

Document 7: Women in the Work Force, 1950–1992

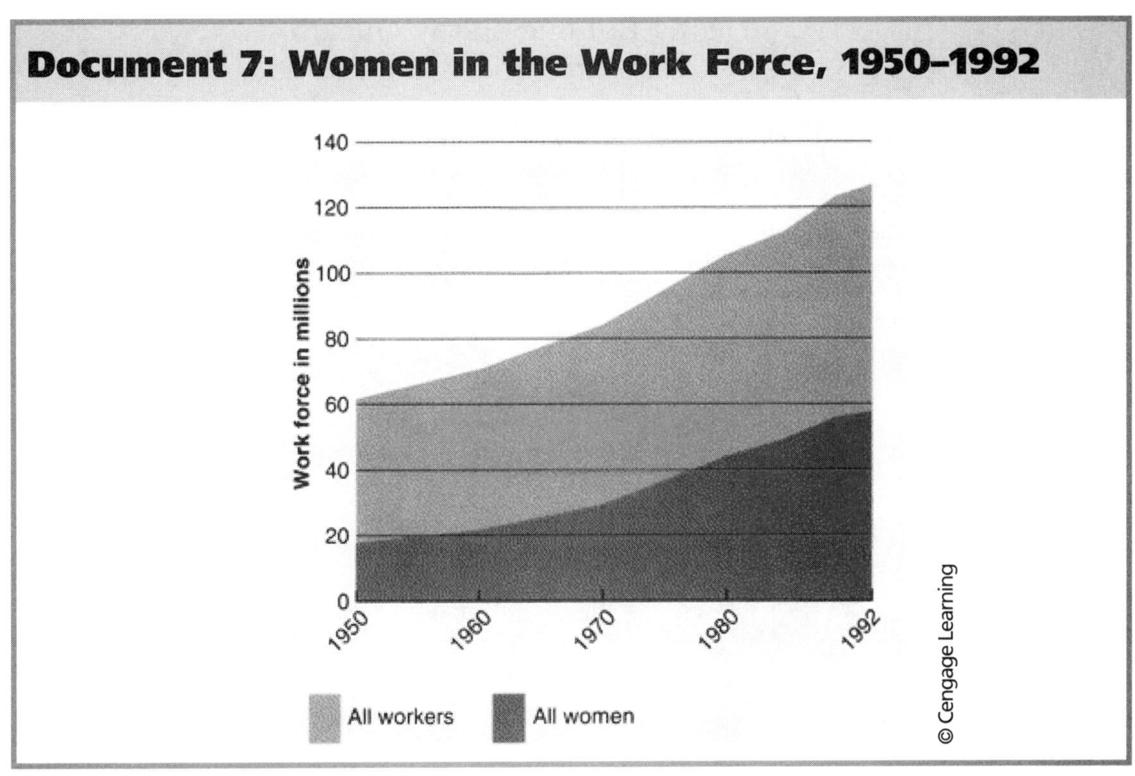

Document 8: Women's Liberation March, 1976

Library of Congress

<u>*End of documents for Question 1.*</u>
<u>*Go on to the next page.*</u>

GO ON TO NEXT PAGE

Part B: Long-Essay Questions
Writing Time—35 minutes

Directions Answer ONE of the following questions. It is recommended that you spend 5 minutes planning each essay and 30 minutes for writing. Write a well-structured, clearly written essay that provides sufficient evidence to support your thesis. Make certain to identify in the test booklet which essay question you have selected.

Question 1. To what extent was the period following the War of 1812 an "Era of Good Feelings"?

Question 2. To what extent was the period following World War II a "Cold War"?

END OF EXAMINATION

ANSWERS FOR SECTION I

ANSWER KEY FOR MULTIPLE-CHOICE QUESTIONS

1. D	12. A	23. C	34. C	45. C
2. C	13. C	24. A	35. A	46. A
3. C	14. C	25. C	36. D	47. B
4. D	15. B	26. B	37. C	48. B
5. B	16. A	27. A	38. B	49. A
6. C	17. D	28. D	39. C	50. D
7. C	18. D	29. B	40. A	51. C
8. B	19. A	30. D	41. B	52. A
9. D	20. B	31. B	42. C	53. B
10. C	21. C	32. B	43. B	54. C
11. B	22. A	33. A	44. D	55. A

PART A: EXPLANATIONS FOR THE MULTIPLE-CHOICE ANSWERS

1. **(D)** Debate over the Mexican War focused on whether the war was based on an attack or simply a "land grab" by President Polk; suspicions regarding the report of shots fired on American troops by the Mexican army; and the United States' role in agitating for conflict by blatantly violating Mexico's stance on Texas. Combined with the rising tensions in the country at that time, these divisions made the war extremely controversial and contentious (*The American Pageant* 14th ed., pp. 407–410/15th ed., pp. 369 372; Learning Objective WOR-5).

2. **(C)** Debates over the war were marked by extremely hostile exchanges over what gaining new land would mean for the expansion of slavery. The Wilmot Proviso, which passed the House but failed in the Senate, attempted to ban slavery in any land won during the war and southern representatives threatened secession if they were barred from bringing slaves into this new land. The land became the subject of the Compromise of 1850, which forestalled the Civil War briefly (*The American Pageant* 14th ed., p. 414/15th ed., p. 376; Learning Objective PEO-3).

3. **(C)** Key figures in the imperialist debates of the 1890s and 1900s used the same language and philosophy to justify American actions in Latin America and in the Pacific, as did President McKinley in deciding to annex the Philippines. In addition, the government and the media focused on the abuses of presidential power in that era—especially regarding Theodore Roosevelt—as

Lincoln did in 1860 (*The American Pageant* 14th ed., pp. 679, 682–683/15th ed., pp. 608–610; Learning Objective WOR-6).

4. **(D)** Though equal protection of the laws and the right to vote had been guaranteed by Reconstruction reformers via the Fourteenth and Fifteenth Amendments, the United States had failed to fulfill those promises a century later (*The American Pageant* 14th ed., p. 533/15th ed., pp. 482–483; Learning Objective POL-3).

5. **(B)** Via presidential mandates (like the desegregation of the military or the support of the Little Rock 9), judicial activism (such as occurred in *Brown* v. *Board*) or legislative action (like the passage of the Civil Rights and Voting Rights Acts)—the federal government was moved to take action by the efforts of reformers, though many complained about the enforcement of those mandates (*The American Pageant* 14th ed., pp. 953, 983/15th ed., pp. 868, 898; Learning Objective POL-7).

6. **(C)** Continued violence against protesters and the reluctance of the federal government to override the justice systems in the South led many frustrated reformers to discount nonviolence and turn to more direct action instead (*The American Pageant* 14th ed., pp. 989–990/15th ed., pp. 904–905; Learning Objective ID-8).

7. **(C)** European explorers' early encounters with Native Americans ended in slavery, bloodshed, and death. Natives were put to work to find the gold that Europeans expected to bring home and were often tortured when they failed to locate gold or other precious metals. Natives also could not withstand European diseases, and many perished—intentionally and accidentally—as a result of exposure to illnesses they could not fight (*The American Pageant* 14th ed., pp. 16–18/15th ed., pp. 15–17; Learning Objective PEO-1).

8. **(B)** Throughout the Western Hemisphere European colonizers and Native Americans engaged in violent struggle from the time of the conquistadores through the late nineteenth century. Native Americans, in fact, were used as slaves in the British colonies before settlers realized that they couldn't withstand the work and started bringing in African slaves (*The American Pageant* 14th ed., pp. 16–18, 283–286, 639–640/15th ed., pp. 15–17, 257–258, 581–584; Learning Objective PEO-4).

9. **(D)** Richard Nixon came into office promising Vietnamization and a new era in U.S. foreign policy. When the public found out about the underhanded way in which he prosecuted the war, it created new doubts about the government and their leaders. Moreover, the deaths of four students at Kent State in Ohio during a protest against the Cambodia raid fueled hatred and mistrust of the government and all of its instruments (*The American Pageant* 14th ed., pp. 1005–1006/15th ed., p. 924; Learning Objective WOR-7).

10. **(C)** Although containment was originally intended as encompassing resources and economic assistance, military action in Korea, Vietnam, and Cambodia shared the rationale of preventing the spread of communism at all costs (*The American Pageant* 14th ed., pp. 928–931/15th ed., pp. 846–847; Learning Objective WOR-7).

11. **(B)** With Henry Kissinger, his secretary of state, Nixon worked to ease tensions between the United States and its communist rivals, becoming the first president to visit China since it became communist in 1949. Nixon negotiated and entered into arms agreements with the Soviet Union in an effort to reduce nuclear weapons stockpiles as well as trading grain. In China, Nixon engaged in "ping-pong diplomacy," with the U.S. and Chinese ping-pong teams traveling to play tournaments against each other in the name of peace (*The American Pageant* 14th ed., pp. 1006–1007/15th ed., pp. 919–920; Learning Objective WOR-7).

12. **(A)** Bacon and his followers were angered by the kind treatment that Berkeley extended to the Native Americans while they struggled to find land and prosper. This led to Bacon's Rebellion, in which Bacon and his followers burned Jamestown down and attempted to overtake the colony. They failed after Bacon died in the middle of the rebellion (*The American Pageant* 14th ed., pp. 70, 74/15th ed., p. 62; Learning Objective POL-1).

13. **(C)** Nonwhites were always at the bottom of the social hierarchy. White farmers, regardless of their wealth, had higher status (Not in text; Learning Objective ID-5).

14. **(C)** Bacon's Rebellion served as a warning to Native Americans and African Americans that whites of any social status would always be superior to them and resist any attempts to better their position (*The American Pageant* 14th ed., pp. 70, 74/15th ed., p. 62; Learning Objective PEO-4).

15. **(B)** Using his "big stick diplomacy," Teddy Roosevelt inserted the United States into several Latin American nations' economic and political affairs. He also intervened in Panama to inspire a rebellion against Colombia and guaranteed U.S. access to the canal zone at the isthmus of Panama. Using his corollary to the Monroe Doctrine, Roosevelt assessed where U.S. support was needed in Latin America; the United States did not wait for Latin American nations to come ask for aid. This inspired resentment throughout Latin America as much as it inspired gratitude among those helped by the United States (*The American Pageant* 14th ed., pp. 690–693/15th ed., pp. 627–629; Learning Objective WOR-7).

16. **(A)** In the Platt Amendment, which the United States inserted into Cuba's constitution after the Spanish-American War, the United States pledged to assist Cuba when that nation was threatened or experiencing economic or political difficulties. The United States used the Platt Amendment to exercise a great deal of influence on Cuba's internal and external dealings until Castro

took over in 1959 (*The American Pageant* 14th ed., p. 683/15th ed., p. 621; Learning Objective WOR-7).

17. **(D)** As the United States' empire and trading activity grew, many came to realize that the nation would benefit from a faster water route between the Atlantic and the Pacific. Despite past failed attempts, a canal through the Isthmus of Panama appeared to be the best solution. After U.S. warships protected Panama during its fight for independence from Colombia, Roosevelt secured the canal zone and began construction (*The American Pageant* 14th ed., pp. 690–692/15th ed., pp. 627–629; Learning Objective WOR-3).

18. **(D)** This speech, a few months after the 9/11 attack, turned attention to Iraq and the weapons of mass destruction that it was allegedly hiding. This reasoning was invoked a year later when the United States invaded Iraq and captured Saddam Hussein. He was tried and sentenced to death for multiple atrocities over the course of his rule (The American Pageant 14th ed., pp. 1070–1073/15th ed., pp. 976–977; Learning Objective WOR-8).

19. **(A)** Since 9/11, much of the U.S. focus has been on defeating terrorists as well as regimes in the Middle East and protecting itself from the nuclear threat posed by nations like Iran (*The American Pageant* 14th ed., pp. 1067–1073/15th ed., pp. 974–979, 986–988; Learning Objective CUL-7).

20. **(B)** After the coalition forces' victory in Operation Desert Storm, the United Nations imposed sanctions on Iraq preventing it from manufacturing or keeping weapons of mass destruction and requiring Iraq to allow UN inspectors into the nation to ensure compliance. After Iraq refused to allow the inspectors access to alleged weapons sites the U.S. military invaded (*The American Pageant* 14th ed., pp. 1070–1071/15th ed., pp. 976–977; Learning Objective WOR-8).

21. **(C)** After the Civil War, the United States transitioned from a primarily agrarian economy to one that looked more towards industry. Thus, different industries grew in different parts of the country. The expansion of the railroad system enabled the transportation of resources and products from one part of the country to another, facilitating production in geographically optimal regions. By the end of the nineteenth century, almost every region of the nation played a significant role in the rapidly industrializing economy (*The American Pageant* 14th ed., pp. 565–574/15th ed., pp. 512–521; Learning Objective WXT-3).

22. **(A)** Although the entire nation was transformed by industrialization, the majority of factories remained in the Northeast. Immigrants who were qualified to work in more specialized areas often looked for such jobs, but many immigrants—men, women, and children—sought a better life through the money they could earn working at jobs that required little to no training. It was also easier for European immigrants to enter the United States through Ellis Island and immigrant

enclaves could be found throughout cities in the Northeast (*The American Pageant* 14th ed., pp. 599–601/15th ed., pp. 542–545; Learning Objective PEO-6).

23. **(C)** One of the major justifications for U.S. imperialism at the beginning of the twentieth century was the need for new markets. As American manufacturing began to produce more than Americans could consume on their own, new ports and peoples were sought for that purpose. In addition, new lands could also provide raw materials that the climate in the United States would not allow (*The American Pageant* 14th ed., p. 669/ 15th ed., p. 608; Learning Objective WXT-6).

24. **(A)** Just as the Progressives had done just a few years previously, Keynes calls for the government to take a lead role in restoring balance to the nation's social and economic status (*The American Pageant* 14th ed., p. 828/15th ed., p. 755; Learning Objective POL-3).

25. **(C)** Culminating in the stock market crash of 1929, episodes of credit and market instability undermined the nation's economic health and led to the Great Depression's spiraling economic decline (*The American Pageant* 14th ed., pp. 812–813/15th ed., pp. 740–741; Learning Objective WXT-8).

26. **(B)** The New Deal programs, while by no means unanimously supported, carved a role for the national government in providing for the nation's weakest citizens and opened the door to large-scale social insurance programs that endure today (*The American Pageant* 14th ed., pp. 849–850/15th ed., pp. 774–775; Learning Objective POL-4).

27. **(A)** Barack Obama's stimulus plan to bring the country out of the Great Recession follows many of the same philosophies as the New Deal (*The American Pageant* 14th ed., Not in text/15th ed., pp. 985–986; Learning Objective WXT-8).

28. **(D)** By the time Thomas Paine published *Common Sense* the Revolutionary War had already started. His pamphlet intended to sway people who weren't convinced that independence was the best course of action. In fact, many of the acts that the colonists rebelled against were passed by Parliament (*The American Pageant* 14th ed., p. 150/15th ed., pp. 135–136; Learning Objective CUL-4).

29. **(B)** Taxation without representation was a rallying cry in the colonies that began with the 1764 Sugar Act and intensified with the Stamp Act a year later. The colonists believed that they had the same rights as Englishmen living in England and Parliament could not pass laws that affected them without their input. Cries of "no taxation without representation" reflect colonists' conception of England and King George III as far away authoritarian powers (*The American Pageant* 14th ed., pp. 129–133/15th ed., pp. 115–119; Learning Objective CUL-4).

30. **(D)** After experiencing oppression under British rule but needing to establish a government as an independent nation, the Continental Congress created the Articles of Confederation. Under the Articles state governments held the majority of power, and a weak national government, consisting of a Congress with one vote per state, oversaw national and international matters. The Framers believed that this would prevent dictatorship in the new United States (*The American Pageant* 14th ed., pp. 179–182/15th ed., pp. 162–165; Learning Objective POL-5).

31. **(B)** Upon leaving office Washington famously urged the United States to remain politically and militarily remote from the rest of the world as it gained its own strength as a nation. With his commitment to protect independent nations in Latin America if they were threatened by an imperial power, Monroe stepped outside of the limits recommended by Washington and began to assert U.S. influence in the Western Hemisphere (*The American Pageant* 14th ed., pp. 267–270/15th ed., pp. 242–243; Learning Objective WOR-5).

32. **(B)** The Monroe Doctrine was frequently invoked by expansionists looking for new land once, as Frederick Jackson Turner stated, the frontier was closed. The United States asserted its right, as the protector of Latin America, to interfere in the economic and political spheres of the nations to ensure their stability. One of the most famous examples of this is the Roosevelt Corollary to the Monroe Doctrine which asserts that if the United States senses instability in a nation it can step in to prop that nation up. This earned Teddy Roosevelt, and the United States, reputations as the policeman of the Western Hemisphere (*The American Pageant* 14th ed., pp. 692–693/15th ed., pp. 616–617, 620; Learning Objective WOR-6).

33. **(A)** The League of Nations, the centerpiece of Wilson's peace plan, included a provision that when one member nation was threatened the other members committed to defend it. Many in the Senate, led by Henry Cabot Lodge, refused to consent to the Treaty of Versailles or join the League of Nations because the United States would be pulled into wars with which it had no concern without the power to vote on whether or not to declare war for itself. Although some senators were willing to ratify the treaty if Wilson consented to changes, Wilson refused. The United States never signed the treaty or joined the League (*The American Pageant* 14th ed., pp. 762–766/15th ed., pp. 694–696; Learning Objective POL-6).

34. **(C)** Woodrow Wilson was so destroyed by the Senate's refusal to ratify the treaty that he ultimately had a stroke and finished his presidency in ailing health. Without Wilson and the United States, the League was ineffective to stop the rise of fascist and totalitarian powers in the 1930s or to prevent their incursions into independent, self-governing countries (*The American Pageant* 14th ed., pp. 765–766/15th ed., p. 695; Learning Objective WOR-7).

35. **(A)** The majority of the Framers were landowners. Many attended college, and many were businessmen and lawyers. Also, some were among the largest slaveholders in the country at that time. Viewing the Constitution as an economic document, then, indicates that the Framers created a structure of government that protected their interests and holdings to the exclusion of those not in their elite company (*The American Pageant* 14th ed., p. 187/15th ed., pp. 169–170; Learning Objective ID-5).

36. **(D)** As a compromise to Antifederalists who opposed the Constitution without guaranteeing individual rights, Madison pledged to introduce amendments in the first Congress. The Bill of Rights, ratified in 1791, includes freedoms of speech, press, and religion, as well as trial by jury and protection from illegal search and seizure, all designed to protect the individual (*The American Pageant* 14th ed., pp. 201–202/15th ed., pp. 181–182; Learning Objective POL-5).

37. **(C)** Many abolitionists looked at provisions like the Fugitive Slave Clause, the 3/5 Clause, and the Commerce Compromise and identifed the Constitution as a document designed to protect the property rights of slaveholders. Among the most prominent abolitionists making that argument was Frederick Douglass, who eventually changed his mind and saw the Constitution as an inclusive document that does not prioritize one race over another (*The American Pageant* 14th ed., p. 189/15th ed., p. 172; Learning Objective POL-5).

38. **(B)** The "Roaring Twenties" were a time of great change as technology allowed people the freedom to travel and pursue interests outside the home. People became more aware of the world through the radio, and newly-enfranchised women began to enjoy more freedom than in the past. These political, social, and cultural reforms created a significant backlash as many more conservative Americans agreed with Harding's emphasis on a return to normalcy. Tennessee was one state that acted on this legislatively, trying to firmly establish its Christian roots by banning the teaching of evolution in 1925. This led to the Scopes Monkey Trial, which became a national sensation (*The American Pageant* 14th ed., pp. 780–781/15th ed., pp. 709–710; Learning Objective CUL-5).

39. **(C)** Dating back to the creation of the Bill of Rights and Jefferson's comments about a wall of separation between religion and government, battles about separation of church and state have yet to cease in the United States as they apply to schools, courthouses, and public spaces with little consistent resolution. The Scopes trial, and the persistent controversy over the role of evolution in the classroom, are an important part of this debate (Not in the text; Learning Objective POL-5).

40. **(A)** *Marbury* v. *Madison* marked the first time that the Court struck down a law passed by a co-equal branch and solidified its power of judicial review, the ability to strike down laws the

Court deems unconstitutional. The Court has used this power innumerable times in the more than two hundred years since *Marbury*. During the 1930s the Court struck down central New Deal measures ruling that the federal government overstepped its boundaries in creating the NIRA and AAA. This led to Franklin Roosevelt's court-packing scheme (*The American Pageant* 14th ed., pp. 232, 836/15th ed., pp. 209, 762; Learning Objective POL-5).

41. **(B)** Article VI of the Constitution states that the document is the highest law in the land. This decision, which establishes that any law that contradicts the Constitution can be struck down, affirms that principle (*The American Pageant* 14th ed., p. A13/15th ed., p. A13; Learning Objective POL-5).

42. **(C)** In *Dred Scott* v. *Sanford*, the Supreme Court ruled that the federal government could not interfere with private property rights, allowing slave owners to bring their slaves anywhere in the nation they wished and striking down the Missouri Compromise. This proved to be one of the major causes leading to the Civil War (*The American Pageant* 14th ed., pp. 445–446/15th ed., pp. 403–404; Learning Objective POL-5).

43. **(B)** Social Darwinists argued that "survival of the fittest" meant that the strongest and ablest businesses would thrive and grow while weaker ventures would succumb to buyouts and competition (*The American Pageant* 14th ed., p. 579/15th ed., p. 525; Learning Objective CUL-5).

44. **(D)** Wealth often translated into power (one of the chief complaints of the Progressives in later years), and government policies of the Gilded Age strongly favored industries with subsidies for transportation and communication as well as near-nonexistent industrial regulation (*The American Pageant* 14th ed., pp. 574–580/15th ed., pp. 520–525; Learning Objective WXT-6).

45. **(C)** This debate yielded Carnegie's "Social Gospel" as well as a rise in labor activism (*The American Pageant* 14th ed., pp. 579–580/15th ed., pp. 524–525; Learning Objective WXT-7).

46. **(A)** Although women were not able to keep the jobs they gained during the war, understanding the possibilities in the workforce and in society and the constraints placed on them as housewives planted the seeds of the women's movement that would happen later. It also led to a significant, if often unspoken, increase in women in the workforce in the 1950s (*The American Pageant* 14th ed., pp. 880–882/15th ed., pp. 803–804; Learning Objective WOR-4).

47. **(B)** The nation rebounded from the Great Depression as a result of World War II. Beginning with the mobilization that happened when the government passed the Lend-Lease Act, factories began manufacturing more goods and turning a profit, spurring the economy. As the war progressed, the sheer quantity of goods necessary for the war kept the factories running and prospering,

changing the nation's fortunes (*The American Pageant* 14th ed., pp. 877, 880/15th ed., pp. 802–803; Learning Objective WOR-3).

48. **(B)** The church was a major fixture in the Second Great Awakening, with preachers all over the country sermonizing against slavery and the "demon rum." Both were viewed as sins and the cause for many of the nation's problems in the home and outside of it. Finney's speech addresses this point, stating that by taking action against consumption and slavery it can play a role in the eradication of both (*The American Pageant* 14th ed., pp. 340–343/15th ed. pp. 307–310; Learning Objective CUL-4).

49. **(A)** The church was a central fixture of the Second Great Awakening, as many of the movements that rose to prominence in that era had their foundation in Christian morality about right and wrong. The civil rights movement in the South, meanwhile, looked to the church as a unifying force and meeting place, with preachers among the highest level of leadership in many organizations (*The American Pageant* 14th ed., pp. 340–343/15th ed. pp. 307–310; Learning Objective CUL-4).

50. **(D)** Throughout American history to that point many churches, especially those in New England, supported maintaining the status quo in social and cultural matters. With the Second Great Awakening, the church became a leading force in advocating for significant changes in American life including temperance, abolition, and prison and mental health reform (*The American Pageant* 14th ed., pp. 348–354/15th ed. pp. 314–317; Learning Objective CUL-4).

51. **(C)** Critics argued that school prayer violated the establishment clause, and that students would feel compelled to participate in a school-sanctioned prayer even if it was optional. They argued that this would violate the precedent set in and upheld since *Engel* v. *Vitale* in 1962 (*The American Pageant* 14th ed., Not in text/15th ed. p. 943; Learning Objective POL-5).

52. **(A)** The Moral Majority was a conservative group founded with the belief that Christianity needed to play a bigger role in daily life in the United States and that the changes the country experienced were largely due to the decreased influence of the church in the U.S. This group spoke out against many changes that they believed interfered with the church's teachings, including abortion. The Moral Majority supported many of Reagan's more conservative ideas, including school prayer (*The American Pageant* 14th ed., p. 1043/15th ed. pp. 951–953; Learning Objective CUL-5).

53. **(B)** Many institutions, including some that are essential parts of the United States government, begin their day with a prayer. Because the figures involved are adults, this has long been considered acceptable. Moreover, the founders relied on Christian principles in making several arguments for independence and state building. These arguments have failed to justify school prayer because children are viewed as too easily

influenced or pressured (Not in the text; Learning Objective POL-5).

54. **(C)** The random nature of accusations created an overwhelming paranoia that prevented people from speaking out against anything they opposed or in favor of anything that might relate to communism or socialism. Although these democratic institutions eventually rebounded, much of the fifties-era conformity and the rebellion of the 1960s can be traced back to the oppressive atmosphere of the McCarthy years (*The American Pageant* 14th ed., pp. 950–951/15th ed., pp. 866–867; Learning Objective POL-7).

55. **(A)** The mass hysteria associated with both the Salem Witch Trials and the McCarthy era meant that an accusation was the equivalent of a sentence. In both events one could accuse others to avoid sentencing, but in both cases the taint of the accusation remained. The similarities between these events, although the McCarthy era lasted significantly longer, are why McCarthyism is often referred to as a witch hunt. Although the McCarthy hearings did lead to the capture of some communists, many others suffered for large portions of their lives after being wrongly accused (*The American Pageant* 14th ed., pp. 83–84, 950–951/15th ed., pp. 73–74, 866–867; Learning Objective CUL-5).

Section I, Part B: Short-Answer Questions

Question 1

Consider first which North American colonies developed a reliance upon African slavery—the Chesapeake and Southern colonies. To answer the question, remember that in these colonies (founded for the purpose of profit), the economy depended on plantation-style agriculture of cash crops. Unlike in New England, these areas did not (at least initially) see large-scale migration of English families looking to create a new life for themselves. Furthermore, consider the social and racial conditions of slavery—perhaps contrasting these with the nature of slavery and labor systems in the colonies of other European nations. Some details worth mentioning include Bacon's Rebellion (a conflict involving indentured servants that led many to prefer slaves), the rise of tobacco farming and John Rolfe, or the settlement of colonists from the Barbados who had prior experience with African slaves.

Question 2

The Second Great Awakening's emphasis on the ability of humans to change their sinful nature (in contrast to Puritan/Calvinist ideas of predestination) led to the rise of many significant reform movements in the mid-nineteenth century. Beyond this ideological shift, the community-based revivals also provided fertile grounds for organizing reformers. Examples you might use include Dorothea Dix's reforms of prisons and asylums, Horace Mann's work in public education, the rise of the temperance movement, or the growth of the women's suffrage movement.

Question 3

This image shows the irony of the children and grandchildren of immigrants—now successful American businessmen—protesting the arrival of new immigrants to the land of opportunity. Based on the time period (1893), you might infer that the immigrant being shunned belongs to the "New Immigrants" from southern and eastern Europe. The New Immigrants were particularly disliked because of fears about their foreign languages, unfamiliar religious practices, and racially or ethnically different appearances. Competition over industrial jobs (the wages of which many believed were driven down by immigrants) and ethnocentric ideas contributed to the clash. You might discuss the rise of the Know-Nothing party or the 1882 legislation to ban Chinese immigration altogether.

In your discussion of causes of immigration, you might include either a "push" or "pull" factor as your choice to explain the influx in the Gilded Age. Unrest in Europe certainly increased the desires of many would-be immigrants to leave their country of origin. On the other hand, rapid industrialization and the promise of jobs, along with the egalitarian principles of the American Constitution made America a beacon of hope.

Question 4

To begin, focus on explaining the root of the problems in your area of choice. In agriculture, overproduction was the root of the disasters of the 1920s and 1930s. The Great Crash caused the skyrocketing rates of unemployment, though the market saturation brought on by a decade of reckless spending and overproduction certainly didn't help. In the banking industry, a lack of regulation had spelled disaster as many lost significant assets in the stock market failure of 1929—the nation's lack of confidence in the banks further complicated this issue.

As you consider which New Deal program to discuss, remember that Part C asks you to also explain one criticism of that plan. New Deal programs abounded—some that fit the categories listed here include the AAA, the CCC, the WPA, the FERA, and the Glass-Steagall Act's creation of the FDIC. Critics were also abundant during the New Deal years, from both the left (arguing, as did Huey Long and Francis Townsend, that the New Deal did not go far enough to help the needy) and the right (arguing, as did the American Liberty League and Hoover supporters, that the New Deal amounted to socialism and would destroy the American social fabric).

Section II, Part A: Document-Based Question (DBQ)

Below are short analyses of the documents. The italicized words suggest what your margin notes might include.

Document 1 This World War II propaganda poster *urging women to join the workforce in support of the war* reflects the importance of women to the war effort. Although they couldn't fight, *women played* *a significant role in the war by working in factories at home, and serving as nurses and supply pilots abroad.* Images like *Rosie the Riveter* and women's satisfaction with working outside the home eventually led to the women's movement of the 1960s.

DOCUMENT 2 This photo shows the *increasing number of women in the workforce, especially in office jobs, in the 1950s.* More women, both married and single, went to work in this decade despite the "housewife" image portrayed in many television shows of the day.

DOCUMENT 3 In her book, *The Feminine Mystique,* Betty Friedan *attacks the view of the American woman as equal to men based solely on the material quality of her life.* She *caustically presents the view that women had no concerns outside those that affected the material happiness of their own families.*

DOCUMENT 4 The designer of this *poster* (possibly created before the ratification of the Nineteenth Amendment) *alerted women that their time for equality was upon them,* as *women's work during World War I brought the appreciation of the nation* and, with it, the right to vote.

DOCUMENT 5 The National Organization for Women (*NOW*) has been one of the primary national organizations for women's rights since it was founded in 1966. Over the years it has *attacked stereotypes, attitudes, and discrimination that have negatively shaped women's lives.* In the document the NOW *statement of purpose indirectly attacks earlier perspectives such as the Cult of Domesticity, Republican Motherhood, and possibly even the Barbie Doll itself.* The political sentiment being expressed is a *demand for equality in politics and government nearly fifty years after the ratification of the Nineteenth Amendment.* Laws change, but attitudes take longer to change. NOW was obviously tired of waiting.

DOCUMENT 6 This *idealistic drawing portrays the varied roles women played in early-twentieth-century* America. *From our perspective it reveals the narrow range of women's work* in this time period. Central to the drawing is the *woman as mother and as caregiver to the helpless and injured.* However there is some recognition of the *manual labor associated with women's work* in the early part of the twentieth century. Perhaps *the little girl* watching her mother caring for the baby *may be seeing how her own life will someday unfold.*

DOCUMENT 7 This chart shows that the number of women in the workforce grew at a rate higher than the rate for general employment. *All workers doubled in number, whereas women in the workforce tripled.* Of course the chart *does not tell* us what *type of labor* women were doing.

DOCUMENT 8 This photograph is quite revealing in that the year is *1976 and women are still demanding "equality" and complaining that they are "second-class citizen(s),"* over half a century after the Nineteenth Amendment. Given the date, it is possible they are advocating in favor of the *Equal Rights Amendment.*

One way to categorize your documents so that they reflect the nature of the question being asked is to group as negative those documents that reflect, say, the way society's attitudes regarding women did not change and group as positive those that reflect change. Some documents reflect both a negative view and a positive view. Also a document may not be identified with one perspective or another, but that does not mean that it cannot be used in defending your thesis. Remember that you provide meaning and perspective to the documents based on your own attitudes and understanding of U.S. history. Below is a categorization of the documents based on changes in attitude:

Negative Documents (Attitudes did not change)	Positive Documents (Attitudes did change)	Neutral Documents
	A	
		B
	C	
	D	
	E	
F		
	G	
H	H	

In developing your essay, you should incorporate the following historical information:

- Attitudes regarding the role of women in American society such as the Cult of Domesticity and Republican Motherhood were common.
- There were antecedents to the twentieth-century women's movement—for example, the Seneca Falls Conference.
- Women's rights, such as the right to vote and the legalization of birth control methods and devices, were national issues in the early twentieth century.
- The Nineteenth Amendment, which gave women the right to vote, was ratified in 1920.
- After World War II, stereotypes of women's place in the family and society were widely expressed in popular culture and consumerism.
- In the 1960s women's rights activists such as Betty Friedan, author of *The Feminine Mystique,* facilitated the challenge to attitudes that left women subordinated despite the educational and professional advances they had made over the years.
- The Equal Rights Amendment was not ratified, and the Supreme Court's ruling in *Roe* v. *Wade* continues to be questioned.

A Sample Essay

If your view is that society's views of women changed in the twentieth century, your essay might look something like this:

Over the course of much of the twentieth century, various reform movements, including the women's rights movement, sought to address the inequalities of American life. Key to gaining political, social, and economic rights was the transformation in attitudes that shaped the American public's views of women. To be sure, women throughout the nation's history have sought to challenge stereotypes, attitudes, and conditions that have shaped their lives. For example, women who organized the Seneca Falls Conference (such as Elizabeth Cady Stanton and Lucretia Mott) sought to challenge attitudes that limited the role of women—for example, the eighteenth-century Cult of Domesticity and in the nineteenth-century Republican Motherhood. In the case of the former, women were expected to develop and adhere to the following characteristics: piety, purity, submissiveness, and domesticity. A small step in the right direction came with the advent of the notion of Republican Motherhood in which women, though disenfranchised, were given a political role: to raise the next generation of politically minded males who fully understood the importance of and responsibility to God, family, and country. Yet, as Document F reveals, the responsibilities of women had not changed that much by the early twentieth century. Women's work was still limited mainly to that of caregiver to the helpless and injured.

By the twentieth century, many women were discontented with the slow pace of change. True, the Nineteenth Amendment enfranchised women (Document D), but given their primary task of bearing and rearing children, most women were unable to improve their lives as a result of traditional stereotypes and unwanted pregnancies. One reformer, Margaret Sanger, took the bold step of publicly advocating for access to birth-control methods, a highly controversial crusade in the first decades of the twentieth century. Later this crusade would expand to the right to have an abortion to end an unwanted pregnancy, which the Supreme Court ruled constitutional in the *Roe* v. *Wade* case of 1973. Access to contraceptives for married couples in all fifty states had been legalized only eight years earlier.

Following ratification of the Nineteenth Amendment in 1920, many women believed that the goal of the women's rights movement had been met; they did not seek to radically challenge the social and ideological attitudes that were so deeply ingrained in American life. Others, such as Elizabeth Paul, took the next step, advocating for an Equal Rights Amendment to the Constitution, an objective that would challenge attitudes in a political battle in the 1970s. Although women's efforts in the workforce and abroad were applauded during World War II (Document A), following the war America seemed to settle back into a sense of conformity in which everyone knew his or her role in the nuclear family. However, women did start moving into the workforce, with many finding employment as secretaries during the economic boom of the 1950s (Document B).

In the early 1960s, society's perceptions and attitudes about women's roles were challenged by Betty Friedan, whose landmark book, *The*

Feminine Mystique, exposed how societal forces such as intellectual and professional oppression left many middle-class women angry and frustrated (Document C). Attitudes, however, were indeed changing. The following year the 1964 Civil Rights Act was passed; this prohibited discrimination on the basis of, among other factors, gender. In 1966 the National Organization for Women was founded in part to "advance the unfinished revolution of women toward true equality now" (Document E). But as more women played an active role in social programs and movements, they found that even within these reform-minded organizations perceptions of women's work reflected a pre-World War II attitude. Consequently it was deemed necessary to resuscitate the crusade for an Equal Rights Amendment (Document H). Unfortunately for advocates of the ERA, attitudes had not changed dramatically enough. Anti-ERA forces led by, among others, Phyllis Schlafly, a conservative Republican, contended that the amendment would break down all differences between the genders.

Undoubtedly attitudes regarding women had changed profoundly in the first five or six decades of the twentieth century. But as is the case with all reform movements, attitudes must change enough so that more democratic legislation can follow. So it is for the women's rights movement.

COMMENT: This essay effectively synthesizes outside information—the writer's knowledge of the nineteenth-century women's rights movement, the ideological influences on women in the eighteenth and nineteenth centuries, as well as twentieth-century movements such as the legalization of birth control and the growing activism of women in the formation of NOW. The document information is also used effectively to depict post–World War II popular and consumer attitudes towards women.

SCORING: Based on the AP U.S. History Document-Based Question Rubric as established by the College Board, you should score your essay as follows (with a maximum possible score of 7).

A. Thesis: 0–1 point

Give 1 point for a stated thesis that directly answers all parts of the question. It must do more than simply restate the question.

B. Analysis of historical evidence and support of argument: 0–4 points

Give 1 point for an essay that offers plausible analysis of the content of a <u>majority</u> of the document, explicitly using that analysis to support the stated thesis or a relevant argument, OR

Give 2 points for an essay that offers plausible analysis of BOTH the content of a <u>majority</u> of the documents, explicitly using this analysis to support the stated thesis or a relevant argument; AND at least one of the following for the majority of the documents: intended audience, purpose, historical context, and/or the author's point of view, OR

Give 3 points for an essay that offers plausible analysis of BOTH the content of all or all but one of the documents, explicitly using this analysis to support the stated thesis or a relevant argument; AND at least one of the following for all or all but one of the documents: intended audience, purpose, historical context, and/or the author's point of view.

PLUS: **Add 1 additional point** for an essay that offers plausible analysis of historical examples beyond or outside of the documents to support the stated thesis or a relevant argument.

C. Contextualization: 0–1 point

Give 1 point for an essay that accurately and explicitly connects historical phenomena relevant to the argument to broader historical events and/or processes.

D. Synthesis: 0–1 point

Give 1 point for an essay that appropriately extends or modifies the stated thesis or argument, OR

Give 1 point for an essay that effectively accounts for disparate, sometimes contradictory evidence from primary sources and/or secondary works in crafting a coherent argument, OR

Give 1 point for an essay that appropriately connects the topic of the question to other historical periods, geographical areas, contexts, or circumstances.

SECTION II, PART B: LONG-ESSAY QUESTIONS

QUESTION 1

Many historians see the years following the War of 1812 as a time when nationalism flourished because Americans unified behind common economic and political objectives. As the nation expanded industrially and as the sections were integrated (especially the North and West) because of the development of national roads and canals, a sense of greater self-sufficiency prevailed. To a certain degree these sentiments and developments generally defined the years immediately after the war. But if there was an Era of Good Feelings, it was very short lived. The elimination of the Federalist Party did much to give Americans the impression that they were unified.

Following the War of 1812 the Federalist Party began to disappear as a viable political alternative to the Democratic-Republicans. The Federalists had only themselves to blame. Well before the war they had passed the undemocratic Alien and Sedition Acts. These pieces of legislation sought to deny Americans their First Amendment right to criticize the government and, by extending the time period before one could become a citizen, neutralized the political power of many new immigrants, who would probably have voted for the Democratic-Republicans. The Federalists further alienated many Americans because of their activities during the War of 1812, which they fervently opposed. In fact some New England Federalists actually sold supplies to the British during the war. Equally controversial was the calling of the Hartford Convention in 1814, at which the delegates discussed the possibility of amending the Constitution to require a two-thirds vote by Congress for a declaration of war. A number of the delegates even discussed secession. With the end of the war many Americans chastised the Federalists for their actions. Soon, at least on the national level, the Federalists imploded, leaving only the Democratic-Republicans. In fact the Democratic-Republican president, James Monroe, was reelected in 1820, having won all but one electoral vote.

Yet, though there was only one major national political party, Americans were still divided as economic and political tensions prevailed, thus limiting the longevity of the assumption that Americans were unified. The issues that had divided the nation before the war continued to shape the political debate after it: the tariff controversy, the establishment of a national bank, tax-supported infrastructural development, the availability of land, and, of course, slavery. The tariff of 1816 (the first in the nation's history) serves as a good example. New England, which had not yet developed a substantial industrial sector, opposed the tariff, whereas the South and West favored it as an expression of national unity and the means for expansion of the nation's economy. (Southern political and economic leaders, however, would condemn subsequent protective tariffs as detrimental to their sectional interests.) The rechartering of the Bank of the United States, a part of Clay's American System, would soon divide the nation as well—the South came to strongly oppose it.

When in 1820 Missouri was prepared to enter the Union as a slave state and thus affect the political balance that prevailed in the Senate, a further sectional division reemerged. The year before this crisis the nation had been devastated by a financial panic, and the focus of the blame was on the Democratic-Republicans, who controlled government. Soon, from the ashes of the old Federalist Party a new political party, the National Republicans, emerged to challenge the power of the Democratic-Republicans. By 1824, although all four candidates for the presidency were Democratic-Republicans, divisions within the party and the nation had emerged. Probably by this point the Era of Good Feelings had run its course.

This approach lays out a clear thesis supported by sufficient background information on the reasons why the Federalist Party collapsed after the War of 1812. It is important to point out that the period was referred to as the Era of Good Feelings because there was only one major national party, the Democratic-Republicans. It is also important to point out that the period was short-lived because of ongoing controversies—the tariff, the Bank of the United States, and the expansion of slavery—and that the tariff and slavery soon replaced a sense of national unity with sectional concerns.

Question 2

Many describe the years following the Second World War as the Cold War—referring to the mounting tensions between the United States—along with other Western (capitalist) nations—and the Soviet Union and its Communist satellite countries. In many respects, this was a "Cold War," particularly when you consider that no open hostilities were ever declared between the Soviet Union and the United States. The tensions were largely diplomatic—though the stakes had been raised by the advent of nuclear weapons—and certainly much of the fear Americans felt at the time can be chalked up to a bit of hysteria. Long periods of relative peace, most notably the era of détente under President Richard Nixon, also demonstrate the ideological nature of this clash. Finally, the end of the "Cold War" came about bloodlessly, brought on by the collapse of the Soviet Union as a result of liberalized internal policies (known as glasnost and perestroika under Soviet Premier Mikhail Gorbachev) and internal dissent—not American intervention.

On the other hand, the idea of a Cold War might also be considered to be an over-simplification. There were many "hot spots" in the Cold War and in many cases, United States troops fought alongside nations battling enemy soldiers supported by Soviet troops. The countries themselves came to the brink of war twice (that we know of): in Berlin in 1948 and later in Cuba in 1962. With crises like the U-2 incident and the revelation of Russian spies in the United States during the HUAC hearings, one could hardly claim that the two nations were not openly at odds. Proxy wars in places like Korea and (especially) Vietnam demonstrate the reality of the conflict for American troops. Supported by the rhetoric of American politicians (including arguments like the Domino Theory), it seems fairly clear that our true targets were the Communist nations and the Soviet Union itself—not the North Koreans or the North Vietnamese.

Regardless of which approach you take, be sure to offer an explanation for the development of the term itself and a reason for its longevity (the period lasted more than half a century).

Scoring: Based on the AP U.S. History Long Essay Question Rubric as established by the College Board, you should score your essay as follows (with a maximum possible score of 6).

A. Thesis: 0–1 point

Give 1 point for a stated thesis that directly answers all parts of the question. It must do more than simply restate the question.

B. Support for argument: 0–2 points

Give 1 point for an essay that supports a stated thesis or makes a relevant argument using specific evidence, OR

Give 2 points for an essay that supports the stated thesis or makes a relevant argument using specific evidence, clearly and consistently stating how the evidence supports the thesis or argument, and establishing clear linkages between the evidence and the thesis or argument.

C. Application of targeted historical thinking skill: 0–2 points

This is a CAUSATION Essay, therefore:

Give 1 point for an essay that describes causes AND/OR effects of a historical development, OR

Give 2 points for an essay that describes causes AND/OR effects of a historical development and analyzes specific examples that illustrate causes AND/OR effects of a historical development.

D. Synthesis: 0–1 point

Give 1 point for an essay that appropriately extends or modifies the stated thesis or argument, OR

Give 1 point for an essay that explicitly employs an additional appropriate category of analysis (e.g., political, economic, social, cultural, geographical, race/ethnicity, gender) beyond that called for by the prompt, OR

Give 1 point for an essay that appropriately connects the topic of the question to other historical periods, geographical areas, contexts, or circumstances.

It is important that you be as objective as possible when evaluating your essays. You might ask a teacher, parent, fellow student, or friend to evaluate your essays for you and to offer advice on areas for improvement.